METHODS FOR BUSINESS ANALYSIS AND FORECASTING: TEXT AND CASES

METHODS FOR BUSINESS ANALYSIS AND FORECASTING: TEXT AND CASES

PETER TRYFOS

York University

JOHN WILEY & SONS, INC.

New York • Chichester • Weinheim • Brisbane • Singapore • Toronto

EDITOR	*Brad Wiley II*
PRODUCTION SERVICE	*J. Carey Publishing Service*
MARKETING MANAGER	*Jay Kirsch*
DESIGN DIRECTION	*Karin Kincheloe*
TEXT DESIGNER	*Nancy Field*
COVER DESIGNER	*Carol C. Grobe*
ILLUSTRATION COORDINATOR	*Sigmund Malinowski*

The book was set in Palatino by Eigentype Compositors and printed and bound by Malloy Lithographers. The cover was printed by Lehigh Press.

Recognizing the importance of preserving what has been written, it is a policy of John Wiley & Sons, Inc. to have books of enduring value published in the United States printed on acid-free paper, and we exert our best efforts to that end.

The paper in this book was manufactured by a mill whose forest management programs include sustained yield harvesting of its timberlands. Sustained yield harvesting principles ensure that the number of trees cut each year does not exceed the amount of new growth.

Library of Congress Cataloging-in-Publication Data

Tryfos, Peter.
    Methods for business analysis and forecasting : text and cases / by Peter Tryfos.
        p.   cm.
    Includes bibliographical references (p.   ) and index.
    ISBN 0-471-12384-6 (alk. paper)
    1. Commercial statistics. 2. Business forecasting.   I. Title.
  HF1017.T79   1998
  519.5–dc21
                                        97-17403
                                           CIP

Printed in the United States of America

10 9 8 7 6 5 4 3 2 1

PREFACE

This book is intended

- primarily as a main text for a one-semester or two-quarter elective course in methods for analysis and forecasting, for students of business or public administration at the upper undergraduate, M.B.A. or Ph.D. level;
- as a text in a "second business statistics" course;
- as a text with an applied orientation in service courses on regression, the linear model, and econometrics offered by departments of mathematics, statistics, and economics; and
- for self-study by professionals in finance, marketing, planning and other areas of business and government.

The text covers the principal methods for analysis and forecasting, which are traditionally included in separate courses with such titles as "Regression," "Linear Models," "Forecasting," and "Econometrics." There is considerable overlap in the content of such courses and mounting pressure in business curricula (especially at the upper undergraduate and graduate level) to utilize efficiently the time devoted to methods courses. This text deals in a balanced way with models for relationships involving quantitative or qualitative dependent and explanatory variables. Its structure can be described schematically as follows:

Dependent variable(s)	Explanatory variables	Method
Single, quantitative	Quantitative	Regression (Chs. 2-3)
Single, quantitative	Qualitative	Dummy variables and ANOVA (Ch. 4)
Single, quantitative	Quant. and qual.	Regression (Chs. 5-10)
Single, qualitative	Quant. and qual.	Classification (Chs. 11-12)
Many, quantitative	Quant. and qual.	Simultaneous equations (Ch. 13)

It is assumed that readers have taken an introductory course in business statistics or general statistics. Since such an introductory course is required by nearly all business schools, this prerequisite ought not be restrictive. Brief reviews of essential statistical concepts are provided in an appendix and in the text proper for readers who do not remember these concepts well.

Some care has been taken, however, to arrange the topics in two "streams" so that most of the text could be used even in a first course in statistical methods or one emphasizing data analysis for exploratory purposes. The recommended sequence for this purpose is described later in this preface.

An interest in quantitative methods is presumed. High school mathematics is adequate for the main text. A second appendix provides selected mathematical derivations for the benefit of students familiar with calculus and linear algebra.

The text is designed to accommodate at least two types of course design. The first (the traditional approach for a technical course) requires students to do exercises and problems and to write exams. Under the second approach (frequently used in business courses), students, perhaps working in groups, read, report, and discuss cases using the text as a resource; they may also do a project and write a paper involving modeling and forecasting in business. The text contains examples, exercises, problems, and small and large cases suitable for either one or for a mixture of these two approaches.

It is generally acknowledged that substantial, real applications of methods are an essential and highly desirable component of a text addressed to an applications-oriented audience. A case is a description of a real situation that lends itself to the application of methods. A case can be thought of as a large problem inviting reflection and providing an opportunity for discussion. Unlike a standard problem, but very much like the real world, the appropriate solution may not be obvious or unique.

Most examples, problems, and cases are based on the author's experience, and their data are real—not contrived. For the purposes of this text, however, actual names, places, and data are sometimes changed, for several reasons. In the first place, and in order to avoid unnecessary obsolescence, dates such as 1992 are written as 19X2, and so on. Secondly, organization names are sometimes changed in order to avoid subjecting the original ones to unnecessary criticism (which students tend to dispense ferociously). Thirdly, the data are occasionally transformed in order to preserve the confidentiality of original sources. Despite these changes, however, the essential integrity of the data, the problem, and the setting has been meticulously preserved.

It is fair to say that none of the methods described in the text (not even simple regression with few observations) is manually executed these days. The computer has made possible not only the implementation of complicated methods, but also the streamlining of the teaching of these methods. In an applied course, there now appears to be little need to dwell on special cases and formulas (for example, analysis of variance) when the general case can be handled easily by the computer. Nor does it appear essential to describe complicated algorithms in detail if the objective of these algorithms can be stated clearly and tersely. For these reasons, the text emphasizes model formulation and interpretation rather than computation.

The text can be understood and many problems solved without the assistance of a computer program. However, the benefit from most of the cases and challenging problems cannot be realized—and the utility of the methods cannot be fully appreciated—without such assistance. It is, therefore, highly desirable that the student have access to a computer program capable of carrying out at least regression. The basic requirement is adequately fulfilled even by such "mainstream" business programs as Lotus and Excel. Programs such as SAS or SPSS are, of course, more than adequate. These or other programs (e.g., Minitab) form the ideal accompaniment to this text. The number of these programs is rapidly growing and their quality continually improving. The programs are becoming more and more user friendly, offering clear instructions, tutorials, and examples for implementing the methods described in the text either on-line or in their manuals. They can often be purchased at very reasonable retail or academic prices. It would consume too much space, therefore, for this text to provide instruction on the use of some of these programs and unwise to single out any one of them. For these reasons, the text is not designed to be supported by or to support any one particular program. The choice is the instructor's.

Supplementary Material

The text is accompanied by a *diskette* containing the data (in ASCII form) used in the text and the cases. The file `readme.txt` in this diskette provides additional information on reading the data files.

An *Instructor's Manual*, available to instructors from the publisher on request, includes solutions to all the problems, teaching notes describing the author's treatment of each case and possible alternatives, and the programs used by the author for the solution of most problems and cases.

Adopters of this text may download the contents of the data diskette and the *Instructor's Manual* from the publisher's Web site at www.wiley.com/college/wave. Also available at this site are two complete *supplementary chapters* on Factor Analysis and Cluster Analysis. These topics round out a survey of the principal methods for business analysis for instructors who share this view. The two chapters are offered as an experiment; if there is sufficient interest, they may be considered for inclusion in any future edition of this text.

A First Course

An introductory course in statistics or business statistics explains probability theory, special distributions, confidence intervals, and statistical tests. This background is necessary for a good understanding of Chapter 3, Sections 4.5 to 4.8, Chapter 9, Sections 10.6 to 10.8, and Section 13.7. These chapters and sections (marked with a † in the table of contents) form a separate stream that is not required elsewhere in the text. Regression and its extensions can be explained, *if* that is necessary or desired, simply as a method of fitting a mathematical model to a set of observations. Chapter 2 explains the method of least squares, measures of fit and contribution, and the statistics appearing in computer output. The remainder of Chapters 4 to 10 can be clearly understood with just this background. Chapters 11 through 13 are largely self-contained and do not rely heavily on statistical inference; a few references to background concepts in these chapters are explained in situ. It is, therefore, possible to use the text even for a first course in statistical methods or one emphasizing data analysis—obviously with a certain sacrifice of rigor but not so much of utility.

ACKNOWLEDGEMENTS

I am indebted to the following organizations and individuals for data and other assistance: NCH Promotional Services, especially Mr. Wayne Mouland, Vice President of Analytical Services; Consumers Gas, especially Ms. Janet Holder, Vice President, Energy Services; Statistics Canada; Decima Research, a division of Hill and Knowlton (Canada) Ltd.; the Insurance Bureau of Canada; and Ontario Hydro. None of the cases, problems or examples in this text, however, should be interpreted as describing the current practices and policies of these organizations.

I have had the pleasure of teaching many good students. Several of their projects became the sources of examples, problems, and cases, as I acknowledge in many places in the text.

I am also grateful to the following people for positive and negative comments on earlier drafts of this book that resulted in significant improvements: Professor Arilee Bagley, SUNY at New Paltz; Professor James Daly, California Polytechnic State University; Professor Marshall Freimer, University of Rochester; Professor Derek Hart, McGill University; Professor George A. Marcoulides, California State University at Fullerton; Professor Kris Moore, Baylor University; Professor Larry Richards, University of Oregon; Professor Gordon S. Roberts, York University; Professor Mack C. Shelley II, Iowa State University; Professor Rafael Solis, California State University at Fresno; Professor Jeff Steagall, University of North Florida; Professor Patrick A. Thompson, University of Florida; Professor N. Tryphonopoulos, York University; and Professor Rudy Wuilleumier, Eastern Kentucky University.

I owe the greatest debt to my wife Barbara, who read critically several drafts of the manuscript and brought clarity to more places than I care to enumerate.

Any errors that remain despite the help of so many are entirely my own.

CONTENTS

PART THREE: APPENDIXES   539

APPENDIX **A:** *STATISTICAL ESSENTIALS*   541

APPENDIX **B:** *MATHEMATICAL NOTES*   559

PART I

TEXT

CHAPTER *1*

INTRODUCTION

1.1 ANALYSIS AND FORECASTING

This, to repeat the title, is a text of methods for business analysis and forecasting. By *analysis* we have in mind the sifting through of available information in order to establish relationships and patterns. By *forecasting* we understand the projection of these relationships and patterns into the future. Analysis and forecasting are essential elements of most business problems.

The methods we shall be dealing with are quantitative, drawn primarily from the field of statistics. These are methods with applications not only in business and economics but also in engineering, the physical and social sciences, medicine, and many other fields.

Before we begin the study of these methods, it is useful to give some simple examples of problems we shall be addressing and to invite the reader to reflect on how he or she would approach these problems. The intention is not that the reader "solve" these problems at this stage; rather, it is hoped that this reflection will bring about some appreciation of the need for methods. The examples themselves are examined at greater length later on in this text.

1.2 CASE: LIFE INSURANCE

The simplest form of life insurance is the one-period term insurance policy: in return for a premium payable in advance, an insurance company agrees to pay the beneficiary of the insured the "face amount" in the event the insured dies during the period (e.g., one year) beginning on the date of issue of the policy. For example, the premium could be $100 and the face amount $20,000. In this case, the insurance company receives $100 on the date the policy is issued and will pay the beneficiary $20,000 if the insured person dies within one year from this date; if the insured does not die, the company does not pay anything.

The company, of course, cannot predict with certainty when the insured will die. If the insured dies within the year, the company will lose $19,900; if the insured does not die, the company gains $100.

An insurance company sells not one but many such policies. Some of its clients will die; some will survive. The company will make a profit if the payments to insureds who die do not exceed the revenue from premiums collected (for simplicity, we ignore the time value of money and other expenses). For example, if N one-year term policies for $20,000 are sold at an annual premium of $100 and we let n stand for the number of insureds who die, the company makes a profit if

$$(100)N - (20,000)n > 0$$

or, if

$$\frac{n}{N} < \frac{100}{20,000} = 0.005$$

—in words, if the death rate among its clients (n/N) is less than 0.5%.

The same reasoning can be used to solve for the break-even premium (or "pure" premium, as it is known in the industry). Let the premium be denoted by P and assume, for example, that the forecast death rate for a certain group of insureds is 0.10, all insured for $20,000. The expected profit is

$$PN - (20,000)(0.1N) = N(P - 2000)$$

The break-even premium (P_0) is such that expected profit is zero—in this case, $P_0 = 2000$.

In practice, the actual premium equals the pure premium times a "mark-up factor," allowing the company to cover other expenses and make a profit. For example, if the markup factor is 1.25, the actual premium for the policy will be (1.25)(2000) or $2500.

A critical element determining the premium for this type of policy, therefore, is the forecast death rate. Since the death rate, as we very well know, varies with age, insurance companies charge different premiums to insureds of different ages. Death rates also depend on gender: much to the envy of men, women tend to live longer. Figure 1.1 shows the observed annual death rates in the past twenty years per thousand men and women in the 40–44 and 60–64 age groups (0 is the current year, −20 stands for twenty years ago). The data can be found in the file `drates.dat` in the diskette accompanying this text.

How would you forecast the death rate for any given gender and age?

1.3 CASE: THE METROPOLITAN TRANSIT COMMISSION

The Metropolitan Transit Commission (MTC) operates streetcars, buses, and a subway in a large metropolitan area. An important part of planning at the MTC is a detailed forecast of monthly revenue. Since a uniform fare is charged

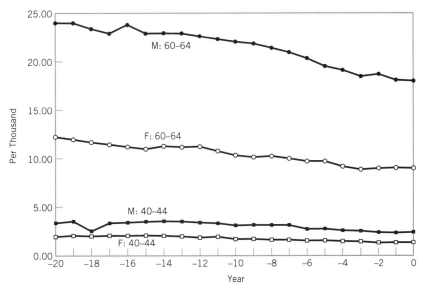

FIGURE 1.1   Death rates by gender and selected age group

for all rides regardless of origin and destination, a forecast is required of the number of passengers to be carried each month over the next year.

A series is available (file `mtc.dat`) showing the number of passengers carried each month in the past six years. A plot of this series is shown in Figure 1.2.

It can be observed that the number of passengers tends to rise over time—the entire series appears to follow an increasing trend. It is also clear that the series follows a fairly stable seasonal pattern; note, for example, that ridership tends to be low in the summer and high in the winter months.

How would you forecast the number of MTC passengers for each month of the next year?

1.4   CASE: SALARY AND EXPERIENCE

Professional organizations of accountants, engineers, systems analysts, and others regularly survey their members for information concerning salaries, pensions, and conditions of employment. One product of these surveys is the so-called salary curve, illustrated in Figure 1.3, which relates salary to years of experience.

The salary curve is said to show the "normal" or "typical" salary of professionals with a given number of years of experience. It is of considerable interest to members of the profession who like to know where they stand

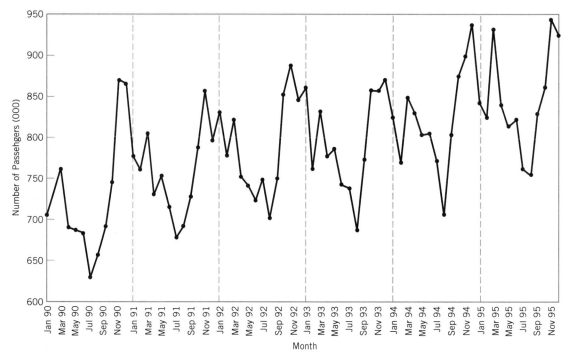

FIGURE 1.2 MTC passengers

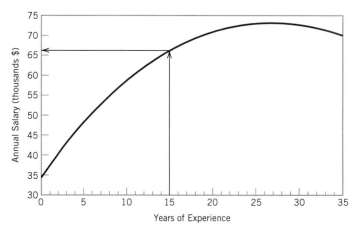

FIGURE 1.3 Salary vs. years of experience

among their peers. It is also valuable to personnel departments of businesses considering salary adjustments or intending to hire new professionals. As shown in Figure 1.3, a firm planning to hire a professional with 15 years of experience may decide that the "normal" salary of about $66,000 for that level of experience is appropriate.

The raw data for this graph, however, come from a survey of professionals (file `profsal.dat`) and look like Figure 1.4.

Each point on this "scatter diagram" represents the pair (salary, years of experience) of one professional. The diagram may show several professionals with the same experience but different salaries. Also, there may be no professional with a given number of years of experience (e.g., 17 years exactly).

How should a salary curve be calculated on the basis of such raw data as that illustrated in Figure 1.4?

1.5   CASE: THE CITY OF WEST YORK

Recent legislation requires that the City of West York—together with other municipalities—switch to the market value system of property assessment (MVA). Under this system, the amount of tax levied against a property is proportional to its market value.

Market value, in turn, is defined as the highest amount that the property can be expected to realize if sold in the open market by a willing seller to a

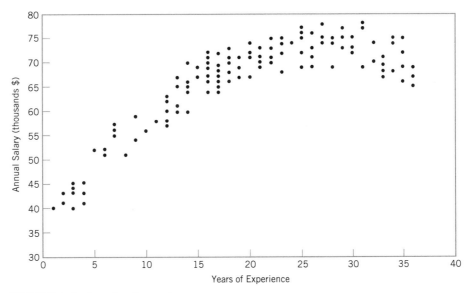

FIGURE 1.4   Raw data from salary survey

willing buyer, with both parties having full knowledge of all the uses to which the property might be put.

When the MVA system comes into effect, therefore, each of the 200,000-odd residential properties in the city must be assessed a market value. These assessed values must be maintained and revised in subsequent years to reflect changing market conditions (resulting, for example, from the deterioration of some neighborhoods). The property tax in a given year will be calculated by multiplying the assessed value by the city's "mill rate," a common rate applicable to all residential properties in the city. For example, if two properties have assessed market values of $150,000 and $300,000 and the mill rate is 1%, their annual property taxes will be $1500 and $3000, respectively.

The problem, of course, is how to determine the market values of all 200,000 properties. Recently sold properties present no difficulty, but only a small fraction of properties are usually sold in a short period of time, such as a month, quarter, or year.

A common method for valuing residential property views the market value of a property as determined by its features. For example, a very simple formula for forecasting market value with the help of just two features is

$$\text{EST. VALUE} = b_0 + b_1(\text{LOT SIZE}) + b_2(\text{FLOOR AREA})$$

b_0, b_1, and b_2 are "parameters," that is, numbers to be specified. Lot size and floor area are measured in square feet. The expression suggests that to forecast the market value of a given residential property, one starts with a base figure (b_0), adds to that so much (b_1) per square foot of the property's lot size, and adds to the result so much (b_2) per square foot of the floor area of the property. This formula may be called "additive," in contrast to the "multiplicative"

$$\text{EST. VALUE} = b_0(\text{LOT SIZE})^{b_1}(\text{FLOOR AREA})^{b_2}$$

In the latter form, the base figure is multiplied by a factor depending on the lot size and another depending on the floor area.

Whichever the form, the key issue is how to determine the values of the parameters b_0, b_1, and b_2. Once these parameters are specified, the estimated market value of every property in the city can be calculated from the formula using lot size and floor area as input.

The city maintains a file for each property, which includes information on such features of the property as its location, lot size and shape, the type and floor area of the house, number of floors, number of rooms, number of bathrooms, type of garage (if any), type of driveway (if any), and so on. In addition, the city has access to the dates of sale and the selling prices of properties sold in the past.

How would you determine the parameters of the preceding (or similar) formulas? Which formula is best? How good is this approach to property valuation?

1.6 CASE: STOCK PRICES

You are considering investing in a given stock—say, ABC common shares. You know today's price of one ABC common share; it is, say, $10. You plan to buy now and sell later. *If* you are certain that the future price will be greater than $10, you will buy; *if* you are certain that the future price will be less than $10, you will not buy. The key to this decision, of course, is the unknown future price. The question is, for forecasting the future price, is it useful to know the past history of the stock's price?

Technical analysts would answer this question affirmatively. In their view, stock prices form trends and patterns. These patterns may be simple or complicated, and their detection may be easy or difficult. However, if correctly detected, patterns can be exploited for better forecasts and decisions. Consider Figure 1.5 by way of illustration.

In all panels, the solid line shows the past history of the price of a stock. The four panels illustrate, respectively, (a) a smooth increasing trend, (b) a smooth decreasing trend, (c) a stable, wavelike pattern, and (d) an upward, wavelike pattern.

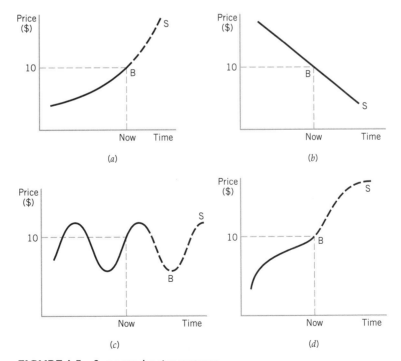

FIGURE 1.5 Some stock price patterns

Some technical analysts would argue that reasonable people should project the observed pattern and forecast the future price of the stock roughly as indicated by the dotted line in each panel. Points in time at which the stock should be bought (B) or sold (S) are also indicated. (In panel b, one could "go short," that is, borrow a share to sell now, repaying the debt by buying later.) For these cases at least, knowledge of the past history of the price of the stock would appear to be useful.

Of course, observed stock price patterns rarely are as simple as those illustrated in Figure 1.5. If they were so obvious, the very actions of investors buying low and selling high would raise the lows and lower the highs, effectively smoothing out the pattern almost before it could be observed. Technical analysts' patterns tend to be more complicated—so complicated, some have protested, as to almost *require* the assistance of a technical analyst for their detection.

The existence of a pattern suggests that the price of a stock "next" period depends on (is a function of) the past prices of the stock. A very simple function, for example—not the type technical analysts have in mind—is as follows:

$$P_{t+1} = b + b_0 P_t + b_1 P_{t-1} + b_2 P_{t-2} + \cdots + b_k P_{t-k}$$

In words, the price of the stock next period (P_{t+1}) depends in a linear fashion on the price of the stock "now" (P_t), and its price one period ago (P_{t-1}), two periods ago (P_{t-2}), and so on, down to the price of the stock k periods ago (P_{t-k}). $b, b_1, b_2, \ldots, b_k$ and k are parameters to be specified.

How does one find out if such patterns do indeed exist? If they do exist, how can they be measured?

1.7   CASE: MORTGAGE LOANS

The main task of a mortgage loan officer is to ensure that the loan is repaid when it matures. The loan application contains information on the applicant's characteristics (gender, age, marital status, occupation, income, number of dependents, etc.), loan characteristics (loan amount, maturity, purpose, interest rate, loan fee, monthly payment, ratio of loan amount to appraised value of the property, etc.), and property characteristics (location, type, construction, lot size, etc.). On the basis of this information, the loan officer must either approve or reject the loan application.

Despite the care with which loan applications are usually evaluated, some mortgage loans become delinquent (that is, the contractual payments fall behind schedule). Among these, some must be foreclosed and the properties repossessed and sold in order to recover the amount loaned. The latter are unpleasant and costly procedures that financial institutions making mortgage loans (commercial banks, savings banks, saving and loan associations) try hard to avoid.

A financial institution has the files of currently delinquent mortgage loans, of loans that were foreclosed during the past two years, and of the mortgage loans currently in good standing. Each of these files contains the original application, with the information on applicant, loan, and property exactly as given to the loan officer at the time of the loan application.

How would you construct a "decision rule" based on this information to assist loan officers in making better decisions in the future? For example, a simple—and *not* recommended—decision rule is to reject all applications by single unmarried persons earning less than $50,000 per year, in which the ratio of loan amount to appraised value of the property is greater than 0.7; approve all other applications.

1.8 EXACT AND APPROXIMATE RELATIONSHIPS

Each of the preceding cases has its own individual distinctive features, but all share two common principal features.

First, forecasts are required: forecasts of death rates in the life insurance case, of the number of passengers to be carried monthly by the MTC, of the normal salary for a given number of years of professional experience, of the market value of a property that has not been sold recently, of the future price of a company's shares, and of the quality of a mortgage loan application.

Second, theory or experience suggests there is a relationship between the variable of interest (the *dependent variable*, as we shall call it from now on) and other variables determining that of interest (the *explanatory variables*): the relationship between death rate, on the one hand, and gender, age, and time, on the other; the relationship between number of passengers, on the one hand, and time and month of the year, on the other; the relationship between salary and years of experience; the relationship between price and features of a property; the relationship between the current and past prices of a given stock; and the relationship between loan quality, on the one hand, and applicant, loan, and property characteristics, on the other.

The key to successful forecasting would seem to be the accurate measurement of the underlying relationships. If a formula could be written in each case describing the relationship well, then one would only need to "plug into" it the values of the explanatory variables in order to forecast the dependent variable.

Indeed, those steeped in the deterministic scientific tradition would say, for every effect there is a cause or causes. For every variable of interest there exist a number of other causal variables and a relationship that specifies how these variables determine the variable of interest.

Imagine, for example, having to forecast (do not ask why) the trajectory of a projectile—an artillery shell, a kicked football, or a struck baseball. Suppose the projectile is launched from a height h, at an angle θ to the ground, with initial speed V, as illustrated in Figure 1.6.

In the absence of air resistance and assuming the acceleration due to gravity is constant, the height y of the projectile at time t after its launch is given by

$$y = h + V\sin(\theta)t - \frac{gt^2}{2} \tag{1.1}$$

where $g \approx 9.8 \, \text{m/sec}^2$ is the gravitational constant.[1] The height y is the variable of interest. Initial speed (V), angle (θ), and height (h), and time (t) are the determining (causal) variables. Eq. 1.1 is the relationship showing how the causal variables determine the height of the projectile.

To predict the height of a projectile launched from a height of, say, 0.5 meters, at speed $V = 20 \, \text{m/sec}$ and angle $\theta = 45°$ to the ground, after $t = 2$ seconds of flight, one simply substitutes these numerical values of the determining variables into Eq. 1.1, to get

$$y = (0.5) + (20)\sin(45°)(2) - (9.8)(2)^2/2 = (0.5) + (20)(0.707)(2) - (9.8)(2)^2/2$$

or 9.18 meters.

In general, a determinist would say, to forecast the value of any variable of interest identify the explanatory variables, determine their relationship to the variable of interest, and enter their values into the resulting formula.

This is not bad advice, but it must be tempered by an awareness that in the world of business and economics the number of determining variables is often very large, many are unknown, some are not measured correctly, the exact form of their relationship to the variable of interest is complicated or poorly understood, and their values are not known when the forecast must be made. In fact, these difficulties are not confined to business and economics.

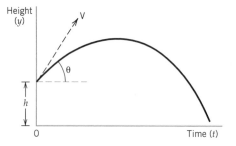

FIGURE 1.6   Trajectory of projectile

[1]See, for example, D. Hart and T. Croft, *Modelling with Projectiles*, Ellis Horwood/Wiley, 1988, Ch. 2.

It is not as easy, for example, to forecast the trajectory of a projectile having irregular shape and subject to air resistance and varying acceleration.

In practice, therefore, we rarely seek to discover exact relationships but good, *approximate* relationships, those involving the more important explanatory variables, the values of which can be known at the time the forecasts are made or themselves forecast with reasonable confidence. In other words, we seek to construct a workable *model* of the exact relationship.

A simple case will illustrate both the difficulties of attempting to estimate an exact relationship and the reasonably good expected performance of approximate ones.

1.9   CASE: GAS CONSUMPTION

You are asked to forecast next month's consumption of natural gas of a small office building.

In this building, gas is used for space heating only (not for water heating, air conditioning, or any other use). The building is one story, detached, constructed of brick. It is located in a northern city and houses a computer software firm. The gas furnace is controlled by a thermostat, which turns the furnace on when the room temperature drops to a certain lower limit and turns the furnace off when the room temperature reaches an upper limit. These limits have not been and will not be altered.

Perhaps your first attempt at forecasting may begin with the observation that a gas furnace consumes gas at a constant rate per unit of time when it is on—for example, at the rate of c cubic meters per hour it is on. This rate can be obtained from the furnace manufacturer or determined by observing the gas meter. Either way, the relationship between gas consumption and time on is exact and very simple:

$$(\text{Gas consumption}) = (c)(\text{Hours on})$$

This relationship would indeed produce an accurate forecast of next month's gas consumption, *provided* that the total time on of the furnace next month could be specified. That, however, is not known in advance.

Knowledge of the exact relationship between the variable of interest and determining variables, therefore, is not sufficient for accurate forecasting if the determining variables themselves must be forecast as well. For the original problem of forecasting gas consumption is transformed into the equally difficult problem of forecasting the total time the furnace will be on.

But you may wish to persevere. *Which* factors determine how long the furnace will be on next month?

The thermostat, you will undoubtedly observe, is triggered by the room temperature. When the furnace is not on, room temperature is determined by the outside temperature: heat is lost and room temperature declines when the outside temperature is less than room temperature, and vice versa. The rate of heat loss or gain depends on wind speed, the building insulation, the number of people in the building, and on such heat-producing appliances as lights, computers, and printers. *If* the outside temperature and the rate of heat loss and gain could be specified for every point in time next month, the time the furnace will be on can be calculated, and the preceding equation can be used to forecast the gas consumption next month.

Obviously, this forecasting attempt is daunting and its requirements formidable. You may be inclined, therefore, to give up the attempt to set up an exact relationship in favor of an approximate but more workable one.

Remembering that the task is to forecast next *month's* gas consumption, you may start by examining past monthly bills from the gas utility. Nearly six years of monthly bills are available. Figure 1.7 shows that the monthly gas consumption varies greatly, from about 0 to nearly 700 cubic meters. The average consumption is 233 m^3. (The data can be found in the file `ogas.dat`.)

Would you use this average (233) as a forecast of next month's gas consumption? You may consider this overall average a reasonable forecast of a month's consumption if the month in question cannot be specified. However,

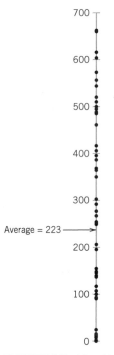

FIGURE 1.7   Monthly gas consumption, in cubic meters

the monthly bills do indicate the month to which they refer, and, almost certainly, the identity of "next" month is known. Figure 1.8 shows the gas consumption by month over the six-year period, beginning with a January and ending with a November bill.

Figure 1.8 confirms—if confirmation were needed—that gas consumption tends to be high in winter months and low in summer months. Figure 1.7, of course, is Figure 1.8 with all the observations projected to the vertical axis. For example, the two largest observations in Figure 1.7 are for January of the first year (663) and December of the fourth year (666). The lines joining the observations have no meaning, but they help guide the eye in detecting the monthly pattern. The gap in the graph is due to a missing observation for February of the fifth year.

Figure 1.9 displays the monthly pattern of gas consumption in a different manner. The pattern is rather stable in that it tends to be repeated—but not, of course, identically—year after year.

To forecast the gas consumption in a given month, therefore, you may consider it reasonable to use as your forecast the average consumption for that month in the past six years. These averages are shown in Figure 1.10, and the forecasts can be read directly from that graph.

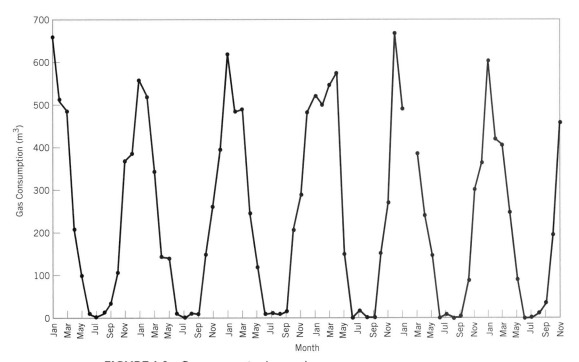

FIGURE 1.8 Gas consumption by month

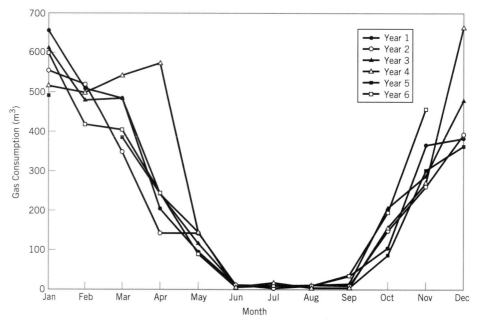

FIGURE 1.9   Monthly pattern of gas consumption

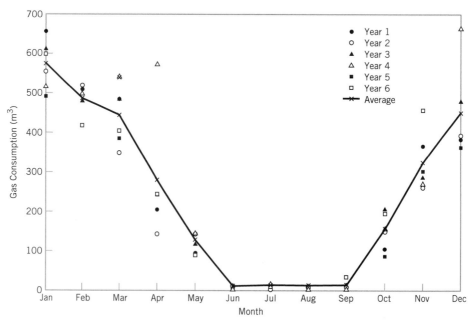

FIGURE 1.10   Average gas consumption by month

For example, a forecast of gas consumption in January (*any* January) would be 576 m³, 487 m³ in February, and so on. Figure 1.10 also shows graphically how good these "forecasts" (more appropriately, "backcasts") would have been in comparison to the actual monthly observations over the past six years. The approximate relationship here is not a formula but a list giving the estimated gas consumption for each month of the year. Let us call this the *first* approach for forecasting gas consumption.

You realize, of course, that the month of the year is not a causal variable (it is not the name *January* that causes consumption to be high) but a surrogate for the principal causal variable: temperature. You may wish to explore, therefore, an alternative model, one relating consumption to temperature.

Figure 1.11 is a simultaneous plot of gas consumption and temperature (to be precise, the monthly average of the average daily temperatures, in °C).

Observe that as temperature increases, gas consumption tends to decrease, and vice versa. This tendency is clearly visible in the scatter diagram shown in Figure 1.12, in which each month's pair of gas consumption and temperature values is shown as a point.

It appears that the straight line shown in Figure 1.12 approximates rather well the relationship between gas consumption and temperature. (We do not

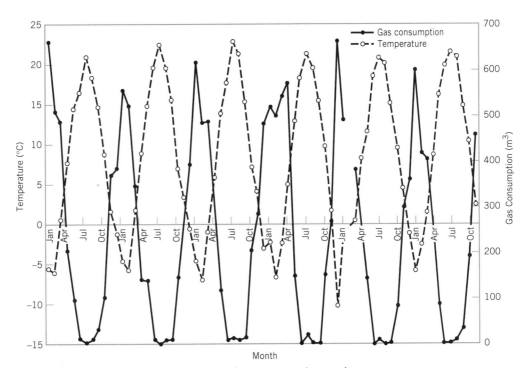

FIGURE 1.11 Gas consumption and temperature, by month

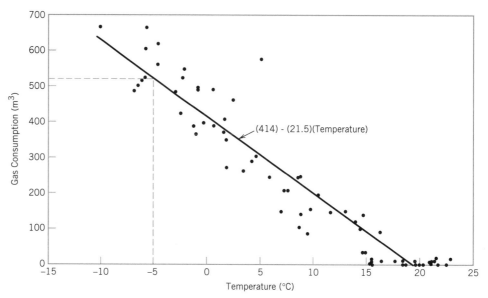

FIGURE 1.12   Scatter diagram of gas consumption and temperature

suggest that a straight line is the only possible approximation or that it is the best one.) This line can be expressed as a formula (we explain why in the next chapter) as follows:

$$\text{(Est. Gas Consumption)} = (414) - (21.5)(\text{Temperature}) \qquad (1.2)$$

For example, if the temperature in a given month is $-5°C$, the estimated gas consumption for that month would be about 520 m³, as shown in Figure 1.12.

Clearly, you would not want to extrapolate this line too far. Figure 1.12 suggests that when temperature exceeds about 19°C, gas consumption ceases. Perhaps then you may consider it reasonable to use the following model for forecasting gas consumption:

$$\text{Est. Gas Consumption} = \begin{cases} (414) - (21.5)(\text{Temperature}), & \text{if Temperature} \leq 19; \\ 0, & \text{otherwise.} \end{cases}$$

$$(1.3)$$

In words, forecast using the line in Figure 1.12 or Eq. 1.2 for temperatures below 19°C, or forecast zero consumption otherwise.

This model, it will be noted, requires a forecast of next month's temperature in order to forecast next month's gas consumption. Until a better method comes along, you may consider it reasonable to use the average temperature in the past as a forecast of that month's temperature in the future.

An alternative method for forecasting a given month's gas consumption, therefore, could proceed in two steps: first, determine the average temperature for that month in the past; second, using Model 1.3, determine the gas consumption corresponding to that temperature. Let us call this the *second* approach.

The average January temperature during the past six years was −3.9°C; the forecast of January gas consumption using Eq. 1.2 would be

$$(414) - (21.5)(-3.9) = 498 \text{ m}^3$$

The average February temperature in the past six years was −5.52; the forecast February gas consumption would be 533 m³. And so on. (Note that these forecasts are different from those obtained with the first approach.) The closeness of the actual observations to the relationship between gas consumption and temperature (Figure 1.12) supports the belief that forecasts based on this second model will be reasonably accurate.

You may have been rather disappointed at the small scale of this case study—after all, how important is it to forecast the gas consumption of an office building? If this is so, consider how you would forecast the *daily* gas consumption for *the utility* that supplies natural gas to the city in which the office building is located. Such forecasts are indeed made by the utility for one, two, and more days ahead in order to estimate the required pipeline flow and any withdrawals from or additions to gas inventories. Figure 1.13 shows the scatter diagram of daily gas consumption (in thousands of cubic meters) and mean daily temperature (in degrees centigrade) observed during a period of thirteen months. (The data can be found in the file norgas.dat.)

It can be noted that there is an approximate relationship between aggregate daily gas consumption and temperature, resembling the one concerning the office building and monthly consumption.

Two similar models may be considered for forecasting the daily gas consumption in the city. In the first model, a given day's observed average gas consumption would be used as the forecast of that day's consumption in the future. The second model would utilize the relationship between daily gas consumption and temperature, and would use the observed average daily temperature in a given day as input to this relationship in order to obtain the forecast of that day's gas consumption in the future.

But there is also a third possibility, which exploits the availability of short-term forecasts of temperature. Government and private weather services regularly provide forecasts of daily weather characteristics one, two, and more days ahead. These forecasts (not always accurate) could be used as input to the model relating daily gas consumption to temperature. In other words,

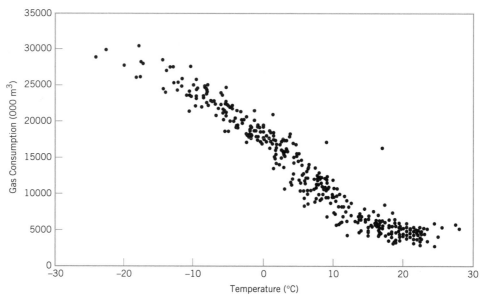

FIGURE 1.13 City daily gas consumption and temperature

this third model would consist of a *system of two equations,* perhaps as follows:

$$T = a + bF$$
$$G = c + dT$$

where F is the forecast of the day's temperature, T; G the daily gas consumption; and a through d are parameters to be specified.

The first equation would give the estimated temperature (T) for a given forecast of that day's temperature (F). The quantity T would then be used as input to the second equation to obtain the estimated gas consumption (G) that day.

The preceding equations are assumed to be linear, but this is not mandatory. For example, an elongated z-shaped curve could better describe the relationship shown in Figure 1.13. The first equation would have to be estimated in a similar fashion from the scatter diagram of actual and forecast daily temperatures. Of course, other weather characteristics such as wind speed, sunshine, and humidity could be added to any one of these models to improve the forecasts.

But we have been carried further than is useful at this stage. Our purpose was not to solve this problem conclusively but to justify our assertion that reasonably good results can often be expected from a model approximating an exact relationship. We shall return to this case later in the text, at which point we shall have the required data and will be equipped with the tools necessary to estimate and evaluate these and other models.

1.10 TO CARRY FORWARD

It would be premature, at this early stage, to advise how to construct a good model. Experience and practice are needed. It would not be at all harmful, however, to keep in mind the following observations and tentative recommendations suggested by the cases examined in the previous sections.

- Even if one agrees that for every effect there exist causes and a mechanism that relates causes to effect, in the large majority of situations in business and economics the number of causal variables, their values, and the form of the mechanism are not known.
- In order to forecast a particular variable, we seek a good approximation— a good *model*—of the exact relationship, involving variables the values of which can be known when the forecast is made or themselves forecast with some confidence.
- The quality of a model should depend on at least two considerations: first, how convincingly the model captures the essentials of the assumed true mechanism, and, second, how well the forecasts approximate the actual values of the variable of interest.
- Finally, and other things being nearly equal, a simple model should be preferable to a more complicated one.

An important—and, in the view of this author, the most important— ingredient is the knowledge of the situation or problem for which the model is intended. This is knowledge that comes from an understanding of economic theory and the theory of the business disciplines. It is also the factual knowledge of the specific situation and problem.

It is this knowledge—and not any technique—that often tells us which variables influence the dependent variable, which are important, in which direction each influences the dependent variable, and what is the general form of the relationship. This is knowledge that academic curricula and experience provide. It is assumed to be shared by all the readers of this text.

Yet this knowledge is often not sufficient. Theory and experience frequently provide only a tentative framework. Often, they cannot specify conclusively and unequivocally the explanatory variables, their importance, or the exact form of the relationships. It is an empirical task to refine the tentative framework on the basis of the available information and data so as to arrive at a specific, usable, and useful model. It is for this task that the methods presented in the text are intended.

I.II THE BOOK IN OUTLINE

In Part I of this book we survey the principal methods for business analysis and forecasting.

We begin in *Chapter 2* with the simplest type of relationship—linear and involving only numeric variables. If the objective is to find the linear relationship providing the best fit to the available observations, the method of least squares (or "regression," as it has come to be called) may be applied. The method also provides measures for judging the quality of fit of the estimated relationship and the contribution of the explanatory variables.

In *Chapter 3* we consider the process that has generated the observations or the population from which the observations were selected. We show that if this process or population has certain special features, the method of least squares has additional desirable properties. It is also possible to test hypotheses concerning the process or population parameters and to construct confidence intervals for these parameters and the model's forecasts.

Next, in *Chapter 4*, we examine how to estimate relationships involving attributes ("qualitative variables"). The market value of a real estate property, for example, depends not only on lot size and floor area (both numeric variables) but also on location (an attribute). Indeed, there is hardly a relationship in business and economics wthat does not involve an attribute, and a method that could not take into account such attributes would be severely limited. We show, however, that the method of least squares can easily deal with attributes by means of special "dummy" or "indicator" variables. This chapter also describes "analysis of variance," a special case of regression in which all explanatory variables are attributes.

One reason for the popularity and widespread use of regression is its ability to handle not only linear but also nonlinear relationships. We shall see in *Chapter 5* that some nonlinear relationships can be estimated simply by applying regression to transformations of the original variables. When these simple solutions fail, the special technique of nonlinear least squares may be utilized.

Very often in business and economics the observations are time series—sequences of yearly, quarterly, monthly, or other season-related data. Time series often exhibit trend (a long-run tendency) and seasonality (a regular variation about the trend associated with the seasons). In *Chapter 6*—and later in *Chapter 10*—we examine special problems associated with the analysis and forecasting of time series and their "adjustment" for seasonality.

When dealing with time series, it happens frequently that the variable of interest depends not only on current but also on past values of the explanatory variables. For example, it is generally held that advertising creates an impression that lasts past the period in which the advertising expenditure is incurred. We can therefore say that the sales of a product depend—among other factors—on advertising expenditures in this and past periods. The measurement of such lagged relationships and of the pattern of lagged effects is the subject of *Chapter 7*.

Chapter 8 deals with a variety of shorter topics in regression, including the possible automation of the search for a good model by means of systematic addition or removal of explanatory variables or attributes, the imposition of equality or inequality constraints on the parameters of a model, the minimization of the sum of absolute deviations as an alternative criterion of fit, and elements of experimental design.

In *Chapter 9* we examine what happens when the special features of the process or population in Chapter 3 are violated and describe simple remedies for some of these violations.

In *Chapters 11* and *12* we consider "dependent attributes". For there are many situations like the mortgage loan case described in Section 1.7 in which we wish to explain and forecast the *category* of an attribute into which an observation belongs with the help of other attributes and variables. In Chapter 11 we examine this classification problem in general, while in Chapter 12 we consider some useful special cases including models for predicting probabilities and for discriminant analysis.

Chapter 13 investigates models consisting of more than one equation (such as the third model for daily gas consumption in Section 1.9) and the special problems of estimation and inference in such multiequation models.

Numerous problems of varying degree of difficulty at the end of each chapter will help test the understanding of the methods surveyed in Part I.

In the real world, however, rarely are problems presented in a way that makes obvious the choice of the method to be used. Often the selection of a suitable method is as much a part of the problem as the implementation of the selected method. The cases in Part II of the book offer an opportunity for selecting and applying the methods studied to concrete situations and problems.

CHAPTER 2

REGRESSION

2.1   INTRODUCTION AND SUMMARY

We saw in the last chapter that successful analysis and forecasting, require approximating as closely as possible the relationship between the variable of interest (the "dependent" variable, as we agreed to call it) and other determining ("explanatory") variables. The approximate relationship is the "model" of the true, but unknown, relationship.

A relationship may be simple or complicated. As we progress through the text, we shall examine ever more complicated relationships, but we begin in this chapter with the simplest type—the linear relationship. For example, the hypothesized relationship described in Section 1.5 between the estimated value of a residential property, on the one hand, and its lot size and floor area, on the other,

$$\text{EST. VALUE} = b_0 + b_1(\text{LOT SIZE}) + b_2(\text{FLOOR AREA})$$

is linear in the parameters b_0, b_1, and b_2.

Regression is a method for determining the parameters of a linear relationship in such a way as to approximate (to fit) the actual values of the dependent variable as closely as possible. The criterion of fit is "least squares," that is, the minimization of the sum of squared deviations between actual and estimated values of the dependent variable. Although other criteria of fit are possible, the method of least squares is widely used because of its ease of use and its desirable properties.

The bulk of this chapter is devoted to a description of the method of least squares and its implementation by computer programs. Our very first case study, however, will show that in practice the best model is rarely obvious at the beginning of the study. Often, a number of models must be considered, involving different subsets of the available explanatory variables. It is thus necessary to examine how to measure the quality of a model and the contribution of one or more explanatory variables. We conclude the chapter with several examples illustrating the application of regression and of these measurements.

2.2 LINEAR RELATIONSHIPS

Knowledge, experience, or intuition may tell us that there is a relationship between a variable, Y, in which we happen to be especially interested and a number of other variables, $X_1, X_2, X_3, \ldots$. We call Y the *dependent variable*, and $X_1, X_2, X_3, \ldots$ the *explanatory variables*. We say that Y is a function of $X_1, X_2, X_3, \ldots$, and write this schematically as

$$\underbrace{Y}_{dependent} = f(\underbrace{X_1, X_2, X_3, \ldots}_{explanatory})$$

The number of possible explanatory variables is usually very large, so that even if there exists an exact relationship between Y and all the X's, that is, a relationship in which for every value of the X's there is one and only one value of Y, the form of the exact relationship $f()$ and many of the explanatory variables may not be known. We hope to approximate Y with a function of k of explanatory variables (perhaps, if we are fortunate, the principal explanatory variables) $X_1, X_2, \ldots, X_k$. We write $Y \approx g(X_1, X_2, \ldots, X_k)$, or

$$Y = g(X_1, X_2, \ldots, X_k) + \varepsilon$$

where ε (called *error* or *disturbance*) represents the combined effect of the omitted variables and the form of the exact relationship. In other words, the error is the difference between actual and approximate Y-value, $\varepsilon = Y - g(X_1, X_2, \ldots, X_k)$. Thus, for every set of values of the k explanatory variables $X_1, X_2, \ldots, X_k$, there corresponds not one but a number of values of Y, depending at least in part on the values of the omitted explanatory variables.

The simplest relationship between Y and $X_1, X_2, \ldots, X_k$ is the *linear* one:

$$Y = \beta_0 + \beta_1 X_1 + \beta_2 X_2 + \cdots + \beta_k X_k + \varepsilon \qquad (2.1)$$

where $\beta_0, \beta_1, \beta_2, \ldots$, and β_k are the $(k+1)$ *parameters* of the model. These parameters must be estimated on the basis of n sets of observations on Y and the explanatory variables $X_1, X_2, \ldots, X_k$. Until further notice, Y and all the X's will be assumed to be variables, not attributes.[1]

---

[1] *Variables* have natural numerical values; *attributes*, or, as they are also called, qualitative variables, are described in terms of categories. For example, age, temperature, distance, and weight are variables; sex (male, female), marital status (single, married, divorced, other) are attributes. Attributes as explanatory variables are treated in Chapter 4; attributes as dependent variables are considered later in Chapters 11 and 12.

One procedure by which the parameters of this relationship are estimated has come to be called called a *regression* of Y on $X_1, X_2, \ldots, X_k$, and the estimated parameters are referred to as the *regression estimates*. These terms will be clarified shortly.

The linear model, 2.1, will be the subject of this and following chapters. Although, obviously, not all relationships are linear, the linear model with its variants can provide a good approximation to a large variety of relationships in business and economics.

EXAMPLE 2.1

According to a widely used definition, the value of a house is the price that it would fetch in a free market if it were offered for sale and sold. This price is commonly assumed to be a function of the features of the house: the size of the lot, the size of the house proper, the number of bathrooms, the location of the property, the type of construction, the type and condition of the driveway and garage, the quality of landscaping, and so on—a large number of features influence the price of a real estate property. Among those just listed, it will be noted, some are variables (e.g., the size of the lot), some are attributes (e.g., the quality of landscaping). If it were possible to identify all the features, then at a given point in time two properties with identical features ought to fetch the same price.

Suppose, however, we can observe only two features—say, the lot area and the floor area. Clearly, we shall not be surprised to find two houses with the same lot and floor area sold at different prices at the same time. Nevertheless, knowing the lot and floor area of a house helps to predict its price; our predictions will be better with this knowledge than without it. In other words, we believe there is an approximate relationship between price, on the one hand, and lot area and floor area, on the other, which we write:

$$PRICE = g(FLOOR\ AREA,\ LOT\ AREA) + \varepsilon$$

It may be reasonable to further assume that the relationship is linear, in which case the price of a house can be expressed as

$$PRICE = \beta_0 + \beta_1(FLOOR\ AREA) + \beta_2(LOT\ AREA) + \varepsilon$$

This linear model may not necessarily be the best, but it is simple and may provide a good starting point.

The model is intended for forecasts in the short run, that is, in a period short enough to justify the assumption that the parameters β_0, β_1, and β_2 are constant. Obviously, a different model is required to explain and forecast house prices over a period in which population, incomes, and tastes—among many other variables—have varied or are expected to vary substantially.

The next question is, how are β_0, β_1, and β_2 to be estimated? Real estate appraisers, who often implicitly use a similar model in assessing properties, rely on recent house sales for information. Usually, a very small proportion of the stock of houses changes hands in a short period of time. Suppose $n = 100$ residential properties were sold within a short period of time, and the information shown in Table 2.1 is available.

The question, once again, is how do we estimate β_0, β_1, and β_2 on the basis of this information? ∎

2.3 ESTIMATION CRITERIA

In general, suppose that n sets of observations are available on the dependent variable Y and the explanatory variables $X_1, X_2, \ldots, X_k$. Let $b_0, b_1, b_2, \ldots, b_k$ be any one set of estimates of the unknown parameters $\beta_0, \beta_1, \ldots, \beta_k$ of Model 2.1. The *estimated value* of Y corresponding to given values of the explanatory variables is

$$\hat{Y} = b_0 + b_1 X_1 + b_2 X_2 + \cdots + b_k X_k \tag{2.2}$$

The terms *expected, fitted, forecast,* or *explained* are also used in place of *estimated,* The *residual,* the difference between actual and estimated value of Y, is

$$\hat{\varepsilon} = Y - \hat{Y} = Y - b_0 - b_1 X_1 - b_2 X_2 - \cdots - b_k X_k \tag{2.3}$$

For a given set of estimates of the parameters, there is a set of n estimated values, $\hat{Y}$, and residuals, $\hat{\varepsilon}$.

To illustrate, suppose that there is only one explanatory variable and that the model is $Y = \beta_0 + \beta_1 X + \varepsilon$. Suppose further there are $n = 3$ pairs of observations on X and Y, as shown in columns 1 and 2 of Table 2.2.

TABLE 2.1   Real Estate Sales

Prop. No.	Price, Y ($000)	Floor area, X_1 (sq ft)	Lot area, X_2 (sq ft)
1	213.75	740	1,854
2	195.00	914	1,256
...	...	...	...
100	305.00	962	2,320

SOURCE: File `rest.dat`

TABLE 2.2 Data Illustrating a Simple Linear Model

Y (1)	X (2)	$b_0 = 1, b_1 = 0.8$ $\hat{Y} = 1 + 0.8X$ (3)	$\hat{\varepsilon} = Y - \hat{Y}$ (4)	$b_0 = 5, b_1 = -1$ $\hat{Y} = 5 - X$ (5)	$\hat{\varepsilon} = Y - \hat{Y}$ (6)
3	3	3.4	−0.4	2	1
5	4	4.2	+0.8	1	4
2	1	1.8	+0.2	4	−2

Suppose that our estimates of β_0 and β_1 are $b_0 = 1$ and $b_1 = 0.8$, respectively. The estimated values of Y are given by $\hat{Y} = (1) + (0.8)X$, and the differences between the actual and estimated value of Y by $\hat{\varepsilon} = Y - \hat{Y}$, as shown in columns 3 and 4 of Table 2.2.

If our estimates of β_0 and β_1 were different, the $\hat{Y}$ and $\hat{\varepsilon}$ would also be different. For example, if $b_0 = 5$ and $b_1 = -1$, the $\hat{Y}$ and $\hat{\varepsilon}$ are shown in columns 5 and 6 of Table 2.2.

The observations, the estimated values, and the residuals for this example are also shown in Figure 2.1.

Each pair of observations (X, Y) is shown as a point in Figure 2.1 (the same three points are shown in both panels). The equation $\hat{Y} = b_0 + b_1 X$ describes a line that can be plotted by locating any two of its points and then joining them with a ruler. For example, to plot the line $\hat{Y} = 1 + 0.8X$, note first that for $X = 0$, $\hat{Y} = 1$, and for $X = 5$, $\hat{Y} = 5$. Therefore, the line passing through the points (0, 1) and (5, 5) is the geometric representation of the equation $\hat{Y} = 1 + 0.8X$. Each residual, $\hat{\varepsilon}$, is equal to the difference between the actual and estimated Y values: the residual is positive if the point lies above the line, negative if it lies below the line, and zero if it lies on the line.

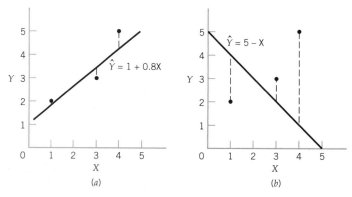

FIGURE 2.1 Illustration of data in Table 2.2

Varying b_0 and b_1 amounts to varying the intercept and the slope of the straight line by which we approximate the relationship between Y and X. Clearly, the line shown in panel (a) of Figure 2.1 would be preferred over that shown in panel (b) since it appears to fit the actual observations better.

What was observed in this simple example applies to the general case as well. By varying b_0, b_1, b_2, ..., b_k in Eq. 2.2, we vary the estimated values, $\hat{Y}$, and the differences between actual and estimated values, $\hat{\varepsilon} = Y - \hat{Y}$. Obviously, there is an infinite number of possible sets of values of $b_0, b_1, ..., b_k$. We wish to find that one set that somehow minimizes these residuals, that is, the set that produces the "best fit" to the actual observations. But best fit in what sense?

Suppose we measure the fit of the estimated model by the sum of the residuals and attempt to find those values of $b_0, b_1, b_2, ..., b_k$ that minimize the sum of residuals:

$$\sum \hat{\varepsilon} = \sum (Y - \hat{Y})$$

The summation notation is explained in Appendix A.1.

Reasonable as this criterion of fit may seem at first thought, it leads to unacceptable results. The problem is illustrated in Figure 2.2. The same three pairs of observations are shown in both panels. The line in panel (a) clearly fits the data well; some residuals are positive, some are negative. However, according to the present criterion, the line in panel (b) would be preferable because in (b) the sum of the residuals (all of which are negative) is algebraically smaller than in (a). (In fact, the sum of the residuals becomes algebraically smaller and smaller as the line is shifted in the northwest direction.)

Consider, then, a different criterion of fit: find $b_0, b_1, b_2, ..., b_k$ that minimize the sum of the absolute values of the residuals,

$$\sum |\hat{\varepsilon}| = \sum |Y - \hat{Y}|$$

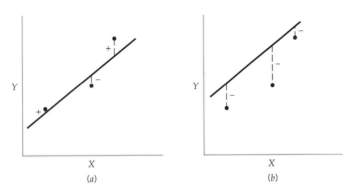

FIGURE 2.2 An unacceptable criterion of fit

This criterion is quite sensible; it is, however, rarely used, but only because it cannot be implemented with ease. The values of the parameters that minimize the sum of absolute deviations may be calculated as the solution to a linear programming problem, but it is not possible to write these solutions in the form of a formula.[2]

The most convenient and widely used criterion of fit is that of *least squares*. It requires that we find $b_0, b_1, b_2, \ldots, b_k$ which minimize the sum of the squared residuals,

$$\sum \hat{\varepsilon}^2 = \sum (Y - \hat{Y})^2 = \sum (Y - b_0 - b_1 X_1 - b_2 X_2 - \cdots - b_k X_k)^2 \qquad (2.4)$$

The values of $b_0, b_1, b_2, \ldots, b_k$ that minimize this sum of squares are called the *least squares (OLS) estimates* of $\beta_0, \beta_1, \beta_2, \ldots, \beta_k$.[3]

2.4 LEAST SQUARES ESTIMATES

Readers familiar with calculus will recognize this as a standard optimization problem, which is solved by taking the partial derivatives of Eq. 2.4 with respect to $b_0, b_1, \ldots, b_k$ and then setting them equal to zero. It can thus be shown (see Appendix B.1 and B.2) that the OLS estimates of the parameters of the linear model are those values of $b_0, b_1, b_2, \ldots, b_k$ that solve the following system of linear equations:

$$
\begin{aligned}
nb_0 + \left(\sum X_1\right)b_1 + \left(\sum X_2\right)b_2 + \cdots + \left(\sum X_k\right)b_k &= \left(\sum Y\right) \\
\left(\sum X_1\right)b_0 + \left(\sum X_1^2\right)b_1 + \left(\sum X_1 X_2\right)b_2 + \cdots + \left(\sum X_1 X_k\right)b_k &= \left(\sum X_1 Y\right) \\
\left(\sum X_2\right)b_0 + \left(\sum X_2 X_1\right)b_1 + \left(\sum X_2^2\right)b_2 + \cdots + \left(\sum X_2 X_k\right)b_k &= \left(\sum X_2 Y\right) \\
\cdots \qquad \cdots \qquad \cdots \qquad \cdots \qquad \cdots \qquad \cdots \\
\left(\sum X_k\right)b_0 + \left(\sum X_k X_1\right)b_1 + \left(\sum X_k X_2\right)b_2 + \cdots + \left(\sum X_k^2\right)b_k &= \left(\sum X_k Y\right)
\end{aligned}
$$

$$(2.5)$$

These are sometimes referred to as the *normal equations*. Formidable as the system of Eq. 2.5 appears at first sight, it is simply a system of $(k + 1)$ equations that are linear in the unknowns $b_0, b_1, \ldots, b_k$. The various sums of X's and Y are given numbers based on n sets observations on Y and the explanatory variables $X_1, X_2, \ldots, X_k$. For example, $\sum X_1$ is the sum of the values of variable X_1; $\sum X_1^2$ is the sum of the squared values of the same variable; and $\sum X_1 X_2$ is the sum of the products of the X_1- and X_2-values. At least $n = k + 1$ observation are needed to estimate uniquely $b_0, b_1, \ldots, b_k$.

---

[2] We examine this criterion later in Section 8.5.

[3] The acronym OLS stands for Ordinary Least Squares. The "ordinary" is to distinguish these from other related estimates to be described in later chapters.

The system can always be solved manually by the method of successive elimination, but this procedure can be painfully slow and tedious when the number of equations is large. In nearly all but the simplest cases the calculations are performed by widely available computer programs, about which more will be said very shortly.

In general, a system of linear equations such as Eq. 2.5 may have no solution, exactly one solution, or multiple solutions. It can be shown, however, that *the system of Eq. 2.5 always has a solution, but that solution may not be unique;* that is, there may exist more than one set of values of $b_0, b_1, \ldots, b_k$ that produce the same minimum sum of squared residuals. In most practical applications in which the values of the explanatory variables are not restricted and do not follow a pattern, there will be exactly one solution. A case of multiple solutions is considered in Chapter 4.

From now on, the symbols $b_0, b_1, b_2, \ldots, b_k$ will be reserved for the OLS estimates, and $\hat{Y}$ and $\hat{\varepsilon}$ for the estimated values and the residuals based on the least squares estimates.

It can be shown that the OLS estimates make the sum and average of the residuals equal to zero; that is, $\sum \hat{\varepsilon} = \frac{1}{n} \sum \hat{\varepsilon} = 0$ always. In words, the deviations $Y - \hat{Y}$ between actual and estimated values cancel out on average.

2.5   SPECIAL CASES: ONE OR TWO EXPLANATORY VARIABLES

Although the OLS estimates are rarely calculated by hand, it is instructive to examine two simple cases as illustrations of the general method. The entire section, however, may be skipped without loss of continuity.

For the special case where there is only **one explanatory variable**, that is, when the model is $\hat{Y} = b_0 + b_1 X$, the system of Eq. 2.5 is reduced to

$$\begin{aligned} nb_0 + \left(\sum X\right) b_1 &= \left(\sum Y\right) \\ \left(\sum X\right) b_0 + \left(\sum X^2\right) b_1 &= \left(\sum XY\right) \end{aligned} \qquad (2.6)$$

Note again that the various sums are calculated from the available observations.

As an example, consider the $n = 3$ observations on X and Y shown in the first two columns of Table 2.3. The required sums are also shown in Table 2.3 (the last column will be used later on).

The least squares estimates b_0 and b_1, then, are the solution to the following system of two linear equations:

$$\begin{aligned} 3b_0 + 8b_1 &= 10 \\ 8b_0 + 26b_1 &= 31 \end{aligned}$$

TABLE 2.3 **Illustration of Calculations When $k = 1$**

X	Y	X^2	XY	Y^2
3	3	9	9	9
1	2	1	2	4
4	5	16	20	25
$\sum X = 8$	$\sum Y = 10$	$\sum X^2 = 26$	$\sum XY = 31$	$\sum Y^2 = 38$

It is easy to verify that the solution is $b_0 = 12/14$, $b_1 = 13/14$. The estimated values of Y are given by

$$\hat{Y} = (12/14) + (13/14)X \approx 0.857 + 0.926X$$

This best-fitting line is plotted in Figure 2.3, together with the observations used in its calculation. b_0 is the Y-intercept and b_1 the slope of the line.

The method of least squares essentially determines that line that fits the observations best, in the sense of minimizing the sum of squared vertical distances between the points and the line. These distances are indicated by dotted lines in Figure 2.3.

In the case of a single explanatory variable, it is possible to develop simple formulas allowing the direct calculation of the OLS estimates from the observations and making unnecessary the solution of the system of Eq. 2.6.

Multiply both sides of the first equation in Eq. 2.6 by $(-\sum X)$ and both sides of the second equation by n, to get

$$-n\left(\sum X\right)b_0 - \left(\sum X\right)^2 b_1 = -\left(\sum X\right)\left(\sum Y\right)$$
$$n\left(\sum X\right)b_0 + n\left(\sum X^2\right)b_1 = n\left(\sum XY\right)$$

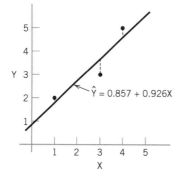

FIGURE 2.3 Best-fitting line for data in Table 2.3

Now add the resulting equations to find

$$b_1 \left[n(\sum X^2) - (\sum X)^2 \right] = n(\sum XY) - (\sum X)(\sum Y)$$

This yields a formula for calculating b_1:

$$b_1 = \frac{(\sum XY) - (\sum X)(\sum Y)/n}{(\sum X^2) - (\sum X)^2/n} \tag{2.7}$$

A simple formula for b_0 can be obtained by first rewriting the second equation in Eq. 2.6,

$$nb_0 = (\sum Y) - b_1(\sum X)$$

and then dividing both sides by n, to get

$$b_0 = \bar{Y} - b_1 \bar{X} \tag{2.8}$$

where $\bar{Y}$ and $\bar{X}$ are the averages of the Y and X values, respectively. The value b_0 can be calculated from Eq. 2.8 after b_1 is calculated from Eq. 2.7.

For example, using the data in Table 2.3, application of Eqs. 2.7 and 2.8 yields

$$b_1 = \frac{(31) - (10)(8)/3}{(26) - (8)^2/3} = \frac{13}{14}$$

and

$$b_0 = (\frac{10}{3}) - (\frac{13}{14})(\frac{8}{3}) = \frac{12}{14}$$

The same solution, of course, was obtained by solving the system of Eq. 2.6.

When the model has only **two explanatory variables**, that is, when $\hat{Y} = b_0 + b_1 X_1 + b_2 X_2$, the system of Eq. 2.5 simplifies to

$$
\begin{aligned}
nb_0 + (\sum X_1)b_1 + (\sum X_2)b_2 &= (\sum Y) \\
(\sum X_1)b_0 + (\sum X_1^2)b_1 + (\sum X_1 X_2)b_2 &= (\sum X_1 Y) \\
(\sum X_2)b_0 + (\sum X_2 X_1)b_1 + (\sum X_2^2)b_2 &= (\sum X_2 Y)
\end{aligned}
$$

This is a system of three linear equations in three unknowns (b_0, b_1, and b_2). Like the simpler system Eq. 2.6, it too can be solved manually.

We noted earlier that when there is only one explanatory variable, the expression giving the estimated values of Y, $\hat{Y} = b_0 + b_1 X$ can be imagined as a *line* in two-dimensional space. With two explanatory variables, the expression $\hat{Y} = b_0 + b_1 X_1 + b_2 X_2$ defines a *plane* in three-dimensional space, as illustrated in Figure 2.4. The location and orientation of this plane depends on the parameters b_0, b_1, and b_2.

Again, as shown in Figure 2.4, each observation (y, x_1, x_2) can be imagined as a point in three-dimensional space with coordinates $Y = y$, $X_1 = x_1$, and $X_2 = x_2$. The estimated value of Y, $\hat{y}$, is the point on the plane with coordinates $X_1 = x_1$ and $X_2 = x_2$, and the residual

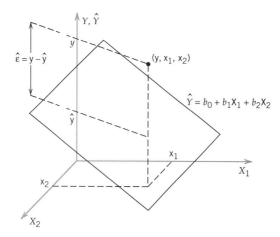

FIGURE 2.4 Two explanatory variables

$\hat{\varepsilon} = y - \hat{y}$ is the signed distance between y and $\hat{y}$. The method of least squares essentially determines that plane that fits best the observations, minimizing the sum of squared vertical distances between the points and the plane.

2.6 AN INTERPRETATION OF THE OLS ESTIMATES

In the general case, the estimated linear relationship between Y and the X's is

$$\hat{Y} = b_0 + b_1 X_1 + b_2 X_2 + \cdots + b_k X_k \tag{2.9}$$

Clearly, b_0 is the estimated value of Y when all the X's are equal to zero. Whether or not this interpretation makes sense depends on the actual situation.

Each b measures the amount (in units of Y) by which the estimated value of Y would change if the associated explanatory variable were to increase by one unit, *other explanatory variables held constant*. To see this, suppose we were to increase X_1 in Eq. 2.9 by one unit, holding all other variables constant. The estimated value of Y would change from $\hat{Y}$ to $\hat{Y}'$, where

$$\begin{aligned}
\hat{Y}' &= b_0 + b_1(X_1 + 1) + b_2 X_2 + \cdots + b_k X_k \\
&= (b_0 + b_1 X_1 + b_2 X_2 + \cdots + b_k X_k) + b_1 \\
&= \hat{Y} + b_1
\end{aligned}$$

that is, $\hat{Y}' - \hat{Y} = b_1$. Therefore, b_1 equals the change in the estimated value of Y due to the unit increase in X_1, other variables held constant. A similar interpretation applies to all other b's.

If it is believed that as an explanatory variable X increases, Y tends to increase, and vice versa (X and Y "positively related"), the OLS coefficient of X can be expected to positive. In the opposite case (X and Y "negatively related"), the OLS coefficient can be expected to be negative. The signs of the OLS estimates are usually among the first items checked to determine whether or not the estimated model is consistent with prior expectations. We shall illustrate these remarks very shortly after a word about computer programs for regression.

2.7 COMPUTER PROGRAMS

When the number of observations and the number of explanatory variables are large, as is frequently the case in practical applications, the manual solution of the system of Eq. 2.5 becomes a formidable task. The difficulty is compounded by the fact that in attempting to measure relationships, a number of models must usually be considered, involving different combinations of explanatory variables. The tedium and drudgery of these numerical calculations are almost entirely eliminated by special computer programs that perform the calculations rapidly, leaving the analyst free to examine the merits of alternative models and to select one that is suited to the purpose of the study.

Although the details will vary with each computer program used, the following steps are generally required to execute a regression: (a) the observations are entered directly or into a file, usually in the form of a table, the columns of which correspond to variables and the rows to observations; (b) for each model to be estimated, the user specifies the dependent and explanatory variables, the desired output and its format. The computer program will then print or display the OLS estimates and, on request, the actual and estimated values of the dependent variable, the residuals, and other measures, which will be described later in this text. The colloquial phrase "to run a regression" means to execute a regression using a computer program, and a "regression run" refers to (the results of) such a regression.

EXAMPLE 2.2

The Norgas Distributing Company is the exclusive supplier of natural gas to residential, commercial, and industrial users in a large metropolitan area. In the winter months, natural gas is used primarily for space heating. It is also used for cooking and water heating in residences and as a source of power in industry. Consumption for the latter two uses depends mainly on household habits and the level of industrial activity and is more or less constant in the short run. Consumption for space heating depends on the weather. Therefore, the total consumption of natural gas during a short period of time in which prices, incomes, and habits are constant is primarily a function of temperature, wind, sunshine, humidity, and other weather factors.

Table 2.4 shows the gas consumption, mean temperature, and wind velocity (hereafter abbreviated to *GASCON, TEMP, WIND*) for the area served by Norgas each Monday during the six-month period from October 1 to March 31. (In the study from which the data were extracted, a longer period was covered and all days were utilized; to simplify the presentation, only the Monday observations are used in this illustration. The price of natural gas was constant throughout the six-month period.)

TABLE 2.4   Daily Natural Gas Consumption and Weather Characteristics

Date (1)	Mean temperature, TEMP (°C) (2)	Wind speed, WIND (mi/hr) (3)	Gas consumption, GASCON (000 m³) (4)
10/01	7.8	8	16,733.0
10/08	6.2	11	16,595.8
10/15	10.1	6	14,665.8
10/22	1.2	5	22,620.9
10/29	4.3	6	20,198.5
11/05	9.4	6	14,848.6
11/12	− 2.0	1	24,085.9
11/19	3.2	9	21,747.5
11/26	3.8	16	24,394.6
12/03	0.4	5	24,035.5
12/10	− 5.3	16	32,919.1
12/17	− 8.0	6	31,712.4
12/24	− 3.9	10	25,435.5
12/31	1.7	14	23,243.3
1/07	−17.2	14	37,280.6
1/14	− 8.3	8	33,338.5
1/21	− 5.1	7	29,773.4
1/28	− 6.8	5	29,835.6
2/04	−17.8	13	40,360.6
2/11	− 8.1	20	32,602.4
2/18	7.4	4	18,333.6
2/25	1.4	16	24,628.1
3/04	0.0	7	26,051.5
3/11	− 1.8	9	25,794.6
3/18	− 8.1	4	30,198.4
3/25	2.6	5	21,262.4

SOURCE: File gascon.dat

We shall first consider the relationship between gas consumption and temperature and examine how a day's gas consumption can be forecast given that day's temperature.

We may begin with the scatter diagram of consumption and temperature shown in Figure 2.5. As expected, the lower the temperature, the greater the consumption. A straight line appears to approximate the relationship well. A reasonable starting model, therefore, is $Y = \beta_0 + \beta_1 X + \varepsilon$, where Y represents the daily consumption of gas, X a day's mean temperature, and ε is an error term. We shall call this Model A.

The OLS estimates of β_0 and β_1 are calculated using the data in columns 2 and 4 of Table 2.4 and a computer program. The format of output varies with the program used. Figure 2.6 shows the edited regression output of program Excel.

The information we need at the moment is in the column labeled Coefficients. Other elements of the computer output will be explained in the remainder of this and in the following chapter. We read, in round figures, $b_0 = 24360$ and $b_1 = -891$.

The estimated consumption ($\hat{Y}$) on a day with mean temperature X can be obtained from

$$\text{Model A:} \qquad \hat{Y} = 24360 - 891X$$

This equation is plotted in Figure 2.5 and appears to fit the observations fairly well. The estimated gas consumption on a day with mean temperature $0°C$ is

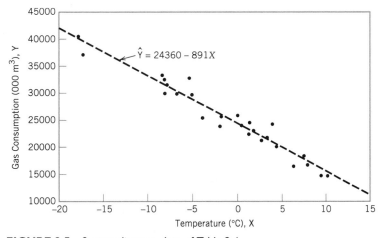

FIGURE 2.5 Scatter diagram, data of Table 2.4

```
Regression Statistics
Multiple R          0.972
R Square            0.945
Adjusted R Square   0.943
Standard Error    1619.763
Observations        26
```

ANOVA

	df	SS	MS	F	Significance F
Regression	1	1079905783	1079905783	411.607	0.000
Residual	24	62967194.72	2623633.114		
Total	25	1142872978			

	Coefficients	Standard Error	t Stat	P-value
Intercept	24359.827	322.492	75.536	0.000
TEMP	-891.507	43.942	-20.288	0.000

FIGURE 2.6 Computer output, Model A, Example 2.2

24,360 (000 m^3); a 1°C increase in mean temperature is estimated to reduce gas consumption by 891 (000 m^3).

The mean temperature on October 1 (the first observation in Table 2.4) was +7.8°C. Using Model A, the estimated consumption for that day would be

$$\hat{Y} = (24360) - (891)(7.8) = 17410 \ (000 \ m^3)$$

In a similar fashion, we may calculate the estimated consumption given the day's mean temperature for all other dates in the period. Actual and estimated values are plotted in Figure 2.7, which provides another basis for judging the fit of the regression model.

Daily gas consumption is also influenced by wind, in that with temperature constant the heat loss of buildings is likely to be greater on windier days. Wind velocity may therefore be used as an additional explanatory variable, and the model (Model B) written as $Y = \beta_0 + \beta_1 X_1 + \beta_2 X_2 + \varepsilon$; X_1 represents temperature and X_2 wind speed. Using the data in Table 2.4 and the same computer program, we get the output shown in Figure 2.8.

The OLS estimates of β_0, β_1, and β_2 are $b_0 = 22952, b_1 = -863$, and $b_2 = 163$. The estimated relationship is

$$\text{Model B:} \quad \hat{Y} = 22952 - 863X_1 + 163X_2$$

The estimated consumption on a day with 0°C mean temperature and no wind is 22,952 (000 m^3). With wind remaining constant, consumption declines by 863 (000 m^3) for each 1°C increase in temperature; with temperature constant, consumption increases by 163 (000 m^3) for each 1-mi/hr increase in wind

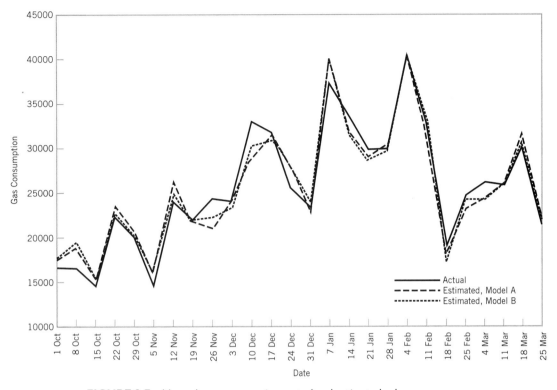

FIGURE 2.7 Natural gas consumption, actual and estimated values

```
Regression Statistics
Multiple R          0.978
R Square            0.957
Adjusted R Square   0.953
Standard Error   1462.906
Observations        26

ANOVA

             df         SS            MS          F      Significance F
Regression    2   1093650821   546825410.3   255.515           0.000
Residual     23   49222157.09  2140093.787
Total        25   1142872978

            Coefficients  Standard Error  t Stat  P-value
Intercept     22951.850        627.289    36.589   0.000
TEMP           -862.720         41.281   -20.899   0.000
WIND            162.574         64.150     2.534   0.019
```

FIGURE 2.8 Computer output, Model B, Example 2.2

velocity. The estimated gas consumption on a day with mean temperature +7.8°C and wind speed 8 mi/hr (the weather characteristics of October 1 in Table 2.4) is

$$\hat{Y} = (22952) - (863)(7.8) + (163)(8)$$
$$= 17525 \quad (000 \text{ m}^3)$$

The estimated consumption for all dates shown in Table 2.4, calculated using Model B, is also plotted in Figure 2.7.

An examination of Figure 2.7 appears to suggest that the use of wind speed as an additional explanatory variable improved the overall fit of the model (that is, on average it reduced the differences between actual and estimated values). In the next section, we confirm this impression using an appropriate summary measure of fit.

Note that the OLS estimate of the coefficient of temperature as well as that of the constant term in Model B are different from those of Model A. In this case the differences are rather small, but in others there can be substantial differences in the value of the coefficient of a given explanatory variable, depending on which other explanatory variables are used in the model.

In order to forecast tomorrow's (or any other future day's) gas consumption, Norgas can (as indeed it does) utilize a weather forecast of the day's mean temperature and wind speed. Of course, the differences between actual and forecast consumption will be due not only to the model's inherent inability to forecast consumption precisely given actual temperature and wind speed but also to the error in forecasting these explanatory variables.   ∎

2.8   MEASURING THE FIT OF A MODEL

The OLS estimates by themselves do not convey any information about how well, overall, the estimated values ($\hat{Y}$) fit the actual values (Y) of the dependent variable.

An obvious candidate for a measure of fit of the model is the average squared residual, more frequently called the *variance of residuals*:

$$S^2 = \frac{1}{n} \sum \hat{\varepsilon}^2 = \frac{1}{n} \sum (Y - \hat{Y})^2 \tag{2.10}$$

The square root of S^2 is called the *root mean square error* or *standard deviation of residuals* and is denoted by S.

The closer the estimated values are to the actual values of Y, the smaller will tend to be the differences between Y and $\hat{Y}$, and the smaller the value of S^2 or S.

To illustrate the calculation of S^2, consider the data of Table 2.3. The least squares estimates were earlier found to be $b_0 = 12/14 \approx 0.857$ and $b_1 = 13/14 \approx 0.9286$.

Y	X	$\hat{Y} = 0.857 + 0.9286X$	$\hat{\varepsilon} = Y - \hat{Y}$	$\hat{\varepsilon}^2$
3	3	3.643	−0.643	0.413
2	1	1.786	0.214	0.046
5	4	4.571	0.429	0.184
			$0.000 = \sum \hat{\varepsilon}$	$0.643 = \sum \hat{\varepsilon}^2$

Therefore, since $n = 3$, $S^2 = 0.643/3 = 0.214$ and $S = \sqrt{0.214} = 0.462$. (Rounding error makes these calculations approximate.)

When there is a single explanatory variable (*but only in this case*) S^2 may be more easily calculated from the following expression:

$$S^2 = \frac{1}{n}\left(\sum Y^2 - b_0 \sum Y - b_1 \sum XY\right) \tag{2.11}$$

For example, using the data of Table 2.3, we find

$$S^2 = \frac{1}{3}\left[38 - \frac{12}{14}(10) - \frac{13}{14}(31)\right] = 0.214$$

The result is the same as in the direct application of the definition.

Incidentally, note that the sum of the residuals is equal to zero. This is a general property of the OLS estimates: $\sum \hat{\varepsilon} = 0$ always, regardless of the number of explanatory variables.

Most computer programs calculate the variance of residuals using $n - k - 1$ in place of n as the divisor, where k is the number of explanatory variables of the model and n the number of observations. We shall denote this variant by $\hat{S}^2$ and its square root by $\hat{S}$. That is,

$$\hat{S}^2 = \frac{1}{n-k-1}\sum(Y - \hat{Y})^2 = \frac{nS^2}{n-k-1} \tag{2.12}$$

We explain the reason in the next chapter: all we need know in the meantime is that the difference with S^2 is likely to be negligible if n is large in relation to k.

EXAMPLE 2.2 (CONTINUED)

As can be seen in Figures 2.6 and 2.8, the standard deviation of the residuals (`Standard Error` in the Excel output) of Model A is 1620 and that for Model B is 1463. The estimated values from Model B, therefore, fit better the actual gas consumption—not a surprising conclusion since Model B makes use of wind speed in addition to temperature for forecasting gas consumption. ∎

Either S^2 or S can be used as the measure of fit of a model; S is often preferred because S^2 tends to be large numerically.

Note that S^2 and S will change if the units in which the dependent variable is measured are changed. For example, if *GASCON* is changed to million m^3 (in which case, the numbers under column 4 of Table 2.4 are divided by 1000) and Model B is reestimated with the new Y values, the new S will be lower (in fact, it will be equal to the old S divided by 1000, or 1.463). S^2 and S are intended for *comparisons* of the fit of models having the same dependent variable. One should not, therefore, attach special meaning to the magnitude of S or compare the S of models in which the dependent variables are different or are measured in different units.

A standardized measure of fit is the *coefficient of determination*, R^2 (read "R-squared"), defined as

$$R^2 = 1 - \frac{\sum(Y - \hat{Y})^2}{\sum(Y - \bar{Y})^2} = 1 - \frac{S^2}{\sum(Y - \bar{Y})^2/n} \tag{2.13}$$

We say R^2 is standardized because it can be shown that R^2 is always in the range from 0 to 1, that is, $0 \le R^2 \le 1$. We explain why and give an additional interpretation to R^2 in the next section.

$\bar{Y}$ is the mean and $\sum(Y - \bar{Y})^2/n$ the ordinary variance of the Y-values (these measures are reviewed in Appendix A.2). The variance of Y does not vary with the model used. Therefore, the magnitude of R^2 of different models using the same observations depends only on S^2: as S^2 approaches 0, R^2 approaches 1; as S^2 increases approaching $\sum(Y - \bar{Y})^2/n$, R^2 approaches 0. Therefore, values of R^2 close to 1 indicate that the model has relatively good fit; values close to 0 suggest the model has relatively poor fit. "Relatively," of course, means "relative to the ordinary variance of the values of the dependent variable." The higher the R^2, the better the relative fit of the model.

To illustrate the calculation of R^2, consider the data in Table 2.3. The denominator in the second term of Eq. 2.13 is

$$\sum(Y - \bar{Y})^2 = (3 - \frac{10}{3})^2 + (2 - \frac{10}{3})^2 + (5 - \frac{10}{3})^2 = 4.667$$

Earlier in this section, we had calculated $\sum(Y - \hat{Y})^2 = 0.643$. Therefore,

$$R^2 = 1 - \frac{\sum(Y - \hat{Y})^2}{\sum(Y - \bar{Y})^2} = 1 - \frac{0.643}{4.667} = 0.862$$

EXAMPLE 2.2 (CONTINUED)

Figures 2.6 and 2.8 show that the addition of wind speed resulted in the R^2 (R Square in the Excel output) increasing from 0.945 to 0.957. This improvement in relative fit parallels that measured by S, which decreased from 1620 to 1463. ∎

In comparing the fit of models using the same dependent variable Y, any one of the three measures of fit (S^2, S, or R^2) may be utilized. In practice, models involving different Y are compared using R^2, as we shall see in later chapters.

2.9 THE CONTRIBUTION OF EXPLANATORY VARIABLES

Occasionally, we want to examine the extent to which a certain subset of explanatory variables is useful in explaining the dependent variable, Y. We have in mind the following situation. A set of explanatory variables is available. From a preliminary analysis or for other a priori reasons, we suspect that some of these variables are not especially helpful in explaining Y. Of course, we do not want to omit vital variables, but, on the other hand, we are not anxious to use irrelevant variables or variables whose explanatory power is negligible. It is not uncommon in practice (especially in cases involving attributes and dummy variables described in Chapter 4) to start with scores of possible explanatory variables and to have no compelling theoretical reasons for establishing their importance.

In this section, we develop a measure of the contribution of one or more explanatory variables. A concrete example will be used to explain the method, but the approach is perfectly general.

Suppose that four explanatory variables, X_1, X_2, X_3, and X_4 are available. We suspect that X_2 and X_4 contribute little toward explaining the dependent variable, Y. The model with all explanatory variables—we shall call it the "full" model—is

$$\text{Full model: } \hat{Y} = b_0 + b_1X_1 + b_2X_2 + b_3X_3 + b_4X_4$$

while the model without X_2 and X_4—we shall call it the "partial" model—is

$$\text{Partial model: } \hat{Y} = b_0 + b_1X_1 + b_3X_3$$

Note that leaving out X_2 and X_4 is equivalent to setting $b_2 = b_4 = 0$ in the full model. (The b's of the full model are not necessarily equal to those of the partial model, though the same symbols are used for simplicity.)

To measure the contribution of the "suspect" explanatory variables X_2 and X_4, begin by running two regressions:

1. Regress Y on all explanatory variables. Calculate the sum of squared residuals, $\sum \hat{\varepsilon}^2 = \sum (Y - \hat{Y})^2$, of this full model. Denote this by SSE_F [remember, $\sum \hat{\varepsilon}^2 = nS^2 = (n - k - 1)\hat{S}^2$].

2. Regress Y on only those explanatory variables that are to be kept, leaving out the suspect variables. Calculate the sum of squared residuals of this partial model. Denote this by SSE_p.

SSE_F and SSE_p are called the *variation* of the full and partial models, respectively. The greater the SSE, the worse the fit of the model. SSE_F and SSE_p are always nonnegative.[4]

It may be clear intuitively that

$$SSE_F \leq SSE_p$$

in other words, that the fit of the full model cannot be worse than that of a model using a subset of the explanatory variables. Since this is an important observation, however, it will be worthwhile to justify it in more detail.

The OLS estimates of the full model are chosen so as to minimize the sum of squared residuals. *One* of the available choices is to make the estimates of the parameters of the suspect variables equal to zero—*if* this choice does indeed yield the minimum value of the SSE_F. But, setting these estimates equal to zero is the same as *not using* the suspect variables, which is precisely what the partial model does. With the full model, there is more freedom of choice; therefore, the fit of the full model is at least as good as that of the partial model. In other words, the addition of explanatory variables (whether useful or irrelevant) will not hurt and, in practice, will improve the fit of the model. The improvement could be, of course, very slight.

Now, the difference $SSE_p - SSE_F$ can be interpreted as the improvement in the fit of the partial model due to the inclusion (addition) of the suspect explanatory variables. In this sense, therefore, $SSE_p - SSE_F$ represents the *contribution* of the suspect explanatory variables; it is the difference between the best attainable fit *without* and the best attainable fit *with* the suspect variables.

SSE_p and SSE_F, as well as the difference $SSE_p - SSE_F$, depend on the units in which Y is measured. It would be useful if we could find a way to standardize

---

[4]The SSE of a model is displayed by computer programs as the `Residual` or `Error SS` in the `Analysis of Variance` or `ANOVA` section of the output. For instance, Figure 2.8 shows that $SSE = 49222157$ for Model B of Example 2.2.

the last quantity, that is, to make $SSE_P - SSE_F$ independent of the units of Y. This is possible. Since

$$0 \leq SSE_P - SSE_F \leq SSE_P$$

dividing the terms of this inequality by SSE_P, we get,

$$0 \leq \frac{SSE_P - SSE_F}{SSE_P} \leq 1$$

Therefore, the ratio Q,

$$Q = \frac{SSE_P - SSE_F}{SSE_P} = 1 - \frac{SSE_F}{SSE_P} \qquad (2.14)$$

is always between 0 and 1 and does not depend on the units in which Y is measured. Q may be interpreted as the *proportion of the variation of the partial model that is explained by the suspect variables*, that is, the proportion by which the fit of the partial model is improved by including the suspect variables in the model. The closer Q is to 1, the greater is the relative contribution of the suspect variables, and vice versa.

To illustrate the calculations, suppose $n = 50$ observations are available. Two regresions were run, with the following results:

Model	Explanatory variables	S	$SSE = nS^2$
Full	X_1, X_2, X_3, X_4	103	530,450
Partial	X_1, X_3	125	781,250

We calculate

$$Q = 1 - \frac{530450}{781250} = 0.321$$

32.1% of the variation of the partial model is explained by X_2 and X_4.

A simpler method for calculating Q is given by Eq. 2.15, described later.

Special Case: The Contribution of All Explanatory Variables, R^2   It is possible to calculate as many Q's as there are different subsets of explanatory variables. One of these Q's, as we shall now see, is a useful measure of the contribution of *all* explanatory variables.

The full model employs all k explanatory variables:

$$\hat{Y} = b_0 + b_1 X_1 + b_2 X_2 + \cdots + b_k X_k$$

The sum of squared residuals of this model is denoted by SSE_F. If all explanatory variables are omitted, the partial model is

$$\hat{Y} = b_0$$

This is the full model with b_1 to b_k equal to zero. The partial model has only one parameter, b_0. The OLS estimate b_0 is that value which minimizes the sum of squared residuals, namely, $\sum(Y - b_0)^2$. It can be shown (see Appendix B.4) that the OLS estimate b_0 is

$$b_0 = \bar{Y} = \frac{1}{n}\sum Y$$

that is, b_0 is equal to the ordinary average of the Y values.

Therefore, since all $\hat{Y} = b_0 = \bar{Y}$, the sum of squared residuals of the partial model is

$$SSE_P = \sum(Y - \bar{Y})^2$$

This particular SSE_P (equal to the sum of squared deviations of the Y's about their mean, $\bar{Y}$) is called the *total variation* of Y. $\sum(Y - \bar{Y})^2/n$ is the ordinary variance of the Y-values.

The proportion of SSE_P that is explained by the variables $X_1, X_2, \ldots, X_k$ is given by

$$Q = 1 - \frac{SSE_F}{SSE_P} = 1 - \frac{\sum(Y - \hat{Y})^2}{\sum(Y - \bar{Y})^2}$$

This special case of Q is, of course, the coefficient of determination, R^2, given by Eq. 2.13 of the previous section.

R^2, then, is the proportion of the total variation of Y that is explained by $X_1, X_2, \ldots, X_k$. Stated otherwise, R^2 is the relative improvement in the fit of a model containing no explanatory variables, an improvement resulting from the addition of the variables $X_1, X_2, \ldots, X_k$ in the model. The closer R^2 is to 1, the greater is the relative contribution of all the explanatory variables, and vice versa. [5]

The Q statistic, Eq. 2.14, measuring the contribution of a set of explanatory variables, may be more conveniently calculated using the R^2 of two regression

---

[5]Our R^2, as defined by Eq. 2.13, is the so-called *unadjusted* R^2. Computer programs also display the *adjusted* R^2, which is defined as follows:

$$R^2(\text{adj.}) = 1 - \frac{SSE_F/(n - k - 1)}{\sum(Y - \bar{Y})^2/(n - 1)}$$

runs—the first (R_F^2) with, and the second (R_P^2) without, the suspect variables. Since

$$R_F^2 = 1 - \frac{SSE_F}{\sum (Y - \bar{Y})^2}$$

and

$$R_P^2 = 1 - \frac{SSE_P}{\sum (Y - \bar{Y})^2}$$

it is easy to verify that

$$Q = \frac{R_F^2 - R_P^2}{1 - R_P^2} \tag{2.15}$$

Special Case: The Contribution of One Explanatory Variable, t-Ratios To measure the contribution of one explanatory variable, the straightforward procedure would be to run two regressions—one with and the other without the variable—and then to calculate the appropriate Q statistic. However, most computer programs for regression calculate and display the so-called t-ratios under such headings as t Ratio, t Value, or t Stat. There is one t-ratio for each explanatory variable and the constant term (see Figures 2.6 and 2.8).

The exact meaning of these t-ratios will be explained in the next chapter, but it can be shown that the t-ratio (t) of a variable (as calculated and displayed by computer programs) is related to its Q statistic as follows:

$$Q = \frac{t^2}{t^2 + (n - k - 1)} \tag{2.16}$$

and

$$t^2 = (n - k - 1) \frac{Q}{1 - Q} \tag{2.17}$$

where k is the total number of explanatory variables in the model and n the number of observations.

We see that, for given k and n, the closer the Q of a variable is to 1—that is, the greater the contribution of the variable—the larger $|t|$ will be; similarly,

---

We shall not explain the purpose of this statistic but note two differences with R^2: (a) while R^2 never decreases, R^2(adj.) may decrease as additional explanatory variables are added to the model; and (b) while R^2 is always between 0 and 1, R^2(adj.) may be outside this range.

the closer Q is to 0, the smaller $|t|$ will be. (A t-ratio always has the same sign as the regression coefficient. For measuring the contribution of a variable, it is its absolute value, $|t|$, that matters.)

In practice, it is not usually worthwhile to convert t-ratios to Q statistics or vice versa. Simply a glance at the list of the t-ratios of the variables as displayed by computer programs will show if any variable has a low $|t|$ and therefore contributes little toward explaining Y. If this is the case, one may consider leaving out this variable and reestimating the model with another regression run.

It should always be borne in mind that the Q statistic (or t-ratio) is a measure of the contribution of a given explanatory variable *under the condition that all other explanatory variables remain in the model*. It is not appropriate to use the low Q's (or $|t|$'s) of a *set* of variables as a justification for dropping them. In business and economic analysis, it is common for some explanatory variables to be related to one another. If these variables as a whole explain Y well, the R^2 of the model will be high, but the individual Q's may be small. That should not be surprising. Since the variables are related to one another, any one variable can be dropped if the other variables are allowed to remain and carry the burden of explaining Y. Dropping *all* these variables, however, may result in a substantial reduction in the fit of the model.

EXAMPLE 2.2 (CONTINUED)

In order to forecast daily gas consumption, two explanatory variables were used: temperature ($TEMP$) and wind speed ($WIND$). The complete regression results (see Figure 2.8) may be presented as follows:

$$\text{Model B}: \quad \widehat{GASCON} = 22952 - 863TEMP + 163WIND \qquad R^2 = 0.957$$
$$(-20.90) \qquad (2.53) \qquad S = 1463$$

This, of course, is Model B, discussed earlier. The numbers in parentheses are the t-ratios of the explanatory variables. This format for presenting regression results is widely used and will be adopted in the rest of this text.

We see that $TEMP$ and $WIND$ together account for 95.7% of the total variation of $GASCON$. A glance at the t-ratios shows that the contribution of $WIND$ (if $TEMP$ remains in the model) is much smaller than that of $TEMP$ (if $WIND$ remains in the model). If it is desired to measure the contribution of $WIND$, another regression should be run without this variable. The following regression results are those of Model A examined earlier (see Figure 2.6):

$$\text{Model A}: \quad \widehat{GASCON} = 24360.3 - 891TEMP \qquad R^2 = 0.945$$
$$(-20.29) \qquad S = 1620$$

TEMP alone explains 94.5% of the total variation of *GASCON*. The contribution of *WIND* can be calculated using Eq. 2.15:

$$Q = \frac{R_F^2 - R_P^2}{1 - R_P^2} = \frac{0.957 - 0.945}{1 - 0.945} = 0.218$$

As a result of including *WIND*, the fit of Model A has been improved by 21.8%. If we use a model with no explanatory variables as the base of comparison, the contribution of *WIND* is simply the difference in the R^2 of the two models: 0.957 − 0.945 or 1.2%; that is, 1.2% of the total variation of *GASCON* is explained by *WIND*.

The contribution of *TEMP* to a model containing *WIND* alone can be measured, if it is so desired, by running a regression of *GASCON* on *WIND*:

$$\text{Model C:} \quad \widehat{GASCON} = 20766 + 531\,WIND \quad \begin{array}{l} R^2 = 0.139 \\ S = 6403 \end{array}$$
$$(1.97)$$

The regression results confirm that dropping *TEMP* from the full model would result in a substantial loss of fit. Using Eq. 2.16, we may calculate the contribution of *TEMP* directly from the regression results of Model B:

$$Q = \frac{t^2}{t^2 + (n - k - 1)} = \frac{(-20.9)^2}{(-20.9)^2 + (26 - 2 - 1)} = 0.95$$

In words, the fit of Model C can be improved by 95% if *TEMP* is included as an additional explanatory variable.

We emphasize that these calculations—which are included here to illustrate formulas presented earlier—would probably be unnecessary in this case. There is little doubt that *TEMP* is the most important factor influencing *GASCON* and that *WIND* contributes in explaining the variation of gas consumption. Model B, therefore, would be the first model estimated. A glance at the signs of the coefficients would have shown them to be sensible, and the R^2 would have indicated a very good fit. Unless further improvements could be made, Model B should be used for forecasting daily gas consumption. ∎

2.10 MORE EXAMPLES

The following applications give a better idea of the type of information sought by means of regression analysis.

EXAMPLE 2.1 (CONTINUED)

Let us return to the model presented at the beginning of this chapter, in which the price of a residential property is assumed to be linearly related to floor and lot area:

$$PRICE = \beta_0 + \beta_1 FLOOR + \beta_2 LOT + \varepsilon$$

β_1 is the "true" price of one square foot of floor area and β_2 that of lot area.

The computer file `rest.dat` contains the price (in $000), floor area (in square feet), lot area (also in square feet), and other features of 100 residential properties that changed hands in a recent three-month period. The file is partially listed in Table 2.1. A regression of price on floor and lot area produced the following results:

$$\widehat{PRICE} = 69.854 + 0.203 FLOOR + 0.022 LOT \qquad R^2 = 0.54$$
$$(8.60) \qquad (6.03) \qquad S = 102.47$$

The numbers in parentheses are t-ratios.

The price of a house is estimated to increase by $203 for each square foot of floor area and by $22 for each square foot of lot area.

As we noted earlier, many other features beside floor and lot area influence the price of a house. It is interesting, therefore, to observe that these two variables alone explain a respectable 54% of the total variation of prices. In the continuation of this example later in the book, we shall examine ways by which the model could be improved. ∎

EXAMPLE 2.3

(Due to Mr. K. Davey) The decision as to which material to use is one of the major problems facing design engineers. The criteria by which a material is judged depend upon the functions it will be called upon to perform, but one important material characteristic is strength. Roughly speaking, strength is the maximum load that a material can bear without breaking. The material studied here is a glass-reinforced polyester, and the objective of the study was to determine how the processing of the material affected its strength. The process employed was injection molding, the most prevalent form of plastic processing in use. In injection molding, the glass-plastic mixture is fed into a hopper and, from there, into a heated chamber. The temperature of the chamber (the barrel temperature) causes the plastic to melt and flow. A plugger then forces the mixture through an orifice at a given injection pressure into a heated mold, where the plastic is cooled and solidified. By varying the injection pressure and the mold and barrel temperatures, the properties of the material can be changed. Table 2.5 shows the results of 27 experiments, in which the strength of

TABLE 2.5 Test Results for Glass-Reinforced Plastic Material

Experiment	Barrel temperature, X_1 (°F)	Mold temperature, X_2 (°F)	Injection pressure, X_3 (psi)	Strength, Y (psi)
1	320	100	7,000	3,877
2	320	100	5,000	3,901
3	320	100	3,000	4,010
4	320	125	7,000	3,706
5	320	125	5,000	3,708
6	320	125	3,000	4,140
7	320	150	7,000	3,749
8	320	150	5,000	3,883
9	320	150	3,000	4,440
10	370	100	7,000	4,017
11	370	100	5,000	4,090
12	370	100	3,000	3,900
13	370	125	7,000	3,947
14	370	125	5,000	4,034
15	370	125	3,000	4,419
16	370	150	7,000	4,003
17	370	150	5,000	3,910
18	370	150	3,000	4,095
19	420	100	7,000	3,885
20	420	100	5,000	4,076
21	420	100	3,000	4,254
22	420	125	7,000	4,123
23	420	125	5,000	4,446
24	420	125	3,000	4,289
25	420	150	7,000	4,151
26	420	150	5,000	4,287
27	420	150	3,000	4,498

SOURCE: File `plmat.dat`

the material was measured at three different barrel temperatures (320°F, 370°F, and 420°F), three different injection pressures (7000, 5000 and 3000 pounds per square inch), and three different mold temperatures (100°F, 125°F, and 150°F).

A linear relationship is assumed between strength (Y), on the one hand, and barrel temperature (X_1), mold temperature (X_2), and injection pressure (X_3), on the other. The regression results are as follows:

$$\hat{Y} = 3081.1 + 2.883X_1 + 2.236X_2 - 0.072X_3 \qquad R^2 = 0.612$$
$$\phantom{\hat{Y} = 3081.1 +} (4.11) \qquad (1.59) \quad (-4.10) \qquad S = 148.7$$

The numbers in parentheses are t-ratios.

An increase by 1°F in barrel temperature (mold temperature and injection pressure held constant) is estimated to increase strength by 2.883 psi. An increase by 1°F in mold temperature (barrel temperature and injection pressure held constant) is estimated to increase strength by 2.236 psi. An increase by 1 psi in injection pressure (barrel and mold temperatures held constant) is estimated to decrease strength by 0.072 psi. The strength of this material, therefore, tends to increase when the barrel or mold temperature increases and tends to decrease when the injection pressure is increased. About 61% of the total variation of strength is explained by the three explanatory variables. ∎

EXAMPLE 2.4

Economic theory tells us that the quantity demanded of a given product (Q) is a function of the price of that product ($P1$), the prices of competing products ($P2$), the prices of all other products ($P3$), and income (I). In symbols, the demand function can be written as

$$Q = f(P1, P2, P3, I, \ldots)$$

The prices of other products are usually represented collectively by a consumer price index, which is divided into the remaining components of the demand function to form "deflated" prices and income, and the demand function is often estimated in the following form:

$$Q = g(\frac{P1}{P3}, \frac{P2}{P3}, \frac{I}{P3}) + \varepsilon = g(DP1, DP2, DI) + \varepsilon$$

where $DP1$, $DP2$, and DI are the deflated prices of the product, of competing products, and the deflated income, respectively. If it is assumed that the demand function is linear, then

$$Q = \beta_0 + \beta_1 DP1 + \beta_2 DP2 + \beta_3 DI + \varepsilon$$

where ε is an error term.

Table 2.6 shows the per capita consumption of beef (QB) and pork (QP); the deflated retail prices of beef (DPB), pork (DPP), and other meats ($DPOM$); and the deflated per capita personal disposable income ($DPDI$) over a 20-year period.[6]

It is assumed that the demand function for each product remained unchanged throughout the period and that the variation of prices and quantities is due entirely to movements of its supply function. As illustrated in Figure 2.9, under this assumption the observations trace the demand function.

The demand functions for beef and pork are estimated as follows:

[6]In Table 2.6, per capita consumption is in pounds. The consumer price index (all items) is used to deflate the retail price index series and the per capita personal disposable income.

TABLE 2.6 Consumption and Prices of Beef and Pork

Year	Per capita consumption of Beef QB	Per capita consumption of Pork QP	Deflated retail price index of Beef DPB	Deflated retail price index of Pork DPP	Deflated retail price index of Other meats DPOM	P.c. deflated pers. disp. income, DPDI
19X1	49.3	58.6	130.23	117.27	134.09	11.996
19X2	54.4	56.0	115.08	100.89	119.95	12.321
19X3	65.1	48.7	105.93	103.91	103.91	12.738
19X4	70.2	45.4	89.21	108.01	97.55	12.353
19X5	69.1	49.2	90.57	97.78	93.01	12.894
19X6	71.4	49.2	90.04	97.15	92.23	13.710
19X7	72.0	44.4	90.88	109.12	94.27	13.579
19X8	68.0	49.4	101.86	104.65	101.86	13.839
19X9	65.6	56.7	107.35	96.12	102.76	13.995
19Y0	70.0	52.6	101.61	95.46	99.90	14.145
19Y1	69.7	49.9	100.00	100.00	100.00	14.249
19Y2	71.1	50.1	108.30	101.68	101.48	14.934
19Y3	74.3	50.7	103.40	100.19	102.04	15.325
19Y4	79.4	51.8	98.28	96.47	99.24	15.691
19Y5	83.6	47.9	99.81	103.72	99.25	16.664
19Y6	84.2	46.9	106.01	113.64	107.81	17.307
19Y7	84.0	53.8	107.63	102.60	104.42	17.717
19Y8	86.5	53.6	105.16	99.75	101.16	18.640
19Y9	87.4	51.9	108.92	108.37	102.47	19.129
19Z0	85.6	56.9	108.48	102.00	104.55	19.326

SOURCE: File: bfpk.dat

(a) Demand for beef:

$$\widehat{QB} = 44.756 - 0.403DPB + 0.171DPP - 0.087DPOM + 4.085DPDI$$
$$\phantom{\widehat{QB} = 44.756\ }(-2.87)\qquad (1.99)\qquad\quad (-0.55)\qquad\quad (17.97)$$
$$R^2 = 0.98 \qquad S = 1.681$$

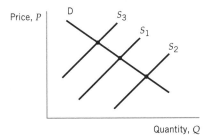

FIGURE 2.9 Demand and supply assumptions, Example 2.4

(b) Demand for pork:

$$\widehat{QP} = 45.235 + 0.124DPB - 0.437DPP + 0.311DPOM + 0.395DPDI$$
$$(0.87) \qquad (-5.04) \qquad (1.95) \qquad (1.72)$$

$$R^2 = 0.85 \qquad S = 1.702$$

Actual and estimated consumption of beef and pork are plotted in Figure 2.10.

Other things being equal, a rise in the price of beef should cause a reduction of beef consumption and an increase of pork consumption. The effect of a drop in the price of beef should be the opposite. The OLS estimate of the coefficient of *DPB* is negative in *QB*, positive in *QP*, and consistent with these expectations. A rise in the price of pork, again other things remaining equal, can be expected to cause an increase of beef consumption and a decrease of pork consumption; the signs of the coefficients of *DPP* in the two equations are consistent with these expectations. A rise in the price of other meats, other things being equal, ought to increase the consumption of both beef and pork; the coefficient of *DPOM* in *QP* is positive, as expected, but is negative and inconsistent in *QB*. Again, other things being equal, a rise in income can be expected to increase the consumption of both beef and pork, and this expectation is borne out by the signs of the coefficients of *DPDI* in the two equations.

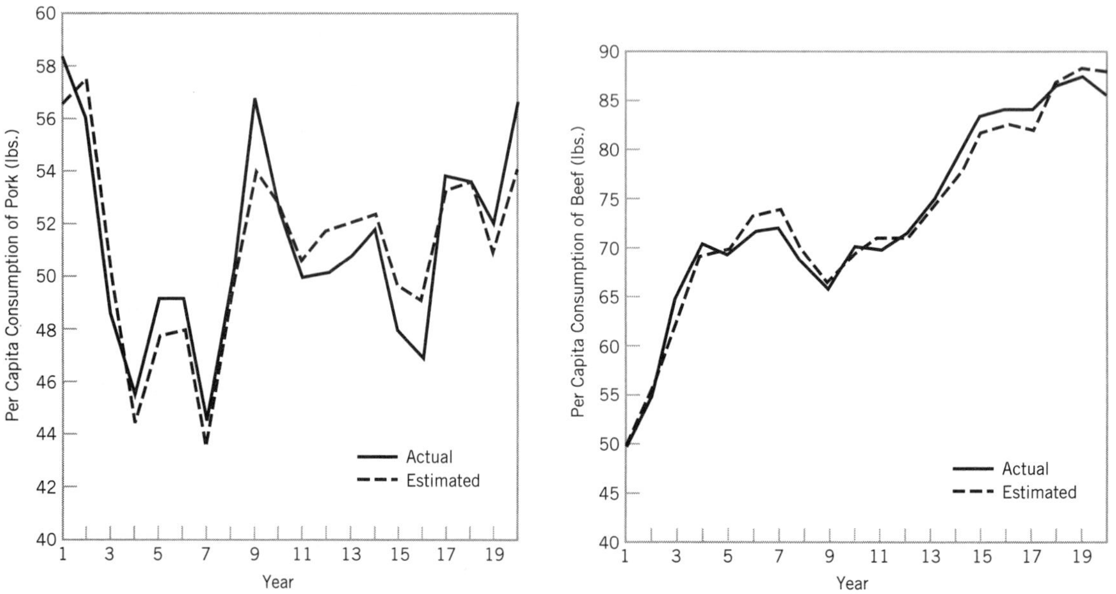

FIGURE 2.10 Consumption of beef (*QB*) and pork (*QP*), actual and estimated values

With one exception, therefore, the regression results are consistent with prior expectations. ∎

2.11 TO SUM UP

- Regression is a method for estimating the parameters of a linear relationship so as to fit the observations as well as possible. The criterion of fit is least squares (that is, the minimization of the sum of squared deviations between actual and estimated values of the dependent variable).

- The least squares (OLS) estimates can be calculated in principle by solving manually a system of linear equations, but in practice the calculations are nearly always done by computers.

- Other useful regression statistics are S^2 (the average of the squared deviations) or its square root S, R^2 (the proportion of the total variation of the dependent variable that is explained by all explanatory variables), Q (measuring the contribution of a subset of explanatory variables), and t (related to Q and measuring the contribution of one explanatory variable).

- Fitting a model to available observations is an objective that has considerable intuitive appeal. Indeed, the concepts, measures, and tools of this chapter are sufficient to begin examining (starting with Chapter 4) the broad range of situations to which regression can be applied with only occasional modifications.

- The OLS estimates, however, have additional desirable properties in the event the observations are produced by a process with specific features or constitute a random sample (a "part") from a population (the "whole") with certain features. These properties, and the additional tools they provide, are described in the next chapter.

PROBLEMS

2.1 Confirm the regression results presented in this chapter using a computer program for regression and the data files in the diskette accompanying this text.

2.2 Table 2.7 shows the one-way airfare, distance, and number of outbound passengers from city A to 17 other cities, as well as the population of these cities. (Problems 2.4 and 2.8 also refer to this set of data.)

Consider first the relationship between airfare and distance. Let

Y: One-way airfare from city A in $ (label: *FARE*),

X: Distance from city A in miles (label: *DIST*).

TABLE 2.7 Fares and Outbound Passengers from City A to Selected Other Cities

Destination city	Fare, FARE ($)	Distance, DIST (miles)	Passengers, PASS (000)	Population, POPU (000)
1	360	1463	85.83	444
2	360	1448	68.78	529
3	207	681	83.05	224
4	111	270	482.43	2798
5	93	190	247.54	626
6	141	393	37.02	499
7	291	1102	29.92	151
8	183	578	20.21	112
9	309	1204	23.34	130
10	300	1138	33.64	132
11	90	184	45.84	154
12	162	502	71.15	112
13	477	1828	18.13	208
14	84	179	46.89	266
15	231	818	117.83	570
16	54	90	11.15	296
17	429	1813	146.57	1137

SOURCE: File `fares.dat`

The 17 pairs of (X, Y) observations are listed in Table 2.7.

(a) In a scatter diagram, plot the 17 pairs of observations. Do you think that the relationship between fare and distance is approximately linear, that is, $\hat{Y} = b_0 + b_1 X$?

(b) The following can be calculated from the data: $\sum X = 13,881$, $\sum Y = 3,882$, $\sum XY = 4,388,343$, $\sum X^2 = 16,881,109$, $\sum Y^2 = 1,155,798$. Calculate the OLS estimates b_0 and b_1, as well as R^2 and S^2. Use the identity $\sum (Y - \bar{Y})^2 = \sum Y^2 - n\bar{Y}^2$. Interpret these statistics.

(c) Plot the estimated relationship in the scatter diagram and visually compare the fit of the model.

(d) City 18 is 300 miles away from city A. What is your estimate of the air fare to city 18? (In case you are curious—the actual airfare was $40.)

(e) In what way can this regression model be useful?

2.3 For a study of the feasibility of constructing storage facilities for liquid cargoes at a Great Lakes port, it was desirable to obtain an estimate of the relationship between the volume of a vessel's cargo and the time required to load or unload this cargo. Table 2.8 shows the cargoes and the times spent in port by each of 35 liquid-carrying vessels that used the port in the summer season. Four shipments of furnace oil are indicated specially; the remaining shipments consisted of animal, vegetable, and marine oils, chemicals, fuels, and so on.

Estimate the relationship between tonnage of cargo and time in port. What would be your forecast of the dock time for a vessel with a cargo of 3000 tons? 10,000 tons?

TABLE 2.8   Liquid-Carrying Vessels, Summer 19X2

Vessel	Hours in port	Tonnage loaded and unloaded	Vessel	Hours in port	Tonnage loaded and unloaded
Atlantic	17	2,213	Atlantic	43	2,790
Orator	24	12,962(F)	Akosombo	15	353
Anette	30	3,256	Anette	28	12,419(F)
Telenikis	68	12,203	Anette	30	2,829
Stuart	64	7,021	Ottawa	20	363
Norness	11	529	Aniara	41	7,084
Orator	55	3,192	Desiree	15	1,328
Minerva	20	547	Clio	13	294
Alor Star	49	4,682	Minerva	11	268
Anina	69	6,112	Aniara	24	1,732
Atlantic	43	10,169(F)	Desiree	11	507
Anette	68	5,375	Anette	28	1,486
Orator	49	6,666	Zeus	22	536
Anette	43	3,930	Atlantic	34	11,012(F)
Crown	31	4,263	Anette	9	851
Orator	17	1,849	Orator	43	6,760
Fian	13	663	Condor	131	15,900
Diana	13	329			

SOURCE: File `glakes.dat`

NOTE: (F) = Furnace oil

2.4   Refer to Table 2.7. It was thought that the number of outbound passengers from city A (*PASS*) should be linearly related to the population of the destination city (*POPU*) and the airfare to that city (*FARE*). The regression results were as follows:

$$\widehat{PASS} = 38.154 + 0.163 POPU - 0.116 FARE \qquad R^2 = 0.87$$
$$\phantom{\widehat{PASS} = 38.154 + }(9.52) \qquad (-1.34) \qquad\quad S = 44.43$$

The numbers in parentheses are *t*-ratios. Interpret and comment on these results.

2.5   A large number of factors influence the gasoline consumption of a car: not only its weight, its shape and wind resistance, and the power of its engine but also the efficiency with which fuel is utilized and power is transmitted from the engine to the wheels. Since not all these factors can be easily ascertained, one attempt was made to approximate the relationship between gasoline consumption and a small number of easily obtainable vehicle characteristics. Thirty-five car models representing a wide spectrum of vehicles were selected from the annual buyer's guide of an automotive magazine. For each car selected, the following characteristics were determined:

MIL :   Average mileage (miles per gallon) attained on a test course reflecting typical city and highway driving conditions.

DIS : Engine displacement (in cubic centimeters). This is a measure of the capacity of an engine. Other things being equal, the greater the displacement, the more powerful the engine.

COM : Compression ratio. Other things being equal, the greater the compression, the more efficient the fuel utilization and the lower the gasoline consumption.

BHP : Brake horsepower (or gross horsepower) has been used over the years by manufacturers to indicate the maximum engine capability.

TOR : Engine torque is a measure of the turning force exerted at the crankshaft. Torque and horsepower are closely related, horsepower being essentially torque per time unit.

WGH : Weight of vehicle in pounds. The greater the weight of the vehicle, the greater the power required to attain and maintain a given speed.

The regression results were as follows:

$$\widehat{MIL} = 30.609 - 0.0016DIS + 0.6204COM + 0.0004BHP -$$
$$\phantom{\widehat{MIL} = 30.609 } (-2.85) \qquad (0.57) \qquad\quad (0.44)$$

$$ - 0.0011TOR - 0.0025WGH \qquad R^2 = 0.81$$
$$ (-1.38) \qquad\quad (-2.51) \qquad\quad S = 2.467$$

The numbers in parentheses are *t*-ratios. Interpret and comment on these results.

2.6 (Due to Mr. J. Schroeder) A study of apartment rents in a large city estimated the following relationships between rent and apartment features.

One-bedroom apartments:

$$\hat{Y} = 184.90 + 22.34X_1 + 12.43X_2 - 1.81X_3 + 1.10X_4 - 0.78X_5$$
$$\phantom{\hat{Y} = 184.90 + } (20.43) \quad (10.34) \quad (-13.24) \quad (1.88) \quad (-3.31)$$

$$R^2 = 0.88 \qquad n = 207$$

Two-bedroom apartments:

$$\hat{Y} = 218.67 + 28.34X_1 + 22.53X_2 - 2.24X_3 - 1.74X_5 + 2.45X_6 - 0.99X_7$$
$$\phantom{\hat{Y} = 218.67 + } (20.66) \quad (17.65) \quad (-10.60) \quad (-3.44) \quad (3.58) \quad (-1.80)$$

$$R^2 = 0.92 \qquad n = 210$$

Three-bedroom apartments:

$$\hat{Y} = 268.33 + 37.93X_1 + 27.99X_2 - 3.13X_3 - 3.90X_5 + 12.94X_8$$
$$\phantom{\hat{Y} = 268.33 + } (11.36) \quad (13.17) \quad (-8.07) \quad (-4.76) \quad (2.86)$$

$$R^2 = 0.94 \qquad n = 85$$

Numbers in parentheses are *t*-ratios. The variables are defined as follows:

Y : Monthly apartment rent ($). Includes parking and utilities.

X_1 : Aesthetic index. Values range from 0 to 3 depending on the quality of landscaping, maintenance and construction, the view, neighborhood, the proximity to a park, etc. (0 = poor, . . . , 3 = very good.)

X_2 : Special features index. Values range from 0 to 4; one point awarded for presence of a doorman, porter, or maid or of a guest suite, air conditioning, or extra bedroom.

X_3 : Age of building (years).

X_4 : Commercial index. Values range from 0 for a building with no commercial facilities to 3 for a building with a complete set of commercial facilities (grocery store plus four or five other stores).

X_5 : Distance from the city center (miles).

X_6 : Recreation index. Values range from 0 for a building with no recreational facilities to 4 for a building with a complete set of recreational facilities (indoor pool, gymnasium, handball and squash courts, sauna, exercise room, games room, etc.).

X_7 : Distance from nearest subway station (miles measured along bus routes).

X_8 : Coded variable = 1 for "adults only" building; 0 otherwise.

Data were obtained from large rental companies, and the values of the explanatory variables were determined subjectively following a personal inspection by the investigator.
Interpret and comment on these results.

2.7 In a study of demand for meat, the following equation was estimated by least squares.

$$\hat{Y} = 47.93 + 0.86X_1 - 1.14X_2 \qquad R^2 = 0.79$$
$$\qquad\qquad (2.36) \quad (-1.72) \qquad n = 20$$

where the numbers in parentheses are t-ratios, and

Y : Annual per capita consumption of meat (lb)

X_1 : Annual per capita personal disposable income ($000)

X_2 : Annual price of meat ($/lb)

Twenty annual observations were used.
For each of the following statements, indicate whether you agree or disagree and briefly explain why.

(a) Income has a more important effect on consumption than price.

(b) If price increased by $1 per lb, other things being equal, per capita consumption would decrease by 1.14 lb.

(c) Price does not have an important influence on consumption.

(d) About 21% of the variation in consumption must be explained by variables other than income and price.

(e) Because the coefficient of X_2 is greater than the coefficient of X_1, we conclude that X_2 explains more of the variation of Y than X_1.

2.8 Refer to Problems 2.2 and 2.4. It was argued that, in addition to *POPU* and *FARE*, the distance to the destination city (*DIST*) should be included as an explanatory variable. The regression results may be summarized as follows:

$$\widehat{PASS} = -16.13 + 0.165POPU + 0.992FARE - 0.245DIST \qquad R^2 = 0.882$$
$$\qquad\qquad (9.57) \qquad\quad (0.89) \qquad\quad (-1.00) \qquad\quad S = 44.43$$

The numbers in parentheses are t-ratios. Compare these results to those of Problem 2.4 and explain any differences that you consider important.

2.9 The measure of the contribution of one or more explanatory variables described in Section 2.9 helps determine whether the coefficients of the "suspect" variables are 0.

(a) More generally, how would you investigate the possibility that the value of the coefficient of a certain explanatory variable is a given number (which could be 0)?

(b) How would you investigate the possibility that the values of the coefficients of certain explanatory variables equal given numbers (which could all be 0)?

(c) Apply your suggestions in (a) to examine whether the unit value of one square foot of lot area in Example 2.1 (Section 2.10) is $20 rather than $22.

(d) Apply your suggestions in (b) to examine whether the unit values of one square foot of floor and lot areas in Example 2.1 (Section 2.10) are $175 and $15, respectively, rather than $203 and $22.

2.10 Able Manufacturing produces one product to order in jobs of varying numbers of units. The total labor content of a job consists of the time required to set up the job, which does not depend on the size of the job, and of a variable component, which is proportional to the number of units of the product in the job. The following table shows the total number of hours required and the size of twelve jobs.

Job No.	Total hours	Number of units
1	280	100
2	250	60
3	180	10
4	320	140
5	260	90
6	245	70
7	300	120
8	290	110
9	240	80
10	340	150
11	200	30
12	220	50

Using a scatter diagram, determine the form of the relationship between total hours and the number of units. Estimate the fixed cost and the variable cost per unit of product (in labor hours). Estimate the total number of hours required to complete a job of 130 units.

2.11 A natural gas utility estimated the following model to explain and forecast sales (= consumption) of natural gas in the local metropolitan area:

$$\widehat{GAS} = 16.42 + 0.24HOM + 0.04DDA \qquad R^2 = 0.82$$
$$\qquad\qquad\quad (1.75) \qquad (1.56) \qquad\qquad n = 60$$

The numbers in parentheses are t-ratios. The variables are defined as follows:

GAS : Monthly total consumption of natural gas (millions of cubic feet).

HOM : Number of houses using natural gas (thousands of housing units).

DDA : Number of days in the month with temperature below 65°F (18°C).

The model was estimated using monthly data for the most recent five-year period. The numbers in parentheses are t-ratios.

(a) Interpret the preceding results.

(b) Of what use could this model be to the gas company?

(c) If you were asked to formulate and estimate a model for explaining and forecasting monthly gas consumption, what changes would you recommend to the above model?

2.12 ProLab is a small engineering company specializing in product testing. Recently it obtained a contract to test 10 regional brands of bias-ply and belted-bias tires for passenger cars. It was estimated that these brands accounted for nearly the entire regional market in this type of tire.

The tires were tested for traction in starting, stopping, and cornering and for their ability to withstand road hazards, but the test revealed negligible differences in performance between brands. There were, however, significant differences in the price and the tread life of these tires. Table 2.9 shows the price (in $) and tread life (in thousands of miles) of the tested tires.

The price is the average retail price in three metropolitan areas. The tread life is the approximate mileage at which tread depth reaches 2/32 in.

Two regression models were estimated, with the following results:

$$\widehat{PRICE} = 99.00 + 1.778LIFE \qquad R^2 = 0.674$$
$$(4.07) \qquad\quad S = 4.63$$

$$\widehat{LIFE} = -30.49 + 0.379PRICE \qquad R^2 = 0.674$$
$$(4.07) \qquad\quad S = 2.14$$

The numbers in parentheses are t-ratios.

TABLE 2.9   ProLab, Tire Test Data

Brand No.	Price, PRICE	Tread life, LIFE
1	121	15
2	138	21
3	148	27
4	144	20
5	141	26
6	125	17
7	145	25
8	138	24
9	135	22
10	139	19

It is often said of competitive products that "you get what you pay for," meaning that, in a competitive market, price differences reflect only quality differences. In view of the test results, would you say that the saying applies to this market of tires?

2.13 Automobile dealers purchase and sell cars at auctions held weekly in various places throughout the city. The prices established at the auctions, as well as influencing the prices at which used car dealers sell to the public, form a base used by banks and other financial institutions in making loans for automobile purchases.

Recently, a study was made of the relationship between used car wholesale prices, on the one hand, and such characteristics of the cars as price when new, age, mileage, and weight, on the other.

(a) Five cars were randomly selected from among those sold at the auctions, and information on two variables was recorded. The variables were

RTO : Ratio of wholesale selling price (used price) to car's original retail list price, expressed as a percentage.
MIL : Mileage of car, in thousands of miles.

The data were as follows:

Car No.	RTO	MIL
1	80	18
2	5	82
3	25	48
4	51	27
5	60	41

(i) Plot these observations in a scatter diagram. Is it reasonable to suppose that the relationship between RTO and MIL is linear?
(ii) Assuming the relationship between RTO and MIL is linear, calculate the least squares estimates and plot the estimated relationship in the scatter diagram (RTO is the dependent variable).
(iii) Calculate the variance of residuals (S^2) and the coefficient of determination (R^2).
(iv) Interpret the above results.
(v) A car sold new for $4000 and has been driven 40,000 miles. What is its estimated used price?

(b) From the records of two automobile auctions, 50 Ford medium- and large-sized cars were randomly selected. For each car selected, the following variables were determined.

RTO : Ratio of wholesale selling price (used price) to car's original retail list price, expressed as a percentage.
AGE : Age of car, in model years.
MIL : Mileage of cars, in thousands of miles.
WGH : Weight of car, in thousands of pounds.

The last variable was used as a proxy for cost of operation, maintenance, and fuel economy, on the argument that heavier cars tend to be less economical to maintain and operate.

(i) The computer results of the regression of *RTO* (the dependent variable) on *AGE, MIL,* and *WGH* are as follows:

$$\widehat{RTO} = 93.726 - 5.196AGE - 0.424MIL - 5.199WGH$$
$$(-5.73) \qquad (-6.73) \qquad (-2.39)$$

$$R^2 = 0.80 \qquad S = 6.64$$

The numbers in parentheses are *t*-ratios.

Calculate the estimated used price of a Ford medium-sized car that is three (model) years old, has been driven for 35,000 miles, weighs 4100 lbs, and was originally purchased for $3800.

(ii) Interpret the regression results in (i).

(iii) Two additional regressions were run with the following results:

$$\widehat{RTO} = 69.626 - 4.660AGE - 0.415MIL \qquad R^2 = 0.78$$
$$(-5.06) \qquad (-6.29) \qquad S = 6.96$$

$$\widehat{RTO} = 65.046 - 0.617MIL \qquad R^2 = 0.65$$
$$(-9.53) \qquad S = 8.56$$

What *additional* information do these results provide?

(c) In addition to the Ford cars, 80 General Motors medium- and large-sized cars were randomly selected in the same manner. The same variables were used, and the results of regressing *RTO* on *AGE, MIL,* and *WGH* are as follows:

$$\widehat{RTO} = 138.844 - 6.083AGE - 0.313MIL - 14.461WGH$$
$$(-9.96) \qquad (-4.97) \qquad (-5.62)$$

$$R^2 = 0.83 \qquad S = 6.96$$

Interpret any additional information that these results provide.

2.14 (Due to Ms. Ruth Sommers) The file `norgas.dat` contains the daily gas consumption, mean temperature, and wind velocity for the area served by Norgas over a recent 13-month period. A partial listing of this file is shown in Table 2.10.

The variables are defined as follows:

DATE: Date (month, day of month). E.g., 1201= December 1.

TEMP: Average day's temperature, in degrees Celsius.

WIND: Average day's wind speed, in miles per hour.

GASCON: Total day's gas consumption, in thousand cubic meters.

(a) Plot scatter diagrams of GASCON and TEMP, GASCON and WIND, and TEMP and WIND.

(b) It is the practice of the industry to relate gas consumption, not to the mean daily temperature, but to "degree days." This variable (call it DEGDAY) is defined as follows:

$$DEGDAY = \begin{cases} 18° - TEMP, & \text{if TEMP} < 18° \\ 0, & \text{otherwise.} \end{cases}$$

TABLE 2.10 File `norgas.dat`,
Partial Listing

DATE	TEMP	WIND	GASCON
1201	4.7	5	15279.3
1202	0.0	22	19228.8
1203	−9.3	13	24722.8
1204	−8.6	4	23305.4
1205	−5.8	3	21263.6
1206	0.0	2	17707.6
1207	3.3	1	15975.0
1208	4.2	11	16940.5
1209	0.0	2	18520.7
1210	−5.7	12	21781.7
...	...	...	...

In words, DEGDAY is equal to the number of degrees below a certain "base temperature" (in this case, +18° C), or zero if the days' mean temperature equals or exceeds the base temperature. It is believed that GASCON is more closely related to DEGDAY than to TEMP. Calculate DEGDAY for each date in the file. Plot a scatter diagram of GASCON against DEGDAY. Do your calculations support industry practice?

(c) Develop and test a regression model to forecast a day's gas consumption given weather forecasts of the day's mean temperature and wind speed. Explain the rationale for your model.

CHAPTER 3

INFERENCE IN REGRESSION

3.1 INTRODUCTION AND SUMMARY

Up to this point, the method of least squares was viewed only as a technique for fitting a linear function to a set of observations; we were not especially concerned about the origin of these observations. We would now like to examine where the observations could come from, whether the OLS estimates can measure characteristics of a "whole" of which the observations form a part, and, if so, how this may be done.

We intend to describe why OLS estimates, in addition to providing the best fit, have the additional desirable properties of unbiasedness, minimum variance among other estimates in their class, and consistency if the observations constitute a random sample from a process or population having certain special features. Exactly what these properties are, why they are desirable, and the nature of the special features must be explained with some care.

We also intend to describe how to form, under some additional conditions, confidence intervals for the parameters and forecasts and to carry out tests of hypotheses concerning these parameters.[1]

3.2 ADDITIONAL PROPERTIES OF OLS ESTIMATORS

Imagine that each of the n observations on Y and the k explanatory variables (Y, $X_1, X_2, \ldots, X_k$) is generated by a process having certain features. The features of this process are as follows.

First, the values of the explanatory variables $X_1, X_2, \ldots, X_k$ are determined in some manner. Then, the value of the dependent variable (Y) is created *as if* by adding to the term $\beta_0 + \beta_1 X_1 + \cdots + \beta_k X_k$ (which can be interpreted as the part of Y *explained* by the X's) an "error" or "disturbance" (ε), which is the result of a random draw with replacement from a population of ε values

---

[1]These issues are rather complicated. We intend to provide only a summary of the principal properties. A more detailed—and mathematically more difficult—treatment can be found in, among other sources, Pindyck and Rubinfeld (1991), Johnston (1984), Theil (1971), or Malinvaud (1980).

having mean $E(\varepsilon) = 0$ and a certain variance, $Var(\varepsilon) = \sigma^2$. The β's and σ^2 (the process parameters) are assumed to be given but unknown numbers.

The emphasis on the words *as if* is deliberate. For the time being, the process can be thought of abstractly as a "black box," the input to which are the X's and the output of which is Y, created as described earlier. In the next section, we describe a concrete situation satisfying the assumptions of this process.

To grasp the mechanism that is supposed to generate the available observations, suppose that there is only one explanatory variable, that is, $Y = \beta_0 + \beta_1 X + \varepsilon$ and that the process parameters are $\beta_0 = 3$ and $\beta_1 = -1$. Imagine further that 10 small identical tags are put in a box, each marked with one of the numbers $-1, 0,$ or $+1$. These numbers, the population of ε values of this illustration, are distributed as follows:

ε	Frequency
-1	3
0	4
$+1$	$\underline{3}$
	10

The mean of these numbers is 0 and the variance $\sigma^2 = 0.6$, as can be easily verified.[2]

Imagine now that the X value of the first observation is 1. The corresponding Y value is created *as if* by adding to the quantity $\beta_0 + \beta_1 X = (3) + (-1)(1) = 2$ the ε value of a tag selected at random from the box. Suppose this ε value is 1. The resulting Y value is $2 + 1$ or 3. Thus, the first observation (X, Y) is the pair $(1, 3)$. The selected tag is put back into the box prior to the following draw.

The following table describes the creation of this and two additional observations corresponding to X values of 2 and 3:

X	$\beta_0 + \beta_1 X$ $= 3 - X$	ε	$Y = \beta_0 + \beta_1 X + \varepsilon$ $= 3 - X + \varepsilon$
1	2	1	3
2	1	-1	0
3	0	0	0

The three sets of (X, Y) observations are the pairs $(1, 3)$, $(2, 0)$, and $(3, 0)$. Of course, different draws would have resulted in different Y values.

---

[2] A review of frequency, relative frequency, and probability distributions can be found in Appendix A.4 and A.5. Joint distributions and independence are reviewed in Appendix A.8 and A.9.

For example, if the three random draws had resulted in ε values of -1, 1, and 0, the three observations would have been (1, 1), (2, 2), and (3, 0).

Clearly, the ε values are not related to (are independent of) the X values. Also, because sampling is with replacement the ε values are independent of one another.

It is this type of process, then, that is assumed to generate the n observations $(Y, X_1, X_2, \ldots, X_k)$ in the general case. Summarizing, the special features of the process are assumed to be

i. $Y = \beta_0 + \beta_1 X_1 + \cdots + \beta_k X_k + \varepsilon$ with $E(\varepsilon) = 0$;

ii. $Var(\varepsilon) = \sigma^2$; and

iii. the ε values are independent of one another and of the X's.

We shall refer to these briefly as the assumptions of (i) linearity, (ii) constant variance, and (iii) independence, respectively. The values of the explanatory variables can be any numbers—we are not concerned about their origin.

If, then, the n observations are generated by such a process, it can be shown that

- the OLS estimators $b_0, b_1, b_2, \ldots, b_k$, are unbiased and consistent estimators of the parameters $\beta_0, \beta_1, \ldots, \beta_k$, respectively;
- the b's have the smallest variance among all unbiased estimators of the β's that are linear functions of the Y's;
- an unbiased and consistent estimator of σ^2 is

$$\hat{S}^2 = \frac{\sum (Y - \hat{Y})^2}{n - k - 1} = \frac{nS^2}{n - k - 1}$$

Before we explain these properties, a note on terminology. By *estimator* we understand a sample statistic used to estimate a population parameter and by *estimate* the value of an estimator. For example, we say that $\hat{S}^2$ is an estimator of σ^2, but its numerical value based on the sample observations is an estimate of σ^2.

Let us now go back to the simple model $Y = \beta_0 + \beta_1 X + \varepsilon$ of the illustration of this section and imagine a large number of experiments, in each of which $n = 3$ pairs of observations (X, Y) are generated, and the OLS estimates b_0, b_1 and $\hat{S}^2$ calculated. For example, the first set of observations generated earlier (1, 3), (2, 0), and (3, 0), yield $b_0 = 4$, $b_1 = -1.5$, and $\hat{S}^2 = 1.5$, as can be easily confirmed. A second set of observations (1, 1), (2, 2), and (3, 0), yields $b_0 = 2$, $b_1 = -0.5$, and $\hat{S}^2 = 1.5$, again as can be confirmed.

Unbiasedness means that in a large number of such experiments the average of the values of b_0 can be expected to equal β_0, the average of b_1 values to equal β_1, and the average of the $\hat{S}^2$ values to equal σ^2. In other words, in the long run and on average, the OLS estimates are expected neither to overstate nor to understate but to equal the process parameters. It should be possible to confirm this property of unbiasedness with experiments involving 5, 10, 100, or any other number of pairs of observations.

Fig. 3.1 illustrates this property. Panel (a) outlines the distribution of the OLS estimator b of a parameter β (this could be β_0 or β_1) in a large number of experiments, each involving the same number n of observations. The distribution can be expected to be "centered" on β, in the sense that the average value of b equals β. By contrast, panel (b) of Fig. 3.1 shows the distribution of a biased estimator, b', of β. The difference between the expected average value of this estimator and β is the *bias* of b'.

Unbiasedness was explained in the context of a large number of experiments. Evidently, we have in mind potential, not real experiments. The expected distribution of an estimator in a large number of potential experiments is, of course, the *probability distribution* of the estimator. The average value of the estimator in a large number of potential experiments is the *expected value* of the estimator. For future reference, therefore, the definition of unbiasedness may be expressed as follows:

- An estimator—say, b—of a process parameter—say, β—is *unbiased* if its expected value equals that parameter, that is, if $E(b) = \beta$.

An estimator b of a process parameter β is consistent if the probability that b will deviate from β by more than a specified positive quantity c, no matter how small the quantity, becomes smaller as the number of observations gets larger. In symbols,

- An estimator b is said to be a *consistent* estimator of a process parameter β if $Pr(|b - \beta| > c) \rightarrow 0$ as $n \rightarrow \infty$.

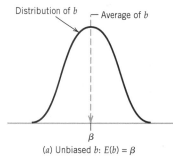

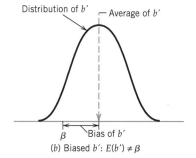

(a) Unbiased b: $E(b) = \beta$

(b) Biased b': $E(b') \neq \beta$

FIGURE 3.1 Unbiasedness illustrated

In practical terms, consistency means that the probability of a deviation exceeding a given amount is small when the number of observations is large.

Fig. 3.2 shows the probability distribution of an OLS estimator b in two cases. In the first, the number of observations n on the basis of which b is calculated is small, while in the second n is large. The probability that b will deviate from β by more than c, that is, will lie outside the range from $\beta - c$ to $\beta + c$, is the sum of the shaded areas to the left of $\beta - c$ and to the right of $\beta + c$. When n is large, we can expect the distribution of b to be more compact and the deviation probability smaller.

The same discussion applies to S^2 as an estimator of the parameter σ^2: the claim is that $\hat{S}^2$ an unbiased and consistent estimator of σ^2.

To complete the explanation of the properties, consider the variability of the OLS estimators. An ideal estimator will have the least variability (the smallest variance) among all unbiased estimators of the process parameter. It is not true that the OLS estimators have this property, but it is possible to show that the b's have the smallest variance among all unbiased estimators that are linear functions of the Y values. Such estimators are called *minimum variance linear unbiased (MVLU)*. The OLS estimators b_0 to b_k, therefore, may not be the very best unbiased estimators but are best in this restricted class of estimators.

Clearly, unbiasedness, minimum variance linear unbiasedness, and consistency are desirable properties. We see that the OLS estimators not only fit the observations best, in the sense of minimizing the sum of squared residuals, but have these *additional* properties in the event the observations are generated by a process having the features described in this section.

3.3   A POPULATION WITH SPECIAL FEATURES

It will be useful to describe at least one concrete situation in which the conditions of the abstract process of the last section are satisfied. The situation

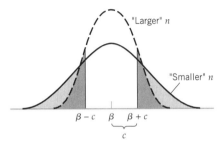

FIGURE 3.2   Consistency illustrated

involves random sampling from a population with certain special features. We shall explain these special features with the help of an example.

We are interested, let us suppose, in the relationship between household savings and income. The population of interest consists of all N households in the country.

Pretend for a moment that a list of all households is available and that the income (X) of and the amount saved (Y) by each household during a given year are known. There are available, therefore, N pairs of (X, Y) values. A joint relative frequency distribution (a "cross-tabulation") of income and savings can be constructed by forming a number of intervals for income and for savings and calculating the proportion of households that fall into each pair of such intervals. If these intervals are narrow enough, the population joint distribution of income and savings, $p(X, Y)$, may be visualized like the smooth joint distribution shown in Fig. 3.3.

Consider now those households that have a specified income level of, say, around ($x_\circ =$) \$10,000. The amount saved by each of these households varies. The relative frequency distribution of savings for households having income $x_\circ$ can be imagined as a scaled "slice" of the joint distribution at $x_\circ$ (see Fig. 3.3). For each income level, therefore, there is a distribution of savings, as shown in Fig. 3.4.

The distribution of savings for households having a given income is called the *conditional distribution* of savings given income. Each of these conditional

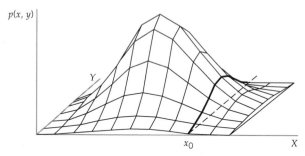

FIGURE 3.3 Bivariate population distribution

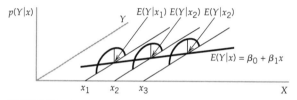

FIGURE 3.4 Conditional distributions of Y given X

distributions (one for each level of income) has a mean and a variance. We shall denote the conditional relative frequency distribution of savings (Y) given income $X = x$ by $p(Y|x)$, and the mean and variance of this distribution by $E(Y|x)$ and $Var(Y|x)$, respectively. In general, these two characteristics of $p(Y|x)$ depend on the value of X. For example, both the average amount saved and the variability of the amount saved by households having an income of \$10,000 are probably different from those of households having an income of \$20,000.

The relationship between $E(Y|x)$ and x can take a variety of forms. The simplest and most convenient is the linear form,

$$E(Y|x) = \beta_0 + \beta_1 x \tag{3.1}$$

where β_0 and β_1 are some constants. Under this assumption, all the means of the conditional distributions of Y given $X = x$ lie on a straight line defined by the parameters β_0 and β_1, as illustrated in Fig. 3.4.

Again, the most convenient assumption concerning the variances of the conditional distributions of Y is that they are all equal and do not depend on the value of X:

$$Var(Y|x) = \sigma^2 \tag{3.2}$$

where σ^2 is a certain constant. This assumption is reflected in the common shape of the conditional distributions shown in Fig. 3.4.

We emphasize that these assumptions concerning the characteristics of the conditional distributions of Y in the population are fairly restrictive. Fig. 3.5 shows a case in which it is true neither that the means of the conditional distributions lie on a straight line nor that the variances of these distributions are equal. Nevertheless, the assumptions are among the simplest possible and are at least approximately satisfied in many practical applications.

Briefly, then, we assume that the joint distribution of income and savings in the population satisfies Eqs. 3.1 and 3.2, but β_0, β_1 and σ^2 are not known

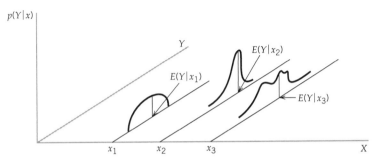

FIGURE 3.5   Nonlinearity and nonconstant variance illustrated

and must be estimated on the basis of a sample. We now turn to the sampling method and distinguish two procedures for selecting a random sample with replacement.

(a) The first procedure is the standard one. Using the available list of households and random numbers, we select a simple random sample of n households and record their savings and income. These sample observations, in turn, will be used to calculate the sample OLS estimates b_0, b_1, and S^2.

(b) A second procedure for selecting a random sample of households is to specify in advance n income levels $x_1, x_2, \ldots, x_n$ (not necessarily all different from one another) and then to select at random and with replacement one household from among those having each specified level of income. Thus, one household will be randomly selected from among those households that have income x_1, one from among those having income x_2, and so on. Since the Y's will vary from one sample to another even when the specified x's remain the same, the OLS estimates will also vary from sample to sample.

The difference between the two methods of sample selection lies in the nature of the observations on the variable X. Under method a, the values of X, as well as those of Y, cannot be predicted in advance. Under method b, the values of X are controlled (as in the experiment to determine the strength of the plastic material described in Example 2.3) or are otherwise determined, and the variability of b_0, b_1, and S^2 from sample to sample is due to the variability of Y alone. Under either method, the Y values are independent of one another by virtue of sampling with replacement. With either procedure, however, we shall end up with n pairs of observations (X, Y) and the least squares estimates b_0, b_1, and S^2 calculated using these observations.

It can be shown that the assumptions of this section are mathematically equivalent to those for the abstract process of Section 3.2. It follows that *for samples selected by either procedure from populations with the above special features, b_0, b_1, and $\hat{S}^2 = nS^2/(n-2)$ are unbiased and consistent estimators of β_0, β_1, and σ^2 respectively. b_0 and b_1 in particular have the lowest variance among all unbiased estimators of β_0 and β_1 that are linear functions of the Y values.*

The conditions and conclusions just described can be restated for the general case, in which we are interested in the relationship between Y, on the one hand, and a number of explanatory variables, $X_1, X_2, \ldots, X_k$, on the other, in a population of N elements. For every set of values of the explanatory variables there exists a conditional population distribution of Y. The conditional distribution of Y given $X_1 = x_1, X_2 = x_2, \ldots, X_k = x_k$ is denoted by $p(Y|x_1, x_2, \ldots, x_k)$.

There are as many conditional distributions of Y as there are different sets of values of explanatory variables. Each such conditional distribution has a mean and a variance, which we may write as $E(Y|x_1, x_2, \ldots, x_k)$ and $Var(Y|x_1, x_2, \ldots, x_k)$, respectively, to make explicit the fact that, in general, they are functions of x_1, $x_2, \ldots, x_k$.

The extension of the assumptions of the simple model is as follows: (i) the means of the conditional distributions of Y are linearly related to $x_1, x_2, \ldots, x_k$,

$$E(Y|x_1, x_2, \ldots, x_k) = \beta_0 + \beta_1 x_1 + \beta_2 x_2 + \cdots + \beta_k x_k \qquad (3.3)$$

where $\beta_0, \beta_1, \beta_2, \ldots$, and β_k are unknown parameters; (ii) the variances of the conditional distributions of Y are all equal:

$$Var(Y|x_1, x_2, \ldots, x_k) = \sigma^2 \qquad (3.4)$$

and (iii) n sets of observations $(Y, X_1, X_2, \ldots, X_k)$ will be available as a result of either (a) taking a simple random sample of size n with replacement from the population or (b) first selecting or otherwise determining n sets of values of the explanatory variables $(X_1, X_2, \ldots, X_k)$ and then randomly selecting one element with replacement from among all population elements having each such set of values. In either case, the Y values are independent of one another by virtue of the random selection. *We refer to these as the assumptions of (i) linearity, (ii) constant variance, and (iii) independence, respectively.*

The OLS estimators $b_0, b_1, b_2, \ldots, b_k$, and S^2 will be based on these sample observations and will be calculated in the standard way.

Under conditions (i) to (iii), it can be shown that $b_0, b_1, \ldots, b_k$, and $\hat{S}^2 = nS^2/(n-k-1)$ are *unbiased and consistent estimators* of the parameters β_0, $\beta_1, \ldots, \beta_k$, and σ^2, respectively; also, that they *have the smallest variance among all unbiased estimators of the parameters that are linear functions of the Y values.*[3]

Since sampling with and sampling without replacement amount essentially to the same method when the population size is large and sample size is small in relation to the population size, we can see that *these desirable properties of OLS estimators hold approximately also for samples without replacement, provided that the population size N is large and the ratio n/N small.*

---

[3]We can now explain why most computer programs prefer to output $\hat{S}$, in place of the more intuitively appealing S: $\hat{S}^2$ is an unbiased estimator of σ^2, S^2 is not. However, S^2 can be shown to be a consistent estimator of σ^2, and when n is large $\hat{S}^2$ and S^2 are approximately equal and have the same properties. Carrying two sets of symbols for essentially the same measure can be quite confusing. From now on, therefore, we shall cease to distinguish between S^2 and $\hat{S}^2$ (or S and $\hat{S}$) and shall use the symbols S^2 and S to refer to the variance and standard deviation of residuals regardless of the manner in which they are calculated.

3.4   A POPULATION WITH DIFFERENT FEATURES

As noted earlier, the assumptions of Section 3.3 are fairly restrictive. It is useful, therefore, to examine the consequences of one departure from these assumptions.

Let us return to the population of households of the last section. We are interested, as before, in the relationship between household savings and income. There are N households in the country. Pretend for a moment that the income (X) of and the amount saved (Y) by each household during a given year are known. There are available, therefore, N pairs of (X, Y) values.

Suppose that a scatter diagram of these observations indicates that the linear model $\hat{Y} = b_0 + b_1 X$ provides a satisfactory *approximate* description of the relationship between income and savings. In contrast to the last section, we do not assume that the means of the conditional distributions of savings are linearly related to income or that the variances of the conditional distributions are constant. The values of b_0 and b_1 that fit the observations best in the sense of the least-squares criterion can be calculated using Eqs. (2.7) and (2.8) and all N available observations. A measure of fit of the model, S^2, can also be calculated from Eq. (2.11) using the N residuals of this regression. Let us refer to these population parameters that are based on all N observations as $\tilde{\beta}_0$, $\tilde{\beta}_1$, and $\tilde{\sigma}^2$.

In reality, of course, these population parameters are not known. They can only be estimated with the help of a sample. Suppose that a simple random sample of n households will be selected, with or without replacement. The income and savings of each household in the sample will be determined, and there will be available n pairs of (X, Y) values. The OLS estimates b_0, b_1, and S^2 will then be calculated, using the same Eqs. (2.7), (2.8), and (2.11), but, this time, the n sample observations.

Since b_0, b_1, and S^2 will be based on the sample observations and since these observations will vary from one sample to another, b_0, b_1, and S^2 will also vary from one sample to another. It is reasonable to use b_0, b_1, and S^2 as estimators of $\tilde{\beta}_0$, $\tilde{\beta}_1$, and $\tilde{\sigma}^2$, respectively, since the former are the sample counterparts of the latter. What, then, can be said about the properties of these estimators?

It can be shown that b_0, b_1, and S^2 are consistent estimators of $\tilde{\beta}_0$, $\tilde{\beta}_1$, and $\tilde{\sigma}^2$ in samples with or without replacement.

In other words, the probability that the estimate will deviate from the corresponding population parameter by more than a given amount—no matter how small that amount may be—tends toward zero as the sample size approaches the population size (in samples without replacement; infinity in samples with replacement). They are *not*, in general, unbiased estimators.

3.5 CONFIDENCE INTERVALS AND TESTS

In this section, we describe how confidence intervals may be formed and tests of hypotheses carried out for the parameters of the process or population if the conditions described in Sections 3.2 or 3.3 *and one more* are satisfied.

We have in mind the general linear model $Y = \beta_0 + \beta_1 X_1 + \beta_2 X_2 + \cdots + \beta_k X_k + \varepsilon$. In order to simplify the notation as much as possible, let X represent a "typical" explanatory variable, β the corresponding process or population parameter, and b its OLS estimator. Since b depends on the n sample observations, its value will depend on these observations. Its probability distribution (its relative frequency distribution in a large number of experiments, as described in Section 3.2) has a certain mean, which we denote by $E(b)$, and a certain variance, denoted by $Var(b)$.

Under the assumptions of Section 3.2 or 3.3, b is unbiased—therefore, $E(b) = \beta$. The variance of the distribution of b, $Var(b)$, can be derived, but it is a complicated expression and will not be written here. It is possible to form an estimator of $Var(b)$ based on the sample observations; this will be denoted by S_b^2. Most computer programs calculate and print the square root, S_b, of these estimates (they appear in the column headed `Standard Error` in Figures 2.6 and 2.8). The t-ratio we referred to in Chapter 2 is simply the ratio b/S_b.

In the special case of one explanatory variable ($Y = \beta_0 + \beta_1 X + \varepsilon$), the variances of the estimators b_0 and b_1 can be shown to be

$$Var(b_0) = \frac{\sigma^2 \sum X^2}{n \sum (X - \bar{X})^2}, \quad \text{and} \quad Var(b_1) = \frac{\sigma^2}{\sum (X - \bar{X})^2}$$

and their estimators

$$S_{b_0}^2 = \frac{S^2 \sum X^2}{n \sum (X - \bar{X})^2}, \quad \text{and} \quad S_{b_1}^2 = \frac{S^2}{\sum (X - \bar{X})^2}$$

respectively.

For the remaining results of this section, it is necessary to assume, *in addition to* (i) linearity, (ii) constant variance, and (iii) independence, that either

iv (a). the population distribution of the ε-values of Section 3.2 is *normal*, or

iv (b). all the conditional distributions of Y, $p(Y|x_1, x_2, \ldots, x_k)$, of Section 3.3 are *normal*.

We shall refer to this briefly as the assumption of (iv) normality. Collectively, conditions i to iv will be said to describe the *classical linear model*.

The probability distribution of a variable Y is said to be *normal* with mean μ and variance σ^2 if it is given by

$$p(Y) = \frac{1}{\sigma\sqrt{2\pi}} e^{-\frac{1}{2}\left(\frac{Y-\mu}{\sigma}\right)^2} \qquad (-\infty < Y < +\infty)$$

The normal distribution is bell-shaped and symmetric about μ, as illustrated in Fig. 3.6.

The normality assumption requires either that the population distribution of the error values, ε, be normal with mean 0 and a certain variance σ^2, or that all conditional distributions of Y (such as those shown in Fig. 3.4) be normal with means $\beta_0 + \beta_1 X_1 + \cdots + \beta_k X_k$ and the same variance σ^2.

A Confidence Interval for a Parameter   Instead of saying "β is estimated to be b," we may say "β is estimated to be in the interval from $b - c$ to $b + c$." This is an interval around b, usually abbreviated as $b \pm c$, with c to be specified. $b \pm c$ is an *interval estimator* of β, and we may on occasion prefer it to the ordinary estimator b (a *point estimator*, as an ordinary estimator is called when contrasted to an interval estimator).

For given values of b and c, the statement "β is in the interval $b \pm c$" is either correct (that is, the interval contains β) or incorrect. Forming an arbitrary interval is not at all difficult, but forming an interval having a given probability of containing β is not trivial. An interval estimator of a process parameter that will contain the parameter with a given probability is called a *confidence interval* and the given probability the *confidence level*.

Under conditions i to iv, it can be shown that a $100(1 - \alpha)\%$ confidence interval for β is the interval

$$b \pm T_{\alpha/2} S_b \tag{3.5}$$

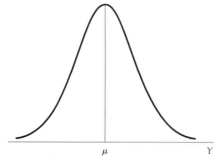

FIGURE 3.6   Normal distribution

Note that this interval is of the form $b \pm c$. α and $T_{\alpha/2}$ depend on the desired confidence level. For example, for a 90% confidence interval, $\alpha = 0.10$ and $\alpha/2 = 0.05$. $T_{\alpha/2}$, often called the "critical t-value," is a number such that the probability that a random variable having the "t distribution" with parameter ("degrees of freedom") $\nu = n - k - 1$ will exceed that number is $\alpha/2$ (as always, k is the number of explanatory variables, n the number of observations). When ν is greater than 30, the t distribution may be well approximated by the standard normal (the normal distribution with mean 0 and variance 1), and commonly used $T_{\alpha/2}$ can be read from Table 3.1.

For given b and S_b, the greater the desired confidence level, the greater is $T_{\alpha/2}$, hence, the wider the confidence interval. Likewise, for given b and confidence level, the smaller the S_b, the narrower the confidence interval.

The calculation of this type of confidence interval (and of other intervals and tests to be described later) is illustrated in Section 3.7.

A Test for a Parameter   A common statistical test in regression is that of the hypothesis that an explanatory variable X has no effect upon Y, against the alternative hypothesis that it has some (positive or negative) effect:

$$H_0: \beta = 0 \quad (X \text{ has no effect on } Y)$$
$$H_A: \beta \neq 0 \quad (X \text{ has some effect on } Y)$$

"Has no effect on Y" means "does not influence Y," "does not contribute toward explaining Y."

Either H_0 is true (and H_A false) or H_0 is false (and H_A true). One of two decisions will be made: Accept H_0 or Reject H_0. "Accept H_0" means "take the action appropriate when H_0 is true," and "Reject H_0" means "take the action appropriate when H_A is true." There are thus two events, two decisions,

TABLE 3.1
Approximate
"Critical
t-Values"

$\alpha/2$	$T_{\alpha/2}$
0.010	2.33
0.025	1.96
0.050	1.64
0.100	1.28
0.250	0.67

and four consequences, which the language of statistical tests describes as follows:

Decisions	Events	
	H_0 true	H_0 false
Accept H_0	No error	Type II error
Reject H_0	Type I error	No error

In general, a statistical test is a decision rule based on the sample observations prescribing when to accept and when to reject H_0 so as to control the probabilities of the two types or error. When the number of observations is given, any decision rule that reduces the probability of one type of error usually increases the probability of the other type. It is reasonable then to look for a decision rule such that the probability of a Type I error (rejecting H_0 when H_0 is true) does not exceed a given number α and that of a Type II error (accepting H_0 when H_0 is false) does not exceed $1 - \alpha$. α is called the "level of significance" of the test. The value of α, in theory at least, ought to depend on the consequences of the two types of error. Thus, when the consequences of a Type I error are more serious than those of a Type II error, we may wish to make α small; in the opposite case, we may want to make $1 - \alpha$ small, that is, let α be relatively large.[4]

Under conditions i to iv, it can be shown that a decision rule for testing $H_0 : \beta = 0$ satisfying the foregoing requirements is to

$$\text{Accept } H_0 \quad \text{if } |t = \tfrac{b}{S_b}| < T_{\alpha/2}$$
$$\text{Reject } H_0 \quad \text{if otherwise}$$

H_0, therefore, should be accepted when the absolute value of the calculated t-ratio ($t = b/S_b$) is small and rejected when it is large. $T_{\alpha/2}$ forms the boundary between "small" and "large" absolute t-ratios. $T_{\alpha/2}$ is the same critical t-value partially tabulated in Table 3.1 for large v.

Many computer programs make such tabulations unnecessary in that they calculate and display the probability of rejecting $H_0 : \beta = 0$ when H_0 is true and the calculated t-ratio is used as the critical t-value. These probabilities are usually displayed under such headings as P, P VALUE, or PROB VALUE.

---

[4] A test satisfying these conditions is known as "unbiased"; see, for example, Wilks (1962, Ch. 13). For the tests described in this section, the decision rules make the probability of a Type I error *equal* to α.

The decision rule, therefore, can be stated more conveniently in terms of these P-VALUEs as follows:

$$\text{Accept } H_0 \text{ if (P-VALUE of } X) > \alpha$$
$$\text{Reject } H_0 \text{ if otherwise}$$

In words, if the P-VALUE of X exceeds α, H_0 should be accepted, otherwise it should be rejected.

A variable for which H_0 is rejected is often called a "significant variable."

A Confidence Interval for a Forecast   Consider now forecasting the value of Y corresponding to a given set of values of the explanatory variables, X_1, X_2, ..., X_k. This forecast, $\hat{Y}$,

$$\hat{Y} = b_0 + b_1 X_1 + b_2 X_2 + \cdots + b_k X_k$$

is based on the OLS estimates b_0, b_1, ..., b_k, which, in turn, are based on the sample observations. Since the latter will vary from one sample to another, so will the b's, hence also $\hat{Y}$.

Under conditions i to iv, it can be shown that a $100(1 - \alpha)\%$ confidence interval for the true value of Y is

$$\hat{Y} \pm T_{\alpha/2} \, S_f \tag{3.6}$$

where S_f is an estimate of the standard deviation of the forecast value, $\hat{Y}$.

In the case of a single explanatory variable (*but only in this case*), S_f is the square root of

$$S_f^2 = S^2 \left[1 + \frac{1}{n} + \frac{(x - \bar{X})^2}{\sum (X - \bar{X})^2} \right]$$

where S^2 is the variance of the residuals, and x the value of X at which the forecast of Y is desired. $\sum (X - \bar{X})^2 / n$ is the ordinary variance of the n X values.

Observe that S_f^2 (and S_f) is least when $x = \bar{X}$. In other words, the interval forecast is narrowest at the average of the observed X values.

In the general case, the formula for S_f is rather complicated and will not be written here. It is stated without proof in Appendix B.3 for the benefit of readers familiar with matrix algebra. S_f as well as confidence interval forecasts are calculated on request by many computer programs for regression for any specified values of the explanatory variables and confidence level.

A Test for a Subset of Parameters We conclude with a formal test of the hypothesis that a subset of explanatory variables has no effect upon the dependent variable. Without loss of generality, we can assume that this set of "suspect" variables consists of the first q of the k available explanatory variables. The hypothesis to be tested is

$$H_0: \quad \beta_1 = \beta_2 = \cdots = \beta_q = 0$$

against the alternative hypothesis H_A that at least one of these β's is not equal to zero. In other words, H_0 is the hypothesis that none of the explanatory variables $X_1, X_2, \ldots, X_q$ influences (contributes toward explaining) Y. The alternative hypothesis is that one or more of these variables does influence Y.

If the probability of a Type I error (rejecting H_0 when H_0 is true) is not to exceed α and that of a Type II error (accepting H_0 when H_0 is false) is not exceed $1 - \alpha$, it can be shown that the decision rule is to

$$\text{Accept } H_0 \quad \text{if } F < F_\alpha$$
$$\text{Reject } H_0 \quad \text{if } F > F_\alpha$$

where

$$F = \frac{n - k - 1}{q} \frac{SSE_P - SSE_F}{SSE_F} = \frac{n - k - 1}{q} \frac{Q}{1 - Q}$$

F is often referred to as "the F statistic." Q, of course, is the Q statistic of Section 2.9. F_α is a "critical value" of the "F distribution" with parameters $v_1 = q$ and $v_2 = n - k - 1$.

For given n, k, and q, the closer Q is to 1 (the greater the relative contribution of the suspect variables), the greater the value of F; the closer Q is to 0, the closer F also is to 0. F is always a positive number. We should want to accept H_0 when F is small and to reject it when F is large. F_α distinguishes "small" from "large" F values.

Major statistical programs calculate on request the F statistic for any specified set of q suspect variables. In addition, they may calculate and display the probability of rejecting H_0 when H_0 is true and the calculated F statistic is used as the critical F value; this probability is shown under such headings as P or P-VALUE. The latter feature is convenient because it makes unnecessary long tabulations of critical F values.[5]

---

[5]These critical values are also produced on request by statistical programs. For example, the Minitab commands invcdf 0.95; f 2 23. produce 3.42, the critical F value for $\alpha = 0.05$, $v_1 = 2$, and $v_2 = 23$.

The last decision rule, expressed in terms of P-VALUEs, reads as follows:

$$\text{Accept } H_0 \quad \text{if (P-VALUE of test)} > \alpha$$
$$\text{Reject } H_0 \quad \text{if otherwise}$$

3.6 ROUGH CHECKS OF THE ASSUMPTIONS OF THE CLASSICAL LINEAR MODEL

We emphasize, once again, that the results of the last section are applicable when the assumptions of the classical linear model are satisfied, that is, (i) linearity, (ii) constant variance, (iii) independence of observations, and (iv) normality.

These conditions are restrictive and should be assumed with care. Scatter diagrams and other simple plots may be used to check roughly the consistency of the observations to these conditions. Let us illustrate.

Suppose there is only one explanatory variable, X. Examine the scatter diagrams of Fig. 3.7. (Fig. 3.7 shows *patterns* suggested by the points in the scatter diagram and not the points themselves.)

Fig. 3.7(a) illustrates the kind of scatter diagram expected if the conditions of linearity and constant variance are satisfied. A plot of the regression residuals against X would appear as in Fig. 3.7(b). Fig. 3.7(c) shows a linear relationship

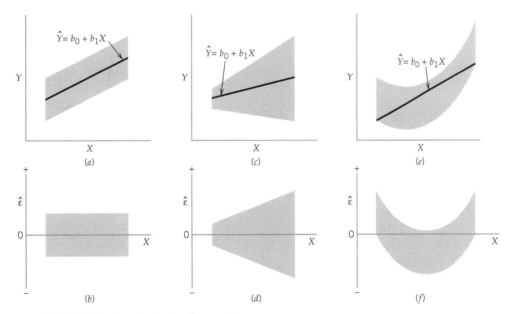

FIGURE 3.7 Simple checks of assumptions

between Y and X, but the variance of Y increases with X. The plot of the regression residuals against X in this case would appear as in Fig. 3.7(d). Fig. 3.7(e) indicates a nonlinear relationship between Y and X; when this relationship is approximated by a linear one, $\hat{Y} = b_0 + b_1 X$, the plot of the regression residuals $\hat{\varepsilon}$ against X would appear as in Fig. 3.7(f).

In models with more than one explanatory variable, plots of the residuals against each explanatory variable X could reveal if the assumptions of linearity and constant variance are approximately satisfied.

Mild violations of the assumptions of linearity and constant variance can be shown to cause little damage. The lack of independence of the observations, however, not only has more serious consequences but also is more difficult to detect. Of course, if the observations are selected at random and with replacement from a population with the features described in Section 3.3, the very method of selection guarantees independence. There is no guarantee of independence, however, when the observations are generated by an unknown process.

A plot of the regression residuals (in the order of the observations) may reveal one form of violation of independence. For if the errors, ε, are indeed random selections with replacement from a population of ε values, there should be *no pattern* in the regression residuals, $\hat{\varepsilon}$; they should appear more or less as in Fig. 3.8(a). Patterns such as the exaggerated ones of Figures 3.8(b), 3.8(c), or 3.8(d), on the other hand, are not consistent with the assumption of independence. This type of plot should be produced and examined especially in the case where the observations are in the form of time series, which are known often not to conform to this assumption. The main weakness of this type of plot, of course, is that a pattern may be more subtle than the plot is capable of detecting.

Finally, a rough check of the normality assumption may be made with the help of a plot of the relative frequency distribution of the regression residuals, which should look symmetric and bell shaped if the distribution of ε is normal. Studies have shown that the confidence intervals described in Section 3.5 and the tests based on the t and F statistics are not very sensitive to mild violations of the normality assumption when the sample size, n, is reasonably large.[6]

3.7 AN ILLUSTRATION

Let us consider once again a model presented in Example 2.1 of Section 2.10, in which the price of a residential property is assumed to be linearly related to floor and lot area:

$$PRICE = \beta_0 + \beta_1 FLOOR + \beta_2 LOT + \varepsilon$$

---

[6]In Chapter 9, we examine in more detail violations of the assumptions of the classical linear model as well as simple remedies.

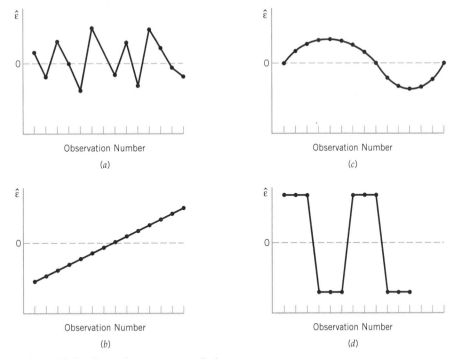

Observation Number

(a)

Observation Number

(c)

Observation Number

(b)

Observation Number

(d)

FIGURE 3.8 Plots of regression residuals

β_1 can be described as the "true" amount by which the price of a property changes with each additional square foot of floor area. Likewise, β_2 is the true amount by which price changes with each additional foot of lot area.

Let us tentatively assume that the errors, ε, representing the combined effect of the neglected property features and the unknown form of the relationship, behave *as if* generated by random draws with replacement from a normal distribution of ε values having mean 0 and some variance σ^2.

The computer file rest.dat, partially listed in Table 3.2, includes the price (*PRICE*, in $000), floor area (*FLOOR*, in square feet), and lot area (*LOT*, also in square feet) of 100 residential properties that changed hands during a three-month period.[7]

A regression of price against floor and lot area using the program Minitab produced the edited computer output shown in Fig. 3.9. In our format, the regression results can be summarized as

$$PRICE = 69.85 + 0.2028FLOOR + 0.0218LOT \qquad R^2 = 0.54$$
$$(8.60) \qquad\qquad (6.03) \qquad\qquad S = 102.5$$

---

[7]The variables *AVESELPR* and *LOC* are explained and used in the continuation of this example in Chapter 4.

TABLE 3.2 File rest.dat, Partial Listing

PRICE	FLOOR	LOT	AVESELPR	LOC
213.750	740	1854	250.500	I
195.000	914	1256	250.500	I
267.500	968	1198	250.500	I
295.000	1983	2667	250.500	I
307.500	1142	3276	281.500	I
. . .	. . .	. . .	. . .	. . .

Fig. 3.10 shows computer plots of the regression residuals, $\hat{\varepsilon}$, against floor area and against lot area. There appears to be no tendency for the residuals or their scatter to vary with either explanatory variable.

Figure 3.11 is a plot of the regression residuals in the order of the observations and does not indicate any glaring violation of the assumption of independence.

Fig. 3.12 shows the relative frequency distribution of the residuals, $\hat{\varepsilon}$; it appears only slightly asymmetric.

All told, these rough checks suggest that the observations are not grossly inconsistent with the tentative assumptions.

```
The regression equation is
PRICE = 69.9 + 0.203 FLOOR + 0.0218 LOT

Predictor          Coef          Stdev       t-Ratio          p
Constant          69.85         29.85          2.34      0.021
FLOOR           0.20284       0.02358          8.60      0.000
LOT            0.021780      0.003613          6.03      0.000

s = 102.5        R-sq = 54.0%       R-sq(adj) = 53.1%

Analysis of Variance

SOURCE           DF            SS            MS           F          p
Regression        2       1196249        598125       56.97      0.000
Error            97       1018483         10500
Total            99       2214732


    . . .

      Fit   Stdev.Fit          95% C.I.          95% P.I.
    260.3        15.7      (229.2,  291.5)   (54.5,  466.1)
```

FIGURE 3.9 Regression results, real estate prices

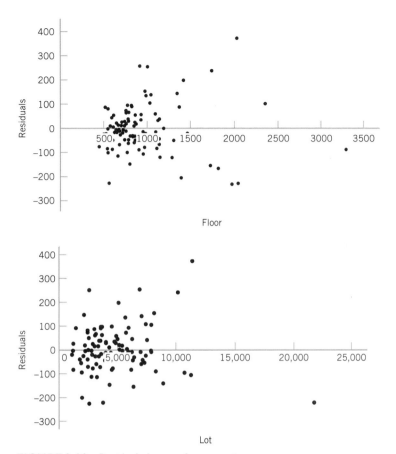

FIGURE 3.10 Residual plots, real estate prices

To construct a, say, 90% confidence interval for β_1 (the true increment in price due to each additional square foot of floor area), we need $T_{0.05}$ for $v = n - k - 1 = 100 - 2 - 1 = 97$. Using the approximate figures in Table 3.1, we find $T_{0.05} \approx 1.64$. Applying Eq. 3.5, the desired confidence interval is

$$(0.203) \pm (1.64)(0.024)$$

or from about 0.164 to 0.242 ($000), that is, from about $164 to $242.

A 90% confidence interval for β_2 (the true increment in price due to each additional square foot of lot area) is $(0.022) \pm (1.64)(0.004)$, or from about $15 to $29.

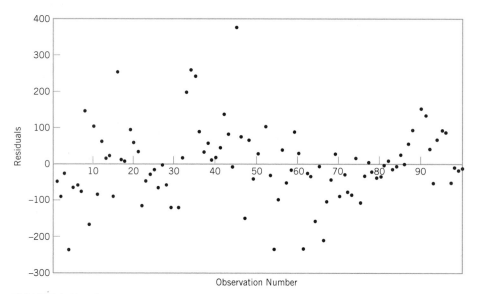

FIGURE 3.11 Ordered residuals, real estate prices

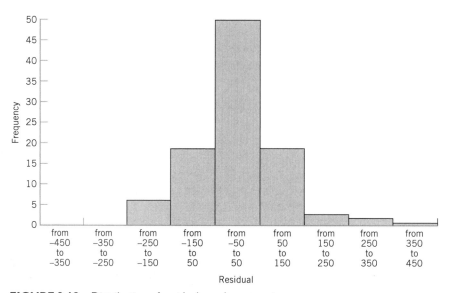

FIGURE 3.12 Distribution of residuals, real estate prices

The forecast value of a property with $FLOOR = 740$ and $LOT = 1854$, the features of the first property in the file `rest.dat`, is

$$PRICE = 69.85 + (0.203)(740) + (0.022)(1854) = 260.3 \; (\$000)$$

This forecast is also shown in Fig. 3.9 under the label `Fit`. This particular program calculates automatically a 95% confidence interval forecast and displays it under the label `95% P.I.`; it is the interval from 54.5 to 466.1.[8] To test the hypotheses $H_0 : \beta_2 = 0$ (lot area has no effect on price) against $H_A : \beta_2 \neq 0$ (lot area has some effect on price), all that need be done is to compare the absolute t-ratio of lot area (6.03) with the critical value, $T_{\alpha/2}$. As always in statistical tests, one must reflect on the meaning and consequences of the two types of error. A Type I error is the conclusion that the lot size has some effect on price when it does not; a Type II error is the opposite conclusion. Which error is more serious? It is rather difficult to say, so let us assume that the two errors are equally serious and set $\alpha = 0.50$. From Table 3.1, $T_{\alpha/2} = T_{0.25} \approx 0.67$. Since $6.03 > 0.67$, H_0 is rejected. The same conclusion is reached comparing the P-VALUE of LOT (0.000, meaning *almost* zero) and $\alpha = 0.50$; since $0.000 < 0.50$, H_0 should be rejected.

Likewise, since the P-VALUE of $FLOOR$, 0.000, is less than $\alpha = 0.50$, we reject the hypothesis $H_0 : \beta_1 = 0$, that is, we conclude that floor area has some effect on price.

As a final illustration, let us formally test the hypothesis that neither floor area nor lot area influences the price of a residential property, $H_0 : \beta_1 = \beta_2 = 0$ *versus* $H_A : \beta_1 \neq 0$ or $\beta_2 \neq 0$.

The Q statistic for this test is equal to the R^2 (why?). Therefore,

$$F = \frac{100 - 2 - 1}{2} \frac{0.54}{1 - 0.54} = 56.97$$

In general, the number under such labels as F or F VALUE in the Analysis of Variance section of the regression output is the F statistic for the test of the hypothesis that no explanatory variable influences Y,

$$H_0 : \beta_1 = \beta_2 = \cdots = \beta_k = 0$$

against the alternative hypothesis that at least one of the variables influences Y. The P VALUE of the test is displayed alongside the F statistic.

---

[8]The Minitab commands that produced the output shown in Fig. 3.9 were `regress 'PRICE' 2 'FLOOR' 'LOT'; predict 740 1854`. The confidence interval shown under the label `95% C.I.` is for the *mean* price of all properties with floor area 740 and lot size 1854.

In this example, this is the test of $H_0 : \beta_1 = \beta_2 = 0$, and the displayed F statistic in Fig. 3.9 agrees with the calculation. The P VALUE of the test is 0.000. If we take α (the maximum tolerable probability of a Type I error) to be 0.5, H_0 should be rejected.

3.8 TO SUM UP

- An estimator of a parameter is unbiased if its expected value equals that parameter.

- An estimator of a parameter is consistent if the probability that it will deviate from that parameter by more than a specified quantity approaches zero as the number of observations increases indefinitely.

- If the process that generates the observations satisfies the conditions of (i) linearity, (ii) constant variance, and (iii) independence, the OLS estimators (the b's) of the model's parameters (β's) are unbiased, consistent, and have the smallest variance among all unbiased estimators that can be expressed as linear functions of the values of the dependent variable.

- If a population of elements is such that the means of the conditional distributions of the dependent variable are linearly related to the values of the explanatory variables, the variances of these conditional distributions are all equal, and either the observations constitute a simple random sample with replacement from the population or one observation is selected randomly from among all population elements having each set of values of the explanatory variables, then the OLS estimators of the parameters of the conditional means are unbiased and consistent.

- Confidence intervals for and tests of hypotheses concerning the linear model's parameters may be constructed if, in addition to the conditions of linearity, constant variance, and independence, the error distribution or the conditional distributions of the dependent variable are normal.

- These conditions are restrictive and are rarely strictly satisfied in practice. Studies have shown, however, that the additional desirable properties of the OLS estimators as well as the confidence intervals and tests are not very sensitive to mild departures from the hypothesized conditions provided that the number of observations is large.

PROBLEMS

3.1 With the help of a computer program, confirm the regression results presented in this chapter.

3.2 Data for $n = 80$ full-time students were available for a study of the relationship between the total score (X) in the Graduate Management Admission Test (GMAT) and performance in the graduate school (the latter variable being measured by the average grade in the first year of study, Y). The assumed model is $Y = \beta_0 + \beta_1 X + \varepsilon$.

The results of regressing Y on X were as follows:

$$\hat{Y} = 1.4932 + 0.0076X \qquad R^2 = 0.27$$
$$\qquad\quad (5.27) \qquad\qquad S = 0.813$$

The number in parentheses is the t-ratio of b_1. Therefore, $S_{b_1} = 0.00144$.

(a) Describe the conditions under which a confidence interval or test concerning the parameter β_1 may be made.

(b) Assuming these conditions are satisfied, form a 90% confidence interval for β_1.

(c) Again assuming these conditions are satisfied, test $H_0 : \beta_1 = 0$ against $H_A : \beta_1 \neq 0$.

(d) Under the same conditions, form a 90% confidence interval for the grade of a student having a GMAT of 600. *Note:* The raw data (not listed here) show $\bar{X} = 542.75$ and $\sum (X - \bar{X})^2 = 336{,}600.8$.

3.3 The results of regressing Y on four explanatory variables, X_1 to X_4, are as follows:

$$\hat{Y} = 3.123 + 1.247X_1 - 2.819X_2 - 0.701X_3 + 10.525X_4 \qquad R^2 = 0.95$$
$$\qquad\quad (0.53) \quad (-0.21) \quad (-0.42) \quad (0.05) \qquad\qquad S = 12.7$$

The results of regressing Y on X_1 and X_4 are as follows:

$$\hat{Y} = 12.863 + 1.654X_1 + 0.398X_4 \qquad R^2 = 0.92$$
$$\qquad\quad (7.34) \quad (10.28)$$

There were $n = 200$ observations. The t-ratios are shown in parentheses.

(a) "As is evident from inspecting the t-ratios of the first regression, none of the explanatory variables contributes much to the model. All should be left out." Comment.

(b) Briefly state the conditions under which it is possible to form confidence intervals and to test hypotheses concerning the parameters of the relationship

$$Y = \beta_0 + \beta_1 X_1 + \beta_2 X_2 + \beta_3 X_3 + \beta_4 X_4 + \varepsilon$$

In the following questions assume that these conditions are met.

(c) Determine the contribution of X_3 in a model that contains the remaining variables.

(d) Determine the contribution of X_2 and X_3 in a model that contains the remaining variables.

(e) Test the hypothesis $\beta_2 = 0$ against $\beta_2 \neq 0$, assuming that the probability of a Type I error should not exceed 5%.

(f) Test the hypothesis $\beta_3 = 0$ against $\beta_3 \neq 0$, assuming that the probability of a Type I error should not exceed 20%.

(g) Test the hypothesis $\beta_2 = 0$ *and* $\beta_3 = 0$, assuming that the probability of a Type I error should not exceed 0.10 (the critical F value is equal to 2.33).

3.4   The following are data on a dependent variable (Y) and two explanatory variables $(X_1$ and $X_2)$:

Y	X_1	X_2
9	3	2
25	8	5
5	2	1
14	5	3
20	7	4

(a) Regress Y on X_1. Calculate b_0, b_1, S, and R^2.

(b) The results of regressing Y on X_2 and Y on X_1 and X_2 are

$$\hat{Y} = -0.700 + 5.100X_2 \qquad R^2 = 0.996$$
$$\qquad\quad (26.63) \qquad\qquad S = 0.469$$

$$\hat{Y} = -0.900 + 1.000X_1 + 3.500X_2 \qquad R^2 = 0.997$$
$$\qquad\quad (1.07) \quad\ (2.32) \qquad\qquad S = 0.374$$

Determine the contribution of X_2: (i) alone; and (ii) over X_1. Explain carefully the method you used and the meaning of the results.

3.5   Refer to Example 2.2 of Section 2.7 concerning the model

$$GASCON = \beta_0 + \beta_1 TEMP + \beta_2 WIND + \varepsilon$$

For the following questions, assume that the assumptions of the classical linear model are satisfied (you will be asked to examine these assumptions in Chapter 9).

(a) Form a 95% confidence interval for β_1. Interpret this interval.

(b) Form a 95% confidence interval for β_2. Interpret this interval.

(c) Test the hypothesis $\beta_1 = 0$ against the alternative $\beta_1 \neq 0$ assuming $\alpha = 0.10$. Interpret this hypothesis.

(d) Test the hypothesis $\beta_2 = 0$ against the alternative $\beta_2 \neq 0$ assuming $\alpha = 0.10$. Interpret this hypothesis.

(e) Test the hypothesis $\beta_1 = \beta_2 = 0$ against the alternative that one of these β's is not equal to zero. Assume $\alpha = 0.10$. Interpret this hypothesis.

(f) Form a 95% confidence interval for $GASCON$ on a day with $TEMP = -1$ and $WIND = 5$. Interpret this interval.

3.6   Refer to Example 2.3 of Section 2.10 concerning the relationship between the strength (Y) of the plastic material, on the one hand, and barrel temperature (X_1), mold temperature (X_2), and injection pressure (X_3), on the other,

$$Y = \beta_0 + \beta_1 X_1 + \beta_2 X_2 + \beta_3 X_3 + \varepsilon$$

For the following questions, assume that the assumptions of the classical linear model are satisfied (you will be asked to examine these assumptions in Chapter 9).

(a) Form a 90% confidence intervals for β_1, β_2, and β_3. Interpret these intervals.

(b) Test in turn the hypotheses $\beta_1 = 0$, $\beta_2 = 0$, and $\beta_3 = 0$ assuming $\alpha = 0.05$. Interpret these hypotheses.

(c) Test the hypothesis $\beta_1 = \beta_2 = \beta_3 = 0$ against the alternative that one of these β's is not equal to zero. Assume $\alpha = 0.05$. Interpret this hypothesis.

(d) Test the hypothesis $\beta_1 = \beta_2 = 0$ against the alternative that one of these β's is not equal to zero. Assume $\alpha = 0.05$ (the critical F value is 3.42). Interpret this hypothesis.

(e) Form a 90% confidence interval for Y given $X_1 = 350$, $X_2 = 130$, and $X_3 = 6,000$. Interpret this interval.

3.7 Refer to Example 2.4 of Section 2.10 concerning the relationship between the per capita consumption of beef (QB), on the one hand, and the deflated prices of beef (DPB), pork (DPP), other meats ($DPOM$), and income ($DPDI$), on the other,

$$QB = \beta_0 + \beta_1 DPB + \beta_2 DPP + \beta_3 DPOM + \beta_4 DPDI + \varepsilon$$

For the following questions, assume that the assumptions of the classical linear model are satisfied (you will be asked to examine these assumptions in Chapter 9).

(a) Form 98% confidence intervals for β_1, β_2, β_3, and β_4. Interpret these intervals.

(b) Test in turn the hypotheses $\beta_1 = 0$, $\beta_2 = 0$, $\beta_3 = 0$, and $\beta_4 = 0$ assuming $\alpha = 0.02$. Interpret these hypotheses.

(c) Test the hypothesis $\beta_1 = \beta_2 = \beta_3 = \beta_4 = 0$ against the alternative that one of these β's is not equal to zero. Assume $\alpha = 0.02$. Interpret this hypothesis.

(d) Test the hypothesis $\beta_1 = \beta_3 = 0$ against the alternative that one of these β's is not equal to zero. Assume $\alpha = 0.02$ (the critical F value is 5.14). Interpret this hypothesis.

(e) Form a 98% confidence interval for QB given $DPB = 110$, $DPP = 105$, $DPOM = 107$, and $DPDI = 20$. Interpret this interval.

3.8 Refer to Example 2.4 of Section 2.10 concerning the relationship between the per capita consumption of pork (QP), on the one hand, and the deflated prices of beef (DPB), pork (DPP), other meats ($DPOM$), and income ($DPDI$), on the other,

$$QP = \beta_0 + \beta_1 DPB + \beta_2 DPP + \beta_3 DPOM + \beta_4 DPDI + \varepsilon$$

For the following questions, assume that the assumptions of the classical linear model are satisfied (you will be asked to examine these assumptions in Chapter 9).

(a) Form 80% confidence intervals for β_1, β_2, β_3, and β_4. Interpret these intervals.

(b) Test in turn the hypotheses $\beta_1 = 0$, $\beta_2 = 0$, $\beta_3 = 0$, and $\beta_4 = 0$ assuming $\alpha = 0.20$. Interpret these hypotheses.

(c) Test the hypothesis $\beta_1 = \beta_2 = \beta_3 = \beta_4 = 0$ against the alternative that one of these β's is not equal to zero. Assume $\alpha = 0.20$. Interpret this hypothesis.

(d) Test the hypothesis $\beta_1 = \beta_3 = 0$ against the alternative that one of these β's is not equal to zero. Assume $\alpha = 0.20$ (the critical F value is 1.80). Interpret this hypothesis.

(e) Form an 80% confidence interval for QP given $DPB = 110$, $DPP = 105$, $DPOM = 107$, and $DPDI = 20$. Interpret this interval.

3.9 Show that Eq. 2.7 can also be written as

$$b_1 = \frac{\sum (X - \bar{X})(Y - \bar{Y})}{\sum (X - \bar{X})^2}$$

3.10 Applying the result of Problem 3.9 or with the help of a numerical example, comment on the following statements.

(a) "Since $\hat{Y} = a + bX$ we can write

$$X \approx -\frac{a}{b} + \frac{1}{b}Y$$

Therefore, if X is regressed on Y to estimate the relationship $\hat{X} = c + dY$, the OLS estimates c and d will be related to a and b as follows:

$$c = -\frac{a}{b} \qquad d = \frac{1}{b}''$$

(b) "The R^2 of a regression of Y on X is equal to the R^2 of the regression of X on Y."

3.11 Refer to the result of Problem 3.9 and Eq. 2.8, which give formulas for calculating b_1 and b_0 of the simple model $\hat{Y} = b_0 + b_1 X$. To answer the following questions, you may use a numerical example or algebra.

(a) Show that the OLS estimates of the model $\hat{Y} = b_0' + b_1' X'$, where $X' = cX$ and c is a constant, are $b_1' = b_1/c$ and $b_0' = b_0$.

(b) Show that the OLS estimates of the model $\hat{Y}' = b_0' + b_1' X$, where $Y' = cY$ and c is a constant, are $b_1' = cb_1$ and $b_0' = cb_0$.

(c) Show that the OLS estimates of the model $\hat{Y}' = b_0' + b_1' X'$ ($Y' = c_1 Y$, $X' = c_2 X$, and c_1 and c_2 are constants) are $b_1' = (c_1/c_2)b_1$ and $b_0' = c_1 b_0$.

3.12 m dependent variables $(Y_1, Y_2, \ldots, Y_m)$ are each linearly related to the *same* explanatory variable, X:

$$Y_1 = \beta_{01} + \beta_{11}X + \varepsilon_1$$
$$Y_2 = \beta_{02} + \beta_{12}X + \varepsilon_2$$
$$\cdots$$
$$Y_m = \beta_{0m} + \beta_{1m}X + \varepsilon_m$$

Denote the OLS estimates of β_{0j} and β_{1j} by b_{0j} and b_{1j} respectively ($j = 1, 2, \ldots, m$).

(a) Show that the sum of the Y's, $Z = Y_1 + Y_2 + \cdots + Y_m$, is also linearly related to X:

$$Z = \beta_0 + \beta_1 X + \tilde{\varepsilon}$$

where $\tilde{\varepsilon}$ is an error term.

(b) Using the result of Problem 3.9 or a numerical example, show that the OLS estimates of β_0 and β_1 in (a) are related to the OLS estimates of β_{0j} and β_{1j} ($j = 1, 2, \ldots, m$) as follows:

$$b_0 = b_{01} + b_{02} + \cdots + b_{0m}$$
$$b_1 = b_{11} + b_{12} + \cdots + b_{1m}$$

(c) On the basis of a survey of n households, the relationships between monthly expenditures on food (*FOOD*), clothing (*CLOTH*), and housing (*HOUS*), on the one hand, and, on the other, monthly household income after taxes (*INC*) are estimated by the method of least squares as follows:

$$\widehat{FOOD}= 60.247 - 0.015INC$$
$$\widehat{CLOTH}= -75.381 + 0.098INC$$
$$\widehat{HOUS}= 87.020 + 0.115INC$$

Total expenditures on food, clothing, and housing may be considered basic expenditures (*BASEX*):

$$BASEX = FOOD + CLOTH + HOUS$$

Estimate the relationship between monthly household basic expenditures (*BASEX*) and monthly household income after taxes (*INC*).

3.13 We noted in Section 2.8 that R^2 is a measure of the *relative* fit of a model, and in Section 2.9 that it measures the relative contribution of all explanatory variables.

Table 3.3 shows three artificial sets of data and related regression results.

For each set of data, we calculate the OLS estimates b_0 and b_1, $\hat{Y} = b_0 + b_1 X$, $\bar{Y}$, $\sum (Y - \bar{Y})^2$, and R^2, as shown in Table 3.3. The data and the estimated lines are plotted in Fig. 3.13. The dotted lines are drawn at the level of the average Y value for each data set.

The data were specially contrived so that in all cases the vertical distances between actual (Y) and estimated ($\hat{Y}$) values are the same. Therefore, $\sum (Y - \hat{Y})^2$, hence also S^2, are the same in all cases. Note, however, that the R^2 are not the same. The greater the $\sum (Y - \bar{Y})^2$, hence also the ordinary variance of the Y-values, the closer is R^2 to 1.

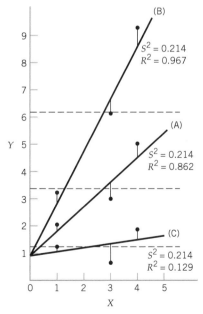

FIGURE 3.13 Illustration of data for Problem 3.13

TABLE 3.3   Data and related results, Problem 3.13

A		B		C	
Y	X	Y	X	Y	X
3	3	87/14	3	9/14	3
2	1	43/14	1	17/14	1
5	4	130/14	4	26/14	4

$\hat{Y} = 0.857 + 0.929X$	$\hat{Y} = 0.857 + 2X$	$\hat{Y} = 0.857 + 0.143X$
$\bar{Y} = 3.333$	$\bar{Y} = 6.190$	$\bar{Y} = 1.238$
$\sum(Y - \bar{Y})^2 = 4.667$	$\sum(Y - \bar{Y})^2 = 19.309$	$\sum(Y - \bar{Y})^2 = 0.738$
$S^2 = 0.214$	$S^2 = 0.214$	$S^2 = 0.214$
$R^2 = 0.862$	$R^2 = 0.967$	$R^2 = 0.129$

What do you conclude from these results?

CHAPTER 4

ATTRIBUTES AS EXPLANATORY VARIABLES

4.1 INTRODUCTION AND SUMMARY

In the two preceding chapters, we examined concepts, measures, and properties common to all models estimated by regression. What makes the method such a valuable tool in practice is the variety of situations to which, with relatively minor modifications, it may be applied. In the following chapters, we shall see, for example, how to work with nonlinear relationships, how to estimate and forecast the trend and seasonality of time series, and how to estimate and forecast lags and their patterns.

In this chapter, we examine how to estimate relationships in which the dependent variable is influenced by one or more attributes. An attribute (or qualitative variable) does not have a natural numerical description. Attributes do influence most business and economic relationships. A method such as regression would be severely handicapped were it unable to take into account attributes when estimating a relationship.

To give just one example, an important feature influencing the value of residential property is its location. With respect to location, properties belong to categories, say, "downtown," "midtown," and "uptown." To forecast the value of a property, we cannot arbitrarily assign numbers to these categories and treat location as a quantitative variable like lot size or lot area in a regression model.

As we shall explain, however, attributes may be handled easily with the use of "dummy" or "indicator" variables, that is, variables taking the values 1 or 0 depending on whether or not an observation falls into a given category of the attribute. Regression may then be applied to these and other quantitative variables in the usual way.

Related (but not exclusively) to the use of dummy variables is the problem of extreme collinearity—the presence of exact linear relationships among explanatory variables. When there is extreme collinearity, the least-squares estimates are not unique, that is, there exist many sets of parameter values minimizing the sum of squared residuals. The problem occurs seldom with "natural" explanatory variables but invariably with dummy variables and gives rise to technical difficulties that can be avoided.

Analysis of variance (a term with historical roots but not operationally descriptive) applies when a dependent variable is a function of one or more attributes only. We shall show that the method is in fact a special case of regression with only dummy variables, to which the general theory of Chapters 2 and 3 applies without change.

4.2 DUMMY VARIABLES

In contrast to a variable, an attribute, it will be recalled, has no natural numerical values. Observations belong to *categories* of an attribute. For example, the sex of a person is an attribute, and persons are classified into the categories "male" and "female." Marital status (single, married, divorced, other), highest level of education attained (elementary school, high school, university, other), whether or not a consumer uses a product (does, does not) are other examples of attributes.

A dependent variable could well be influenced by an attribute. For example, a person's annual income can be assumed to depend on age, years of experience, level of education, and occupation; the first two are variables, the last two are attributes. A way must be found to take into account attributes when estimating relationships.

It should be clear that attributes must not, in general, be arbitrarily converted to variables. For example, in estimating the above income relationship, it may be tempting to convert occupation into a variable taking, say, the code value 1 for the category "clerical," 2 for "professional," 3 for "manual work," and 4 for "other." A similar conversion could be performed on the level of education and a linear relationship estimated by regressing income against age, experience, level of education code, and occupation code. The first problem with this approach is that the codes used are arbitrary (why 1, 2, 3, 4 and not, say, 10, 5, −4, and 20—or any other set of numbers?). Secondly, any numerical codes used assume a ranking and a scale for the categories; for example, the first codes used earlier imply that professionals earn twice as much as clerical workers. In general, we want the *data* to tell us how the various occupations rank in terms of income and what the income differentials among occupations are—we do not want to begin by forcing on the data more or less arbitrary assumptions.

Dummy (also called *binary* or *indicator*) variables are specially constructed variables that are allowed to take only the values 0 or 1 and may be employed to measure in general the effects of attributes. The term *dummy* is used in the sense of "artificial." Dummy variables, as we shall soon see, are among the most useful constructs in regression analysis. A simple example will illustrate their essential features.

Suppose we wish to forecast the resale price of used cars. We take as the dependent variable the resale ratio, that is, the ratio of the resale price over the price at which the car was sold when new. It is reasonable to assume that at any point in time the resale ratio is related to the age, mileage, and make of the car. The first two explanatory variables, age and mileage, are quantitative. The third, the make of the car, is qualitative: it is intended to represent the market's evaluation of the manufacturer's reputation for cost of operation, the frequency and extent of required repairs, the quality of service of the dealer organization, and so on.

To measure the relationship between the resale ratio and the three explanatory variables, one alternative is to separate the observations into groups according to the make of the car and, for each group, to estimate the model

$$\hat{Y} = b_0 + b_1 X_1 + b_2 X_2$$

where Y is the resale ratio, X_1 is the age, and X_2 the mileage of the car. There will thus be a number of models, one for each make of car. The constant (b_0) and coefficients of age (b_1) and mileage (b_2) need not be the same for cars of different makes. These models can be estimated in a straightforward way by running a number of separate regressions, assuming, of course, that there are enough sales for each make to allow reliable estimates of the parameters.

If we suppose, however, that the coefficients of age and mileage are the same for all makes, it is reasonable to use all the observations in estimating b_1 and b_2, provided that a way can be found to incorporate into the model the effects of the various car makes.

A reasonable model may be one expressing the estimated resale ratio of a car with age $X_1 = x_1$ and mileage $X_2 = x_2$ as

$$\hat{Y} = (b_0 + b_1 x_1 + b_2 x_2) + (\text{car make effect})$$

where the "car make effect" is a number depending on the make of the car. The first term, $b_0 + b_1 x_1 + b_2 x_2$, is assumed to depend on age and mileage but not on the car make.

A regression model may be formulated by introducing one dummy variable for each car make, in the following manner. Assume for simplicity that all cars are classified into three makes: VW, Ford, and "Other." Consider the model

$$\hat{Y} = b_0 + b_1 X_1 + b_2 X_2 + b_3 X_3 + b_4 X_4 + b_5 X_5 \tag{4.1}$$

where X_1 and X_2 represent age and mileage and X_3, X_4, and X_5 are dummy variables defined as follows:

$$X_3 = \begin{cases} 1 & \text{if the car is a VW,} \\ 0 & \text{if not;} \end{cases}$$

$$X_4 = \begin{cases} 1 & \text{if the car is a Ford,} \\ 0 & \text{if not;} \end{cases}$$

$$X_5 = \begin{cases} 1 & \text{if the car is classified as Other,} \\ 0 & \text{if not.} \end{cases}$$

The data appear in Table 4.1 (the column labeled "Constant, X_0" will be explained shortly).

Consider a car with given age ($X_1 = x_1$) and mileage ($X_2 = x_2$). If the car is a VW, $X_3 = 1$, $X_4 = 0$, $X_5 = 0$, and the estimated resale ratio is given by Eq. 4.1, which becomes

$$\hat{Y} = (b_0 + b_1 x_1 + b_2 x_2) + b_3$$

If the car is a Ford, $X_3 = 0$, $X_4 = 1$, $X_5 = 0$, and

$$\hat{Y} = (b_0 + b_1 x_1 + b_2 x_2) + b_4$$

For any car classified as Other, $X_3 = 0$, $X_4 = 0$, $X_5 = 1$, and

$$\hat{Y} = (b_0 + b_1 x_1 + b_2 x_2) + b_5$$

The estimated resale ratio differs only with respect to the last term: b_3, b_4 or b_5. The first term, $b_0 + b_1 x_1 + b_2 x_2$, is the same in all three cases. This is precisely the model we had in mind.

Therefore, the OLS estimates b_3, b_4, and b_5 can be interpreted as the *effects* of car makes upon the resale ratio. They estimate the "bonus" (positive b) or

TABLE 4.1 Data Illustrating the Use of Dummy Variables

Car no.	Description	Resale price ($)	New car price ($)	Resale ratio, Y	Constant, X_0	Age (years), X_1	Mileage (000), X_2	VW, X_3	Ford, X_4	Other, X_5
1	Toyota station wagon	3,500	4,200	0.83	1	3	52	0	0	1
2	VW Beetle	2,300	2,900	0.79	1	1	25	1	0	0
...	...	...	...	...	...	...	...	...	...	...
124	Ford Mustang	3,200	4,500	0.71	1	2	27	0	1	0

"penalty" (negative b) that the market attaches to cars of a certain make, over and above the constant term (b_0) and the effects of age ($b_1 x_1$) and mileage ($b_2 x_2$).

The OLS estimates could be obtained by regressing Y on X_1 to X_5, using all available observations. There is, however, a technical problem we need to address before we complete this illustration.

4.3 A DIGRESSION: EXTREME COLLINEARITY

Let us go back to the basic model described in Chapter 2 and assume a linear relationship between Y and any k explanatory variables X_1, X_2, ..., X_k. An alternative way of writing the model

$$\hat{Y} = b_0 + b_1 X_1 + \cdots + b_k X_k$$

is

$$\hat{Y} = b_0 X_0 + b_1 X_1 + \cdots + b_k X_k$$

where X_0 is an explanatory variable that always takes the value 1. It will be useful to think of the n sets of observations arranged in the format shown in Table 4.2. X_{ij} denotes the value of the jth observation of variable X_i.

The constant (b_0) can thus be viewed as the coefficient of an explanatory variable (X_0), just like any other b.[1]

Let X represent collectively the "matrix" (or "block") of observations of the explanatory variables (including the column of 1's), as illustrated in Table 4.2.

We noted earlier in Section 2.4 that the OLS estimates $b_0, b_1, \ldots, b_k$ always exist but may not be unique. Whether or not they are unique depends on the

TABLE 4.2 Table of Observations

Y	X_0	X_1	X_2	...	X_k	
Y_1	1	X_{11}	X_{21}	...	X_{k1}	
Y_2	1	X_{12}	X_{22}	...	X_{k2}	—— Matrix X
...	...	...	...	...	...	
Y_n	1	X_{1n}	X_{2n}	...	X_{kn}	

[1] It follows that there is a standard error, S_{b_0} and a t-ratio associated with b_0. Computer programs do display these statistics under such headings as `Standard Error` and `t-ratio`—see, for example, Figures 2.6 and 2.8. Assuming that the relationship satisfies the assumptions of the classical linear model, these statistics can be used, if so desired, to construct a confidence interval for β_0 or to test the hypothesis $H_0 : \beta_0 = 0$ in the manner of Section 3.5.

characteristics of the matrix X. It can be shown that *the OLS estimates are unique if no one column of X can be expressed as a linear function of other columns of X.* Conversely, if one or more columns of X can be written as linear functions of other columns (for example, $X_1 = X_2 + X_3$, $X_1 = 1.6X_2$, etc.) the OLS estimates are not unique.

To illustrate, let us suppose that four sets of observations are available on Y and two explanatory variables, X_1 and X_2, as follows:

Y	X_0	X_1	X_2	
8	1	2	3	
15	1	5	0	Matrix X
10	1	3	2	
13	1	4	1	

Note that the X_2 column can be reproduced by multiplying the X_0 column by 5 and subtracting the X_1 column, element by element:

$$\begin{pmatrix} 3 \\ 0 \\ 2 \\ 1 \end{pmatrix} = 5 \begin{pmatrix} 1 \\ 1 \\ 1 \\ 1 \end{pmatrix} - \begin{pmatrix} 2 \\ 5 \\ 3 \\ 4 \end{pmatrix}$$

In this case, $X_2 = 5X_0 - X_1$ and the model

$$\hat{Y} = b_0 + b_1 X_1 + b_2 X_2 = b_0 X_0 + b_1 X_1 + b_2 X_2$$

can be written as

$$\begin{aligned} \hat{Y} &= b_0 X_0 + b_1 X_1 + b_2 (5X_0 - X_1) \\ &= (b_0 + 5b_2) X_0 + (b_1 - b_2) X_1 \\ &= c_0 + c_1 X_1 \end{aligned}$$

Any set of values of b_0, b_1, and b_2 such that $b_0 + 5b_2$ equals the same value c_0 and $b_1 - b_2$ equals the same c_1 yields the same $\hat{Y}$'s. In effect, then, the sum of squared residuals $\sum(Y - \hat{Y})^2$ is $\sum(Y - c_0 - c_1 X_1)^2$. If c_0^* and c_1^* minimize $\sum(Y - c_0 - c_1 X_1)^2$, any set of values of b_0, b_1, and b_2 such that $b_0 + 5b_2 = c_0^*$ and $b_1 - b_2 = c_1^*$ yields the same minimum $SSE = \sum(Y - \hat{Y})^2$.

It can be verified that $c_0^* = 3.1$, $c_1^* = 2.4$, and the minimum SSE is equal to 0.2. Three—among the very many—sets of b's giving the same optimal fit are, as can be easily verified,

b_0	b_1	b_2
0.0	3.02	0.62
3.1	2.40	0.00
15.1	0.00	−2.40
. . .	. . .	. . .

The presence of an exact linear relationship among columns of X is called *collinearity* or *extreme collinearity*. The columns could represent variables or attributes.

Two problems created by collinearity should be noted. First, the non-uniqueness of the OLS estimates means we cannot interpret any one set as *the* estimated changes in $\hat{Y}$ due to a unit increase in each X, others held constant. Consider, for example, the numbers under b_2 in the just presented table. Which of the numbers listed (0.62, 0, −2.4, . . .) is *the* estimated change in $\hat{Y}$ due to a unit increase in X_2?

The second problem relates to the calculation of the OLS estimates. Manual computations are not hindered by collinearity, but computer programs sometimes are because they usually rely on procedures for solving systems of linear equations that require the absence of linear relationships between the columns of X. If the computer program encounters such a relationship, it may print a warning or error message and may not even attempt any calculations. Some programs display just one solution, occasionally without an indication that many other solutions exist.

The technical problem can be corrected by one of two methods. The easier solution is simply not to use (to "drop," leave out from the model) a redundant column or columns, that is, any column that can be expressed as a linear function of some of the remaining columns. A second method, on which we shall not elaborate right now, is to impose appropriate restrictions on the OLS estimates (the b's) to ensure their uniqueness, for example, to require that they add up to or average zero. We describe this approach in Sections 4.5 and 4.6.

In cases where the explanatory variables vary freely and may take a large number of distinct values, the chance of an *exact* linear relationship between the columns of the matrix X is very small.[2] But when dummy variables are introduced in the model, collinearity is created automatically, as we shall see immediately.

---

[2]However, *approximate* linear relationships between explanatory variables are often present in business and economic relationships. Such a presence is known as *multicollinearity*. We examine multicollinearity and its consequences later in Section 8.6.

4.4 DUMMY VARIABLES, CONTINUED

Note that the columns in Table 4.1 corresponding to the dummy variables and the constant are linearly related since $X_3 + X_4 + X_5 = X_0$ ($X_0 = 1$, always) for all observations. This exact linear relationship is present no matter how large or small the number of observations.

Collinearity can be avoided (and unique OLS estimates assured) simply by dropping (leaving out of the model) one—any one—of the related variables. If we wish to keep X_0, as in most cases we do, we can drop any one of the three dummy variables. For example, if we drop X_5 (that is, if we force b_5 to be zero), the model becomes

$$\hat{Y} = b_0 + b_1 X_1 + b_2 X_2 + b_3 X_3 + b_4 X_4 \qquad (4.2)$$

and Y can be regressed on X_1 to X_4.

A slight change is necessary in the interpretation of the parameters b_3 and b_4. For all VWs, Model 4.2 reduces to

$$\hat{Y} = b_0 + b_1 X_1 + b_2 X_2 + b_3$$

for all Fords,

$$\hat{Y} = b_0 + b_1 X_1 + b_2 X_2 + b_4$$

and for all Other cars, Model 4.2 becomes

$$\hat{Y} = b_0 + b_1 X_1 + b_2 X_2$$

which can also be written as

$$\hat{Y} = b_0 + b_1 X_1 + b_2 X_2 + 0$$

Therefore, b_3 and b_4 should be interpreted as the effects of VW and Ford cars *over the effect of Other makes* (b_5, the effect of Other makes, is zero). They measure the amounts (in terms of the resale ratio) by which VWs and Fords are valued over or under cars of Other makes.

EXAMPLE 4.1

In Chapter 2, we began developing a model relating the price of a residential property to its features. We started with two of these features, floor area and lot size—both variables—and obtained (see Sections 2.10 and 3.7) the following regression results:

$$\widehat{PRICE} = 69.854 + 0.203FLOOR + 0.022LOT \qquad R^2 = 0.54$$
$$\text{(2.34)} \qquad \text{(8.60)} \qquad \text{(6.03)} \qquad S = 102.47$$

An important factor influencing real estate prices—some would even say the most important—is location. Location is an attribute. The data file `rest.dat` used for the last regression, distinguishes three locations, coded 1, 2, and 3 as indicated in Table 4.3.

One possible model relating price to floor area, lot size, and location is

$$\widehat{PRICE} = b_0 + b_1 FLOOR + b_2 LOT + \text{(location effect)}.$$

In this formulation, the unit values of floor area (b_1) and lot size (b_2) do not depend on location. By "location effect" we understand a certain dollar figure (say, c_1) for all properties in location 1, a different figure (c_2) for properties in location 2, and a third (c_3) for properties in location 3. These figures modify the "base price," b_0. A regression model meeting these specifications is

$$\widehat{PRICE} = b_0 + b_1 FLOOR + b_2 LOT + c_1 L1 + c_2 L2 + c_3 L3, \qquad (4.3)$$

where $L1$, $L2$, and $L3$ are dummy variables representing locations 1, 2, and 3, respectively, as shown in Table 4.3.

For example, the estimated price of a property in location 1 is

$$\widehat{PRICE} = b_0 + b_1 FLOOR + b_2 LOT + c_1;$$

the effect of location 1 is c_1 and it is added to the base price b_0. Likewise for c_2 and c_3.

TABLE 4.3 Real Estate Sales

Property no.	Price ($000) PRICE	Floor area (sq ft) FLOOR	Lot size (sq ft) LOT	Location code	Dummy variables		
					L1	L2	L3
1	213.75	740	1854	1	1	0	0
...	...	...	...	...	...	...	...
9	415.00	1823	6452	2	0	1	0
...	...	...	...	...	...	...	...
21	500.00	1135	7575	3	0	0	1
...	...	...	...	...	...	...	...

SOURCE: File `rest.dat`

Leaving out $L3$ to avoid collinearity, Model 4.3 is estimated as follows:

$$\widehat{PRICE} = 159.59 + 0.203FLOOR + 0.015LOT - 111.03L1 - 36.26L2$$
$$(3.90) \qquad (9.24) \qquad\qquad (3.79) \qquad (-3.61) \quad (-1.32)$$
$$R^2 = 0.61 \quad S = 95.66$$

The estimated base price is now \$159,590 (note the change in this and other OLS estimates as explanatory variables are added to the model). The estimated value of one square foot of floor space is \$203 and that of land \$15. Properties in location 1 are estimated to be worth \$111,030 less, and those in location 2 \$36,260 less, than properties in location 3. By including the location dummy variables, R^2 increased from 0.54 to 0.61.

Those who consider location the most important explanatory factor will probably find this modest improvement surprising and may suggest that the problem lies in the manner in which location was taken into account. Location may influence the *unit value* of lot size rather than the base price. In other words, a reasonable model might be

$$\widehat{PRICE} = b_0 + b_1 FLOOR + b_2 LOT$$

as before, but now

$$b_2 = c + \text{(location effect)}$$

where c is a constant and location effect is a number, different for each location. This new formulation can be accommodated by writing

$$b_2 = c + c_1 L1 + c_2 L2 + c_3 L3$$

where $L1$, $L2$, and $L3$ are the three dummy variables representing locations 1, 2, and 3, respectively. For properties in location 1, $b_1 = c + c_1$; for those in location 2, $b_2 = c + c_2$; while for those in location 3, $b_2 = c + c_3$. c_1, c_2, and c_3, therefore, are the effects of location on the price of one square foot of land.

Substituting this last equation in place of b_2 in the root model, we get

$$\widehat{PRICE} = b_0 + b_1 FLOOR + [c + c_1 L1 + c_2 L2 + c_3 L3]LOT$$
$$= b_0 + b_1 FLOOR + cLOT + c_1(LOT)(L1) + c_2(LOT)(L2)$$
$$+ c_3(LOT)(L3)$$
$$= b_0 + b_1 FLOOR + cLOT + c_1(LOT1) + c_2(LOT2) + c_3(LOT3)$$

$LOT1$ is the product of the variables LOT and $L1$; likewise for $LOT2$ and $LOT3$. The values of the explanatory variables are illustrated in Table 4.4.

TABLE 4.4   Real Estate Sales, Continued

Prop. no.	PRICE	FLOOR	LOT	L1	L2	L3	LOT1	LOT2	LOT3
1	213.75	740	1854	1	0	0	1854	0	0
...	...	...	...	...	...	...	...	...	...
9	415.00	1823	6452	0	1	0	0	6452	0
...	...	...	...	...	...	...	...	...	...
21	500.00	1135	7575	0	0	1	0	0	7575
...	...	...	...	...	...	...	...	...	...

It can be noted that $LOT1 + LOT2 + LOT3 = (LOT)(L1 + L2 + L3) = LOT$. To avoid collinearity, therefore, one of these variables ($LOT3$) is left out. The regression results are as follows:

$$\widehat{PRICE} = 90.89 + 0.200FLOOR + 0.021LOT - 0.013LOT1 - 0.0002LOT2$$
$$(2.85) \quad (8.69) \quad (5.97) \quad (-2.26) \quad (-0.05)$$
$$R^2 = 0.57 \quad S = 100.11$$

Since $c = 0.021, c_1 = -0.013, c_2 = -0.0002$, we conclude that the estimated value of one square foot of land in location 1 is \$13 less, and in location 2 \$0.20 less, than that in location 3; the latter is estimated to be \$21.

The second model, however, was not an improvement over the last. On the contrary, R^2 declined from 0.61 to 0.57.

There is, of course, yet another way of taking location into account and that is simply to divide the observations into three sets corresponding to the three locations and to estimate three models, each of the form

$$\widehat{PRICE} = b_0 + b_1 FLOOR + b_2 LOT$$

The OLS estimates b_0, b_1, and b_2 (the estimates of the base price and the unit values of floor area and lot size) will, in all likelihood, be different for each location. We let the reader investigate these and other issues in the case on the city of West York in the cases section of Part II.[3] ∎

[3]The relatively poor performance of the models could well be due to the manner in which location is defined. We should have explained that the local real estate association divides the metropolitan area in which the residential properties of Table 4.3 are located into 25 districts. To compile the data for this example, four residential properties were randomly selected from among those sold in each such district during a three-month period, giving a total of 100 observations. Instead of the district number, the file rest.dat contains the average selling price (*AVESELPR*) of all properties sold in the district during the immediately preceding nine-month period. The three locations of this illustration were formed as follows: location 1 consists of districts with *AVESELPR* less than \$300,000; location 2 of districts with *AVESELPR* in the range from \$300,000 to 400,000; and location 3 of districts with *AVESELPR* greater than \$400,000. The three locations, therefore, do not consist of geographically

This is then the way in which dummy variables are used to estimate the effects of attributes. If there are several attributes, one set of dummy variables is introduced for each attribute. The number of dummy variables in each set is equal to the number of mutually exclusive and collectively exhaustive categories of the attribute. One dummy variable is dropped from each set in order to prevent redundancy among the columns of the matrix of explanatory variables.

Dummy variables can also be used to estimate the effects of *interactions* between attributes, that is, effects of combinations of categories of pairs of attributes. To illustrate, suppose we want to relate expenditures on reading (books, magazines, newspapers, etc.) to two attributes, gender and level of education. We distinguish two gender categories (male, female) and three educational levels (university, high school only, elementary school only). If we assume that expenditures on reading tend to be different in each gender education category, we may introduce six dummy variables, as follows:

| | **Level of education** | | |
Gender	*Elementary*	*High school*	*University*
Male	X_1	X_2	X_3
Female	X_4	X_5	X_6

where

$$X_1 = \begin{cases} 1 & \text{if person is male with elementary school education,} \\ 0 & \text{if not;} \end{cases}$$

$$X_2 = \begin{cases} 1 & \text{if person is male with high school education,} \\ 0 & \text{if not;} \end{cases}$$

and so on. The model can now be written as

$$\hat{Y} = b_0 + b_1 X_1 + b_2 X_2 + \cdots + b_6 X_6$$

where Y represents expenditures on reading. The parameters b_1 to b_6 are the effects of each combined gender/education category. Once one of the dummy variables is dropped, the modified model can be estimated in the standard way. Assuming that, say, X_6 is left out of the model, b_0 can be interpreted as the estimated reading expenditure of a female with university education (the base category), b_1 as the estimated reading expenditure of a male with elementary education over or under that of a female with university education, and so on.

adjacent districts. Perhaps, then, all 25 original locations should be distinguished or combined in a different way.

4.5 ONE-WAY ANALYSIS OF VARIANCE

Analysis of variance is a method for estimating the effects of one or more attributes on a variable and for determining whether these effects are significant (in the statistical sense). The term *analysis of variance* (ANOVA to initiates) is due to the fact that the method partitions the total variation of the observations according to the sources of variation (the attributes). However, the problems to which this method is applied can also be analyzed by means of the linear regression model. Indeed, as we shall soon see, *analysis of variance can be considered a special case of regression with dummy variables and the procedure of decomposing the total variation can be considered an application of the F-test of Section 3.5 that a subset of parameters is equal to zero.*

The objective of this and remaining sections in this chapter is to explain the connection between regression and analysis of variance—two methods often perceived as unrelated. Strictly speaking, we shall not be saying anything new. Readers may therefore skip the remainder of this chapter without fear of losing continuity.[4]

We consider first the case in which there is only one attribute. "One-way" means involving one attribute, one source of variation. The following sections describe extensions to two or more sources.

EXAMPLE 4.2

Let us suppose that four machine operators are clocked on three different occasions for the time (in minutes) required to complete a certain task, with the results shown in Table 4.5.

The overall mean (the average of all 12 timings) is 16.5 minutes. We assume that the raw materials, working conditions, and other factors causing

TABLE 4.5 Task Times by Operator

	Operator			
	1	2	3	4
	14	16	16	15
	15	17	18	15
	16	18	20	18
Means:	15	17	18	16

[4]A more extensive treatment of analysis of variance can be found in, among many good sources, Neter, Wasserman, and Kutner (1990).

task times to vary remained stable throughout the experiment, leaving the operator as the principal "source of variation" of the task completion times.

Some questions we may wish to ask are the following: What are the effects of the operators on the task completion time? Do the operators tend to differ in the time they need to perform this task? In other words, do all operators tend to work at the same speed, or are some operators faster than others? If so, by how much?

We assume, of course, that the timings constitute a random sample from a population of potential timings and that the questions refer to this population. For if we restrict ourselves to the available observations only, obviously the three operators do differ in the average time they need to complete the task, with Operator 1 being the fastest (average time 15 minutes) and 3 the slowest (18 minutes on average).

Let us estimate the operator effects as we would those of any other attribute. Let Y represent the task completion time, and consider the following model:

$$Y = \beta_0 + \beta_1 X_1 + \beta_2 X_2 + \beta_3 X_3 + \beta_4 X_4 + \varepsilon \tag{4.4}$$

where X_1, X_2, X_3, and X_4 are dummy variables corresponding to the four operators and ε is an error term. X_1, for example, equals 1 if the timing refers to Operator 1, and 0 otherwise. β_1 to β_4 are the effects of the operators upon the task completion time. If β_1 to β_4 are all equal, there are no differences between operators.

This is a linear model, and the least-squares estimates of its parameters can be obtained by regressing Y on the X's. The data for this example appear in Table 4.6.

It is clear from Table 4.6 that the values of *all* the explanatory variables are either 0 or 1. Furthermore, the 1's are not arranged in any odd way but form a pattern—the "staircase" pattern apparent in Table 4.6. Intuitively, we can expect a simple solution for the OLS estimators in this special case. This is indeed so, as we shall soon see.

Note that any one column of the matrix of values of the explanatory variables (the block of numbers under the headings X_0 to X_4) can be reproduced as a linear combination of the other columns. For example, the X_0 column is equal to the sum of all other columns; the X_1 column is equal to the X_0 column minus the sum of columns X_2 to X_4; and so on. As always happens when dummy variables are introduced, there exists (extreme) collinearity, and the OLS estimates of the parameters are not unique (that is, there are many sets of values of $b_0, b_1, \ldots, b_4$ that produce the same minimum sum of squared residuals).

Unique OLS estimates can be obtained in general either by dropping one or more of the redundant X's or by imposing suitable restrictions on the OLS estimators. Leaving out a variable is, of course, the same as requiring that its

**TABLE 4.6   Data for
Regression Model, Example 4.2**

Y	β_0 X_0	β_1 X_1	β_2 X_2	β_3 X_3	β_4 X_4
14	1	1	0	0	0
15	1	1	0	0	0
16	1	1	0	0	0
16	1	0	1	0	0
17	1	0	1	0	0
18	1	0	1	0	0
16	1	0	0	1	0
18	1	0	0	1	0
20	1	0	0	1	0
15	1	0	0	0	1
15	1	0	0	0	1
18	1	0	0	0	1

coefficient be zero. Let us follow the first approach and leave out one of the X's from the model. As any X will do, let us drop X_4. The model now becomes

$$Y = \beta_0 + \beta_1 X_1 + \beta_2 X_2 + \beta_3 X_3 + \varepsilon \tag{4.5}$$

Regressing Y against X_1 to X_3, we obtain

$$\hat{Y} = 16.0 - 1.00X_1 + 1.00X_2 + 2.00X_3$$

The estimated task completion time for Operator 1 is

$$\hat{Y} = 16.0 - 1.00(1) + 1.00(0) + 2.00(0) = 16.0 - 1.0 = 15$$

The estimated task completion time for Operator 2 is 17 minutes, for Operator 3 18 minutes, and for Operator 4 (all X's equal 0) 16 minutes.   ∎

So far, we have not said anything new. Our next task is to determine if there tend to be any differences between operators. Before doing that, however, let us generalize.

Suppose that n observations on a variable Y are classified into J categories according to a certain attribute. We assume that each category contains the same number (I) of observations. Let Y_{ij} denote the ith observation in the jth category, $Y_{\cdot j}$ the mean of the observations in the jth category, and $Y_{\cdot\cdot}$ the overall mean—the mean of all observations. The $n = IJ$ observations can be visualized in the form of a table with I rows and J columns, as shown in Table 4.7 (the row means will be used in the next section).

We assume that the relationship between Y and the attribute can be described by the model

$$Y = \beta_0 + \beta_1 X_1 + \beta_2 X_2 + \cdots + \beta_{J-1} X_{J-1} + \beta_J X_J + \varepsilon \tag{4.6}$$

where the X_j are dummy variables corresponding to the categories of the attribute, and the β_j represent the effects of these categories. The last X is dropped to obtain unique OLS estimates, so the model becomes

$$Y = \beta_0 + \beta_1 X_1 + \beta_2 X_2 + \cdots + \beta_{J-1} X_{J-1} + \varepsilon \tag{4.7}$$

Dropping X_J is, of course, equivalent to setting $\beta_J = 0$.

If $\beta_1 = \beta_2 = \cdots = \beta_{J-1} = 0$, Y does not depend on the X's, that is, the attribute has no effect on Y.

The contribution of the variables $X_1, X_2, \ldots, X_{J-1}$ can always be measured by calculating the Q statistic based on two regressions—one *with* $X_1, X_2, \ldots, X_{J-1}$ and the other *without* these variables. No special assumptions are needed for using this measure.

But let us assume—and here we shall repeat the assumptions of Section 3.2—that the ε value in Model 4.7 is generated *as if* by a random draw with replacement from a normal distribution with mean 0 and variance σ^2.

The test of the hypothesis of no column effects

$$H_0 : \beta_1 = \beta_2 = \cdots = \beta_{J-1} = 0$$

TABLE 4.7 Notation in One- and Two-Way Classification

Rows	Columns				Row means
	1	2	...	J	
1	Y_{11}	Y_{12}	...	Y_{1J}	$Y_{1.}$
2	Y_{21}	Y_{22}	...	Y_{2J}	$Y_{2.}$
...	...	...	...	...	...
I	Y_{I1}	Y_{I2}	...	Y_{IJ}	$Y_{I.}$
Column means	$Y_{.1}$	$Y_{.2}$	...	$Y_{.J}$	Overall mean $Y_{..}$

against the alternative hypothesis that at least one of the β's is not equal to zero is based on the F statistic, which in this case is (why?)

$$F = \frac{n-J}{J-1}\frac{SSE_P - SSE_F}{SSE_F} = \frac{n-J}{J-1}\frac{Q}{1-Q}$$

SSE_F is the sum of squared residuals of the "full" Model 4.7, while SSE_P that of Model 4.7 with β_1 to β_{J-1} all equal to zero. The latter is the model $Y = \beta_0 + \varepsilon$, and we know that $SSE_P = \sum_i \sum_j (Y_{ij} - Y_{..})^2$.

H_0 should be rejected when F is large. If the probability of Type I error is not to exceed α, and that of Type II error not to exceed $1 - \alpha$, then the boundary point between "large" and "not large enough" F values is the "critical F value," F_α, for $v_1 = J - 1$ and $v_2 = n - J$. H_0 should be rejected if $F > F_\alpha$. Alternatively, reject H_0 if the P-VALUE of the test is less than α.

EXAMPLE 4.2 (CONTINUED)

To test the hypothesis that the effects of all operators in Model 4.5 are equal to zero, first we establish from the regression output that $SSE_F = 18$ and $SSE_P = 33$. Thus, the F statistic is

$$F = \frac{12 - 4}{3}\frac{33 - 18}{18} = 2.222$$

The critical F value for $v_1 = 3$, $v_2 = 8$, and, say, $\alpha = 0.05$ is $F_{0.05} = 4.07$ (calculated by a computer program). Therefore, since $F = 2.22 < F_\alpha = 4.07$, the hypothesis that there are no operator effects is accepted. The conclusion is, in other words, that there are no differences between the operators. ∎

Again, nothing we have said so far is new. The problem was analyzed by techniques that apply to any regression model.

But let us go back to the general Model 4.6, and, instead of dropping one of the X's to ensure a unique set of OLS estimates, let us impose a different restriction. Specifically, let us require that $b_1 + b_2 + \cdots + b_J = 0$.[5] The least-squares problem then is to find $b_0, b_1, \ldots, b_J$ that minimize $\sum_i \sum_j (Y_{ij} - \hat{Y}_{ij})^2$ subject to $\sum_{j=1}^J b_j = 0$, where

$$\hat{Y}_{ij} = b_0 + b_1 X_1 + \cdots + b_J X_J$$

It can be shown that this one restriction is sufficient to ensure uniqueness. Using calculus, it can also be shown (see Appendix B.5) that there is a very

[5]Other restrictions also achieve the same objective. See, for example, Scheffé (1959, Ch. 1).

simple solution to the problem: the restricted OLS estimate b_0 is the overall mean of the observations,

$$b_0 = Y_{..} \tag{4.8}$$

while the OLS estimate of the effect of the jth category, b_j, is equal to the difference between the jth column mean and the overall mean of the observations,

$$b_j = Y_{.j} - Y_{..} \qquad (j = 1, 2, \ldots, J) \tag{4.9}$$

The estimated value of any observation in the jth category is

$$\hat{Y}_{ij} = b_0 + b_1(0) + \cdots + b_j(1) + \cdots + b_J(0) = b_0 + b_j = Y_{.j} \tag{4.10}$$

that is, the average of the observations in the jth category.

EXAMPLE 4.2 (CONTINUED)

The following quantities were calculated earlier in Table 4.5.

$$Y_{.1} = 15, \; Y_{.2} = 17, \; Y_{.3} = 18, \; Y_{.4} = 16, \; Y_{..} = 16.5$$

Therefore, the estimated operator effects are $b_1 = 15 - 16.5 = -1.5$, $b_2 = 17 - 16.5 = 0.5$, $b_3 = 18 - 16.5 = 1.5$, and $b_4 = 16 - 16.5 = -0.5$. (Note that $b_1 + b_2 + b_3 + b_4 = 0$.) The estimated task-completion time is 15 for Operator 1, 17 for Operator 2, 18 for Operator 3, and 16 for Operator 4; these estimates are identical to those of the first regression model. ∎

The sum of squared residuals of the full Model 4.6 is

$$SSE_F = \sum_i \sum_j (Y_{ij} - \hat{Y}_{ij})^2 = \sum_i \sum_j (Y_{ij} - Y_{.j})^2$$

The sum of squared residuals of the "partial" model is still

$$SSE_P = \sum_i \sum_j (Y_{ij} - Y_{..})^2$$

The restricted OLS estimators $b_0, b_1, \ldots, b_J$, and the F statistic, therefore, can be calculated simply from the table of observations (Table 4.7). Statistical programs for the analysis of variance usually present the components of the F statistic in the format of Table 4.8.

Of all the quantities displayed, *only* the F statistic and P-VALUE (shown in the last columns of Table 4.8) are normally of practical interest. All the

TABLE 4.8   Analysis of Variance: One-Way Classification

Source of variation	Degrees of freedom	Sum of squares	Mean square	F statistic	P-value
Columns	$J - 1$	$SSC = SSE_p - SSE_F$	$MSC = SSC/(J - 1)$	$F = MSC/MSE$	$\cdots$
Residual (error)	$n - J$	SSE_F	$MSE = SSE_F/(n - J)$		
Total	$n - 1$	SSE_p			

other quantities have little meaning by themselves. The terms used in Table 4.8 (*source of variation, degrees of freedom, mean square*) have a historical justification that need not concern us here. It is sufficient that the reader know where in this table the various components of F are located and how, in principle, they are calculated.

EXAMPLE 4.2 (CONTINUED)

The results shown in Figure 4.1 will be found among the output of most computer programs for analysis of variance applied to the data of Example 4.2.

Note that the F statistic and the two sums of squared residuals (SSE_F and SSE_p) are identical to those of the regression model.

To test the hypothesis of no operator effects for Model 4.4, H_0: $\beta_1 = \cdots = \beta_4 = 0$, we compare the P-VALUE (0.1631) with the maximum tolerable probability of Type I error, α. If it is assumed that $\alpha = 0.05$, H_0 should be accepted as $0.1631 > 0.05$. This conclusion is the same as for the regression model. ∎

Let us sum up. To estimate the effects of an attribute upon a variable, Model 4.6 is appropriate. Unique OLS estimates can be obtained by leaving out of the model one dummy variable. Leaving out one variable is tantamount to restricting its coefficient to zero. Alternatively, a different restriction may be imposed, namely, that the sum of all effects be equal to zero, that is, $b_1 + b_2 + \cdots + b_J = 0$. This is mathematically convenient because in this case the estimates as well as the sums of squares and the F statistic can all be calculated

```
DEPENDENT VARIABLE: Y

   SOURCE    DF     SS      MS      F     P-VALUE

  COLUMNS     3    15.0    5.00    2.22    0.1631
 RESIDUAL     8    18.0    2.25
    TOTAL    11    33.0
```

FIGURE 4.1   One-way ANOVA, computer output, Example 4.2

very simply—even by hand, if necessary. In the days before computers, this approach had an obvious practical advantage, but even now it results in faster calculations.

4.6 TWO-WAY ANALYSIS OF VARIANCE

Suppose that n available observations on a variable Y are classified into J categories according to one attribute and into I categories according to a second attribute. We assume that there is one observation in each cross-classification. The $n = IJ$ observations can be arranged into a table with I rows and J columns as shown in Table 4.7. "Two-way" means two sources of variation—two attributes.

The notation is the same as in the one-way classification. The typical row mean is denoted by $Y_{i.}$ and the typical column mean by $Y_{.j}$. The mean of all observations is denoted by $Y_{..}$.

EXAMPLE 4.3

Suppose that the timings for each operator given in Example 4.2 have a special meaning in that each operator was timed once in the morning, once at noon, and once in the afternoon. The same observations, classified now according to two attributes (operator and time of day), are shown in Table 4.9.

The order of the observations now *does* matter. The question is, Is the time required to perform the task influenced by the operator and by the time of day? If so, by how much?

We may begin as we would when estimating the effects of two attributes. Consider the model

$$Y = \beta_0 + \beta_1 X_1 + \beta_2 X_2 + \beta_3 X_3 + \beta_4 X_4 + \gamma_1 Z_1 + \gamma_2 Z_2 + \gamma_3 Z_3 + \varepsilon \qquad (4.11)$$

TABLE 4.9   Task Times by Operator and Time of Day

Time of day	Operator 1	2	3	4	Row means
Morning	14	16	16	15	15.25
Noon	15	17	18	15	16.25
Afternoon	16	18	20	18	18.00
Column means:	15	17	18	16	16.50

Y is the task completion time. The X's are dummy variables corresponding to the operators (the columns), and the Z's are dummy variables corresponding to the times of day (the rows of Table 4.9). β_1 to β_4 are the effects of the operators and γ_1 to γ_3 the effects of the times of day. The data are shown in Table 4.10.

Note that one—any one—of columns X_0 to X_4 and one of $X_0, Z_1, \ldots, Z_3$ can be expressed as a linear function of the other columns. For example, X_1 equals X_0 minus the sum of X_2 to X_4 and Z_1 equals X_0 minus the sum of Z_2 to Z_3. As in the previous section, there are many sets of values of the OLS estimators which yield the same minimum sum of squared residuals. ∎

In general, to estimate the effects of two attributes, the first with J and the second with I categories, the simplest model is

$$Y = \beta_0 + \beta_1 X_1 + \beta_2 X_2 + \cdots + \beta_J X_J + \gamma_1 Z_1 + \gamma_2 Z_2 + \cdots + \gamma_I Z_I + \varepsilon \qquad (4.12)$$

The X's and Z's are dummy variables corresponding to the categories of the first and second attribute respectively. The categories of the first attribute correspond to the columns, and those of the second to the rows of the table of observations, Table 4.7. Unique OLS estimates $(b_0, b_1, \ldots b_J, c_1, \ldots, c_I)$ of the model's parameters may be obtained either by dropping one of the X's and one of the Z's, or by imposing *two* restrictions on the OLS estimators: $b_1 + b_2 + \cdots + b_J = 0$

TABLE 4.10   Data for Regression Model, Example 4.3

Y	β_0 X_0	β_1 X_1	β_2 X_2	β_3 X_3	β_4 X_4	γ_1 Z_1	γ_2 Z_2	γ_3 Z_3
14	1	1	0	0	0	1	0	0
15	1	1	0	0	0	0	1	0
16	1	1	0	0	0	0	0	1
16	1	0	1	0	0	1	0	0
17	1	0	1	0	0	0	1	0
18	1	0	1	0	0	0	0	1
16	1	0	0	1	0	1	0	0
18	1	0	0	1	0	0	1	0
20	1	0	0	1	0	0	0	1
15	1	0	0	0	1	1	0	0
15	1	0	0	0	1	0	1	0
18	1	0	0	0	1	0	0	1

and $c_1 + c_2 + \cdots + c_I = 0$. If the latter approach is followed, it can be shown (see Appendix B.5) that the OLS estimators are very simply:

$$b_0 = Y_{..}$$
$$b_j = Y_{.j} - Y_{..} \quad (j = 1, 2, \ldots, J)$$
$$c_i = Y_{i.} - Y_{..} \quad (i = 1, 2, \ldots, I)$$

(4.13)

It follows that the estimated value of Y in cell (i, j) is

$$\hat{Y}_{ij} = b_0 + b_1(0) + \cdots + b_j(1) + \cdots + b_J(0) + c_1(0) + \cdots + c_i(1) + \cdots + c_I(0)$$
$$= b_0 + b_j + c_i$$
$$= Y_{i.} + Y_{.j} - Y_{..}$$

EXAMPLE 4.3 (CONTINUED)

Referring to Table 4.9, we calculate $b_0 = 16.5$, $b_1 = 15 - 16.5 = -1.5$, $b_2 = 17 - 16.5 = 0.5$, $b_3 = 18 - 16.5 = 1.5$, $b_4 = 16 - 16.5 = -0.5$, $c_1 = 15.25 - 16.5 = -1.25$, $c_2 = 16.25 - 16.5 = -0.25$, and $c_3 = 18 - 16.5 = 1.5$. The estimated task completion time for operator 1 in the morning, cell (1,1), is calculated as

$$\hat{Y}_{11} = b_0 + b_1 + c_1 = 16.5 - 1.5 - 1.25 = 13.75$$

or

$$\hat{Y}_{11} = Y_{1.} + Y_{.1} - Y_{..} = 15.25 + 15 - 16.5 = 13.75 \quad \blacksquare$$

The sum of squared residuals of the full Model 4.12 is

$$SSE_F = \sum_i \sum_j (Y_{ij} - \hat{Y}_{ij})^2 = \sum_i \sum_j (Y_{ij} - Y_{i.} - Y_{.j} + Y_{..})^2$$

From here on, it will be assumed that the error ε in Model 4.12 is generated *as if* by a random draw with replacement from a normal population distribution with mean 0 and variance σ^2.

The dual classification gives rise to tests of two kinds of hypotheses.

(a) The Hypothesis of No Row Effects   This is a test of the hypothesis that all row effects are zero

$$H_0: \gamma_1 = \gamma_2 = \cdots = \gamma_I = 0$$

against the alternative hypothesis that at least one of the row effects is not equal to zero.

If all $\gamma_i = 0$ in Model 4.12, the model becomes one with column effects only. As we saw in the previous section, the sum of squares of this partial model is

$$SSE_R = \sum_i \sum_j (Y_{ij} - Y_{.j})^2$$

We denote this sum of squares by SSE_R instead of SSE_P because, as we shall see shortly, there are two partial models in this case—one with zero row effects and the other with zero column effects.

To test H_0 we use the F statistic, which is (why?)

$$F_R = \frac{(I-1)(J-1)}{I-1} \frac{SSE_R - SSE_F}{SSE_F}$$

H_0 should be rejected when $F_R > F_\alpha$. F_α is the critical value of the F distribution with parameters $v_1 = I - 1$ and $v_2 = (I - 1)(J - 1)$. Alternatively, H_0 is rejected if the P-VALUE of the test is less than α.

(b) The Hypothesis of No Column Effects   This is the hypothesis that all column effects are equal to zero:

$$H_0: \beta_1 = \beta_2 = \cdots = \beta_J = 0$$

The alternative hypothesis is that at least one of these β_j is not equal to zero. By analogy with (a), the F statistic for this test is

$$F_C = \frac{(I-1)(J-1)}{J-1} \frac{SSE_C - SSE_F}{SSE_C}$$

where

$$SSE_C = \sum_i \sum_j (Y_{ij} - Y_{i.})^2$$

Again, H_0 should be rejected when $F_C > F_\alpha$. F_α is the critical value of the F distribution with parameters $v_1 = J - 1$ and $v_2 = (I - 1)(J - 1)$. Again, the alternative is to reject H_0 if the P-VALUE of the test is less than α.[6]

The components of these F statistics are usually displayed by computer programs in the format of Table 4.11. Again note that only the last two columns

---

[6]There is, of course, a third kind of hypothesis: that β_1 to β_J *and* γ_1 to γ_I are all equal to zero (that is, neither attribute has any effect on the variable). We will let the reader develop the appropriate test of this hypothesis as an exercise.

TABLE 4.11   Analysis of Variance: Two-way Classification with One Observation per Cell

Source of variation	Degrees of freedom	Sum of squares	Mean square	F statistic	P-value
Rows	$I - 1$	$SSR = SSE_R - SSE_F$	$MSR = SSR/(I - 1)$	$F_R = MSR/MSE$	...
Columns	$J - 1$	$SSC = SSE_C - SSE_F$	$MSC = SSC/(J - 1)$	$F_C = MSC/MSE$	...
Residual (error)	$(I - 1)(J - 1)$	SSE_F	$MSE = SSE_F/(I - 1)(J - 1)$		
Total	$IJ - 1$	SST			

of the table, giving the F statistics and P-VALUES for the above two tests, are normally of interest in practice. The other numbers are simply the components of the F statistics.

EXAMPLE 4.3 (CONTINUED)

The results shown in Fig. 4.2 will be found among the output of most computer programs for two-way analysis of variance.

For, say, $\alpha = 0.05$, the critical F value for testing the hypothesis of no row effects ($v_1 = 2$, $v_2 = 6$) is 5.143, while the critical F for testing the hypothesis of no column effects ($v_1 = 3$, $v_2 = 6$) is 4.757 (calculated by a computer program). Thus, under the routine assumptions in analysis of variance, both hypotheses should be rejected because the calculated F statistics exceed the critical values. Exactly the same conclusion is reached on observing that the P-VALUES of both tests are less than $\alpha = 0.05$. In other words, the conclusion is that both the time of day and the operator influence the time required to perform the task.

It is interesting to compare these conclusions with those of the one-way analysis of the same set of data, where it was concluded that there were *no* differences between operators. The apparent inconsistency can be explained. The variability of each operator's timings is so great that differences between operators are obscured. When a part of this variability is systematically explained by the time of day at which the measurements were taken, the effects of the operators are allowed to stand out more clearly. ∎

```
DEPENDENT VARIABLE: Y
    SOURCE   DF      SS       MS       F      P-VALUE
       ROW    2    15.5    7.750    18.6     0.0027
   COLUMNS    3    15.0    5.000    12.0     0.0060
  RESIDUAL    6     2.5    0.417
     TOTAL   11    33.0
```

FIGURE 4.2   Two-way ANOVA, computer output, Example 4.3

EXAMPLE 4.4

(Due to Mr. C. Nathan) In order to find out if appreciable differences between cities existed in the prices of various meat products, a study was made of the retail prices of six meat cuts in eight cities across the country over a period of 10 years.

The following meat cuts were considered: beef sirloin steak, beef round steak, pork shoulder, sliced bacon, leg roast of lamb, and veal loin chop. For each meat cut, the retail price (in cents per pound) was recorded in each city for the months of January and July of each year from 19X0 to 19X9. The retail price in each city and month is the average of the retail prices recorded in monthly surveys of selected retail establishments.

In order to illustrate the approach followed, consider one of these meat cuts, pork shoulder, and imagine the retail prices arranged in the form of a table with eight rows, one for each city, and 20 columns, one for each January and July from 19X0 to 19X9, as follows:

City	Jan. 19X0	$\cdots$	$\cdots$	Jul. 19X9	City average
1	51.8	$\cdots$	$\cdots$	70.8	54.6
$\cdots$	$\cdots$	$\cdots$	$\cdots$	$\cdots$	$\cdots$
8	54.8	$\cdots$	$\cdots$	67.1	59.9
Average for month:	50.5	$\cdots$	$\cdots$	66.5	57.8

A number of factors account for the variability of these prices—the population of the city, local tastes, the level of competition between the retail outlets, the ease with which stock is transported from one city to another, variations in the timing of the survey and the establishments surveyed, and so on. These factors do not necessarily remain constant from month to month. It may not be a question, therefore, of simply comparing the *observed* average city prices because the observations and the averages may have been different under different circumstances. It may be more appropriate to consider the observations as a sample and to ask if there is any evidence that retail prices *tend to* vary between cities.

Figure 4.3 shows the price of pork shoulder by city in the period 19X0 to 19X9. The retail prices appear to form a band that moves up or down reflecting changes in demand and supply for the entire country. Within this band of prices, however, the city prices do not always maintain their relative positions. The price in City 3, for example, is sometimes among the highest and sometimes among the lowest.

Let Y be the price of pork shoulder. We use Model 4.12 with γ_i the city and β_j the period effects. Under the assumptions of this section, two hypotheses may be tested.

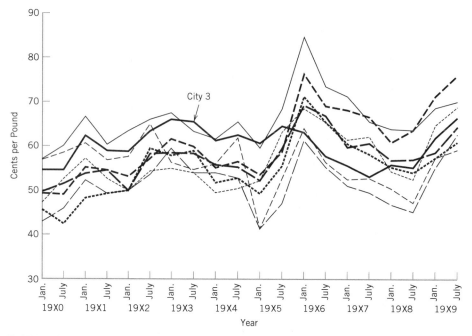

FIGURE 4.3 Pork shoulder prices by city

The first hypothesis is that city prices tend to be the same, which is the hypothesis that all city effects are equal to zero:

$$H_0: \gamma_1 = \gamma_2 = \cdots = \gamma_8 = 0 \qquad \text{(No city effects)}$$

The second hypothesis to be tested (although perhaps we already have a good idea of what the conclusion will be) is that pork shoulder prices tend to be the same across periods, which is the hypothesis that all period effects are zero:

$$H_0: \beta_1 = \beta_2 = \cdots = \beta_{20} = 0 \qquad \text{(No period effects)}$$

Our problem is clearly a special case of a two-way classification with one observation per cell. The number of observations ($n = 180$) is large. The two hypotheses are tested by comparing the F statistics with the critical F values. From the output of the computer program used (there is no point in listing the entire output), we find

$$F_R = 24.02$$

for testing the hypothesis of no city effects, and

$$F_C = 11.97$$

for testing the hypothesis of no period effects.

The critical F value for testing the hypothesis of no city effects at, say, $\alpha = 0.05$ with $v_1 = I - 1 = 7$ and $v_2 = (I - 1)(J - 1) = 133$ is 2.08 (from a computer program). Similarly, the critical F value for testing the hypothesis of no period effects at $\alpha = 0.05$ for $v_1 = 19$ and $v_2 = 133$ is 1.67. Both hypotheses, therefore, should be rejected: the observed differences between the cities and periods cannot be attributed to random variation.

The same procedure was followed to examine differences between cities and between periods for each of the remaining five meat cuts. The results are summarized as follows:

Meat cut	Calculated F statistic	
	F_R	F_C
Beef sirloin steak	67.85	57.22
Beef round steak	48.11	48.55
Pork shoulder	24.02	11.97
Bacon	22.39	44.48
Lamb leg roast	15.80	7.04
Veal loin chops	4.26	8.11

In each case, the observations form a table with eight rows (cities) and 20 columns (periods). The critical F values are the same as in the analysis of pork shoulder prices: at $\alpha = 0.05$, these are 2.08 (for testing the hypothesis of no city effects) and 1.67 (for the hypothesis of no period effects). Clearly, in all cases, we conclude that there are differences between cities and periods. ∎

As in all problems of inference in regression, four assumptions must be checked before applying the tests just discussed—the assumptions of linearity, constant variance, independence, and normality. The simple plots of residuals described in Section 3.6 ought to screen out gross violations of these assumptions. Two more warnings. First, as in all statistical tests, the meaning and likely consequences of Type I and II errors should be examined and the value of α selected appropriately. Second, the hypotheses in analysis of variance are very strict (for example, the hypothesis of no column effects means that all the column effects are precisely equal to zero); in most practical situations, rejection of these hypotheses is inevitable if the sample is large enough.

4.7 INTERACTIONS IN ANALYSIS OF VARIANCE

Suppose that, in addition to the separate effects of two attributes, there exist effects due to their interaction. A suitable model is

$$Y = \beta_0 + \beta_1 X_1 + \cdots + \beta_J X_J + \gamma_1 Z_1 + \cdots + \gamma_I Z_I$$
$$+ \delta_{11} W_{11} + \cdots + \delta_{IJ} W_{IJ} + \varepsilon \tag{4.14}$$

As before, the X's and Z's are dummy variables corresponding to the categories of the two attributes and the β's and γ's their effects. The W's are also dummy variables, and there is one for each of the IJ cross-classifications (cells). For example, if the first attribute has two categories and the second three, there are six cells and W's as follows:

First	*Second attribute*		
attribute	*C1*	*C2*	*C3*
R1	W_{11}	W_{12}	W_{13}
R2	W_{21}	W_{22}	W_{23}

W_{11} takes the value 1 for observations falling into category 1 of the first attribute and category 1 of the second and the value 0 otherwise. W_{21} equals 1 for observations in category 2 of the first and category 1 of the second attribute. And so on.

Model 4.14 has $(I + 1)(J + 1)$ parameters, and to estimate them we must have more than one observation in each cell. The parameters may be estimated by regression (after dropping one of the X's, Z's, and W's) or more simply calculated by formulas similar to those in the previous sections (obtained by requiring that appropriate restrictions be satisfied). Tests of the hypotheses that all the β's apart from β_0, all the γ's, or all the δ's equal zero may be developed based on appropriate F statistics.

4.8 MULTI-WAY ANALYSIS OF VARIANCE

The approach described earlier for analyzing the effects of a classification according to one or two attributes can be easily extended to classifications according to three, four, or more attributes. Each multiple classification (cell) may contain one or more observations. Interactions between the attributes—that is, special effects attributed to cells, over and above the sum of the corresponding attribute effects—can also be accommodated. All these models can be analyzed either as special cases of the linear regression model or using results obtained by taking advantage of their special features in the manner illustrated in this chapter.

4.9   TO SUM UP

- Dummy (binary, indicator) variables are specially constructed variables that are allowed to take the values 0 or 1 only.

- Attributes are normally taken into account by introducing a dummy variable for each category of the attribute. The dummy variable takes the value 1 if the category is present in the observation or the value 0 otherwise. One of the dummy variables in the set may be left out of the model to avoid extreme collinearity. The regression coefficients of the dummy variables measure the effects of the categories of the attribute in relation to the effect of the category of the omitted dummy variable.

- The presence of an exact linear relationship between the columns of the matrix of values of the explanatory variables is called collinearity or extreme collinearity. When there is collinearity, there exists an infinite number of solutions to the least-squares problem.

- A unique solution to the least-squares problem may be obtained either by not using one of the related variables or by imposing other suitable restrictions on the OLS estimates.

- Analysis of variance is a special case of regression with attributes only as explanatory variables. One-way analysis of variance, for example, is regression with one explanatory attribute only, two-way one with two attributes only, and so on. It is customary in analysis of variance to ensure uniqueness of the OLS estimates by requiring that the sum of an attribute's effects equals zero. This requirement is mathematically convenient because the estimates as well as the components of the F statistics can be simply calculated.

PROBLEMS

4.1   Using a computer program, confirm the results presented in this chapter.

4.2   (a) Using a computer program and the following data,

Y	X_0	X_1	X_2
7	1	2	3
15	1	5	0
10	1	3	2
13	1	4	1

regress Y against X_1 and X_2 to find out how your program handles extreme collinearity.

(b) Verify that the two sets of estimates, (i) $b_0 = 1.8, b_1 = 2.7, b_2 = 0$, and (ii) $b_0 = 15.3, b_1 = 0$, $b_2 = -2.7$, both give $\sum (Y - \hat{Y})^2 = 0.3$.

(c) Find another set of estimates also giving $\sum (Y - \hat{Y})^2 = 0.3$.

4.3 (a) Using the data file `rest.dat`, confirm the results presented in Example 4.1.

(b) Suppose location influences the unit value of floor space rather than lot size as assumed in Example 4.1. That is, suppose $b_1 = c + c_1 L1 + c_2 L2 + c_3 L3$. Formulate and estimate the implied regression model. Is the assumption justified?

4.4 Regression was used to identify the determinants of the size of the audience for theatrical films when they were first shown on television. The regression results were reported as follows:

$$\widehat{RTG} = 14.72 + 6.56AWD + 0.05LEN - 3.31QU2 - 3.47MUS - 2.81SCF \qquad R^2 = 0.65$$
$$\quad\;\; (5.66) \quad\;\; (5.89) \quad\;\;\; (2.01) \quad\;\;\; (-2.32) \quad\;\; (-1.73) \quad\;\; (-1.38) \qquad\quad S = 3.35$$

where

RTG: Film's rating (percentage of adults who watched the film)

AWD: Number of major Academy Awards won by film

LEN: Running time of the film (minutes)

QU2: =1 if film was shown in April, May, or June; =0 otherwise

MUS: =1 if a musical; =0 otherwise

SCF: =1 if a science fiction film; =0 otherwise

Interpret and comment on these results.

4.5 Consider once again the example of Section 4.4, in which expenditures on reading are assumed to be related to gender and the level of education. A type of model frequently used in such a case is the following:

$$\hat{Y} = b_0 + \underbrace{c_1 U_1 + c_2 U_2}_{Gender} + \underbrace{d_1 V_1 + d_2 V_2 + d_3 V_3}_{Education} + \underbrace{b_1 X_1 + b_2 X_2 + \cdots + b_6 X_6}_{Interactions}$$

where U_1 and U_2 are dummy variables representing males and females; V_1 to V_3 dummy variables representing elementary, high school, and university education; and X_1 to X_6 dummy variables representing the six gender/education categories listed in Section 4.4. The c's and d's of this model are called "main effects" and the b's "interaction effects."

(a) Which dummy variables should be dropped to ensure unique OLS estimates of the remaining effects?

(b) Interpret the estimates of the remaining effects.

(c) Is this model better than the one in Section 4.4?

4.6 A national survey of household expenditures provided, among other things, some information on the relationship between annual household savings and certain explanatory variables. 580 heads of households across the country were interviewed and supplied information on the following variables:

Y: Amount saved by household during the previous calendar year ($000);

X_1: Number of persons in the household;

X_2: Number of persons in the household under 18 years of age;

X_3: Total household income during the previous calendar year ($000);

X_4: Highest level of education attained by head of household, coded as follows: 1 for elementary school, 2 for high school, and 3 for university;

X_5: Dummy variable, = 1 for urban household, 0 otherwise.

The regression results were as follows:

$$\hat{Y} = 2.121 + 0.718X_1 - 0.605X_2 + 0.044X_3 + 0.156X_4 - 1.315X_5 \qquad R^2 = 0.68$$
$$\qquad (1.05) \qquad (-0.75) \qquad (2.05) \qquad (1.87) \quad (-1.65) \qquad n = 580$$

(a) Interpret these results.

(b) Estimate the annual savings of an urban household consisting of two adults and one child eight years of age, in which the head is a high school graduate and the total annual income is $16,000.

(c) If the survey were to be repeated, what changes would you recommend to the coding of the variables and the form of the model? Explain.

4.7 (Due to Alain Roy and Jim Knighton) Equity in real estate property taxation is commonly taken to mean that the tax per dollar of value of the property is the same for all properties in the taxing district. "Value," in turn, is usually understood as the selling price of the property under free-market conditions. The main obstacle to a fair taxation system is that relatively few properties change hands in a month, quarter, or year, hence the selling price of the large majority of properties cannot be determined.

In the municipality considered in this study, each real estate property pays an annual tax equal to the product of the "mill rate" (the same for all properties) and the "assessed value" of the property. The mill rate is 0.2031, so that a property assessed at $5000 pays a tax of about $1015. Assessed values are supposed to reflect 1945 property prices and are determined by assessors when construction is completed and only occasionally revised for any building alterations. If the assessed values were proportional to market prices, the taxes would also be proportional to market prices. That, however, is suspected not to be the case.

A random sample without replacement of 70 properties was selected from among all properties sold in a given year. The data can be found in the file proptax.dat and are outlined in Table 4.12.

TABLE 4.12 File proptax.dat, Partial Listing

PRICE	ASSM	TYPE	TAX
53000	4757	D	965.91
58500	3500	S	710.67
89900	4460	S	905.60
179900	7000	S	1421.35
78500	4058	C	823.98
. . .	. . .	. . .	. . .

The variables are defined as follows:

PRICE: Selling price ($)

ASSM: Assessed value ($)

TYPE: Type of property (D = detached, S = semidetached or townhouse, C = condominium apartment, X = duplex, M = multiple use, O = Other)

TAX: Annual property tax ($)

(a) Calculate the tax rate, TR=TAX/PRICE, for every property. Plot the distribution of this variable. Calculate its mean and standard deviation.

(b) Using a scatter diagram of tax rate and price, examine whether there is any relationship between these two variables.

(c) Regress TR against PRICE. Is the property tax system of this municipality fair, or does it discriminate on the basis of property values? State clearly any assumptions you are forced to make.

(d) Show graphically any relationship between the tax rate and the type of the property.

(e) Does the property tax system discriminate with respect to the type of property? State clearly any assumptions you are forced to make.

(f) Does the property tax system discriminate with respect to property value *and* the type of property? State clearly any assumptions you are forced to make.

4.8 (Due to Mr. Tony Smith) In a study of the determinants of a baseball team's attendance, the dependent variable was the team's total paid admission during the year (the number of persons who paid to view the team's games, in thousands). Twenty-six major league baseball teams were considered over a period of four years, thus yielding 104 observations. Attendance ranged from about 700,000 to 3,500,000 during the period.

(a) A number of models were estimated, but the preferred one ($R^2 = 0.90$) is detailed in Table 4.13.

The World Series score variable gave the team 2 points for each prior year it was a World Series champion and 1 point for each prior year it was a World Series finalist.

TABLE 4.13   Baseball Attendance, Explanatory Model, Problem 4.8

Explanatory variable	Coefficient	t-value
Constant	−634.639	−3.87
Time trend (= 1 for year 1, $\cdots$, = 4 for year 4)	56.857	3.25
Number of wins this year	21.762	4.12
Number of wins last year	−9.060	−2.85
Last year's attendance	0.650	5.02
Dummy variable (=1 if team was division champion last year)	381.849	4.95
Dummy variable (= 1 if team was in penant race this year)	221.091	3.46
World Series score (see text)	4.679	1.45

The population of the team's home city (divided by the number of teams in cases where the city was home to more than one team) and its location (east/west) were considered but found not to be significant explanatory variables.

Interpret the results. Comment on their managerial implications.

(b) It was recognized that the model in (a) could not be used for forecasting as some of the explanatory variables are determined simultaneously with attendance. For forecasting purposes, the model specified in Table 4.14 was estimated ($R^2 = 0.72$).

Interpret and comment on these results.

4.9 (Due to Mr. Peter Geub) "Over/Under" is the name of a betting game managed by the Ontario Lottery Corporation (OLC). A player selects 3, 4, 5, or 6 sports games from among those listed on a daily selection slip and, for each selected game, indicates whether the total score of the game will be over or under the total score predicted by the OLC and posted on the previous day. The listed sports games are between professional baseball, ice hockey, and football teams. The player may wager an amount ranging from $2 to $100 per selection slip. All the player's predictions must be correct in order to win. The payout is 4, 7, 14, or 25 times the amount wagered if all 3, 4, 5, or 6 predictions, respectively, are correct.

You are asked to determine if information publicly available prior to the wager can be utilized to forecast the total score of an ice hockey game and to guide a bettor. The file hockey1.dat contains the prior information and total score for the 100 most recently played ice hockey games. The data are partially listed in Figure 4.4.

TABLE 4.14   Baseball Attendance, Forecasting Model, Problem 4.8

Explanatory variable	Coefficient	t-value
Constant	654.490	0.29
Time trend	66.295	1.81
Last year's attendance	0.715	3.79
Population of home city	43.513	1.72

OBS	HOME	VIS	SCORE	AGFH	AGFV	AGAH	AGAV	DIV	CONF	FAVH	FIRST	LOP
1	PITT	STL	12	4.58	2.70	3.50	3.14	0	0	1	1	1
2	NYI	WASH	8	2.81	2.85	3.91	2.82	1	0	0	0	1
3	DALL	WINN	10	2.79	3.40	3.38	3.62	0	0	0	0	0
4	WASH	ANA	3	2.85	2.82	2.60	3.10	0	0	1	1	0
5	FLOR	OTT	7	3.29	2.32	2.89	3.64	0	1	1	1	1
6	NYR	EDM	5	3.46	2.93	2.81	3.74	0	0	1	1	1
7	VAN	COL	7	3.44	3.93	3.45	2.89	1	0	0	0	1
8	BUFF	MONT	5	2.91	3.26	3.11	3.01	1	0	0	0	1
9	DET	COL	7	3.94	3.92	2.23	3.40	0	1	1	1	0
10	NJ	CHI	6	2.59	3.40	2.38	2.67	0	0	0	0	0

FIGURE 4.4   File hockey1.dat, partial listing

The labels of the variables should be interpreted as follows:

HOME: Home team

VIS: Visiting team

SCORE: Total score of the game

AGFH: Average number of goals per game for home team

AGFV: Average number of goals per game for visiting team

AGAH: Average number of goals per game against home team

AGAV: Average number of goals per game against visiting team

DIV: $= 1$ if game is interdivisional; $= 0$ otherwise

CONF: $= 1$ if game is interconference; $= 0$ otherwise

FAVH: $= 1$ if home team is ranked higher than the visiting one; $= 0$ otherwise

FIRST: $= 1$ if one of the teams is ranked first; $= 0$ otherwise

LOP: $= 1$ if the proportion of wins to losses of one team is greater, and that of the other less than 0.5; $= 0$ otherwise

Consider the first entry in Figure 4.4 by way of illustration. Prior to that game, the home team (Pittsburgh) had scored 4.58 goals per game and allowed 3.50 goals per game on average. The corresponding statistics for the visiting team (St. Louis) were 2.7 for and 3.14 against, respectively. Professional hockey teams are divided into two conferences and each conference into a number of divisions. The game was neither interdivisional nor interconference. The home team was ranked higher than the visiting one—in fact, the home team was ranked first. Pittsburgh's win/loss proportion was greater than 0.5, while St. Louis's was less. The actual total number of goals scored in this game was 12 (this could have been the result of a 7-5 win by Pittsburgh).

(a) On the reasoning that the total score of a game tends to be higher the greater the scoring record of the opposing teams, a regression of SCORE against the four goals-per-game variables yielded the following results:

$$\widehat{SCORE} = \quad -13.295 \quad + 1.614AGFH + 1.854AGFV + 1.787AGAH$$
$$(-5.27) \qquad (4.52) \qquad (4.59) \qquad (4.66)$$
$$+ 0.877AGAV \quad R^2 = 0.400$$
$$(2.28) \qquad S = 1.774$$

Figure 4.5 shows the prior information, the total score predicted by OLC (under the label PRED), and the actual total score for the first 10 of 30 subsequent hockey games. The complete set of data can be found in the file `hockey2.dat`.

Using these regression results, forecast the total score of each game in Figure 4.5. Assuming it is possible to place bets on individual games, determine whether a bet should be Under or Over. Assuming further that each individual bet is for $1 and that a win returns $2, calculate the proportion of winning bets and the return on your investment. Explain any reservations you may have about the validity of the model and its usefulness.

(b) Using the full data in the file `hockey1.dat`, improve the model used in (a). Under the assumptions in (a), test your model against the full set of data in the file `hockey2.dat`. Explain clearly any suggestions you may have for improving the data and the model.

```
OBS  HOME  VIS    AGFH AGAH AGFV AGAV DIV CONF FAVH LOP FIRST PRED SCORE

  1  BOST  MONT  3.45 3.35 3.27 3.00  1    0    0   0    0    6.5    7
  2  DALL  ANA   2.80 3.83 2.80 3.08  0    1    0   0    0    5.5    4
  3  STL   NJ    2.72 2.96 2.66 2.49  0    0    0   0    0    5.5    8
  4  FLOR  PITT  3.23 2.89 4.55 3.46  0    1    0   0    1    7.5    5
  5  VAN   CHIC  3.42 3.45 3.34 2.63  0    1    0   0    1    6.5    7
  6  EDM   WINN  2.93 3.60 3.40 3.62  0    1    0   0    0    6.5    5
  7  WASH  OTT   2.82 2.54 2.32 3.59  0    1    1   1    0    5.5    5
  8  COL   SJ    3.89 2.79 3.11 4.28  1    0    1   1    1    7.5   11
  9  BUFF  PHIL  2.93 3.15 3.40 2.58  0    1    0   1    0    5.5   11
 10  CALG  LA    2.95 2.82 3.08 3.71  1    0    1   0    0    5.5    7
```

FIGURE 4.5   File hockey2.dat, partial listing

(c) Refer to the file hockey2.dat. How accurate is OLC in predicting the total score of a hockey game? Does the success of a wager depend only on the accuracy of the forecast of the total score of a game?

4.10   Refer to Problem 2.14 and the file norgas.dat. In the light of the material presented in this chapter, can you improve your model for forecasting a day's gas consumption given weather forecasts of the day's mean temperature and wind speed? Explain clearly the rationale for your new model and examine its performance.

4.11   The Oshawa Ambulance Service (OAS) is a centralized dispatch center coordinating ambulance service in five adjacent municipalities. Table 4.15 shows the response time and

TABLE 4.15   Data for Problem 4.11

Priority 3		Priority 4	
Response	Distance	Response	Distance
8	1.21	6	0.39
10	2.35	8	2.21
8	0.83	7	2.12
9	2.50	5	1.14
5	0.91	4	1.14
3	0.45	5	1.30
11	1.06	5	2.35
9	1.14	4	1.29
4	0.53	9	2.80
7	1.21	8	2.12
12	2.12	7	1.36
5	0.45	10	3.03
9	1.29		
5	0.53		

SOURCE: File ambul.dat

distance to the scene of the accident or other emergency for a sample of 14 "Priority 3" and 12 "Priority 4" calls.

The response time is the period in minutes that elapses between the time the call is received by the OAS dispatcher and the time the ambulance arrives at the site of the accident. Distance is straight line, not the actual distance traveled, between the ambulance station and the site and is measured in miles. A call is classified by the dispatcher as Priority 3 if it involves a minor, not-life-threatening medical emergency; the ambulance responds immediately but without flashing lights or siren. A Priority 4 call involves threat to life or death; the ambulance responds immediately with flashing lights and siren. The observations in Table 4.15 were randomly selected for the purpose of this problem from OAS records of 1612 Priority 3 and 2772 Priority 4 calls in one year.

Do distance and the class of the call affect the ambulance response time? Explain in detail your answer, the method used, and any assumptions you were forced to make. Forecast the response time to a Priority 3 and 4 call 2.5 miles from the station.

4.12 (Due to Mr. H. Grouni) Before construction begins, a bridge project goes through a number of stages of production, one of which is the design stage. This phase is composed of various activities each of which contributes directly to the overall design time. Some of the major design activities are calculations, drafting, quantity takeoffs, preparation of tender documents, and checking. The duration of each of these activities and consequently the overall design time is a highly indeterminate variable affected by a number of other variables, a significant portion of which are related to the size, type, and configuration of the structure to be designed.

For two reasons it is important to be able to predict this service time reasonably accurately before starting the actual design: first, to estimate and control the cost of design production and, secondly, to verify or set design completion dates so that other sections in the Department of Transportation may carry on the overall production function toward the ultimate objective of constructing the designed project. In short, predicting the design time is helpful for budgeting and internal as well as external scheduling purposes.

Detailed information on 45 bridge projects was compiled for use in this study. The data are contained in the file bridge.dat and partially listed in Table 4.16.

The variables have the following interpretation:

TIME: Design time, in person-days

DAREA: Deck area of bridge (000 sq. ft)

CCOST: Construction cost ($0000)

TABLE 4.16 File bridge.dat, Partial Listing

TIME	DAREA	CCOST	DWGS	LENGTH	SPANS	DDIFF	TYPE
47.8	1.01	30.0	4	35	1	0	1
57.0	2.52	65.5	5	70	1	0	1
111.7	3.43	67.4	5	70	1	1	0
418.1	7.21	336.2	11	285	3	1	1
59.4	2.16	63.7	5	60	1	0	1
...	...	...	...	...	...	...	...

DWGS: Number of structural drawings

LENGTH: Length of bridge, in feet

SPANS: Number of spans

DDIFF: Degree of difficulty of bridge design ($= 0$ easy, $= 1$ complex)

TYPE: Type of structure ($= 0$ concrete, $= 1$ structural steel)

The deck area is the area of the bridge surface. Construction cost is estimated at the start of the design once the general layout of the structure is decided. The length of a bridge is the length from one abutment to the other and is dictated by the type and width of the crossing. The number of spans indicates the number of intermediate piers that are needed to support the bridge as a whole. The number of structural drawings is dictated by the combination of size, area, length, number of spans, and complexity of the structure; it can be estimated accurately at the outset of the design stage. It is expected that steel or complex structures will require more time to design than concrete or simple ones.

Some time ago scheduling and budgeting techniques were initiated in the department. The mean value of the design time per structural drawing is currently used for estimating the design time. That value was found to be 20 person-days per drawing.

Can you improve the estimation of bridge design time?

4.13 The file opers.dat, partially listed in Table 4.17, contains the data of Examples 4.2 and 4.3. The labels have the following interpretation:

TIME: Task completion time

OPER: Operator number

TOD: Time of day (1=Morning, 2=Noon, 3=Afternoon)

(a) With the help of a computer program, confirm the regression and one-way analysis of variance results presented in Example 4.2.

(b) With the help of a computer program, confirm the two-way analysis of variance results presented in Example 4.3.

TABLE 4.17   File opers.dat, Partial Listing

TIME	OPER	TOD
14	1	1
15	1	2
16	1	3
16	2	1
17	2	2
. . .	. . .	. . .

4.14 A certain type of plastic material was tested for strength at three levels each of temperature and injection pressure. The results, measured in hundreds of pounds per square inch (psi), are as follows.

Injection pressure	Temperature		
	A	B	C
a	41.1	41.9	44.6
b	39.7	40.5	42.8
c	38.3	38.8	41.4

(a) Assume that the conditions for the application of analysis of variance are satisfied and ignore for the moment the injection pressure of the observations. Test the hypothesis that temperature has no effect on strength, assuming that the probability of a Type I error should not exceed 5%. Interpret the meaning and describe the likely consequences of the two types of error in this case. Redo the test under the assumption that the probability of a Type II error should not exceed 5%. Estimate the effects of and calculate the estimated strength $(\hat{Y})$ at each level of temperature.

(b) Same as (a), except test the hypothesis that injection pressure has no effect on strength, ignoring temperature. Estimate the effects of and calculate the estimated strength of the material at each level of pressure.

(c) Again assuming that the conditions for the application of analysis of variance are satisfied, test the hypotheses that (i) temperature and (ii) pressure have no effect on strength, this time recognizing that strength is related to both attributes. Estimate the effects of each level of temperature and pressure, and calculate the estimated strength of the material at each temperature/pressure level. Compare these tests with those in (a) and (b) and explain the differences.

(d) For each of cases a, b, and c, estimate the appropriate model with dummy variables and verify that the effects of temperature and pressure are consistent with those calculated under the analysis of variance model.

(e) State the conditions for the application of the analysis of variance model. Check roughly whether or not these conditions appear to be satisfied in case c.

4.15 Consider the data of Example 2.3 of Section 2.10 (file plmat.dat), which showed the results of tests for strength of a plastic material at selected barrel temperatures, mold temperatures, and injection pressures.

(a) Regress strength (Y) on barrel temperature (X_1) and injection pressure (X_2) to estimate the model: $\hat{Y} = b_0 + b_1 X_1 + b_2 X_2$. Interpret the results.

(b) Regress strength on dummy variables representing the three levels each of barrel temperature and injection pressure. Write and interpret the estimated regression equation.

(c) Compare your results in (a) and (b). In particular, explain why the S and R^2 of the two models differ. Should one model always have better fit than the other?

(d) Can you test the hypotheses that (i) barrel temperature and (ii) injection pressure have no effect on strength?

(e) Calculate the effects of barrel temperature and injection pressure using the results of this chapter, and show that they are consistent with those of (b).

(f) Regress strength on dummy variables representing the three levels each of barrel temperature, mold temperature, and injection pressure. Write and interpret the estimated regression equation. Compare your results with those shown in Example 2.3.

(g) The following is an analysis of variance table for testing the hypotheses that (i) barrel temperature, (ii) mold temparature, and (iii) injection pressure have no effect on the strength of the plastic material. Try to specify clearly H_0 and H_1 in each case and, by analogy with the two-way classification, try to guess how these tests can be carried out.

SOURCE	DF	SS	MS	F	P
Barrel temperature	2	380625	190312	7.89	0.0030
Mold temperature	2	62847	31423	1.30	0.2941
Injection pressure	2	384659	192330	7.97	0.0028
Error	20	482676	24134		
Total	26	1310806	50416		

4.16 Under the standard assumptions of the linear model, develop a test of the hypothesis that β_1 to β_J and γ_1 to γ_I of Model 4.12 are all equal to zero, against the alternative hypothesis that at least one of these β's or γ's is not equal to zero.

4.17 Savings and loan associations are financial intermediaries: they make loans—generally long-term loans in residential real estate—and derive their funds primarily from deposited savings and from the liquidation of their loan portfolios through amortization and pre-payments. When a loan is made, an agreement is reached through bargaining between the association and the borrower on the *loan fee* (expressed as a percentage of the loan amount covering closing expenses, title clearance, etc.), the *loan term* (the number of years to the date of the last payment), the *loan-to-appraisal ratio* (the loan amount expressed as a percentage of the appraised value of the property offered as security for the loan), and the *interest rate*.

It has been argued that associations (for reasons similar to those of other oligopolistic firms) are reluctant to change the ("visible") interest rates and rely instead on the other ("hidden") charges to achieve some degree of price flexibility. For example, instead of raising interest rates, associations could increase the loan fees, reduce the loan-to-appraisal ratios, or decrease the loan terms in order to ration scarce funds. If this argument is correct, a change in the scope of the regulation would be appropriate.

The records of 23 savings and loan associations located in the Bay Area allowed the calculation of the average interest rate of all loans made by each of these associations in each of 18 consecutive months. Similarly, the average fee, average loan-to-appraisal ratio, and average loan term were calculated for each association and month.

This period of 18 months was one of crisis for the Bay Area associations. Savings withdrawals exceeded savings deposits by far, and loan funds had to be reduced drastically—from $130 million at the beginning to $30 million at the end of the period.

The data were arranged in four tables, each having 18 columns corresponding to months and 23 rows corresponding to firms. The typical cell entry, Y_{ij}, stood, in turn, for the average interest rate, average loan term, average loan fee, and average loan-to-appraisal ratio of firm i in month j. In each case it was assumed that

$$Y_{ij} = \beta_0 + \beta_j + \gamma_i + \varepsilon_{ij}$$

where γ_i $(i = 1, 2, \ldots, 23)$ is the firm effect, β_j $(j = 1, 2, \ldots, 18)$ the month effect, and ε_{ij} the error. Two hypotheses were tested in each case:

$$\text{(a)} \quad H_0: \beta_1 = \beta_2 = \cdots = \beta_{18} = 0,$$
$$\text{(b)} \quad H_0: \gamma_1 = \gamma_2 = \cdots = \gamma_{23} = 0.$$

The following table shows the calculated F statistics:

Source of variation	Degrees of freedom	Interest rate	Loan term	Loan fee	Loan/appraisal ratio
Firms	22	10.18	35.74	14.87	18.89
Months	17	30.96	1.46	1.61	1.04
Error	374				

For $\alpha = 0.05$, the critical value for testing (a) is 1.65 and that for testing (b) is 1.57. Interpret and comment on these findings.

4.18 (Due to Mr. Scott Anderson) The file mfunds.dat contains the annual rates of return for 54 equity mutual funds over a 14-year period. The data are arranged in a table with the following format:

	Rate of return (%)			
Fund no.	Year 1	Year 2	$\cdots$	Year 14
1	23.2	2.6	$\cdots$	1.6
2	33.6	16.5	$\cdots$	2.0
$\cdots$	$\cdots$	$\cdots$	$\cdots$	$\cdots$
54	36.1	23.5	$\cdots$	0.1

A fund's rate of return for year t is defined as

$$\text{Rate of return} = \frac{(P_t - P_{t-1}) + D_t}{P_t}$$

where P_t is the fund's share price at the end of year t and D_t the dividends distributed by the fund during year t.

(a) Calculate the average $(\bar{Y})$ and standard deviation (S_Y) of the annual rates of return for each of the 54 funds in the file mfunds.dat.

(b) Financial theory suggests there is a relationship between the expected return and the risk of an asset, in the sense that riskier assets require a higher expected return in order to attract investors. This relationship holds *ex ante*, but it is also suggested that it applies *ex post*. For this case in particular, it is suggested that riskier funds (ones with greater standard deviation) tend to have greater average return. In a scatter diagram, plot the 54 pairs of $(\bar{Y}, S_Y)$ values. Does there appear to be a relationship between S_Y and $\bar{Y}$?

(c) Regress $\bar{Y}$ against S_Y to investigate whether or not there is a linear relationship between the two variables. Comment on the features of the estimated relationship.

(d) The data can be used to measure the quality of financial management of the funds. It can be hypothesized that the rate of return of fund i in year t, Y_{it}, is

$$Y_{it} = \delta + \beta_i + \gamma_t + \varepsilon_{it},$$

where δ can be interpreted as a base figure, β_i as the effect of fund i, γ_t as the effect of year t, and ε_{it} as the error. If all funds were managed equally well, all the β's would be equal. Likewise, if all the years were equally prosperous for mutual funds, all γ's would be equal.

Formulate the appropriate regression or analysis of variance model.

(e) Were all funds managed equally well? Were all years equally prosperous? Explain clearly your reasoning and assumptions.

(f) If you have not done so under (e), assume that the errors (ε) can be considered as random draws with replacement from a normal population of ε-values having mean 0 and a certain variance σ^2. Test the hypotheses: (i) all β's are equal and (ii) all γ's are equal. Explain clearly any additional assumptions you are forced to make.

(g) In view of (b) and (c), which of the assumptions in (f) may be violated?

(h) Comment on any other aspects of the problem that were not specifically covered in the preceding questions.

CHAPTER **5**

NONLINEAR RELATIONSHIPS

5.1   INTRODUCTION AND SUMMARY

When the relationship between the dependent and the explanatory variables is not linear, the results of the previous chapters obviously do not apply.

As we shall now see, however, in some cases simple transformations of the variables yield a linear relationship between the transformed variables, and the method of least squares may be used to obtain estimates of the parameters of the transformed and original models.

For example, a relationship between Y and X exhibiting a moderate curvature can often be approximated by regressing Y against the explanatory variable X and the squared values of the same variable, X^2. This model is a special case of a polynomial. A polynomial of appropriately high degree (the terms will be explained later) may be used to approximate any nonlinear function of X and may be estimated by regressing Y against X, X^2, X^3, and so on.

Other nonlinear relationships that may be estimated by applying regression to transformed variables include certain inverse and logarithmic models, which will described in more detail later. Relationships that are not linear over the entire range of values of an explanatory variable but are linear within each of a number of intervals of the variable may also be easily estimated with the help of dummy and transformed variables.

If all these simple methods fail, it is still possible to estimate directly the best-fitting values of the parameters of a nonlinear relationship by utilizing special algorithms—iterative numerical procedures that search for and, in well-behaved cases at least, find estimates of the parameters that minimize the sum of squared residuals.

5.2   POLYNOMIALS

Examine the scatter diagram shown in Figure 5.1, which is based on the data listed in the first two columns of Table 5.1.

Evidently, there is a fairly close relationship between Y and X, but the relationship is not linear. We note that as X increases, Y decreases up to a point, beyond which it again increases. A relationship of this type (shaped like the

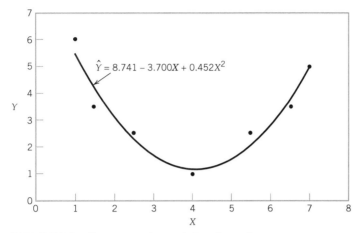

FIGURE 5.1   Illustration of a parabolic relationship

letter U or an inverted U) may be approximated by a *parabola* (or *"polynomial of the second degree"*):

$$\hat{Y} = b_0 + b_1 X + b_2 X^2 \tag{5.1}$$

Eq. 5.1 is a linear function in X and X^2. To see this, replace X by X_1 and X^2 by X_2; then,

$$\hat{Y} = b_0 + b_1 X_1 + b_2 X_2$$

We may treat X_1 and X_2 as any other explanatory variables and obtain the OLS estimates b_0, b_1, and b_2 by regressing Y against X_1 and X_2.

TABLE 5.1   Data Illustrating a Parabolic Approximation

Y	$X (= X_1)$	$X^2 (= X_2)$
2.5	2.5	6.25
3.5	6.5	42.25
6.0	1.0	1.00
1.0	4.0	16.00
3.5	1.5	2.25
2.5	5.5	30.25
5.0	7.0	49.00

As can be easily verified, the OLS estimates are $b_0 = 8.741$, $b_1 = -3.700$, and $b_2 = 0.452$. The estimated values of Y can be calculated from

$$\hat{Y} = 8.741 - 3.700X + 0.452X^2$$

This equation is plotted in Figure 5.1.

In Model 5.1, if X is increased by one unit, the estimated value of Y changes to

$$\begin{aligned}\hat{Y'} &= b_0 + b_1(X+1) + b_2(X+1)^2 \\ &= (b_0 + b_1X + b_2X^2) + (b_1 + b_2) + 2b_2X \\ &= \hat{Y} + (b_1 + b_2) + 2b_2X\end{aligned}$$

Therefore, the effect of a unit increase in X is

$$\hat{Y'} - \hat{Y} = (b_1 + b_2) + 2b_2X$$

which, in contrast to the linear model, is not constant but depends on the level of X.

It can be shown that a parabola $\hat{Y} = b_0 + b_1X + b_2X^2$ achieves its maximum (or minimum) value at the point $x_0 = -b_1/2b_2$. In our example, the minimum value of $\hat{Y}$ occurs at

$$x_0 = \frac{-(-3.700)}{(2)(0.452)} = 4.093$$

EXAMPLE 5.1

It is widely believed that an individual's income tends to increase with age up to a certain point, beyond which it begins to decrease. Table 5.2, showing average income by age group, and Figure 5.2, in which average income (INC) is plotted against the midpoints of age intervals (AGE), tend to support this view.

It would appear from Figure 5.2 that a parabolic relationship between income and age would fit the data well. Two such relationships are estimated, one for men and the other for women, with the following results.

Men: $\widehat{INC} = -33194 + 2822.7(AGE) - 31.174(AGE)^2$ $R^2 = 0.99$

Women: $\widehat{INC} = -2143 + 662.4(AGE) - 7.804(AGE)^2$ $R^2 = 0.90$

These two relationships are plotted in Figure 5.2. Men achieve maximum income at age 45.28 and women at age 42.44. The corresponding maximum average income of men is \$30,716 and that of women is \$11,913.   ∎

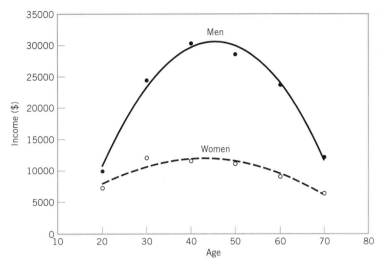

FIGURE 5.2 Relationship between income and age

In a model with several explanatory variables, the effects of some of these may be linear while those of others may be nonlinear. For example, the model

$$\hat{Y} = b_0 + b_1 X_1 + b_2 X_2 + b_3 X_2^2$$

is linear in X_1 but nonlinear in X_2. It implies that a unit increase in X_1, X_2 held constant, changes $\hat{Y}$ by the quantity b_1, but one in X_2, X_1 held constant, changes $\hat{Y}$ by an amount that depends on the level of X_2. The OLS estimates are obtained by regressing Y against X_1, X_2, and X_2^2.

TABLE 5.2 Average Income of Individuals by Age Group and Sex

Age group	Midpoint, AGE	Average income, INC ($) Male	Average income, INC ($) Female
24 and under	20	10,090	7,270
25 to 34	30	24,524	12,068
35 to 44	40	30,408	11,662
45 to 54	50	28,742	11,032
55 to 64	60	23,890	9,100
65 and over	70	11,998	6,378

EXAMPLE 5.2

(Due to Prof. K. Weiermair) In a survey of hiring practices, 165 firms were randomly selected from the latest edition of the Trade Index. The purpose of the survey was to collect information on starting salaries, educational requirements, and experience required for different occupations. Questionnaires were directed to the employing unit of the firms, requesting the following information for each of the firm's last 20 hirings prior to the time of the survey: the job title and job description, the educational background of the hired person, the amount of job-related and general experience that an individual brought to the job, and the starting monthly gross salary. In addition, the firms provided information with respect to their location, industry classification, total number of employees, and the like. One hundred firms responded, and 80 provided usable questionnaires for a total of 1488 hirings.

Of interest is the relationship of starting salary to educational level and experience and the implied value of education and experience as judged by the job market. The model used is

$$\hat{Y} = b_0 + b_1 E + b_2 SH + b_3 CH + b_4 SU + b_5 UD + b_6 GUD$$
$$+ b_7 SE + b_8 (SE)^2 + b_9 GE + b_{10}(GE)^2$$

The dependent variable is

$$Y = \text{Monthly starting salary, in dollars.}$$

The first group of explanatory variables refers to the highest level of education attained by the hired person:

$E = 1$ if attended elementary school; $=0$ otherwise;
$SH = 1$ if attended high school; $=0$ otherwise;
$CH = 1$ if completed high school; $=0$ otherwise;
$SU = 1$ if attended unversity; $=0$ otherwise;
$UD = 1$ if obtained a first university degree; $=0$ otherwise;
$GUD = 1$ if obtained second university degree; $=0$ otherwise.

In addition, two types of experience are distinguished.

SE: Number of years of work experience related to the job for which the person is hired;

GE: Number of years of work experience not considered specific experience.

Squared values of specific and general experience are also included in the model in the belief that the value of experience increases but at a decreasing rate with the number of years of experience. The dummy variables describe six mutually exclusive and collectively exhaustive categories. One of these variables is redundant. Any one may be dropped. It was decided to drop E; therefore, hired persons with at most elementary school education provide the base for measuring the effects of the other variables. The regression results are shown in Table 5.3.

The overall fit of the model is only fair (why?), with about 50% of the variation in starting salaries explained by education, specific experience, and general experience. The OLS estimates of the parameters of the model are generally consistent with prior expectations. Some interesting results are worth noting.

First, experience held constant, salaries tend to increase with the level of education, the only exception being persons with some high school education, who tend to earn slightly less ($3.61 less per month to be exact) than those with elementary school education only. For example, the average starting salary of persons who completed high school only is $108.54 higher than that of persons with elementary school education only and the same amount of specific and general experience; persons with a second university degree earn $133.53 (= $490.20 − $356.67) more than those with one university degree only and the same experience.

Second, starting salaries are clearly influenced by the number of years of specific and/or general experience. The effect of specific experience is given by

$$27.62SE - 0.55(SE)^2$$

TABLE 5.3 Determinants of Starting Salaries

Variable	Symbol	Estimate	t-ratio
Constant		270.83	
Some high school	SH	−3.61	−1.11
Completed high school	CH	108.54	3.00
Some university	SU	193.11	4.37
First university degree	UD	356.67	7.46
Second university degree	GUD	490.20	9.11
Specific experience	SE	27.62	16.73
(Specific experience)^2	$(SE)^2$	−0.55	−9.42
General experience	GE	14.53	6.86
(General experience)^2	$(GE)^2$	−0.33	−4.99
$R^2 = 0.49$		$n = 1,448$	

The effect of general experience is

$$14.53GE - 0.33(GE)^2$$

These two effects are plotted in Figure 5.3.

It can be seen that for a given level of education the market value of either type of experience is an increasing function of the number of years of experience, but the market value increases at a decreasing rate and reaches a peak at 25 years in the case of specific experience and 22 years in the case of general experience. Beyond these points, the value of experience declines, but this could very well be the result of the decline in productivity with increasing age.

In order to estimate the starting salary of persons with specified characteristics, one must add the effects of education, specific experience, and general experience to the constant term. For example, to find the estimated starting salary of persons with a first university degree only, three years of specific experience, and two years of general experience, we set $UD = 1$, $SE = 3$, $GE = 2$, and all other variables equal to zero, to get

$$\hat{Y} = 270.83 + 356.67 + (27.62)(3) - (0.55)(3)^2 + (14.53)(2) - (0.33)(2)^2$$

or $733.15 per month. ∎

Polynomials of higher degree may be estimated in a similar fashion. For example, to fit a polynomial of the third degree,

$$\hat{Y} = b_0 + b_1 X + b_2 X^2 + b_3 X^3 \tag{5.2}$$

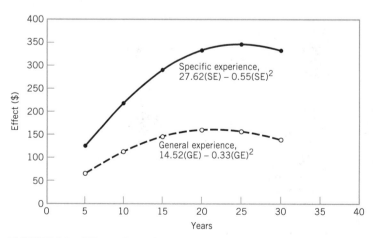

FIGURE 5.3 Effects of specific and general experience

let $X_1 = X$, $X_2 = X^2$, and $X_3 = X^3$. Then,

$$\hat{Y} = b_0 + b_1 X_1 + b_2 X_2 + b_3 X_3$$

The OLS estimates b_0, b_1, b_2, and b_3 can be obtained as in the case where X_1, X_2, and X_3 are distinct explanatory variables.

In general, a polynomial of degree m in X is the function

$$b_0 + b_1 X + b_2 X^2 + b_3 X^3 + \cdots + b_m X^m$$

Figure 5.4 shows the patterns of polynomials of low degree, the polynomials more often used in practice. The exact pattern, of course, depends on the values of the coefficients $b_0, b_1, \ldots, b_m$. A polynomial of degree 1 is the straight line.

It can be shown that any (continuous) nonlinear function may be approximated to a desired degree of accuracy by a polynomial of a suitably high

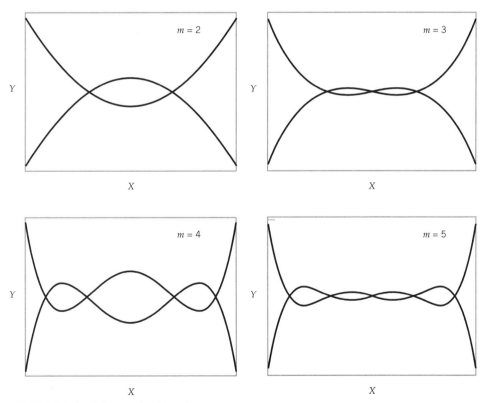

FIGURE 5.4 Polynomials of low degree

degree.[1] In practice, it is hoped that a polynomial of low degree (perhaps two or three) will provide a satisfactory approximation.

Polynomials may also be used to approximate nonlinear relationships involving two or more explanatory variables. For example, a nonlinear relationship between Y and two explanatory variables, X_1 and X_2, may be approximated by

$$\hat{Y} = b_0 + b_1 X_1 + b_2 X_2 + b_3 X_1^2 + b_4 X_2^2 + b_5 X_1 X_2 \tag{5.3}$$

This model consists of the sum of two polynomials in X_1 and X_2, and includes an "interaction" term involving the product of X_1 and X_2. Because of this interaction term, the effect of a change in X_1 will depend on the level of X_2, and vice versa.

Again, the model is linear in $b_0, b_1, \ldots, b_5$ and may be written as

$$\hat{Y} = b_0 + b_1 X_1 + b_2 X_2 + b_3 X_3 + b_4 X_4 + b_5 X_5$$

where $X_3 = X_1^2$, $X_4 = X_2^2$ and $X_5 = X_1 X_2$. The OLS estimates $b_0, b_1, \ldots, b_5$ are obtained by regressing Y on X_1 to X_5. Models of more than two explanatory variables may be formulated in a similar fashion.

To estimate these models using a computer program, it is not usually necessary to calculate and input the powers $X^2, X^3, \ldots$, or cross-products $X_1 X_2, \ldots$. Nearly all statistical programs allow the user to create with simple commands additional explanatory variables that are functions of basic variables. In the case of Model 5.3, for example, the user would input (directly or into a file) the values of Y, X_1, and X_2, and the program would create X_1^2, X_2^2, and $X_1 X_2$. The form of the commands for achieving this depends, of course, on the program used.

5.3 INVERSE RELATIONSHIPS

Consider the following relationship between Y and X,

$$\hat{Y} = b_0 + b_1 \frac{1}{X} \tag{5.4}$$

[1] If there are n distinct observations on Y and at least one explanatory variable X, it can be shown that a polynomial of degree $m = n - 1$ in X will pass through every single observation, that is, will produce a perfect fit, regardless of the contribution of X alone. For example, a polynomial of degree 3 in X will produce a perfect fit to four distinct observations on Y and X, no matter what Y and X represent. The pursuit of fit without regard to underlying theory is not wise, for what confidence can one attach to forecasts from a model that utilizes essentially $n - 1$ different forms of the same explanatory variable?

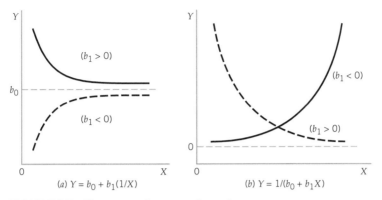

FIGURE 5.5 Illustration of inverse relationships

The general form of this relationship for positive X is shown in Figure 5.5(a).

Note that as X increases, Y approaches the value b_0 either from above (when $b_1 > 0$) or from below ($b_1 < 0$). The parameters b_0 and b_1 of 5.4 can be estimated by regressing Y on X', where $X' = 1/X$.

To illustrate, consider the three observations on Y and X listed in the first two columns of Table 5.4. The values of $X' = 1/X$ are shown in the third column.

Regressing Y on X', we get, as can be easily verified,

$$\hat{Y} = 10 + 2X' = 10 + \frac{2}{X}$$

A slightly different model that may be estimated in a similar fashion is

$$Y \approx \frac{1}{b_0 + b_1 X}$$

TABLE 5.4 Data Illustrating an Inverse Transformation

Y	X	X' = 1/X
12	1	1
10.4	5	0.20
10.2	10	0.10

which implies

$$Y' = \frac{1}{Y} \approx b_0 + b_1 X$$

It is assumed that $Y \neq 0$. The form of this model is illustrated in Figure 5.5(b) for the case where $b_0 + b_1 X > 0$. The model may be estimated by regressing $Y' = 1/Y$ against X.

The multivariable analogue of this model is

$$Y \approx \frac{1}{b_0 + b_1 X_1 + b_2 X_2 + \cdots + b_k X_k}$$

which can be estimated by regressing $Y' = 1/Y$ against $X_1, X_2, \ldots, X_k$.

5.4 PIECEWISE LINEAR MODELS

Continuous, piecewise linear relationships of the type illustrated in Figure 5.6(a) can be easily estimated with the help of dummy variables.

The relationship between Y and X is not linear over the entire range of values of X but linear within each of the intervals $X \leq x_0$ and $X > x_0$, where x_0 is a given number. In symbols,

$$\hat{Y} = \begin{cases} b_{01} + b_{11}X, & \text{if } X \leq x_0 \\ b_{02} + b_{12}X, & \text{if } X > x_0 \end{cases} \tag{5.5}$$

The two linear "pieces" must be joined at $X = x_0$, that is, $b_{01} + b_{11}x_0 = b_{02} + b_{12}x_0$.

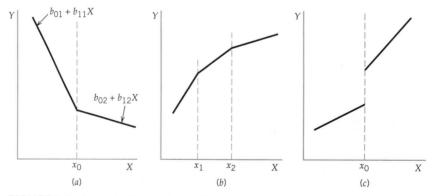

FIGURE 5.6 Piecewise linear relationships

Consider now the following model:

$$\hat{Y} = b_0 + b_1 X + b_2 (X - x_0) D \qquad (5.6)$$

where D is a dummy variable having the value 1 if $X \le x_0$ or the value 0 if $X > x_0$. $(X - x_0)D$ is a variable obtained by multiplying $X - x_0$ by D. If $X \le x_0$, $D = 1$, and Model 5.6 reduces to

$$\hat{Y} = b_0 + b_1 X + b_2 (X - x_0) = (b_0 - b_2 x_0) + (b_1 + b_2) X$$

which is of the form $\hat{Y} = b_{01} + b_{11} X$. At $X = x_0$, it will be noted, $\hat{Y} = b_0 + b_1 x_0$.
On the other hand, if $X > x_0$, Model 5.6 becomes simply

$$\hat{Y} = b_0 + b_1 X$$

which is also of the form $\hat{Y} = b_{02} + b_{12} X$. At $X = x_0$, $\hat{Y} = b_0 + b_1 x_0$, the same value as in the first piece. The two pieces, therefore, are joined at $X = x_0$. In other words, Model 5.6 *is* 5.5, and its parameters may be estimated very simply by regressing Y against X and $(X - x_0)D$.

The procedure is illustrated with the artificial data shown in Table 5.5; here x_0 is assumed to be equal to 5.

Using the data of Table 5.5, a regression of Y against X and $(X - x_0)D$ yields

$$\hat{Y} = 7.5 - 1.5X - 0.5(X - x_0)D$$

The estimated value of Y for $X = 3$ is

$$\hat{Y} = (7.5) - (1.5)(3) - (0.5)(3 - 5)(1) = 4$$

TABLE 5.5   Data Illustrating a Piecewise Linear Relationship $(x_0 = 5)$

Y (1)	X (2)	X − 5 (3)	D (4)	(X − 5)D (5)
6	2	−3	1	−3
2	4	−1	1	−1
−3	7	2	0	0
−7.5	10	5	0	0

while that for $X = 6$ is

$$\hat{Y} = (7.5) - (1.5)(6) - (0.5)(3 - 5)(0) = -2.5$$

EXAMPLE 5.3

In Example 2.2, we noted that the uses for natural gas fall into two categories: space heating and other (cooking, water heating, fuel for industry). Over relatively short periods of time, the daily gas consumption for the latter uses may be assumed constant, while that for space heating depends on temperature. Indeed, as we saw in Example 2.2, the regression of gas consumption against mean temperature gave rather good results.

But the estimated downward-sloping linear relationship between gas consumption and temperature shown in Figure 2.5 implies that estimated consumption declines steadily as temperature increases, no matter how high the temperature. This, obviously, cannot be the case: when temperature reaches a certain level, gas consumption for space heating ceases and is not resumed at temperatures exceeding that level. This "critical" level is thought to be about 18°C (about 64°F), the so-called home comfort level. This argument suggests that the relationship between gas consumption (Y) and temperature (X) ought to look like Figure 5.6(a), with $x_0 \approx 18$ and with the right linear piece nearly horizontal.

The data in Table 2.4 cannot be used to estimate a piecewise linear relationship between daily gas consumption and temperature because the selected dates cover the period from October to March, and on no such date did the mean daily temperature exceed 18°C. However, the file `norgas.dat`, from which the data in Table 2.4 were selected, covers a period of 396 consecutive days. This file is partially listed in the first four columns of Table 5.6.

The scatter diagram of *GASCON* against *TEMP* is shown in Figure 5.7.

If it is assumed that

$$\widehat{GASCON} = \begin{cases} b_{01} + b_{11}TEMP, & \text{if } TEMP \leq 18 \\ b_{02} + b_{12}TEMP, & \text{if } TEMP > 18 \end{cases}$$

TABLE 5.6   File `norgas.dat`, Partial Listing

Date	*TEMP*	*WIND*	*GASCON*	*D*	*(TEMP − 18)D*
1201	4.7	5	15279.3	1	−13.3
1202	0.0	22	19228.8	1	−18.0
. . .	. . .	. . .	. . .	. . .	. . .

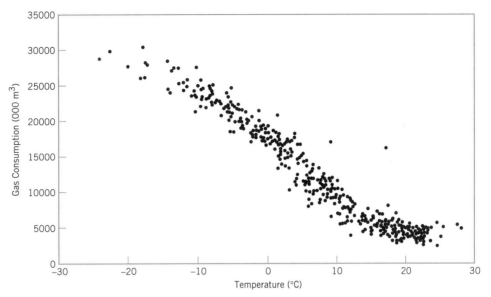

FIGURE 5.7 Gas consumption and temperature, Example 5.3

the model to be estimated is

$$GA\widehat{SC}ON = b_0 + b_1 TEMP + b_2 (TEMP - 18)D$$

where D is a dummy variable having the value 1 if TEMP$\leq$18 and 0 otherwise. The last two columns of Table 5.6 illustrate the coding of these variables.

The regression results are as follows:

$$GA\widehat{SC}ON = 3876 + 35.11TEMP - 741(TEMP - 18)D \qquad R^2 = 0.95$$
$$\qquad\qquad (3.22) \qquad (0.57) \qquad\qquad (-11.16) \qquad\qquad S = 1644$$

The coefficient of *TEMP* appears inconsistent with prior expectations, but its low *t*-ratio suggests that the fit of the model would probably not suffer greatly if that variable was left out of the model (that is, if b_1 is forced to be 0). Regressing *GASCON* against *Z* only, we get the following results:

$$GA\widehat{SC}ON = 4560 - 703(TEMP - 18)D \qquad R^2 = 0.95$$
$$\qquad\qquad (35.16) \qquad (-85.47) \qquad\qquad S = 1644$$

The fit of the model did not indeed suffer as a result of leaving out *TEMP*. The estimated piecewise linear model can be written as

$$GA\widehat{SC}ON = \begin{cases} 17210 - 703TEMP, & \text{if } TEMP \leq 18 \\ 4556, & \text{if } TEMP > 18 \end{cases}$$

The reader is asked to consider other possible model improvements in the Norgas Distributing Company case in Part II. ∎

A continuous, piecewise linear relationship with two "breaks" at $X = x_1$ and $X = x_2$, illustrated in Figure 5.6(b), may be estimated using the model

$$\hat{Y} = b_0 + b_1 X + b_2(X - x_1)D_1 + b_3(X - x_2)D_2 \tag{5.7}$$

where D_1 is a dummy variable having the value 1 for $X \leq x_1$ and 0 otherwise, while D_2 equals 1 for $X \leq x_2$ or 0 otherwise. x_1 and x_2 ($x_1 < x_2$) are assumed to be known numbers. Extensions to three or more breaks are similar.

A discontinuous, piecewise linear model with a single break at $X = x_0$, as illustrated in Figure 5.6(c), may be estimated with the use of the model

$$\hat{Y} = b_0 + b_1 X + b_2 DX + b_3 D \tag{5.8}$$

where, as before, the dummy variable D has the value 1 for $X \leq x_0$, 0 otherwise. For $X \leq x_0$, $D = 1$, and

$$\hat{Y} = (b_0 + b_3) + (b_1 + b_2)X$$

while for $X > x_0$, $D = 0$ and

$$\hat{Y} = b_0 + b_1 X$$

The two pieces, therefore, have different slopes and produce different $\hat{Y}$ at $X = x_0$, as intended.[2]

5.5 LOGARITHMIC MODELS

Consider the scatter diagram shown in Figure 5.8, which is based on the observations listed in the first two columns of Table 5.7.

---

[2]We note in passing that piecewise linear models are special cases of *spline models*, in which the pieces are typically described by polynomials of degrees two, three, or higher.

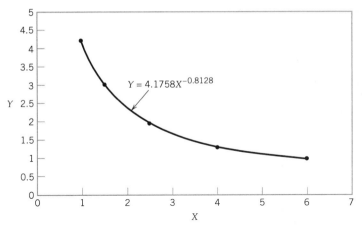

FIGURE 5.8   A logarithmic model

There is evidence of a strong but nonlinear relationship between Y and X. As X increases, Y decreases, but—unlike in Figure 5.1—it does not appear that Y ever increases again. This type of relationship may be approximated by

$$Y = b_0 X^{b_1} \qquad (5.9)$$

For simplicity, we treat Eq. 5.9 temporarily as an exact relationship. If Y, X, and b_0 are positive, we may take the logarithms—natural or common—of both sides of Eq. 5.9 to obtain

$$\log Y = \log b_0 + b_1 (\log X) \qquad (5.10)$$

TABLE 5.7   Data Illustrating a Logarithmic Transformation

Y	X	$Y' = \log Y^a$	$X' = \log X^a$
3.0	1.5	0.477	0.176
1.3	4.0	0.114	0.602
4.2	1.0	0.623	0.000
2.0	2.5	0.301	0.398
1.0	6.0	0.000	0.778

^{a}Logarithms are to the base 10.

Letting $Y' = \log Y$, $X' = \log X$, and $b_0' = \log b_0$, the estimated values of $\log Y$ may be written as

$$Y' = b_0' + b_1 X'$$

which is linear in b_0' and b_1. In reality, of course, the relationship is approximate, not exact, giving the estimated values of Y as

$$\hat{Y} = b_0' + b_1 X'$$

The OLS estimates b_0' and b_1 can be obtained by regressing $Y' = \log Y$ on $X' = \log X$. Using the data in the last two columns of Table 5.7, it is easy to verify that $b_0' = 0.621$ and $b_1 = -0.813$. An estimate of b_0 is the antilogarithm of b_0', which is $10^{0.621}$, or $b_0 = 4.178$. The estimated values of Y can be obtained either directly from

$$\hat{Y} = (4.178)X^{-0.813} \tag{5.11}$$

or by taking the antilogarithms of $\hat{Y}'$, where

$$\hat{Y}' = 0.621 - 0.813 \log X$$

Eq. 5.11 is plotted in Figure 5.8.

Eq. 5.9 is one of three types of nonlinear relationships that may be converted into linear ones in the logarithms of the original variables. The three models are summarized in Table 5.8.

Model B is Eq. 5.9 and was just illustrated. In all three models, the nonlinear relationship between Y and X is converted into a linear relationship between Y or the logarithm of Y, and X or the logarithm of X. This linear relationship can be written as $\hat{Y}' = b_0' + b_1' X'$. In A we regress $\log Y$ on X; in B we regress $\log Y$ on $\log X$; and in C we regress Y on $\log X$. Estimates of the parameters b_0 and b_1 of the original model, when they are not calculated directly, can be obtained by transforming the OLS estimates b_0' and b_1'. For example, in Model

TABLE 5.8 Logarithmic Models

Original model	Transformed model	Restrictions
A: $Y = b_0 b_1{}^X$	$\log Y = \log b_0 + (\log b_1)X$	$Y > 0, b_0 > 0, b_1 > 0$
B: $Y = b_0 X^{b_1}$	$\log Y = \log b_0 + b_1 (\log X)$	$Y > 0, X > 0, b_0 > 0$
C: $X = b_0 b_1{}^Y$	$Y = -\frac{\log b_0}{\log b_1} + \left(\frac{1}{\log b_1}\right)\log X$	$X > 0, b_0 > 0, b_1 > 0$

C, $b_1' = 1/\log b_1$; therefore, $b_1 = \text{antilog}(1/b_1')$; similarly, $b_0 = \text{antilog}(-b_0'/b_1')$. Figure 5.9 shows the general form of these relationships.

In practical applications, a comparison of the scatter diagram of the original (X, Y) observations with Figure 5.9 is occasionally the starting point in deciding which particular model may best approximate the relationship between X and Y. It will be noted, however, that the three models look very similar over certain ranges of values of the parameters and X. Consequently, often two or more of the models listed in Table 5.8 are estimated and the one with the best fit selected.

At times, the choice between Models A, B, and C is made on the basis of their particular features.

Consider Model A and the effect of increasing X by one unit. Y changes from Y to Y', where

$$Y' = b_0 b_1^{X+1} = (b_0 b_1^{X})b_1 = Yb_1$$

In other words, $b_1 = Y'/Y$. Model A, therefore, is appropriate when it is believed that a unit increase in X results in a constant (b_1) percentage change in Y.

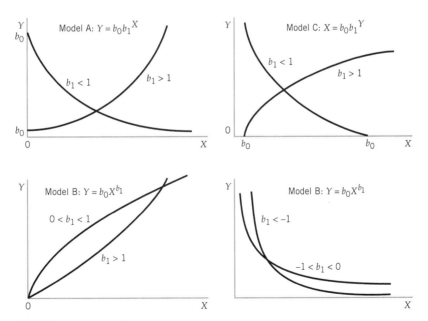

FIGURE 5.9 Logarithmic models

In Model B, a given percentage increase in X results in a constant percentage change in Y. To see this, observe that if X is increased to cX ($c > 0$), Y changes to Y', where

$$Y' = b_0(cX)^{b_1} = (b_0 X^{b_1})c^{b_1} = Yc^{b_1}$$

The relative change in Y, $(Y'/Y) = c^{b_1}$ does not depend on X.

Finally, as can be inferred by analogy with Model A, Model C implies the same arithmetic change in Y for a given percentage increase in X, that is, increasing X from X to cX results in Y changing from Y to $Y' = Y + d$, where d does not depend on X.

The logarithmic models can be modified easily to accommodate any number of explanatory variables. For example, the multivariable analogue of Model B is

$$Y = b_0 X_1^{b_1} X_2^{b_2} \cdots X_k^{b_k} \tag{5.12}$$

Taking the logarithms of both sides of Eq. 5.12, we get

$$\log Y = \log b_0 + b_1 \log X_1 + b_2 \log X_2 + \cdots + b_k \log X_k$$

which suggests a linear relationship between $\log Y$ and the logarithms of the explanatory variables. For evident reasons, this model is referred to as the *log-log, double-log,* or *log-linear* model. Model B and its multivariable extension are popular among economists (who know them as the *Cobb-Douglas* models) because each b_i can be shown to be an estimate of the *elasticity* of Y with respect to X_i (elasticity being defined as the percentage change in Y due to a small percentage increase in X_i).

EXAMPLE 5.4

In order to examine the relationship between electricity consumption and size of refrigerators, the following models were estimated.

$$\widehat{ENER} = 118.01 + 2.83RVOL - 4.47FVOL \qquad R^2 = 0.70$$
$$(4.60) \qquad (-4.63) \qquad\quad S = 20.50$$

$$\log \widehat{ENER} = 4.457 + 0.079 \log RVOL + 0.127 \log FVOL \qquad R^2 = 0.82$$
$$(1.23) \qquad\qquad (3.64) \qquad\qquad S = 0.514$$

Only two-door, automatic-defrost refrigerators with top-mounted freezers were considered. *ENER* represents the monthly electricity consumption of the refrigerator (in kwh) measured under controlled test conditions. *RVOL* is the volume of the refrigerator compartment (in cu ft), and *FVOL* is the volume of the freezer compartment (also in cu ft). Seventy-nine sets of observations and natural logarithms were used.

The logarithmic model has a better fit (as revealed by R^2, *not S*; the latter also reflects the change in the dependent variable). The estimated monthly electricity consumption of a refrigerator with a 10-cu ft refrigerator volume and a 3-cu ft freezer volume is obtained by first calculating:

$$\log \widehat{ENER} = 4.457 + (0.079)(2.302) + (0.127)(1.099) = 4.778$$

and then the antilogarithm of 4.778, $e^{4.778}$, which is 119 (kwh/month). ∎

5.6 NONLINEAR REGRESSION

The simple models of the preceding sections can be used to approximate a wide range of nonlinear relationships. In all cases, the parameters of the models are estimated by applying regression to transformed variables such as $\log X$, X^2, and so on. The transformed variables can be easily created and the required calculations quickly carried out by computer programs.

When the dependent variable is transformed, the OLS estimators minimize the sum of squared deviations between actual and estimated values of the *transformed* dependent variable. In Model A, for example, the b_0' and b_1' obtained by regressing $\log Y$ on X minimize $\sum(\log Y - \widehat{\log Y})^2$. Therefore, $b_0 = \text{antilog}(b_0')$ and $b_1 = \text{antilog}(b_1')$ do not necessarily minimize $\sum(Y - \hat{Y})^2$. Note the difference between $\widehat{\log Y}$ and $\log \hat{Y}$. The first is the estimated value of the variable "logarithm of Y"; the second is the logarithm of the estimated value of variable Y—there *is* a difference.

In many situations in practice, the convenience of applying a single familiar method (linear regression) compensates for the suboptimal fit. There are, however, situations where the best possible fit is desired or required. The method of *nonlinear regression* obtains the values of the parameters of a nonlinear model minimizing the sum of the squared residuals of the original dependent variable.

A simple numerical example will illustrate the method. The first two columns of Table 5.9 show four pairs of observations on Y and X.

Suppose it is desired to use Model A, $Y = b_0 b_1^X$, to approximate the relationship between Y and X. A regression of $\log Y$ against X yields the following results:

$$\widehat{\log Y} = 1.692 + 0.667X \qquad R^2 = 0.995$$
$$(19.37) \ (20.91) \qquad S = 0.0504$$

TABLE 5.9 Nonlinear Model, Approximate Solution

Y (1)	X (2)	log Y (3)	$\widehat{\log Y}$ (4)	$\hat{Y}$ (5)	$\hat{\varepsilon} = Y - \hat{Y}$ (6)	$\hat{\varepsilon}^2$ (7)
11	1	2.398	2.359	10.577	0.422	0.178
19	2	2.944	3.026	20.608	−1.608	2.587
42	3	3.738	3.693	40.151	1.848	3.417
78	4	4.537	4.360	78.228	−0.228	0.052
					0.435	6.234

Natural logarithms are used. $b_0' = 1.692$ and $b_1' = 0.667$ minimize $\sum(\log Y - \widehat{\log Y})^2$. The estimates of the original parameters are $b_0 = e^{1.692} = 5.429$ and $b_1 = e^{0.667} = 1.948$. Columns 4 to 7 of Table 5.9 show $\widehat{\log Y}$, calculated from the preceding regression results, $\hat{Y} = e^{\widehat{\log Y}}$, $\hat{\varepsilon} = Y - \hat{Y}$, and $\hat{\varepsilon}^2$. It can be noted that $\sum \hat{\varepsilon}^2 = 6.234$.

Let us now attempt to estimate Model A directly by seeking values of b_0 and b_1 that minimize

$$\sum \hat{\varepsilon}^2 = \sum(Y - \hat{Y})^2 = \sum(Y - b_0 b_1^X)^2 \tag{5.13}$$

The problem is of the same type as the original least-squares problem of Sections 2.3 and 2.4. It can be shown (by taking partial derivatives of Eq. 5.13 with respect to b_0 and b_1 and equating these to zero) that the least-squares estimates b_0 and b_1 must satisfy the following equations:

$$b_0 \sum b_1^{2X} = \sum b_1^X Y$$
$$b_0^2 \sum X b_1^{2X-1} = b_0 \sum XY b_1^{X-1} \tag{5.14}$$

The various sums involve the two unknowns (b_0, b_1) and the n observations (X, Y). This system of two equations is not linear in b_0 and b_1 and is much more difficult to solve than the linear system Eq. 2.6. Unlike the linear system, it is not possible to express the solution of Eqs. 5.14 by means of formulas.

However, the system 5.14 can always be solved numerically. A number of algorithms are available. Advanced statistical programs search numerically for the values of the parameters of a nonlinear model that minimize the sum of squared residuals, $\sum \hat{\varepsilon}^2$.

These algorithms follow an iterative process. A candidate solution is tested to determine if it satisfies optimality conditions such as those specified by Eqs. 5.14 of our illustration. If it does, the process stops. If it does not, another improved candidate solution is generated and again tested in the same manner. The process continues until successive candidate solutions do not differ perceptibly from one another or the number of iterations exceeds a set limit.

The manner in which new candidate solutions are generated depends on the algorithm ("Gauss-Newton," "Marquardt," and "steepest descent" being the most popular).

For well-behaved models such as our Model A, an algorithm is likely to find the optimal solution in relatively few iterations, the number depending on the nearness of the initial candidate solution to the optimal one. In general, however, *the algorithm may find a suboptimal solution or may not converge at all.* The reason for the former is that the optimality conditions are necessary, not sufficient. That is, an optimal solution must satisfy these conditions, but a solution that satisfies them is not necessarily optimal. As for the latter danger, it is possible for the algorithm to keep cycling through the same set of candidate solutions.[3]

```
              Non-linear Least Squares Iterative Phase
           Dependent Variable Y    Method: Gauss-Newton
      Iter              b0               b1  Sum of Squares
        0          5.429000         1.948000        6.266630
        1          5.517735         1.941410        6.099524
        2          5.516868         1.941569        6.099331
        3          5.516896         1.941567        6.099331
   NOTE: Convergence criterion met.
```

```
Non-linear Least Squares Summary Statistics    Dependent Variable Y

   Source                 DF Sum of Squares      Mean Square
   Regression              2    8323.9006685     4161.9503343
   Residual                2       6.0993315        3.0496657
   Uncorrected Total       4    8330.0000000
   (Corrected Total)       3    2705.0000000
```

```
   Parameter     Estimate     Asymptotic            Asymptotic 95%
                              Std. Error         Confidence Interval
                                                 Lower          Upper
       b0    5.516895775 0.61157391013   2.8854767119   8.1483148381
       b1    1.941566668 0.05794139176   1.6922622412   2.1908710938
```

```
              Asymptotic Correlation Matrix
        Corr                    b0                    b1
        ---------------------------------------------------
          b0                     1         -0.984980316
          b1          -0.984980316                    1
```

FIGURE 5.10 Output of program *SAS*

---

[3]For a rigorous treatment of nonlinear regression, see, for example, Seber and Wild (1989).

Let us return to the numerical illustration of this section. The computer program SAS produced the output shown in Figure 5.10.[4]

From Figure 5.10 we read the following solution to the nonlinear least-squares problem Eq. 5.13, reached after three iterations:

$$b_0 = 5.517, \text{ and } b_1 = 1.941$$

The estimated values of Y can be calculated directly from

$$\hat{Y} = (5.517)(1.941)^X$$

as shown in Table 5.10. The sum of squared residuals, $\sum \hat{\varepsilon}^2$, is 6.099.

We see that the model estimated by regressing $\log Y$ against X came reasonably close but, as expected, did not minimize $\sum (Y - \hat{Y})^2$. That model's sum of squared residuals was 6.234, compared with the optimal 6.099.

5.7 TO SUM UP

- Any continuous nonlinear function may be approximated to a desired degree of accuracy by a polynomial of a suitably high degree. In practice, it is hoped that a polynomial of a low degree (perhaps two or three) will provide a satisfactory approximation.

TABLE 5.10 Nonlinear Model, Optimal Solution

Y	$\hat{Y}$	$\hat{\varepsilon} = Y - \hat{Y}$	$\hat{\varepsilon}^2$
11	10.711	0.289	0.083
19	20.797	−1.797	3.229
42	40.379	1.621	2.629
78	78.398	−0.398	0.158
		−0.285	6.099

[4]Nonlinear least-squares algorithms usually require from the user the specification of the partial derivatives of the dependent variable with respect to each parameter. For the model of this section, $Y = b_0 b_1^X$, these partial derivatives are $\partial Y / \partial b_0 = b_1^X$ and $\partial Y / \partial b_1 = b_0 X b_1^{X-1}$. The SAS statements that produced the output of Figure 5.10 are `proc nlin; parms b0=5.429 b1=1.948; model y = b0*b1**x; der.b0 = b1**x; der.b1 = b0*x*b1**(x-1);` the `parms` statement specifies the parameters of the model and optionally assigns as starting values for the iterative process the estimates based on the first approximate solution. The reader should also note that the additional properties, confidence intervals, and tests of Chapter 3 require large samples. We examine these topics of inference later in Section 9.2, where we also explain some of the other output shown in Figure 5.10.

- In some cases, regression applied to transformations of the original variables provides a simple method for estimating a nonlinear model. Examples of such transformations can be found among the inverse, piecewise linear, and logarithmic models examined in this chapter.

- The method of nonlinear regression directly obtains the values of the parameters of a nonlinear model minimizing the sum of the squared residuals of the original dependent variable. These values are calculated by an iterative numerical procedure. In well-behaved cases the procedure is likely to find the optimal solution in a few itereations, but in others it may find a suboptimal solution or may not find a solution at all.

PROBLEMS

5.1 Using a computer program, confirm the results presented in this chapter.

5.2 Using the data of Table 5.11, estimate polynomial models of order 1, 2, 3, and 4. Select the best of these models, plot actual and estimated values, and forecast Y for $X = 5$.

5.3 Use the data in Table 5.12 to estimate the polynomial Model 5.3 of degree 2 in X_1 and X_2. Plot actual and estimated values of Y, and forecast Y for $X_1 = 1$ and $X_2 = 3$.

5.4 In Section 1.4, we described a survey of professionals from which a "salary curve" was estimated relating salary to years of experience. The survey data were plotted in Figure 1.4 and the salary curve in Figure 1.3. The data can be found in the file profsal.dat, and are partially listed in Table 5.13.

    Estimate the salary curve. Use it to calculate the "normal" salary of a professional with 17 years of experience. To which factors is due the shape of the salary curve? How would you explain more precisely the meaning of "salary curve" and "normal salary"?

TABLE 5.11
Data for
Problem 5.2

X	Y
3	37.5
4	87.6
−2	9.1
6	601.0
8	1812.2
9	3041.5
2	12.9
−4	108.6

TABLE 5.12
Data for
Problem 5.3

X_1	X_2	Y
−3.1	3.3	−35.9
2.9	9.4	−48.0
4.9	5.5	14.9
−0.6	6.2	−49.7
−1.5	5.8	−52.0
5.0	1.4	29.6
−4.1	6.7	−85.2
2.5	3.4	2.9
−2.4	5.1	−50.8
3.5	9.4	−38.4

5.5 Refer to Example 5.1 concerning the relationship between income, on the one hand, and age and gender, on the other. It is suggested that the following single model is preferable to the two presented in Example 5.1:

$$\widehat{INC} = b_0 + b_1(AGE) + b_2(AGE)^2 + b_3(GENDER)$$

where *GENDER* is a dummy variable taking the value 1 for a male or the value 0 for a female income.

Estimate this model. Do you agree it is superior to the two models of Example 5.1?

5.6 (a) Determine which of the models (i) $b_0 + b_1/X$ or (ii) $1/(b_0 + b_1 X)$ best describe the relationship between Y_1 and X given the data in Table 5.14. Plot actual and estimated values, and forecast Y_1 for $X = 2$.

(b) Same as (a), except replace Y_1 by Y_2.

5.7 (a) Using the data of Table 5.15, estimate the piecewise linear Model 5.6 of Section 5.4, assuming $x_0 = 30$. Forecast Y at $X = 35$.

TABLE 5.13 File
profsal.dat, Partial
Listing

Years of experience	Annual salary ($000)
26	71
19	69
22	73
17	69
13	65
...	...

TABLE 5.14
Data for
Problem 5.6

X	Y_1	Y_2
2.46	4.07	0.11
3.70	3.86	0.07
1.09	4.83	0.20
2.03	4.19	0.12
1.59	4.40	0.15
4.31	3.80	0.07
1.77	4.30	0.14

(b) Using the data of Table 5.15, estimate the piecewise linear Model 5.7 of Section 5.4, assuming $x_1 = 20$ and $x_2 = 40$. Forecast Y at $X = 35$.

(c) Using the data of Table 5.15, estimate the piecewise linear Model 5.8 of Section 5.4, assuming $x_0 = 30$. Forecast Y at $X = 35$.

5.8 **(a)** Refer to the data in part a of Table 5.16. Determine which of the Models A, B, or C defined in Table 5.8 best fit the data. Forecast Y for $X = 5.5$.

(b) Same as (a), except use the data in part b of Table 5.16.

(c) Same as (a), except use the data in part c of Table 5.16.

5.9 The savings and loan associations operating in the Bay Area have an almost monopolistic position in the market for residential real estate loans: their closest competitors—chartered banks—have a small portion of the market, and savings and loan associations located outside the region are prevented by law from making loans in the Bay Area. The data shown in Table 5.17 were gathered in order to estimate the short-run demand function of mortgage loans.

TABLE 5.15
Data for
Problem 5.7

X	Y
27.2	7120
49.8	43092
15.6	1343
33.6	13419
43.6	29083
49.0	41158
24.5	5152
10.7	467
32.1	11664
13.4	889

TABLE 5.16 Data for Problem 5.8

(a)		(b)		(c)	
X	Y	X	Y	X	Y
1	9	1	1	2	1
5	3	4	7	6	3
3	4	2	4	4	2
9	1	9	10	9	6
6	2	7	9	7	4

TABLE 5.17 Market data, Bay Area Savings and Loan Associations

Year	Month	Interest rate, Y (%)	Amount of loans closed, X_1 ($ million)	Vacancy index, X_2 (%)
19X5	Jun.	6.25	127.9	3.03
	Jul.	6.30	114.2	3.14
	Aug.	6.30	99.0	3.25
	Sep.	6.31	87.1	3.08
	Oct.	6.31	85.9	2.90
	Nov.	6.34	88.9	2.73
	Dec.	6.32	95.0	2.55
19X6	Jan.	6.37	70.8	2.55
	Feb.	6.37	69.8	2.54
	Mar.	6.37	95.7	2.54
	Apr.	6.56	65.0	2.54
	May	6.69	35.7	2.59
	Jun.	6.80	25.4	2.65
	Jul.	6.92	21.5	2.70
	Aug.	7.04	28.2	2.76
	Sep.	6.96	29.8	2.57
	Oct.	7.08	31.2	2.37
	Nov.	7.08	28.3	2.17
	Dec.	7.12	38.9	1.96

SOURCE: File `bareal.dat`

It is assumed that the demand function (D) remains unchanged during this period and that the supply function (S) is inelastic. All funds available for lending in any one month are placed in the market and loaned at whatever interest rate can be obtained. The situation is pictured in Figure 5.11.

The demand for mortgage loans is derived from the demand for housing. When demand for housing is strong, demand for loans is also strong, and vice versa. An indication of the strength of the housing demand is the percentage of properties that are vacant. When

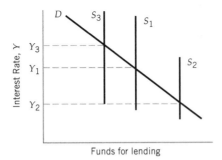

FIGURE 5.11 Loan demand and supply

housing demand is weak, vacancies would be high and demand for loans weak. Vacancies, in turn, are measured by the percentage of idle electric meters, and this is the variable denoted by X_2.

(a) Plot Y against X_1 in a scatter diagram for a preliminary check of the relationship between Y and X_1.

(b) Estimate the parameters of the following models relating Y to X_1 and X_2:

$$
\begin{array}{lll}
\text{(i)} & \hat{Y} & = & b_0 + b_1 X_1 \\
\text{(ii)} & \hat{Y} & = & b_0 + b_1 X_1 + b_2 X_2 \\
\text{(iii)} & \hat{Y} & = & b_0 + b_1 X_1 + b_2 X_2 + b_3 X_1^2 \\
\text{(iv)} & \hat{Y} & = & b_0 + b_1 \log X_1 + b_2 X_2 \\
\text{(v)} & \hat{Y} & = & b_0 + b_1 \log X_1 + b_2 \log X_2 \\
\text{(vi)} & \widehat{\log Y} & = & b_0 + b_1 \log X_1 + b_2 \log X_2 \\
\end{array}
$$

For each model show b_0, b_1, b_2, S, and R^2. Do the signs of the regression coefficients make sense?

(c) Of the six models just given, select two that you judge to be best. Show in a diagram the exact form of the relationship between Y and X_1, assuming X_2 remains constant at $X_2 = 2.50$. Which of the two models would you choose? Why?

(d) Use the best model in (c) to predict the interest rates in the year 19X7, using the values of the explanatory variables shown in Table 5.18. Obviously, these predictions utilize information not normally available at the time the forecasts are required. How could "pure" forecasts be obtained?

(e) In a time diagram, compare actual and predicted interest rates for the entire period of June 19X5 to December 19X7. Is there any practical value to this quantitative exercise?

5.10 (Due to B. Hackett and T. Lawson) Table 5.19 shows the long-distance telephone rates between a given city and 15 others in the same region.

(a) Plot each of the rate variables in Table 5.19 against distance.

(b) Estimate the relationships between each of the rates and distance.

(c) Comment on the results in (b).

TABLE 5.18   Supplementary Data, Problem 5.9

Year	Month	Interest rate (%)	Amount of loans closed ($ million)	Vacancy rate (%)
19X7	Jan.	7.12	27.0	1.90
	Feb.	6.99	36.3	1.85
	Mar.	6.87	53.4	1.79
	Apr.	6.82	49.7	1.73
	May	6.72	66.3	1.76
	Jun.	6.66	79.8	1.79
	Jul.	6.68	66.0	1.82
	Aug.	6.65	80.0	1.84
	Sep.	6.65	75.7	1.69
	Oct.	6.60	76.4	1.53
	Nov.	6.69	69.2	1.37
	Dec.	6.77	61.1	1.22

SOURCE: File `barea2.dat`

TABLE 5.19   Long Distance Telephone Rates

Distance (miles)	Customer dialed 1st min.	After[a]	Station-to-station 1st min.	After[a]	Person-to-person 1st min.	After[a]
55	0.27	0.24	0.95	0.24	1.9	0.24
42	0.23	0.18	0.75	0.18	1.5	0.18
160	0.38	0.33	1.35	0.33	2.7	0.33
69	0.27	0.24	0.95	0.24	1.9	0.24
114	0.35	0.30	1.25	0.30	2.5	0.30
340	0.52	0.45	1.75	0.45	3.5	0.45
208	0.41	0.36	1.45	0.36	2.9	0.36
248	0.44	0.39	1.55	0.39	3.1	0.39
81	0.29	0.26	1.05	0.26	2.1	0.26
423	0.52	0.45	1.75	0.45	3.5	0.45
210	0.41	0.36	1.45	0.36	2.9	0.36
241	0.44	0.39	1.55	0.39	3.1	0.39
860	0.60	0.50	1.95	0.50	3.9	0.50
432	0.52	0.45	1.75	0.45	3.5	0.45
234	0.44	0.39	1.55	0.39	3.1	0.39

[a]Each additional minute.

SOURCE: File `telrates.dat`

5.11 (Due to Ms. J. Smith) Portland cement, one of the most widely employed construction materials, is a powder used with water and sand to make mortar and with water, sand, and crushed stone to make concrete. The common raw materials in the manufacture of cement are limestone and clay or shale. These are ground and heated in kilns to produce clinker of marble size or larger, which is then finely ground to produce the cement powder. In the grinding of raw materials, two processes are used: the dry process, in which raw materials are dried and then ground, and the wet process, in which the raw materials are ground with the addition of water to form pulp or "slurry."

Tables 5.20 and 5.21 show the total cost, fuel usage, electricity usage, and labor usage as a function of the volume of production.

(a) Using the data for dry process plants, determine the best-fitting functions relating each of the following variables to the volume of production (the single explanatory variable): total cost, average cost per ton of production, fuel usage, electricity usage, and labor usage. *Note: Five* models need be estimated.

(b) Do as in (a) but use the data for wet process plants.

(c) Of what use could these models be?

TABLE 5.20   Operating Data, Dry Process Plants

Production (000 tons)	Total cost ($000)	Fuel (million Btu per ton)	Electricity (kwh per ton)	Labor (man-hours per ton)
200	30,960	4.4	155	0.675
300	34,600	4.1	150	0.570
400	39,100	3.8	145	0.505
500	45,200	3.6	140	0.470
600	52,880	3.5	135	0.435
700	60,030	3.4	132	0.415
800	67,620	3.4	130	0.400
900	74,060	3.3	128	0.395
1,000	80,570	3.3	128	0.390

SOURCE: File dplants.dat

TABLE 5.21   Operating Data, Wet Process Plants

Production (000 tons)	Total cost ($000)	Fuel (million Btu per ton)	Electricity (kwh per ton)	Labor (man-hours per ton)
200	23,860	6.3	122	0.600
300	28,660	5.6	115	0.490
400	34,330	5.2	109	0.440
500	40,590	4.9	107	0.400
600	47,840	4.8	105	0.370
700	54,570	4.7	104	0.355
800	61,940	4.7	103	0.335
900	69,050	4.7	103	0.325
1,000	75,810	4.7	103	0.325

SOURCE: File wplants.dat

5.12 It has been the experience of manufacturers in various industries that the amount of labor required to make one unit of a product decreases with each unit manufactured, although the reduction is at a decreasing rate. This is attributed to the improvement of the workers' efficiency with practice, to better organization of production by supervisors, to successful modifications of equipment suggested by experience, and to other factors.

The relationship between the number of hours of labor per unit of product (Y) and cumulative production (X) is summarized in the so-called *learning curve*, which is often expressed as

$$\hat{Y} = b_0 X^{b_1}$$

$\hat{Y}$ is the estimated number of labor hours required to produce the Xth unit, and b_0 and b_1 are parameters.

One company's experience with the manufacture of a particular product over a six-month period is shown in Table 5.22.

(a) Show that the form of the learning curve provides a good description of the relationship between X and Y.

(b) Estimate the parameters (b_0 and b_1) of the learning curve.

(c) Estimate the number of labor hours required to produce the 250th unit of this product.

(d) Show that a doubling of cumulative production from X to $2X$ results in a change of the unit labor input from $\hat{Y}$ to $\hat{Y}' = (2^{b_1})\hat{Y}$. If, for example, $b_1 = -0.52$, this implies that a doubling of cumulative production results in a 30% reduction of unit labor input ($2^{-0.52} \approx 0.70$). Because of this property, this particular learning curve is called *a 70% learning curve*. By implication, a 70% learning curve is better than an 80% one. Using your estimates in part b calculate the estimated unit labor input for cumulative production levels of 100, 200, and 400 units.

5.13 In actuarial studies, the relationship between the annual death rate (expressed as a percentage, Y) and age (X) is often approximated by

$$\hat{Y} = b_0 b_1{}^X.$$

For example, if $b_0 = 0.005$ and $b_1 = 1.1$, $\hat{Y} = (0.005)(1.1)^{50} = 0.586$. That is, 0.586% (a little more than one-half of 1%) of 50-year-old people are estimated to die in one year.

TABLE 5.22 Data, Problem 5.12

Month	Month's production (units)	Total labor hours	Cumulative production, X	Labor hours per unit, Y
Jan.	28	1,395	28	49.81
Feb.	18	649	46	36.04
Mar.	28	828	74	29.58
Apr.	36	967	110	26.86
May	40	809	150	20.23
Jun.	76	1,357	226	17.85

The following data are extracted from a mortality/life table used by insurance companies to determine pensions:

Age, X	Death rate (%), Y
20	0.024
40	0.092
60	0.639
80	6.381

(a) Plot the observations in a scatter diagram. Does the expression for $\hat{Y}$ appear suitable?

(b) Calculate the least-squares estimates b_0 and b_1. Carry out your calculations to at least four decimal places.

(c) Calculate the estimated death rate, $\hat{Y}$, at selected ages. Plot these in the scatter diagram. Is the model appropriate?

5.14 (Due to Ms. Sharon Kim) Purchase of a Lotto 6/49 lottery ticket costing $1 entitles a player to select 6 numbers from 1 to 49. Twice weekly on Wednesdays and Saturdays, the lottery draws 7 numbers from 1 to 49 at random and without replacement; the first 6 are called "main" and the seventh a "bonus" number. Players who match these numbers share one of five prizes, as follows:

Prize	Number of matches
Jackpot	6 main
Second	5 main plus bonus number
Third	5 main
Fourth	4 main
Fifth	Players matching 3 main win $10

If there is no jackpot winner, a portion of the jackpot prize is "rolled over" to the next draw. The jackpot thus may continue to grow until at least one player succeeds in matching the six main numbers.

It has been observed that rollovers and the associated publicity help stimulate sales of Lotto 6/49 tickets, as the lure of a greater first prize attracts additional wagerers.

Prior to each draw, the lottery provides an estimate of the jackpot. It is not known how this estimate is arrived at; the public relations department simply informs inquirers that the estimate is based on the staff's experience with this lottery.

Currently, the lottery guarantees a jackpot of $1 million when there are no rollovers, $5 million for one, and $10 million for two rollovers. There is no guaranteed jackpot for more than two rollovers.

The file lotto.dat contains data concerning the 160 most recent draws of Lotto 6/49 (80 weeks). A partial list of the data is given in Table 5.23.

EJACK is the estimated jackpot, SALES the revenue from the sale of Lotto 6/49 tickets, and AJACK the actual jackpot (first prize), all in millions of dollars. The first line of data refers to a Wednesday draw, the second to a Saturday draw, and so on for 80 weeks.

TABLE 5.23 File lotto.dat, Partial Listing

EJACK	SALES	AJACK
10.0	28.23	9.34
14.0	42.96	14.43
2.4	17.17	2.65
2.4	19.18	2.76
5.4	21.97	6.00
...	...	...

(a) Estimate the relationship between estimated and actual jackpot. Comment on the lottery staff's forecasting ability.

(b) Estimate the relationship between the estimated jackpot and sales. Comment on the effect of rollovers on revenue and their implication for the lottery.

5.15 (Due to Mr. Bubb-Clarke) Some years after the study reported in Problem 2.5, a new set of data was collected regarding the gasoline consumption and characteristics of 116 car models. The data can be found in the file mpg.dat and are partially listed in Table 5.24.

The interpretation of the variables is as follows:

ED: Engine displacement (liters)

CYL: Number of cylinders

HP: Horsepower

DES: Engine design (1= inline configuration of cylinders, 2= V or flat configuration)

VALV: Valvetrain design (1= pushrod, 2= single overhead cam, 3= double overhead cam)

WEIGHT: Weight (lbs.)

TYPE: Type (1= 2-door, 2= 4-door, 3= convertible, 4= truck or minivan)

DRIVE: Drivetrain (1= front wheel, 2= rear wheel, 3= four wheel)

TRANS: Transmission (1= manual, 2= automatic)

IND: Induction system (1= naturally aspirated, 2= forced induction)

MPG: Fuel mileage (miles per gallon)

TABLE 5.24 File mpg.dat, Partial Listing

OBS	ED	CYL	HP	DES	VALV	WEIGHT	TYPE	DRIVE	TRANS	IND	MPG
1	1.8	4	170	1	3	2825	1	1	1	1	26.0
2	3.2	6	230	2	2	3735	1	1	1	1	20.0
3	3.0	6	270	2	3	3175	1	2	1	1	18.0
4	2.5	5	176	1	2	3430	2	1	2	1	21.0
5	3.0	6	230	2	3	3565	2	1	1	1	17.5
6	2.2	5	227	1	3	3990	2	3	1	2	16.0
...	...	...	...	...	...	...	...	...	...	...	...

(a) A regression of MPG against all available explanatory variables using the program SAS gave the edited results shown in Figure 5.12.

E1, V1-V2, T1-T3, D1-D2, S1, and N1 are dummy variables representing the categories of DES, VALV, TYPE, DRIVE, TRANS, and IND, respectively (the last category of each attribute was left out of the regression).

Interpret these results. Are the regression coefficients consistent with prior expectations?

(b) The study opted instead for the "simpler and nearly as good" model shown with edited results in Figure 5.13, where IHP=1/HP and IED=1/ED.

Comment on the form of the model and interpret the results. Explain why a model with so few explanatory variables appears to be "nearly as good" as the one in (a).

(c) Verify and, if possible, improve the models in (a) and (b).

5.16 (Due to Ms. Danielle Landry) The Department of Transportation regularly forecasts the number of passengers departing from and arriving at each of the 60 or so major airports under its jurisdiction. These forecasts are used for the planning of airport facilities and services.

The department's forecasts are based on an "origin/destination (OD)" model that explains the number of air trips from airport i to airport j. Although there are 3600 such

```
Model: MODEL1
Dependent Variable: MPG


            Root MSE        2.13725     R-square      0.8453
            Dep Mean       20.44741     Adj R-sq      0.8238
            C.V.           10.45241


                        Parameter Estimates


                     Parameter      Standard    T for H0:
Variable    DF        Estimate         Error    Parameter=0    Prob > |T|

INTERCEP     1       31.582931    3.44524555        9.167        0.0001
ED           1       -0.056599    0.50163175       -0.113        0.9104
CYL          1       -0.202366    0.24084939       -0.840        0.4028
HP           1       -0.017603    0.00445955       -3.947        0.0001
E1           1        1.663273    0.58862288        2.826        0.0057
V1           1       -0.397902    1.05330467       -0.378        0.7064
V2           1        0.031793    0.51659238        0.062        0.9510
WEIGHT       1       -0.002553    0.00077628       -3.289        0.0014
T1           1        1.911580    1.57303034        1.215        0.2271
T2           1        0.954014    1.42675060        0.669        0.5052
T3           1       -0.172720    1.80201003       -0.096        0.9238
D1           1        1.035551    0.92016434        1.125        0.2631
D2           1       -0.483046    0.94454339       -0.511        0.6102
S1           1       -0.074004    0.63832882       -0.116        0.9079
N1           1        1.217182    0.81729221        1.489        0.1395
```

FIGURE 5.12 Regression results, Problem 5.15(a)

```
Model: MODEL2
Dependent Variable: MPG

                    Root MSE        1.89819      R-square      0.8671
                    Dep Mean       20.44741      Adj R-sq      0.8610
                    C.V.            9.28328

                          Parameter Estimates

                    Parameter         Standard     T for H0:
Variable   DF        Estimate            Error    Parameter=0    Prob > |T|

INTERCEP    1        7.317499       0.67950167       10.769         0.0001
IHP         1      944.509429     180.95705201        5.220         0.0001
IED         1       16.218160       2.67607281        6.060         0.0001
T1          1        0.938633       0.36748358        2.554         0.0120
D1          1        1.198497       0.45780255        2.618         0.0101
N1          1        1.736031       0.55854024        3.108         0.0024
```

FIGURE 5.13   Regression results, Problem 5.15(b)

OD pairs, the model that follows is estimated with data for 310 OD pairs only because the remaining ones have negligible air traffic:

$$\log(\widehat{PASS}) = -1.944 + 0.877\log(GDPI) + 0.782\log(GDPJ) + 0.380LOS$$
$$\quad\quad\quad\quad\quad\quad (31.28) \quad\quad\quad\quad\quad (28.74) \quad\quad\quad\quad (8.01)$$
$$\quad\quad\quad -0.234\log(COMP) -0.773\log(DIST) \quad\quad R^2 = 0.922$$
$$\quad\quad\quad\quad (-2.88) \quad\quad\quad\quad (-15.05) \quad\quad\quad\quad n = 310$$

Natural logarithms are used. The variables are defined as follows:

PASS: Number of trips from airport i to airport j

GDPI: Gross domestic product of the region served by airport i ($million)

GDPJ: Gross domestic product of the region served by airport j ($million)

LOS: Level of service for travel by air between airports i and j (= 1 if the number of daily nonstop flights between airports i and j is six or greater, = 0 otherwise)

COMP: Measure of competition to air by surface travel modes (bus, train, automobile); equals the ratio of the average air travel time to the average surface travel time between airports i and j

DIST: Great circle distance between airports i and j (miles)

(a) Comment on the model used by the department. Does it omit relevant explanatory variables? Does it include irrelevant ones? What difficulties, if any, arise if the model is to be used to forecast the number of air trips from one airport to another *next year*?

(b) Estimate the number of air trips from airport i to airport j given that $GDPI = 116,774$, $GDPJ = 72,330$, $LOS = 1$, $COMP = 0.368$, and $DIST = 315$.

(c) It has been suggested that more accurate forecasts may be obtained by replacing the preceding single model with two—one for business and the other for nonbusiness trips. Are the variables influencing business travel different from those influencing nonbusiness travel? If not, is there any advantage to estimating two models? If they are different, in what ways do they differ?

5.17 (Due to Ms. Ann Edwards) The Utility Employees' Pension Fund (UEPP) has more than 23,000 members and assets exceeding $5 billion. Each year an actuarial valuation is carried out to ensure that the assets of the fund are sufficient to meet its current and future liabilities. In order to assess the liabilities of the plan, forecasts must be made of economic (e.g., salary changes, investment yields) and noneconomic factors (e.g., rates of mortality, retirement, and disability). Forecasts of mortality rates are especially important as they are used to estimate how long pensions will be payable.

The UEPP has been compiling mortality data for its members over a period of 10 years. The data can be found in the file `mortal.dat` and are partially listed in Table 5.25.

If the data represented one year's experience, NM and NF would be the number of male and female members, respectively, of the given age at the start of the year and DM and DF the number who died during the year. As it is, these variables represent the sums of the number of members and deaths at the given age over each of the 10 years.

(a) Calculate the male (RM), female (RF), and total (RT) death rate for each age level: RM = DM/NM, RF = DF/NF, and RT = (DM + DF)/(NM + NF). Plot RM, RF, and RT as a function of age.

(b) Among the models found in the actuarial literature relating the death rate (Y) to age (X) is

$$\text{Model A:} \qquad \hat{Y} = b_0 b_1^{\,X}.$$

Estimate this model separately for male, female, and all plan members. Pay particular attention to death rates at low and high age levels, explaining carefully the rationale for any assumptions you made. Show graphically actual and estimated death rates.

(c) Another model found in the actuarial literature relating the death rate (Y) to age (X) is

$$\text{Model B:} \qquad \hat{Y} = b_0 b_1^{\,X} + b_2 X + b_3.$$

TABLE 5.25 Mortality Experience, UEPP

Age	Male Number (NM)	Male Deaths (DM)	Female Number (NF)	Female Deaths (DF)
16	0	0	1	0
17	3	0	15	0
18	65	0	123	0
19	374	1	389	0
20	994	3	763	0
...	...	...	...	...

One way of estimating b_2 and b_3 is to regress the residuals of Model A against X:

$$(Y - \widehat{b_0 b_1}{}^X) = b_2 X + b_3,$$

where b_0 and b_1 are as estimated in (b).

Apply this method to estimate Model B separately for male, female, and all plan members. Show graphically actual and estimated death rates.

(d) Can you think of a better method for estimating Model B? If so, apply the method separately for male, female, and all plan members. Show graphically actual and estimated death rates.

(e) Which of models A and B better describes the relationship between death rate and age? Is a model really necessary? Why not take the actual death rate as an estimate of the probability that a plan member of a given age will die?

CHAPTER 6

REGRESSION AND TIME SERIES

6.1 INTRODUCTION AND SUMMARY

A time series is a sequence of observations arranged in time. Annual time series consist of observations recorded once a year, monthly time series of observations taken once a month, and so on for weekly, daily, hourly, or any other time series.

In the business and economic world, many time series exhibit a trend, a tendency associated with time, and/or seasonality, a recurring variation about the trend associated with particular seasons of the year (such as quarters, months, weeks, days, or even the hours of a day).

For example, if we examine the aggregate hourly electricity consumption in a region, we will observe that it follows a pattern during each 24-hour period, reaching a peak during the early evening hours and a trough in the early morning hours. In addition, the level of consumption is generally higher on weekdays than on Saturdays or Sundays, higher during the colder and darker months, and lower during the warmer months with longer daylight. The level of consumption also tends to increase gradually in the long run as the population of the region and the number of industries increase over time.

In many cases in business practice, trend and seasonality may be estimated and forecasts of the time series obtained by regressing the series against a function of a variable measuring time and dummy variables representing the seasons. The regression results may also be used to adjust the series for seasonality, thereby enabling comparisons of the values of the series at different points in time. When the trend cannot be simply described by a function of time, the method of moving averages may be used to estimate the seasonal pattern of the series and to adjust it for seasonality.

6.2 TREND

Trend is the long-run tendency of the series, expressed as a function (often a smooth function) of time.

EXAMPLE 6.1

Figure 6.1 is based on the data in Table 6.1 and shows the annual sales of a company over a 20-year period. Figure 6.1 can be viewed as a scatter diagram in which time (in years) serves as the explanatory variable. The increasing trend is obvious.

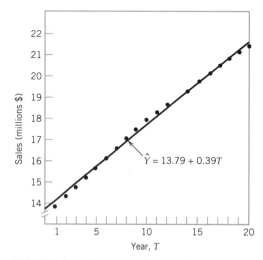

FIGURE 6.1   Company sales, trend

TABLE 6.1   Company Sales, Example 6.1

Year, T	Sales, Y ($ million)	Year, T	Sales, Y ($ million)
1	14.01	11	18.24
2	14.46	12	18.58
3	14.84	13	18.93
4	15.29	14	19.29
5	15.70	15	19.64
6	16.08	16	20.01
7	16.61	17	20.40
8	17.08	18	20.74
9	17.48	19	21.06
10	17.87	20	21.38

SOURCE: File csales1.dat

Perhaps the simplest description of this trend is the straight line $\hat{Y} = b_0 + b_1 T$, where Y is annual sales and T is a variable representing the year ($T = 1, 2, \ldots, 20$). Regressing Y on T, we get the following results.

$$\hat{Y} = 13.793 + 0.390T \qquad R^2 = 0.997$$
$$(238.73) \quad (80.80) \qquad S = 0.124$$

The trend line is plotted in Figure 6.1. The fit of the model, as indicated by R^2, is quite good.

Sales forecasts made in Year 20 for Years 21, 22, $\ldots$, 26 were calculated using the above model and $T = 21, 22, \ldots, 26$. These forecasts lie on the extension of the trend line and are plotted in Figure 6.2 together with the actual sales for these years.

It is easy to see that these forecasts are not close to the actual sales for the Years 21 to 26. With the benefit of hindsight, it could be argued that the trend appears to have shifted in Year 9, so that better results may have been obtained by fitting one trend line to the data for the Years 1 to 8 and another line to sales in Years 9 to 20; the latter could then be projected to Years 21 to 26. All this is, of course, hindsight—a forecast must be evaluated on the basis of information available at the time it is made. ∎

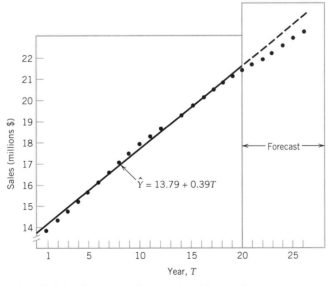

FIGURE 6.2 Company sales, trend and forecasts

Time (T) may be measured in a number of ways. For example, suppose that annual data are available for the years 1990 to 1993. Time may be represented by any one of the variables T_1, T_2, T_3, or T_4, as follows, or by other similar variables:

Year	T_1	T_2	T_3	T_4
1990	1990	1	−2	−1
1991	1991	2	−1	0
1992	1992	3	0	1
1993	1993	4	1	2

T_2 is the variable used in Example 6.1 and is the simplest possible. T_1 equals $T_2 + 1989$. T_3 equals $T_1 - 1992$ or $T_2 - 3$. T_4 equals $T_1 - 1991$ or $T_2 - 2$ or $T_3 + 1$. Indeed, any transformation of the form $T = T_2 + c$, where c is positive, zero, or negative simply changes the origin of the time variable. It can be shown that the OLS estimator of the coefficient of T in the regression—the slope of T—will be the same and only the constant term will change. Any one form of measuring time can be used, therefore, but whichever is used must be used consistently.

In general, depending on the situation, the trend can be represented by a linear or some nonlinear function of the time variable. Some common examples are

Linear trend:	$\hat{Y} = b_0 + b_1 T$
Logarithmic trends:	$\hat{Y} = b_0 + b_1 \log T$
	$\widehat{\log Y} = b_0 + b_1 T$
	$\widehat{\log Y} = b_0 + b_1 \log T$
Parabolic trend:	$\hat{Y} = b_0 + b_1 T + b_2 T^2$
Trend approximated by polynomial of degree k:	$\hat{Y} = b_0 + b_1 T + b_2 T^2 + \cdots + b_k T^k$

In the last case, the appropriate value of k can be established by experimentation. See Figure 5.4 for the patterns generated by polynomials of low degree.

Other things being equal, simpler trend functions are preferable to more complicated ones. Excessive attention to the mathematical form of the trend often obscures the purpose of the analysis, which is to obtain a good and convenient approximation, not a very precise description, of the long-run tendency of the time series.

6.3 TREND AND SEASONALITY

Seasonality, as noted earlier, is the regular variation of a time series associated with calendar periods, such as quarters, months, days of the week, or hours of the day. The following examples illustrate models for estimating trend and seasonality.

EXAMPLE 6.2

(Due to S. Stewart and N. Diluccio) Figure 6.3 shows a plot of the average daily number of passengers on transatlantic flights for each month from January 19X1 to December 19X5.

The series shows a steady upward trend and a regular, recurring pattern associated with the months of the year. A number of factors may account for the upward trend, such as an increase in population, in income, in leisure time, or in popularity of travel. The monthly variation can be accounted for by the regularity of a host of factors having to do with the weather and people's work and leisure habits.

In order to describe the seasonal pattern, we may imagine a certain number (positive or negative) to be associated with each month, this number representing the "effect" of that particular month. The estimated value of the series in a given month can be thought of as generated by adding to the trend value for that month the appropriate monthly effect. For example, assuming a linear

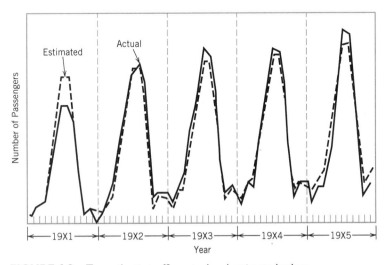

FIGURE 6.3 Transatlantic traffic, actual and estimated values

trend, $b_0 + b_1 T$, the estimated number of transatlantic passengers in February 19X2 can be imagined as being the result of the following calculation:

$$\hat{Y} = b_0 + b_1(14) + (\text{February effect})$$

Similarly, for March 19X2,

$$\hat{Y} = b_0 + b_1(15) + (\text{March effect})$$

The numbers 14 and 15 are the values of the variable T, which measures time in months beginning with January, 19X1.

Consider now the model

$$\hat{Y} = b_0 + b_1 T + c_1 M_1 + c_2 M_2 + \cdots + c_{12} M_{12}$$

where $M_1, M_2, \ldots, M_{12}$ are dummy variables such that

$$M_1 : = 1 \text{ for a January observation; } = 0 \text{ otherwise;}$$
$$M_2 : = 1 \text{ for a February observation; } = 0 \text{ otherwise;}$$
$$\cdots$$
$$M_{12} : = 1 \text{ for a December observation; } = 0 \text{ otherwise.}$$

For all January observations, $M_1 = 1$, $M_2 = M_3 = \ldots = M_{12} = 0$, and the model becomes

$$\hat{Y} = b_0 + b_1 T + c_1$$

For all February observations, the model is

$$\hat{Y} = b_0 + b_1 T + c_2$$

And so on. The model behaves as desired; $b_0 + b_1 T$ is the trend component, and $c_1, c_2, \ldots, c_{12}$ are the effects of the months January, February, ..., and December, respectively. Table 6.2 illustrates the coding of the explanatory variables (the data can be found in the file `airline.dat`, described in Problem 6.12).

As usual when dummy variables are used, one (in this example, the January dummy variable, M_1) is dropped to avoid perfect collinearity. Another dummy variable is included to account for the effect of the moving Easter holiday:

$$Z = 1 \text{ if Easter holiday occurred in month; } = 0 \text{ otherwise.}$$

The regression results are shown in Table 6.3.

TABLE 6.2 Illustration of the Coding of Explanatory Variables, Transatlantic Traffic

Year	Month	Ave. daily number of passengers	T	M_1	M_2	$\cdots$	M_{12}
19X1	Jan.	1,089	1	1	0	$\cdots$	0
	Feb.	972	2	0	1	$\cdots$	0
	...	...	...	...	...	$\cdots$	...
	Dec.	1,225	12	0	0	$\cdots$	1
19X2	Jan.	721	13	1	0	$\cdots$	0
...	...	...	...	...	...	$\cdots$	...
19X5	Dec.	1,910	60	0	0	$\cdots$	1

TABLE 6.3 Regression Results, Example 6.6

Variable	Estimate	t-ratio
Constant	952.2	
Time (T)	17.6	7.51
February (M_2)	−265.2	−1.37
March (M_3)	267.1	1.19
April (M_4)	559.9	1.64
May (M_5)	1,441.3	7.43
June (M_6)	2,538.8	13.08
July (M_7)	3,595.4	18.52
August (M_8)	3,573.4	18.38
September (M_9)	2,661.3	13.68
October (M_{10})	905.9	4.65
November (M_{11})	−180.1	−0.92
December (M_{12})	109.4	0.56
Mov. holiday (Z)	−264.0	−0.94
$R^2 = 0.97$	$S = 306.2$	$n = 60$

The OLS estimates measure the increase or decrease in the average daily number of passengers *in relation to the January base*. For example, in February, about 265 fewer passengers per day fly on transatlantic flights than in January; in March, 267 more than in January. The OLS estimates describe the seasonal pattern of this case, as shown in Figure 6.4.

To obtain forecasts, we substitute the appropriate values of the explanatory variables in the estimated model:

$$\hat{Y} = 952.2 + 17.6T - 265.2M_2 + \cdots + 109.3M_{12} - 264.0Z$$

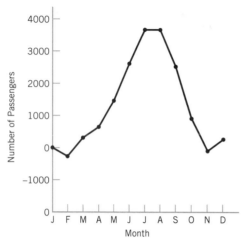

FIGURE 6.4 Seasonal pattern, transatlantic traffic

The forecast for January 19X6 is calculated by setting $T = 61$ and all other variables equal to zero:

$$\hat{Y} = 952.2 + (17.6)(61) = 2026$$

The February 19X6 forecast is found by setting $T = 62$, $M_2 = 1$, and all other variables equal to zero:

$$\hat{Y} = 952.2 + (17.6)(62) - 265.2 = 1778$$

and so on for other months. The effect of the moving holiday should be included in the April forecast if Easter occurs in April in 19X6. ■

EXAMPLE 6.3

The quarterly sales of a company are shown in the third column of Table 6.4 and plotted in Figure 6.5.

There appears to be an increasing trend but also increasing seasonality—that is, the quarterly variations appear to increase with time. It would be inappropriate to use the model

$$\hat{Y} = b_0 + b_1 T + c_1 Q_1 + c_2 Q_2 + c_3 Q_3 + c_4 Q_4$$

where the Q's are dummy variables representing the quarters because this model implies that the quarterly effects (c's) are constant. A simple remedy is

TABLE 6.4 Data for Example 6.3

Year	Quarter	Sales, Y	T	Q_1	Q_2	Q_3	Q_4	TQ_1	TQ_2	TQ_3	TQ_4
1	4	7.0	1	0	0	0	1	0	0	0	1
2	1	4.2	2	1	0	0	0	2	0	0	0
2	2	7.1	3	0	1	0	0	0	3	0	0
2	3	6.6	4	0	0	1	0	0	0	4	0
2	4	10.9	5	0	0	0	1	0	0	0	5
3	1	5.2	6	1	0	0	0	6	0	0	0
3	2	9.8	7	0	1	0	0	0	7	0	0
3	3	8.7	8	0	0	1	0	0	0	8	0
3	4	15.0	9	0	0	0	1	0	0	0	9
4	1	6.3	10	1	0	0	0	10	0	0	0
4	2	12.5	11	0	1	0	0	0	11	0	0
4	3	10.7	12	0	0	1	0	0	0	12	0
4	4	18.9	13	0	0	0	1	0	0	0	13
5	1	7.6	14	1	0	0	0	14	0	0	0
5	2	15.1	15	0	1	0	0	0	15	0	0
5	3	12.4	16	0	0	1	0	0	0	16	0

SOURCE: File `csales2.dat`

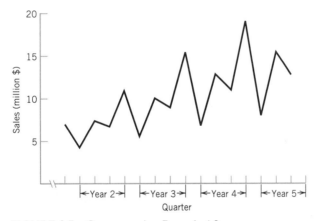

FIGURE 6.5 Company sales, Example 6.3

to make the quarterly effects functions of time—linear functions will do for a start:

$$c_1 = d_1 + e_1 T$$
$$c_2 = d_2 + e_2 T$$
$$c_3 = d_3 + e_3 T$$
$$c_4 = d_4 + e_4 T$$

The d's and e's are new parameters to be estimated. Substituting, we get

$$\hat{Y} = b_0 + b_1 T + (d_1 + e_1 T)Q_1 + (d_2 + e_2 T)Q_2$$
$$+(d_3 + e_3 T)Q_3 + (d_4 + e_4 T)Q_4$$

or

$$\hat{Y} = b_0 + b_1 T + d_1 Q_1 + d_2 Q_2 + d_3 Q_3 + d_4 Q_4$$
$$+e_1(TQ_1) + e_2(TQ_2) + e_3(TQ_3) + e_4(TQ_4)$$

All the parameters of this model can be estimated by regressing Y on Q_1 to Q_4 and TQ_1 to TQ_4. TQ_i is a new variable obtained by multiplying T by Q_i. The values of these variables are shown in Table 6.4.

To ensure unique OLS estimates, one of the Q's is left out, since the Q's sum is always equal to 1. Also, one of the TQ's is left out, since the sum of TQ_1 through TQ_4 equals T. In this case, Q_1 and TQ_1 are left out. The regression results are as follows.

$$\hat{Y} = 3.565 + 0.282T + 1.552Q_2 + 1.185Q_3 + 2.420Q_4$$
$$(35.69) \quad (25.92) \quad (10.47) \quad (7.61)$$
$$+ 0.385TQ_2 + 0.202TQ_3 + 0.712TQ_4 \quad R^2 = 0.999$$
$$(24.98) \quad (13.14) \quad (46.23) \quad S = 0.097$$

The forecast of sales in Quarter 4 of Year 5 is

$$\hat{Y} = (3.565) + (0.282)(17) + (2.42) + (0.712)(17) = 22.883$$

Other forecasts are calculated in the same manner.   ■

EXAMPLE 6.4

(Due to Mr. W. B. Kipkie) Figure 6.6 shows the quarterly shoe store sales for the period ending in 19Y0. The trend appears to be curvilinear, and the seasonal fluctuations appear to increase with time.

One possible model for this pattern would be that of the previous example but with a curvilinear trend (e.g., $b_0 + b_1 T + b_2 T^2$) in place of the linear one.

A simple alternative worth trying is to regress the (common or natural) logarithm of the original dependent variable on time and dummy variables representing the quarters. This model can be written as

$$\log Y = b_0 + b_1 T + c_1 Q_1 + c_2 Q_2 + c_3 Q_3 + c_4 Q_4 \tag{6.1}$$

Y represents shoe store sales, T is the time variable ($T = 1$ for Quarter 1, 19X0; ...; $T = 44$ for Quarter 4, 19Y0), and the Q's are dummy variables representing

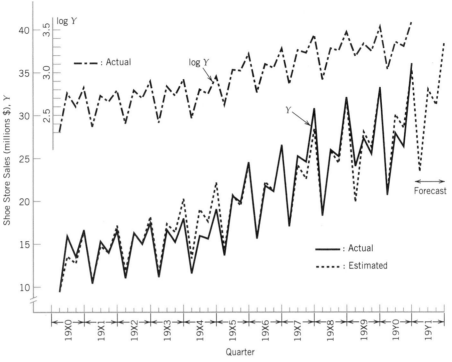

FIGURE 6.6 Quarterly shoe store sales

the four quarters. c_1, c_2, c_3, and c_4 are the quarterly effects. The data can be found in the file shoes.dat. The values of the variables employed are outlined in Table 6.5.

TABLE 6.5 Illustration of Values of Variables, Shoe Store Sales

Year	Quarter	Shoe store sales, Y ($ million)	log Y	Time T	Dummy variables Q_1	Q_2	Q_3	Q_4
19X0	1	9.8	2.282	1	1	0	0	0
	2	16.1	2.779	2	0	1	0	0
	3	13.8	2.625	3	0	0	1	0
	4	16.6	2.809	4	0	0	0	1
19X1	1	10.5	2.351	5	1	0	0	0
...	...	...	...	...	...	...	...	...
19Y0	4	35.6	3.572	44	0	0	0	1

NOTE: log Y is the natural logarithm of Y

Model 6.1 is appropriate when the series shows a curvilinear trend and the seasonal effects are multiplicative—rather than additive, as in the previous models. To see this, note that Eq. 6.1 is based on

$$Y = e^{b_0 + b_1 T + c_1 Q_1 + \cdots + c_4 Q_4}$$

after taking the logarithms of both sides. This last model can be written as

$$Y = e^{b_0 + b_1 T} e^{c_1 Q_1} \cdots e^{c_4 Q_4}$$

The first term, $e^{b_0 + b_1 T}$, is the (curvilinear) trend component. For any given quarter, the corresponding Q is equal to 1, while all other Q's equal zero. For example, the approximate value of a first-quarter observation is

$$Y = e^{b_0 + b_1 T} e^{c_1}$$

$e^{c_1}, e^{c_2}, \ldots, e^{c_4}$, therefore, are the quarterly effects, multiplying the trend component of this model.

Observe in Figure 6.6 that the time plot of log(Sales) shows a linear trend and constant seasonality—a confirmation that Model 6.1 describes the series well.

One of the dummy variables is redundant. We drop Q_1 and regress log Y on T, Q_2, Q_3, and Q_4. The regression results are as follows.

$$\widehat{\log Y} = 2.223 + 0.020T + 0.343Q_2 + 0.256Q_3 + 0.461Q_4 \qquad R^2 = 0.95$$
$$\qquad (20.94) \quad (10.14) \quad (7.57) \quad (13.58) \qquad S = 0.079$$

The estimated values of log Y are calculated by substituting the appropriate values of T, Q_2, Q_3, and Q_4 in the preceding expression. For example, for Quarter 1, 19X1, we have $T = 5$, $Q_2 = Q_3 = Q_4 = 0$, and

$$\widehat{\log Y} = (2.223) + (0.020)(5) = 2.323$$

The estimated value of Y is the antilogarithm (to the base e) of 2.323, which is $e^{2.323}$, or 10.206. Actual and estimated shoe store sales are shown in Figure 6.6.

Also shown in Figure 6.6 are the forecast shoe store sales in 19Y1, calculated as shown in Table 6.6. ∎

As with all other regression problems, the coding of the time and dummy variables and any required transformations of the original variables are conveniently performed by computer programs. These operations, the estimation of the models, and the display of the results can be carried out rapidly by simply invoking the appropriate commands.

TABLE 6.6 Calculation of Forecasts, Example 6.4

Year	Quarter	Forecast log(Sales)			Forecast sales
19Y1	1	2.223 + (0.020)(45)		= 3.123	22.71
	2	2.223 + (0.020)(46)	+0.343	= 3.486	32.65
	3	2.223 + (0.020)(47)	+0.256	= 3.419	30.54
	4	2.223 + (0.020)(48)	+0.461	= 3.644	38.24

6.4 SEASONAL ADJUSTMENT OF TIME SERIES

Occasionally, a time series is "adjusted" for seasonal variation. The purpose of such an adjustment is usually to compare values of the series at different points in time in order to determine whether the observed change can be explained by the regular seasonal variation. For instance, we may be interested in knowing whether the decline in the number of transatlantic passengers between December 19X1 and January 19X2 (see Table 6.2) can be accounted for by the fact that there are normally fewer passengers in January than in December.

The *seasonally adjusted series* in the examples of the last section is the original series minus the estimated seasonal effect. For example, the seasonally adjusted transatlantic traffic of Example 6.2 is obtained by subtracting the appropriate monthly effect from each observation. The calculations are illustrated in Table 6.7, using the data of Table 6.2 and the estimated monthly effects of Table 6.3.

On a seasonally adjusted basis, transatlantic traffic increased between January and February of 19X1 (though the actual series showed a decline) but declined between December 19X1 and January 19X2 (though the reduction was less than that of the actual series). Of course, values of the series corresponding

TABLE 6.7 Seasonal Adjustment of Transatlantic Traffic

Year	Month	Ave. daily number of passengers, Y	Monthly effect, c	Seasonally adjusted number of passengers, $Y - c$
19X1	Jan.	1,089	0.0	1,089.0
	Feb.	972	−265.5	1,237.5
	...	...	...	...
	Dec.	1,224	109.0	1,115.0
19X2	Jan.	721	0.0	721.0
...	...	...	...	...
19X5	Dec.	1,910	109.0	1,801.0

to distant periods can also be compared. For example, on a seasonally adjusted basis, traffic increased by 712 between January 19X1 and December 19X5.

The seasonally adjusted shoe store sales of Example 6.4 are calculated as in Table 6.8.

The procedure here is only slightly more complicated because the dependent variable is expressed in logarithms. The last column is obtained by taking the antilogarithms (to the base e) of column 6 and rounding these off to the same degree of precision as the original series. We see, for example, that on a seasonally adjusted basis, shoe store sales actually declined between Quarters 3 and 4 of 19X0; even though actual sales increased, they increased less than they normally do between third and fourth quarters.

6.5 METHOD OF MOVING AVERAGES

The approaches described so far are appropriate for modeling a time series that consists of a seasonal pattern and a trend that can be described mathematically by a function of a time variable. For some series, however, the trend is very difficult to describe by a simple function. As an example, consider Figure 6.7, which shows the monthly unemployment rate over a five-year period. Some would describe the trend by the dotted line labeled "12-month, centered moving average" in Figure 6.7—a line that "goes through" the clear pattern of seasonality. This line cannot be described accurately by a simple formula.

A widely applied technique for measuring trend and seasonal effects in such cases is the *method of moving averages*. Variants of this method are used for the seasonal adjustment of economic time series by government agencies. For these reasons, the method deserves mention at this point, even though it is not directly related to regression.

TABLE 6.8   Seasonal Adjustment of Shoe Store Sales

Year (1)	Quarter (2)	Shoe store sales, Y (3)	log Y (4)	Quarterly effect, c (5)	log Y − c (6)	Seasonally adjusted sales (7)
19X0	1	9.8	2.282	0	2.282	9.8
	2	16.1	2.779	0.343	2.436	11.8
	3	13.8	2.625	0.256	2.369	10.7
	4	16.6	2.809	0.461	2.348	10.5
19X1	1	10.5	2.351	0	2.351	10.5
. . .	. . .	. . .	. . .	. . .	. . .	. . .
19Y0	4	35.6	3.572	0.461	3.111	22.4

At the simplest level, the method of moving averages comes in two versions and proceeds by the following steps, which we shall first describe and then illustrate. (The reader may wish to read Example 6.5 along with the description of the method.)

Step 1: Calculate the consecutive moving averages of the observations. The span of the moving average should be that of the seasonal pattern: use a twelve-month moving average for monthly data, a four-quarter moving average for quarterly data, a seven-day moving average for daily data, and so on. *The calculated moving average is taken as the measure of trend at the center of the moving span.* If the span consists of an odd number of periods (e.g., a seven-day moving average), the moving average is the trend value at the middle (e.g., the fourth day) of the span. If the span consists of an even number of periods, the moving average measures the trend at the middle of the two middle periods.

Step 1a: When the span consists of an even number of periods, calculate a centered moving average of the uncentered moving averages in step 1. This centered moving average then becomes the measure of trend for the middle period.

Step 2: Calculate the deviation (D) of each observation (Y) from the trend (centered moving average, W), either as the difference

$$\text{(i)} \quad D = Y - W \qquad \text{(additive version)},$$

or as the ratio

$$\text{(ii)} \quad D = Y/W \qquad \text{(multiplicative version)}.$$

Step 3: *The seasonal effects are the averages of the deviations for the season.* For example, if the data are quarterly, the effect of the first quarter is equal to the average of all Quarter 1 deviations, and the effect of the second quarter is equal to the average of all Quarter 2 deviations.

Step 4: The *seasonally adjusted series* is obtained by either (i) subtracting from or (ii) dividing into each observation (y) the estimate of the appropriate seasonal effect calculated in step 3, depending on whether the additive or multiplicative version was used.

It can be shown that the averages of step 3 are the OLS estimators obtained by regressing the deviations, D, on the appropriate seasonal dummy variables but without a constant term. For example, if the data are quarterly and we regress D on $Q_1, Q_2, Q_3,$ and Q_4

$$\hat{D} = c_1 Q_1 + c_2 Q_2 + c_3 Q_3 + c_4 Q_4$$

the OLS estimator c_i equals the average of the deviations in Quarter i.

EXAMPLE 6.5

Column 1 of Table 6.9 shows the number of job vacancies in a region quarterly over a five-year period.

The first four-quarter moving average (37.40) is the average of 25.1, 40.4, 44.3, and 39.8 and is placed between Quarters 2 and 3; the second four-quarter moving average (42.10) is the average of 40.4, 44.3, 39.8, and 43.9 and is placed between Quarters 3 and 4; the other uncentered moving averages are similarly calculated from observations in a moving span of four quarters. The first centered moving average (39.75) is the average of the first two uncentered moving averages (37.40 and 42.10) and corresponds to Quarter 3 of 19X1; the second (43.66) is the average of 42.10 and 45.22 and corresponds to Quarter 4 of 19X1, and so on. This centered moving average is the measure of the trend. The differences between the observations and the centered moving average are shown in column 4 and in Table 6.10, while the ratios of the observations divided by the centered moving average are shown in column 6 and in Table 6.11.

Four of these deviations—two at the beginning and two at the end—are missing because the moving average cannot be calculated for these quarters. The quarterly effects are the ordinary averages of the deviations for each quarter separately. If the deviations are measured as differences, we note from Table 6.10 that Quarter 1 job vacancies average 10,470 below the trend and Quarter 2 job vacancies average 1320 above the trend. If deviations are measured as ratios, Table 6.11 shows that Quarter 1 job vacancies are on average 85.7% of the trend and Quarter 2 vacancies are on average 101% of trend. These averages are the estimates of the quarterly effects.

To adjust seasonally the series of job vacancies, the calculated quarterly effects are subtracted from (in the case of differences) or divided into (in the case of ratios) the observations. For example, using differences, the seasonally adjusted job vacancies in Quarter 1, 19X1, are equal to $25.1 - (-10.47)$ or 35.57 (slight differences from the values shown in Table 6.9 are due to rounding); in Quarter 2, 19X2, $52.9 - (1.32)$ or 51.58; in Quarter 3, 19X4, $130.9 - 15.0$ or 115.9, and so on. Using ratios, the seasonally adjusted job vacancies for the same quarters are $25.1/0.857$ or 29.29, $52.9/1.010$ or 52.37, $130.9/1.196$ or 109.45, respectively. The seasonally adjusted job vacancies may now be compared in the usual way. ∎

TABLE 6.9 Quarterly Job Vacancies

Year	Qtr.	Job vacancies, Y (000) (1)	4-quarter mov. aver. (uncentered) (2)	Centered mov. aver., W (3)	Additive version Deviation, D = Y − W (4)	Additive version Seas. adj. series (5)	Multip. version Deviation, D = Y/W (6)	Multip. version Seas. adj. series (7)
19X1	1	25.1				35.56		29.30
	2	40.4				39.08		39.99
	3	44.3	37.40	39.75	4.55	29.30	1.114	37.05
	4	39.8	42.10	43.66	−3.86	45.37	0.912	43.22
19X2	1	43.9	45.22	50.79	−6.89	54.36	0.864	51.24
	2	52.9	56.35	61.21	−8.31	51.58	0.864	52.37
	3	88.8	66.15	69.72	19.08	73.80	1.274	74.26
	4	79.0	73.30	77.72	1.28	84.57	1.016	85.78
19X3	1	72.5	82.15	83.19	−10.69	82.96	0.871	84.62
	2	88.3	84.22	84.99	3.31	86.98	1.039	87.41
	3	97.1	85.75	87.66	9.44	82.10	1.108	81.20
	4	85.1	89.57	92.15	−7.05	90.67	0.923	92.41
19X4	1	87.8	94.72	98.95	−11.15	98.26	0.887	102.48
	2	108.9	103.17	102.45	6.45	107.58	1.063	107.80
	3	130.9	101.72	98.41	32.49	115.90	1.330	109.47
	4	79.3	95.10	90.25	−10.95	84.87	0.879	86.11
19X5	1	61.3	85.40	77.92	−16.62	71.76	0.787	71.55
	2	70.1	70.45	66.89	3.21	68.78	1.048	69.39
	3	71.1	63.32	61.67	9.43	56.10	1.153	59.46
	4	50.8	60.02	58.09	−7.29	56.37	0.875	55.16
19X6	1	48.1	56.15	55.05	−6.95	58.56	0.874	56.14
	2	54.6	53.95	52.64	1.96	53.28	1.037	54.05
	3	62.3	51.32			47.30		52.10
	4	40.3				45.87		43.76

TABLE 6.10 Calculation of Quarterly Effects Based on the Additive Version, Job Vacancies

Year	Quarter 1	2	3	4
19X1	–	–	4.55	−3.86
19X2	−6.89	−8.31	19.08	1.28
19X3	−10.69	3.31	9.44	−7.05
19X4	−11.15	6.45	32.49	−10.95
19X5	−16.69	3.21	9.43	−7.29
19X6	−6.95	1.96	–	–
Total	−52.37	6.62	74.99	−27.87
Average	−10.47	1.32	15.00	−5.57

TABLE 6.11 Calculation of Quarterly Effects Based on the Multiplicative Version, Job Vacancies

Year	Quarter 1	2	3	4
19X1	–	–	1.114	0.912
19X2	0.864	0.864	1.274	1.016
19X3	0.871	1.039	1.108	0.923
19X4	0.887	1.063	1.330	0.879
19X5	0.787	1.048	1.159	0.875
19X6	0.874	1.037	–	–
Total	4.283	5.051	5.979	4.605
Average	0.857	1.010	1.196	0.921

Essentially, then, the method averages out the seasonal fluctuations and uses the centered moving average as a measure of the trend. The average of the deviations from the trend for a given season is the effect of that season. The seasonal effects are subtracted from or divided into the observations to obtain the seasonally adjusted series. The result of this last step is to "raise" observations that tend to lie below the trend and to "lower" observations that tend to lie above the trend.

In any application of this method, of course, the deviations are measured either as differences or as ratios—not in both ways. Neither approach is inherently better than the other, but ratios are often employed in practice on the grounds that they tend to be more stable over time than differences.

Forecasting with the method of moving averages requires an extrapolation of the trend (the centered moving average). In most cases, one must use one's judgment for this extrapolation, based on whatever information is available at the time. Given this trend forecast, however, the forecast of the series is obtained by (i) adding to the trend forecast the appropriate seasonal effect (additive version) or (ii) multiplying the trend forecast by the appropriate seasonal effect (multiplicative version).

EXAMPLE 6.6

Figure 6.7 shows the monthly unemployment rate among men and women in the labor force who are 15 years old or older, the centered 12-month moving average, and the seasonally adjusted rate, from 19X2 to 19X6. The calculations were carried out by a special computer program and are based on the ratios of the series to the moving average. The monthly effects are shown in Figure 6.8. They show clearly that the unemployment rate tends to decrease steadily until August then rises steadily again until it peaks in January.

To forecast the trend, one must come to an informed judgment concerning the state of the economy as well as other factors influencing the size of the labor force, the participation rate, and the future demand for labor. No simple technique can replace this judgment. Given this forecast, however, the unemployment rate in any one month can be estimated by multiplying the forecast of the trend by the appropriate monthly effect.

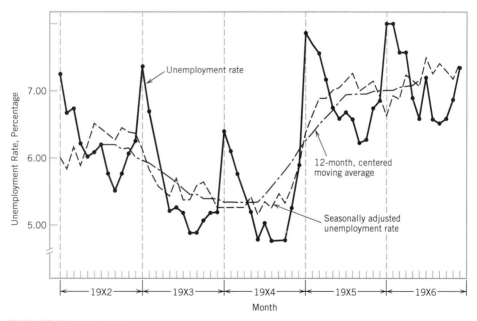

FIGURE 6.7 Unemployment rate

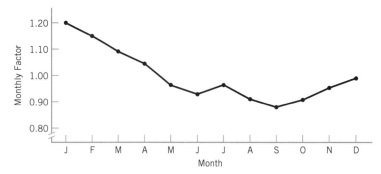

FIGURE 6.8   Seasonal factors, Example 6.6

To illustrate, let us suppose that the level of unemployment in the near future is expected to remain stable and the 12-month centered moving average projected to remain constant at about 7.00 (that is, 7%; see Figure 6.7). The forecast of the unemployment rate in January 19X7 is 7.00×1.21, or 8.47%, that in February 19X7, 7.00×1.15 or 8.05%, and so on. ∎

6.6 TIME SERIES MODELS IN PERSPECTIVE

The common feature of the time series models described in this chapter is the assumption that all the information required for the analysis of a series is contained in the series itself. No attempt is made to bring in other explanatory variables or to identify relationships between the series of interest and other series. This is, at the same time, the most convenient feature and the most serious shortcoming of the models.

For instance, consider the case of airline traffic described in Example 6.2. The number of airline passengers in a given period of time should depend on the price of air travel, the prices of alternative modes of transportation, the level of national income, people's tastes for travel in general and air travel in particular, the number and size of available aircraft, foreign competition and the international situation, and a host of other factors. A logically satisfactory model should relate the volume of air traffic to the most important of these factors.

The fact that airline traffic follows as stable a pattern as that shown in Figure 6.3 is, in a way, remarkable and begs to be exploited. The reason, of course, for this pattern is that the factors influencing air travel did not change or changed only gradually over the period considered, leaving the travelers' habits over the year as the principal cause of variation in air travel in the short run. But who would blindly extrapolate this pattern in the face of an announcement of a drastic fare increase?

Time series models, therefore, should be used with reasonable caution for as long as important, omitted explanatory variables remain stable, and forecasts from these models should be modified as common sense dictates when the stable conditions are expected to change.

In Chapter 10, we present an alternative method for the analysis of time series, a method extending and combining regression and moving averages but again resting on the assumption that the required information is contained in the series itself. The preceding remarks will apply, as we shall see, to this method as well.

6.7 TO SUM UP

- Trend is the long-run tendency of a series and may be estimated by regressing the series against an appropriate function of time.
- Seasonality is the regular variation of a time series associated with calendar periods, such as quarters, months, days of the week, or hours of the day. Many types of seasonality can be estimated with the use of dummy variables that represent the calendar periods.
- The main purpose of adjusting a series for seasonality is to allow a comparison of the series at different points in time and to determine whether or not the observed change can be explained by the regular seasonal variation.
- The method of moving averages may be used to estimate the seasonal pattern of a series with an irregular trend and to adjust the series for seasonality.
- The common feature of time series models is the assumption that all the information required for the analysis of the series is contained in the series itself. Such models should be used with reasonable care as long as important neglected variables remain stable.

PROBLEMS

6.1 With the help of a computer program, confirm the regression results presented in this chapter.

6.2 Refer to Example 6.1 and the data in the file `csales1.dat`. Estimate a parabolic trend model, $\hat{Y} = b_0 + b_1 T + b_2 T^2$. Forecast the company sales in years 21 to 26. Is this a better model than the linear one?

6.3 Estimate the trend of the annual series Y_1 shown in Table 6.12. Forecast the value of the series in the years 1997 to 2000.

TABLE 6.12 Data for Problems 6.3 to 6.5

Year	Y_1	Y_2	Y_3
1987	182.0	65.8	43.947
1988	232.4	40.9	32.870
1989	314.0	80.2	30.220
1990	387.8	104.9	26.520
1991	448.9	143.5	28.461
1992	513.5	194.6	24.869
1993	537.5	222.3	26.737
1994	614.9	311.8	21.868
1995	694.8	400.5	19.429
1996	727.5	483.7	18.630

SOURCE: File `tser1.dat`

6.4 Same as Problem 6.3, except use the series Y_2 in Table 6.12.

6.5 Same as Problem 6.3, except use the series Y_3 in Table 6.12.

6.6 The file `drates.dat` contains the observed annual death rates in the past twenty years per thousand men and women in the 40-44 and 60-64 age groups. The data were plotted in Figure 1.1 and are partially listed in Table 6.13.

   Forecast the death rate for each gender and age group in each of the next five years.

6.7 (a) Estimate the trend and seasonality of the quarterly series Y_1 shown in Table 6.14.

   (b) Forecast the series in Quarters 3 and 4 of year 4 and Quarters 1 and 2 of Year 5.

   (c) Seasonally adjust the series.

6.8 Same as Problem 6.7, except use the series Y_2 in Table 6.14.

6.9 Same as Problem 6.7, except use the series Y_3 in Table 6.14.

TABLE 6.13 File `drates.dat`, Partial Listing

Years ago	Men, 40-44	Men, 60-64	Women, 40-44	Women, 60-64
20	3.4	24.0	2.0	12.2
19	3.6	24.0	2.1	11.9
18	2.5	23.4	2.0	11.7
17	3.4	23.0	2.1	11.5
16	3.5	23.7	2.1	11.2
...	...	...	...	...

TABLE 6.14 Data for Problems 6.7 to 6.9

Year	Quarter	Y_1	Y_2	Y_3
1	3	108	7.0	25
1	4	132	4.2	45
2	1	133	7.1	32
2	2	110	6.5	52
2	3	133	10.9	80
2	4	151	5.2	120
3	1	162	9.8	80
3	2	131	8.7	123
3	3	141	15.0	238
3	4	182	6.3	399
4	1	169	12.5	262
4	2	153	10.7	452

SOURCE: File tser2.dat

6.10 The series of the number of passengers carried each month by the Metropolitan Transit Commission (MTC) during the past six years was plotted in Figure 1.2 and can be found in the file mtc.dat. The file is partially listed in Table 6.15.

Forecast the number of MTC passengers each month of the next year.

6.11 The file ogas.dat contains the monthly gas consumption of the office building described in Section 1.9 and the average temperature at the building's location over a period of nearly six years. The file is partially listed in Table 6.16.

(a) Confirm the relationship between temperature and gas consumption shown in Figure 1.12.

(b) Forecast the building's gas consumption in each of the next twelve months.

6.12 In addition to the data for Example 6.2, the file airline.dat contains the average daily number of passengers on transcontinental flights each month from January 19X1 to December 19X5. A partial listing of the file is shown in Table 6.17.

TABLE 6.15 File mtc.dat, Partial Listing

Year	Month	Number of passengers (000)
1	1	705
1	2	734
1	3	762
1	4	689
1	5	686
. . .	. . .	. . .

TABLE 6.16 File ogas.dat, Partial Listing

Year	Month	Gas consumption (m³)	Monthly temperature (°C)
1	1	663	− 5.6
1	2	510	− 6.1
1	3	487	0.6
1	4	207	7.6
1	5	99	14.3
. . .	. . .	. . .	. . .

TABLE 6.17 File airline.dat, Partial Listing

YEAR	MONTH	EASTER	TATL	TCONT
19X1	Jan	0	1089	21772
19X1	Feb	0	972	22097
19X1	Mar	0	1267	23395
19X1	Apr	1	1333	23678
19X1	May	0	2317	23242
. . .	. . .	. . .	. . .	. . .

TATL is the average daily number of passengers on transatlantic flights used in Example 6.2 and TCONT that on transcontinental flights. EASTER equals 1 if the Easter holiday occurred in the month or 0 if it did not.

(a) In the manner of Figure 6.3, plot TCONT as a function of time.

(b) Construct a model explaining the trend and seasonality of TCONT.

(c) Plot the seasonal pattern of TCONT.

(d) Forecast TCONT for each month in 19X6.

6.13 As an analyst for an electric utility, you are interested in forecasting energy consumption over the next year. A time series is available that shows how much electricity was produced and consumed each *hour* in the past years.

A plot of the series suggests that there is a fairly clear linear long-run trend. In addition to trend, there appear to be three sources of seasonal variation: (i) a monthly variation reflecting changes in temperature and daylight over the year; (ii) a variation associated with the day of the week; and (iii) a variation associated with the hour of the day. In case (ii), it may not be necessary to distinguish all days of the week but only weekdays, Saturdays, and Sundays. Figure 6.9 illustrates the typical hourly pattern of electricity consumption by day of the week for a given month in two selected years. Patterns in other months are similar.

Explain precisely how you would analyze the time series by means of a regression model. Show how to forecast energy consumption for a given hour of a given Saturday in February of next year. Use arbitrary figures to illustrate the calculations.

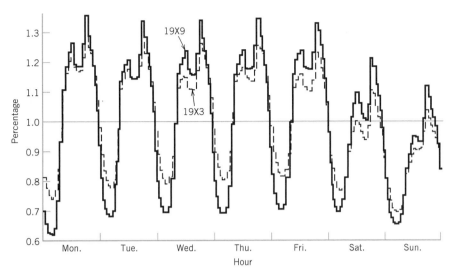

FIGURE 6.9 Hourly pattern of electricity consumption

6.14 Sales of passenger cars vary considerably throughout the year. A study was made to determine if this variability could be exploited for forecasting purposes and if the patterns of monthly variation are different for different types of passenger cars.

Five categories of passenger cars were distinguished: full-sized, medium-sized, and small-sized cars, all cars (equals the sum of the previous three categories), and imported cars (most of which also fall into the "small-sized" category). Five regression models were estimated, each of the following form:

$$\hat{Y} = b_0 + b_1 T + c_1 X_1 + \cdots + c_{12} X_{12}$$

where

Y : Number of total registrations of new (i) full-sized, (ii) medium-sized, (iii) small-sized, (iv) total, and (v) imported passenger cars;

T : Time variable (=1 for Oct. 19X5, . . . , =60 for Sept. 19Y0);

X_1-X_{12} : Dummy variables for January to December, respectively.

Note that the dependent variable is not sales but registrations. It is thought, however, that new car registrations are nearly identical to new car sales. Sixty monthly observations were obtained, covering a period of five full consecutive model years from October 19X5 to September 19Y0. Total new car registrations are plotted in Figure 6.10. The October dummy variable, X_{10}, was dropped in all regressions. The results are summarized in Table 6.18.

Compare the monthly patterns of sales for the five categories. Forecast sales of total new car registrations in the first six months following September 19Y0. Discuss any improvements of the model you may wish to suggest.

TABLE 6.18 New Passenger Car Registrations

Explanatory variable	Full-sized Estimate	t	Medium-sized Estimate	t	Small-sized Estimate	t	Total Estimate	t	Imported Estimate	t
Constant	46669	7.33	9992	8.93	9241	8.69	65386	8.79	7107	9.35
Time, T	− 260	−6.17	112	6.45	165	9.89	22	0.40	126	9.70
January, X$_1$	− 8079	−2.30	−3988	−2.75	−6886	−4.97	−20590	−4.54	−5728	−6.41
February, X$_2$	−12380	−3.53	−4424	−3.05	−6283	−4.54	−22490	−4.96	−5196	−5.81
March, X$_3$	− 8023	−2.28	−1502	−1.04	−4161	−3.00	−13270	−2.92	−3787	−4.23
April, X$_4$	165	0.05	3071	2.11	−1017	−0.73	2810	0.62	− 1545	−1.72
May, X$_5$	1888	0.54	6293	4.33	1606	1.16	10389	2.28	− 278	−0.31
June, X$_6$	− 1721	−0.49	4639	3.19	648	0.47	3956	−0.87	− 961	−1.07
July, X$_7$	− 8233	−2.33	1196	0.82	− 870	−0.62	7499	0.87	− 1805	−2.01
August, X$_8$	−11660	−3.30	− 755	−0.52	− 352	−0.25	−12380	−2.71	− 1505	−1.67
September, X$_9$	−13700	−3.87	−3875	−2.65	−1149	−0.82	−18350	−4.02	−1019	−1.13
November, X$_{11}$	− 1134	−0.32	−1664	−1.15	−2772	−2.00	− 5112	−1.13	− 2350	−2.63
December, X$_{12}$	− 1736	−0.49	−1824	−1.26	−5049	−3.65	− 8150	−1.80	−4377	−4.90
R^2	0.69		0.79		0.82		0.85		0.71	
n	60		60		60		60		60	

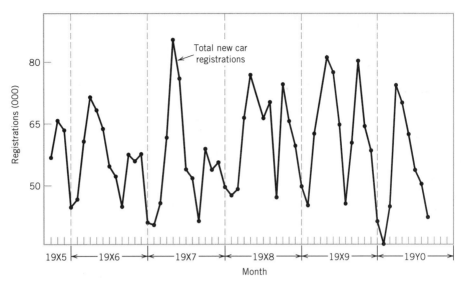

FIGURE 6.10 New car registrations

6.15 The following models were estimated in order to forecast the monthly sales of three major household appliances.

$$\text{(a)} \quad \hat{Y} = b_0 + b_1 T \qquad\quad + c_2 X_2 + c_3 X_3 + \cdots + c_{12} X_{12}$$
$$\text{(b)} \quad \hat{Y} = b_0 + b_1 T + c_1 X_1 + c_2 X_2 + c_3 X_3 + \cdots + c_{12} X_{12}$$

where

Y : Monthly sales of washers, dryers, or refrigerators (number of units);

T : Time trend (=1 for January 19X1, ..., =60 for December 19X5);

X_1 : Number of housing units completed, monthly;

X_2 : Dummy variable (=1 for February; =0 otherwise);

X_3: Dummy variable (=1 for March; =0 otherwise); $\cdots$

X_{12} : Dummy variable (=1 for December; =0 otherwise).

The only difference between Models a and b is that X_1, the number of housing completions, is included in (b) but not in (a).

The regression coefficients and t-ratios for Model a are shown in Table 6.19, while those for Model b are shown in Table 6.20. These results are based on 60 monthly observations for the period January 19X1 to December 19X5.

(a) Comment on the models and results presented.

(b) Using these results, forecast the sales of washers, dryers, and refrigerators for the first six months of 19X6.

(c) How would you construct a model for forecasting the monthly sales of these appliances? Explain carefully and justify your proposal.

TABLE 6.19 Appliance Sales, Problem 6.15, Model a

Explanatory variable	Washers Estimate	t	Dryers Estimate	t	Refrigerators Estimate	t
Constant	29495	9.22	21620	8.15	32047	10.50
Time trend, T	5	0.10	43	1.04	135	2.85
February, X_2	2056	0.49	−603	−0.17	2471	0.62
March, X_3	5721	1.37	−212	−0.06	9797	2.46
April, X_4	4551	1.09	−3088	−0.89	7127	1.79
May, X_5	5590	1.34	−3800	−1.10	9385	2.36
June, X_6	7887	1.89	−2409	−0.70	15341	3.85
July, X_7	6953	1.66	−591	−0.17	15721	3.95
August, X_8	6435	1.54	957	0.28	7524	1.89
September, X_9	18466	4.41	13185	3.80	17814	4.46
October, X_{10}	18115	4.32	16847	4.85	11984	3.00
November, X_{11}	10239	2.44	11061	3.18	8632	2.16
December, X_{12}	8509	2.02	7527	2.16	5790	1.44
R^2	0.46		0.67		0.52	
n	60		60		60	

TABLE 6.20 Appliance Sales, Problem 6.15, Model (b)

Explanatory variable	Washers Estimate	t	Dryers Estimate	t	Refrigerators Estimate	t
Constant	9355	1.42	4486	0.83	4978	0.91
Time trend, T	−39	−0.83	6	0.15	78	1.99
Completions, X_1	1.42	3.40	1.21	3.51	1.91	5.53
February, X_2	5671	1.45	2469	0.77	7323	2.26
March, X_3	10282	2.57	3665	1.11	15919	4.82
April, X_4	7441	1.93	−632	−0.20	11003	3.45
May, X_5	3158	0.82	−5870	−1.86	6115	1.93
June, X_6	8719	2.31	−1704	−0.55	16452	5.27
July, X_7	8270	2.18	527	0.17	17483	5.57
August, X_8	6193	1.64	749	0.24	7192	2.30
September, X_9	15928	4.13	11023	3.47	14396	4.52
October, X_{10}	13288	3.29	12739	3.82	5494	1.64
November, X_{11}	5752	1.43	7242	2.19	2597	0.78
December, X_{12}	8595	2.26	7595	2.43	5893	1.88
R^2	0.57		0.74		0.71	
n	60		60		60	

6.16 Figure 6.11 shows a monthly index of shipments of spirits by distilleries for the period January 19X0 to December 19X4.

Without doing any calculations, describe clearly the *regression model using time and dummy variables* that best explains the pattern of the series. Define precisely all variables used. List the first 15 values of all explanatory variables.

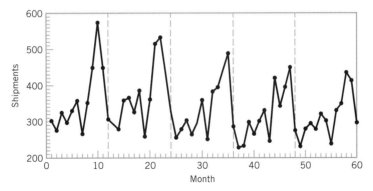

FIGURE 6.11 Monthly shipments of spirits, Problem 6.16

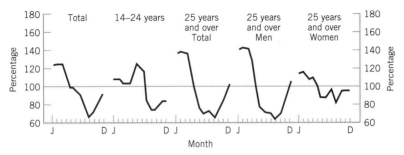

FIGURE 6.12 Seasonal factors by age and sex, Problem 6.17

6.17 Figure 6.12 shows the seasonal factors (multiplied by 100) for the total number unemployed and the number unemployed in several categories. These seasonal factors were based on the moving average method (multiplicative model).

Interpret and comment on the results presented.

6.18 The quarterly earnings of Lake Michigan Cement Co. are shown in Table 6.21.

TABLE 6.21   Lake Michigan Cement, Quarterly Earnings

Year	Quarter	Earnings ($000)	Year	Quarter	Earnings ($000)
19X6	1	(838)[a]	19X7	1	(1,145)
	2	1,338		2	1,237
	3	748		3	1,405
	4	237		4	511

[a]Numbers in parentheses are losses.

Calculate the quarterly effects using the additive and multiplicative moving average models. Calculate the seasonally adjusted earnings. Forecast the earnings in Quarter 1, 19X8.

6.19 Table 6.22 is a worksheet for applying the method of moving averages (multiplicative model) to an index of quarterly sales of a company. Parts of the worksheet (indicated by a question mark) are purposely left blank. *Note:* Slight discrepancies due to rounding should be expected.

(a) Calculate the entries marked by a question mark in Table 6.22. Briefly explain your calculations.

(b) "How can one possibly claim that sales went up between Quarter 4, 19X0, and Quarter 1, 19X1, 'on a seasonally adjusted basis' when everyone can see that sales went *down*—from 280 to 110?" Comment on this statement.

6.20 (Due to Mr. Zaimin Lu) Table 6.23 shows a partial listing of the file `liquor.dat`. The file contains 60 observations from January 19X0 to December 19X4.

The variables have the following interpretation:

MONTH: Month number

DSHIP: Shipments of distilled spirits, in current $000

BSHIP: Shipments of beer, in current $000

WSHIP: Shipments of wine, in current $000

DIND: Price index of distilled spirits

TABLE 6.22 Worksheet, Problem 6.19

Year	Quarter	Sales index	Centered mov. ave.	Ratio	Seas. adj. sales
19X0	2	131	-	-	166.854
	3	134	-	-	?
	4	280	163.625	1.711	161.886
19X1	1	110	164.250	?	?
	2	130	167.500	0.776	165.980
	3	140	170.500	0.821	171.712
	4	300	171.625	1.748	?
19X2	1	114	?	?	?
	2	135	170.000	0.794	?
	3	136	168.000	0.810	166.806
	4	290	-	-	167.668
19X3	1	108	-	-	?

Quarter	Quarterly effect
1	?
2	0.785
3	0.815
4	1.730

TABLE 6.23 File `liquor.dat`, Partial Listing

MONTH	DSHIP	BSHIP	WSHIP	DIND	BIND	WIND
1	44400	68321	8415	148.1	242.8	196.0
2	40515	75213	8538	147.8	257.8	196.0
3	48001	87297	9772	149.1	257.8	198.6
4	46574	103200	12309	158.9	259.7	212.4
5	51948	121061	12668	158.8	260.8	212.8
...	...	...	...	...	...	...

BIND: Price index of beer

WIND: Price index of wine

(a) Plot DSHIP, BSHIP, and WSHIP against time. What do these plots tell you about the trend and seasonality of each series?

(b) Plot DIND, BIND, and WIND against time. What do these plots tell you about the trend and seasonality of each series?

(c) Calculate three new variables: DSHIP/DIND, BSHIP/BIND, and WSHIP/WIND, which can be interpreted as indexes of real shipments of distilled spirits, beer and wine respectively. Plot the new variables against time. Do these plots tell the same story as those in (a)?

(d) For each new variable in (c) determine the best model explaining the trend and seasonality of the variable. Forecast these three variables each month in 19X5.

6.21 (Due to Ms. Laura Parker) A mid-year review of sales of Direct Drugs (DD), a chain of drugstores with numerous outlets in the region, showed below budget company sales and a negative sales trend. Of additional concern to DD was the effect of a law that came in force just four weeks ago and which prohibited the sale of cigarettes and other tobacco products by drugstores. Also of concern was the response to flyer sales which are held frequently in designated weeks.

DD undertook an analysis of sales both at the company and the individual store level. This problem deals with the sales of a particular member of the chain known as Store #7.

Store sales data are available for the last 80 weeks. The data can be found in the file `drugstor.dat`, a partial listing of which is shown in Table 6.24.

The variables are to be interpreted as follows:

WEEK: Week number

MONTH: Month (1 = January, ..., 12 = December)

SALES: Week's sales (in $)

RXNO: Number of pharmacy customers

FSNO: Number of "front shop" (non-pharmacy) customers

SWEEK: $= 1$ if there is a flyer sale that week; $= 0$ otherwise

NOCIGS: $= 1$ if tobacco products cannot be sold that week; $= 0$ otherwise

TABLE 6.24 File `drugstor.dat`, Partial Listing

WEEK	MONTH	SALES	RXNO	FSNO	SWEEK	NOCIGS
1	8	73666	455	3030	0	0
2	8	103373	539	4475	1	0
3	8	74285	527	3120	0	0
4	8	92587	538	4613	1	0
5	9	87144	545	4644	0	0
6	9	90245	490	4325	1	0
...	...	...	...	...	...	...

(a) As part of the analysis of the weekly sales of Store #7, the following regression model was estimated:

$$\widehat{SALES} = 77205 \quad -45\,WEEK \quad -1886\,AUG \quad +2632\,SEP \quad +4852\,OCT$$
$$(14.47) \quad (-0.87) \quad (-0.32) \quad (0.45) \quad (0.84)$$
$$+7340\,NOV \quad +10316\,DEC \quad +4802\,JAN \quad -11462\,FEB$$
$$(1.28) \quad (1.80) \quad (0.84) \quad (-2.00)$$
$$-14563\,MAR \quad -9022\,APR \quad +3195\,MAY \quad -3367\,JUN$$
$$(-2.18) \quad (-1.36) \quad (0.48) \quad (-0.51)$$
$$+16280\,SWEEK \quad -1388\,NOCIGS \quad R^2 = 0.65$$
$$(7.56) \quad (-0.19) \quad S = 9349$$

AUG to JUN are dummy variables representing the months August to June, respectively. Interpret these results.

(b) Confirm the regression results in (a) using the data in the file `drugstor.dat` and a computer program.

(c) What else do the data in the file `drugstor.dat` tell Direct Drugs about the weekly sales of Store #7 and its customers?

6.22 (Due to Mr. Lou Carbone) Figure 6.13 is a plot of the monthly retail sales in a region over a five-year period. The data can be found in the file `rsales.dat`, a partial listing of which is given in Table 6.25.

(a) To which factors is due the pattern revealed in Figure 6.13? Are these factors likely to remain stable next year?

(b) In the manner of Figure 6.4, estimate and plot the seasonal pattern of retail sales.

(c) Forecast the retail sales for each month of Year 6.

(d) Explain any reservations or suggestions for improvement you may have about the methods used in (b) and (c).

6.23 (Due to Mr. John Innes) Table 6.26 is a partial listing of the file `mvacc1.dat` showing the number of motor vehicle accidents for each day of the week during the period 1988 to 1992 in the province of Manitoba.
Three types of accident are distinguished.

FATAL: Accidents resulting in the death of one or more persons within 30 days from the accident date

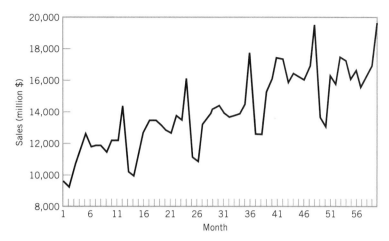

FIGURE 6.13 Retail sales, Problem 6.22

TABLE 6.25 File rsales.dat, Partial Listing

Year	Month	Retail Sales
1	1	9689
1	2	9217
1	3	10547
1	4	11590
1	5	12683
1	6	11790
1	7	11899
1	8	11893
1	9	11501
1	10	12222
...	...	...

SOURCE: File rsales.dat

INJURY: Accidents resulting in nonfatal injury to one or more persons

PROP: Accidents resulting in damage to the vehicle and/or property of $500 or more but not in death or injury

The variable TOTAL is the sum of the three types of accidents and is plotted in Figure 6.14.

(a) Comment on the pattern of seasonality apparent in Figure 6.14. To which factors is it due? Are these factors likely to remain stable in 1993?

(b) Forecast the total number of accidents for each day of the week in 1993.

TABLE 6.26 Accidents by Day of the Week

Year	Day	FATAL	INJURY	PROP	TOTAL
1988	Sun	32	986	2840	3858
1988	Mon	9	1110	3630	4749
1988	Tues	11	1148	3639	4798
1988	Wed	14	1014	3570	4598
. . .	. . .	. . .	. . .	. . .	. . .

SOURCE: File mvacc1.dat

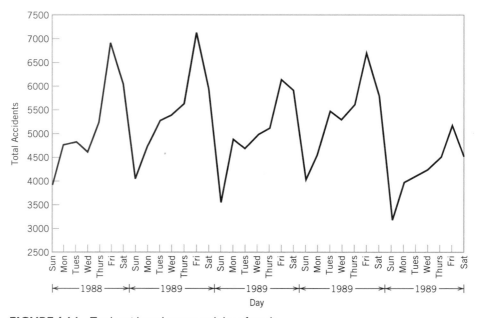

FIGURE 6.14 Total accidents by year and day of week

(c) Forecast the number of fatal, personal injury, and property damage accidents for each day of the week in 1993. Compare these forecasts with those in (b).

(d) The file mvacc2.dat stores the number of fatal, personal injury, and property accidents each month from 1988 to 1992. A partial listing of the file is given in Table 6.27.

Forecast the total number of accidents for each month in 1993.

(e) Forecast the number of fatal, personal injury, and property accidents for each month in 1993. Compare these forecasts with those in (d).

TABLE 6.27 Accidents by month

Year	Month	FATAL	INJURY	PROP	TOTAL
1988	Jan	5	877	3581	4463
1988	Feb	5	789	2994	3788
1988	Mar	6	581	2099	2686
1988	Apr	10	470	1521	2001
1988	May	11	644	1844	2499
1988	June	14	736	2175	2925
...	...	...	...	...	...

SOURCE: File `mvacc2.dat`

CHAPTER 7

LAGGED VARIABLES

7.1 INTRODUCTION AND SUMMARY

In economic and business relationships involving time series, the current value of the dependent variable is often related to the current and lagged values of one or more explanatory variables.

For example, an advertising campaign may succeed in creating a favorable image for the product in the minds of consumers, the effects of which may persist over time. Thus, advertising expenditures during one period of the campaign can be expected to influence sales of the product in the next period, the period after, and so on. Alternatively, we can say that a given period's sales depend on advertising expenditures in this and past periods.

The simplest models of such relationships may be estimated in a straightforward way by regressing the current values of the series against lagged explanatory variables, that is, variables created by lagging the explanatory variables one or more periods.

Occasionally, it is desirable to require that the effects of the lagged variables follow a pattern suggested by theory or experience. Such a pattern may always be satisfactorily approximated by a polynomial of a suitable degree, and the models so created can be estimated by regressing the current values of the series against specially constructed explanatory variables.

In the special case where the effects of lagged explanatory variables follow a simple declining pattern, the final model can be estimated by regressing the current values of the series against the current value of the explanatory variable and the values of the series lagged one period. This is known as the "geometric lag model," which is also implied by two different arguments concerning the formation of the series known as "adaptive expectations" and "stock adjustment." We explain these terms in the following sections.

7.2 DISTRIBUTED LAGS

Suppose there is a linear relationship between the current value of the dependent variable, on the one hand, and the current and k lagged values of one explanatory variable, on the other. The model may be written as

$$\hat{Y} = b + b_0 X + b_1 X_{-1} + b_2 X_{-2} + \cdots + b_k X_{-k} \tag{7.1}$$

For example, Y could represent the number of houses completed "this" month, X the number of houses started this month, and $X_{-1}, X_{-2}, \ldots, X_{-k}$ the monthly housing starts $1, 2, \ldots, k$ months ago. Model 7.1 is based on the reasonable assumption that some of the houses completed this month were started this month, others were started one month ago, still others two months ago, and so on. This is the same as saying that some of the houses whose construction started this month will be completed this month, while others will be completed next month, others the month after, and so on. The effect of starts upon completions is said to be *distributed* over k periods, and Model 7.1 is a *distributed lag model*.

The values of $X_{-1}, X_{-2}, \ldots, X_{-k}$ are the values of X lagged $1, 2, \ldots, k$ periods, and the parameters of the model may be estimated by regressing Y on $X, X_{-1}, \ldots, X_{-k}$. ($X_{-1}$ should be read as "X lagged one period," not as "X minus 1"; likewise for the other lagged variables.)

Another way of writing Model 7.1 is

$$\hat{Y}_t = b + b_0 X_t + b_1 X_{t-1} + b_2 X_{t-2} + \cdots + b_k X_{t-k} \tag{7.2}$$

This notation refers to the observations and makes explicit the current period, t: in words, the number of houses completed in period t depends on the number of houses started in periods $t, t-1, t-2, \ldots, t-k$. We shall find this notation useful for clarifying some models that appear later in this chapter.

EXAMPLE 7.1

The first recorded stage of residential construction is the issuance of a building permit. The permit is a form of approval confirming that the proposed construction conforms to various bylaws, land-use designations, official plans, environmental considerations, building codes, and the like. A permit must be acquired prior to the start of construction; therefore, housing starts follow the issuance of building permits. The delay between the issue of a permit and the start of construction depends on such factors as weather conditions, the developers' financial position, and market conditions. In what follows, we shall describe a model developed to forecast monthly housing starts on the basis of permits issued in past months.

Table 7.1 shows the number of residential units started (Y) and the number of permits issued (X) each month over a five-year period. The remaining columns of the table show the number of permits issued one (X_{-1}), two (X_{-2}), three (X_{-3}), $\ldots$ months previously. It can be noted that these lagged variables are in effect the variable X "shifted down" the appropriate number of periods. The missing observations could be obtained from the original sources; alternatively, the regressions could be based on the months for which complete data are available. The latter course is followed here.

TABLE 7.1 Housing Starts and Permits Issued

Year	Month	Starts, Y	Permits, X	X_{-1}	Lagged variables X_{-2}	X_{-3}	
19X2	Oct.	10,046	7,916	-	-	-	...
	Nov.	7,436	8,371	7,916	-	-	...
	Dec.	5,263	6,619	8,371	7,916	-	...
19X3	Jan.	5,186	5,616	6,619	8,371	7,916	...
	Feb.	3,676	6,704	5,616	6,619	8,371	...
...	...	...	...	...	...	...	...
19X7	Aug.	7,207	7,215	8,311	9,380	10,007	...
	Sep.	6,263	6,924	7,215	8,311	9,380	...

Because there was no information concerning the proper number (k) of lagged variables to be used, a number of regression runs were executed and the R^2 noted (OLS estimates and other statistics are omitted):

k	Lagged variables	R^2	n
1	X_{-1}	0.737	59
2	X_{-1}, X_{-2}	0.783	58
3	X_{-1}, X_{-2}, X_{-3}	0.792	57
4	$X_{-1}, X_{-2}, X_{-3}, X_{-4}$	0.813	56
5	$X_{-1}, X_{-2}, X_{-3}, X_{-4}, X_{-5}$	0.813	55

The inclusion of current permits (X) would probably have improved the fit of the model, but the values of this variable are not normally known when the forecast of next month's housing starts is made.

As lagged variables were added to the model R^2 increased, but the increments diminished with k. It was judged that a model with four lagged variables was satisfactory. The complete regression results for this model were as follows.

$$\hat{Y} = 876 + 0.529X_{-1} + 0.259X_{-2} + 0.155X_{-3} + 0.047X_{-4} \qquad R^2 = 0.813$$
$$\phantom{\hat{Y} = 876 +} (8.20) \quad\;\; (3.31) \qquad (0.60) \qquad (2.40) \qquad\qquad S = 941$$

A forecast of the number of residential units to be started in October 19X7 (the first month following the period covered in Table 7.1) is

$$\hat{Y} = 876 + (0.529)(6924) + (0.259)(7215) + (0.155)(8311) + (0.047)(9380)$$

or, 8136 residential housing units.

It is reasonable to expect the OLS estimates of the coefficients of X_{-1} to X_{-4} to be between 0 and 1 and to interpret these as the proportions of lagged permits resulting in current starts. Indeed, the regression results show that 52.9% of permits issued one month ago, 25.9% of permits issued two months ago, 15.5% and 4.7% of permits issued three and four months ago, respectively, are estimated to start construction in the current month. This consistency with prior expectations, however, is fortuitous because the method of least squares in general cannot ensure that the estimates will be between 0 and 1. ■

7.3 THE POLYNOMIAL LAG MODEL

It is often reasonable to suppose (and occasionally to require) that the coefficients (b_j) of the lagged variables in Model 7.1 follow a pattern.

For example, the estimated coefficients (b_j) of lagged housing permits in Example 7.1 ($b_1 = 0.529$, $b_2 = 0.259$, $b_3 = 0.155$, and $b_4 = 0.047$) when plotted against j suggest the declining pattern indicated by the solid curve in Figure 7.1: the proportion of a given month's issued permits that result in starts this month declines as the month of issue becomes more distant.

It can be shown that any pattern of the b_j can be approximated by a polynomial in j of a suitably high degree. A polynomial of degree m in j, it will be recalled, is the function

$$d_0 + d_1 j + d_2 j^2 + d_3 j^3 + \cdots + d_m j^m$$

where the d's are constants. For example, a parabola

$$d_0 + d_1 j + d_2 j^2$$

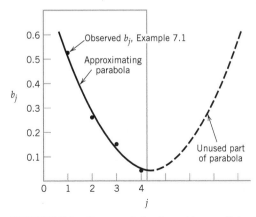

FIGURE 7.1 Pattern of distributed lag coefficients

is a polynomial of degree 2. Figure 5.4 shows the general shape of the curves generated by polynomials of low degree.

In approximating the pattern of the b_j, we may use only a part of the polynomial. For example, the solid curve in Figure 7.1 is the declining portion of a parabola, the extension of which is indicated by the dotted line. In this case, it is understood that the parabola will give the pattern of the b_j for $j = 1, 2, 3,$ and 4 only. (In the next section, we examine an alternative representation of a declining pattern that may be extended to j's beyond their observed range.)

In general, the higher the degree of the polynomial, the better the approximation. However, as will be made clear later, the usefulness of this approach rests on the hope that a polynomial of fairly low degree (say, 2 to 5) will provide a satisfactory approximation.

To explain how polynomials are applied, suppose that $k = 3$, so that the distributed lag model is

$$\hat{Y} = b + b_0 X + b_1 X_{-1} + b_2 X_{-2} + b_3 X_{-3} \tag{7.3}$$

Assume that a polynomial of degree $m = 2$ will be used to approximate the pattern of the b_j, that is,

$$b_j = d_0 + d_1 j + d_2 j^2 \tag{7.4}$$

Substituting for j the values 0, 1, 2, and 3 in Eq. 7.4, we get

$$\begin{aligned}
b_0 &= d_0 + d_1(0) + d_2(0)^2 = d_0 \\
b_1 &= d_0 + d_1(1) + d_2(1)^2 = d_0 + d_1 + d_2 \\
b_2 &= d_0 + d_1(2) + d_2(2)^2 = d_0 + 2d_1 + 4d_2 \\
b_3 &= d_0 + d_1(3) + d_2(3)^2 = d_0 + 3d_1 + 9d_2
\end{aligned} \tag{7.5}$$

Substituting these last expressions into Eq. 7.3, we get

$$\hat{Y} = b + d_0 X + (d_0 + d_1 + d_2)X_{-1} + (d_0 + 2d_1 + 4d_2)X_{-2} \\ + (d_0 + 3d_1 + 9d_2)X_{-3}$$

or, combining terms,

$$\hat{Y} = b + d_0 \underbrace{[X + X_{-1} + X_{-2} + X_{-3}]}_{Z_0} + d_1 \underbrace{[X_{-1} + 2X_{-2} + 3X_{-3}]}_{Z_1}$$
$$+ d_2 \underbrace{[X_{-1} + 4X_{-2} + 9X_{-3}]}_{Z_2}$$
$$= b + d_0 Z_0 + d_1 Z_1 + d_2 Z_2$$

b and the "artificial" parameters d_0, d_1, and d_2 can be estimated by regressing Y against the "artificial" variables Z_0, Z_1, and Z_2, where

$$Z_0 = X + X_{-1} + X_{-2} + X_{-3}$$
$$Z_1 = X_{-1} + 2X_{-2} + 3X_{-3} \tag{7.6}$$
$$Z_2 = X_{-1} + 4X_{-2} + 9X_{-3}$$

The estimates of the d_j can then be substituted into Eq. 7.5 to obtain estimates of the original parameters, b_j.

A simple example will illustrate the calculations. Suppose that the values of Y and of X, X_{-1}, X_{-2}, and X_{-3} are as shown in the first five columns of Table 7.2.

Ordinarily, the first values of the lagged variables (indicated by an asterisk in Table 7.2) would be missing. It is assumed here that the missing entries were filled in by consulting the original sources of data.

The values of the artificial variables, calculated according to Eq. 7.6, are shown in the last three columns of the table.

To estimate the d_j, we regress Y against Z_0, Z_1, and Z_2 and obtain

$$\hat{Y} = -0.8137 + 2.4971Z_0 - 2.3711Z_1 + 0.5937Z_2$$

that is, $b = -0.8137$, $d_0 = 2.4971$, $d_1 = -2.3710$, and $d_2 = 0.5937$. Substitution of these values into Eq. 7.5 yields the following estimates of the original parameters, b_j;

$$b_0 = d_0 = 2.4971$$
$$b_1 = d_0 + d_1 + d_2 = 0.7198$$
$$b_2 = d_0 + 2d_1 + 4d_2 = 0.1299$$
$$b_3 = d_0 + 3d_1 + 9d_2 = 0.7274$$

TABLE 7.2   Data Illustrating a Polynomial Model

Y	X	X_{-1}	X_{-2}	X_{-3}	Z_0	Z_1	Z_2
16	5	3*	1*	2*	11	11	25
15	4	5	3*	1*	13	14	26
18	7	4	5	3*	19	23	51
30	8	7	4	5	24	30	68
25	6	8	7	4	25	34	72
20	5	6	8	7	26	43	101
25	5.5	5	6	8	24.5	41	101

so that the estimated value of Y may also be calculated from

$$\hat{Y} = -0.8137 + 2.4971X + 0.7198X_{-1} + 0.1299X_{-2} + 0.7274X_{-3}$$

In general, the purpose of a *polynomial model* is to force a pattern on the parameters of the original distributed lag model. When the number of original parameters (k) is large and the degree of the approximating polynomial (m) is low, there can be substantial economy in the number of parameters that must be estimated.

Special computer programs are available to create the artificial variables and perform the required calculations. These programs allow experimentation with different values of k and m, so that the model that best describes the data may be conveniently selected. The programs also calculate the standard errors and t-ratios of the original distributed lag coefficients as functions of those of the artificial variables.

EXAMPLE 7.2

The main features of a study of the relationship between mortgage disbursements and approvals by life insurance companies are best described in the authors' own words[1]:

> The relationship beween the commitment and disbursement of mortgage funds is complicated both by the timing of mortgage disbursements after commitments and by the problem of commitment attritions, i.e., the failure of borrowers to exercise commitments. A typical mortgage lending sequence begins with an application by a borrower for a mortgage commitment. After a period of from a week to three months—the length of the lag depending on the lending institution, the degree of tightness in the capital markets, the borrower, and the nature of the project—an institution will approve or refuse a loan. If a commitment is granted, a timetable for the disbursement of funds is then established. The timetable will depend on the type and size of the loan. Loans on existing properties are usually disbursed within a few weeks; loans for new construction are disbursed in stages over the construction period, which may be as long as two years in the case of large-scale multiple dwellings and large commercial structures. The granting of a mortgage commitment does not insure that it will be ex ercised. A commitment may not be exercised because scheduled construction is postponed or cancelled; similarly a project may be altered so as to reduce the value and hence the size of the mortgage, or funds may become available elsewhere on better terms.

---

[1]L. B. Smith and G. R. Sparks, *Institutional Mortgage Lending in Canada, 1954–1968: An Econometric Analysis*, Bank of Canada, Staff Research Study No. 9, 1973, pp. 17-19.

Smith and Sparks approximated the relationship between aggregate disbursements and approvals by the model

$$\hat{D} = b_0 A + b_1 A_{-1} + b_2 A_{-2} + \cdots + b_k A_{-k}$$

where D represents monthly disbursements and $A, A_{-1}, \ldots, A_{-k}$ represent current and lagged monthly approvals (commitments). The constant term (b) of this model was suppressed.[2]

Smith and Sparks experimented with various lag periods (k) and degrees of the approximating polynomial (m). The selected model had a lag period of $k = 8$ months and the approximating polynomial was of degree $m = 3$. The artificial variables (Z_j) and the results of regressing D against the Z_j are not listed here since they are of little interest in themselves. Substitution of the coefficients of the artificial variables into equations similar to Eq. 7.5 yields estimates of the original parameters (b_j). All these calculations, of course, are carried out by the computer. The final results are as follows:

$$D = 0.139A + 0.150A_{-1} + 0.145A_{-2} + 0.129A_{-3} + 0.105A_{-4}$$
$$(3.34) \qquad (7.89) \qquad (6.29) \qquad (5.49) \qquad (5.96)$$
$$+ 0.077A_{-5} + 0.048A_{-6} + 0.024A_{-7} + 0.006A_{-8},$$
$$(5.90) \qquad (2.79) \qquad (1.08) \qquad (0.34)$$

$$R^2 = 0.72, \quad S = 8.76, \quad n = 96.$$

These results are based on 96 monthly observations. R^2 and s are those of the regression against the artificial variables. The lag coefficients and the approximating polynomial are plotted in Figure 7.2.

A forecast of next month's approvals, it will be noted, is required to forecast next month's disbursements. ∎

The same principles apply when the model includes several lagged explanatory variables, perhaps each with a different lag period. For example, housing starts may be explained not only by lagged housing permits but also by lagged interest rates, lagged constructions costs, and other variables. Each lagged variable may have a separate approximating polynomial, set of artificial variables, and set of artificial parameters, the last being related to the original variables and parameters by means of equations similar to 7.6 and 7.5.

[2]Suppressing the constant term means leaving out of the model the variable X_0 consisting of 1's (as described in Section 4.3) or forcing the restriction $b = 0$ on Model 7.1. This is a special case of least–squares estimation with equality restrictions, which will be described later in Section 8.2.

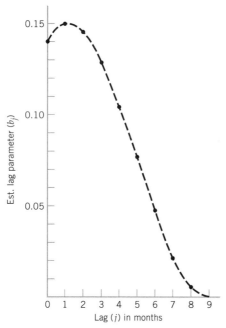

FIGURE 7.2 Estimates of lag parameters and polynomial approximation, mortgages

7.4 THE GEOMETRIC LAG MODEL

The polynomial distributed lag model rests on the assumption that the lag parameters, b_j, can be approximated by a polynomial, preferably one of a low degree. A stronger assumption is made by the *geometric lag model*.

This model begins by assuming that *all* previous lagged values of the explanatory variable X influence the current value of Y; that is,

$$Y = a + b_0X + b_1X_{-1} + b_2X_{-2} + b_3X_3 + \cdots \qquad (7.7)$$

The lag sequence does not terminate in k periods, as was the case with Model 7.1. It is convenient initially to treat Eq. 7.7 as describing an exact relationship between Y and the lagged variables.

The geometric model further assumes that the parameters b_j can be approximated by

$$b_j = bc^j \qquad (7.8)$$

where b and c $(0 < c < 1)$ are constants. In other words, it is assumed that

$$b_0 = bc^0 = b$$
$$b_1 = bc^1 = bc$$
$$b_2 = bc^2$$

and so on. Figure 7.3 shows the form of Eq. 7.8 for $b = 1$ and selected values of c.

Essentially, Eq. 7.8 asserts that the parameters of the lagged explanatory variables decline by a constant proportion, c, each period, since

$$b_j = (bc^{j-1})c = b_{j-1}c$$

Model 7.7, therefore, can be written as

$$Y = a + bX + (bc)X_{-1} + (bc^2)X_{-2} + (bc^3)X_{-3} + \cdots \tag{7.9}$$

In the alternative notation, the last equation is

$$Y_t = a + bX_t + (bc)X_{t-1} + (bc^2)X_{t-2} + \cdots$$

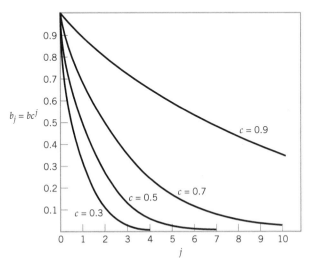

FIGURE 7.3 Coefficients of geometric lag model ($b = 1$)

This relationship holds for any period t, hence also for $t = t - 1$, in which case we have

$$Y_{t-1} = a + bX_{t-1} + (bc)X_{t-2} + (bc^2)X_{t-3} + \cdots$$

or, going back to the original notation,

$$Y_{-1} = a + bX_{-1} + (bc)X_{-2} + (bc^2)X_{-3} + \cdots \qquad (7.10)$$

Now, multiply both sides of Eq. 7.10 by c to get

$$cY_{-1} = ac + (bc)X_{-1} + (bc^2)X_{-2} + (bc^3)X_{-3} + \cdots \qquad (7.11)$$

Subtract Eq. 7.11 from 7.9 to get

$$Y - cY_{-1} = a(1 - c) + bX$$

or

$$Y = a(1 - c) + bX + cY_{-1}$$

At this stage, we stop treating the model as an exact relationship and write it as

$$\hat{Y} = a' + bX + cY_{-1} \qquad (7.12)$$

The three parameters of the model, $a' = a(1 - c)$, b, and c, can be estimated by regressing Y against X, the current values of the explanatory variable, and Y_{-1}, the values of the dependent variable lagged one period. The estimate of c is the regression coefficient of Y_{-1}; the estimate of b is the coefficient of X, and an estimate of a can be calculated by dividing the OLS estimate a' by one minus the estimate of c. (It should be kept in mind that the method of least squares does not guarantee that the estimate of c will satisfy the restriction $0 < c < 1$. If the calculated c does not meet this restriction, the model may be reestimated using constrained least squares, a method we shall describe later in Section 8.3.)

The estimation of the geometric lag model is illustrated using the artificial data shown in Table 7.3.

**TABLE 7.3
Artificial Data
Illustrating a
Geometric Lag
Model**

Y	X	Y_{-1}
12	4	7*
15	3	12
6	2	15
3	1	6
6	2	3
7	3	6

We prepare the Y_{-1} column by lagging the first column one period, fill in the missing entry (indicated with an asterisk), and then regress Y against X and Y_{-1} with the following results:

$$\hat{Y} = -2.280 + 3.289X + 0.272Y_{-1}$$

The estimate of c is equal to 0.272, the estimate of b is equal to 3.289, and an estimate of a is equal to $-2.280/(1 - 0.272)$, or -3.132.

Going back to Eq. 7.9, we see that if X is increased by one unit in a given period, Y will change by an amount b in this period, bc next period, bc^2 two periods hence, and so on. The total effect of this unit increase is equal to the sum

$$b + bc + bc^2 + bc^3 + \cdots$$

or

$$b(1 + c + c^2 + c^3 + \cdots)$$

The term in parentheses in the last expression is the sum of a geometric series and (assuming always that $0 < c < 1$) is equal to $1/(1 - c)$.[3] We conclude that the total effect of increasing X by one unit in one period is $b/(1 - c)$.

The geometric lag model achieves great simplicity but at the expense of a rather strong assumption about the pattern of the b_j, which are constrained to follow Eq. 7.8. Nevertheless, this assumption is plausible in many cases where

---

[3]Let $T = 1 + c + c^2 + c^3 + \cdots$. The successive terms of this series approach 0. Then, $cT = c + c^2 + c^3 + c^4 + \cdots$ and $T - cT = 1$. Therefore, $T = 1/(1 - c)$.

it can be assumed that the lagged effects decline steadily with the number of periods.

It is sometimes desirable to let the geometric lag begin after a certain number of periods. For example, if it is believed that the geometric lag pattern begins after two periods, the model can be written as

$$\hat{Y} = a + b_0X + b_1X_{-1} + \underbrace{b_2X_{-2} + (b_2c)X_{-3} + (b_2c^2)X_{-4} + \cdots}_{\text{geometric lag}}$$

The reader can verify in Problem 7.7 that this can be written in the form

$$\hat{Y} = a(1 - c) + b_0X + (b_1 - b_0c)X_{-1} + (b_2 - b_1c)X_{-2} + cY_{-1}$$

and its parameters estimated by regressing Y against X, X_{-1}, X_{-2}, and Y_{-1}.

If there are two explanatory variables, X and Z, and it is assumed that each follows a geometric model *with the same parameter c*, we have

$$\hat{Y} = a + bX + bcX_{-1} + (bc^2)X_{-2} + \cdots + dZ + (dc)Z_{-1} + (dc^2)Z_{-2} + \cdots$$

from which we get (Problem 7.8) after some algebra,

$$\hat{Y} = a(1 - c) + bX + dZ + cY_{-1}$$

This last model may be estimated by regressing Y against X, Z, and Y_{-1}. Extensions to three or more variables are similar.

EXAMPLE 7.3

The measurement of the effect of advertising on sales from time series data is usually difficult because it is not easy to separate the effects of advertising from those of price changes, price discounts, changes in the sales force or the package design, the actions of competitors, and so on. These complicating factors were said to not be present in the interesting case of the Lydia E. Pinkham Company, whose sales and advertising expenditures were studied by K. S. Palda[4].

The company sold mainly a vegetable compound designed to relieve menopausal malaise and menstrual pain. The product had no close substitutes and did not change substantially over time, the price did not change frequently, and changes in the marketing organization and in the policies of the company were minor. The firm did spend a large proportion (40 to 60%) of its sales on advertising. The annual domestic sales and advertising expenditures of the

[4]"The Measurement of Cumulative Advertising Effects," *The Journal of Business*, April 1965, pp. 162–179.

company over the period studied (1907–60) are shown in Figure 7.4 (the data can be found in the file `lydia.dat.`)

In measuring the relationship between advertising and sales, it is often assumed that advertising has a "lingering" effect on sales, that is, the effect of advertising continues beyond the period of expenditure.

For the Pinkham case, it is assumed that the effects of advertising expenditures (ADV) on sales ($SALES$) can be approximated by a geometric lag model:

$$SALES = a + (b)ADV + (bc)ADV_{-1} + (bc^2)ADV_{-2} + \cdots$$

which, as we know, can be estimated as

$$\widehat{SALES} = a(1 - c) + bADV + cSALES_{-1} \tag{7.13}$$

In addition to advertising, three dummy variables were introduced directly into Eq. 7.13 to represent four different eras of advertising copy at Lydia Pinkham.

> A historical incident drew attention to copy "quality" as a possible exogenous variable influencing sales. In November of 1925, the Food and Drug Administration ordered the company to stop using its current label claims. From the beginning of 1926 the labels—and advertising copy, which had to follow suit—recommended the compound only as vegetable tonic; claims that it acted

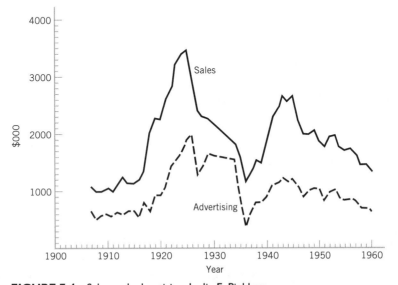

FIGURE 7.4 Sales and advertising, Lydia E. Pinkham

directly upon female organs were abandoned. Sales immediately declined. There are three turning points in the character of the claims that were used to advertise the compound. Before 1914 it was touted as an almost universal remedy. After the intervention of federal authorities the copy concentrated mainly on the relief of "female troubles." These claims, as already explained, had to be restricted further. But from the middle of 1940 the Federal Trade Commission was compelled to allow Pinkham to restore its previous appeals, for the company was by then able to adduce medical evidence for them. Since sales appeared to have been influenced by the character of the copy claims, it was decided to approximate the four copy periods with the use of dummy variables. (ibid., pp. 168–69)

The dummy variables are

$$D1 : = 1 \text{ for the period 1907–14}; \; = 0, \text{ otherwise};$$
$$D2 : = 1 \text{ for the period 1915–25}; \; = 0, \text{ otherwise};$$
$$D3 : = 1 \text{ for the period 1926–40}; \; = 0, \text{ otherwise}.$$

A fourth dummy variable for the period 1941–60 was dropped as redundant, and the period 1941–60 forms the base in the interpretation of the coefficients of the other dummy variables.

A number of models were estimated, but Model 7.13 with the dummy variables provided relatively good results. As reported by Palda, these were

$$\widehat{SALES} = 212 + 0.537ADV + 0.628SALES_{-1} - 102D1 + 181D2 - 203D3$$
$$(3.76) \qquad (7.39) \qquad (-1.04) \quad (2.66) \quad (-2.90)$$

$$R^2 = 0.922, \quad S = 185, \quad n = 53$$

The coefficient of $SALES_{-1}$, 0.628, is the estimate c; that is, the effects of advertising are estimated to decline by about 37% each year. The current effect, b, is estimated to be 0.537, that is, for each dollar spent on advertising Pinkham gets about 54 cents back in current sales.

If the effect of advertising is exhausted in the year in which the expenditure is incurred, the preceding would imply that the company pays out more than it gets back in revenue. According to the model, however, this year's advertising also affects sales one, two, three, and so on, years hence. The total advertising effect is given by

$$b + bc + bc^2 + \cdots = \frac{b}{1-c} = \frac{0.537}{1-0.628} = 1.44$$

In other words, an increase of this year's advertising expenditure by $1 will bring back a total of $1.44 in current and future sales.

Pinkham's expenses, excluding advertising, averaged 25% of sales. It would appear, therefore, that in return for an outlay of $1 in advertising, the company received (0.75)(1.44), or $1.08, making the apparent rate of return of advertising 8%.

These calculations, however, ignore the time value of money. Let f represent net sales as a proportion of gross sales ($f = 0.75$, in this case). The true rate of return is that discount rate, r, which makes the present value of future additional net sales equal to a current advertising increase of $1:

$$1 = fb + \frac{fbc}{1+r} + \frac{fbc^2}{(1+r)^2} + \frac{fbc^3}{(1+r)^3} + \cdots$$

or

$$1 = fb[1 + (\frac{c}{1+r}) + (\frac{c}{1+r})^2 + (\frac{c}{1+r})^3 + \cdots]$$

or

$$1 = fb\frac{1}{1 - c/(1+r)} = \frac{fb(1+r)}{1+r-c}$$

Solving for r, we get

$$r = \frac{fb + c - 1}{1 - fb}$$

In this case, it is estimated that $f = 0.75$, $c = 0.628$, and $b = 0.537$. Therefore, $r = 0.051$, that is, the rate of return of advertising is estimated to be about 5%. ∎

7.5 THE ADAPTIVE EXPECTATIONS MODEL

A model of the form

$$\hat{Y} = b_0 + b_1 X + b_2 Y_{-1}$$

is, as we saw in the last section, implied by the geometric lag model. A very similar final model is also implied by two quite different arguments, leading to the *adaptive expectations model*, examined in this section, and the *stock adjustment model*, described in the next section.

The adaptive expectations model begins by assuming that the current value of Y is linearly related, not to the current actual value of X, but to the "anticipated" value of X, X^*,

$$Y = a + bX^* \tag{7.14}$$

or, in the alternative notation,

$$Y_t = a + bX_t^* \tag{7.15}$$

It is again convenient temporarily to think of Eqs. 7.14 or 7.15 as describing an exact linear relationship; we shall remove this assumption at a later stage.

X^* is assumed to be unobservable but formed according to

$$X_t^* - X_{t-1}^* = c(X_t - X_{t-1}^*), \qquad (0 < c < 1)$$

or

$$X_t^* = cX_t + (1 - c)X_{t-1}^* \tag{7.16}$$

In words, the anticipated value of X at the end of period t is assumed to be a weighted average of the actual value of X during, and the anticipated value of X at the beginning of, period t (end of period $t - 1$).[5]

For example, it may be reasonable to suppose that the current aggregate production in an industry (Y_t) depends not on current sales (X_t) but on anticipated sales (X_t^*). In the absence of other information, it may also be reasonable to assume that sales expectations are adapted each period t in the light of the latest actual sales (X_t) and in the manner indicated by Eq. 7.16.

Substituting Eq. 7.16 into 7.15, we get

$$Y_t = a + b[cX_t + (1 - c)X_{t-1}^*]$$
$$= a + (bc)X_t + b(1 - c)X_{t-1}^*$$

But, according to Eq. 7.16, which holds for any period t including $t = t - 1$

$$X_{t-1}^* = cX_{t-1} + (1 - c)X_{t-2}^*$$

Substituting this last expression, we find

$$Y_t = a + (bc)X_t + b(1 - c)[cX_{t-1} + (1 - c)X_{t-2}^*]$$
$$= a + (bc)X_t + (bc)(1 - c)X_{t-1} + b(1 - c)^2 X_{t-2}^*$$

Substituting like expressions for $X_{t-2}^*, X_{t-3}^*, X_{t-4}^*, \ldots$, we get, after some algebra,

$$Y_t = a + (bc)X_t + (bc)(1 - c)X_{t-1} + (bc)(1 - c)^2 X_{t-2} + \cdots \tag{7.17}$$

[5]If X_t is not known at the time expectations are formed, it may be replaced by X_{t-1} in Eq. 7.16 (see Problem 7.9).

Lagging this last expression one period, we have

$$Y_{t-1} = a + (bc)X_{t-1} + (bc)(1-c)X_{t-2} + (bc)(1-c)^2 X_{t-3} + \cdots \qquad (7.18)$$

Multiplying Eq. 7.18 by $1 - c$ and subtracting from Eq. 7.17, we find all terms canceling out except for

$$Y_t - (1-c)Y_{t-1} = (ac) + (bc)X_t$$

that is,

$$Y_t = (ac) + (bc)X_t + (1-c)Y_{t-1} \qquad (7.19)$$

Recognizing at this stage that the relationship can only be an approximate one, we see that the last expression is of the form

$$\hat{Y} = b_0 + b_1 X + b_2 Y_{-1} \qquad (7.20)$$

and its parameters may be estimated by regressing Y against X and Y_{-1}. The regression coefficient of Y_{-1} is the estimate of $(1-c)$, from which the estimate of c can be obtained; the estimate of b can be obtained by dividing the coefficient of X by the estimate of c; to estimate a, divide the intercept b_0 by the estimate of c.[6]

EXAMPLE 7.4

An important element of the adaptive expectations model is the manner according to which expectations are assumed to change,

$$X^* - X^*_{-1} = c(X - X^*_{-1})$$

where $0 < c < 1$. Kopalle and Lehmann carried out two experiments to investigate the validity of this model.[7]

In the first experiment, subjects were asked to imagine that they were forced to buy car tires with an advertised useful life of L miles. The subjects were asked to record their expectation, X^*_{-1}, of the life of the tires in light of some information about the brand and the manufacturer provided in the experiment. In the next stage of the experiment, some time had elapsed, and the tires had to be replaced after lasting X miles. The subjects again recorded

---

[6]Remember, however, that OLS cannot guarantee that c will indeed satisfy the restriction $0 < c < 1$.

[7]Praveen K. Kopalle and Donald R. Lehmann, "The Effects of Advertised and Observed Quality on Expectations about New Product Quality," *Journal of Marketing Research*, Vol. 32, August 1995, pp. 280–90.

their expectation, X^*, of the useful life of the tires. The quantities L and X varied for each subject. Some 155 MBA students at a northeastern university participated in this simulated experiment. The results of regressing $(X^* - X^*_{-1})$ against $(X - X^*_{-1})$ with no intercept were as follows:

$$(X^* - X^*_{-1}) = 0.86(X - X^*_{-1}) \qquad R^2 = 0.81$$
$$(21)$$

The second experiment was very similar to the first except that the product was a car battery and expectations were recorded of its useful life in months. Subjects were 242 undergraduate business students at a southwestern university. The regression results were

$$(X^* - X^*_{-1}) = 0.80(X - X^*_{-1}) \qquad R^2 = 0.73$$
$$(22.5)$$

Overall, then, the adaptive expectations model appears to describe fairly well the change in expectations of the subjects of this experiment. ∎

7.6 THE STOCK ADJUSTMENT MODEL

This model also has a different origin but, in its final form, is identical to the geometric lag model. The stock adjustment model begins by assuming a linear relationship between the "desired" level of the dependent variable Y, Y^*, and an explanatory variable X. Again, temporarily assuming an exact relationship, this means that

$$Y^* = a + bX$$

or, in the alternative notation of this chapter,

$$Y^*_t = a + bX_t \tag{7.21}$$

Y^* could be, for example, the desired aggregate inventory level in an industry and X the current aggregate orders for the industry's products. In contrast to the adaptive expectations model, it is the *dependent* variable that is unobservable in this model. Y^* is assumed to influence the observable Y according to

$$Y_t - Y_{t-1} = c(Y^*_t - Y_{t-1})$$

where $0 < c < 1$, or,

$$Y_t = cY_t^* + (1 - c)Y_{t-1} \qquad (7.22)$$

In a manner similar to the adaptive expectations model, the actual current value of Y is assumed to be a weighted average of the current period's desired, and last period's actual, values of Y. If c is close to 1, then $Y_t \approx Y_t^*$, and Y can be said to adjust rapidly to the desired level; if c is close to 0, $Y_t \approx Y_{t-1}$ and the desired level has little effect on the actual level.

Substituting Eq. 7.21 into 7.22, we get

$$\begin{aligned} Y_t &= c[a + bX_t] + (1 - c)Y_{t-1} \\ &= (ac) + (bc)X_t + (1 - c)Y_{t-1} \end{aligned}$$

Restoring the approximate nature of the original relationship, the model can be written as

$$\hat{Y} = b_0 + b_1 X + b_2 Y_{-1}$$

and its parameters estimated by regressing Y against X and Y_{-1}.[8] Minor variations of the formulation produce slightly different versions of the stock adjustment model, as the following example illustrates.

EXAMPLE 7.5

Eppli and Shilling make use of the stock adjustment model to estimate the speed of adjustment of the stock of commercial retail space in the United States to desired levels.[9] They begin by assuming that the desired stock of retail space in quarter t, Y_t^*, is a linear function of employment in the retail sector k quarters before, X_{t-k},

$$Y_t^* = a + bX_{t-k}$$

with k to be determined. The actual stock of retail space, Y_t, is assumed to adjust to the desired level according to

$$Y_t - Y_{t-1} = c(Y_t^* - Y_{t-1}) \qquad (0 < c < 1)$$

---

[8]The final form of the models in Sections 7.4 to 7.6 contains Y_{-1} as an explanatory variable. It can be shown that the OLS estimators of the parameters of such models are consistent but not unbiased. In addition, the usual tests and confidence intervals concerning the parameters and forecasts are applicable only when the number of observations is large.

[9]Mark J. Eppli and James D. Shilling, "Speed of Adjustment in Commercial Real Estate Markets," *Southern Economic Journal*, Vol. 61, No. 4, April 1995, 1127–45.

These assumptions imply

$$\hat{Y}_t = (ac) + (bc)X_{t-k} + (1-c)Y_{t-1}$$

or, in the notation for variables,

$$\hat{Y} = b_0 + b_1 X_{-k} + b_2 Y_{-1}$$

Eppli and Shilling introduced into the last model three dummy variables, Q_2, Q_3, and Q_4, representing, respectively, quarters 2, 3, and 4, and they experimented with different values of k, finding best results for $k = 12$. The regression results are

$$\hat{Y} = -2584 + 0.0324X_{-12} + 0.9608Y_{-1} - 1718Q_2 - 1255Q_3 - 1996Q_4 \qquad R^2 = 0.997$$
$$\phantom{\hat{Y} =} (-0.83) \quad (3.24) \qquad (48.04) \qquad (-1.52) \quad (-0.11) \quad (-1.72) \qquad S = 2652$$

The estimate of c is $1 - 0.9608$ or 0.0392, suggesting that the stock of commercial retail space adjusts slowly to desired levels.   ∎

7.7   TO SUM UP

- An unrestricted distributed lag model can be estimated by regressing the dependent variable against the current and lagged values of the explanatory variable.

- It is occasionally reasonable to suppose that the parameters of the lagged values of the explanatory variable follow a pattern and to impose restrictions on these parameters.

- Under a polynomial lag model the pattern of the parameters is approximated by a polynomial of an appropriate degree. The parameters of this model are estimated by regressing the dependent variable against "artificial" explanatory variables, which are linear combinations of the lagged values of the explanatory variable.

- When the parameters of the original distributed lag model decline steadily as the lag increases, a geometric lag model may be applicable. This model is estimated simply by regressing the dependent variable against the explanatory variable and the dependent variable lagged one period.

- The adaptive expectations and stock adjustment models are based on different assumptions but can be put into a final form very similar to that of the geometric lag model.

PROBLEMS

7.1 With the help of a computer program, confirm the results presented in this chapter.

7.2 Table 7.4 shows the values of a dependent variable (Y) and an explanatory variable (X) in each of 11 periods.

(a) Estimate the model $\hat{Y} = b + b_0 X + b_1 X_{-1} + b_2 \mu c X_{-2} + b_3 X_{-3}$.

(b) Approximate the parameters of the model in (a) by a polynomial of degree $m = 2$, that is, $b_j = d_0 + d_1 j + d_2 j^2$.

(c) Approximate the parameters of the model in (a) by the geometric model $b_j = bc^j$.

7.3 Same as in Problem 7.2, except use the data in Table 7.5.

7.4 Refer to the Lydia E. Pinkham case described in Example 7.3.

(a) Using the data in the file `lydia.dat`, reestimate Palda's model. Do your results agree with Palda's? If not, what is your estimate of the rate of return of advertising?

(b) Construct the appropriate geometric lag model (that is, the appropriate versions of the equation preceding Eq. 7.13), which imply the following models:

(i) $SALES = a(1 - c) + bADV_{-2} + cSALES_{-1}$
(ii) $\log SALES = a(1 - c) + bADV + c \log SALES_{-1}$
(iii) $SALES = a(1 - c) + b \log ADV + cSALES_{-1}$

(c) Implicit in the description of the case is the assumption that advertising *causes* sales—that sales, in other words, are influenced by advertising and not the other way round. Yet it could be argued that the close relationship between advertising and sales shown in Figure 7.4 is due to the fact that the company's sales in this and earlier years determine how

TABLE 7.4
Data for
Problem 7.2

X	Y
11.4	18.2
17.3	20.1
10.7	16.4
17.8	20.2
18.0	21.8
18.7	23.6
19.6	24.1
11.3	18.5
16.1	19.0
17.6	20.9
14.5	20.3

SOURCE: File
`lag1.dat`

TABLE 7.5
Data for
Problem 7.3

X	Y
15.7	15.4
15.2	14.7
21.1	16.2
21.1	20.0
19.4	20.5
19.2	19.4
20.8	19.4
21.2	20.6
24.9	22.2
23.2	24.2
23.8	23.9

SOURCE: File
`lag2.dat`

much will be spent on advertising this year: when sales are high, advertising outlay is high; when sales are low, the company can afford to spend less on advertising.

Indeed, a regression of A on S, S_{-1}, and D1, D2, D3 yields good results:

$$A = -165.0 + 0.463S + 0.093S_{-1} + 132.0D1 - 45.0D2 + 257.0D3$$
$$\quad\quad (3.93) \quad (0.084) \quad\quad (1.60) \quad (-0.65) \quad (4.53)$$

$$S = 164 \quad R^2 = 0.825 \quad n = 53$$

Can the regression results be used to determine the direction of causality in this case? In general?

7.5 Suppose there is a relationship between the current value of Y, on the one hand, and the current and two lagged values of an explanatory variable X, on the other:

$$Y = b + b_0 X + b_1 X_{-1} + b_2 X_{-2}$$

Assume that a polynomial of degree 1 can approximate the pattern of the b_j, that is,

$$b_j = d_0 + d_1 j \quad\quad (j = 0, 1, 2)$$

(a) Derive the polynomial distributed lag model of this case, which takes the form

$$Y = b + d_0 Z_0 + d_1 Z_1$$

Show the relationships between Z_0 and Z_1, on the one hand, and X, X_{-1}, and X_{-2}, on the other.

(b) Given the following data

Y	X
16	5
15	4
18	7
30	8

calculate the values of Z_0 and Z_1, and describe how the distributed lag model will be estimated.

7.6 Consider the model $\hat{Y} = b + b_0 X + b_1 X_{-1} + b_2 X_{-2} + b_3 X_{-3} + b_4 X_{-4}$ and suppose its parameters are approximated by a polynomial of degree $m = 3$, $b_j = d_0 + d_1 j + d_2 j^2 + d_3 j^3$.

Derive the equations relating the b_j to the d_j and the artificial to the lagged variables. Explain how the d's and b's will be estimated.

7.7 Suppose the geometric lag model begins after two periods, that is,

$$\hat{Y} = a + b_0 X + b_1 X_{-1} + \underbrace{b_2 X_{-2} + (b_2 c)X_{-3} + (b_2 c^2)X_{-4} + \cdots}_{\text{geometric lag}}$$

Show that this can be written as

$$\hat{Y} = a(1 - c) + b_0 X + (b_1 - b_0 c)X_{-1} + (b_2 - b_1 c)X_{-2} + cY_{-1}$$

7.8 Suppose two explanatory variables, X and Z, follow a geometric lag model with the same parameter c, $0 < c < 1$. That is,

$$\hat{Y} = a + bX + bcX_{-1} + (bc^2)X_{-2} + \cdots + dZ + (dc)Z_{-1} + (dc^2)Z_{-2} + \cdots$$

Show that this model can be written as

$$\hat{Y} = a(1 - c) + bX + dZ + cY_{-1}$$

7.9 Consider the adaptive expectations model described in Section 7.5 but suppose that the anticipated value of X, X_t^*, is formed according to

$$X_t^* - X_{t-1}^* = c(X_{t-1} - X_{t-1}^*).$$

All other assumptions being the same as in Section 7.5, show how Eq. 7.19 should be modified. Briefly interpret these modifications.

7.10 Consider the stock adjustment model described in Section 7.6 but suppose that the desired value of Y, Y_t^*, is formed according to

$$Y_t^* = a + bX_{t-1}$$

All other assumptions being the same as in Section 7.6, derive the final form of the stock adjustment model. Explain how to estimate the parameters of this model.

7.11 The computer file `housing.dat` contains the number of housing permits issued (*PERMITS*), the number of housing units started (*STARTS*), and the number of housing units completed

TABLE 7.6   File `housing.dat`, Partial Listing

OBS	PERMITS	STARTS	COMPLETIONS
1	2161	2126	4472
2	2999	1402	3156
3	4795	2271	4061
4	8584	4075	3655
5	10470	8213	3875
6	7908	8054	3015
7	8065	6326	4057
8	6085	6128	4618
9	6452	6622	4644
10	6639	6209	5713
...	...	...	...

(*COMPLETIONS*) in each of 312 consecutive months in a certain region. The first 10 observations in this file are listed in Table 7.6, and the general patterns of the three series are shown in Figure 7.5. (These are not the same data used in Example 7.1.)

(a) Estimate an appropriate unrestricted regression model relating housing starts to current and lagged permits issued.

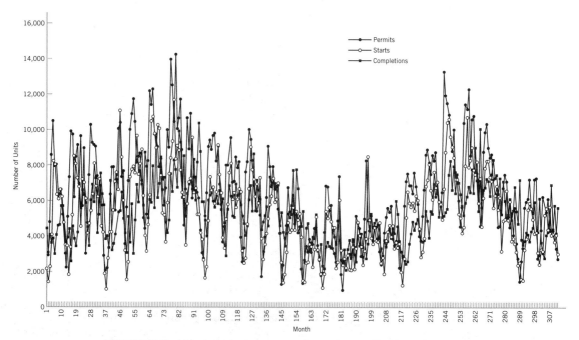

FIGURE 7.5   Housing permits, starts and completions, Problem 7.11

(b) Estimate an appropriate unrestricted regression model relating housing completions to current and lagged housing starts.

(c) Estimate an appropriate unrestricted regression model relating housing completions to current and lagged permits issued.

(d) Interpret your findings in (a) through (c). Are there other important explanatory variables that influence the dependent variable in each case?

(e) Reformulate (a) through (c), if necessary, so that the regression models are suitable for forecasting.

(f) For each of (a) through (c), investigate the desirability of a polynomial distributed lag model. Explain the advantages and disadvantages of these models in relation to the unrestricted models in (a) through (c).

(g) For each of (a) through (c), investigate the desirability of a geometric lag model. Explain the advantages and disadvantages of these models in relation to the unrestricted ones in (a) through (c) and the polynomial models in (f).

7.12 (Due to Mr. B. Cooke) When the holder of an insurance policy (life, automobile, home, etc.) makes a claim, the amount of the claim and the time at which it will be paid may not be known. Consider, for example, a car accident involving personal injuries as well as property damage; the payments by the insurance companies may have to be settled in court, and that could be several years after the accident.

When a claim is not settled in the year in which it arises, the insurance company charges that year's revenue with an *estimate* of the amount of the claim and sets up a reserve of equal amount. The sum of these reserves is the *loss reserve* for the year. Separate loss reserves are set up for different lines of insurance (e.g., automobile—bodily injury, automobile—property damage, fire, etc.). These reserves are reduced when claims are settled and payments made but may also be increased if it is determined that the original estimate was low.

Accurate forecasts of payments from the loss reserve are valuable because they allow the company to invest the reserve in assets of suitable maturity rather than entirely in low-yielding liquid assets.

(a) Table 7.7 shows an insurance company's loss reserves for automobile property damage claims over a period of 11 years.

For example, at the end of Year 2, the company established a loss reserve of $2881 (000) for claims arising but not settled in Year 2. At the end of Year 3, this particular reserve was reduced to $527 (000), indicating a net change of $2354 (000) for Year 2 claims settled in Year 3.

Forecast the total remaining loss reserve at the end of Year 12 due to the loss reserves set up in Years 2 to 11. Explain in detail the method you used and any assumptions you made.

(b) Same as (a), except use the data of Table 7.8 showing the same company's loss reserves for automobile bodily injury claims.

Note that some loss reserves increase in later years because adjustments for originally low estimates exceed payments.

TABLE 7.7   Loss Reserves, Automobile, Property Damage ($000)

Year set up	1	2	3	4	Reserve at end of year 5	6	7	8	9	10	11
1	2656	488	212	90	38	28	11	2	2	8	0
2		2881	527	190	110	57	12	9	6	2	1
3			3407	446	136	88	35	19	7	5	1
4				3174	442	232	227	123	92	6	3
5					4068	498	164	77	18	4	0
6						3691	718	406	296	35	20
7							3415	420	214	58	41
8								3836	664	309	212
9									5003	997	450
10										4571	754
11											4823

SOURCE: File `reserv1.dat`

TABLE 7.8   Loss Reserves, Automobile, Bodily Injury ($000)

Year set up	1	2	3	4	Reserve at end of year 5	6	7	8	9	10	11
1	5001	3989	2952	1514	751	514	340	389	396	394	392
2		3755	3910	2853	2011	952	394	416	268	175	167
3			4404	4317	3306	2387	1301	650	285	214	210
4				4282	3835	3657	2635	1214	1228	420	265
5					4456	5203	4031	3010	2093	1139	572
6						5477	6665	4968	5187	1882	2301
7							5683	7483	7979	6282	5008
8								10729	13599	12735	10438
9									18413	19032	15700
10										15214	15990
11											16865

SOURCE: File `reserv2.dat`

CHAPTER 8

REGRESSION MISCELLANEA

8.I INTRODUCTION AND SUMMARY

We now plan to look at a number of special problems in regression and the methods for solving some of them.

In certain situations, common sense suggests that the estimate of the dependent variable should be equal to zero when the values of all explanatory variables are zero. For example, in a linear model relating aggregate commissions to aggregate sales, commissions are normally expected to be zero when there are no sales. Such situations call for regression with no intercept, the first of the special methods examined in this chapter.

We shall see that regression with no intercept is a special case of least-squares estimation subject to a set of linear equality constraints on the model's parameters. The requirements that the estimates of two parameters be equal or that the sum of the estimates of a set of parameters be equal to 1 are other examples of such constraints.

Even more general is the problem of least-squares estimation that is subject to a set of linear equality *and* inequality constraints, which is considered next in this chapter. In a given situation, for example, we may expect certain parameters to be positive and others negative. We may thus want to find the values of the parameters that best fit the observations but also conform to these expectations.

The objective of least-squares estimation is to minimize the sum of the squared deviations (residuals, errors). An equally appealing goal, however, is the minimization of the sum of *absolute* deviations. Estimates of a linear model's parameters that satisfy this objective can be obtained by the least absolute deviations method, which, as we shall see, can be implemented with a little more effort than OLS.

As we observed in Chapter 4, exact linear relationships between "natural" explanatory variables do not occur frequently in practice, but approximate ones do. The presence of such approximate relationships is called "multicollinearity," and as a rule it cannot be avoided. Awareness of the consequences of multicollinearity, however, helps to prevent unwarranted conclusions from being drawn from the regression results.

Stepwise regression is a technique by which explanatory variables are brought into or removed from the model one at a time according to their contribution to the model at each step. Stepwise regression and kindred methods can assist in selecting from a large number of available explanatory variables.

Experiments, in contrast to other sources of information, let the experimenter control the number of observations and the values of the explanatory variables. Experimental design is a large and complicated subject that we cannot treat justly within the limits of this text. In the final section of this chapter, however, we develop some simple rules for designing experiments that ought to serve reasonably well at least until an experimenter understands the criteria by which even better rules are constructed.

8.2 REGRESSION WITH ZERO INTERCEPT

Consider the linear model

$$\hat{Y} = b_0 + b_1 X_1 + b_2 X_2 + \cdots + b_k X_k \tag{8.1}$$

and recall from Section 2.6 the interpretation of b_0 (the Y-intercept) as the estimated value of Y when all the X's are equal to zero. In some situations, $\hat{Y}$ *ought* to be zero when all the X's are zero, in which case an appropriate model is

$$\hat{Y} = b_1 X_1 + b_2 X_2 + \cdots + b_k X_k \tag{8.2}$$

This is, of course, a special case of Eq. 8.1 with $b_0 = 0$. The least-squares problem is now to find values of $b_1, b_2, \ldots, b_k$ in 8.2 that minimize

$$\sum (Y - \hat{Y})^2 = \sum (Y - b_1 X_1 - b_2 X_2 - \cdots - b_k X_k)^2$$

When there is only one explanatory variable—that is, $\hat{Y} = bX$—the least-squares estimate b can be shown to be (see Appendix B.6)

$$b = \frac{\sum XY}{\sum X^2}$$

For the general Model 8.2, the least-squares estimates $b_1, b_2, \ldots, b_k$ are calculated by computer programs providing the so-called no-intercept option (sometimes described as "forcing the Y-intercept to equal zero"). It will be recalled from Section 4.3 that the term b_0 can be regarded as the parameter of a variable X_0 that always takes the value 1. Thus, forcing b_0 to equal zero is nothing other than not using X_0.

EXAMPLE 8.1

In Example 2.1 of Section 2.10, we had related the price of a residential real estate property (*PRICE*, in $000) to its floor area (*FLOOR*) and lot size (*LOT*). Using the data on 100 properties contained in the file rest.dat, we had estimated this relationship as follows:

$$\widehat{PRICE} = 69.854 + 0.203\,FLOOR + 0.022\,LOT \qquad R^2 = 0.54$$
$$(2.34)(8.60)(6.03)S = 102.469$$

Strictly speaking, we should conclude that $69,854 is the estimated price of a property with zero floor and lot area. Of course, almost by definition, a residential property must have a positive lot size and, if the study is restricted to nonvacant lots, a positive floor area as well. It is understood, therefore, that the model applies in the neighborhood of the observations, in which case the strict interpretation does not apply. But suppose we wish to estimate instead the model

$$\widehat{PRICE} = b_1\,FLOOR + b_2\,LOT$$

Figure 8.1 shows the edited output of program Minitab for the regression of PRICE against FLOOR and LOT with no intercept.[1]

The regression results can also be summarized as follows:

$$\widehat{PRICE} = 0.243\,FLOOR + 0.027\,LOT \qquad S = 104.8$$
$$(14.72)(8.74)$$ ∎

Two additional remarks should be made about models with zero intercept. First, the sum of the residuals $\hat{\varepsilon}$ of such a model—unlike that of the unrestricted model—is not necessarily equal to zero. Second, the coefficient of

```
The regression equation is
price = 0.243 floor + 0.0266 lot

Predictor        Coef        Stdev      t-ratio          p
Noconstant
floor         0.24306      0.01652      14.72        0.000
lot          0.026580     0.003041       8.74        0.000

s = 104.8
```

FIGURE 8.1 Minitab output, Example 8.1

[1]The Minitab statements are regress 'price' 2 'floor' 'lot'; noconst.

determination, the (unadjusted) R^2, cannot be interpreted as a measure of the contribution of all explanatory variables. This is so because the "partial model" of Section 2.9 (the result of omitting all explanatory variables) is not defined. When the model has no intercept, an R^2 calculated according to Eq. 2.13 may be negative, something that cannot happen in a model with intercept. For the last reason, most computer programs do not print or display the R^2 of a model with no intercept.

8.3 LINEAR EQUALITY CONSTRAINTS

Regression with no intercept is an instance of least-squares estimation subject to one or more linear equality constraints on the model's parameters. For example, it may be desired to find the values of the parameters b_0, b_1, b_2, and b_3 of the model

$$\hat{Y} = b_0 + b_1 X_1 + b_2 X_2 + b_3 X_3$$

that minimize $\sum (Y - \hat{Y})^2$ subject to the constraint that $b_1 + b_2 + b_3 = 1$. Or, the constraint could be $b_1 = b_2$, that is, $b_1 - b_2 = 0$. Or, it may be required that the following two linear constraints be satisfied:

$$b_1 + b_2 + b_3 = 1$$

and

$$b_1 - b_2 = 0$$

In regression with zero intercept, the constraint is $b_0 = 0$.

In general, the problem is to find the values of the parameters $b_0, b_1, b_2, \ldots, b_k$ of the model

$$\hat{Y} = b_0 + b_1 X_1 + b_2 X_2 + \cdots + b_k X_k$$

that minimize

$$\sum (Y - \hat{Y})^2 = \sum (Y - b_0 - b_1 X_1 - b_2 X_2 - \cdots - b_k X_k)^2$$

subject to r constraints of the form

$$c_{0i} b_0 + c_{1i} b_1 + c_{2i} b_2 + \cdots + c_{ki} b_k = c_i, \qquad (i = 1, 2, \cdots, r)$$

where the c's are given numbers.

Readers familiar with advanced calculus will recognize this as a constrained optimization problem that can be solved with the use of Lagrange multipliers.[2] Several statistical programs implement this method and perform the calculations.

EXAMPLE 8.2

Table 8.1 shows the number of housing units started (X) and completed (Y) in a certain region each month during a five-year period.

As in Example 7.1, it is reasonable to assume that of the housing units started this month, some are completed this month, others next month, still others two, three, ..., k months hence. Put differently, of the housing units completed this month, some were started this month, others last month, still others two, three, ..., k months ago. This reasoning suggests the model

$$\hat{Y} = b + b_0 X + b_1 X_{-1} + b_2 X_{-2} + \cdots + b_k X_{-k}$$

where X_{-j} denotes the number of housing units started j months ago. For example, if it is assumed that $k = 2$, the least-squares estimates of the model

$$\hat{Y} = b + b_0 X + b_1 X_{-1} + b_2 X_2$$

are as follows:

$$\hat{Y} = -401 + 0.162\,X + 0.455\,X_{-1} + 0.250\,X_{-2}, \quad R^2 = 0.77$$
$$(-0.78) \quad (2.24) \quad\quad (5.08) \quad\quad\quad (3.38) \quad\quad\quad S = 970$$

The model is based on $n = 58$ observations (the first two observations in Table 8.1 are not used because the values of X_{-2} are missing for March and April, 19X4). For future reference, we note that the sum of squared residuals of this model is $SSE = 50,855,235$.

TABLE 8.1 Housing Starts and Completions, Example 8.2

Year	Month	Starts, X	Completions, Y
19X4	Mar.	4102	3731
	Apr.	4845	2939
...	...	...	...
19X9	Feb.	3659	5947

SOURCE: File stcomp.dat

[2]See, for example, Johnston (1984, Ch. 6) and Theil (1971, Ch. 1).

The results indicate that 16.2% of the housing starts this month, 45.5% of those one month ago, and 25% of the starts two months ago are completed this month.

Now, if all housing starts are completed within two months of their start, we should expect $b = 0$ and $b_0 + b_1 + b_2 = 1$.[3] A model consistent with these expectations, therefore, is

$$\hat{Y} = b + b_0 X + b_1 X_{-1} + b_2 X_2$$

```
Model: MODEL1
NOTE: Restrictions have been applied to parameter estimates.
Dependent Variable: COMPL
```

Analysis of Variance

Source	DF	Sum of Squares	Mean Square	F Value	Prob>F
Model	1	55221478.26	55221478.26	18.503	0.0001
Error	56	167133937.9	2984534.6053		
C Total	57	222355416.16			

Root MSE	1727.58056	R-square	0.2483	
Dep Mean	6101.87931	Adj R-sq	0.2349	
C.V.	28.31227			

Parameter Estimates

Variable	DF	Parameter Estimate	Standard Error	T for H0: Parameter=0	Prob > |T|
INTERCEP	1	-1.54394E-13	0.00000000	.	.
START	1	0.223235	0.11840245	1.885	0.0646
STL1	1	0.449332	0.15813491	2.841	0.0063
STL2	1	0.327433	0.12245409	2.674	0.0098
RESTRICT	-1	-80762	13150.181360	-6.142	0.0001
RESTRICT	-1	-632474862	101576573.28	-6.227	0.0001

FIGURE 8.2 SAS output, Example 8.2

[3]For the b's to be interpreted as proportions, it is also necessary that $b_0 \geq 0$, $b_1 \geq 0$, and $b_2 \geq 0$. We do not impose these inequality constraints explicitly in the hope that they will be satisfied in fact. We consider inequality constraints in the next section.

where $b = 0$ and $b_0 + b_1 + b_2 = 1$. Figure 8.2 shows the output of program SAS giving the restricted least-squares estimates for this problem and the data outlined in Table 8.1.[4]

In the more familiar format, the results can be presented as follows:

$$\hat{Y} = \underset{(1.88)}{0.223\,X} + \underset{(2.84)}{0.449\,X_{-1}} + \underset{(2.67)}{0.328\,X_{-2}} \qquad S = 1728$$

∎

In general, the fit of the constrained model cannot be better than that of the unconstrained one. A substantial loss of fit is an indication that the constraints and the implied assumptions are not supported by the evidence. We may measure the effect of the constraints by calculating a modified Q-statistic,

$$Q = \frac{SSE_C - SSE_U}{SSE_C}$$

where SSE_C is the sum of squared residuals of the constrained model and SSE_U that of the unconstrained model. In effect, Q measures the relative improvement in the fit of the constrained model resulting from abandoning the constraints.

EXAMPLE 8.2 (CONTINUED)

For the unconstrained model, we have $SSE_U = 50,855,235$; for the constrained model, $SSE_C = 167,133,938$. Therefore,

$$Q = \frac{167,133,938 - 50,855,235}{167,133,938} = 0.696$$

The fit of the constrained model would improve by about 70% if the two constraints were lifted. This rather large figure indicates that the constraints are very costly in terms of fit. Thus, the assumption that all housing units are completed within two months of their start should probably be rejected. ∎

EXAMPLE 8.3

In Example 4.3, we assumed that the task-completion time (Y) is a function of two attributes, operator and time of day, and wrote

$$\hat{Y} = b_0 + b_1 X_1 + b_2 X_2 + b_3 X_3 + b_4 X_4 + c_1 Z_1 + c_2 Z_2 + c_3 Z_3 \qquad (8.3)$$

---

[4]The SAS statements are `proc reg; model compl = start stl1 stl2; restrict intercept=0, start+stl1+stl2=1;`. The t-ratios have the same interpretation as in OLS. For our purposes, the two lines in the output beginning with `RESTRICT` can be ignored.

where the X's and Z's are dummy variables representing the four operators and the three times of day, respectively. The data are shown in Table 4.9.

We noted that unique OLS estimates are obtained by imposing two constraints:

$$b_1 + b_2 + b_3 + b_4 = 0$$
$$c_1 + c_2 + c_3 = 0 \tag{8.4}$$

The restricted (and unique) OLS estimates can be easily calculated from the row and column means of the observations when these are arranged in the form of a two-way table.

These calculations can also be confirmed by applying the framework of this section. Specifically, we seek values of $b_0, b_1, \ldots, b_4, c_1, \ldots, c_3$ that minimize $\sum (Y - \hat{Y})^2$, where $\hat{Y}$ is given by Eq. 8.3, subject to the constraints shown in Eq. 8.4. Figure 8.3 shows the output of program SAS for this problem.[5]

We see that $b_0 = 16.5$, $b_1 = -1.5$, $c_1 = -1.25$, and so on, in agreement with the calculations of Example 4.3.   ∎

8.4   LINEAR EQUALITY AND INEQUALITY CONSTRAINTS

In this version of the regression problem, the task is to find the values of the parameters $b_0, b_1, b_2, \ldots, b_k$ of the model

$$\hat{Y} = b_0 + b_1 X_1 + b_2 X_2 + \cdots + b_k X_k$$

that minimize

$$\sum \hat{\varepsilon}^2 = \sum (Y - \hat{Y})^2 = \sum (Y - b_0 - b_1 X_1 - b_2 X_2 - \cdots - b_k X_k)^2$$

subject to r constraints of the form

$$c_{0i} b_0 + c_{1i} b_1 + c_{2i} b_2 + \cdots + c_{ki} b_k \quad (\leq, =, \text{ or } \geq) \quad c_i, \qquad (i = 1, 2, \cdots, r)$$

where the c's are given numbers.

Minimizing a quadratic function of the parameters subject to a set of linear equality or inequality constraints is known as a *quadratic programming problem*

---

[5]The SAS statements are `proc reg; model time = x1 -- x4 z1 -- z3; restrict x1+x2+x3+x4=0, z1+z2+z3=0;`.

```
Model: MODEL1
NOTE: Restrictions have been applied to parameter estimates.
Dependent Variable: TIME
```

Analysis of Variance

Source	DF	Sum of Squares	Mean Square	F Value	Prob>F
Model	5	30.50000	6.10000	14.640	0.0026
Error	6	2.50000	0.41667		
C Total	11	33.00000			

Root MSE	0.64550	R-square	0.9242	
Dep Mean	16.50000	Adj R-sq	0.8611	
C.V.	3.91210			

Parameter Estimates

Variable	DF	Parameter Estimate	Standard Error	T for H0: Parameter=0	Prob > |T|
INTERCEP	1	16.500000	0.18633900	88.548	0.0001
X1	1	-1.500000	0.32274861	-4.648	0.0035
X2	1	0.500000	0.32274861	1.549	0.1723
X3	1	1.500000	0.32274861	4.648	0.0035
X4	1	-0.500000	0.32274861	-1.549	0.1723
Z1	1	-1.250000	0.26352314	-4.743	0.0032
Z2	1	-0.250000	0.26352314	-0.949	0.3794
Z3	1	1.500000	0.26352314	5.692	0.0013
RESTRICT	-1	0	0.00000000	.	.
RESTRICT	-1	2.775558E-16	0.00000001	0.000	1.0000

FIGURE 8.3 SAS output, Example 8.3

and can be solved with the help of special computer programs.[6] Such a problem arises, for example, when there are strong a priori reasons for requiring that some parameters of the model have a specified sign.

---

[6]The quadratric programming problem and its better-known relation, the *linear programming problem,* are special cases of the *mathematical programming problem,* which involves the minimization or maximization of an objective function subject to a set of linear or nonlinear equality or inequality constraints. Linear, quadratic, and mathematical programming are described in introductory operations research and management science texts.

EXAMPLE 8.4

In Example 2.4, we had estimated the demand for beef by regressing the per capita consumption of beef (QB) against the deflated retail price indexes of beef (DPB), pork (DPP), and other meats ($DPOM$) and the per capita deflated personal disposable income ($DPDI$). The data, consisting of 20 annual observations, are shown in Table 2.6 and can be found in the file `bfpk.dat`. The unrestricted regression results are reproduced below:

$$\widehat{QB} = 44.756 - 0.403DPB + 0.171DPP - 0.087DPOM + 4.085DPDI$$
$$\quad (6.08) \qquad (-2.87) \qquad (1.99) \qquad (-0.55) \qquad (17.97)$$

$$R^2 = 0.98 \quad S = 1.456$$

As we observed in Example 2.4, when other variables are held constant, a rise in beef consumption is expected to result from a drop in the price of beef, a rise in the price of pork, a rise in the price of other meats, or a rise in income. The estimate of the coefficient of $DPOM$ is inconsistent with this expectation.

We may be willing to sacrifice some goodness of fit in order to obtain estimates conforming to these expectations. We may therefore seek to find values of $b_0, b_1, \ldots, b_4$ of the model

$$\widehat{QB} = b_0 + b_1 DPB + b_2 DPP + b_3 DPOM + b_4 DPDI$$

that minimize $\sum \hat{\varepsilon}^2$ subject to the constraints $b_1 \leq 0, b_2 \geq 0, b_3 \geq 0$, and $b_4 \geq 0$.

Figure 8.4 shows the problem formulation in terms of the Solver tool of Microsoft Excel. PQB is $\widehat{QB}$, SSE is $\sum \hat{\varepsilon}^2$, and the initial values of $b_0, b_1, \ldots, b_4$ are the unconstrained OLS estimates. We note that $SSE = 42.427$ (slight differences are due to rounding).

The solution to the constrained problem (not shown in Figure 8.4) is

$$QB = 44.756 - 0.476DPB + 0.145DPP - 0DPOM + 4.171DPDI$$

$$SSE = 43.242 \qquad S = 1.470$$

In the constrained solution, it can be noted, the retail price of other meats is estimated to have no effect on the per capita consumption of beef.   ∎

As in regression with equality constraints only, the fit of the constrained model cannot be better than that of the unconstrained one. The same modified Q-statistic,

$$Q = \frac{SSE_C - SSE_U}{SSE_C}$$

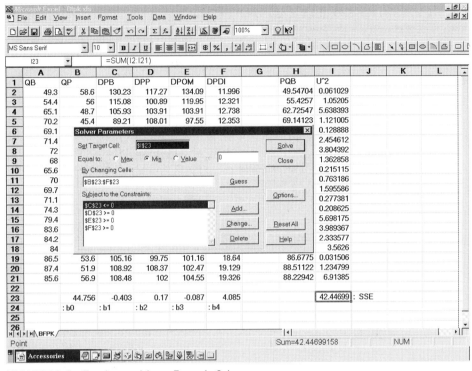

FIGURE 8.4 Excel spreadsheet, Example 8.4

can be used to measure the effect of the constraints on the fit of the model. In the last expression, SSE_C is the sum of squared residuals of the constrained model and SSE_U that of the unconstrained model. The constraints and the implied assumptions should be rejected if the loss of fit is substantial.

EXAMPLE 8.4 (CONTINUED)

The effect of requiring that the coefficients of the demand function agree with a priori expectations is measured by

$$Q = \frac{SSE_C - SSE_U}{SSE_C} = \frac{43.242 - 42.427}{43.242} = 0.019$$

In other words, the fit of the constrained model would improve by only 1.9% if the constraints were lifted. As this figure is rather low, we should probably accept the assumption that $b_1 \leq 0$, $b_2 \geq 0$, $b_3 \geq 0$, and $b_4 \geq 0$. ∎

8.5 LEAST ABSOLUTE DEVIATIONS

The least-squares problem, as we so often repeated, is to find the values of the parameters $b_0, b_1, \ldots, b_k$ that minimize the sum of the squared deviations

$$\sum (Y - \hat{Y})^2 = \sum (Y - b_0 - b_1 X_1 - b_2 X_2 - \cdots - b_k X_k)^2$$

In Section 2.3, we observed that another criterion of fit, the minimization of the sum of absolute deviations, is also reasonable but not popular because it is not mathematically convenient. Under this criterion, we seek the values of the parameters $b_0, b_1, \ldots, b_k$ that minimize the sum of the absolute deviations

$$\sum |Y - \hat{Y}| = \sum |Y - b_0 - b_1 X_1 - b_2 X_2 - \cdots - b_k X_k|$$

We shall call this the *least absolute deviations (LAD)* problem and the resulting estimates the *LAD estimates* of the parameters.

Since the LAD criterion does not magnify the deviations as much as the least-squares one, the LAD estimates are not as sensitive to outliers (observations deviating substantially from the model) as the OLS estimates.

For given values of the parameters $b_0, b_1, \ldots, b_k$, the difference between the actual and estimated Y-value of the ith observation is

$$Y_i - b_0 - b_1 X_{1i} - b_2 X_{2i} - \cdots - b_k X_{ki} \qquad (i = 1, 2, \ldots, n)$$

This difference—whatever its sign—can be written as the difference between two *nonnegative* numbers, u_i and v_i, that is

$$Y_i - b_0 - b_1 X_{1i} - b_2 X_{2i} - \cdots - b_k X_{ki} = u_i - v_i \qquad (i = 1, 2, \ldots, n)$$

For example, if, for a given observation, the left-hand side is equal to -3, this can be expressed as $-3 = 5 - 8$, $-3 = 0 - 3$, $-3 = 6 - 9$, $-3 = 1 - 4$, and so on; if the left-hand side is, say, $+3$, it can be expressed as $+4 = 25 - 21$, $+4 = 4 - 0$, and so on.

Among the many choices for the pair (u_i, v_i), the one in which one of the elements is zero minimizes the sum $u_i + v_i$. For example, among all pairs (u_i, v_i) such that $u_i - v_i = -3$, the pair $(0, 3)$ clearly minimizes $u_i + v_i$. In such a pair, the nonzero element is equal to the absolute deviation of the observation,

$$|Y_i - b_0 - b_1 X_{1i} - b_2 X_{2i} - \cdots - b_k X_{ki}|$$

The LAD problem, therefore, can be formulated as follows. Find the values of $b_0, b_1, \ldots, b_k$ *and* of the u_i and v_i that minimize

$$\sum_{i=1}^{n} (u_i + v_i),$$

subject to

$$Y_i - b_0 - b_1 X_{1i} - b_2 X_{2i} - \cdots - b_k X_{ki} = u_i - v_i$$

and

$$u_i \geq 0, \qquad v_i \geq 0$$

for $i = 1, 2, \ldots, n$.

This is a *linear programming problem* and can be solved easily with the help of widely available computer programs.

EXAMPLE 8.5

To illustrate the formulation, let us consider a small artificial example involving one explanatory variable and three observations:

Y	X
3	3
5	4
2	1

We introduce one pair of variables (u_i, v_i) for each of the three observations, and write the constraints as

$$
\begin{aligned}
3 - b_0 - 3b_1 &= u_1 - v_1 \\
5 - b_0 - 4b_1 &= u_2 - v_2 \\
2 - b_0 - 1b_1 &= u_3 - v_3
\end{aligned}
$$

The linear programming problem is to minimize

$$0 b_0 + 0 b_1 + 1 u_1 + 1 v_1 + 1 u_2 + 1 v_2 + 1 u_3 + 1 v_3$$

subject to

$$
\begin{aligned}
3 - 1b_0 - 3b_1 - 1u_1 + 1v_1 + 0u_2 + 0v_2 + 0u_3 + 0v_3 &= 0 \\
5 - 1b_0 - 4b_1 + 0u_1 + 0v_1 - 1u_2 + 1v_2 + 0u_3 + 0v_3 &= 0 \\
2 - 1b_0 - 1b_1 + 0u_1 + 0v_1 + 0u_2 + 0v_2 - 1u_3 + 1v_3 &= 0
\end{aligned}
$$

and all $u_i \geq 0$ and $v_i \geq 0$. ∎

EXAMPLE 8.6

In Example 2.2, we had estimated by the method of least-squares the following relationship between daily gas consumption (*GASCON*), on the one hand, and temperature (*TEMP*) and wind speed (*WIND*), on the other

$$\widehat{GASCON} = 22952 - 863\,TEMP + 163\,WIND \qquad R^2 = 0.96$$
$$(36.59) \qquad (-20.90) \qquad (2.53) \qquad S = 1376$$

The data in the file `gascon.dat` are now used to calculate the estimates of the parameters that minimize the sum of absolute deviations. Figure 8.5 displays the problem formulation using the Solver tool of Microsoft Excel.

The starting values of the parameters ($b_0 = 23000$, $b_1 = -850$, and $b_2 = 150$) are arbitrary. *ESTIMATED* stands for

$$\widehat{GASCON} = b_0 + b_1\,TEMP + b_2\,WIND$$

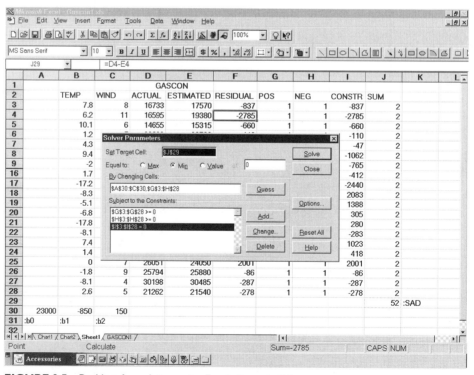

FIGURE 8.5 Problem formulation using Excel, Example 8.6

and *RESIDUAL* for

$$GASCON - \widehat{GASCON}$$

The u_i and v_i are given the arbitrary value 1 and are listed under the labels *POS* and *NEG*, respectively. *CONSTR* stands for

$$GASCON - \widehat{GASCON} - POS + NEG$$

and *SUM* is equal to *POS* + *NEG*. The sum of the *SUM* values (:*SAD*) is the objective function to be minimized. The constraints are as explained in Example 8.5.

Solving the problem gives the LAD estimates (not shown in Figure 8.5), which are

$$\widehat{GASCON} = 23182 - 882\,TEMP + 114\,WIND$$

For this example, the LAD and OLS estimates are fairly close. The average absolute deviation (the counterpart of S under least-squares) is 1004. Figure 8.6 shows the actual gas consumption and the LAD estimates, which can be compared with those of Model B shown in Figure 2.7. ∎

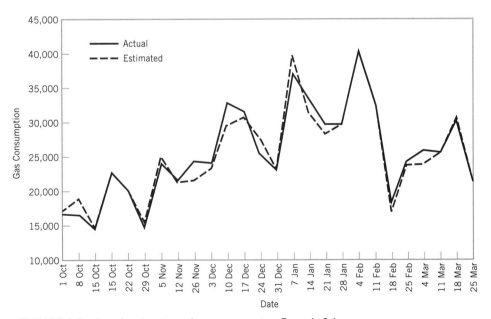

FIGURE 8.6 Actual and estimated gas consumption, Example 8.6

8.6 MULTICOLLINEARITY

In Section 4.3, we described extreme collinearity, the presence of an exact linear relationship between explanatory variables and two problems its presence creates. As noted there, extreme collinearity is unlikely to arise in situations where the observations are many and the explanatory variables are not artificially created. Often in practice, however, we encounter situations where one or more columns of the matrix X of explanatory variables or attributes (see Section 4.3) can be closely *approximated* by a linear combination of other columns.

Consider, for example, the relationship between the value of a residential property (as measured by its selling price, Y) and two of its features: lot size (X_1) and floor area (X_2). Most of us probably believe that large houses tend to be built in large, and small houses in small, lots. There are exceptions, of course, so we do not expect the relationship between X_1 and X_2 to be exact, but approximate and perhaps linear, $X_1 \approx c + dX_2$.

The presence of such approximate linear relationships between the columns of X is called *multicollinearity*. Multicollinearity occurs quite frequently in economic and business studies. Three consequences of multicollinearity may be mentioned briefly.

- It may be difficult to estimate with precision the effect of each related explanatory variable. Roughly speaking, if some explanatory variables are related to one another, each such variable serves as a close substitute for the others. Although we can tell how well these explanatory variables *collectively* help explain the dependent variable, it is difficult to determine precisely the individual effect of each. Chances are that small changes to the OLS estimates of the parameters of the related variables will not result in a substantial reduction of the fit of the model.

- Leaving out one of the related variables may alter substantially the estimated values of the parameters of the remaining variables.

- Small changes or additions to the observations may produce substantial changes in the regression estimates.

To illustrate, suppose four sets of observations are available on Y and two explanatory variables, X_1 and X_2, as follows:

Y	X_0	X_1	X_2	
8	1	2	3.00	
15	1	5	0.01	Matrix X
10	1	3	2.00	
13	1	4	1.00	

The example is identical to that of Section 4.3, except that the second observation on X_2 has the value 0.01 rather than 0 as in that section. There is now no *exact* linear relationship between the columns of the matrix X, but an *approximate* one: $X_2 \approx 5X_0 - X_1$, as can be verified in the manner of Section 4.3. Consequently, there is no technical problem in calculating unique OLS estimates of the model $\hat{Y} = b_0 + b_1 X_1 + b_2 X_2$, which are as follows:

$$\hat{Y} = 169.5 - 30.8333X_1 - 33.3333X_2 \qquad R^2 = 0.994$$
$$\phantom{\hat{Y} = }(0.46) \quad (-0.42) \qquad (-0.45) \qquad S = 0.408$$

Observe the low t-ratios and the very large R^2. It would be a mistake, of course, to conclude that *all* explanatory variables contribute little to the model because each t-ratio measures the contribution of the associated explanatory variable under the condition that the other explanatory variables remain in the model. The large R^2 provides evidence that the X's collectively explain a large proportion of the total variation of Y.

Table 8.2 shows five sets of values of b_0, b_1, and b_2 and the associated $SSE = \sum(Y - \hat{Y})^2$. The first is the set of OLS estimates, and 0.1667 is the minimum SSE. Set no. 3 is that of the OLS estimates of a model without X_2,

$$\hat{Y} = 3.1 + 2.4X_1 \qquad R^2 = 0.993$$
$$\phantom{\hat{Y} = }(5.97) \ (16.97) \qquad S = 0.316$$

Set no. 4 consists of the OLS estimates of a model without X_1,

$$\hat{Y} = 15.117 - 2.407X_2 \qquad R^2 = 0.993$$
$$\phantom{\hat{Y} = }(57.64) \ (-17.17) \qquad S = 0.313$$

The other two sets were arbitrarily determined to produce an SSE close to the minimum.

Note the disparity between these values as estimates of the effects of unit increases in X_1 and X_2. Yet the overall fit of each set is not perceptibly worse than the minimum, nor, as shown in Figure 8.7, are the $\hat{Y}$'s produced by each

TABLE 8.2 Multicollinearity Effects Illustrated

Set no.	b_0	b_1	b_2	SSE
1	169.5	−30.8333	−33.3333	0.1667
2	0	3.02	0.62	0.2013
3	3.1	2.4	0	0.2000
4	15.117	0	−2.407	0.1958
5	8.1	1.4	−1	0.1981

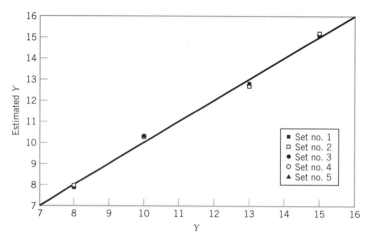

FIGURE 8.7   Actual and estimated Y, multicollinearity

set perceptibly different from the OLS ones (perfectly accurate estimates, i.e., all $\hat{Y} = Y$, would lie along the 45° line).

Now suppose the second observation on X_2 is changed to -0.01 from $+0.01$. The results of regressing Y against X_1 and X_2 are now

$$\hat{Y} = -163.833 + 35.833X_1 + 33.333X_2 \qquad R^2 = 0.994$$
$$(-0.44) \qquad (0.48) \qquad (0.45) \qquad S = 0.408$$

This very small change in one of the observations, therefore, produced radically different estimates of the effects of the explanatory variables.

The preceding example is rather extreme but makes clear that the presence of multicollinearity mandates caution in interpreting the OLS estimates. As we observed earlier, in most studies in practice the explanatory variables are related to one another to a greater or lesser degree. Unless the values of the variables can be controlled in advance (as in the experiments described in Example 2.3 and later in Section 8.8), not much can be done about these correlations.

At the very least, users of regression should be aware of the possibility that values of the parameters in the neighborhood of the OLS estimates may fit the observations almost as well as the latter. An examination of the correlation coefficients of all pairs of explanatory variables is recommended in cases where some explanatory variables are believed to be strongly related to one another. If the correlation coefficient of a pair of explanatory variables is very close to

1 in absolute value, the case can be treated as one of extreme collinearity and one of the related variables can be left out of the model.[7]

EXAMPLE 8.7

Let us return to the model first presented in Example 2.1,

$$\widehat{PRICE} = b_0 + b_1(FLOOR) + b_2(LOT)$$

relating the price of a residential real estate property to the floor area of the house and the size of the lot. The data in the file `rest.dat` allow us to calculate the correlation coefficient of *FLOOR* and *LOT*; it is equal to $+0.0336$.

Contrary to expectations, therefore, there is only a slight tendency for the floor area of the house to increase with the size of the lot. Since the two explanatory variables are not strongly correlated, the interpretation of the regression results in the continuation of Example 2.1 in Section 2.10 can be allowed to stand. ∎

8.7 STEPWISE AND ALL SUBSETS REGRESSION

Additional insight into the relationship between dependent and explanatory variables can sometimes be gained by building up the model, introducing one explanatory variable at a time, instead of regressing Y directly on all k available explanatory variables. *Stepwise regression* is actually a series of k regressions. At each step, that variable is introduced that contributes most in terms of the Q-statistic (Eq. 2.14) to the model of the previous step. The order in which the explanatory variables are introduced can be shown to result in the greatest possible increase in R^2 at each step. Stepwise regression is implemented by most computer programs for regression.

EXAMPLE 8.8

In Example 2.4, the per capita consumption of beef (QB) was assumed to be determined by the deflated price of beef (DPB), the price of pork (DPP), the price of other meats (DPOM), and personal per capita disposable income (DPDI). Figure 8.8 shows the Minitab output of stepwise regression applied to the data in Table 2.6 (file `bfpk.dat`).[8]

---

[7]The definition and interpretation of the correlation coefficient are reviewed in Appendix A.6. Later in Section 9.8 of this text, we describe "ridge regression," a technique said to produce more precise estimates of the regression parameters. For more on multicollinearity and possible remedies see, for example, Belsley (1991) and Chatterjee and Hadi (1988).

[8]The Minitab statements were `stepwise 'qb' 'dpb' ... 'dpdi'; fremove=0; fenter=0`.

```
STEPWISE REGRESSION OF     qb    ON   4 PREDICTORS, WITH N = 20
```

STEP	1	2	3	4
CONSTANT	13.35	56.27	44.76	44.76
dpdi	3.97	4.15	4.17	4.08
T-RATIO	8.75	23.60	25.84	17.97
dpb		-0.441	-0.476	-0.403
T-RATIO		-10.21	-11.05	-2.87
dpp			0.145	0.171
T-RATIO			2.07	1.99
dpom				-0.09
T-RATIO				-0.55
S	4.66	1.80	1.64	1.68
R-SQ	80.95	97.33	97.89	97.93

FIGURE 8.8   Minitab output, Example 8.8

The explanatory variables enter the model in the order DPDI, DPB, DPP, and DPOM. Among all explanatory variables, the one contributing most to the explanation of QB is DPDI (Step 1). Among the remaining variables, the one contributing most to the model having DPDI as the only explanatory variable is DPB (Step 2). DPP, among the remaining variables, contributes most to the model having QB and DPB as explanatory variables (Step 3). The last variable is DPOM, and the results of Step 4 are as first presented in Example 2.4.   ■

Stepwise regression can also be performed in reverse order. We begin with a regression that includes all available explanatory variables, then drop these variables from the model, one at a time, the order of exclusion being that which results in the smallest possible reduction in R^2 at each step.

Other criteria for exclusion or inclusion of variables are sometimes employed, but these are usually related to incremental R^2. Some stepwise programs will include variables only as long as the maximum possible increase in R^2 exceeds a predetermined number or until R^2 reaches a certain predetermined value. Still other computer programs check the variables in the model at the end of each step and remove any that become nearly redundant by the variable most recently included.

One limitation of stepwise regression should be noted: the m variables included in the model at the mth step are not necessarily those m of the available variables that yield the greatest R^2. In stepwise regression, only one variable is included or excluded at a time on the basis of its contribution to a model using the previously selected variables; thus, the procedure that maximizes the increment or minimizes the decrement in R^2 at the mth step does not necessarily find the subset of m variables that maximizes R^2 overall.

Some statistical programs provide procedures ("all subsets regression," "all possible regressions") designed to overcome this one limitation of stepwise regression. These programs examine the R^2 of each possible subset of 1, 2, 3, ... explanatory variables and display the regression results for the subset of variables maximizing R^2 at each step. Other statistics related to R^2 are also used.

When the number of available explanatory variables is large, stepwise or all subsets regression may help in deciding which subset of these variables to select for the final model. These mechanical methods, however, should not be considered substitutes for knowledge and experience, which in the large majority of cases in practice can be relied on for guidance regarding which explanatory variables are relevant or important. Injudicious use of stepwise and all subsets regression often results in little more than a large heap of computer output.

8.8 ELEMENTS OF EXPERIMENTAL DESIGN

A distinguishing feature of an experiment is that the number of observations and the values of the explanatory variables are not predetermined (as, say, with many time series) but can be controlled by the experimenter.

In Example 2.3, for instance, we described an experiment designed to estimate the relationship between the strength of a plastic material, on the one hand, and three factors influencing strength, on the other. The experiment consisted of subjecting pieces of the plastic material to 27 different combinations of three levels each of barrel temperature (320°, 370°, and 420°), mold temperature (100°, 125°, and 150°), and injection pressure (7000, 5000, and 3000 psi).

In the vocabulary of experimental design, a *factor* is an explanatory variable and a *level* is a value of such a variable. Observing or otherwise measuring the variable of interest (the *response*) at given factor levels is called a *trial*.

In this example and in Problems 3.6 and 4.15, we examined different forms of the relationship *given* the results of the experiment. Let us step back a moment, however, to consider how this experiment could be *designed*. For it is clear that before the experiment was conducted, decisions were made concerning the number of trials, the levels of each factor, and the particular combinations of factor levels used in each trial. A different design, for example, could have distinguished only two levels for each factor (say, 300° and 450° for barrel temperature, 120° and 160° for mold temperature, and 4000 and 6000 psi for injection pressure) and called for 16 trials in total—two at each of the eight different combinations of factor levels. In another design, the levels of injection pressure, barrel temperature, and mold temperature at each trial could be selected randomly from the range of possible values of each factor. Many other designs are possible. Are some designs better than others?

Let us consider first the simplest case in which the variable of interest (Y) is assumed to be influenced primarily by only one factor, the variable X. For example, Y could be the strength of the plastic material and X the injection pressure.

The range of values of X to be considered is the *experimental region* of this case. For example, it could be that the relevant range of injection pressures is from 2000 to 8000 psi because injection pressures outside this range are not feasible or are known to produce undesirable results.

Suppose that the ranges of the possible values of Y at each level of X within the experimental region form the shaded area shown in Figure 8.9(a). For example, the possible values of Y at $X = x_0$ lie in the interval from y_0' to y_0''.

Suppose further that only two trials will be conducted, that is, Y will be measured at two levels of X. In our example, the strength of the plastic material will be measured at two levels of injection pressure. What should these two levels be?

In Figure 8.9(b), the two levels of X, x_1 and x_2, are close to one another. The corresponding Y-values will lie along the dotted lines at x_1 and x_2. If the Y-values happened to be y_1'' and y_2', the relationship between Y and X would be estimated by line AA' in Figure 8.9(b), and the forecast of Y at any value of X would lie along this line. If the observed Y-values happened to be y_1' and y_2'', the forecasts of Y would lie along line BB'. Any other pair of Y-values would result in a forecast line lying in the shaded area $Ay_1''y_2''B'A'y_2'y_1'B$ of Figure 8.9(b). Observe that the range of forecasts is wider than the actual range at all levels of X outside the interval from x_1 to x_2. Actual and forecast ranges coincide for values of X in the interval from x_1 to x_2.

It seems reasonable, therefore, to select as the two levels of X the end points of the experimental region, as shown in Figure 8.9(c). Then, the actual and forecast ranges coincide for all levels of X in that region.

The same argument suggests that if there are to be more than two trials—in our example, if the strength of the plastic material is to be measured at more than two levels of injection pressure—then some of these trials should be at the low (x_1), and the others at the high (x_2), end of the experimental region, again as shown in Figure 8.9(c).

With such a design, however, there is the danger that the true form of the relationship will not be recognized. For if there are no observations in the interior of the experimental region, there is no way of detecting a nonlinear relationship between Y and X. As Figure 8.9(d) illustrates, if all the trials are carried out at the ends of the experimental region in the belief that the relationship is linear, the forecast region may not even be in contact with the actual one over certain intervals of X-values when the true relationship is nonlinear. To guard against this kind of error, it is prudent to select levels of the factor X between—as well as at—the two ends of the experimental region.

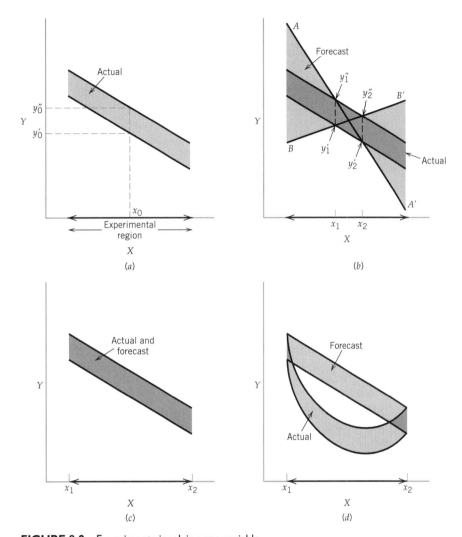

FIGURE 8.9 Experiments involving one variable

Three levels are sufficient to detect a parabolic relationship, four a polynomial of degree 3, and so on. Unless the relationship between Y and X is expected to be complicated, a simple and reasonably good design is to use three or four more or less equally spaced levels of X and an equal number of trials at each level. Figure 8.10(a), for example, shows four equally spaced levels of X within the experimental region. If there are to be, say, eight trials, two could be placed at each of the levels indicated in Figure 8.10(a).

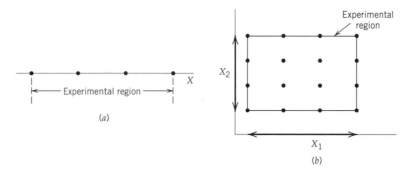

FIGURE 8.10 Reasonably good designs involving (a) one and (b) two variables

We are led to similar conclusions when the variable of interest, Y, depends on two factors, X_1 and X_2, as when the strength of the plastic material is thought to be influenced primarily by injection pressure and mold temperature. The experimental region shown in Figure 8.10(b) is the rectangular set of points (X_1, X_2) formed by the intervals of feasible X_1- and X_2-values. A prudent design would be to select levels of X_1 and X_2 that correspond to the four corners of the experimental region as well as to points within the region. Again, when the relationship between Y, on the one hand, and X_1 and X_2, on the other, is not expected to be unduly complicated, a simple and reasonably good design is to carry out an equal number of trials at each combination of three or four more or less uniformly spaced levels of the variables X_1 and X_2. Figure 8.10(b), for example, shows such a placement of 16 trials within the rectangular experimental region. If there are to be, say, 32 trials, two could be placed at each of the 16 marked points. Experimental designs for more than two variables can be similarly constructed.

We see that the experiment of Example 2.3, involving three trials at each combination of three levels of injection pressure, barrel temperature, and mold temperature, can be considered reasonably good if these levels were indeed chosen at the ends and middle of the feasible range of each factor (320° to 420° for barrel temperature, 100° to 150° for mold temperature, and 3000 to 7000 psi for injection pressure). The 27 observations are more than sufficient to estimate the parameters of even of polynomial of degree 2 in the three variables with interactions:

$$\hat{Y} = b_0 + b_1 X_1 + b_2 X_2 + b_3 X_3 + b_4 X_1^2 + b_5 X_2^2 + b_6 X_3^2 + b_7 X_1 X_2 + b_8 X_1 X_3 + b_9 X_2 X_3$$

By "reasonably good" design we mean, of course, a reasonable compromise between forecast accuracy and the means for detecting an uncomplicated nonlinear relationship. We have not attempted to be rigorous in defining these objectives or the suggested design. A reasonably good design, we suggested, should span the experimental region, but this can be done in many ways; for example, the levels of a variable need not be exactly evenly spaced, and the lower and upper levels need not be placed precisely at the ends of the feasible region.

Let us now turn our attention to the case where all the factors in an experiment are attributes. For example, suppose that a coffee distributor is considering changing its 8-oz. package of coffee. Three types of container (jar, can, pouch) and three color schemes for the container (intense, neutral, and subdued) are considered. In addition to container type and color scheme, the distributor also plans to examine the effect of shelf placement on sales. Three placement positions are to be distinguished: high (eye-level), medium (waist-level), and low (knee-level). The cooperation of a supermarket chain with several stores in the region has been secured. The plan is to use each combination of container, color, and shelf position at one participating store for a period of one month. At the end of the month, the sales of the new package will be ascertained and expressed as a percentage of the average monthly sales of the old package in the same store. The variable of interest, therefore, is

$$Y = \frac{\text{Sales of new package in store}}{\text{Average sales of old package in same store}}$$

For brevity, we shall call Y simply "sales."

A simple relationship between sales, on the one hand, and container, color scheme, and shelf position, on the other, is

$$(\widehat{\text{Sales}}) = (\text{base}) + (\text{container effect}) + (\text{color effect}) + (\text{position effect})$$

or, in symbols,

$$\hat{Y} = b_0 + \underbrace{b_1 X_1 + b_2 X_2 + b_3 X_3}_{container} + \underbrace{c_1 V_1 + c_2 V_2 + c_3 V_3}_{color} + \underbrace{d_1 W_1 + d_2 W_2 + d_3 W_3}_{position}$$

where $\hat{Y}$ is estimated sales, X_1 to X_3 are dummy variables representing the three kinds of container (jar, can, and pouch, respectively), V_1 to V_3 are dummy variables representing the color schemes (intense, neutral and subdued), and W_1 to W_3 are dummy variables representing the three shelf positions (high, medium, and low, respectively). To ensure unique estimates, one dummy variable from each group should be left out of the model, or equivalent restrictions should be placed on the coefficients of the dummy variables. Leaving out, say, X_1, V_1, and W_1 is the same as requiring that $b_1 = c_1 = d_1 = 0$, in which case the model reads

$$\hat{Y} = b_0 + b_2 X_2 + b_3 X_3 + c_2 V_2 + c_3 V_3 + d_2 W_2 + d_3 W_3 \qquad (8.5)$$

Thus, the coefficient b_0 can be interpreted as the estimated sales of a jar with an intense color scheme placed at eye level. The other coefficients represent the estimated attribute effects relative to this base.

There are altogether $3 \times 3 \times 3$ or 27 different combinations of type of container, color scheme, and shelf position: (jar, intense, high), (jar, intense, medium), ..., (pouch, subdued, low).

The straightforward approach would be to use each of these combinations in a different store. Twenty-seven stores would be needed for this experiment. If the supermarket chain has more than 27 stores and cost is not of concern, it is possible to use some combinations in more than one store. The assignments of combinations to stores could be done randomly. At the end of the experiment, there will be 27 or more observations on Y and the dummy variables. Twenty-seven observations are more than sufficient to estimate the parameters of Model 8.5, but just sufficient to estimate the parameters of a model with interactions,

$$\hat{Y} = b_0 + b_1 V_1 + b_2 V_2 + \cdots + b_{27} V_{27}$$

after one of the V's is dropped to ensure unique estimates of the remaining parameters. The V's are, of course, dummy variables representing the 27 combinations of type of container, color scheme, and shelf position.

In general, then, a reasonably good design for experiments involving attributes only is to carry out one or more trials at each combination of categories of the attributes. For experiments involving variables and attributes, there could be one or more trials for each combination of categories of the attributes and levels of the variables spanning the experimental region.

These designs, however, may require many more trials than the minimum needed to estimate the simplest model and may be costly if the number of attributes and categories are large. For example, if there are just four attributes, each with five categories, the number of required trials is 4^5 or 1024. Similar comments apply to designs involving variables or variables and attributes.

On the other hand, if the number of trials is drastically reduced, it may not be possible to estimate at all some parameters of models that may be suggested by the results of the experiment.

There is a large literature on experimental design, and there exist methods for finding designs with any given number of trials that are optimal according to specific criteria. The criteria, however, are not entirely compatible with one another, and a design that is optimal according to one may not be optimal according to another criterion. The subject is large and we cannot do it justice in the confines of this book. The interested reader may consult, among many other good sources, Hinkelmann and Kempthorne (1994); Pukelsheim (1993); Atkinson and Donev (1992); or Raktoe, Hedayat, and Federer (1981).

8.9   TO SUM UP

- Regression with no intercept ensures that the estimated value of the dependent variable is zero when the values of all explanatory variables are equal to zero.

- Regression with no intercept is a special case of least-squares estimation subject to a set of linear equality constraints on the linear model's parameters.

- Least-squares estimation subject to a set of linear equality and inequality constraints on a linear model's parameters is a quadratic programming problem.

- The least absolute deviations (LAD) problem is to find the values of a linear model's parameters that minimize the sum of the absolute deviations (not the squared deviations, as in OLS). It is a linear programming problem and can be solved with the help of special computer programs.

- The presence of approximate linear relationships between the values of the explanatory variables is called multicollinearity and occurs quite frequently in economic and business studies. When there is multicollinearity, it may be difficult to estimate with precision the effects of the related explanatory variables. These effects may be altered substantially by leaving out of the model one of the related variables or by making small changes to the observations or their number.

- Stepwise regression is actually a series of regressions. In forward stepwise regression, the explanatory variables are introduced one at a time to arrive ultimately at a model using all available explanatory variables. Backward stepwise regression begins with a model utilizing all explanatory variables, then drops these variables one at a time. A number of criteria are used in practice for the inclusion or exclusion of variables, but these are usually related to incremental R^2.

- A design spanning the experimental region offers a reasonably good compromise between forecast accuracy and the means for detecting an uncomplicated nonlinear relationship in experiments involving variables. A reasonably good design for experiments involving attributes only is to carry one or more trials at each combination of categories of the attributes. For experiments involving variables and attributes, there could be one or more trials at each combination of categories of the attributes and levels of the variables spanning the experimental region. Such designs, however, may require more trials than is neccessary to estimate the simplest models.

PROBLEMS

8.1 Using a computer program, confirm as many as possible of the results presented in this chapter.

8.2 Refer to Problem 2.2 concerning the relationship between airfare (Y) and distance from a city (X). The data are listed in Table 2.7 (file `fares.dat`) and summarized in Problem 2.2(b).

  (a) Is it reasonable to suppose that airfare is equal to zero when the distance is zero?

  (b) Estimate the model $\hat{Y} = bX$ and forecast the airfare to a destination 300 miles away.

8.3 Refer to Problem 2.3 concerning the relationship between the volume of a vessel's liquid cargo (X) and the time required to load or unload that cargo (dock time, Y). The data are shown in Table 2.8 (file `glakes.dat`).

  (a) Is it reasonable to require that the dock time be zero when the volume is equal to zero?

  (b) Estimate the model $\hat{Y} = bX$ and forecast the dock time for cargoes of 3000 and 10,000 tons.

8.4 The XYZ Company is engaged in the distribution of beauty supplies to beauty salons. It employs 18 salespeople, who call directly on beauty salons and are paid on a commission basis consisting of five different rates. The rates vary from 5% of sales to 15% of sales depending on the types of products sold. Obviously, the amount that a salesperson earns depends not only on the amount of sales but also on the composition of and the rates that apply to those sales.

  The following is a partial list of the recorded sales of and commissions paid to salespersons in the months of October, November, and December:

Sale No.	Salesperson	Month	Sales, X ($)	Commission, Y ($)
1	A	Oct.	10,959	1,555
2	A	Nov.	13,903	1,990
...	...	...	...	...
39	J	Dec.	4,226	586

From these data we calculate: $n = 39$; $\sum X = 268{,}609$; $\sum Y = 35{,}720$; $\sum (Y/X) = 5.192$; $\sum XY = 270{,}703{,}172$; $\sum X^2 = 2{,}035{,}207{,}387$.

  On the basis of the preceding data, the company would like to calculate an "average commission rate," which it plans to apply to next month's expected sales so as to estimate next month's commissions. Two methods were suggested for calculating this "average rate":

$$\text{(i)} \quad \frac{\text{Total commissions}}{\text{Total sales}} = \frac{\sum Y}{\sum X}$$

$$\text{(ii)} \quad \text{Average of all individual commission rates} = \frac{1}{n} \sum \frac{Y}{X}$$

  Can you suggest a third method for estimating the average commission rate? Which method is best? Does it make much difference which method is used in this particular problem?

8.5 Refer to Example 4.2 in Section 4.5. The completion time of the task (Y) was estimated by

$$\hat{Y} = b_0 + b_1 X_1 + b_2 X_2 + b_3 X_3 + b_4 X_4$$

where the X's are dummy variables representing the four operators. The data are shown in Table 4.6 and can be found in the file `opers.dat`.

Confirm the calculations in Example 4.2 by determining the values of $b_0, b_1, \ldots, b_4$ that minimize $\sum(Y - \hat{Y})^2$ subject to the constraint $b_1 + b_2 + b_3 + b_4 = 0$.

8.6 Refer to Example 6.2 and the data in the file `airline.dat` concerning the number of passengers on transatlantic flights (Y). As in Example 6.2, estimate the model

$$\hat{Y} = b_0 + b_1 T + c_1 M_1 + c_2 M_2 + \cdots + c_{12} M_{12} + dZ$$

where Z is a dummy variable representing the Easter holiday, but subject to the constraint $c_1 + c_2 + \cdots + c_{12} = 0$. Plot the seasonal pattern and compare it to the one shown in Figure 6.4. Forecast the number of passengers on transatlantic flights in January and February 19X6, and compare these forecasts with those in Example 6.2.

8.7 Consider the data in the following table:

X_1	X_2	Y
−1.2	13.1	−2.6
−4.0	14.8	−5.2
1.0	14.8	0.2
4.0	12.9	0.6
3.8	11.2	2.8

(a) Determine the OLS estimates of the model $\hat{Y} = b_0 + b_1 X_1 + b_2 X_2$.

(b) Determine the parameters of the model $\hat{Y} = b_0 + b_1 X_1 + b_2 X_2$ that minimize $\sum(Y - \hat{Y})^2$ subject to the constraints $b_1 \geq 0$, $b_2 \geq 0$, and $b_1 + b_2 = 1$.

(c) Measure the effect of the constraints on the model in (a).

8.8 Calculate the least absolute deviations (LAD) estimates of the model $\hat{Y} = b_0 + b_1 X_1 + b_2 X_2$ using the data of Problem 8.7.

8.9 With the help of a computer program for linear programming, determine the LAD estimates in Example 8.5.

8.10 Refer to Example 2.3 regarding the strength of the plastic material and the data in the file `plmat.dat`. Estimate the model of this example using the least absolute deviations (LAD) method. Compare the results with those of Example 2.3.

8.11 Refer to Example 2.4 concerning the per capita consumption of beef and pork and the data in the file `bfpk.dat`. Estimate the models of this example using the least absolute deviations (LAD) method. Compare the results with those of Example 2.4.

8.12 Consider the following data, which are only slightly different from those used in Section 8.6.

Y	X_0	X_1	X_2
8	1	2.01	3
15	1	5	0
10	1	3	2
13	1	4	1

(a) Regress Y against X_1 and X_2 to investigate how your computer program handles multicollinearity.

(b) Regress Y against X_1 only and Y against X_2 only. Show that these two models give approximately the same $\sum(Y - \hat{Y})^2$ as in (a).

(c) Which consequences of multicollinearity does this numerical example illustrate? Discuss.

8.13 (Due to Mr. Joseph Chan) The circulation of a public library is in many respects like the revenue of a private organization. Library success is often measured by and libraries are often compared on the basis of circulation. Finding the determinants of circulation and forecasting it is of interest to administrators faced with the task of allocating operating funds and deciding if new branches should be created or old ones closed due to changes in the determining factors.

The library system involved in this study serves a region with a population exceeding 9 million. There are 372 public libraries in the region. These are operated and largely funded by local municipalities but also receive grants from the regional government. The very large majority of these libraries have one or two "service points," that is, permanent or mobile outlets from which service is offered directly to the public. The largest library, however, serves a population of more than half a million from more than 70 service points. The average annual circulation per library is 57,600 items.

The objective of the study was to estimate the relationship between a library's circulation, on the one hand, and variables influencing circulation, on the other. Information was available on the following variables.

CIRC:	Number of items (books, records, tapes, etc.) charged out from the library's collection during the year of study
POP:	Population of municipality or community in which the library is located
HHLDS:	Number of households in municipality or community
SERVP:	Service points, as explained previously
FLRSP:	Total floor area used by the library, in square meters
HRS:	Number of hours in which library was open during the year
VOL:	Number of items in the collection of the library
STAFF:	Number of full-time equivalent paid staff members
FUNDS:	Total revenue of the library from all sources (municipal and regional grants, fees, fines, etc.)

The first model considered yielded the following results:

$$\widehat{CIRC} = 2995 \quad + 7.54POP \quad + 1.08HHLDS + 10320SERVP$$
$$(0.71) \qquad (15.16) \qquad (0.74) \qquad (9.16)$$
$$-11.53FLRSP \quad - 319HRS \quad - 0.64VOL$$
$$(-2.00) \qquad (-3.58) \qquad (-4.37)$$
$$-83.18STAFF + 0.07FUNDS \quad R^2 = 0.99$$
$$(-0.55) \qquad (7.46) \qquad S = 57567$$

Interpret the regression results. Explain possible reasons for any inconsistencies. Indicate possible improvements to the model.

8.14 Refer to Problem 4.12 regarding the design time of bridges. The data are partially listed in Table 4.16 and can be found in the file `bridge.dat`.

Figure 8.11 shows the output of program Minitab and the results of stepwise regression of design time against all available explanatory variables. Interpret these results.

8.15 Refer to Problem 4.9 regarding the scores of hockey games. The data are partially listed in Figure 4.4 and can be found in the file `hockey1.dat`.

```
STEPWISE REGRESSION OF    TIME    ON  7 PREDICTORS, WITH N =    45

       STEP        1        2        3        4        5        6        7
   CONSTANT    -39.50   -37.53   -42.28   -43.94   -42.99   -45.41   -42.88

       DWGS      26.1     19.8     20.1     20.6     20.4     21.0     20.7
    T-RATIO      8.65     5.90     5.88     5.28     5.06     4.51     4.33

      SPANS               19.2     18.8     19.0     18.1     18.2     16.3
    T-RATIO               3.25     3.15     3.12     2.50     2.47     1.56

       TYPE                         11       11       12       13       11
    T-RATIO                       0.62     0.59     0.61     0.65     0.53

      DDIFF                                  -5       -6       -8       -7
    T-RATIO                                -0.24    -0.29    -0.34    -0.28

      DAREA                                           0.3      0.6      0.6
    T-RATIO                                          0.21     0.32     0.34

      CCOST                                                 -0.015   -0.025
    T-RATIO                                                  -0.25    -0.34

     LENGTH                                                            0.03
    T-RATIO                                                            0.26
          S      59.1     53.5     53.9     54.5     55.2     55.8     56.5
       R-SQ     63.49    70.82    71.09    71.14    71.17    71.21    71.27
```

FIGURE 8.11   Minitab output, Problem 8.14

Use a computer program for stepwise regression to get a rough indication of the importance of all available explanatory variables. Find out and explain the criterion used by your program for adding or deleting an explanatory variable at each step. Discuss the usefulness of stepwise regression in addressing the main question of this problem.

8.16   Same as Problem 8.15, except refer to Problem 5.15 and the file `mpg.dat` regarding the gasoline consumption of passenger cars.

8.17   An agency of the federal government owns 2153 real estate properties located throughout the country. These properties are relatively small and were acquired at various times during the 1900s; the average floor area of all 2153 buildings is 293 m² and their average year of construction or acquisition is 1963.

Until now, the agency did not carry in its financial statements the value of each property individually but only in the aggregate under two separate items: the total value of the land (shown as $504 million) and the total depreciated value of the buildings ($612 million).

A recent change in the law made it necessary for the agency to estimate the value of each building and parcel of land individually. Such estimates, of course, *could* be made by having every property individually appraised, but the cost of this approach is so high as to make it impractical.

On the advice of a consultant, the agency selected a simple random sample without replacement of 100 properties and had them appraised by real estate experts. The appraisal results and two characteristics of the selected properties can be found in the file `govpro.dat`, which is partially listed in Table 8.3.

The interpretation of the variables in Table 8.3 is as follows:

SIZE:	Floor area of the building, in m²
YEAR:	Year of acquisition or construction of building, last two digits
VREPL:	Building replacement value ($000)
VDEPR:	Depreciated building replacement value ($000)
VLAND:	Land value ($000)
VTOTAL:	Total value, VTOTAL = VDEPR + VLAND, in $000

(a)   The results of regressing VREPL against SIZE and YEAR are

$$VREPL = 31.880 + 0.963SIZE + 0.515YEAR \qquad R^2 = 0.948$$
$$\qquad (0.37) \quad (41.12) \qquad\quad (0.39) \qquad\qquad S = 244$$

Interpret these results. Are they consistent with your expectations?

TABLE 8.3   File `govpro.dat`, Partial Listing

SIZE	YEAR	VREPL	VDEPR	VLAND	VTOTAL
2478.9	52	2225.70	1391.06	293.00	1684.06
2405.3	7	2349.80	1174.90	56.00	1230.90
2041.2	59	2108.80	790.80	166.00	956.80
1904.7	61	2157.20	1186.46	44.70	1231.16
1899.0	60	2115.50	1586.63	55.00	1641.63
. . .	. . .	. . .	. . .	. . .	. . .

(b) Is it reasonable to require that the constant term of this model be equal to zero? Is there any evidence that it is indeed zero? Reestimate the model in (a), forcing the intercept to equal zero. Interpret this model.

(c) Calculate the difference between replacement and depreciated replacement value, DEPR = VREPL − VDEPR. Regress DEPR against SIZE and YEAR. Interpret the results. Are they consistent with your expectations?

(d) The consultant's advice is to estimate a building's depreciated replacement value with the help of a regression of VDEPR against SIZE and YEAR. Implement this suggestion. Explain your implementation and results. Estimate the depreciated replacement value of the first building listed in Table 8.3.

(e) It was pointed out that the sum of the estimates of the depreciated building replacement values of all 2153 properties would not necessarily equal their aggregate book value ($612 million). Can you suggest a method for estimating the regression model's parameters that will ensure that the sum of the estimates will equal $612 million? If so, explain your recommendations and carry them out.

(f) How would you estimate the land value of each property and ensure that the sum of the estimates equals the aggregate book value of $504 million? Explain your recommendations and, if possible, carry them out.

(g) Comment on any other aspects of the problem that were not specifically covered in the preceding questions.

8.18 (a) The variable Y of interest is thought to be influenced primarily by a single explanatory variable X. An experiment is planned to estimate the relationship between Y and X and to forecast the values of Y at various levels of X in the interval from 10 to 20. The plan is to observe Y at five levels of X. What should these levels be and why?

(b) Same as (a), except that two variables, X_1 and X_2, are believed to primarily influence Y. Forecasts of Y will be made for values of X_1 in the interval from −5 to 5, and values of X_2 in the interval from 0 to 10. Ten trials are planned. Where should these trials be placed and why?

8.19 Consider an experiment in which the variable of interest Y is thought to be linearly related to a single explanatory variable X and the model $Y = \beta_0 + \beta_1 X + \epsilon$ satisfies the conditions of the classical linear model. In Section 3.5, we stated that a $100(1 - \alpha)\%$ confidence interval for the value of Y at $X = x$ is given by $\hat{Y} \pm T_{\alpha/2} S_f$, that is,

$$(b_0 + b_1 x) \pm T_{\alpha/2} S \sqrt{1 + \frac{1}{n} + \frac{(x - \bar{X})^2}{\sum (X - \bar{X})^2}}$$

where S^2 is the variance of residuals and $\sum (X - \bar{X})^2 / n$ is the ordinary variance of the n X-values used to estimate b_0 and b_1. For the following questions, assume you are free to select the n X-values in the interval (experimental region) from c to d.

(a) If the purpose of the experiment is to arrive at the narrowest possible confidence interval for Y at $X = x$, show that the n X-values can be chosen in any manner as long as $\bar{X} = x$.

(b) It follows from (a) that all n X-values could be equal to x. What is a problem with such an experiment?

(c) If it is anticipated that several confidence intervals for Y will be constructed at various values of X in the interval from c to d, how do you suggest that the n X-values be selected?

8.20 Consider the experiment described in Section 8.8 to estimate the relationship between sales, on the one hand, and the type of container, color scheme, and shelf position, on the other, given by Eq. 8.5.

Suppose there are only nine stores in the region. Examine the experimental design shown in Table 8.4.

Each cell of Table 8.4 shows a combination of type of container, color scheme, and shelf position to be used at one of the nine stores. In Store 1 (upper left cell), the combination (jar, intense, high) will be used; in Store 2 (next right), the combination is (jar, neutral, high); and so on.

(a) Show the values of the dummy variables corresponding to this design in the form of a table the rows of which are the stores.

(b) What is a problem with this design?

(c) Can the effects, the coefficients of the dummy variables in Model 8.5, be estimated uniquely?

(d) Is Design A a good design? Does your answer depend on the fact that there are only nine trials in this design?

8.21 Same as Problem 8.20, except the design is as shown in Table 8.5.

(a) Show the values of the dummy variables corresponding to this design in the form of a table the rows of which are the stores.

(b) Is there any problem with this design?

(c) Can the effects, the coefficients of the dummy variables in Model 8.5, be estimated uniquely?

(d) Is Design B a good design? Does your answer depend on the fact that there are only nine trials in this design?

8.22 Medlabs Inc. is a pharmaceutical company. One of its products is Tenderdent toothpaste, designed to relieve the pain or discomfort from sensitive teeth. Tenderdent has never been marketed directly to consumers but rather to dentists, drugstores, and hospitals through a promotional package that covers all the products of the company. Medlabs now plans to imitate the successful promotional strategy of its main competitor and address the public

TABLE 8.4   Design A, Problem 8.20

| | Color scheme | | |
Container	Intense	Neutral	Subdued
Jar	High[a]	High	High
Can	Medium	Medium	Medium
Pouch	Low	Low	Low

[a] Cell entries indicate shelf position.

TABLE 8.5   **Design B, Problem 8.21**

| Container | Color scheme | | |
	Intense	Neutral	Subdued
Jar	High[a]	Low	Medium
Can	Low	Medium	High
Pouch	Medium	High	Low

[a]Cell entries indicate shelf position.

directly by means of television advertising. Medlabs has no solid experience concerning what sales increase to expect from a given advertising outlay and is considering measuring the consumers' response to its advertising in a number of test markets before embarking on a national campaign.

Medlabs' market research consultants divide the country into 140 "Television Markets (TMs)." These are nonoverlapping regions, each centered around a population center, and are similar to the "Areas of Dominant Influence (ADI)" or "Designated Marketing Areas (DMA)" used by television ratings services. Roughly speaking, each TM consists of counties where the majority of people view the television stations that broadcast in that market.

Figure 8.12 shows selected characteristics for the first few of these markets. The complete set of data can be found in the file `tender.dat`.

The variables are defined as follows:

TM:	Television market identification number
HHLDS:	Number of households
POPTOT:	Total population
MADULT:	Number of male adults (20 years old and older)
FADULT:	Number of female adults (20 years old and older)
AVAGE:	Average age of all adults
UN:	Percentage of adults with some university education
AVINC:	Average household income ($000)
AVVDW:	Average value of residential dwellings ($000)
DR:	Percentage of owned dwellings
COMM:	Average cost of broadcasting a 30-second commercial ($)

TM	HHLDS	POPTOT	MADULT	FADULT	AVAGE	UN	AVINC	AVVDW	DR	COM
1	54805	170105	56825	62685	42.49	33	39.23	99.21	67	100
2	7890	25230	8335	8760	44.24	18	32.41	65.91	77	50
3	3445	10825	3685	3865	41.91	27	42.83	95.07	67	50
4	10725	33735	11440	12035	43.88	22	34.14	77.43	76	50
5	3375	11380	3645	3425	38.27	21	53.17	42.61	77	50
...	...	...	...	...	...	...	...	...	..	...

FIGURE 8.12   File `tender.dat`, partial listing

The plan is to select 20 of the 140 TMs and broadcast in each TM a different number of 30-second commercials in the range of 1 to 120 per month.

On behalf of Medlabs, select the 20 TMs and specify the number of commercials to be broadcast in each. Carefully explain your reasoning. Do not overlook the cost of this experiment.

CHAPTER 9

MORE ON INFERENCE IN REGRESSION

9.1 INTRODUCTION AND SUMMARY

In Sections 3.2 and 3.3, we described several desirable properties that OLS estimators of a linear model's parameters possess if three conditions are met. These conditions are, it will be recalled, (i) linearity, (ii) constant variance, and (iii) independence. Under these conditions, the OLS estimators are unbiased, are consistent, and have the least variance among all estimators of the parameters that can be written as linear functions of the Y-values. If, in addition, the condition of (iv) normality is met, then tests of hypotheses and confidence intervals concerning the model's parameters and forecasts can be carried out as described in Section 3.5. Conditions (i) to (iv) describe the classical linear model. Of course, the OLS estimators always yield the best fit, in the sense of minimizing the sum of squared residuals, $\sum \hat{\varepsilon}^2 = \sum (Y - \hat{Y})^2$.

These properties and the relative ease with which the required calculations are carried out by computers explain in large part the popularity of the method of least squares.

In this chapter, we consider how to form unbiased and consistent estimators as well as confidence intervals and tests when these conditions (linearity, constant variance, independence, or normality) are not met. We shall find that it may then be necessary to estimate the model's parameters by methods other than least squares. Consequently, these estimates may no longer fit the observations as well as the OLS according to the criterion of least squares.

It should be clear that when a condition is violated, it may be violated in many ways. It is impossible to examine all conceivable violations. We shall concentrate, therefore, on simple, one-at-a-time departures from the initial conditions and shall examine simple remedies.

In this chapter we also examine the consequences of some types of specification error, that is, the error associated with estimating a model different from the true one. We also examine ridge regression, a method of estimation said to produce more accurate estimates than OLS.[1]

---

[1] This chapter is by necessity more technical than the preceding ones. On occasion we shall have to make use of some results that are more fully explained in Appendixes A and B.

9.2   NONLINEARITY

We saw in Chapter 5 that some nonlinear models are or become linear in their parameters after the original variables are transformed. For example, a parabolic relationship between Y and X is captured by the model

$$Y = \beta_0 + \beta_1 X + \beta_2 X^2 + \varepsilon$$

which is linear in the parameters β_0, β_1, and β_2. Also, the "log-log" model described in Section 5.5,

$$Y = \beta_0 X_1^{\beta_1} X_2^{\beta_2} \cdots X_k^{\beta_k} \varepsilon$$

becomes linear in the parameters $\beta_1, \beta_2, \ldots, \beta_k$ after the logarithmic transformation

$$\log Y = \log \beta_0 + \beta_1 \log X_1 + \beta_2 \log X_2 + \cdots + \beta_k \log X_k + \tilde{\varepsilon}$$

where $\tilde{\varepsilon} = \log \varepsilon$. If the errors, ε or $\tilde{\varepsilon}$, satisfy the conditions of constant variance, independence, and normality, the OLS estimators of the parameters are minimum variance linear unbiased and consistent, and confidence intervals and tests concerning these parameters can be formed as described in Chapter 3. Similar conclusions apply to other nonlinear models described in Chapter 5.

For any nonlinear model, the method of *nonlinear regression* described in Section 5.6 provides estimators with properties similar to OLS when the number of observations is large. Let us explain.

Assume that the dependent variable is a certain function of k explanatory variables and $l + 1$ parameters

$$Y = g(X_1, X_2, \ldots, X_k; \beta_0, \beta_1, \ldots, \beta_l) + \varepsilon$$

Available are n observations in the form $(Y_i, X_{1i}, \ldots, X_{ki})$. The least-squares estimators $b_0, b_1, \cdots, b_k$ are those values of the parameters that minimize the sum of squared residuals

$$\sum_{i=1}^{n} \hat{\varepsilon}_i^2 = \sum_{i=1}^{n} [Y_i - g(X_{1i}, \ldots, X_{ki}; b_0, b_1, \ldots, b_k)]^2$$

For the illustration given in Section 5.6, for example, it was assumed that

$$Y = \beta_0 \beta_1^X + \varepsilon$$

Given n observations (Y_i, X_i), the least-squares estimators b_0 and b_1 minimize

$$\sum_{i=1}^{n} \hat{\varepsilon}_i^2 = \sum_{i=1}^{n} [Y_i - b_0 b_1^{X_i}]^2$$

As noted in Section 5.6, these estimators are calculated by an iterative numerical procedure.

If the errors ε_i are generated *as if* by random draws with replacement from a population of ε-values having mean 0 and variance σ^2, it can be shown that the least-squares estimators $b_0, b_1, \ldots, b_k$ are consistent but not in general unbiased. If, in addition, the distribution of the ε-values is normal and the number of observations large, it is possible to form confidence intervals and carry out tests concerning the model's parameters in the same manner as in linear regression.[2] Advanced statistical programs for nonlinear regression calculate an estimate S_b of the standard deviation of the estimator b of each parameter β. *These calculations require that the number of observations be large,* although some programs do not check that this is indeed the case. Just as in linear regression, a $100(1 - \alpha)\%$ confidence interval for β is

$$b \pm T_{\alpha/2} S_b$$

where $T_{\alpha/2}$ is the "critical t-value" with $\nu = n - (l + 1)$ "degrees of freedom." For large ν, $T_{\alpha/2}$ can be approximated by the standard normal critical values shown in Table 3.1. Under the same assumptions, the decision rule for the test of $H_0 : \beta = 0$ against $H_A : \beta \neq 0$ at the α level of significance is to reject H_0 if $|t = b/S_b| > T_{\alpha/2}$.

EXAMPLE 9.1

In the illustration in Section 5.6, only the four observations (Y, X) shown in Table 5.9 were available. Since the number of observations is very small, confidence intervals and tests should not be considered. Nevertheless, and strictly in order to illustrate the calculations, we shall pretend that the SAS results of Figure 5.10 are based on large n, in which case they could be presented in the following more familiar format:

Parameter, β	Estimate, b	Std. Dev., S_b	t-ratio
β_0	5.517	0.611	9.03
β_1	1.941	0.058	33.46

[2]For the derivation of these results, see, for example, Seber and Wild (1989).

An approximate 95% confidence interval for β_0 would be

$$(5.517) \pm (1.96)(0.611)$$

or from about 4.32 to 6.71.[3]

Again pretending that the number of observations is large, the hypothesis $H_0 : \beta_1 = 0$ should be rejected at the 0.05 level because $t = 33.46 > 1.96$. ∎

9.3 NONCONSTANT VARIANCE

One of the assumptions of the classical linear model, it will be recalled, is that the errors ε are generated as if by random draws with replacement from a common population of error values having mean 0 and a certain variance σ^2.

Let us consider first a linear model with a single explanatory variable,

$$Y = \beta_0 + \beta_1 X + \varepsilon \tag{9.1}$$

If the assumption of constant variance is satisfied, that is, if $Var(\varepsilon) = \sigma^2$, a scatter diagram of the regression residuals $\hat{\varepsilon}$ against X should look like Figure 3.7(b); there should be no visible tendency for the scatter of the $\hat{\varepsilon}$ to vary with X. By contrast, scatter diagrams having the appearance of Figure 9.1(b) or 9.1(d) show a tendency for the scatter of $\hat{\varepsilon}$ to increase with X and suggest that $Var(\varepsilon)$ depends on X.

In Figure 9.1(b), the scatter appears to increase faster than X and is consistent with the assumption that

$$Var(\varepsilon) = \sigma^2 X^2$$

We can think of the error ε as the outcome of a random draw with replacement from separate populations of ε-values, one for every possible value of X, each population of ε-values having mean 0 and variance $\sigma^2 X^2$.

This model violates the constant variance condition, but it is possible to cast it in terms that permit estimators of the parameters to have all the desirable properties described in Chapter 3. Assuming $X \neq 0$, divide Eq. 9.1 by X to get

$$\frac{Y}{X} = \beta_0 \frac{1}{X} + \beta_1 + \frac{\varepsilon}{X}$$

---

[3]Note that this interval is quite different from the one shown in Figure 5.10. The reason is that SAS `proc nlin` utilizes the critical t-value corresponding to $v = n - (l + 1) = 4 - 2 = 2$ degrees of freedom, $T_{\alpha/2} = 4.30$, to produce the interval from about 2.88 to 8.15, overlooking the fact that the number of observations is small.

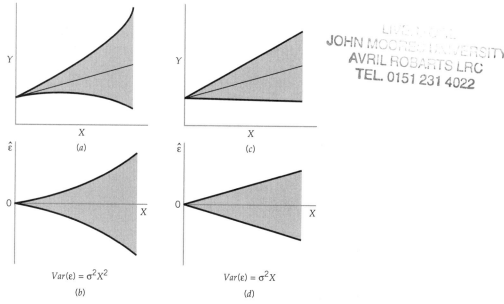

FIGURE 9.1 Error variance as a function of X

or

$$Y' = \beta_1 + \beta_0 X' + \varepsilon' \tag{9.2}$$

Writing

$$\varepsilon' = \frac{\varepsilon}{X} = 0 + \frac{1}{X}\varepsilon$$

we see that ε' is a linear function of ε of the form $\varepsilon' = a + b\varepsilon$, where $a = 0$ and $b = 1/X$. Applying the results of Appendix A.3, we find

$$E(\varepsilon') = 0 + \frac{1}{X}E(\varepsilon) = 0 + \frac{1}{X}0 = 0$$

and

$$Var(\varepsilon') = (\frac{1}{X})^2 Var(\varepsilon) = (\frac{1}{X})^2(\sigma^2 X^2) = \sigma^2$$

In words, Y' is a linear function of X', the mean of ε' is zero, and the variance of ε' is constant—it does not depend on X. Since the ε-values are unrelated to one another, so are the ε'-values, which are simply the ε-values divided by constants. We conclude that Model 9.2 satisfies the conditions of linearity, independence, and constant variance. Therefore, minimum variance linear unbiased and consistent estimators of β_0 and β_1 can be obtained by regressing $Y' = Y/X$ against $X' = 1/X$. Keep in mind, however, that the estimate of β_1 is the regression intercept, and the estimate of β_0 is the coefficient of X'.

EXAMPLE 9.2

We illustrate the calculations using the artificial data in the first two columns of Table 9.1.

The plot of the observations in Figure 9.2 appears consistent with the model $Y = \beta_0 + \beta_1 X + \varepsilon$, where $E(\varepsilon) = 0$ and $Var(\varepsilon) = \sigma^2 X^2$.

TABLE 9.1   Data for Example 9.2

Y	X	$Y' = Y/X$	$X' = 1/X$
1	1	1.00000	1.00000
2	2	1.00000	0.50000
3	4	0.75000	0.25000
4	3	1.33333	0.33333
4	6	0.66667	0.16667
7	5	1.40000	0.20000

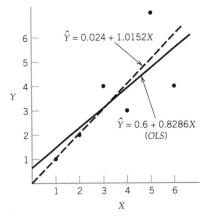

FIGURE 9.2 Data and estimated relationships, Example 9.2

$Y' = Y/X$ and $X' = 1/X$ are calculated in the last two columns of Table 9.1. Regressing Y' against X' we get

$$\hat{Y}' = 1.0152 + 0.024X' \qquad R^2 = 0.10$$
$$\quad\;\; (4.30) \qquad (0.05) \qquad\quad S = 0.332$$

Thus, the estimate of β_0 is 0.024 and that of β_1 is 1.0152. The forecast of Y for $X = 4$ is $\hat{Y} = 0.024 + (1.0152)(4) = 4.0848$.

In contrast, had we regressed Y against X we would have obtained the OLS estimates

$$\hat{Y} = 0.6000 + 0.8286X \qquad R^2 = 0.56$$
$$\quad\;\; (0.42) \qquad (2.25) \qquad\quad S = 1.54$$

The forecast of Y for $X = 4$ would be $\hat{Y} = 0.6 + (0.8286)(4) = 3.9144$.

Note the different estimates and t-ratios. The two estimated relationships are plotted in Figure 9.2. If we want our estimators to have the properties described in Chapter 3, we should use the first set of estimates. Tests and confidence intervals concerning the parameters β_0 and β_1 should also be based on the first set of results—not the second—provided, of course, that the assumptions of independence and normality are satisfied. ∎

Scatter diagrams of Y and the OLS residuals $\hat{\varepsilon}$ against X having the appearance of Figures 9.1(c) and 9.1(d) are consistent with the model $Y = \beta_0 + \beta_1 X + \varepsilon$, in which $E(\varepsilon) = 0$ and $Var(\varepsilon) = \sigma^2 X$. In Problem 9.5 we let the reader show that estimators of β_0 and β_1 with the desirable properties described in Section 3.2 are obtained by regressing $Y' = Y/\sqrt{X}$ against $X_1 = 1/\sqrt{X}$ and $X_2 = \sqrt{X}$ with zero intercept. The estimate of β_0 is the coefficient of X_1 and that of β_1 the coefficient of X_2.

For the general case involving k explanatory variables,

$$Y = \beta_0 + \beta_1 X_1 + \beta_2 X_2 + \cdots + \beta_k X_k + \varepsilon \qquad (9.3)$$

it may be reasonable to suppose that the condition of independence is satisfied but that the variance of ε depends on a known variable Z. Z could be one of the explanatory variables $X_1, X_2, \ldots, X_k$ or an altogether different variable not used in explaining Y. This tendency may be detected by plotting the OLS residuals $\hat{\varepsilon}$ of Model 9.3 against Z.[4]

---

[4] We remark in passing that the presence of constant variance is called *homoscedasticity* and its absence *heteroscedasticity*.

Suppose that the relationship between $Var(\varepsilon)$ and Z is of the form

$$Var(\varepsilon) = \sigma^2 Z^2$$

Dividing Eq. 9.3 by Z, we find

$$\frac{Y}{Z} = \beta_0 \frac{1}{Z} + \beta_1 \frac{X_1}{Z} + \beta_2 \frac{X_2}{Z} + \cdots + \beta_k \frac{X_k}{Z} + \frac{\varepsilon}{Z} \qquad (9.4)$$

Letting $Y' = Y/Z$, $X_0' = 1/Z$, $X_1' = X_1/Z$, $X_2' = X_2/Z$, $\ldots$, $X_k' = X_k/Z$, and $\varepsilon' = \varepsilon/Z$, we write Eq. 9.4 as

$$Y' = \beta_0 X_0' + \beta_1 X_1' + \beta_2 X_2' + \cdots + \beta_k X_k' + \varepsilon' \qquad (9.5)$$

The results of Appendix A.3 can again be applied to show that $E(\varepsilon') = 0$ and $Var(\varepsilon') = \sigma^2$. Therefore, minimum variance linear unbiased and consistent estimators of $\beta_0, \beta_1, \beta_2, \ldots, \beta_k$ are obtained by regressing Y' against $X_0', X_1', X_2', \ldots, X_k'$ but with no intercept. If, in addition, the errors ε' of Model 9.5 satisfy the normality assumption, confidence intervals and tests concerning these parameters can be constructed in the usual manner.

The reader may wonder at this point what the consequences are of applying OLS to Model 9.3, that is, overlooking the nonconstant variance of the error term. It can be shown[5] that the OLS estimators are unbiased and consistent but do not have the smallest variance among estimators that can be written as linear functions of the Y-values. It can also be shown that standard tests and confidence intervals concerning the model's parameters and forecasts based on the OLS estimates are inappropriate.

Our next example illustrates a situation where nonconstant variance can be expected on theoretical grounds.

EXAMPLE 9.3

Consider a very simple model of the relationship between a person's annual income (Y), on the one hand, and his or her age (X_1) and level of education, on the other. Let X_2 be a dummy variable such that $X_2 = 1$ if the person is university educated or $X_2 = 0$ otherwise. A simple model (too simple perhaps) is

$$Y = \beta_0 + \beta_1 X_1 + \beta_2 X_2 + \varepsilon \qquad (9.6)$$

To estimate such a model, one could survey a number of persons, determine their income, age, and education level and then regress Y against X_1 and X_2.

---

[5]See, for example, Johnston (1984, Ch. 8).

This approach is likely to be costly and may be difficult to implement because people are often reluctant to reveal their income accurately. Suppose, however, that data are available from the most recent census giving the average personal income and age and the proportion of persons with university education by census tract, enumeration area, or other region. The available data, for example, could be in the form shown in Table 9.2.

We shall show that the census data can be used to estimate the parameters of Model 9.6. According to Eq. 9.6, for the ith person in a given census tract the relationship between income, age, and education is $Y_i = \beta_0 + \beta_1 X_{1i} + \beta_2 X_{2i} + \varepsilon_i$. If there are N persons in the tract, the average income of all persons in the tract is

$$\frac{1}{N} \sum_{i=1}^{N} Y_i = \frac{1}{N} \sum_{i=1}^{N} [\beta_0 + \beta_1 X_{1i} + \beta_2 X_{2i} + \varepsilon_i]$$

$$= \beta_0 + \beta_1 \frac{1}{N} \sum_{i=1}^{N} X_{1i} + \beta_2 \frac{1}{N} \sum_{i=1}^{N} X_{2i} + \frac{1}{N} \sum_{i=1}^{N} \varepsilon_i$$

This can be written more simply as

$$\bar{Y} = \beta_0 + \beta_1 \bar{X}_1 + \beta_2 \bar{X}_2 + \bar{\varepsilon} \qquad (9.7)$$

where $\bar{Y}$ is the average income, $\bar{X}_1$ the average age in the tract, and $\bar{X}_2$ the proportion of persons in the tract having university education. These are, respectively, the variables INC, AGE, and EDU of Table 9.2. The parameters β_0, β_1, and β_2 of Model 9.7 are the same as those of Model 9.6. Clearly, then, these parameters can be estimated by regressing INC against AGE and EDU.

But is OLS the best estimation method in this case? Suppose that Model 9.6 satisfies the conditions of independence, linearity, and constant variance. This means, in particular, that $E(\varepsilon) = 0$ and $Var(\varepsilon) = \sigma^2$. Since

$$\bar{\varepsilon} = \frac{1}{N}\varepsilon_1 + \frac{1}{N}\varepsilon_2 + \cdots + \frac{1}{N}\varepsilon_N$$

TABLE 9.2 Census Tract Data, Example 9.3

Census tract number	Number of persons, POP	Average personal income ($000), INC	Average age, AGE	Proportion of persons with university education, EDU
. . .	. . .	. . .	. . .	. . .
102	1725	26.231	33.7	0.09
. . .	. . .	. . .	. . .	. . .

$\bar{\varepsilon}$ is a linear function of N independent variables $\varepsilon_1, \varepsilon_2, \ldots, \varepsilon_N$, all of which have the same mean 0 and variance σ^2. Applying the results of Appendix A.11, we find

$$E(\bar{\varepsilon}) = \frac{1}{N}0 + \frac{1}{N}0 + \cdots + \frac{1}{N}0 = 0$$

$$Var(\bar{\varepsilon}) = \frac{1}{N^2}\sigma^2 + \frac{1}{N^2}\sigma^2 + \cdots + \frac{1}{N^2}\sigma^2 = \frac{N\sigma^2}{N^2} = \frac{\sigma^2}{N}$$

In other words, $Var(\bar{\varepsilon}) = \sigma^2 Z^2$, where $Z = 1/\sqrt{N}$.

We saw earlier in this section that minimum variance linear unbiased and consistent estimators of β_0, β_1, and β_2 are obtained by regressing $Y' = \bar{Y}/Z = \bar{Y}\sqrt{N}$ against $X'_0 = 1/Z = \sqrt{N}$, $X'_1 = \bar{X}_1/Z = \bar{X}_1\sqrt{N}$, and $X'_2 = \bar{X}_2/Z = \bar{X}_2\sqrt{N}$ with no intercept. These variables are transformations of the variables listed in Table 9.2; their calculation is outlined in Table 9.3.

If the errors $\bar{\varepsilon}$ satisfy the normality condition, confidence intervals and tests may be carried out using the results of this regression.   ∎

9.4   NONINDEPENDENCE, SERIAL CORRELATION

The OLS estimators of a linear model's parameters are minimum variance linear unbiased and consistent if the observations are generated by a process satisfying the assumptions of linearity, constant variance, and independence. Independence is satisfied if the observations are selected at random and with replacement from a population of elements described in Section 3.3, in which the means of the conditional distributions are linearly related to the explanatory variables and the variances of these distributions are equal.

However, the observations are not independent when the sample from such a population is without replacement and are often not independent when they constitute a time series. If the population is large and the sample is small, sampling without replacement is, for all practical purposes, the same as sampling with replacement. Time series are by far the more common source of dependence, and it is to time series that the rest of this section is devoted.

TABLE 9.3   Required Data, Example 9.3

N	$\bar{Y}$	$\bar{X}_1$	$\bar{X}_2$	$Y' = \bar{Y}\sqrt{N}$	$X'_0 = \sqrt{N}$	$X'_1 = \bar{X}_1\sqrt{N}$	$X'_2 = \bar{X}_2\sqrt{N}$
. . .	. . .	. . .	. . .	. . .	. . .	. . .	. . .
1725	26.231	33.7	0.09	1089	41.533	1400	3.738
. . .	. . .	. . .	. . .	. . .	. . .	. . .	. . .

Several questions arise and will be addressed in this section. What form can this dependence take? How does one detect a particular form of dependence? What are the consequences of a given form of dependence? How does one circumvent any ill consequences?

We shall use the alternative notation of Section 7.2 to describe relationships involving time series. As usual, we begin with one explanatory variable, X, and assume that the value of the dependent variable in period t, Y_t, is related to the value of X in the same period, X_t, as follows:

$$Y_t = \beta_0 + \beta_1 X_t + \varepsilon_t \qquad (9.8)$$

Let us suppose that the errors ε_t are not independent but related to one another. Specifically, suppose that

$$\varepsilon_t = \rho \varepsilon_{t-1} + \tilde{\varepsilon}_t \qquad (9.9)$$

ρ is another parameter, like β_0 and β_1, and $\tilde{\varepsilon}_t$ are errors like the ε_t. Let us further suppose that the $\tilde{\varepsilon}_t$ are independent of one another, with mean $E(\tilde{\varepsilon}_t) = 0$ and common variance $Var(\tilde{\varepsilon}_t) = \sigma^2$. In this case, Eq. 9.9 describes a first-order model of *serial correlation*.[6]

It is clear that if $\rho = 0$, the ε_t are identical to the $\tilde{\varepsilon}_t$ and are therefore independent of one another. If $\rho \neq 0$, ε_t is related to ε_{t-1} and hence to all prior ε's.

To understand better the mechanism that is assumed to generate the observations, let us revisit the illustration of Section 3.2 and assume that $Y = 3 - X + \varepsilon$, where $\varepsilon = 0.7\varepsilon_{-1} + \tilde{\varepsilon}$ and $\tilde{\varepsilon}$ is the outcome of a random draw with replacement from the following population of $\tilde{\varepsilon}$-values:

$\tilde{\varepsilon}$	Frequency
−1	2
0	6
+1	2
	10

It is assumed that the ε-values are created as if by selecting at random and with replacement an $\tilde{\varepsilon}$-value and adding it to the product of 0.7 and the preceding ε-value. Assuming $\varepsilon_0 = 0$, $X_1 = 1$, and that a random draw produced $\tilde{\varepsilon}_1 = -1$, we have $\varepsilon_1 = 0.7\varepsilon_0 + \tilde{\varepsilon}_1 = -1$ and $Y_1 = 3 - X_1 + \varepsilon_1 = 1$. These and two more assumed sets of values of X and $\tilde{\varepsilon}$ shown in the first and third columns imply the Y-values shown in the last column of the following table.

---

[6]Referred to also as a *first-order* model of *autocorrelation* or *autoregression*. The terminology varies. The term *first-order* indicates that the current error depends only on the preceding error. This is not, of course, the only possible form of dependence. We look briefly at some other forms toward the end of this section.

X	3 − X	$\tilde{\varepsilon}$	$\varepsilon = (0.7)\varepsilon_{-1} + \tilde{\varepsilon}$	Y
1	2	−1	−1	1.00
2	1	1	0.3	1.30
3	0	0	0.21	0.21

Thus, the three pairs of observations (X, Y) are $(1, 1.00)$, $(2, 1.30)$, and $(3, 0.21)$.

When the ε_t are related to one another, so are the Y_t. To see this, first lag Eq. 9.8 one period:

$$Y_{t-1} = \beta_0 + \beta_1 X_{t-1} + \varepsilon_{t-1} \tag{9.10}$$

Multiply Eq. 9.10 by ρ and subtract from Eq. 9.8 to get

$$Y_t - \rho Y_{t-1} = \beta_0(1 - \rho) + \beta_1(X_t - \rho X_{t-1}) + (\varepsilon_t - \rho \varepsilon_{t-1})$$

or

$$Y_t - \rho Y_{t-1} = \beta_0(1 - \rho) + \beta_1(X_t - \rho X_{t-1}) + \tilde{\varepsilon}_t \tag{9.11}$$

or

$$Y_t = \beta_0(1 - \rho) + \rho Y_{t-1} + \beta_1 X_t - (\rho \beta_1)X_{t-1} + \tilde{\varepsilon}_t \tag{9.12}$$

In other words, when $\rho \neq 0$, Y_t is related to Y_{t-1} and X_{t-1} as well as to X_t. Note that Model 9.12 is nonlinear in its parameters β_0, β_1, and ρ.

This simple model of serial correlation can be generalized to accommodate any number of explanatory variables:

$$Y_t = \beta_0 + \beta_1 X_{1t} + \beta_2 X_{2t} + \ldots + \beta_k X_{kt} + \varepsilon_t \tag{9.13}$$

where

$$\varepsilon_t = \rho \varepsilon_{t-1} + \tilde{\varepsilon}_t \tag{9.14}$$

and the $\tilde{\varepsilon}_t$ are independent with $E(\tilde{\varepsilon}_t) = 0$ and $Var(\tilde{\varepsilon}_t) = \sigma^2$. As in the model with a single X, when $\rho \neq 0$ Y_t can be shown to be related to Y_{t-1} and last period's X's as well as to the current period's X's.

Testing for Serial Correlation   The first question that arises is how to determine whether or not serial correlation is present. The hypotheses to be tested are:

$$H_0 : \rho = 0$$
$$H_A : \rho \neq 0$$

If H_0 is true, the ε_t are identical to the $\tilde{\varepsilon}_t$; hence they, as well as the Y_t, are independent of one another.

Since ρ is the coefficient of ε_{t-1} in the relationship $\varepsilon_t = 0 + \rho\varepsilon_{t-1} + \tilde{\varepsilon}_t$, a reasonable test statistic may be obtained as follows. First, regress Y against the explanatory variables $X_1, X_2, \ldots, X_k$, and calculate the OLS residuals $\hat{\varepsilon}_t = Y_t - \hat{Y}_t$. Second, regress the $\hat{\varepsilon}_t$ against the $\hat{\varepsilon}_{t-1}$, forcing the intercept to equal zero, to obtain an estimate of ρ. It is not difficult to show (see Appendix B.6) that this estimate of ρ is given by

$$r = \frac{\sum_{t=2}^{n} \hat{\varepsilon}_t \hat{\varepsilon}_{t-1}}{\sum_{t=2}^{n} \hat{\varepsilon}_t^2} \tag{9.15}$$

We should want to accept H_0 when r is close to 0 and to reject it when r is not close to zero.

In place of r, a related statistic is often used. The *Durbin-Watson statistic,*[7] denoted by d or DW, is defined as

$$DW = d = \frac{\sum_{t=2}^{n}(\hat{\varepsilon}_t - \hat{\varepsilon}_{t-1})^2}{\sum_{t=1}^{n} \hat{\varepsilon}_t^2}$$

For large n, it can be shown that

$$d \approx 2(1 - r)$$

When $\rho = 0$, we expect r to be close to 0 and d close to 2. Thus, a rough test is to reject H_0 when r is not close to 0 or d not close to 2.

A more formal test based on d *under the additional condition that the distribution of $\tilde{\varepsilon}$ is normal* is described in most econometric texts. This test involves critical values for d that depend on the number of observations, n, the number of explanatory variables, k, and the maximum tolerable probability of a Type I error, α.

Consequences of Ignoring Serial Correlation   It is useful to know how serious are the consequences of ignoring serial correlation, that is, of estimating the parameters of the linear model as if the observations were independent.

It can be shown[8] that when there is serial correlation, that is, when $\rho \neq 0$ in Eq. 9.14, the OLS estimators of the parameters $\beta_0, \beta_1, \beta_2, \ldots, \beta_k$ are still unbiased and consistent—as they are when there is no serial correlation. However, in some situations likely to be encountered in practice, the estimates of the

[7]J. Durbin and G. S. Watson, "Testing for Serial Correlation in Least Squares Regression," *Biometrika*, Vol. 37, December 1950, pp. 409–28, and Vol. 38, June 1951, pp. 159–78.

[8]See, for example, Johnston (1984, Ch. 8) and Theil (1971, Ch. 6).

standard deviations of the parameters, S_b, as calculated by computer programs when there is no serial correlation (see Section 3.5), will tend to underestimate the true standard deviations. Consequently, the ordinary t-ratios of the parameters will tend to be inflated, creating the impression that the explanatory variables are significant when in fact they are not.

The OLS estimators, therefore, maintain their properties of unbiasedness and consistency and, as always, provide the best fit even when serial correlation is present. However, the standard tests and confidence intervals concerning the model's parameters based on the OLS estimates should not be applied.

Estimation Procedure   If there is evidence of serial correlation, is there a better method than OLS for estimating the parameters of the model? A number of estimation methods are available that, when the number of observations is large, can be shown to yield estimators with lower variance than OLS and permit interval estimates to be made and tests carried out in the usual manner.[9] We shall describe two alternate estimation methods using the simple Model 9.9 with one explanatory variable as an illustration.

The starting point of these methods is Eq. 9.11:

$$(Y_t - \rho Y_{t-1}) = \beta_0(1 - \rho) + \beta_1(X_t - \rho X_{t-1}) + \tilde{\varepsilon}_t$$

which can be written as

$$Y_t^* = \beta_0' + \beta_1 X_t^* + \tilde{\varepsilon}_t \tag{9.16}$$

where $\beta_0' = \beta_0(1 - \rho)$, $Y_t^* = Y_t - \rho Y_{t-1}$, and $X_t^* = X_t - \rho X_{t-1}$.

Model 9.16 satisfies the assumptions of linearity, constant variance, and independence. If ρ were known, its parameters could be estimated by regressing Y^* against X^*.

Of course, ρ is not known and must be replaced by an estimate. The two methods described next obtain this estimate in different ways.

(a) *The Durbin procedure* takes two steps.[10] Since ρ is the coefficient of Y_{t-1} in Eq. 9.12,

$$Y_t = \beta_0(1 - \rho) + \rho Y_{t-1} + \beta_1 X_t - (\rho\beta_1)X_{t-1} + \tilde{\varepsilon}_t$$

---

[9]For a rigorous treatment of these methods and the conditions under which they apply, see Theil (1971, Ch. 8).

[10]J. Durbin, "Estimation of Parameters in Time Series Regression Models," *Journal of the Royal Statistical Society, Series B,* Vol. 22, 1960, pp. 139–53.

an estimator of ρ is the OLS coefficient of Y_{-1} in the regression of Y against Y_{-1}, X, and X_{-1}. In the first step of the Durbin procedure, Y is regressed against Y_{-1}, X, and X_{-1}. The regression coefficient of Y_{-1}, call it r, is used to create the new variables $Y_t^* = Y_t - rY_{t-1}$ and $X_t^* = X_t - rX_{t-1}$. In the second step, the OLS estimators of β_0' and β_1, b_0', and b_1, are obtained by regressing Y^* against X^*. The estimate of β_0 is $b_0'/(1-r)$.

(b) The *Cochrane-Orcutt procedure* is iterative.[11] First, Y is regressed against X. The residuals of this regression, $\hat{\varepsilon}_t = Y_t - \hat{Y}_t$, are used to obtain an estimate of ρ according to Eq. 9.15. Y^* and X^* are calculated, and a regression is run of Y^* against X^*. This regression will yield estimators b_0 and b_1 of β_0 and β_1, respectively. A new set of residuals, $\hat{\varepsilon}_t = Y_t - (b_0 + b_1 X_t)$ is obtained, and a new estimate of ρ is calculated according to Eq. 9.15. That estimate is used to calculate once again Y^* and X^*, and another regression is run of Y^* against X^*. The process can be repeated for as many iterations as desired, but in practice it is terminated when successive estimates of ρ do not differ by more than a predetermined amount or the number of iterations exceeds a predetermined number.

Advanced statistical programs implement these and other estimation methods, which can be extended to other forms of serial correlation, such as

$$\varepsilon_t = \rho_1 \varepsilon_{t-1} + \rho_2 \varepsilon_{t-2} + \tilde{\varepsilon}_t$$
$$\varepsilon_t = \rho_1 \varepsilon_{t-1} + \rho_2 \varepsilon_{t-2} + \rho_3 \varepsilon_{t-3} + \tilde{\varepsilon}_t$$

and so on.[12] These methods, it should be kept in mind, are known to be superior to OLS when the number of observations is large. Unfortunately, it cannot be specified exactly how large n must be for the superiority to hold. Practice and convention suggest n should be at least 30, but this must be treated purely as a rule of thumb.

EXAMPLE 9.4

In Example 6.1, we found that a linear trend approximated quite well the annual sales (Y) of a company over a 20-year period. The data are shown in

---

[11]D. Cochrane and G. H. Orcutt, "Applications of Least Squares Regressions to Relationships Containing Autocorrelated Error Terms," *Journal of the American Statistical Association*, Vol. 44, 1949, pp. 32–61.

[12]These forms are referred to as *second-* and *third-order* models, respectively, of serial correlation, autocorrelation, or autoregression.

Table 6.1 and can be found in the file `csales1.dat`. The OLS results are as follows:

$$\hat{Y} = 13.793 + 0.390T \qquad R^2 = 0.997$$
$$(238.73) \quad (80.80) \qquad S = 0.124$$

where $T = 1, 2, \ldots, 20$. The residuals of this model, $\hat{\varepsilon} = Y - \hat{Y}$, are plotted in Figure 9.3.

It is clear that the residuals are not randomly distributed about zero (see Figure 3.8) but appear to have a pattern indicating that there may be a relationship between current and earlier ε's. Figure 9.4 is a plot of $\hat{\varepsilon}_t$ against $\hat{\varepsilon}_{t-1}$, which suggests a linear relationship between ε and ε_{-1}.

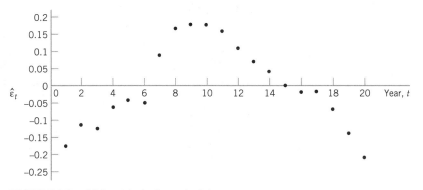

FIGURE 9.3 OLS residuals, Example 9.4

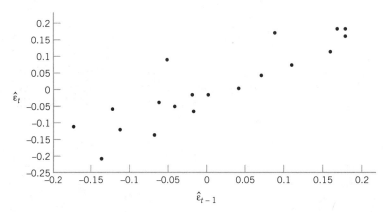

FIGURE 9.4 Plot of $\hat{\varepsilon}$ vs. $\hat{\varepsilon}_{-1}$, Example 9.4

It could be assumed, therefore, that the true relationship is $Y = \beta_0 + \beta_1 T + \varepsilon$, where $\varepsilon = \rho\varepsilon_{-1} + \tilde{\varepsilon}$. The SAS `proc autoreg` was applied to the data of Table 6.1, and its output is shown in Figure 9.5.[13]

The first part of Figure 9.5 shows the OLS results. It can be noted, for example, that the Durbin-Watson statistic is 0.19 and substantially different from 2. SAS employs an iterative estimation method similar to Cochrane-Orcutt. We cannot—and need not—interpret all the output in the second part of Figure 9.5. Suffice it to point out that the new estimates of the relationship between annual sales and time are

$$\hat{Y} = 13.755 + 0.389T$$
$$(153.39) \quad (56.30)$$

For technical reasons peculiar to this program, the estimate of ρ is the negative of the value shown under `Coefficient`, that is, $r = 0.7738$.

In this illustration, the number of observations is not large, and the new estimates of β_0 and β_1 are not appreciably different from the OLS estimates. If the number of observations was indeed large and confidence intervals or tests were required, however, these should be based on the second part of Figure 9.5.

For the sake of illustrating the calculations, let us pretend that $n = 20$ is large enough. The hypothesis, say, $H_0 : \beta_1 = 0$ should be rejected at the 0.05 level since $t = 56.30 > 1.96$. To form a 95% confidence interval for β_0, we calculate first $S_b = b_0/t_a = 13.755/153.39 = 0.0897$ and then the interval $(13.755) \pm (1.96)(0.0897)$, or from about 13.58 to 13.93. ∎

9.5 SPECIFICATION ERROR

As we pointed out in Section 1.8, we may not be able to predict accurately a variable of interest even when it is known to be related exactly to a number of explanatory variables. This is so for three reasons: (a) we may not know the form of the relationship, (b) we may not know all explanatory variables, and/or (c) we may not be able to measure without error some of the variables. For these reasons, we can expect a difference (an error, ε) between the dependent variable Y and whatever can be explained by the employed function $g()$ of the used explanatory variables $X_1, X_2, \ldots, X_k$. In symbols,

$$Y = g(X_1, X_2, \ldots, X_k) + \varepsilon$$

[13]The SAS statements were `proc autoreg; model Y=T/nlag=1;` the `nlag=1` option specifies a first-order model of serial correlation.

```
                            Autoreg Procedure

Dependent Variable = SALES

                    Ordinary Least Squares Estimates
           SSE              0.278432      DFE                 18
           MSE              0.015468      Root MSE    0.124372
           SBC            -22.7373        AIC         -24.7287
           Reg Rsq          0.9973        Total Rsq    0.9973
           Durbin-Watson    0.1924


Variable    DF      B Value    Std Error    t- Ratio    Approx Prob

Intercept    1    13.7927368    0.05777     238.733        0.0001
YR           1     0.3896917    0.00482      80.800        0.0001

--------------------------------------------------------------------

                 Estimates of Autocorrelations

Lag Covariance Correlation -1 9 8 7 6 5 4 3 2 1 0 1 2 3 4 5 6 7 8 9 1
 0   0.013922    1.000000 |                    |*******************|
 1   0.010772    0.773768 |                    |**************     |

                 Preliminary MSE = 0.005587

           Estimates of the Autoregressive Parameters

        Lag           Coefficient          Std Error            t-Ratio
         1           -0.77376774          0.15363890          -5.036275

                      Yule-Walker Estimates

           SSE              0.065091      DFE                 17
           MSE              0.003829      Root MSE    0.061878
           SBC            -47.8963        AIC         -50.8835
           Reg Rsq          0.9947        Total Rsq    0.9994
           Durbin-Watson 0.8917


Variable    DF     B Value    Std Error    t-Ratio    Approx Prob

Intercept    1   13.7553159    0.08968     153.387       0.0001
YR           1    0.3886561    0.00690      56.296       0.0001
```

FIGURE 9.5   SAS output, Example 9.4

Any assumptions made as a result of our ignorance concerning (a), (b), and/or (c) may lead to *specification error*, the error associated with failing to use the true relationship and variables.

It is almost inevitable that a specification error of some type will occur in practice. Thus, it is useful to be aware of the consequences of at least some kinds of specification error when the true relationship satisfies in other respects the conditions of linearity, constant variance, and independence.[14]

(A) Inclusion of Irrelevant Variables   Suppose that the true relationship is

$$Y = \beta_0 + \beta_1 X_1 + \varepsilon$$

but we mistakenly include a variable X_2 in the model and estimate

$$\hat{Y} = b_0 + b_1 X_1 + b_2 X_2$$

by regressing Y against X_1 and X_2. The true model can also be written as

$$Y = \beta_0 + \beta_1 X_1 + 0 X_2 + \varepsilon$$

and X_2 can be described as an irrelevant variable in that it does not influence Y.

It can be shown that the OLS estimators b_0 and b_1 are unbiased and consistent estimators of β_0 and β_1, respectively, and that the expected value of b_2 (its average value in a large number of repetitions of the process described by the true model) is zero. These results also hold for models with any number of explanatory variables. In this sense, therefore, no harm is done by including irrelevant variables in the model. This comforting conclusion, however, does not hold for other kinds of specification error, as we shall see next.

(B) Omission of Relevant Variables   Suppose that the true model is

$$Y = \beta_0 + \beta_1 X_1 + \beta_2 X_2 + \varepsilon$$

but we inadvertently omit X_2 and regress Y against X_1 only to obtain $\hat{Y} = b_0 + b_1 X_1$.

Obviously, no estimate can be made of β_2. It can be shown that b_0 and b_1 are biased and inconsistent estimators of β_0 and β_1 respectively. This conclusion holds for models with any number of variables: the omission of relevant variables makes the OLS estimators biased and inconsistent estimators of the true coefficients of the included variables.

(C) Overlooking a Nonlinear Relationship   Suppose that the true relationship between Y and X is parabolic:

$$Y = \beta_0 + \beta_1 X + \beta_2 X^2 + \varepsilon$$

[14]For a more rigorous treatment of specification error, see, for example, Johnston (1984, Ch. 6).

but it is mistakenly assumed to be linear and estimated by regressing Y against X to obtain $\hat{Y} = b_0 + b_1 X$.

It is clear that this case is like (B) in that a relevant variable, X^2, is left out of the model. We know, therefore, that the OLS estimators b_0 and b_1 are biased and are inconsistent estimators of β_0 and β_1.

The least harmful of the three types of specification error is the inclusion of irrelevant variables, an error that does not affect the unbiasedness and consistency of the OLS estimators of the relevant variables. To some critics, the conclusions in (B) and (C) considerably weaken the classical linear model and its desirable properties, for rarely can it be claimed that an applied study accounted for all relevant variables or discovered the true form of the relationship. Critics conclude that OLS estimators are nearly always biased and inconsistent, the only question being the extent of the bias or inconsistency. Unfortunately, the degree of bias and inconsistency cannot be determined or estimated in advance.

9.6 GENERALIZED LEAST SQUARES (GLS)

When the errors $\varepsilon_1, \varepsilon_2, \ldots, \varepsilon_n$ associated with the n sets of observations of the linear model are independent of one another and have the same variance σ^2, their covariance matrix (see Appendix A.10) can be written as

	ε_1	ε_2	$\cdots$	ε_n
ε_1	σ^2	0	$\cdots$	0
ε_2	0	σ^2	$\cdots$	0
$\cdots$	$\cdots$	$\cdots$	$\cdots$	$\cdots$
ε_n	0	0	$\cdots$	σ^2

Because of independence, all covariances (the off-diagonal elements of the matrix) are equal to zero. The diagonal elements reflect the equal variances. In such a case, as we know well by now, the OLS estimators are minimum variance linear unbiased and consistent.

When the ε_i's are independent but with variances $\sigma^2 Z_i^2$ (Z_i being constants as assumed in Section 9.3), the variance covariance matrix is

	ε_1	ε_2	$\cdots$	ε_n
ε_1	$\sigma^2 Z_1^2$	0	$\cdots$	0
ε_2	0	$\sigma^2 Z_2^2$	$\cdots$	0
$\cdots$	$\cdots$	$\cdots$	$\cdots$	$\cdots$
ε_n	0	0	$\cdots$	$\sigma^2 Z_n^2$

We noted in Section 9.3 that OLS applied to the transformed variables of Eq. 9.4 yields minimum variance linear unbiased and consistent estimators of the model's parameters. Indeed, it is also possible to obtain minimum variance linear unbiased and consistent estimators when the variances and covariances of the ε_i's are equal to a multiple of *any known* constants C_{ij}:

	ε_1	ε_2	$\cdots$	ε_n
ε_1	$\sigma^2 C_{11}$	$\sigma^2 C_{12}$	$\cdots$	$\sigma^2 C_{1n}$
ε_2	$\sigma^2 C_{12}$	$\sigma^2 C_{22}$	$\cdots$	$\sigma^2 C_{2n}$
$\cdots$	$\cdots$	$\cdots$	$\cdots$	$\cdots$
ε_n	$\sigma^2 C_{1n}$	$\sigma^2 C_{2n}$	$\cdots$	$\sigma^2 C_{nn}$

In other words, estimators with the desirable properties described in Chapter 3 can be obtained even when the errors are correlated, provided their variances and covariances are known apart from the common multiplier σ^2.

The method by which such estimators are derived is known as *generalized least squares (GLS)*, and the resulting estimators are called *GLS* or *Aitken* estimators. We do not make use of GLS in this text except to refer to it briefly later in Chapter 13. Computer programs implementing this method require input of the C_{ij} in addition to the observations. The expressions for the GLS estimators are given without proof in Appendix B.8; their derivation can be found in, among other sources, Johnston (1984, Ch. 8).

9.7 NONNORMALITY, THE GENERALIZED LINEAR MODEL (GLM)

Normality—or at least approximate normality—is necessary for the standard tests and confidence intervals concerning the model's parameters when the number of observations is small.

A plot of the relative frequency distribution of the model's residuals, which should look symmetric and bell shaped, can be used for a rough check of this assumption, as described in Sections 3.6 and 3.7.

The normal distribution plays a prominent role in statistics in part because of the relative ease with which it can be handled mathematically. Other distributions are not as tractable, and derivations and results tend to be more complicated.

Yet, the normal distribution—symmetric about its mean, bell shaped, and suitable for variables that take on any positive or negative value—is a poor model in situations where, say, Y or ε can take positive integer values only or their distributions are strongly asymmetric.

In recent years, considerable literature has accumulated regarding an extension of the classical linear model known as the *generalized linear model (GLM)*.

According to the alternate description of the classical linear model in Sections 3.3 and 3.5, it will be recalled, each observation Y_i is assumed to be selected at random and with replacement from a normal conditional population distribution $p(Y|X_{1i}, X_{2i}, \cdots, X_{ki})$ having mean $\mu_i = \beta_0 + \beta_1 X_{1i} + \beta_2 X_{2i} + \cdots + \beta_k X_{ki}$ and variance σ^2.

Under the GLM, each observation Y_i is assumed to be selected at random and with replacement from a population conditional distribution that is a member of the *exponential family of distributions* having mean μ_i and variance σ_i^2. The normal is a member of the exponential family, but members are also the Gamma, exponential, Bernoulli, binomial, and Poisson distributions familiar to students of introductory statistics.

It is further assumed under the GLM that a function of the mean is linearly related to the values of the explanatory variables:

$$g(\mu_i) = \beta_0 + \beta_1 X_{1i} + \beta_2 X_{2i} + \cdots + \beta_k X_{ki}$$

where the β's are parameters to be estimated.

The particular member of the exponential family as well as the function $g(\mu_i)$ must be specified in advance.

The parameters of the GLM are estimated by the maximum likelihood method (see Appendix B.7) and calculated by advanced statistical programs using an iterative numerical procedure.

It can be shown that the maximum likelihood estimators are consistent. When the number of observations is large, confidence intervals and tests based on these estimators can be calculated in the usual manner using estimates of the standard deviations of the parameters and t-ratios calculated by GLM programs.

This, in a nutshell, is the GLM. It is more general than the classical linear model in that the form of the population distribution of the Y_i can be other than the normal, its variance σ_i^2 need not be the same for all i, and the function $g(\mu_i)$ can be other than the identity $g(\mu_i) = \mu_i$.

A thorough description of the GLM is beyond the scope of this text. We illustrate with a single example and refer the interested reader to McCullagh and Nelder (1989) for additional information.

EXAMPLE 9.5

Let us suppose that the amount of the claim (Y) made on an automobile insurance policy tends to depend on the policyholder's age (X_1) and gender ($X_2 = 0$ for male, $X_2 = 1$ for female), and let us speculate on the form of the distribution of the claim amount for given X_1 and X_2.

Table 9.4 shows the distribution of the amount of third-party liability claim for 21,121 policies of an automobile insurance company against which claims were made in a given year.

Of the 21,121 policies that made a claim, 19,592 (or 92.76%) claimed an amount less than $1000, 948 (or 4.49%) claimed between $1000 and $5000, and so on. The mean claim size is about $100.

It is clear from Table 9.4 that the distribution of the amount of the claim is not at all symmetric about the mean claim or bell shaped. Furthermore, the claim amount cannot be negative. Of course, Table 9.4 does not shed any light on the distributions of the claim amount for policyholders having a given age and gender, but it suggests that these distributions are likely to have the shape shown in Figure 9.6.

TABLE 9.4   Distribution of Claim Amount, Example 9.5

Claim amount ($000)	Number of policies	Percentage of policies
to 1	19,592	92.76
1 to 5	948	4.49
5 to 10	300	1.42
10 to 25	181	0.86
25 to 50	61	0.29
50 to 100	27	0.13
100 to 250	8	0.04
250 to 500	3	0.01
500 to 1000	1	0.00

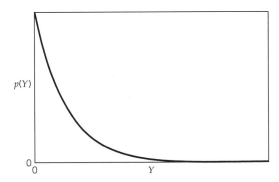

FIGURE 9.6 Exponential distribution of claim amount

Figure 9.6 is the plot of an *exponential distribution*, itself a special case of a *Gamma distribution*, defined as

$$p(Y) = \frac{1}{(v-1)!Y}\left(\frac{vY}{\mu}\right)^{v}\exp\left(-\frac{vY}{\mu}\right) \qquad (Y > 0)$$

where v and μ are parameters; μ is equal to the mean of the distribution. When $v = 1$, the Gamma becomes the exponential distribution $p(Y) = (1/\mu)\exp(-Y/\mu)$.

Let us further suppose that the mean μ of $p(Y)$ is a function of X_1 and X_2. Evidently, the simplest function is the linear one $\mu = \beta_0 + \beta_1 X_1 + \beta_2 X_2$. A linear function, however, may produce negative values of μ for certain values of the variables and parameters of the right-hand side. This awkward formulation can be avoided if it is assumed instead that

$$\mu = e^{\beta_0 + \beta_1 X_1 + \beta_2 X_2}$$

which is always positive and implies

$$\log(\mu) = \beta_0 + \beta_1 X_1 + \beta_2 X_2$$

Finally, let us suppose that the 10 claims presented in Table 9.5 were generated by the GLM process. That is, we regard each claim as a random draw with replacement from a Gamma population distribution of claim amount, one for each possible set of values of X_1 and X_2, the mean of which is such that $\log(\mu) = \beta_0 + \beta_1 X_1 + \beta_2 X_2$.

TABLE 9.5   Data for Example 9.5

Age, X_1	Gender, X_2	Claim, Y
20	1	100
37	0	525
26	0	2277
44	1	55
38	0	480
34	1	1262
31	0	981
47	0	360
45	1	152
42	0	97

SOURCE: File `glm1.dat`

A computer program was applied to the data of Table 9.5 and yielded the following results:[15]

$$\widehat{\log(\mu)} = 9.591 - 0.087X_1 - 0.514X_2$$
$$(6.74) \quad (-2.27) \quad (-0.95)$$

To forecast the claim by a 40-year-old female policyholder, we calculate first

$$\widehat{\log(\mu)} = 9.591 - (0.087)(40) - (0.514)(1) = 5.597$$

and then $e^{5.597}$ or \$269.62.

The numbers in parentheses are, as usual, t-ratios—that is, ratios of the estimates of the coefficients and their standard deviations, $t = b/S_b$. The latter are given by $S_b = b/t$.

If these results were based on a large number of observations (they are not), the hypothesis, say, $H_0 : \beta_2 = 0$ would be accepted at the 0.05 level since $|t| = 0.95 < 1.96$. Under the same conditions, a, say, 95% confidence interval for β_1 would be $(-0.087) \pm (1.96)(-0.087/ - 2.29)$, or from about -0.162 to -0.012. ∎

9.8 RIDGE REGRESSION

The goal of ridge regression is to estimate more accurately than the method of least squares the parameters of the linear model

$$Y = \beta_0 + \beta_1 X_1 + \beta_2 X_2 + \ldots + \beta_k X_k + \varepsilon$$

particularly when multicollinearity is present.

Ridge regression essentially consists of adding an arbitrary positive constant c to the coefficients of the parameters in the diagonal terms of the normal equations defined in Section 2.4. For example, when there is only one explanatory variable, the normal equations (Eq. 2.6) are modified as follows:

$$(n + c)b_0 + (\sum X)b_1 = \sum Y$$
$$(\sum X)b_0 + (\sum X^2 + c)b_1 = \sum XY$$

In the general case of the system Eq. 2.5 of normal equations, the modification consists of changing the coefficient of b_0 in the first equation from n to

---

[15]Program SAS with the statements `proc genmod; model y = x1 x2 / dist = gamma link = log;`.

$(n + c)$, that of b_1 in the second equation from $\sum X_1^2$ to $(\sum X_1^2 + c)$, and so on. The constant c can be any positive number. The values of $b_0, b_1, b_2, \ldots, b_k$ that solve the modified system of normal equations are called the *ridge estimators*.

The calculations are carried out by computer programs and need not concern us here. In a moment we shall illustrate, but first let us explain the rationale of ridge regression.

If the process that generates the observations of the linear model satisfies the conditions of linearity, constant variance, and independence described in Section 3.2, it can be shown that the ridge estimators of the parameters $\beta_0, \beta_1, \ldots, \beta_k$ are biased but have smaller variance than the OLS estimators.[16] In other words, if b is the OLS estimator of a parameter β and b' the ridge estimator of the same parameter, it can be shown that $E(b') \neq \beta$ but $Var(b') < Var(b)$. The situation is pictured in Figure 9.7.

Shown in Figure 9.7 are the probability distributions of the estimators, that is, their expected relative frequency distributions in a large number of the experiments described in Section 3.2.

Let us digress for a moment and consider how to compare two estimators, one of which is unbiased but with relatively larger variance while the other is biased but with relatively smaller variance.

A reasonable criterion is the *mean square error (MSE)*, which is defined as the expected long run average value of the squared error $(b - \beta)^2$ of an estimator b of β. The mean square error, in turn, can be shown to be equal to the sum of the variance and the squared bias of the estimator; in symbols,

$$MSE(b) = Var(b) + [E(b) - \beta]^2$$

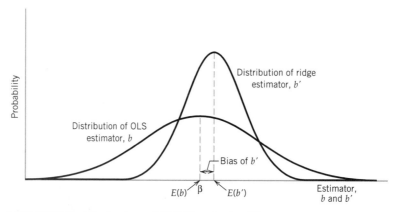

FIGURE 9.7 Distributions of OLS (b) and ridge (b') estimators

[16]See, for example, Gruber (1990).

Evidently, $MSE(b) = Var(b)$ if b is unbiased. In comparing two estimators of a parameter based on the same number of observations it is reasonable to prefer the estimator with the smaller mean square error.

Returning to ridge regression, it can be shown that there is a value of c at which the MSE of a ridge estimator is smaller than the MSE of the corresponding OLS estimator. The problem is that this value depends on unknown process parameters and cannot be determined in advance. If estimates of these parameters are used to estimate c, it cannot be guaranteed that the estimated value of c is one at which the ridge estimator is superior to the OLS estimator. Further, that value may be different for ridge estimators of different parameters.

A technique is sometimes suggested according to which the ridge estimators are calculated for a number of values of c. A plot of these estimates as a function of c often indicates that the estimates tend to stabilize as c increases. One is advised to select the minimum value of c at which all ridge estimates appear stabilized.

EXAMPLE 9.6

In Example 3.1, we examined the relationship between the price of a residential property, on the one hand, and its floor area and lot size, on the other. The data can be found in the file `rest.dat`. The statistical program SAS was used to calculate ridge estimates for values of c ranging from 0.0 to 20 in increments of 0.5.[17] The values of c are shown under the label _RIDGE_ and the ridge estimates under the labels INTERCEP to LOT in the partial listing of the output shown in Figure 9.8.

In this output, _RMSE_ is S. The ridge estimates for $c = 0.0$ are, of course, the OLS estimates. S and the ridge estimates are plotted in Figures 9.9 and 9.10 as functions of c.

OBS	_MODEL_	_TYPE_	_DEPVAR_	_RIDGE_	_PCOMIT_	_RMSE_	INTERCEP	FLOOR	LOT	PRICE
1	MODEL1	PARMS	PRICE	.	.	102.469	69.854	0.20284	0.021780	−1
2	MODEL1	RIDGE	PRICE	0.0	.	102.469	69.854	0.20284	0.021780	−1
3	MODEL1	RIDGE	PRICE	0.5	.	108.693	167.384	0.13626	0.014748	−1
4	MODEL1	RIDGE	PRICE	1.0	.	116.137	216.921	0.10259	0.011148	−1
5	MODEL1	RIDGE	PRICE	1.5	.	121.775	246.895	0.08226	0.008960	−1
6	MODEL1	RIDGE	PRICE	2.0	.	125.964	266.983	0.06866	0.007490	−1
...	...	...	...	...	...	...	...	...	...	...
42	MODEL1	RIDGE	PRICE	20.0	.	147.146	354.057	0.00988	0.001084	−1

FIGURE 9.8 Partial listing of SAS output, Example 9.6

[17]The SAS statements were `proc reg ridge = 0.0 to 20.0 by 0.5 outest = temp;` `model price = floor lot;`. The temporary file `temp` stores the results of ridge regression.

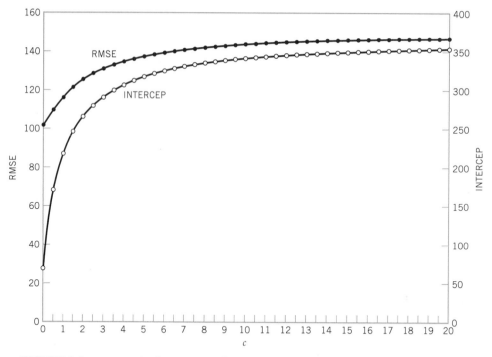

FIGURE 9.9 RMSE and ridge estimate of intercept, Example 9.6

It would appear that S and the ridge estimates are stabilized by $c = 20$, suggesting that the relationship between price, floor area, and lot size can be estimated as

$$PRICE = 354.057 + 0.0099FLOOR + 0.0011LOT \qquad S = 147.146$$

It can be noted that these estimates are quite different from the OLS ones ($c = 0.0$). The ridge estimate of the intercept is nearly five times the OLS estimate. The ridge estimates of the value of one square foot of floor and lot area are about 5% of the corresponding OLS estimates. The fit of the ridge estimates, as measured by S^2, is only half as good as that of the OLS estimates. ∎

There is no guarantee, it must be pointed out again, that the ridge estimators produced by this technique have better properties than the OLS estimators. The ridge estimators, of course, do not fit the observations as well as the OLS estimators. One must conclude, therefore, that there are no compelling reasons for preferring ridge estimation to OLS.

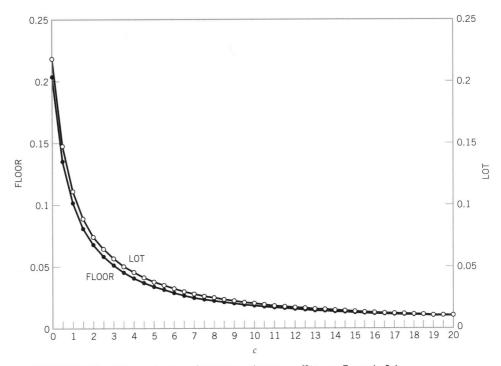

FIGURE 9.10 Ridge estimates of FLOOR and LOT coefficients, Example 9.6

9.9 TO SUM UP

- If a nonlinear model can be made linear after the variables are transformed and the linear model satisfies the conditions of the classical linear model, the OLS estimators of the parameters of the linear model have all the desirable properties described in Chapter 3. Nonlinear regression estimators have similar properties to the OLS estimators when the number of observations is large.

- The OLS estimators of a model with nonconstant variance are unbiased and consistent but not minimum variance linear unbiased. In some cases explained in Section 9.3, models violating the constant variance condition can be recast in terms of transformed variables, so that the OLS estimators of the parameters have the desirable properties described in Chapter 3.

- Values of r close to 0 or of the Durbin-Watson statistic close to 2 are indications that first-order serial correlation is not present. OLS estimators remain unbiased and consistent even when serial correlation is present, but the standard tests and confidence intervals should not be applied. A number of methods (including the Durbin and Cochrane-Orcutt procedures) are available for estimating models with serial correlation.

- The least harmful kind of specification error is the inclusion of irrelevant variables, but the omission of relevant variables results in biased and inconsistent estimation of the parameters of the included variables.

- Minimum variance linear unbiased and consistent estimators of a linear model's parameters can be obtained by generalized least squares (GLS) even when the errors are correlated, provided their variances and covariances are known apart from a common multiplier.

- The GLM is more general than the classical linear model in that the distribution from which each observation is drawn can be other than normal and the relationship between the mean of these distributions and the explanatory variables can be other than linear. The maximum likelihood estimators of the parameters of the GLM are consistent, and tests and confidence intervals can be constructed when the number of observations is large.

- Ridge estimators are neither unbiased nor necessarily more accurate (in terms of mean squared error) than the OLS estimators.

PROBLEMS

9.1 Refer to Example 5.2 concerning the relationship between starting salary, on the one hand, and educational level and experience, on the other.

(a) Under what conditions can confidence intervals be constructed and tests concerning the model's parameters carried out? Describe how these conditions may be roughly checked.

(b) Assuming the conditions in (a) are satisfied, test the hypothesis that the effect of specific experience is linear (and not quadratic). Use an appropriate level α.

(c) Assuming the conditions in (a) are satisfied, test the hypothesis that the effect of general experience is linear (and not quadratic). Use an appropriate level α.

(d) How would you test the hypothesis that the effects of *both* specific and general experience are linear? Describe clearly.

9.2 Refer to Example 5.3 and the relationship between gas consumption (GASCON) and temperature (TEMP),

$$GASCON = \beta_0 + \beta_1 TEMP + \beta_2(TEMP - 18)D + \varepsilon$$

where D is a dummy variable taking the value 1 if $TEMP \leq 18$ or 0 otherwise.

(a) Under what conditions can confidence intervals be constructed and tests concerning the model's parameters carried out? Describe how these conditions may be roughly checked.

(b) Using the data in the file norgas.dat, determine whether or not the conditions in (a) are satisfied.

(c) Assuming the conditions in (a) are satisfied, test the hypothesis that temperature has no effect on gas consumption at an appropriate level α of significance.

9.3   Consider the following nonlinear models:

$$
\begin{aligned}
A: &\quad Y = \beta_0 \beta_1^X + \varepsilon \\
B: &\quad Y = \beta_0 X^{\beta_1} + \varepsilon \\
C: &\quad Y = \beta_0 + \beta_1 \log X + \varepsilon
\end{aligned}
$$

The models are listed in slightly different form in Table 5.8.

In what manner and under what conditions can one obtain consistent estimators, and form confidence intervals and carry out tests concerning the parameters β_0 and β_1 of each model?

9.4   In Example 5.4, the following model was estimated of the relationship between electricity consumption (Y), on the one hand, and refrigerator (X_1) and freezer (X_2) volumes, on the other.

$$
\widehat{\log Y} = 4.457 + \log 0.079 X_1 + \log 0.127 X_2 \qquad R^2 = 0.82
$$
$$
\quad\quad\quad\quad\quad (1.23) \quad\quad\quad\quad (3.64) \quad\quad\quad\quad S = 0.514
$$

(a) Show that this model is derived from the nonlinear model $Y = \beta_0 X_1^{\beta_1} X_2^{\beta_2} \varepsilon$.

(b) Under what conditions can confidence intervals be constructed and tests concerning the model's parameters carried out? Describe how these conditions may be roughly checked.

(c) Assuming that these conditions are satisfied, calculate 95% confidence intervals for β_1 and β_2.

(d) Test the hypothesis that $\beta_1 = 0$ at the 0.05 level.

9.5   **(a)** Suppose that $Y = \beta_0 + \beta_1 X + \varepsilon$, $E(\varepsilon) = 0$, and $Var(\varepsilon) = \sigma^2 X$. Think of the error ε as the outcome of a random draw with replacement from separate populations of ε-values, one for each possible value of X, each such population of ε-values having mean 0 and variance $\sigma^2 X$. Show that estimators of β_0 and β_1 with the desirable properties described in Section 3.2 can be obtained by regressing $Y' = Y/\sqrt{X}$ against $X_1 = 1/\sqrt{X}$ and $X_2 = \sqrt{X}$ with zero intercept. Show that the estimate of β_0 is the regression coefficient of X_1 and that of β_1 the regression coefficient of X_2.

(b) Using the data of Table 9.1, estimate the model in (a). Plot the estimated relationship in the manner of Figure 9.2. Compare your results with those in Example 9.2.

9.6   Table 9.6 shows the population (POP), average personal income (INC), average age (AGE), and proportion of persons with university education (EDU) in 15 census tracts selected at random and with replacement from among 580 census tracts comprising a metropolitan area.

Assume that the relationship between a person's income (Y), on the one hand, and the person's age (X_1) and education (X_2) is $Y = \beta_0 + \beta_1 X_1 + \beta_2 X_2 + \varepsilon$, where $X_2 = 1$ if a person has university education and $X_2 = 0$ otherwise, and the ε's are independent with $E(\varepsilon) = 0$ and $Var(\varepsilon) = \sigma^2$.

(a) Estimate the model by OLS.

(b) Estimate the model's parameters using the method of Example 9.2.

TABLE 9.6   Data for Problem 9.6

CT No.	POP	INC	AGE	EDU
1	1461	37.9	29.0	0.078
2	532	39.4	28.1	0.089
3	2168	38.5	28.8	0.060
4	1167	39.3	27.0	0.047
5	3119	35.2	26.7	0.080
6	2863	35.2	27.7	0.057
7	248	34.2	27.2	0.058
8	1544	34.5	29.5	0.045
9	3049	34.8	26.1	0.068
10	657	37.9	30.6	0.090
11	1009	38.9	27.0	0.069
12	350	35.2	28.7	0.033
13	307	34.0	27.0	0.045
14	742	34.1	26.0	0.052
15	925	35.2	28.1	0.067

SOURCE: File `ctracts.dat`

(c) Compare the results in (a) and (b). What is the advantage—if any—of the method in (b) over that in (a)?

9.7 Refer to Example 9.4 and the data in the file `csales1.dat`. Estimate ρ, β_0, and β_1 by the Durbin procedure. Compare your estimates with those given in Example 9.4.

9.8 Same as Problem 9.7, except use two iterations of the Cochrane-Orcutt procedure.

9.9 Refer to Example 9.4 and the data in the file `csales1.dat`. Can you account for the pattern of the residuals with a different model? If so, estimate this model and compare your results to those in Example 9.4.

9.10 Refer to Example 2.2 of Section 2.7 concerning the model

$$GASCON = \beta_0 + \beta_1 TEMP + \beta_2 WIND + \varepsilon$$

Check whether or not the assumptions of the classical linear model are approximately satisfied. Re-estimate the model if they are not.

9.11 Refer to Example 2.3 of Section 2.10 concerning the relationship between the strength (Y) of the plastic material, on the one hand, and barrel temperature (X_1), mold temperature (X_2), and injection pressure (X_3), on the other,

$$Y = \beta_0 + \beta_1 X_1 + \beta_2 X_2 + \beta_3 X_3 + \varepsilon$$

Check whether or not the assumptions of the classical linear model are approximately satisfied. Re-estimate the model if they are not.

9.12 Refer to Example 2.4 of Section 2.10 concerning the relationship between the per capita consumption of beef (QB), on the one hand, and the deflated prices of beef (DPB), pork (DPP), other meats ($DPOM$), and income ($DPDI$), on the other,

$$QB = \beta_0 + \beta_1 DPB + \beta_2 DPP + \beta_3 DPOM + \beta_4 DPDI + \varepsilon$$

Check whether or not the assumptions of the classical linear model are approximately satisfied. Re-estimate the model if they are not.

9.13 Refer to Example 2.4 of Section 2.10 concerning the relationship between the per capita consumption of pork (QP), on the one hand, and the deflated prices of beef (DPB), pork (DPP), other meats ($DPOM$), and income ($DPDI$), on the other,

$$QP = \beta_0 + \beta_1 DPB + \beta_2 DPP + \beta_3 DPOM + \beta_4 DPDI + \varepsilon$$

Check whether or not the assumptions of the classical linear model are approximately satisfied. Re-estimate the model if they are not.

9.14 Refer to Problem 5.9 regarding the relationship between the interest rate (Y), on the one hand, and the amount of loans closed (X_1) and vacancy index (X_2), on the other. The data are in the file `bareal.dat`.

(a) Estimate by OLS the model $Y = \beta_0 + \beta_1 X_1 + \beta_2 X_2 + \beta_3 X_1^2 + \varepsilon$. Asssuming that the model satisfies the conditions of the classical linear model, form approximate 90% confidence intervals for β_1, β_2, and β_3.

(b) Is there any evidence in (a) of first-order serial correlation? If so, estimate the model's parameters by an appropriate method. Form approximate 90% confidence intervals for β_1, β_2, and β_3.

(c) Comment on the results in (a) and (b).

9.15 (a) Refer to Example 6.2 and the data in the file `airline.dat` concerning the average daily number of passengers on transatlantic flights (Y). Estimate again by OLS the model $Y = \beta_0 + \beta_1 T + \beta_2 M_2 + \cdots + \beta_{12} M_{12} + \varepsilon$ to determine if first-order serial correlation is present. If so, reestimate the model using any suitable method. Compare your results with those in Example 6.2.

(b) Same as (a), except let Y stand for the average daily number of passengers on transcontinental flights, also included in the file `airline.dat`.

9.16 Refer to Example 6.4 and the data in the file `shoes.dat` concerning the quarterly shoe store sales (Y). Estimate again by OLS the model $\log Y = \beta_0 + \beta_1 T + \beta_2 Q_2 + \cdots + \beta_4 Q_4 + \varepsilon$ to determine if first-order serial correlation is present. If so, reestimate the model using any suitable method. Compare your results with those in Example 6.4.

9.17 Refer to Section 9.5 and the conclusion that no harm is done by including in the model irrelevant variables. Does this mean that every conceivable variable should be thrown into the model? What would you say if in Example 9.4 the company's annual sales were expressed as a function of time *and* the population of Nepal, the number of home runs scored in professional baseball games, the mean temperature in Burundi, and other variables of the same nature?

9.18 Suppose the true relationship between Y and X_1 and X_2 is

$$Y = \beta_0 + \beta_1 X_1 + \beta_2 X_2 + \beta_3 X_1 X_2 + \varepsilon$$

but instead the following linear model is estimated,

$$\hat{Y} = b_0 + b_1 X_1 + b_2 X_2$$

What are the consequences of this specification error?

9.19   Describe a type of specification error other than (A), (B), or (C) in Section 9.5. Speculate on the likely consequences of such an error.

9.20   Suppose $Y_i = \beta_0 + \beta_1 X_i + \varepsilon_i$, $i = 1, 2, \ldots, n$, where the ε_i are independent, with mean 0 and variance $Var(\varepsilon_i) = \sigma^2 X_i^2$. Write the variance covariance matrix of the ε's.

9.21   Same as Problem 9.20, except that $Var(\varepsilon_i) = \sigma^2 X_i$.

9.22   Consider the first-order model of serial correlation described in Section 9.4:

$$Y_t = \beta_0 + \beta_1 X_t + \varepsilon_t \qquad (t = 1, 2, \ldots, n)$$

where $\varepsilon_t = \rho \varepsilon_{t-1} + \tilde{\varepsilon}_t$, and the $\tilde{\varepsilon}_t$ are independent with $E(\tilde{\varepsilon}_t) = 0$ and $Var(\tilde{\varepsilon}_t) = \sigma^2$.

(a) Through successive substitutions, show that

$$\varepsilon_t = \tilde{\varepsilon}_t + \rho \tilde{\varepsilon}_{t-1} + \rho^2 \tilde{\varepsilon}_{t-2} + \rho^3 \tilde{\varepsilon}_{t-3} + \cdots$$

(b) Assuming $|\rho| < 1$, apply the results of Appendix A.11 to show that

$$Var(\varepsilon_t) = \frac{\sigma^2}{1 - \rho^2}$$

Hint: The sum of a geometric series $1 + c + c^2 + c^3 + \cdots$ is $1/(1 - c)$ if $0 < c < 1$ (see another application of this result in Section 7.4).

(c) Apply the results of Appendix A.12 to show that

$$Cov(\varepsilon_t, \varepsilon_{t-j}) = \sigma^2 \frac{\rho^j}{1 - \rho^2}$$

(d) In view of the results in (b) and (c), write the variance covariance matrix of $\varepsilon_1, \varepsilon_2, \ldots, \varepsilon_n$. Explain why this model cannot be estimated by GLS.

9.23   If you have access to a computer program for estimating the GLM, confirm the results of Example 9.5 using the data in the file `glm1.dat`.

9.24   Refer to Example 9.5 and the data in the file `glm1.dat`.

(a) Estimate by OLS the model $Y = \beta_0 + \beta_1 X_1 + \beta_2 X_2 + \varepsilon$.
(b) Estimate by OLS the model $\log Y = \beta_0 + \beta_1 X_1 + \beta_2 X_2 + \varepsilon$.
(c) If you have access to a suitable computer program, estimate a GLM model assuming the population distribution is normal and $\mu = \beta_0 + \beta_1 X_1 + \beta_2 X_2$.
(d) Same as (c), except $\log(\mu) = \beta_0 + \beta_1 X_1 + \beta_2 X_2$.
(e) Comment on the results in (a) to (d) and in Example 9.5.

9.25   With the help of a computer program, apply ridge regression to estimate the model of Example 2.2 using the data file `gascon.dat`. Plot the actual and estimated values obtained by OLS and ridge regression. Comment.

9.26 With the help of a computer program, apply ridge regression to estimate the model of Example 2.3 using the data file `plmat.dat`. Plot the actual and estimated values obtained by OLS and ridge regression. Comment.

9.27 With the help of a computer program, apply ridge regression to estimate the models of Example 2.4 using the data file `bfpk.dat`. Plot the actual and estimated values obtained by OLS and ridge regression. Comment.

CHAPTER 10

AUTOREGRESSIVE MODELS

10.1 INTRODUCTION AND SUMMARY

We examined time series first in Chapter 6, where we applied regression to estimate the trend and seasonality of a series. As we noted in Section 6.6, a feature of time series analysis is the assumption that the entire information required for the analysis and forecasting of the series is contained in the series itself. This, we pointed out, is the most convenient feature but also the most serious shortcoming of the approach.

Regression against time trend and dummy variables, however, is not the only means for exploiting the information provided by the series. In this chapter we shall examine a class of models relating the current value to past values of the series. As the starting method for estimating such relationships is regression of the series against the same series lagged one, two, and so on periods, the models we shall examine are called "autoregressive," or AR for short. Further refinements lead to the so-called autoregressive integrated (ARI), autoregressive moving average (ARMA), and autoregressive integrated moving average (ARIMA) models, which we intend to describe in the following sections.

10.2 AUTOREGRESSION

We have in mind a time series Y of hourly, daily, weekly, or other periodic observations. Using the alternative notation introduced in Section 7.2, we let Y_t denote the value of the series in period t.

An extremely simple forecasting model could use as the forecast of the current value of the series the actual value of the series in the previous period (assumed to be known when the forecast is made):

$$\hat{Y}_t = Y_{t-1} \tag{10.1}$$

Another simple model could add to the value of the series in the last period a certain multiple or fraction of the change in the value of the series over the past two periods,

$$\hat{Y}_t = Y_{t-1} + c(Y_{t-1} - Y_{t-2}) = (1+c)Y_{t-1} - cY_{t-2} \qquad (10.2)$$

where $c > 0$.

A slightly more complicated model could use the moving average of the past k values of the series as the forecast of the current value,

$$\hat{Y}_t = \frac{1}{k}(Y_{t-1} + Y_{t-2} + \cdots + Y_{t-k}) = \frac{1}{k}Y_{t-1} + \frac{1}{k}Y_{t-2} + \cdots + \frac{1}{k}Y_{t-k} \qquad (10.3)$$

The weights applied to the past values of the series, rather than being equal to $1/k$, could vary:

$$\hat{Y}_t = w_1 Y_{t-1} + w_2 Y_{t-2} + \cdots + w_k Y_{t-k} \qquad (10.4)$$

where all $w_j \geq 0$ and $\sum_j w_j = 1$. It could also be required that the weights decline with distance from the current period, that is, $w_1 > w_2 > \cdots > w_k$. The weights could be further specified as functions of other basic parameters. For example, it could be required that

$$w_j = b^j$$

where b is the single basic parameter. This implies that $w_1 = b^1 = b$, $w_2 = b^2, \ldots, w_k = b^k$. Substituting these into Eq. 10.4, we find

$$\hat{Y}_t = bY_{t-1} + b^2 Y_{t-2} + \cdots + b^k Y_{t-k} \qquad (10.5)$$

If $0 < b < 1$, then $b > b^2 > \cdots > b_k$, and the weights would decline with the time lag. For instance, if $b = 0.7$, then $b^2 = 0.49$, $b^3 = 0.34$, and so on. Model 10.5 is one of several extant versions of *exponential smoothing* that are quite popular in certain business fields.

In Models 10.1 and 10.3 the values of the parameters are specified by the model; in all other models the parameters are estimated so as to best fit the past observations of the series.

Models 10.1 to 10.5, as well as variations of these models, are constrained cases of the *autoregressive model*

$$\hat{Y}_t = b_0 + b_1 Y_{t-1} + b_2 Y_{t-2} + \cdots + b_k Y_{t-k} \qquad (10.6)$$

or, in the notation for variables,

$$\hat{Y} = b_0 + b_1 Y_{-1} + b_2 Y_{-2} + \cdots + b_k Y_{-k} \tag{10.7}$$

By "constrained" we mean special cases of the autoregressive model in which the model's parameters must satisfy certain constraints. For example, we see that Model 10.1 is an autoregressive model with $k = 1$, $b_0 = 0$, and $b_1 = 1$; likewise, Model 10.2 is the autoregressive model with $k = 2$, $b_0 = 0$, $b_2 < 0$, and $b_1 + b_2 = 1$; Model 10.5 is 10.7 subject to the constraints that $b_0 = 0$, and $b_j = b^j$, $0 < b < 1$, for $j = 1, 2, \ldots, k$, and so on.

As there are usually no compelling theoretical reasons for imposing the constraints and good practical reasons for seeking heuristically the best-fitting unconstrained values of the parameters, the autoregressive model may be estimated by regressing the time series Y against the same series lagged one (Y_{-1}), two $(Y_{-2}), \ldots, k\,(Y_{-k})$ periods.

The maximum lag, k, is usually determined empirically. We begin with $k = 1$, and observe the R^2 or S of the model. Next, we estimate a second model with $k = 2$, and observe the R^2 or S of this model. We then proceed to estimate models with $k = 3, k = 4$, and so on. As k increases, R^2 increases and S declines, but beyond a certain point the improvement of fit is likely to be small. The maximum lag is that value of k beyond which there is no further noticeable improvement.

EXAMPLE 10.1

The third column of Table 10.1 shows a monthly series of federal funds interest rates, Y. These are the rates at which federally chartered banks borrow from and lend to one another funds temporarily in excess of the regulatory requirements. The remaining columns of Table 10.1 show the series of interest rates lagged one to six months.

Thus, the column labeled Y_{-1} is column Y "pushed down" one line, Y_{-2} is Y pushed down two lines (or, Y_{-1} pushed down one line), and so on.

Following are selected regression results for $k = 1$ to $k = 6$.

k	n	S	R^2
1	47	0.6313	0.9417
2	46	0.5588	0.9562
3	45	0.4814	0.9678
4	44	0.4806	0.9681
5	43	0.4915	0.9668
6	42	0.4824	0.9688

TABLE 10.1 **Federal Funds Interest Rates, Example 10.1**

Year	Month	Y	Y_{-1}	Y_{-2}	Y_{-3}	Y_{-4}	Y_{-5}	Y_{-6}
19X3	May	7.95						
	Jun.	8.59	7.95					
	Jul.	10.58	8.59	7.95				
	Aug.	10.79	10.58	8.59	7.95			
	Sep.	10.84	10.79	10.58	8.59	7.95		
	Oct.	9.90	10.84	10.79	10.58	8.59	7.95	
	Nov.	10.09	9.90	10.84	10.79	10.58	8.59	7.95
	Dec.	9.52	10.09	9.90	10.84	10.79	10.58	8.59
...	...	...	...	...	...	...	...	...
19X7	Apr.	4.82	4.74	4.74	4.72	4.66	4.90	4.99

SOURCE: File ffunds.dat

Each model uses all complete sets of observations. As a result, n varies, and S and R^2 do not improve uniformly with n. Best were thought to be the results with $k = 3$, which were in full as follows:

$$\hat{Y} = 0.3278 + 1.2617Y_{-1} - 0.1104Y_{-2} - 0.2074Y_{-3}$$
$$(1.43) \quad (9.60) \quad (-0.50) \quad (-1.58)$$

Actual and estimated interest rates are shown in Figure 10.1.

At first glance, the fit appears remarkably good. On closer inspection, however, it is clear that the model is at its worst at points where the series changes direction abruptly (the "turning points" of the series). At these points, the estimated values appear to fall behind the actual values of the series.

To forecast the rate for May 19X7, we apply the estimated model with Y_{-1} equal to the rate for April 19X7, Y_{-2} equal to the rate for March 19X7, and Y_{-3} equal to the rate for February 19X7:

$$\hat{Y} = 0.3278 + (1.2617)(4.82) - (0.1104)(4.74) - (0.2074)(4.74) = 4.90$$

The model cannot forecast more than one month ahead because the required actual values of the lagged variables are not known. One possibility is to use the *forecasts* of these values produced by the model. For example, the forecast for June 19X7 would be

$$\hat{Y} = 0.3278 + (1.2617)(4.90) - (0.1104)(4.82) - (0.2074)(4.74) = 4.99$$

As successive monthly observations become available, one-period forecasts can be made in at least three ways: (a) using the model as estimated

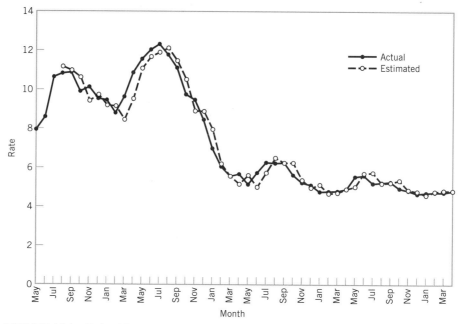

FIGURE 10.1 Federal funds interest rates, Example 10.1

above; (b) reestimating the parameters of the model using the most recent n observations and then forecasting; or (c) first modifying the model to find the best k, estimating the parameters of that model, and then forecasting. ∎

10.3 SERIES WITH TREND AND NO SEASONALITY

Often in practice, the number of lagged terms (k) is heuristically determined, and the OLS estimates of the model's parameters are used for forecasting with little concern about their numerical values. It is useful, however, to consider the values of k and of the OLS estimates implied by series that follow certain common patterns of trend and seasonality.

To begin, let us suppose that a series Y exhibits a linear trend but no seasonality, that is,

$$Y_t \approx c_0 + c_1 t$$

where c_0 and c_1 are some constants and t is the number of the time period. The symbol $\approx$ means "approximately equal to." Since

$$Y_{t-1} \approx c_0 + c_1(t-1)$$

it follows that

$$Y_t - Y_{t-1} \approx c_1 t - c_1(t-1) = c_1$$

In words, the first difference of a series with linear trend is approximately constant. This suggests

$$\hat{Y}_t = c_1 + Y_{t-1}$$

and an autoregressive model with $k = 1$,

$$\hat{Y}_t = b_0 + b_1 Y_{t-1}$$

In the alternative notation, this last model can be written as

$$\hat{Y} = b_0 + b_1 Y_{-1}$$

For a series with linear trend, the estimate b_1 can be expected to be close to 1.

EXAMPLE 10.2

In Example 6.1, we used a model with linear trend to forecast the annual sales of a company. A partial listing of the data is reproduced in column 2 of Table 10.2. The remaining columns will be explained shortly.

Applying an autoregressive model with $k = 1$, we obtain the following results:

$$\hat{Y} = 0.6876 + 0.9831 Y_{-1} \qquad R^2 = 0.9997 \qquad n = 19$$
$$(227.06) \qquad\qquad S = 0.0407$$

The forecast of sales in Year 21 is

$$\hat{Y} = 0.6876 + 0.9831(21.38) = 21.71$$

Actual and estimated sales based on this autoregressive model are shown in Figure 10.2. ∎

TABLE 10.2   Company Sales, Example 10.2

Year (1)	Sales, Y (2)	Y_{-1} (3)	$Z = Y - Y_{-1}$ (4)	Z_{-1} (5)	$V = Z - Z_{-1}$ (6)	Y_{-2} (7)
1	14.01	-	-	-	-	-
2	14.46	14.01	0.45	-	-	-
3	14.84	14.46	0.38	0.45	−0.07	14.01
4	15.29	14.84	0.45	0.38	0.07	14.46
5	15.70	15.29	0.41	0.45	−0.04	14.84
6	16.08	15.70	0.38	0.41	−0.03	15.29
7	16.61	16.08	0.53	0.38	0.15	15.70
...	...	...	...	...	...	...
19	21.06	20.74	0.32	0.34	−0.02	20.40
20	21.38	21.06	0.32	0.32	0.00	20.74

SOURCE: File csales1.dat

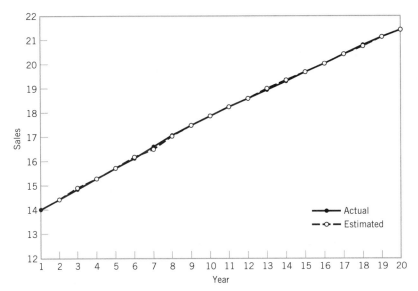

FIGURE 10.2   Company sales, Example 10.2

If a series follows a parabolic trend and shows no seasonality, then

$$Y_t \approx c_0 + c_1 t + c_2 t^2$$

and

$$Y_{t-1} \approx c_0 + c_1(t-1) + c_2(t-1)^2$$

The first difference of this series, $Z_t = Y_t - Y_{t-1}$, is

$$
\begin{aligned}
Z_t = Y_t - Y_{t-1} &\approx [c_0 + c_1 t + c_2 t^2] - [c_0 + c_1(t-1) + c_2(t-1)^2] \\
&\approx c_1 t + c_2 t^2 - c_1 t + c_1 - c_2(t^2 - 2t + 1) \\
&\approx (c_1 - c_2) + 2c_2 t
\end{aligned}
$$

In words, the first difference of the series follows a linear trend. The second difference of the series (the first difference of the first difference), V_t, is

$$
V_t = Z_t - Z_{t-1} \approx [c_1 + 2c_2 t - c_2] - [c_1 + 2c_2(t-1) - c_2] = 2c_2
$$

In words, the second difference of the series is approximately constant,

$$
(Y_t - Y_{t-1}) - (Y_{t-1} - Y_{t-2}) \approx c
$$

where c is a constant, and

$$
Y_t \approx c + 2Y_{t-1} - Y_{t-2}
$$

This suggests that an autoregressive model with $k = 2$

$$
\hat{Y} = b_0 + b_1 Y_{-1} + b_2 Y_{-2}
$$

may be appropriate for a series with parabolic trend. It can be expected that $b_1 \approx 2$ and $b_2 \approx -1$.

EXAMPLE 10.2 (CONTINUED)

Let us take a closer look at the data of Table 10.2. The first difference of the series (the change in annual sales) is shown in column 4 and is plotted in Figure 10.3.

It appears that the first difference follows a linear trend, as expected for a series the original values of which follow a parabolic trend. In such a case, the second difference tends to be constant. This expectation appears to be borne out in the plot of the second difference of company sales shown in Figure 10.4, which is based on the data in column 6 of Table 10.2.

An autoregressive model with $k = 2$, therefore, should be better than one with $k = 1$, although, as we saw earlier, the latter had a very good fit. The regression results are as follows:

$$
\hat{Y} = 0.5771 + 1.1479 Y_{-1} - 0.1622 Y_{-2} \quad R^2 = 0.9996 \quad n = 18
$$
$$
\phantom{\hat{Y} = 0.5771 + }(4.50) \quad\quad (-0.65) \quad\quad S = 0.0427
$$

■

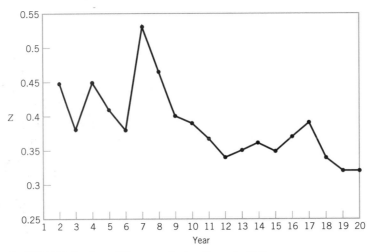

FIGURE 10.3 First difference of sales, Example 10.2

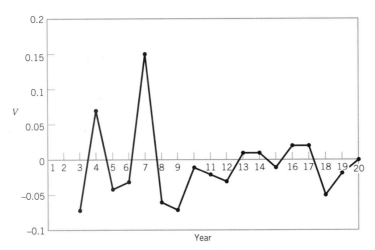

FIGURE 10.4 Second difference of sales, Example 10.2

In general, if the trend of a series can be described by a polynomial of degree d,

$$Y_t \approx c_0 + c_1 t + c_2 t^2 + \cdots + c_d t^d$$

the dth difference of the series can be expected to be approximately constant, and an autoregressive model with $k = d$ may be appropriate for forecasting such a series.

10.4 SERIES WITH SEASONALITY

Let us now turn to series with seasonality. The simplest case is a series with stable seasonality but no trend. Again, for simplicity assume that the series of interest consists of quarterly observations, as illustrated in Figure 10.5.

Observe that each quarter's observations tend to vary about a common level, as can be seen in the pattern of Quarter 2 and Quarter 4 observations marked in Figure 10.5.

In this case, the current value of the series can be expected to be close to the value of the series four quarters ago,

$$Y_t \approx Y_{t-4}$$

which suggests an autoregressive model with $k = 4$

$$\hat{Y}_t = b_0 + b_1 Y_{t-1} + b_2 Y_{t-2} + b_3 Y_{t-3} + b_4 Y_{t-4}$$

The OLS estimates b_0, b_1, b_2, and b_3 of this model can be expected to be close to 0 and b_4 close to 1.

If the quarterly series shows stable seasonality and a linear trend, then

$$Y_t \approx c + Y_{t-4}$$

This suggests the same autoregressive model with $k = 4$,

$$\hat{Y}_t = b_0 + b_1 Y_{t-1} + b_2 Y_{t-2} + b_3 Y_{t-3} + b_4 Y_{t-4}$$

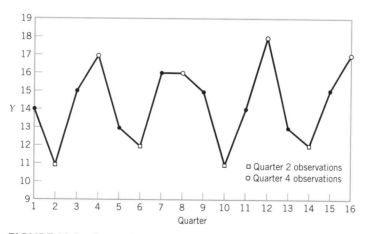

FIGURE 10.5 Quarterly series with stable seasonality and no trend

The OLS estimates b_1, b_2, and b_3 can be expected to be close to zero and b_4 close to one. The OLS estimate b_0 can be expected to be positive for a series with positive trend or negative for a series with negative trend. When these expectations agree with preliminary results, it is not unusual to see the restricted model

$$\hat{Y}_t = b_0 + b_4 Y_{t-4}$$

estimated directly in place of the unrestricted model.

Similar models may be used for daily, monthly, and other series that exhibit stable seasonality and a linear trend.

EXAMPLE 10.3

In Example 6.2, we used a regression model with linear trend and dummy variables to forecast the average daily number of passengers each month on transatlantic flights (Y). Sixty observations were available; these are partially listed in Table 6.2 and can be found in the file `airline.dat`.

The plot of the series shown in Figure 6.3 and the following Figure 10.6 shows a clear linear trend and stable monthly pattern. An alternative forecasting model, therefore, is an autoregressive model with $k = 12$. Using 48 complete sets of observations, we obtain the following results:

$$\hat{Y} = \underset{(1.85)}{1484.2} + \underset{(1.85)}{0.24Y_{-1}} - \underset{(-1.20)}{0.16Y_{-2}} + \underset{(0.07)}{0.01Y_{-3}} - \underset{(-0.76)}{0.10Y_{-4}}$$

$$\underset{(-0.23)}{-0.03Y_{-5}} + \underset{(0.09)}{0.01Y_{-6}} - \underset{(-0.17)}{0.02Y_{-7}} - \underset{(-0.96)}{0.13Y_{-8}}$$

$$\underset{(-0.81)}{-0.11Y_{-9}} + \underset{(0.30)}{0.04Y_{-10}} + \underset{(0.73)}{0.10Y_{-11}} + \underset{(5.11)}{0.67Y_{-12}}, \quad \begin{array}{l} R^2 = 0.97 \\ S = 319 \end{array}$$

A much simpler model, using Y_{-12} as the only explanatory variable and the same number of observations, yields about as good a fit:

$$\hat{Y} = 137.48 + \underset{(28.06)}{1.03Y_{-12}}, \quad \begin{array}{l} R^2 = 0.94, \\ S = 366 \end{array} \quad n = 48$$

Figure 10.6 shows the actual and estimated number of passengers based on this last model. ∎

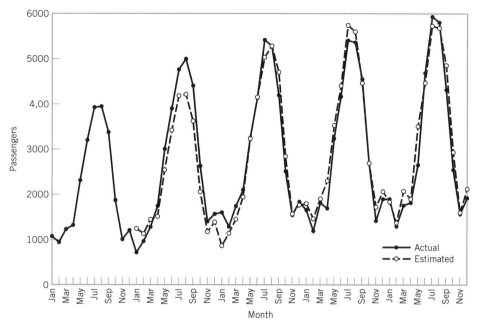

FIGURE 10.6 Transatlantic traffic, autoregressive model

For a quarterly series with increasing seasonality and trend, it could be that the second difference of observations four quarters apart is approximately constant, suggesting that

$$(Y_t - Y_{t-4}) - (Y_{t-4} - Y_{t-8}) \approx c$$

which implies

$$Y_t \approx c + 2Y_{t-4} - Y_{t-8}$$

and in turn suggests an autoregressive model with $k = 8$. A simpler version of that model is

$$\hat{Y} = b_0 + b_4 Y_{-4} + b_8 Y_{-8}$$

The OLS estimates b_4 and b_8 can be expected to be close to 2 and -1, respectively.

EXAMPLE 10.4

Let us reconsider Example 6.3, which dealt with a company's quarterly sales. The data are reproduced in Table 10.3.

TABLE 10.3   Company Sales, Example 10.4

Year	Quarter	Sales, Y	Y_{-4}	Y_{-8}
1	4	7.0	-	-
2	1	4.2	-	-
2	2	7.1	-	-
2	3	6.6	-	-
2	4	10.9	7.0	-
3	1	5.2	4.2	-
3	2	9.8	7.1	-
3	3	8.7	6.6	-
3	4	15.0	10.9	7.0
4	1	6.3	5.2	4.2
4	2	12.5	9.8	7.1
4	3	10.7	8.7	6.6
4	4	18.9	15.0	10.9
5	1	7.6	6.3	5.2
5	2	15.1	12.5	9.8
5	3	12.4	10.7	8.7

SOURCE: File `csales2.dat`

It can be seen from Figure 6.5 and the following Figure 10.7 that the series shows increasing trend and seasonality. Using the eight complete sets of observations, the results of regressing Y against Y_{-4} and Y_{-8} are as follows:

$$\hat{Y} = 0.436 + 2.101Y_{-4} - 1.197Y_{-8} \qquad R^2 = 0.999$$
$$\quad\quad\;\;\; (38.08) \quad\;\; (-15.38) \qquad S = 0.014$$

It can be noted that the OLS estimates of the coefficients of Y_{-4} and Y_{-8} are indeed close to 2 and -1, as expected.

As can be seen in Figure 10.7, estimated sales fit nearly perfectly actual sales.

The forecast sales for Quarter 4 of Year 5 and Quarters 1 to 3 of Year 6 are calculated as follows:

Year	Quarter	Forecast sales
4	4	$0.436 + 2.101(18.9) - 1.197(15.0) = 22.19$
5	1	$0.436 + 2.101(\;7.6) - 1.197(\;6.3) = \;\;8.86$
5	2	$0.436 + 2.101(15.1) - 1.197(12.5) = 17.20$
5	3	$0.436 + 2.101(12.4) - 1.197(10.7) = 13.68$

■

Another approach that often works well for series showing increasing trend and seasonality is to apply an autoregressive model to the logarithm of the series.

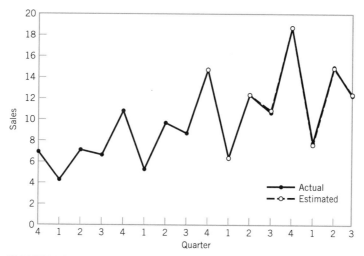

FIGURE 10.7   Company Sales, Example 10.4

EXAMPLE 10.5

If we examine the time series of shoe store sales (Y) of Example 6.4 shown in Figure 6.6, we shall note the increasing seasonality and curvilinear trend of the original series but the constant seasonality and linear trend of the logarithm of shoe store sales. We expect, therefore, that

$$\log Y_t \approx c + \log Y_{t-4}$$

which suggests applying to $\log Y$ an autoregressive model with $k = 4$. A simpler version of this model is

$$\hat{Y}' = b_0 + b_4 Y'_{-4}$$

where $Y' = \log Y$. A partial listing of the data is shown in Table 10.4. The logarithms are natural (to the base e).

There are 40 complete sets of observations. The regression results are as follows:

$$\hat{Y}' = 0.128 + 0.978 Y'_{-4} \qquad R^2 = 0.928$$
$$(22.10) \qquad\qquad S = 0.087$$

TABLE 10.4 Shoe Store Sales, Y, Example 10.5

Year	Quarter	Sales, Y	$Y' = \log Y$	Y'_{-4}
19X0	1	9.8	2.282	-
19X0	2	16.1	2.779	-
19X0	3	13.8	2.625	-
19X0	4	16.6	2.809	-
19X1	1	10.5	2.351	2.282
...	...	...	...	...
19Y0	4	35.6	3.572	3.254

SOURCE: File `shoes.dat`

The estimate of shoe store sales in a given quarter is calculated by first determining $\hat{Y}' = \widehat{\log Y}$ and then taking the antilogarithm of this last figure. For example, the estimate of $\log Y$ for Quarter 1, 19X1, is

$$\widehat{\log Y} = 0.128 + 0.978(2.282) = 2.3598$$

and its antilogarithm gives

$$\hat{Y} = e^{2.3598} = 10.59$$

Actual and estimated sales for all quarters are shown in Figure 10.8. ∎

10.5 AUTOREGRESSIVE MODELS IN PERSPECTIVE

The examples presented so far appear to suggest that an autoregressive model can capture the pattern of a time series as well as, or on occasion better than, a model involving trend and dummy seasonal variables. However, one should not lose sight of the fact that the autoregressive model does not explain *why* a series behaves as it does. Neither, of course, does the alternative model, but the latter at least is more transparent in communicating that trend and dummy variables are surrogates for habits, customs, and phenomena that themselves tend to have a trend and to vary predictably with the seasons. For series with trend and seasonality, an autoregressive model is an alternative to one involving time and dummy variables and may be evaluated by the degree of its success in fitting the past values of the series.

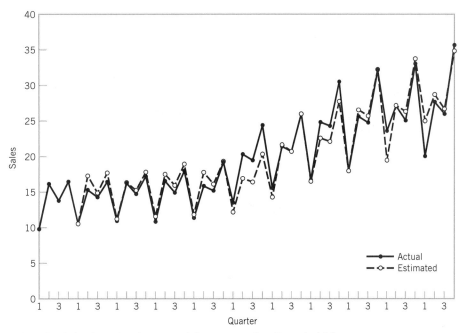

FIGURE 10.8   Actual and estimated shoe store sales, Example 10.5

For series showing no trend or seasonality, the apparent success of autoregressive models can often be explained by their tendency not to vary substantially from one period to the next, making the current value of the series or some simple function of recent values a reasonably good predictor of the value of the series in the following period. Whether or not any profitable use can be made of this tendency must be decided for each series separately.

EXAMPLE 10.6

For some years now, the question of whether the history of a stock's price is relevant, useful, or profitable in forecasting the future price of the stock has been a subject of controversy among academics and stock market professionals.

On the one hand, there are those who argue that stock prices are no more predictable than the outcomes of a series of tosses of a coin, rolls of a die, or spins of a roulette wheel. In the stock market, proponents of this view say, the price of a stock is determined by its demand and supply. These are influenced by individuals' expectations of the future earnings of the company. A change in the price of a stock will occur as a result of new information becoming available that is related to the future earnings of the company or a reappraisal of existing information. Since this information is unlikely to have any connection to past prices, the study of the past should be of no value to the market analyst or investor—their efforts might more enjoyably be devoted to another pastime.

On the other hand, there are those who believe that stock prices tend to follow certain patterns. These patterns may be simple or complex, easy or difficult to identify, but they are nonetheless predictable. Careful study of past prices, it is claimed, will reveal these patterns, which can then be used to forecast future prices, thereby providing profits for traders who buy or sell on the basis of the forecasts.

As we noted in Section 1.6, a pattern arises if the price of a stock at the end of period t, P_t, is a function of the prices of the stock in prior periods P_{t-1}, P_{t-2}, P_{t-3}, ... It is generally recognized, however, that stock prices tend to follow trends, especially over long periods of time, so that such a relationship can be expected. For example, if the trend is linear and $P_t \approx c_0 + c_1 t$, then, as we saw earlier, $P_t \approx c_1 + P_{t-1}$ and P would indeed be related to P_{-1}. For this reason, empirical studies of stock prices usually examine relationships between *price changes* rather than price levels. A simple form of such a relationship is the linear one

$$Y_t = b_0 + b_1 Y_{t-1} + b_2 Y_{t-2} + \cdots + b_k Y_{t-k}$$

where $Y_t = P_t - P_{t-1}$ and k depends on the situation.

It should be clear that if it is possible to somehow forecast price changes, it is also possible to forecast price levels. For example, if the known current price of a stock is P_{t-1} and the forecast price change is $\hat{Y}_t$, then the forecast price at the end of period t is $\hat{P}_t = P_{t-1} + \hat{Y}_t$; the forecast price at the end of period $t+1$ is $\hat{P}_{t+1} = \hat{P}_t + \hat{Y}_{t+1} = P_{t-1} + \hat{Y}_t + \hat{Y}_{t+1}$; and so on.

Figure 10.9 shows the closing price of a stock at the end of each of 378 trading days[1].

Table 10.5 shows the closing price P_t, the price change $Y_t = P_t - P_{t-1}$, and the lagged price changes Y_{t-1} and Y_{t-2} for the first few trading days, t.

TABLE 10.5   Closing Prices and Price Changes, Example 10.6

Trading day, t	Closing price, P_t	Price change, $Y_t = P_t - P_{t-1}$	Y_{t-1}	Y_{t-2}
1	14.50	-	-	-
2	15.00	0.50	-	-
3	16.00	1.00	0.50	-
4	16.50	0.50	1.00	0.50
. . .	. . .	. . .	. . .	. . .

[1]This stock is the first of five, the closing prices of which are stored in the file `stocks.dat`. The data for the other stocks are used in Problem 10.14. The data are from Professor P. Karagiannopoulos.

FIGURE 10.9 Closing price of stock, Example 10.6

We begin with $k = 1$ and regress Y against Y_{-1} to obtain

$$\hat{Y}_t = 0.0096 + 0.0845Y_{t-1} \qquad R^2 = 0.007$$
$$\quad (0.65) \qquad (1.63) \qquad\qquad S = 0.2827$$

The results indicate a positive relationship between successive price changes, but the relationship is very weak, as evidenced by the very low R^2. It may be, however, that the current price change is influenced by more distant price changes. Table 10.6 shows selected regression results for $k = 1, 2, \ldots, 5$. (All regressions use 372 sets of observations; S is the standard deviation of residuals with n rather than $n - k - 1$ in the denominator.)

We observe that the relationship remains very weak even when five lagged price changes are included in the model. We could, of course, continue to investigate still larger models but shall not do so for the following reasons.

First, the results concerning the stock of this example are consistent with numerous larger studies, which generally conclude that price changes tend to be very weakly linearly related to past price changes and that commissions and other trading costs tend to offset any potential gains from exploiting these

**TABLE 10.6
Regression Results,
Example 10.6**

k	R^2	S
1	0.007	0.2827
2	0.008	0.2826
3	0.013	0.2819
4	0.013	0.2819
5	0.018	0.2811

relationships. Second, it is not possible to prove conclusively that there is no relationship between current and past price changes because it is impossible to enumerate all possible relationships—linear and nonlinear. For this last reason, the debate between those who do and others who do not believe that past prices or price changes are useful in forecasting future prices is likely to continue, and the claims of one study are likely to be routinely disputed by the other.[2]   ■

10.6   AR MODELS

The autoregressive models of the preceding sections were estimated by applying the method of least squares. We know from Chapter 3 that the OLS estimators, in addition to fitting the observations best, have under certain conditions the desirable properties of unbiasedness, minimum variance, and consistency. Under further conditions, it is also possible to form interval estimates and forecasts and to carry out statistical tests for the model's parameters. It is useful, therefore, to examine if the same properties and results hold for time series generated by a process similar to that of the classical linear model of Chapter 3.[3]

[2]The literature on the subject is quite large. For references to earlier as well as more recent work see, for example, Paul H. Cootner (ed.), *The Random Character of Stock Market Prices*, rev. ed., M.I.T. Press, 1967; James H. Lorie and Richard A. Brealey (eds.), *Modern Developments in Investment Management: A Book of Readings*, Praeger, 1972; R. M. C. Guimaraes, B. G. Kingsman, and S. J. Taylor (eds.), *A Reappraisal of the Efficiency of Financial Markets*, NATO ASI Series, Springer-Verlag, 1988; B. G. Malkiel, *A Random Walk down Wall Street*, 6th ed., Norton, 1996; Thomas R. DeMark, *The New Science of Technical Analysis*, Wiley, 1994; and G. S. Wagner and Bradley L. Matheny, *Trading Applications of Japanese Candlestick Charting*, Wiley, 1994.

[3]Our intention is to provide a brief introduction and summary of the principal results. Even so, this and the remaining sections are more technical than the preceding sections of this chapter. The material that follows may be omitted without fear of losing continuity.

It is easier if we begin with the simplest model and assume that

$$Y_t = \beta_0 + \beta_1 Y_{t-1} + \varepsilon_t \tag{10.8}$$

where ε_t are independent and such that $E(\varepsilon_t) = 0$ and $Var(\varepsilon_t) = \sigma^2$.

In other words, we assume that the current value of the series is determined *as if* to the term $\beta_0 + \beta_1 Y_{t-1}$ (a term that can be described as the part of Y_t that is explained by Y_{t-1}) an error (ε_t) is added, itself the value of a random draw with replacement from a population of ε-values having mean zero and a certain variance σ^2.

We see immediately from Eq. 10.8 that Y_t depends on Y_{t-1}. Unlike the situation contemplated by the classical model, therefore, the Y-values are not independent of one another even when the errors ε_t are. Now, since

$$Y_{t-1} = \beta_0 + \beta_1 Y_{t-2} + \varepsilon_{t-1}$$

substitution into Eq. 10.8 gives

$$\begin{aligned} Y_t &= \beta_0 + \beta_1[\beta_0 + \beta_1 Y_{t-2} + \varepsilon_{t-1}] + \varepsilon_t \\ &= (\beta_0 + \beta_0\beta_1) + \beta_1^2 Y_{t-2} + (\varepsilon_t + \beta_1\varepsilon_{t-1}) \end{aligned} \tag{10.9}$$

Again, since

$$Y_{t-2} = \beta_0 + \beta_1 Y_{t-3} + \varepsilon_{t-2}$$

substitution into Eq. 10.9 yields

$$Y_t = (\beta_0 + \beta_0\beta_1 + \beta_0\beta_1^2) + \beta_1^3 Y_{t-3} + (\varepsilon_t + \beta_1\varepsilon_{t-1} + \beta_1^2\varepsilon_{t-2}) \tag{10.10}$$

Continuing in this fashion and substituting into Eq. 10.10 in turn the appropriate expressions for Y_{t-3}, Y_{t-4}, ..., Y_{t-m}, we get, after m substitutions and a great deal of algebra,

$$\begin{aligned} Y_t &= (\beta_0 + \beta_0\beta_1 + \beta_0\beta_1^2 + \cdots + \beta_0\beta_1^m) + \beta_1^{m+1} Y_{t-m+1} \\ &\quad +(\varepsilon_t + \beta_1\varepsilon_{t-1} + \beta_1^2\varepsilon_{t-2} + \cdots + \beta_1^m\varepsilon_{t-m}) \end{aligned} \tag{10.11}$$

It may be reasonable to assume that m can be made infinitely large (in other words, that the series has been in existence infinitely long) and convenient to assume that Y_{t-m+1} (the starting value of the series) is zero, in which case,

$$Y_t = \beta_0(1 + \beta_1 + \beta_1^2 + \beta_1^3 + \cdots) + (\varepsilon_t + \beta_1\varepsilon_{t-1} + \beta_1^2\varepsilon_{t-2} + \beta_1^3\varepsilon_{t-m} + \cdots) \tag{10.12}$$

We observe that Y_t is a linear function of the independent errors ε_t, ε_{t-1}, $\varepsilon_{t-2}, \ldots$, the coefficients of these errors being constants. It can be shown (see Appendix A.11) that the expected value and variance of Y_t are

$$E(Y_t) = \beta_0(1 + \beta_1 + \beta_1^2 + \beta_1^3 + \cdots)$$
$$Var(Y_t) = \sigma^2(1 + \beta_1^2 + \beta_1^4 + \beta_1^6 + \cdots)$$

If $|\beta_1| > 1$, each term of the series in parentheses is larger in absolute value than the preceding term, implying that both the expected value and variance of Y_t are infinitely large. Such a model could not describe series normally encountered in practice, all observations of which are finite. For Model 10.8 to be plausible, therefore, we must require that $|\beta_1| < 1$. In this case, the expressions within parentheses in $E(Y_t)$ and $Var(Y_t)$ are sums of terms that are ever declining in absolute value. It is well known that the sums of such series are finite,[4] and

$$E(Y_t) = \frac{\beta_0}{1 - \beta_1}$$

$$Var(Y_t) = \frac{\sigma^2}{1 - \beta_1^2}$$

Observe that neither the expected value nor the variance of Y_t depends on the time period t. We conclude that Model 10.8 with $|\beta_1| < 1$ is not appropriate for a series with trend, seasonality, or variability that increases or decreases with time, t.

The covariance of values of the series one period apart can also be determined. Since

$$Y_t = \frac{\beta_0}{1 - \beta_1} + \varepsilon_t + \beta_1\varepsilon_{t-1} + \beta_1^2\varepsilon_{t-2} + \beta_1^3\varepsilon_{t-3} + \cdots$$

$$Y_{t-1} = \frac{\beta_0}{1 - \beta_1} + \quad\quad +\varepsilon_{t-1} + \beta_1\varepsilon_{t-2} + \beta_1^2\varepsilon_{t-3} + \cdots$$

using a result of Appendix A.12, we find

$$\begin{aligned} Cov(Y_t, Y_{t-1}) &= \beta_1 Var(\varepsilon_{t-1}) + \beta_1^3 Var(\varepsilon_{t-2}) + \beta_1^5 Var(\varepsilon_{t-3}) + \cdots \\ &= \beta_1\sigma^2 + \beta_1^3\sigma^2 + \beta_1^5\sigma^2 + \cdots \\ &= \sigma^2\beta_1(1 + \beta_1^2 + \beta_1^4 + \cdots) \\ &= \sigma^2\frac{\beta_1}{1 - \beta_1^2} \end{aligned}$$

[4]See footnote 3 of Section 7.4.

In a similar fashion, we can show that the covariance of observations j periods apart is

$$Cov(Y_t, Y_{t-j}) = \sigma^2 \frac{\beta_1^j}{1 - \beta_1^2}$$

The correlation coefficient of observations j periods apart is

$$Cor(Y_t, Y_{t-j}) = \frac{Cov(Y_t, Y_{t-j})}{\sqrt{Var(Y_t)}\sqrt{Var(Y_{t-j})}} = \frac{\frac{\sigma^2 \beta_1^j}{1 - \beta_1^2}}{\sqrt{\frac{\sigma^2}{1 - \beta_1^2}}\sqrt{\frac{\sigma^2}{1 - \beta_1^2}}} = \beta_1^j$$

The correlation coefficient, therefore, is smaller in absolute value the further apart the observations. Note that neither the covariance nor the correlation coefficient depend on t.

A time series with such properties (that is, one with mean, variance, covariances and correlations coefficients that do not depend on t) is called *stationary*.[5]

The simple model can be extended. An AR(k) model (acronym for *autoregressive model of order k*) is defined as

$$Y_t = \beta_0 + \beta_1 Y_{t-1} + \beta_2 Y_{t-2} + \cdots + \beta_k Y_{t-k} + \varepsilon_t \qquad (10.13)$$

where ε_t are independent and such that $E(\varepsilon_t) = 0$ and $Var(\varepsilon_t) = \sigma^2$.

Clearly, Model 10.8 is an AR(1) model. If the expected value and variance of Y_t under the AR(k) model are to be finite for the same reasons as with the AR(1) model, it is necessary that the parameters $\beta_1, \beta_2, \ldots, \beta_k$ satisfy certain constraints. (The constraints cannot be described simply, but one of these is that the sum of these β's be less than 1.) If these constraints are satisfied, it can be shown that $E(Y_t)$, $Var(Y_t)$, and $Cor(Y_t, Y_{t-j})$ do not depend on t. This means that the constrained AR(k) model—like its special case AR(1)—is appropriate for a stationary time series and not for a series with trend, seasonality, or variability that tends to increase or decrease with t.

In the next section we shall see how the AR(k) model can be made to apply to non-stationary series, but first let us state the properties of the OLS estimators when the process that generates the observations satisfies the assumptions of the constrained AR(k) model.

It will be recalled that the OLS estimators of the classical linear model are unbiased (in fact, minimum variance linear unbiased) and consistent. The AR(k) model resembles the classical, but its explanatory variables are lagged

---

[5]This is a weak definition of stationarity. Stronger definitions will be encountered in advanced statistical texts.

values of the dependent variable Y. We noted earlier that the Y's cannot be independent of one another even when the ε's are. It may not be surprising, therefore, that the properties of the OLS estimators are different under the two models.

Indeed, it can be shown that when the parameters β_0, β_1, ..., β_k of an AR(k) model are estimated by regressing Y against Y_{-1}, Y_{-2}, ..., Y_{-k}, the OLS estimators *are consistent but not unbiased.* That is, the expected value of the estimate is not equal to the target parameter, but, as the number of observations increases, the probability that the OLS estimate b will deviate from the parameter β by more than a specified amount—however small that amount—approaches zero. One desirable property of the OLS estimators, therefore, disappears, but the remaining one justifies the continued use of the least-squares method for estimating the parameters of an AR(k) model when the number of observations is large. It can also be shown that when the number of observations is large, the standard confidence intervals and tests of hypotheses concerning the model's parameters and forecasts are valid.[6]

10.7 NONSTATIONARY SERIES, ARI MODELS

We noted earlier that the AR(k) model cannot describe a nonstationary series. This conclusion would rule out the model as a descriptor of many economic time series that show trend, seasonality, increasing or decreasing variability, or combinations of these features. One way of circumventing this difficulty is to assume that the AR(k) describes a function of the series rather than the original series itself.

Consider first a series following a linear trend and for which the AR(k) model is not appropriate. We saw in Section 10.3 that the first difference of such a series

$$Z_t = Y_t - Y_{t-1}$$

tends to be approximately constant. If the variability of the first difference is also constant, an AR(k) model

$$Z_t = \beta_0 + \beta_1 Z_{t-1} + \beta_2 Z_{t-2} + \cdots + \beta_k Z_{t-k} + \varepsilon_t$$

may explain the first difference of the series. The parameters of this model can be estimated by regressing Z against Z_{-1}, Z_{-2}, ..., Z_{-k}. As we know, given an estimate of a first difference, $\hat{Z}_t$, from such a model the estimate of the value of the series is $\hat{Y}_t = Y_{t-1} + \hat{Z}_t$.

---

[6]See, for example, Theil (1971, Ch. 8) and Johnston (1984, Ch. 9).

If a series follows a parabolic trend, the second difference $V_t = Z_t - Z_{t-1}$ tends to be constant. If the variability of the second difference also tends to be constant, an AR(k) model may be used to model these differences and its parameters estimated by regressing V against $V_{-1}, V_{-1}, \ldots, V_{-k}$. Given an estimate of the second difference, $\hat{V}_t$, the estimate of the first difference is $\hat{Z}_t = Z_{t-1} + \hat{V}_t$ and that of the value of the series is $\hat{Y}_t = Y_{t-1} + \hat{Z}_t$.

An AR(k) model applied to the dth difference of the original series is known as an ARI(k, d) model (acronym for *autoregressive integrated model of order k and d*).

For series showing seasonality but no trend, one could consider whether an AR(k) model describes the difference between periodic terms; for example, if a series consists of quarterly observations, an autoregressive model could be considered for the difference $Y_t - Y_{t-4}$. If a series shows increasing variability, a possible remedy is to apply an AR(k) model to the logarithm of the original series. For series exhibiting combinations of these nonstationary features, combinations of the simple prescriptions may be appropriate.

10.8 NONINDEPENDENCE, ARMA AND ARIMA MODELS

The ordinary OLS estimators of the parameters of an AR(k) model, we remarked earlier, are not unbiased but are consistent. Even this last desirable property, however, is lost if the errors ε_t are not independent of one another.

Consider the general AR(k) model

$$Y_t = \beta_0 + \beta_1 Y_{t-1} + \beta_2 Y_{t-2} + \cdots + \beta_k Y_{t-k} + \varepsilon_t \tag{10.14}$$

but now relax the assumption that the ε_t are independent. If the errors are not independent, they may be related to one another in an infinite number of ways. Simplest is the linear relationship,

$$\varepsilon_t = \tilde{\varepsilon}_t + \gamma_1 \tilde{\varepsilon}_{t-1} + \gamma_2 \tilde{\varepsilon}_{t-2} + \cdots + \gamma_l \tilde{\varepsilon}_{t-l} \tag{10.15}$$

where it is the $\tilde{\varepsilon}$'s that are now assumed to be independent and such that $E(\tilde{\varepsilon}_t) = 0$ and $Var(\tilde{\varepsilon}_t) = \sigma^2$. The γ's are additional parameters of the model, to be estimated along with the β's. This model is known as an ARMA(k, l) model, an acronym for *autoregressive moving average model of order k and l*.

To see that Eq. 10.15 implies a relationship between the ε's, suppose $l = 1$, in which case

$$\varepsilon_t = \tilde{\varepsilon}_t + \gamma_1 \tilde{\varepsilon}_{t-1}$$

Lagging one period, we find

$$\varepsilon_{t-1} = \tilde{\varepsilon}_{t-1} + \gamma_1 \tilde{\varepsilon}_{t-2}$$

Observe that $\tilde{\varepsilon}_{t-1}$ is common to both expressions, hence it influences both ε_t and ε_{t-1}. Therefore, ε_t and ε_{t-1} are related if $\gamma_1 \neq 0$. A similar argument will show that all the ε's are related.

Clearly, the AR(k) is a special case of the ARMA(k, l) model with all γ's equal to zero. In this case, the ε_t's are identical to the $\tilde{\varepsilon}_t$'s, by definition independent of one another, and have the common mean zero and variance σ^2.

The parameters $\beta_0, \beta_1, \ldots, \beta_k$ of the ARMA(k, l) model *could* be estimated by regressing Y against $Y_{-1}, Y_{-2}, \ldots, Y_{-k}$. It can be shown[7], however, that *the OLS estimators are neither unbiased nor consistent*. The absence of independence, therefore, removes one remaining desirable property of the OLS estimators.

Consistent estimators of the parameters of the ARMA(k, l) model can be obtained if it can be further assumed that the errors $\tilde{\varepsilon}_t$ are *normally* distributed. Such estimators can be derived by applying the method of maximum likelihood outlined in Appendix B.7 and are calculated using an iterative numerical procedure implemented by major statistical computer programs. When the number of observations is large, tests of hypotheses and confidence intervals concerning the model's parameters can be based on these estimates.[8]

EXAMPLE 10.1 (CONTINUED)

An autoregressive model with $k = 3$ was used earlier to forecast the series of federal funds interest rates. The OLS results are repeated in Table 10.7.

Next in Table 10.7 are the maximum likelihood estimates of an ARMA($3, 0$) model, that is, one in which all the γ's in Eq. 10.15 are equal to zero—in effect assuming that the errors ε are independent. The maximum likelihood estimates and associated t-ratios, it can be noted, are very similar to OLS.

The third and fourth sets of results in Table 10.7 are the maximum likelihood estimates of the ARMA($3, 1$) and ARMA($3, 2$) models, respectively; c_1 and c_2 are the estimates of the parameters γ_1 and γ_2.[9]

If the assumptions of this section are satisfied, the hypothesis $H_0 : \gamma_2 = 0$ in the ARMA($3, 2$) model could be accepted since the t-ratio of c_2 is very close to zero. Thus, ARMA($3, 1$) appears best among the models considered, and it is the third set of results that should be used for any inferences concerning the

---

[7]See, for example, Theil (1971, Ch. 8) or Johnston (1984, Ch. 9).

[8]For details see, for example, Nelson (1973, Ch. 5), Pindyck and Rubinfeld (1991, Ch. 17), and Janacek and Swift (1993).

[9]The maximum likelihood estimates were obtained using program SAS and the commands `proc arima; identify rate; estimate p=3 method=ml; estimate p=3 q=1 method=ml; estimate p=3 q=2 method=ml;`. rate is the label of the time series of interest rates and ml specifies maximum likehood. The data are in the file `ffunds.dat`.

TABLE 10.7 Comparison of Estimation Methods, Example 10.1

Model/ Method	b_0	Estimates / t-ratios				
		b_1	b_2	b_3	c_1	c_2
Autoregressive OLS	0.328 (1.43)	1.262 (9.60)	−0.110 (−0.50)	−0.207 (−1.58)		
ARMA(3,0) ML	0.438	1.309 (9.27)	−0.102 (−0.43)	−0.270 (−1.91)		
ARMA(3,1) ML	0.672	0.649 (4.11)	0.845 (6.63)	−0.591 (−5.11)	0.749 (4.46)	
ARMA(3,2) ML	0.662	0.667 (3.47)	0.856 (6.70)	−0.619 (−3.27)	0.722 (2.88)	−0.040 (−0.16)

model's parameters. Observe the differences with the OLS and ARMA(3, 0) results; these are due to the presence of serial correlation among the errors. ∎

One last piece of nomenclature. An ARMA(k, l) model applied to the dth differences of the series Y is called an *autoregressive integrated moving average model of order k, d, and l*, and is abbreviated as ARIMA(k, d, l). It is the most general in this class of models, in the sense that all previously examined models are its special cases. For example, an ARMA(k, l) model is an ARIMA(k, d, l) model with $d = 0$.

Suggestions concerning how to identify the ARIMA(k, d, l) model appropriate for a particular time series—that is, how to select suitable values of the parameters k, d, and l—can be found in advanced texts of time series analysis.

10.9 TO SUM UP

- A number of heuristic forecasting methods often used in practice are special cases of the autoregressive model and can be estimated by regressing the current values of the variable of interest against the lagged values of the same variable.

- The autoregressive model is an alternative to one involving time and dummy variables for series exhibiting trend and seasonality. For series without trend or seasonality, the apparent success of the autoregressive model is often due to the tendency of business and economic series not to vary substantially from one period to the next, making the current value of the series or some function of recent values a reasonably good predictor of the next value of the series.

- An AR(k) model is not appropriate for series with trend, seasonality, or variability that tends to increase or decrease with time. However, an AR(k) model applied to the dth difference of the series—an ARI(k, d) model— may be appropriate for series with trend. Other simple modifications often make the model suitable for series with seasonality or non-constant variability.

- The OLS estimators of the parameters of an AR(k) model are consistent but not unbiased. When the number of observations is large, tests and confidence intervals based on the OLS estimates may be calculated in the usual manner.

- The OLS estimators are neither unbiased nor consistent when the errors are not independent, the case envisaged by the ARMA(k, l) and ARIMA(k, d, l) models.

- One should not lose sight of the fact that autoregressive models do not explain *why* a series behaves as it does. Neither, of course, do regression models involving time and dummy variables, but the latter are at least more transparent in communicating that trend and dummy variables are surrogates for habits, customs, and other phenomena that themselves tend to have a trend or to vary predictably with the seasons.

PROBLEMS

10.1 With the help of a computer program, confirm as many as possible of the results presented in this chapter.

10.2 Refer to Table 6.12 and the data file `tser1.dat`. Estimate the best autoregressive model for series Y_1 and forecast the series in the years 1997 to 2000.

10.3 Same as Problem 10.2, except use the series Y_2.

10.4 Same as Problem 10.2, except use the series Y_3.

10.5 Refer to Table 6.14 and the data file `tser2.dat`. Estimate the best autoregressive model for the series Y_1. Forecast the series in Quarters 3 and 4 of Year 4, and Quarters 1 and 2 of Year 5.

10.6 Same as Problem 10.5, except use the series Y_2.

10.7 Same as Problem 10.5, except use the series Y_3.

10.8 The file `airline.dat`, partially listed in Table 6.17, contains the values of TCONT, the average daily number of passengers on transcontinental flights monthly from January 19X1 to December 19X5. Estimate the autoregressive model that best describes the series. Forecast TCONT for each month in 19X6.

10.9 Refer to Problem 6.20 and the data file `liquor.dat`. Estimate the autoregressive models that best describe the indexes of the real shipments of (a) distilled spirits, DSHIP/DIND; (b) beer, BSHIP/BIND; and (c) wine, WSHIP/WIND. Forecast the series each month in 19X5.

10.10 Refer to Problem 6.21 and the data in the file `drugstor.dat` concerning the weekly sales and the number of customers of a drugstore.

(a) Estimate the autoregressive model that best describes the weekly sales, SALES. Forecast the series in weeks 81 to 84.

(b) Estimate the autoregressive model that best describes the number of pharmacy customers, RXNO. Forecast the series in weeks 81 to 84.

(c) Estimate the autoregressive model that best describes the number of non-pharmacy customers, FSNO. Forecast the series in weeks 81 to 84.

10.11 Refer to Problem 6.22 and the data in the file `rsales.dat` concerning the monthly retail sales in a region. Estimate the autoregressive model that best describes the series. Forecast retail sales each month in year 6.

10.12 Refer to Problem 6.23 and the file `mvacc1.dat` outlined in Table 6.26 regarding the number of (a) fatal, (b) nonfatal injury, and (c) property damage accidents by day of week from 1988 to 1992. Estimate the autoregressive models that best describe the series. Forecast the series for each day of the week in 1993.

10.13 Refer to Problem 6.23 and the file `mvacc2.dat` outlined in Table 6.27 regarding the number of (a) fatal, (b) nonfatal injury, and (c) property damage accidents monthly from 1988 to 1992. Estimate the autoregressive models that best describe the series. Forecast the series for each month in 1993.

10.14 The file `stocks.dat` contains the daily closing price of each of five stocks over 378 consecutive trading days. A partial listing of this file is shown in Table 10.8.

(a) The data for Stock 1 were used in Example 10.6. Confirm the regression results presented in that example.

(b) Plot the daily closing price and price change of Stock 2 over the period. In the manner of Example 10.6, estimate a number of autoregressive models to determine the extent to which past price changes can be used to forecast next day's price change.

(c) Same as (b), except use the data for (i) Stock 3, (ii) Stock 4, and (iii) Stock 5. In the case of Stock 3, be aware that the stock was split at about the middle of the period considered in

TABLE 10.8 File stocks.dat, Partial Listing

Day	Stock 1	Stock 2	Stock 3	Stock 4	Stock 5
1	14.500	33.125	17.250	24.000	8.750
2	15.000	33.500	18.500	23.750	9.250
3	16.000	35.500	19.750	23.750	9.500
4	16.500	36.125	19.625	24.000	9.625
5	16.750	37.375	20.250	23.875	9.875
...	...	...	...	...	...

the ratio 3 (new shares) : 1 (old share); in other words, each stockholder received three new shares in return for each old share owned.

10.15 Figure 10.10 shows the per capita consumption of beer monthly over the 12-year period from January 19X4 to December 19Y5. The data can be found in the file `pcbeer.dat`, a partial listing of which is shown in Table 10.9.

(a) Estimate the model that best describes the pattern of the series. The model could be one involving regression against time and dummy variables, autoregression, or another

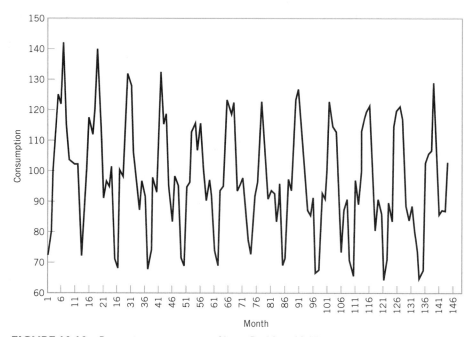

FIGURE 10.10 Per capita consumption of beer, Problem 10.15

TABLE 10.9 File `pcbeer.dat`, Partial Listing

Month	Per capita consumption of beer
Jan	71.03
Feb	80.42
Mar	100.93
Apr	113.75
May	124.91
. . .	. . .

method. Show graphically the seasonal pattern of the series, if one is present. Forecast the series in each month of 19Y6.

(b) How confident are you about these forecasts? Explain how you would provide better forecasts.

10.16 (Due to Mr. A. Hutchinson) Table 10.10 shows a partial listing of the file `vehicles.dat` concerning the sales of passenger and commercial vehicles in a region monthly from January 19X0 to December 19X5.

The variables should be interpreted as follows:

MONTH: Month number, 1 to 72.

PCARNA: Number of sold passenger cars manufactured in North America

PCAROS: Number of sold passenger cars manufactured overseas

COMMNA: Number of sold commercial vehicles manufactured in North America

COMMOS: Number of sold commercial vehicles manufactured overseas

(a) Create two new variables, PCARTOT = PCARNA + PCAROS and COMMTOT = COMMNA + COMMOS, representing the total sales of passenger and commercial vehicles.

(b) Plot all six series against time.

(c) Estimate the model that best describes the pattern of (i) PCARNA, (ii) PCAROS, (iii) COMMNA, (iv) COMMOS, (v) PCARTOT, and (vi) COMMTOT. The model could be one involving regression against time and dummy variables, autoregression, or another method. Show graphically the seasonal pattern of the series, if one is present. Forecast the series in each month of 19X6.

(d) How confident are you about these forecasts? Explain how you would provide better forecasts.

10.17 (Due to Mr. David Lee) Table 10.11 shows a partial listing of the file `socass.dat` containing the number of persons receiving unemployment and maternity benefits in a region and the number of weeks of such benefits monthly from January 19X9 to June 19Y5.

The variables have the following interpretation:

NOUNE: Number of persons receiving unemployment benefits

NOMAT: Number of persons receiving maternity benefits

TABLE 10.10   File `vehicles.dat`, Partial Listing

MONTH	PCARNA	PCAROS	COMMNA	COMMOS
1	50929	12324	24080	1404
2	61594	15150	25418	1654
3	75575	14034	30339	1496
4	75144	15689	31889	1749
5	67302	16610	27802	1787
...	...	...	...	...

TABLE 10.11 File `socass.dat`, Partial Listing

MONTH	NOUNE	NOMAT	WKSUNE	WKSMAT
Jan	198576	12290	959670	65094
Feb	209996	12666	837614	51406
Mar	205917	12721	849614	53226
Apr	186056	13493	843836	54652
May	153083	13436	726348	61229
...	...	...	...	...

WKSUNE: Weeks of benefits received by unemployment beneficiaries

WKSMAT: Weeks of benefits received by maternity beneficiaries

(a) Create two additional variables, AVEUNE = WKSUNE/NOUNE and AVEMAT = WKS-MAT/NOMAT, representing, respectively, the average number of weeks of benefits received by unemployment and maternity beneficiaries.

(b) Plot the six time series of this problem against time.

(c) Estimate the model that best describes the pattern of (i) NOUNE, (ii) NOMAT, (iii) WK-SUNE, (iv) WKSMAT, (v) AVEUNE, and (vi) AVEMAT. The model could be one involving regression against time and dummy variables, autoregression, or another method. Show graphically the seasonal pattern of the series, if one is present. Forecast the series in each of the twelve months following June 19Y5.

(d) How confident are you about these forecasts? Explain how you would provide better forecasts.

10.18 You may occasionally be impressed by the success of an autoregressive model in forecasting a series with no apparent trend or seasonality. Consider, for example, Example 10.6 and Figure 10.9, showing the daily closing price of a stock. The data can be found in the file `stocks.dat`.

Figure 10.11 shows the actual closing price of the same stock (solid line) and a one-day-ahead forecast of that price (dotted line). The two lines are so close to one another that they appear indistinguishable. In fact, the forecast of "tomorrow's" price is none other than "today's" actual price, that is, $\hat{P}_t = P_{t-1}$. The behavior of these forecasts can be seen better in Figure 10.12, which is an enlargement of Figure 10.11 for days 200 to 250.

(a) Is there a lesson to be learned from this demonstration? How useful are such forecasts? What would be a reasonable standard against which to compare the performance of any forecasting model?

(b) Examine the performance of the "naive" forecasting model $\hat{P}_t = P_{t-1}$ for each of the other four stocks in the file `stocks.dat`. See note in Problem 10.14(c) regarding Stock 3. Comment on the results.

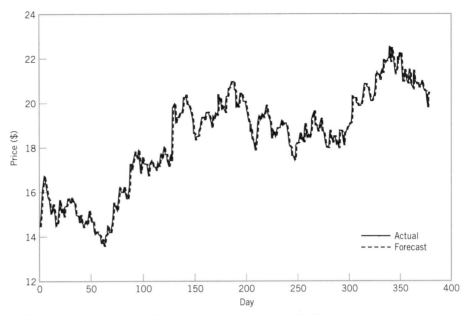

FIGURE 10.11 Closing stock price and forecast, Problem 10.18

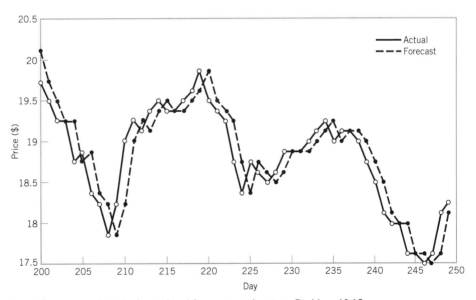

FIGURE 10.12 Detail of actual and forecast stock prices, Problem 10.18

CHAPTER 11

THE CLASSIFICATION PROBLEM

11.1 INTRODUCTION AND SUMMARY

In all the models we have considered so far, the objective was to explain and forecast a *variable*. In this and the next chapter, we examine how to explain and forecast an *attribute* as a function of other attributes and variables.

Attributes, of course, are not described numerically. In models with a dependent attribute, we seek to predict the *category* of the attribute by means of a *rule* assigning an element to one or another category depending on given values and categories of the explanatory variables and attributes.

A credit manager, for example, may use such a rule to classify an applicant for credit as a "good risk" or a "poor risk" on the basis of the applicant's age, gender, income, job status, and so on, at the time of application. The rule could be of the following form: all male, single applicants under 21 years of age and earning less than $30,000 per year are classified as poor credit risks and (presumably) refused credit; all other applicants are classified as good risks and given credit. Clearly, this is not the only possible, nor necessarily the optimal, rule. Whatever rule is used, there is always the possibility that a potentially "Good" applicant will be classified as a poor credit risk and that a potentially "Bad" applicant will be classified as a good risk. In this case, these errors have monetary consequences: the opportunity loss of profit from rejecting a Good applicant and the real loss from accepting a Bad one.

We assume there is some experience in the form of observations on the variables and attributes to be used in the study. In our example, we assume that a number of credit applications are available and, for each such application, the applicant's age, gender, income, job status, and current account standing (Good or Bad) recorded. This experience will be utilized in the construction of a rule for classifying other credit applicants as good or bad credit risks on the basis of their age, gender, income, and job status.

In what follows, we shall investigate ways to find optimal rules, that is, rules that minimize the expected loss or probability of misclassification. We begin with the simplest case—that of a dependent attribute with two categories—and then extend the results to the general case where the attribute can take any number of categories.

11.2 AN ILLUSTRATION

A simple artificial example will illustrate the derivation of an optimal classification rule.

EXAMPLE 11.1

A bank plans to construct a rule to assist the evaluation of new applicants for checking accounts.

Until now, the bank's policy has been to accept all applicants. The large majority of accounts are "Good accounts," accounts in good standing. With some accounts, the bank has experienced difficulties, such as overdrafts, returned deposited checks, and the like; these we call "Bad accounts."

At the time of application, applicants complete a form giving their name, address, gender, age, marital status, occupation, personal annual income, and so on. The bank is considering classifying new applicants as potentially Good or Bad accounts on the basis of their income and marital status at the time of application. New applicants classified as Good will be accepted, while those classified as Bad will be rejected.

A new applicant will be either Good or Bad (it is, of course, the *account* held by the applicant—not the applicant—that will be Good or Bad, but we shall use the imprecise phraseology for the sake of brevity). If an applicant is Good and is classified as Good, no error is made. Likewise, no error is made if an applicant is Bad and is classified as Bad. But an error is made if an applicant is Good and classified as Bad or is Bad and classified as Good. These errors have different consequences. If a Good applicant is classified as Bad and rejected, the bank loses a potentially profitable account; if a Bad applicant is classified as Good and accepted, the bank will suffer the consequences of bad checks and overdrafts. In general, the monetary values of these consequences may be difficult to estimate, but for this example they are assumed to be as shown in Table 11.1.

In other words, it is assumed that the bank loses $10 for every Good applicant classified as Bad and $15 for every Bad applicant classified as Good. The losses resulting from correct classifications are assumed to be zero.

TABLE 11.1 Classification Losses, Example 11.1

Account standing	Actions	
	Classify as Good	**Classify as Bad**
Good	$0	$10
Bad	$15	$0

As a first step toward developing an optimal rule, the application forms of 4000 recent applicants for a checking account were pulled out and each applicant's income and marital status at the time of application as well as the current standing of the account (Good or Bad) recorded. The raw data have the format shown in Table 11.2.

The bank arbitrarily formed two categories for marital status and three for income, and assigned codes to each as follows:

Income category	Code, X_1
Under \$20,000	0
\$20,000 to \$50,000	1
Over \$50,000	2

Marital status category	Code, X_2
Not married	0
Married	1

The available data were tabulated according to account standing, income, and marital status, with the results shown in Tables 11.3 and 11.4.

TABLE 11.2 Raw Data from 4000 Recently Opened Accounts

Account no.	Current standing	Marital status	Annual income ($000)
1	Good	Married	25
2	Bad	Single	56
3	Good	Divorced	40
...	...	...	...
4000	Good	Married	36

TABLE 11.3 Good Accounts, Number of Applicants by Income and Marital Status

Annual income (X_1)	Marital status (X_2) Not married (0)	Married (1)	Total
Under \$20,000 (0)	180	540	720
\$20,000 to \$50,000 (1)	720	1080	1800
Over \$50,000 (2)	540	540	1080
Total	1440	2160	3600

TABLE 11.4 Bad Accounts, Number of Applicants by Income and Marital Status

Annual income (X_1)	Marital status (X_2) Not married (0)	Married (1)	Total
Under $20,000 (0)	140	100	240
$20,000 to $50,000 (1)	80	40	120
Over $50,000 (2)	20	20	40
Total	240	160	400

We see that 3600 accounts (90% of the 4000 selected accounts) were Good and 400 (10%) Bad; 180 accounts were Good and were held by customers who were not married and had income under $20,000; 100 accounts were Bad and were held by customers who were married and had income under $20,000; and so on.

A new applicant will have one of six possible sets of characteristics, that is, combinations of marital status and income categories corresponding to the cells of Tables 11.3 and 11.4: not married, with income under $20,000; married, with income under $20,000; . . . ; and married, with income over $50,000.

We begin by examining how to classify a new applicant who is not married and has income under $20,000 (that is, one coded $X_1 = 0$, $X_2 = 0$). We shall then repeat the procedure for all other sets of characteristics.

As Tables 11.3 and 11.4 show, 180 Good and 140 Bad applicants (320 applicants in total) had this set of characteristics. The probability is $180/320 = 0.5625$ that a new applicant with this set of characteristics will be Good and $140/320 = 0.4375$ that such an applicant will be Bad. In other words, we expect that out of every, say, 10,000 new applicants with this set of characteristics 5625 will be Good and 4375 will be Bad.

Table 11.5 shows the possible events (future account standing categories) and their probabilities, the possible actions, and the consequences of each event/action combination. All these, of course, refer to a new applicant who is not married and has income under $20,000.

If such an applicant is classified as Good, the expected loss is

$$(0)(0.5625) + (15)(0.4375) = 6.5625$$

If the applicant is classified as Bad, the expected loss is

$$(10)(0.5625) + (0)(0.4375) = 5.625$$

TABLE 11.5 Decision Table for New Applicant with $X_1 = 0, X_2 = 0$ (Not Married, Income under $20,000)

Account standing	Probability	Action Classify as good	Classify as bad	
Good	0.5625	0	10	
Bad	0.4375	15	0	
	1.0000	6.5625	5.625*	:Expected loss

In different words, if every one of, say, 10,000 new applicants who are not married and have income under $20,000 is classified as Good, the bank's total loss is expected to be

$$(0)(5625) + (15)(4375) = 65,625$$

and the average loss per applicant $65,625/10,000 = 6.5625$. Likewise, if all 10,000 applicants are classified as Bad, the expected average loss per applicant is 5.625.

The optimal action is the one with the lowest expected loss. Thus, a new applicant who is not married and has income under $20,000 should be classified as Bad and rejected.

Exactly the same procedure is applied to determine the optimal action for each of the other five sets of applicant characteristics. The results are summarized in Table 11.6.

The first line corresponds to the set of characteristics examined earlier. The other results can be easily confirmed. An asterisk in this and similar tables marks the lower expected loss for each set of characteristics.

TABLE 11.6 Applicant Characteristics and Optimal Actions, Example 11.1

Income code, X_1	Marital status code[a], X_2	Probability Good	Bad	Expected loss Classify as Good	Classify as Bad	Optimal action: Classify as
0	0	0.5625	0.4375	6.5625	5.6250*	Bad
0	1	0.8437	0.1563	2.3437*	8.4375	Good
1	0	0.9000	0.1000	1.5000*	9.0000	Good
1	1	0.9643	0.0357	0.5355*	9.6430	Good
2	0	0.9643	0.0357	0.5355*	9.6430	Good
2	1	0.9643	0.0357	0.5355*	9.6430	Good

[a] 1 = married, 0 = not married.

We see, for instance, that the probability a married applicant will be Good is greater than or equal to that of an unmarried applicant in every income category; the probability that an unmarried applicant will be Good increases with income; and so on.

We see also that the bank—in this artificial example, of course—should reject all applicants for checking accounts who are not married and earn less than $20,000 and accept all others.

This classification rule minimizes the expected loss of misclassification for *each* set of applicant characteristics, hence also the overall expected misclassification loss. It is, therefore, the optimal classification rule for this example.

The form of this rule is shown graphically in Figure 11.1. There are six possible pairs of values of X_1 and X_2. The rejection region consists of the point $(0, 0)$; the acceptance region consists of all other possible points. ∎

11.3 CLASSIFICATION INTO TWO CATEGORIES

Let us generalize. We have in mind a population of elements, each of which belongs to one of two mutually exclusive and collectively exhaustive categories or groups, C_1 and C_2. In Example 11.1, this population consists of new applicants for a checking account, and the two categories are "Good account" and "Bad account."

With each element there is associated a set of known values of k explanatory variables or attributes $X_1, X_2, \ldots, X_k$. In Example 11.1, the marital status and income of an applicant are the $k = 2$ attributes represented by X_1 and X_2, respectively.

We wish to construct a rule based on $X_1, X_2, \ldots, X_k$. The rule will take the following form: if an element has such and such values of $X_1, X_2, \ldots, X_k$, classify it as C_1; if not, classify it as C_2.

If an element actually belongs to C_1 but is classified as C_2, an error is made; let L_1 be the loss associated with misclassifying a member of C_1. Similarly, if an element belongs to C_2 but is classified as C_1, another error is made; let L_2 be the loss of misclassifying a member of C_2. We may assume that the losses associated with correct classifications are equal to zero.

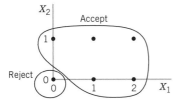

FIGURE 11.1 Classification regions, Example 11.1

Consider now an element with a given set of characteristics $x = [X_1 = x_1, X_2 = x_2, \ldots, X_k = x_k]$. The key components of the classification problem are the probabilities that such an element belongs to C_1 and C_2 given that it has the set of characteristics x. We denote these (conditional) probabilities by $Pr(C_1|x)$ and $Pr(C_2|x)$, respectively. Of course, $Pr(C_1|x) + Pr(C_2|x) = 1$, so only one of these need be estimated. Table 11.7 illustrates the notation.

If an element with the set of characteristics x is classified as C_1, the expected loss is

$$(0)Pr(C_1|x) + (L_2)Pr(C_2|x) = L_2 Pr(C_2|x)$$

If the element is classified as C_2, the expected loss is

$$(L_1)Pr(C_1|x) + (0)Pr(C_2|x) = L_1 Pr(C_1|x)$$

The element should be classified into the category with the smaller expected loss. If $L_1 Pr(C_1|x) > L_2 Pr(C_2|x)$, the element should be classified as C_1. If $L_1 Pr(C_1|x) < L_2 Pr(C_2|x)$, the element should be classified as C_2. If $L_1 Pr(C_1|x) = L_2 Pr(C_2|x)$, the element may be assigned to either category; we assume this category is C_1.

Summarizing, an element with the set of characteristics $x = [X_1 = x_1, X_2 = x_2, \ldots, X_k = x_k]$ should be classified as C_1 if

$$L_2 Pr(C_2|x) \leq L_1 Pr(C_1|x) \tag{11.1}$$

and into C_2 otherwise.

If this rule is applied to all possible sets of characteristics, it will minimize the overall expected loss, since it minimizes the expected loss for *each* set of characteristics. The rule Eq. 11.1 is therefore the optimal classification rule.

TABLE 11.7 States, Actions, and Consequences

Actual state	Probability	Action Classify as C_1	Classify as C_2	
Belongs to C_1	$Pr(C_1|x)$	0	L_1	
Belongs to C_2	$Pr(C_2|x)$	L_2	0	
	1	$L_2 Pr(C_2|x)$	$L_1 Pr(C_1|x)$	:Expected loss

Provided that $Pr(C_2|x) \neq 0$, the rule can be written in a different form: classify an element with the set of characteristics x as C_1 if

$$\frac{Pr(C_1|x)}{Pr(C_2|x)} \geq \frac{L_2}{L_1} \tag{11.2}$$

and as C_2 otherwise.

It will be noted that the optimal rule does not require exact knowledge of L_1 and L_2 but only of their ratio. In practical applications it is usually far easier to determine this ratio than both its components.

EXAMPLE 11.2

An insurance company plans to offer a one-year term life insurance policy for $20,000 to "qualified adults" for an annual premium of $200. An applicant for such a policy will be either accepted or rejected on the basis of such characteristics as age, gender, occupation, place of residence, and the like. The possible states, actions, and consequences are as shown in Table 11.8.

An applicant will either die or survive the one-year term. The insurance company has two options: classify the applicant as one who will die during the term of the policy (and reject the application) or as one who will survive (and accept the application). If the applicant is accepted and dies, the company receives $200 and pays $20,000, for a net revenue of −$19,800; if the applicant is accepted and survives, the company's net revenue is +$200. Thus, if the applicant is accepted and dies, the company's loss is 19,800; if the applicant is rejected and survives, the company's loss (the foregone profit) is 200.

An applicant should be classified as C_2 and rejected if $EL_2 < EL_1$, or

$$(200)[1 - Pr(C_1|x)] < (19800)Pr(C_1|x)$$

or

$$Pr(C_1|x) > 0.01$$

TABLE 11.8   Decision Table, Example 11.2

Actual state	Probability	Action: Classify as C_1 (Accept)	C_2 (Reject)	
C_1: Dies	$Pr(C_1|x)$	19,800	0	
C_2: Survives	$1 - Pr(C_1|x)$	0	200	
	1	EL_1	EL_2	:Expected loss

In words, an applicant with a given set of characteristics should be rejected if the probability that he or she will die within a year is greater than 1%. ■

Let us now consider the case where the misclassification losses are equal, that is, $L_1 = L_2 = L$. In view of Eq. 11.1, an element with the set of characteristics x should be classified as C_1 if

$$Pr(C_2|x) \leq Pr(C_1|x)$$

or as C_2 if

$$Pr(C_2|x) > Pr(C_1|x)$$

In the case of equal misclassification losses, therefore, the optimal classification rule is especially simple: classify an element into the more likely of the two categories.

If the misclassification losses in Example 11.1 were equal, we would simply examine the probabilities of a Good or Bad account for each combination x of income and marital status listed in Table 11.6. Since $Pr(Good|x) > Pr(Bad|x)$ for all x, the optimal classification rule would have the bank accept *all* new applicants for a checking account.

11.4 MEASURING THE QUALITY OF A CLASSIFICATION RULE

We have not said anything yet about measuring the quality of a classification rule. Since the objective is to minimize the expected loss of misclassification, the quality of a classification rule should be measured by the overall expected loss resulting from the application of the rule. Let us return to Example 11.1 to show how this is determined.

EXAMPLE II.I (CONTINUED)

The optimal classification rule was developed earlier: classify as Bad all new applicants coded $X_1 = 0$ and $X_2 = 0$—that is, applicants who are not married and have income under $20,000; classify as Good all other applicants.

The probability that an applicant will be Good and misclassified is the probability that an applicant will be Good, unmarried, and earning less than $20,000. Referring to Table 11.3, we see that there were 180 such applicants in the sample of 4000. Therefore, the probability can be estimated as 180/4000, or 0.045. The probability of correctly classifying a Good applicant is (3600 − 180)/4000, or 0.855. Similarly, the probability an applicant will be Bad and correctly classified is (see Table 11.4) 140/4000, or 0.035. The probability that an applicant will be Bad and misclassified is $(400 - 140)/4000$, or 0.065. These probabilities are shown in Table 11.9.

Therefore, the probability of classifying an applicant incorrectly (the overall probability of misclassification) is $0.045 + 0.065$, or 0.11; the probability of correct classification is 0.89. The overall expected loss (per applicant) is

$$(0.045)L_1 + (0.065)L_2 = (0.045)(10) + (0.065)(15) = \$1.425 \qquad \blacksquare$$

Clearly, if the misclassification losses are equal, the overall expected misclassification loss is proportional to the misclassification probability. In Example 11.1, for instance, if $L_1 = L_2 = L$, the overall expected loss is

$$(0.045 + 0.065)L = 0.11L$$

These measures of the quality of a classification rule may be applied to examine the *contribution* of one or more explanatory variables or attributes. In Example 11.1, for instance, we may wish to consider whether or not, say, marital status is useful for classifying new applicants. Using both explanatory attributes (income and marital status), the overall expected loss is $1.425. It should be clear that without the use of one of these attributes the overall expected loss cannot be less than 1.425. Thus, to determine the contribution of income, we would begin by calculating the optimal rule and the overall expected loss using marital status as the only explanatory attribute. In Problem 11.2, the reader is asked to confirm that this amounts to $1.50. By using income as an additional explanatory attribute, therefore, the overall expected loss is reduced from 1.50 to 1.425, or by $(1.50 - 1.425)/1.50$, that is, by 5%.

In general, then, a procedure for determining the contribution of one or more explanatory variables or attributes is to first calculate the optimal rule and the associated overall expected loss without using these variables and then to compare that with the overall expected loss when all explanatory variables are used. The relative reduction in the overall expected loss is a measure of the

TABLE 11.9 Probabilities of Correct and Incorrect Classification, Example 11.1

Account standing	Action Classify as Good	Classify as Bad	Total
Good	0.855	0.045	0.900
Bad	0.065	0.035	0.100
Total	0.920	0.080	1.000

contribution of the variables or attributes in question. If the misclassification losses L_1 and L_2 are equal or not known, the overall misclassification probability may be used in place of the overall expected loss.

EXAMPLE 11.3

In a study of personal loan applications made to a bank in New York City, a random sample was taken from all applications submitted in a particular year.[1] The sample consisted of 774 applications, of which 385 were good loans (G) and 389 were bad loans (B). Such a large bad loan rate is rather unusual but appears to have been the reality in this case. There were eight attributes included in the study, and each of the attributes was either present (coded 1) or absent (coded 0). The attributes were

X_1: Income more than $6000 X_5: Own home
X_2: Residence in good area X_6: More than 3 years at present work
X_3: Owe less than $300 X_7: White collar
X_4: Have telephone X_8: Single

The optimal classification rule and misclassification probabilities were calculated for different sets of explanatory attributes and values of the ratio L_2/L_1, as shown in Table 11.10.

L_1 is the loss of classifying a good loan as bad and L_2 that of classifying a bad loan as good. As one would expect, the greater the ratio L_2/L_1, the smaller the probability of misclassifying a bad loan but also the greater the probability of misclassifying a good loan.

To determine the contribution of a particular explanatory attribute or set of attributes, the misclassification probabilities with and without the use of

TABLE 11.10 Percentage of Misclassified Applications for Given Relative Losses and Classification Attributes, Example 11.3

Attributes included	$L_2/L_1 = 1$ G	B	$L_2/L_1 = 2$ G	B	$L_2/L_1 = 3$ G	B	$L_2/L_1 = 0.5$ G	B	$L_2/L_1 = 0.3$ G	B
1-8	21	20	32	10	44	7	11	40	6	47
1-7	22	27	41	13	48	7	11	40	6	56
1, 3-8	26	25	39	9	49	7	11	53	3	56
2-8	22	25	37	13	47	7	14	44	6	56
3-8	16	36	39	15	64	5	8	54	5	62
1-6	27	31	31	18	50	11	12	39	9	57

[1]S. Chatterjee and S. Barcun, "A Nonparametric Approach to Credit Screening," *Journal of the American Statistical Association*, Vol. 65, March 1970, pp. 150–54.

these attributes can be compared. For example, when $L_2/L_1 = 1$ and all eight explanatory attributes are used, 21% of the good loans and 20% of the bad loans are misclassified; without X_8, the corresponding relative frequencies are 22% and 27%; without X_7 and X_8, the proportions of good and bad loans misclassified increase to 27% and 31%, respectively. ■

11.5 MORE ON THE CONDITIONAL PROBABILITIES

Important elements of the classification problem are $Pr(C_1|x)$ and $Pr(C_2|x)$, the probabilities that an element having the set of characteristics x will belong to category C_1 or C_2. How these probabilities are estimated depends on the situation.

In some situations, these probabilities can be estimated directly—for example, by carrying out experiments with different sets of characteristics x and observing the proportions of elements falling into C_1 and C_2.

In other situations, a simple random sample is selected from a population of elements, and the proportions of elements belonging to C_1 and C_2 for each set of characteristics are taken as estimates of $Pr(C_1|x)$ and $Pr(C_2|x)$. This was the approach used in Example 11.1, where we treated the 4000 recently opened accounts essentially as a simple random sample from the population of all accounts.

In still other situations, the available information comes from simple random samples, one from each category. Sampling, in other words, is stratified random. In the remainder of this section, we shall show how to estimate $Pr(C_1|x)$ and $Pr(C_2|x)$ in such a situation.

Let us return to Example 11.1. Suppose 90% of all accounts are known to be Good and 10% Bad. Rather than select 4000 recently opened accounts, let us suppose the bank selects a simple random sample of 400 Good accounts and another simple random sample of 200 Bad accounts. The application forms corresponding to the 600 selected accounts are pulled out from the files and the data tabulated as shown in Tables 11.11 and 11.12.

For example, 5% of the 400 selected Good accounts were held by customers who were not married and had income under $20,000; 35% of the selected Bad accounts had the same set of characteristics; and so on. Tables 11.11 and 11.12 show the estimated joint probability distributions $p_1(X_1, X_2)$ and $p_2(X_1, X_2)$ of income and marital status among Good and Bad accounts, respectively.[2]

---

[2]The numbers in Tables 11.11 and 11.12 were deliberately made consistent with Tables 11.3 and 11.4. In reality, of course, such exact consistency cannot be expected because the results will vary from sample to sample.

TABLE II.II   Good Accounts, Distribution of Income and Marital Status, $p_1(X_1, X_2)$

Annual income (X_1)	Marital status (X_2) Not married (0)	Married (1)	Total
Under $20,000 (0)	0.05	0.15	0.20
$20,000 to $50,000 (1)	0.20	0.30	0.50
Over $50,000 (2)	0.15	0.15	0.30
Total	0.40	0.60	1.00

TABLE II.12   Bad Accounts, Distribution of Income and Marital Status, $p_2(X_1, X_2)$

Annual income (X_1)	Marital status (X_2) Not married (0)	Married (1)	Total
Under $20,000 (0)	0.35	0.25	0.60
$20,000 to $50,000 (1)	0.20	0.10	0.30
Over $50,000 (2)	0.05	0.05	0.10
Total	0.60	0.40	1.00

Let us estimate the probabilities that a new applicant with the set of characteristics $x = [X_1 = 0, X_2 = 0]$—that is, not married and having income under $20,000—will be Good or Bad. We shall use the symbol $\tilde{x}$ to mean "not having the set of characteristics x." Figure 11.2 illustrates the calculations.

It will be recalled that 90% of the accounts are Good and 10% Bad. The proportion of Good accounts having the set of characteristics x is 0.05 (Table 11.11). The proportion of Bad accounts with this set of characteristics is 0.35 (Table 11.12). The proportion of accounts that are Good *and* have these characteristics is (0.90)(0.05), or 0.045. The proportion of accounts that are Bad and have these characteristics is (0.10)(0.35), or 0.035. Thus, the proportion of

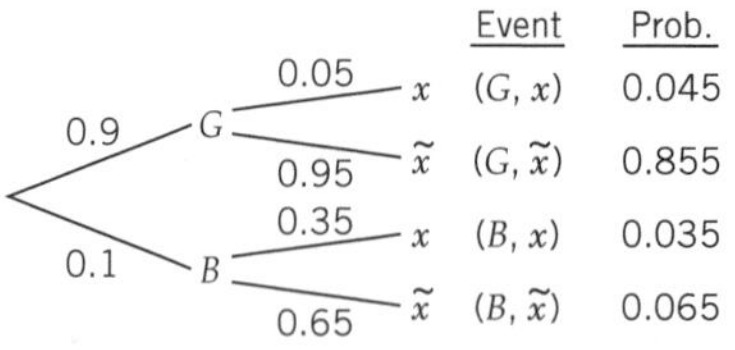

FIGURE II.2   Derivation of $Pr(C_j|x)$, illustrated

accounts that have the set of characteristics x is $0.045 + 0.035$, or 0.080. Among accounts having these characteristics, the proportion Good is $0.045/0.080$, or 0.5625, and the proportion Bad is $0.035/0.080$, or 0.4375. These are estimates of the probabilities that a new applicant who is not married and has income under \$20,000 will be Good or Bad, respectively.

We can generalize. Let q_1 be the probability that an element belongs to C_1 and q_2 that it belongs to C_2. Let $p_1(X_1 = x_1, X_2 = x_2, \ldots, X_k = x_k)$ or, more simply, $p_1(x)$ be the probability that a member of C_1 will have a given set of characteristics $x = [x_1, x_2, \ldots, x_k]$; similarly, let $p_2(x) = p_2(X_1 = x_1, X_2 = x_2, \ldots, X_k = x_k)$ be the probability that a member of C_2 will have the set of characteristics $x = [x_1, x_2, \ldots, x_k]$. Figure 11.3 illustrates the notation.

The probability that an element will belong to C_1 *and* have the given set of characteristics is $q_1 p_1(x)$. The probability that an element will belong to C_2 and have the given characteristics is $q_2 p_2(x)$. The probability that an element will have the given set of characteristics is $q_1 p_1(x) + q_2 p_2(x)$. The probability that an element having the set of characteristics x will belong to C_1, is

$$Pr(C_1|x) = \frac{q_1 p_1(x)}{q_1 p_1(x) + q_2 p_2(x)} \tag{11.3}$$

Similarly, the probability that an element will belong to C_2 given that it has the set of characteristics x is

$$Pr(C_2|x) = \frac{q_2 p_2(x)}{q_1 p_1(x) + q_2 p_2(x)} \tag{11.4}$$

Replacing $Pr(C_1|x)$ and $Pr(C_2|x)$ in Eq. 11.1 with their equals from Eqs. 11.3 and 11.4, and simplifying, we find that an element with the set of characteristics $x = [x_1, x_2, \ldots, x_k]$ should be classified as C_1 if

$$L_2 q_2 p_2(x) \le L_1 q_1 p_1(x) \tag{11.5}$$

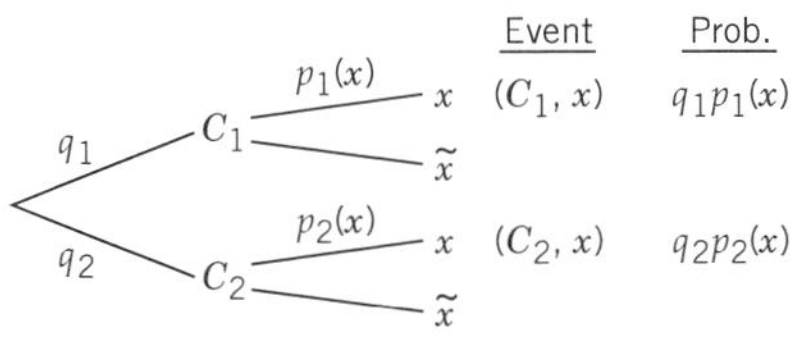

FIGURE 11.3 Derivation of $Pr(C_j|x)$

or as C_2 if otherwise. Alternatively, and provided that $p_2(x) \neq 0$, classify as C_1 if

$$\frac{p_1(x)}{p_2(x)} \geq \frac{q_2 L_2}{q_1 L_1} \tag{11.6}$$

or as C_2 otherwise.

11.6 CLASSIFICATION INTO MORE THAN TWO CATEGORIES

The preceding results can be easily extended to the case where an element is classified into one of m mutually exclusive and collectively exhaustive categories $C_1, C_2, \ldots, C_m$ on the basis of k known explanatory variables or attributes $X_1, X_2, \ldots, X_k$. Table 11.13 illustrates the notation.

Let L_{ij} be the loss of misclassifying an element into C_j when in fact it belongs to C_i. We assume that the losses of correct classification are zero, that is, that all $L_{ii} = 0$. Let $Pr(C_i|x)$ be the conditional probability that an element belongs to C_i given that it has the set of characteristics $x = [X_1 = x_1, X_2 = x_2, \ldots, X_k = x_k]$.

If an element with the set of characteristics $x = [x_1, x_2, \ldots, x_k]$ is classified as C_1, the expected loss is

$$EL_1 = L_{21} Pr(C_2|x) + \cdots + L_{m1} Pr(C_m|x)$$

In general, if the element is classified as C_j the expected loss is

$$EL_j = \sum_{i=1}^{m} L_{ij} Pr(C_i|x) \qquad (i \neq j) \tag{11.7}$$

TABLE 11.13 Classification into More than Two Categories

Actual state	Probability	Action: Classify as			
		C_1	C_2	$\cdots$	C_m
C_1	$Pr(C_1|x)$	0	L_{12}	$\cdots$	L_{1m}
C_2	$Pr(C_2|x)$	L_{21}	0	$\cdots$	L_{2m}
$\cdots$	$\cdots$	$\cdots$	$\cdots$	$\cdots$	$\cdots$
C_m	$Pr(C_m|x)$	L_{m1}	L_{m2}	$\cdots$	0
	1	EL_1	EL_2	$\cdots$	EL_m	:Expected loss

To determine the category into which the element should be classified, we calculate the expected loss for each possible action and select that action for which Eq. 11.7 is minimized. The calculations are repeated and the optimal action determined for each other set of characteristics x. Since this method minimizes the expected loss for each possible set of characteristics, it minimizes the overall expected loss and yields the optimum classification rule.

EXAMPLE 11.4

Consider once again the situation described in Example 11.1 but suppose that checking accounts are classified into three categories:

C_1: Good accounts
C_2: Accounts with minor problems
C_3: Accounts with serious problems

A checking account with a small temporary overdraft is classified as C_2, while an account with a substantial and/or prolonged overdraft is classified as C_3.

A new applicant classified as C_2 (i.e., as an account with minor problems in the future) will pay a higher service fee, while an applicant classified as C_3 is refused. For the purpose of this illustration, let us suppose that the misclassification losses are as follows:

Actual	Action: Classify as		
category	C_1	C_2	C_3
C_1	$0	10	20
C_2	15	0	5
C_3	5	2	0

The application forms of the 4000 most recent applicants and accounts were tabulated as shown in Tables 11.14, 11.15, and 11.16.

TABLE 11.14 Good Accounts, Number of Applicants by Income and Marital Status

Annual income (X_1)	Marital status (X_2)		Total
	Not married (0)	Married (1)	
Under $20,000 (0)	140	420	560
$20,000 to $50,000 (1)	560	840	1400
Over $50,000 (2)	420	420	840
Total	1120	1680	2800

TABLE 11.15   Accounts with Minor Problems, Number of Applicants by Income and Marital Status

Annual income (X_1)	Marital status (X_2)		Total
	Not married (0)	Married (1)	
Under $20,000 (0)	120	120	240
$20,000 to $50,000 (1)	160	160	320
Over $50,000 (2)	120	120	240
Total	400	400	800

TABLE 11.16   Accounts with Major Problems, Number of Applicants by Income and Marital Status

Annual income (X_1)	Marital status (X_2)		Total
	Not married (0)	Married (1)	
Under $20,000 (0)	140	100	240
$20,000 to $50,000 (1)	80	40	120
Over $50,000 (2)	20	20	40
Total	240	160	400

For example, 140 accounts were Good and held by persons who had income less than $20,000 and were not married, and so on.

Consider now an applicant who has an annual income greater than $50,000 ($X_1 = 2$) and is not married ($X_2 = 0$).

Referring to Tables 11.14, 11.15, and 11.16, we see that 420 good accounts, 120 accounts with minor problems, and 20 accounts with major problems (560 accounts in all) had this set of characteristics. Thus, the probability that an account with this set of characteristics will be good is $Pr(C_1|x) = 420/560 = 0.75$; that it will be one with minor problems is $Pr(C_2|x) = 120/560 = 0.214$; that it will be one with major problems is $Pr(C_3|x) = 20/560 = 0.036$.

The possible states and their probabilities together with the actions and their consequences are shown in the following table:

Actual state	Probability, $Pr(C_i|x)$	Action: Classify as		
		C_1	C_2	C_3
C_1	0.750	$0	10	20
C_2	0.214	15	0	5
C_3	0.036	5	2	0
	1.000	3.390*	7.572	16.070

If the applicant is classified as C_1, the expected loss is

$$(0.750)(0) + (0.214)(15) + (0.036)(5) = \$3.390$$

if the applicant is classified as C_2, the expected loss is

$$(0.750)(10) + (0.214)(0) + (0.036)(2) = \$7.572$$

if the applicant is classified as C_3, the expected loss is

$$(0.750)(20) + (0.214)(5) + (0.036)(0) = \$16.070$$

Therefore, an applicant who has income greater than \$50,000 and is not married should be classified as C_1 (Good) since the expected loss of that action is least.

In a similar manner, the conditional probabilities, $Pr(C_i|x)$, and expected losses are calculated for all possible sets of applicant characteristics, as shown in Table 11.17.

According to the optimal classification rule, therefore, applicants who are not married and earn less than \$20,000 should be classified as C_2; all others should be classified as C_1. ∎

If all misclassification losses are equal, that is, all $L_{ij} = L$, then the expected loss of classifying as C_j, Eq. 11.7, is

$$EL_j = L \sum_{i \neq j}^{m} Pr(C_i|x) = L[1 - Pr(C_j|x)] \tag{11.8}$$

For example,

$$EL_1 = L[Pr(C_2|x) + \cdots + Pr(C_m|x)] = L[1 - Pr(C_1|x)]$$

TABLE 11.17 Conditional Probabilities and Expected Losses, Example 11.4

x_1	x_2	Conditional probabilities $Pr(C_1|x)$	$Pr(C_2|x)$	$Pr(C_3|x)$	Expected loss C_1	C_2	C_3	Optimal action
0	0	0.350	0.300	0.350	6.250	4.200*	8.500	C_2
0	1	0.656	0.188	0.156	3.600*	6.872	14.060	C_1
1	0	0.700	0.200	0.100	3.500*	7.200	15.000	C_1
1	1	0.808	0.154	0.038	2.500*	8.156	16.930	C_1
2	0	0.750	0.214	0.036	3.390*	7.572	16.070	C_1
2	1	0.750	0.214	0.036	3.390*	7.572	16.070	C_1

The optimal action is the one for which $1 - Pr(C_j|x)$ is minimum, or, what amounts to the same thing, the one for which $Pr(C_j|x)$ is maximum. Quite reasonably, *when the misclassification losses are equal, an element with a given set of characteristics should be classified into the most likely category.*

EXAMPLE 11.4 (CONTINUED)

If the misclassification losses in this example were equal, the optimal action for each set of characteristics listed in Table 11.17 is the one associated with the greatest conditional probability, $Pr(C_j|x)$. Thus, when $x = [X_1 = 0, X_2 = 0]$ one should be indifferent between classifying x as C_1 or as C_3. For all other x, the optimal action is C_1. ∎

As in the case of two categories, the quality of the optimal classification rule is measured by the overall expected misclassification loss or, in the event the misclassification losses are equal, by the overall misclassification probability resulting from the application of the rule.

EXAMPLE 11.4 (CONTINUED)

Table 11.18 shows the probabilities of correct and incorrect classification if the optimal rule of Table 11.17 is followed. In parentheses are the associated losses. Note that only two actions are indicated: classify as C_1 and classify as C_2; the third action, classify as C_3, was ruled out in all cases.

For example, the probability that an applicant will be a member of C_1 and classified as C_2 is the probability that an account will be good and held by an unmarried person having income less than \$20,000 (i.e., Good, $X_1 = 0$, $X_2 = 0$). This probability (see Table 11.14) is 140/4000, or 0.035. The remanining probabilities in Table 11.17 are similarly calculated.

TABLE 11.18   Probabilities of Classification and Losses, Example 11.4

Actual state	Action: Classify as	
	C_1	C_2
C_1	0.665 (0)	0.035 (10)
C_2	0.170 (15)	0.030 (0)
C_3	0.065 (5)	0.035 (2)
Total	0.900	0.100

The probability that an applicant will be misclassified (the overall probability of misclassification) is

$$(0.035) + (0.170) + (0.065) + (0.035) = 0.305$$

and the overall expected loss of misclassification

$$(0.035)(10) + (0.170)(15) + (0.065)(5) + (0.035)(2) = \$3.295 \qquad \blacksquare$$

Again, as in the case of two categories, the conditional probabilities $Pr(C_i|x)$ may be estimated by experiment, by means of a simple random sample of elements selected from the entire population, or by means of separate simple random samples of elements belonging to each category.

In the example of this section, we applied the second approach, treating the most recent 4000 applications as a simple random sample from the population of all applications. The calculations in the case of separate samples are best explained with a numerical example.

EXAMPLE 11.5

The situation is identical to Example 11.4, except that instead of examining the most recent 4000 applications and accounts, the bank selected a simple random sample of 200 good accounts (C_1), another of 200 accounts with minor problems (C_2), and a third independent random sample of 200 accounts with major problems (C_3). The application forms of the selected accounts were pulled out and the applicant's income (X_1) and marital status (X_2) categories detetermined. The results are tabulated in Table 11.19.

For example, 5% of the 200 selected good accounts (C_1) were held by persons who, at the time of their application, had income less than $20,000

TABLE 11.19 Distributions of Income and Marital Status, Example 11.5

x:		C_1:	C_2:	C_3:
x_1	x_2	$p_1(x_1,x_2)$	$p_2(x_1,x_2)$	$p_3(x_1,x_2)$
0	0	0.05	0.15	0.35
0	1	0.15	0.15	0.25
1	0	0.20	0.20	0.20
1	1	0.30	0.20	0.10
2	0	0.15	0.15	0.05
2	1	0.15	0.15	0.05
		1.00	1.00	1.00

$(X_1 = 0)$ and were not married $(X_2 = 0)$; 0.05 is used as the estimate of $p_1(X_1 = 0, X_2 = 0)$. The remaining entries of Table 11.19 are similarly interpreted.

Suppose that the proportions of accounts in the three categories C_1, C_2, and C_3 are $q_1 = 0.7$, $q_2 = 0.2$, and $q_3 = 0.1$.

Consider now an applicant who is not married and has income less than \$20,000 (i.e., one with characteristics $x = [X_1 = 0, X_2 = 0]$). The probabilities that an account with such applicant characteristics will turn out good or with minor or major problems can be calculated with the help of Figure 11.4.

To avoid cluttering Figure 11.4, only the needed numbers are shown. The probability that an applicant will have the set of characteristics x is $0.035 + 0.030 + 0.035$, or 0.10. The probability that an applicant with characteristics x will be good (C_1) is $Pr(C_1|x) = 0.035/0.10 = 0.35$. Likewise, $Pr(C_2|x) = 0.030/0.10 = 0.30$ and $Pr(C_3|x) = 0.035/0.10 = 0.35$.

It can be confirmed that these probabilities and those corresponding to all other sets of characteristics are as shown in Table 11.17. (This is because the numbers in Table 11.19 were deliberately made consistent with those of Tables 11.14, 11.15, and 11.16. In reality, of course, it is unlikely that random samples of accounts selected in different ways will yield identical results.) Thus, the optimal actions and classification rule are the same as in Example 11.4. ■

In general, let $q_1, q_2, \ldots, q_m$ be the probabilities that an element will belong to $C_1, C_2, \ldots, C_m$, respectively, and $p_i(X_1, X_2, \ldots, X_k)$ be the joint probability distribution of the explanatory variables $X_1, X_2, \ldots, X_k$ in C_i. The probability that an element of C_i will have the set of characteristics $x = [x_1, x_2, \ldots, x_k]$ will be written as $p_i(x)$ for brevity. Figure 11.5 illustrates the notation and the calculations.

The probability that an element belongs to C_i *and* has the set of characteristics x is $q_i p_i(x)$. The probability that an element has the set of characteristics x

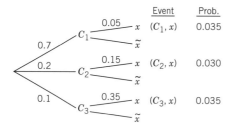

FIGURE II.4   Calculations, Example II.5

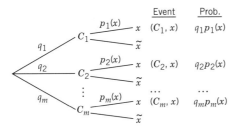

FIGURE 11.5 Calculation of $Pr(C_i|x)$, separate samples

is $\sum_{j=1}^{m} q_j p_j(x)$. The conditional probability that an element having the set of characteristics x belongs to C_i is

$$Pr(C_i|x) = \frac{q_i p_i(x)}{\sum_{j=1}^{m} q_j p_j(x)} \qquad (11.9)$$

11.7 TO SUM UP

The method described in this chapter for determining the optimal classification rule is quite general and easily implemented. No special assumptions need be satisfied.

The method is most appropriate when the rule is based on attributes only. It is clear, however, that the computational burden increases rapidly with the number of possible sets of characteristics. For example, when there are eight explanatory attributes, each with three possible categories, the number of possible sets of characteristics is 3^8 or 6561. Modern computers, of course, can handle such numbers with hardly any exertion. It is also clear, however, that as the number of possible sets of characteristics increases, the proportion of elements having a given set of characteristics tends to decrease, so that the size of a sample required to yield elements with a given set of characteristics increases.

If the classification rule involves variables as well as attributes, the variables must be turned into attributes for the method of this chapter to apply. In Example 11.1, for instance, annual income was treated as an attribute with three categories: under $20,000, $20,000 to $50,000, and over $50,000. Some judgment is necessary in forming these categories and perhaps some experimentation with different limits is desirable, but otherwise the method of this chapter can be applied without change.

Nevertheless, often in practice rules are sought that can be stated, estimated, and implemented more simply. Consider, for example, the case in which applicants for credit will be classified as good or bad risks on the basis of their income (X_1) and age (X_2). A simple classification rule is a linear one, roughly described as follows. Assign b_1 "points" for each \$1 of income and b_2 points for each year of age. Calculate the applicant's "score" $Y = b_1 X_1 + b_2 X_2$. If Y exceeds a given cutoff value Y_0, classify the applicant as Good and give credit; otherwise, classify as Bad and refuse credit. The points b_1 and b_2 as well as the cutoff Y_0 will be based on the available observations and designed to make the rule perform well. Although not necessarily optimal in the sense of this chapter, such a rule is indeed simpler than one that assigns a category to each possible set of values of X_1 and X_2.

In the following chapter, we examine some special cases where linear rules are optimal and others where additional information about the elements of the classification problem may be exploited to produce simpler classification rules.

PROBLEMS

11.1   Confirm the calculations of Table 11.6.

11.2   Refer to Example 11.1 but suppose the bank is considering classifying new applicants on the basis of marital status only. Using the data in Tables 11.3 and 11.4, determine the optimal classification rule. Show that the associated overall expected loss and probability of misclassification are \$1.50 and \$0.10, respectively.

11.3   Refer to Example 11.1 but suppose that the bank is considering classifying new applicants on the basis of income only. Using the data in Tables 11.3 and 11.4, determine the optimal classification rule. Calculate the associated overall expected loss and probability of misclassification. Determine the contribution of marital status as an explanatory variable in addition to income.

11.4   Same as Problem 11.2, but suppose that the loss from classifying a Bad applicant as Good is \$70 rather than \$15.

11.5   Same as Problem 11.3, but suppose that the loss from classifying a Bad applicant as Good is \$70 rather than \$15.

11.6   Refer to Section 11.3 and assume that the misclassification losses are equal (that is, $L_1 = L_2 = L$). Show that the optimal classification rule is to classify as C_1 if $Pr(C_1|x) \geq 0.5$.

11.7   Refer to Example 11.4. Confirm the results shown in Table 11.17.

11.8   Refer to Example 11.5. Confirm the entries of Table 11.17. Explain your calculations.

11.9   A study was made to determine the characteristics of regular listeners of the two FM radio stations broadcasting in a region.

From a simple random sample of regular listeners of station A, the following relative frequency distribution of level of education and age was obtained:

Station A

Level of education	Age Young	Old
Low	0.6	0.1
High	0.1	0.2

For example, 60% of the regular listeners of Station A were young and had a low level of education, and so on.

Similarly, from a simple random sample of regular listeners of Station B, the following distribution was determined:

Station B

Level of education	Age Young	Old
Low	0.2	0.1
High	0.1	0.6

Assume that, among those who regularly listen to Stations A or B, 70% listen to A and 30% to B and that the costs of misclassification are equal.

Develop a rule for classifying listeners that minimizes the expected misclassification probability. Determine the performance of this rule.

11.10 The diskette accompanying this text contains the computer program `classify` to assist in the calculation of problems in this chapter. The instructions for this program can be found in the file `classify.txt` and the source code in the file `classify.c`.

(a) Apply `classify` to confirm the calculations of Example 11.1.

(b) Apply `classify` to confirm the calculations of Example 11.5.

11.11 A random sample of persons 18 years old and older was taken, and the selected persons were asked for their age, level of education, and household income, as well as whether or not they owned a personal computer. Their responses were coded as follows:

AGE: Age of respondent

> = 1, 18-24 years old

> = 2, 25-64 years old

> = 3, 65 or more years old

EDUC: Highest level of education attained by respondent

> = 1, elementary

> = 2, secondary

> = 3, postsecondary

HINC: Annual household income

> = 1, less than $20,000

$= 2, \$20{,}000 \text{ to } \$40{,}000$

$= 3, \$40{,}000 \text{ to } \$60{,}000$

$= 4, \text{more than } \$60{,}000$

Altogether, 1306 persons responded to all four questions. Table 11.20 shows the number of respondents and the proportion of respondents owning a personal computer for each observed combination of age, education, and income codes.

TABLE 11.20 Responses, Problem 11.11

AGE	EDUC	HINC	Number of respondents	Proportion owning PC
1	1	2	1	0.00000
1	2	1	11	0.00000
1	2	2	22	0.27273
1	2	3	8	0.37500
1	2	4	3	0.33333
1	3	1	24	0.33333
1	3	2	26	0.38462
1	3	3	27	0.55556
1	3	4	16	0.68750
2	1	1	22	0.00000
2	1	2	29	0.24138
2	1	3	16	0.00000
2	1	4	1	0.00000
2	2	1	81	0.14815
2	2	2	170	0.19412
2	2	3	127	0.30709
2	2	4	71	0.47887
2	3	1	45	0.28889
2	3	2	128	0.36719
2	3	3	163	0.45399
2	3	4	178	0.69101
3	1	1	11	0.00000
3	1	2	8	0.00000
3	1	4	1	1.00000
3	2	1	34	0.02941
3	2	2	34	0.02941
3	2	3	7	0.14286
3	2	4	3	0.00000
3	3	1	7	0.14286
3	3	2	15	0.26667
3	3	3	6	0.16667
3	3	4	11	0.27273

SOURCE: File `pcsurv.dat`

One of the objectives of the study was to develop a rule for classifying persons as potential owners or nonowners of a personal computer on the basis of their age, level of education, and household income.

To begin with, assume that the sample is a simple random sample from the population of all persons 18 years old and older and that the misclassification losses are equal.

(a) Determine the optimal classification rule for each combination of age, level of education, and household income categories. Determine the overall expected loss and misclassification probability associated with this rule.

(b) Determine the optimal classification rule, the overall expected misclassification loss, and the misclassification probability using (i) age only, (ii) level of education only, and (iii) household income only. In what way does the probability that a person is a PC owner depend on these variables?

(c) Determine the optimal classification rule, the overall expected misclassification loss, and the misclassification probability using (i) age and education only, (ii) age and household income only, and (iii) level of education and household income only.

(d) In view of your calculations in (a) to (c), determine the contribution of age, level of education, and household income to the classification rule.

(e) Repeat (a) to (d) but now assuming that the loss of misclassifying a nonowner is four times that of an owner. Comment on the effect of the misclassification losses in this case.

(f) How would you select a simple random sample of persons 18 years old and older in a city? In the country? How else can a random sample be selected? Does the method of selection matter?[3]

---

[3]This problem is based on the Johnson & Phillips case described in Part II of the text.

CHAPTER 12

MORE ON CLASSIFICATION

12.1 INTRODUCTION AND SUMMARY

In this chapter, we examine special cases of the classification problem described in Chapter 11, in which additional information or a different criterion is exploited to produce simple classification rules.

We begin with situations involving classification into two categories and consider cases where the probability that an element with a given set of characteristics belongs to a category can be expressed as a function of the explanatory variables and attributes. The simplest such function is, of course, linear, but linear functions may produce probability estimates outside the range from 0 to 1. The so-called logit, complementary log-log, and probit models we shall soon examine are designed to overcome this one shortcoming of the linear probability model.

Next, we examine the case in which the joint distribution of the explanatory variables among the elements of each category is multivariate normal. The multivariate normal distribution is an extension of the familiar normal distribution to joint distributions of any number of variables. We shall see that under certain conditions the classification rule minimizing the overall expected misclassification loss is linear in the explanatory variables and therefore especially easy to implement.

Multivariate normality is a rather restrictive condition. We shall see, however, that the optimal classification rule under normality is also optimal under a different criterion that does not require normality but seeks to achieve the greatest possible separation of the mean linear "scores" in favor of the two categories.

Similar results apply to classification problems involving more than two categories, albeit under more restrictive conditions. We examine such situations in the last two sections of this chapter.

12.2 PROBABILITY MODELS, TWO CATEGORIES

Important elements of the classification problem examined in Chapter 11, it will be recalled, are the probabilities, $Pr(C_1|x)$ and $Pr(C_2|x)$, that an element with the set of characteristics $x = [X_1, X_2, \ldots, X_k]$ belongs to category C_1 or C_2.

In the special case where the misclassification losses are equal, the element should be classified into the category with the greater such probability.

On some occasions, we may have reasons to believe that $Pr(C_i|x)$ is a given function of $X_1, X_2, \ldots, X_k$. Estimation of this function often gives a better understanding of the relationship between the classification probability and the explanatory variables.

To simplify the notation, let us denote by P—rather than $Pr(C_i|x)$—the probability that an element with the set of characteristics $x = [X_1, X_2, \ldots, X_k]$ belongs to a given category (this could be C_1 or C_2). We assume that P is a certain function of $X_1, X_2, \ldots, X_k$.

We shall consider some functions frequently used in practice and how these may be estimated.

The simplest function, of course, is linear:

$$P = \beta_0 + \beta_1 X_1 + \beta_2 X_2 + \cdots + \beta_k X_k \tag{12.1}$$

Model 12.1 is the *linear probability model*.

P cannot be observed. If, for each set of characteristics x, there are f elements belonging to the category of interest in a simple random sample of n elements having the set of characteristics x, we may use f/n as an estimate of P and estimate the parameters $\beta_0, \beta_1, \ldots, \beta_k$ of the linear model by regressing f/n against $X_1, X_2, \ldots, X_k$.

To illustrate, suppose an insurance company recorded the gender and age at the start of a year of each person insured for life and whether or not the insured died during the year. Suppose further that only four distinct sets of age values and gender categories were observed, as shown in columns 1 to 3 of Table 12.1.

For each set of characteristics, the number of insureds alive at the start of the year, n, and the number who died during the year, f, are shown in columns 4 and 5.

TABLE 12.1 Illustrative Data for Forecasting the Probability of Death

Set no. (1)	Age, X_1 (2)	Gender[a], X_2 (3)	Number of insureds, n (4)	Number who died, f (5)	f/n (6)	$\log \frac{f}{n-f}$ (7)	$\log[-\log(1 - \frac{f}{n})]$ (8)
1	35	1	30	1	0.033	−3.367	−3.384
2	50	0	40	1	0.025	−3.663	−3.676
3	55	0	20	2	0.100	−2.197	−2.250
4	60	1	10	1	0.100	−2.197	−2.250

[a] 1 = male, 0 = female.

For example, there were thirty 35-year-old male insureds at the start of the year, one of whom died during the year. If it is assumed that the 30 insureds were selected at random from the population of all 35-year-old males, then 1/30 is an estimate of the probability that a 35-year-old male insured will die during a one-year period.

The relationship between the probability of death, on the one hand, and age and gender, on the other, can be estimated by regressing f/n in column 6 against X_1 and X_2. The regression results are

$$\hat{P} = -0.102 + 0.003X_1 + 0.020X_2$$

For example, the probability that a 45-year-old male will die in a one-year period is estimated to be $-0.102 + (0.003)(45) + (0.020)(1) = 0.053$. The probability of death, we observe, increases with age and is higher for males than for females.

It is clear, however, that the linear model must be used with care because for sufficiently large or small values of the explanatory variables the forecast value of P, $\hat{P}$, will exceed 1 or be less than 0, whereas probabilities must always be in the range from 0 to 1. In our example, the estimate of the probability that, say, a 20-year-old female will die is $-0.102 + (0.003)(20) + (0.020)(0)$, or -0.042, which, of course, does not make sense.

Applied with caution near the range of observed values of the explanatory variables, the linear model can be (and is) used, but its very form makes it unsuitable when the dependent variable is restricted to lie within a given range of values.

A model designed for dependent variables constrained to lie in the interval from 0 to 1 is the *logit model*, defined as

$$P = \frac{e^Y}{1 + e^Y} \tag{12.2}$$

where

$$Y = \beta_0 + \beta_1 X_1 + \beta_2 X_2 + \cdots + \beta_k X_k$$

and $e = 2.71828\ldots$ is the familiar mathematical constant. Note that $0 < P < 1$, because e^Y is always positive. Eq. 12.2 is plotted in Figure 12.1, where it can be compared with the linear ($P = Y$) and other models to be described later.

Y can be interpreted as a "score" in favor of the category of interest. The score is linear in the X's. The greater the score, the greater the probability P.

The logit model implies $1 - P = 1/(1 + e^Y)$, and

$$\frac{P}{1 - P} = e^Y$$

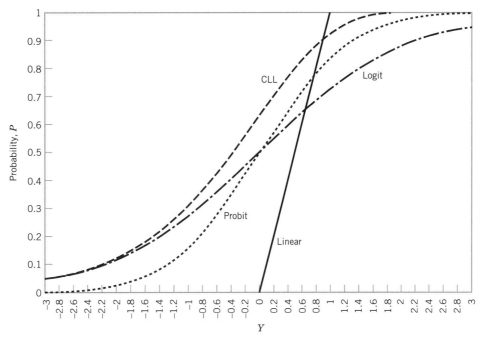

FIGURE 12.1 Probability models

Taking natural logarithms, we find

$$\log \frac{P}{1-P} = Y = \beta_0 + \beta_1 X_1 + \beta_2 X_2 + \cdots + \beta_k X_k$$

If the f are such that $0 < f < n$ for all sets of values of the explanatory variables, then the logit model can be estimated by regressing

$$\log \frac{(f/n)}{1-(f/n)} = \log \frac{f}{n-f}$$

against $X_1, X_2, \ldots, X_k$.

For the example of this section, the values of the dependent variable are shown in column 7 of Table 12.1, and the regression results are

$$\hat{Y} = -5.885 + 0.056 X_1 + 0.429 X_2$$

Thus, to forecast the probability of death of a 45-year-old male, we would calculate first

$$\hat{Y} = -5.885 + (0.056)(45) + (0.429)(1) = -2.936$$

and then

$$\hat{P} = \frac{e^{-2.936}}{1 + e^{-2.936}} = 0.050$$

The logit is not the only model suitable for dependent variables restricted to the range from 0 to 1. Another is the *complementary log-log (CLL) model*, under which the relationship between P and the X's is

$$P = 1 - exp[-exp(Y)] \qquad (12.3)$$

where, again,

$$Y = \beta_0 + \beta_1 X_1 + \beta_2 X_2 + \cdots + \beta_k X_k$$

For simplicity, we have written e^Y as $exp(Y)$. Because $e^Y > 0, -e^Y < 0, exp[-e^Y] < 1$, and P and $1 - P$ always lie in the interval from 0 to 1.

Eq. 12.3 is plotted in Figure 12.1, where it can be compared with the logit model. As in the logit model, Y can be interpreted as a score in favor of the category of interest and such that the greater the score, the greater the probability P. It can be seen from Figure 12.1 that the logit and CLL models have similar S shapes, except that the CLL (unlike the logit) model tends to approach 1 at a different rate than it approaches 0.

The CLL model implies $1 - P = exp[-exp(Y)]$. Taking natural logarithms, we get $\log(1 - P) = -exp(Y)$, and

$$\log[-\log(1 - P)] = Y = \beta_0 + \beta_1 X_1 + \beta_2 X_2 + \cdots + \beta_k X_k$$

When the number f of elements in the category of interest among the n elements having each set of characteristics x is such that $0 < f < n$, the CLL model can be estimated by regressing

$$\log[-\log(1 - \frac{f}{n})]$$

against $X_1, X_2, \ldots, X_k$.

For the numerical example of this section, the values of the dependent variable are shown in column 8 of Table 12.1. The regression results are

$$\hat{Y} = -5.829 + 0.055X_1 + 0.419X_2$$

The score for a 45-year-old male is

$$\hat{Y} = -5.829 + 0.055(45) + 0.419(1) = -2.935$$

and the forecast of the probability of death

$$\hat{P} = 1 - exp[-exp(-2.935)] = 0.052$$

Neither the logit nor the CLL model can be estimated using regression if an f is equal to 0 or n, for in such a case the value of the dependent variable is not defined. This would be the case, for example, if all x's are distinct, so that all $n = 1$ and all f are equal to 0 or 1.

There is, however, another method of estimation that can be applied whether or not all $0 < f < n$ and whether or not all sets of characteristics are distinct. The method, the *maximum likelihood method*, is outlined in Appendix B.7.

Roughly speaking, the maximum likelihood method seeks to find the values of the parameters (the β's, in the case of the models of this section) that make it most likely that the observations (in this section, the observed f for each set x) would have occurred. The method relies on an iterative numerical procedure for the calculation of the estimates and is implemented by major statistical programs. For the linear, logit, and CLL models of this section, the maximum likelihood method does not make any requirements other than that the observations are independent of one another.[1]

For the example of this section and the data in Table 12.1, the maximum likelihood estimates of the parameters of the linear, logit, and CLL models are as follows:[2]

$$
\begin{array}{lrl}
\text{Linear:} & \hat{Y} = & -0.168 + 0.004X_1 + 0.054X_2 \\
\text{Logit:} & \hat{Y} = & -6.088 + 0.061X_1 + 0.418X_2 \\
\text{CLL:} & \hat{Y} = & -6.009 + 0.059X_1 + 0.391X_2
\end{array}
$$

---

[1]For additional information regarding the application of the maximum likelihood method to the models of this section see, for example, McCullagh and Nelder (1989, Ch. 4) and Agresti (1990, Ch. 4).

[2]Obtained using program SAS. For example, the CLL results were obtained with the statements `proc genmod; model f/n = x1 x2 / dist=bin link=cll;`.

It can be verified that the estimate of the probability that a 45-year-old male insured will die during a one-year period is 0.066 (linear model), 0.051 (logit), or 0.050 (CLL).

Major statistical programs offer yet another alternative for modeling the relationship between a probability and explanatory variables. Under the *probit model*, the probability that an element belongs to the category of interest is the probability that a standard normal variable, Z, will take a value less than or equal to the score Y, where, as before,

$$Y = \beta_0 + \beta_1 X_1 + \beta_2 X_2 + \cdots + \beta_k X_k$$

As shown in Figure 12.2(a), the probability that an element with score Y belongs to the category of interest is assumed to be equal to the area under the standard normal distribution to the left of Y. Alternatively, this probability can be read directly from the graph of the cumulative standard normal distribution shown in Figure 12.2(b). The greater the score Y, the greater this probability P.

The cumulative normal distribution is also plotted in Figure 12.1 under the label "Probit." Note the similar shapes of the cumulative normal distribution and of the logit and CLL models.

To see how the probit model can be estimated, consider again the data for the example of this section, reproduced for convenience in columns 1 to 4 of Table 12.2.

To begin, suppose that the parameter values are given numbers—say, $\beta_0 = -3.0$, $\beta_1 = 0.05$, and $\beta_2 = 0.30$. The scores for each set of characteristics are given by

$$Y = -3.0 + 0.05X_1 + 0.30X_2$$

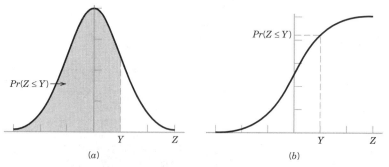

FIGURE 12.2 Standard normal distribution and the probit model

TABLE 12.2   Illustration of the Probit Model

Set no. (1)	Age, X_1 (2)	Gender[a], X_2 (3)	f/n (4)	Arbitrary Y (5)	Arbitrary P (6)	Probit Y (7)	Probit P (8)
1	35	1	0.033	−0.95	0.171	−1.894	0.029
2	50	0	0.025	−0.50	0.308	−1.689	0.046
3	55	0	0.100	−0.25	0.401	−1.544	0.061
4	60	1	0.100	+0.30	0.618	−1.169	0.121

[a] 1 = male, 0 = female.

and are shown in column 5 of Table 12.2. The probability that a standard normal variable will take a value less than or equal to Y can be calculated with the help of a table (to be found in nearly all introductory statistics texts) or a function for calculating cumulative standard normal probabilities provided by statistical and other computer programs. These probabilities are shown in column 6 of Table 12.2.

If the probit is indeed the appropriate model and the preceding are the true values of the parameters, we would expect the probabilities in column 6 to be close to the observed relative frequencies in column 4 of Table 12.2. They are not. Therefore, we want to find values of the β's that bring the estimated probabilities as close as possible to the observed relative frequencies. We could, for example, look for β's that minimize the sum of the absolute deviations $|P - (f/n)|$ or some other reasonable criterion.

In the implementation of the probit model by major statistical programs, however, the method used is maximum likelihood. The maximum likelihood estimates, it will be recalled, are those values of the β's that make it most likely that the observed f's would have occurred. For the data of Table 12.2, the maximum likelihood estimates (obtained using the SAS `proc genmod` with `link=probit`) yield

$$Y = -3.139 + 0.029X_1 + 0.230X_2$$

The scores Y and the estimated normal probabilities are shown in columns 7 and 8 of Table 12.2.[3]

---

[3]There is, of course, no special reason why the probability of interest ought to be cumulative standard normal. The cumulative standard normal distribution is one of several possible models of the relationship between P and Y. In fact, *any* cumulative distribution of a variable that can take values from $-\infty$ to $+\infty$ can serve as a model of this relationship.

12.3 JOINT NORMAL DISTRIBUTIONS, TWO CATEGORIES

In some situations, it may be reasonable to suppose that the joint probability distributions $p_1(X_1, X_2, \ldots, X_k)$ and $p_2(X_1, X_2, \ldots, X_k)$—the joint distributions of the explanatory variables among the elements belonging to the categories C_1 and C_2 (see Section 11.5)—are *multivariate normal* or at least approximately so.

To gain insight into the meaning of this assumption, let us suppose first that there are only two explanatory variables. Recall Example 11.1, and consider Figure 12.3.

Figure 12.3(a) shows the estimated joint probability distribution of income (X_1) and marital status (X_2) codes among good accounts given in Table 11.11.

Imagine now a different situation where the possible values of X_1 and X_2 are more numerous and the joint distribution of these variables among the elements in a given category is as shown in Figure 12.3(b).

The discrete distribution of Figure 12.3(b) can be approximated by the continuous joint distribution shown in Figure 12.3(c). One can think of the latter as a sheet draped over the "Manhattan skyscape" of Figure 12.3(b).

Figure 12.3(c), in turn, is the plot of a *bivariate normal distribution*, defined as

$$p(X_1, X_2) = \frac{1}{2\pi \sigma_1 \sigma_2 \sqrt{1 - \rho^2}} \exp \left\{ -\frac{1}{2(1 - \rho^2)} \left[(\frac{X_1 - \mu_1}{\sigma_1})^2 \right. \right.$$
$$\left. \left. -2\rho(\frac{X_1 - \mu_1}{\sigma_1})(\frac{X_2 - \mu_2}{\sigma_2}) + (\frac{X_2 - \mu_2}{\sigma_2})^2 \right] \right\}$$
$$-\infty < X_1, X_2 < +\infty \qquad (12.4)$$

The parameters μ_1 and μ_2 are the means, σ_1^2 and σ_2^2 the variances, and $\rho = \sigma_{12}/\sigma_1\sigma_2$ the correlation coefficient (σ_{12} is the covariance) of X_1 and X_2.

Figure 12.4(a) shows the contours of a bivariate normal distribution. The distribution is centered at the point of means (μ_1, μ_2), but its orientation and shape depend on the variances (σ_1^2, σ_2^2) and covariance (σ_{12}). If $p_1(X_1, X_2)$ and $p_2(X_1, X_2)$ are two bivariate normal distributions with different means but the same variances and covariance, then, as Figure 12.4(b) shows, they are centered at different points, but their shape and orientation are the same.

The normality assumption is, of course, quite restrictive and should be made with care. There is no compelling reason why it should be satisfied in any given situation. Statistical programs and texts, however, give normality prominent consideration, so it is worthwhile to summarize the conclusions that can be drawn from this assumption.

Suppose $p_1(X_1, X_2)$ and $p_2(X_1, X_2)$ are bivariate normal with the same variances (σ_1^2, σ_2^2) and covariance σ_{12}. Two simple random samples of elements

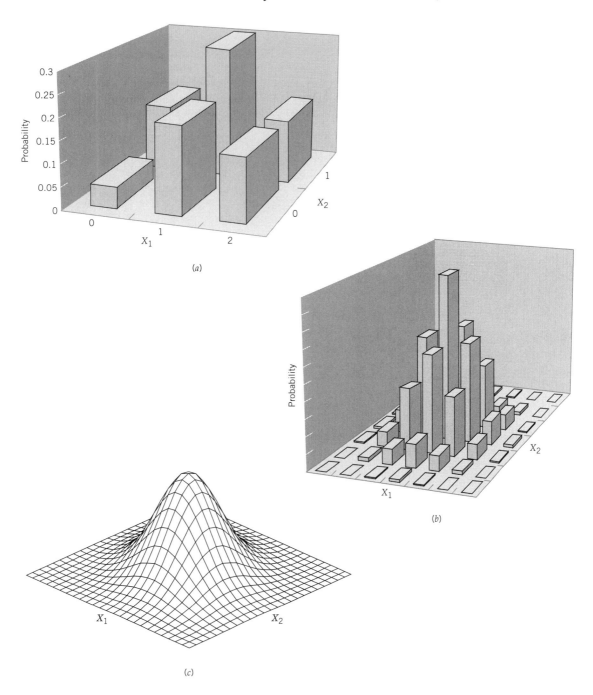

FIGURE 12.3 Bivariate normal approximation of a discrete distribution

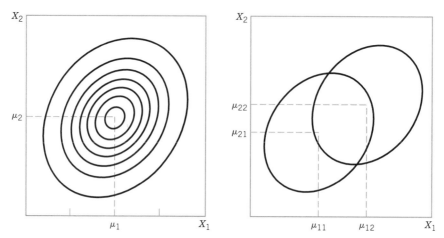

FIGURE 12.4 Bivariate normal distributions

are available, one drawn from among the elements belonging to C_1 and the other from among the elements belonging to C_2. It can be shown that the optimal classification rule (that is, the rule that minimizes the overall expected misclassification loss) is implemented in two steps:

1. *Construct two classification functions, one for each category:*

$$\hat{Y}_1 = b_{01} + b_{11}X_1 + b_{21}X_2 + \log(q_1 L_1)$$
$$\hat{Y}_2 = b_{02} + b_{12}X_1 + b_{22}X_2 + \log(q_2 L_2)$$

(12.5)

The coefficients b_{ij} of these two functions are calculated from the sample observations. q_1 and q_2 are the proportions of population elements belonging to C_1 and C_2. L_1 and L_2 are the losses of misclassifying an element belonging to C_1 and C_2, respectively. The last terms in the preceding equations are the natural logarithms of $q_1 L_1$ and $q_2 L_2$.

2. *An element with characteristics X_1, X_2 should be classified into C_1 if $\hat{Y}_1 \geq \hat{Y}_2$, or into C_2 if $\hat{Y}_1 < \hat{Y}_2$.*

q_1 and q_2 are also called the *prior probabilities* of C_1 and C_2. The classification functions, it will be observed, are *linear* in the X's. The coefficients b_{ij} can be thought of as the *weights* of the variables X_1 and X_2 and the *linear classification function* $\hat{Y}_i$ as defining a *score in favor of* category C_i for an element with characteristics X_1 and X_2. The element is classified into the category with the higher score.

Very shortly, we shall extend this result to the general case involving any number k of explanatory variables and indicate how the rule is derived and the coefficients calculated. First, however, an example.

EXAMPLE 12.1

An insurance company is considering developing a rule to classify prospective automobile insurance policies according to whether or not they are likely to have an accident during the term of the policy. (It is, of course, the insured drivers—not the policy—that may have accidents, but we shall be deliberately inaccurate for the sake of brevity.)

Two policy characteristics are considered especially relevant: the number of years of driving experience of the principal driver and the horsepower of the insured automobile.

The company examined all annual policies that had expired by a certain date and classified them as not having (C_1) or having (C_2) an accident. Some 85% of these policies were C_1 and 15% C_2. A simple random sample of 11 policies was selected from among the policies classified as C_1 and another simple random sample of 10 policies selected from among those classified as C_2. (In practice, of course, much larger samples would be used.)

For each selected policy, the number of years of driving experience of the principal driver (X_1) and the car's horsepower (X_2) were recorded, as shown in columns 2 and 3 of Table 12.3. Column 4 shows the category to which the policy belongs. Columns 5 and 6 will be explained shortly.

Let us assume that the joint probability distribution of driving experience and horsepower among policies in both C_1 and C_2 is approximately bivariate normal. Let us also suppose that the variances and covariance of the two distributions are the same and that the misclassification losses, L_1 and L_2, are equal.

In the notation of this section, $\log q_1 = \log(0.85) = -0.1625$ and $\log q_2 = \log(0.15) = -1.8971$. A computer program[4] was used to obtain the coefficients of the classification functions, which are

$$\hat{Y}_1 = -30.7454 + 0.4315X_1 + 0.3862X_2 - 0.1625 + \log L$$
$$= -30.9079 + 0.4315X_1 + 0.3862X_2 + \log L$$
$$\hat{Y}_2 = -49.5378 + 0.3832X_1 + 0.5079X_2 - 1.8971 + \log L$$
$$= -51.4349 + 0.3832X_1 + 0.5079X_2 + \log L$$

Since the term $\log L$ is common to $\hat{Y}_1$ and $\hat{Y}_2$, it will be ignored from now on.

---

[4]Program SAS. The SAS statements were `proc discrim; class categ; var x1 x2; priors '1'=0.85 '2'=0.15;`. `categ` is the label of column 4 of Table 12.3. The `priors` statement specifies the proportions of elements in categories 1 and 2.

TABLE 12.3 Characteristics of Policies and Scores, Example 12.1

Policy no. (1)	Driving experience, X_1 (2)	Horsepower X_2 (3)	Category[a] (4)	Classification scores, $\hat{Y}_1$ (5)	$\hat{Y}_2$ (6)
1	23	153	1	38.1052*	35.0874
2	18	142	1	31.6995*	27.5845
3	16	184	1	47.0569	48.1499*
4	25	105	1	20.4306*	11.4746
5	32	160	1	44.6921*	42.0915
6	8	142	1	27.3845*	23.7525
7	15	129	1	25.3844*	19.8322
8	2	128	1	19.3887*	14.3427
9	27	120	1	27.0866*	19.8595
10	28	138	1	34.4697*	29.3849
11	23	108	1	20.7262*	12.2319
12	15	181	2	45.4668	46.2430*
13	18	170	2	42.5131*	41.8057
14	4	186	2	42.6513	44.5673*
15	2	205	2	49.1261	53.4510*
16	22	194	2	53.5079	55.5281*
17	14	204	2	53.9179	57.5415*
18	23	160	2	40.8086*	38.6427
19	18	193	2	51.3957	53.4874*
20	8	174	2	39.7429	40.0053*
21	12	181	2	44.1723	45.0934*

[a] 1 = No accident, 2 = One or more accidents. The asterisks are explained in the text.

SOURCE: File `discr1.dat`

An applicant for automobile insurance having 15 years' driving experience and a car with 181 hp (the characteristics of policy no. 12 in Table 12.3) would receive the following scores:

$$\hat{Y}_1 = -30.9079 + 0.4315(15) + 0.3862(181) = 45.4668$$

and

$$\hat{Y}_2 = -51.4349 + 0.3832(15) + 0.5079(181) = 46.2430$$

Since $\hat{Y}_1 < \hat{Y}_2$, the applicant would be classified as C_2.

To evaluate the quality of this classification rule we begin by calculating the classification scores, $\hat{Y}_1$ and $\hat{Y}_2$, for all sampled policies. These scores are shown in columns 5 and 6 of Table 12.3. The greater of the two scores is indicated with an asterisk. Each observation is classified into the category associated with the higher score. Based on Table 12.3, we construct the following summary table of correct and incorrect classifications:

Actual state	Action: Classify as		Total
	No accident, C_1	Accident, C_2	
C_1: No accident	10	1	11
C_2: Accident	2	8	10
Total	12	9	21

Had the classification functions been applied to the available observations, therefore, 10 of the 11 policies in C_1 and 8 of the 10 policies in C_2 would have been correctly classified. The proportions of incorrect classifications are thus 9% for the "no accident" category and 20% for the "accident" one. ∎

When the same sample is used to derive the optimal classification functions and to determine their quality, the estimates of the misclassification probabilities can be shown to be biased in favor of the classification rule. However, the bias will not be significant if the sample sizes are large. In any event, unbiased estimates of the misclassification probabilities can be obtained by applying the classification functions to a different sample. That is, one sample (the "analysis sample") can be used to estimate the coefficients of the classification functions and another (the "holdout sample") to estimate the probabilities of misclassification.

The linear classification rule Eq. 12.5 can also be written in a different form. Since $\hat{Y}_1 \geq \hat{Y}_2$ implies $\hat{Y}_1 - \hat{Y}_2 \geq 0$, we need only examine the difference

$$
\begin{aligned}
\hat{Y}_1 - \hat{Y}_2 &= (b_{01} + b_{11}X_1 + b_{21}X_2 + \log q_1 L_1) \\
&\quad - (b_{02} + b_{12}X_1 + b_{22}X_2 + \log q_2 L_2) \\
&= (b_{01} - b_{02}) + (b_{11} - b_{12})X_1 + (b_{21} - b_{22})X_2 \\
&\quad + (\log q_1 L_1 - \log q_2 L_2) \\
&= c_0 + c_1 X_1 + c_2 X_2 - \log(q_2 L_2 / q_1 L_1)
\end{aligned}
$$

where $c_j = b_{j1} - b_{j2}$.

Therefore, the optimal classification rule in the normal case can also be expressed as follows:

An element with characteristics X_1, X_2 should be classified as C_1 if

$$
\hat{Y} = c_0 + c_1 X_1 + c_2 X_2 \geq \log \frac{q_2 L_2}{q_1 L_1} \tag{12.6}
$$

Otherwise, it should be classified as C_2.

The coefficients c_j are—like the b_{ji}—given numbers calculated from the sample observations. The function $\hat{Y} = c_0 + c_1 X_1 + c_2 X_2$ is a *linear discriminant function*.[5] It too can be considered as a score for an element with characteristics X_1 and X_2, but different from the scores of the classification functions. If the discriminant score $\hat{Y}$ is "high," the element is classified as C_1; if "low," it is classified as C_2. The point $\log(q_2 L_2 / q_1 L_1)$ marks the boundary between high and low scores. The two forms—Eq. 12.5 and 12.6—of the classification rule, of course, always yield the same results.

EXAMPLE 12.1 (CONTINUED)

A automobile insurance policy in which the principal driver has X_1 years of driving experience and the automobile has horsepower X_2 should be classified as C_1 if

$$[(-30.7454) - (-49.5378)] + (0.4315 - 0.3832)X_1 + (0.3862 - 0.5079)X_2$$

that is, if

$$\hat{Y} = 18.7924 + 0.0483X_1 - 0.1217X_2$$

is greater than or equal to

$$\log \frac{q_2 L}{q_1 L} = \log \frac{q_2}{q_1} = \log \frac{0.15}{0.85} = -1.7346$$

In other words, the policy should be classified as C_1 (will have no accident) if

$$0.0483X_1 - 0.1217X_2 \geq -20.527 \tag{12.7}$$

Otherwise, the policy should be classified as C_2 (will have an accident).

Observe that as X_1—the number of years of driving experience—increases, the score in favor of classifying into the no-accident category increases, which is as many would expect. Likewise, as X_2—the car's horsepower—increases, the score in favor of classifying into the no-accident category decreases, which is as some would expect.

As shown in Figure 12.5, the line

$$0.0483X_1 - 0.1217X_2 = -20.527$$

---

[5]There are *two* classification functions—one for each category—but only *one* discriminant function. Computer programs sometimes print the *b*-coefficients of the classification functions, sometimes the *c*-coefficients of the discriminant function, sometimes both. Practice and terminology vary.

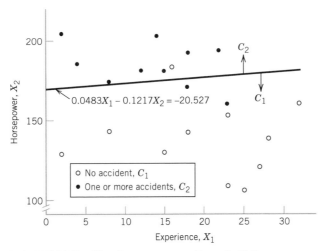

FIGURE 12.5 Classification regions, Example 12.5

divides the (X_1, X_2) space into two regions. All points (X_1, X_2) that lie on or below the line satisfy the inequality Eq. 12.7 and should be classified as C_1. All points above the line should be classified as C_2. ∎

The optimal classification rule can be extended to the general case where there are k explanatory variables, the joint distributions of which, $p_1(X_1, X_2, \ldots, X_k)$ and $p_2(X_1, X_2, \ldots, X_k)$, are *multivariate normal*.

Suppose $p_1(X_1, X_2, \ldots, X_k)$ and $p_2(X_1, X_2, \ldots, X_k)$ are multivariate normal with the same variances σ_i^2 and covariances σ_{ij}. Two simple random samples of elements are available, one selected from among the elements belonging to C_1 and the other from among those belonging to C_2. It can be shown that the optimal classification rule (that is, the rule that minimizes the overall expected loss of misclassification) is implemented in two steps:

1. *Construct two linear classification functions, one for each category:*

$$\hat{Y}_1 = b_{01} + b_{11}X_1 + b_{21}X_2 + \cdots + b_{k1}X_k + \log(q_1 L_1)$$
$$\hat{Y}_2 = b_{02} + b_{12}X_1 + b_{22}X_2 + \cdots + b_{k2}X_k + \log(q_2 L_2) \tag{12.8}$$

2. *An element with characteristics $X_1, X_2, \ldots, X_k$ should be classified as C_1 if $\hat{Y}_1 \geq \hat{Y}_2$ or as C_2 if $\hat{Y}_1 < \hat{Y}_2$.*

The definition of the multivariate normal distribution and an outline of the derivation of the optimal classification rule and of the b-coefficients can be found in Appendix B.9. The derivation is worth at least a glance, for it will show that the rule follows directly from Eq. 11.6 in Section 11.5 after substituting for $p_1(x)$ and $p_2(x)$ the appropriate expressions defining multivariate normal probabilities.[6]

Alternatively, the optimal classification rule, Eq. 12.8, can be written in terms of the discriminant function.

An element with characteristics $X_1, X_2, \ldots, X_k$ should be classified as C_1 if

$$\hat{Y} = c_0 + c_1 X_1 + \cdots + c_k X_k \geq \log \frac{q_2 L_2}{q_1 L_1} \qquad (12.9)$$

where $c_j = b_{j1} - b_{j2}$. Otherwise, the element should be classified as C_2.

EXAMPLE 12.2

In a pioneering study, Altman used discriminant analysis to explain and forecast business bankruptcy.[7] Two samples, each with 33 observations, were available. The first consisted of manufacturing firms that had declared bankruptcy in the period from 1946 to 1965. The second sample consisted of nonbankrupt firms selected to match those in the first sample by industry and size. Five financial ratios served as explanatory variables:

X_1: Working capital / Total assets
X_2: Retained earnings / Total assets
X_3: Earnings before interest and taxes / Total assets
X_4: Market value of equity / Book value of total debt
X_5: Sales / Total assets

These ratios were selected from 22 considered on the basis of statistical significance, low intercorrelations, predictive accuracy, and judgment. The following linear discriminant function was estimated:

$$\hat{Y} = 1.2X_1 + 1.4X_2 + 3.3X_3 + 0.6X_4 + 1.0X_5$$

---

[6]It is possible to derive a classification rule for the case where the variances and covariances of the explanatory variables in the two categories are not equal; in this case, the classification functions are *quadratic* in the X's. For additional information on the models of this section, see, for example, Lachenbruch (1975, Ch. 1) and Johnson and Wichern (1992, Ch. 11).

[7]E. I. Altman, "Financial Ratios, Discriminant Analysis, and the Prediction of Corporate Bankruptcy," *Journal of Finance*, Vol. 23, September 1968, pp. 589–609. Numerous similar studies followed. For references to these studies see, for example, E. I. Altman, *Corporate Financial Distress and Bankruptcy*, 2d ed., Wiley, 1993.

The model was found to be 95% overall accurate in its predictions when using values of financial ratios one year prior and 83% accurate with values two years prior to bankruptcy. ∎

Multivariate normal distributions are not encountered frequently in practice. The normality assumption is particularly inappropriate when the explanatory variables are dummy variables taking values of 0 or 1 or are codes for attributes. The linear classification or discriminant functions, however, which are optimal under normality, have strong appeal because of their simplicity and ease of interpretation. One often observes in practice a willingness to proceed *as if* normality prevailed even when it does not. In such situations, one should recognize that Eqs. 12.8 or 12.9 provide just one (not necessarily the optimal) classification rule. In the next section, however, we describe a different interpretation of Eq. 12.9 that does not require the normality assumption.

12.4 AN ALTERNATIVE JUSTIFICATION OF THE LINEAR DISCRIMINANT FUNCTION

The linear discriminant function (the left-hand side of Eq. 12.9) can also be justified on entirely different grounds that do not require the normality assumption. For it can be shown that its coefficients $c_0, c_1, \ldots, c_k$ also maximize a standardized squared difference between the mean linear scores of the observations in the two categories. Let us explain.

EXAMPLE 12.3

Let us revisit Example 12.1 and consider forming some sort of "points system" for rating automobile insurance applications. We could award c_1 points for each year of driving experience X_1, c_2 points for each unit of power of the automobile X_2, and add these points to a base figure c_0 to form a linear score for each application

$$Y = c_0 + c_1 X_1 + c_2 X_2$$

The intent may be to accept applications with high scores and to reject those with low scores. What should be the values of $c_0, c_1,$ and c_2? What should be the "cutoff" score separating low from high scores?

To begin, let us arbitrarily select $c_0 = 1$, $c_1 = -0.05$, and $c_2 = 0.005$. The linear score

$$Y = 1 - 0.05X_1 + 0.005X_2$$

for each policy in Example 12.1 is shown in Table 12.4. X_1 denotes the number of years of driving experience and X_2 the horsepower of the vehicle.

The scores Y are shown in Figure 12.6 separately for each category (all scores should be plotted along the Y-axis, but for clarity the scores of C_1 policies are plotted above and those of C_2 policies below the axis).

Also plotted in Figure 12.6 are the average scores for policies in categories C_1 ($\bar{Y}_1 = 0.699$) and C_2 ($\bar{Y}_2 = 1.244$). It can be observed that the scores based on the arbitrary values of the coefficients c_0, c_1, and c_2 do not differentiate the two categories very well. There is not much separation between $\bar{Y}_1$ and $\bar{Y}_2$, and there is considerable overlap of the Y-scores in the two categories.

We realize, however, that by varying c_0, c_1, and c_2, we vary each Y-score, hence also $\bar{Y}_1$ and $\bar{Y}_2$ and the squared distance between $\bar{Y}_1$ and $\bar{Y}_2$, $(\bar{Y}_1 - \bar{Y}_2)^2$. Suppose then we try to find values of c_0, c_1, and c_2 maximizing $(\bar{Y}_1 - \bar{Y}_2)^2$, that

TABLE 12.4 Characteristics of Policies and Linear Scores, Example 12.3

No.	Category C_1^a			No.	Category C_2^a		
	X_1	X_2	Y		X_1	X_2	Y
1	23	153	0.615	12	15	181	1.155
2	18	142	0.810	13	18	170	0.950
3	16	184	1.120	14	4	186	1.730
4	25	105	0.275	15	2	205	1.925
5	32	160	0.200	16	22	194	0.870
6	8	142	1.310	17	14	204	1.320
7	15	129	0.895	18	23	160	0.650
8	2	128	1.540	19	18	193	1.065
9	27	120	0.250	20	8	174	1.470
10	28	138	0.290	21	12	181	1.305
11	23	108	0.390				
Ave.:	19.727	137.182	0.699		13.600	184.800	1.244

$^a C_1$: No accident; C_2: One or more accidents; $Y = 1 - 0.05X_1 + 0.005X_2$.

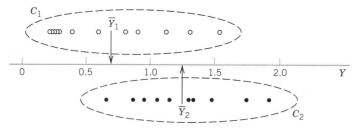

FIGURE 12.6 Linear scores Y, Table 12.4

is, separating as much as possible $\bar{Y}_1$ from $\bar{Y}_2$. This does not guarantee there will be no overlap of the Y-scores in the two categories, but it is hoped that the overlap will be minimal, as illustrated in Figure 12.7.

In the case of Figure 12.7, we could say that the scoring system differentiates and separates the two categories reasonably well. We could then classify a new policy into C_1 or C_2 depending on whether its Y-score is closer to $\bar{Y}_1$ than to $\bar{Y}_2$. This is the same as using the middle of the distance between $\bar{Y}_1$ and $\bar{Y}_2$ for the cutoff score.   ∎

In general, for any given set of coefficients $c_0, c_1, c_2, \ldots, c_k$, the linear score of an element with characteristics $X_1, X_2, \ldots, X_k$ is $Y = c_0 + c_1 X_1 + \cdots + c_k X_k$. Let $\bar{Y}_1$ be the average of these scores for all elements in C_1 and $\bar{Y}_2$ the average of the scores for all elements in C_2. The larger the squared difference of the two averages, $(\bar{Y}_1 - \bar{Y}_2)^2$, the greater can be said to be the differentiation between the two categories. Thus, it appears reasonable to look for those values of $c_0, c_1, \ldots, c_k$ that make $(\bar{Y}_1 - \bar{Y}_2)^2$ as large as possible.

The maximization of $(\bar{Y}_1 - \bar{Y}_2)^2$, however, is not a workable objective because it is *always* possible to make $(\bar{Y}_1 - \bar{Y}_2)^2$ infinitely large.

To see this, suppose $k = 2$ and note that for any $c_0, c_1,$ and $c_2,$

$$\bar{Y}_1 = c_0 + c_1 \bar{X}_{11} + c_2 \bar{X}_{21}$$
$$\bar{Y}_2 = c_0 + c_1 \bar{X}_{12} + c_2 \bar{X}_{22}$$

where $\bar{X}_{ij}$ is the mean of variable X_i in category j. These relationships are justified in Appendix A.11 but can also be verified using the data of Table 12.4, where $\bar{X}_{11} = 19.727$, $\bar{X}_{21} = 137.182$, $\bar{X}_{12} = 13.6$, and $\bar{X}_{22} = 184.8$. It follows that

$$(\bar{Y}_1 - \bar{Y}_2)^2 = [c_1(\bar{X}_{11} - \bar{X}_{12}) + c_2(\bar{X}_{21} - \bar{X}_{22})]^2$$

Let Z be the value of this expression associated with given $c_0, c_1,$ and c_2. Now, multiply the c-coefficients by any constant d. The resulting value of the objective function is

$$Z' = (\bar{Y}_1' - \bar{Y}_2')^2 = [dc_1(\bar{X}_{11} - \bar{X}_{12}) + dc_2(\bar{X}_{21} - \bar{X}_{22})]^2 = d^2 Z$$

Clearly, Z' increases without limit as d increases.

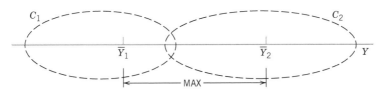

FIGURE 12.7 Hypothetical pattern of scores Y

For this reason, we look for values of the coefficients that maximize a standardized squared distance between the mean scores. More precisely, the problem can be stated as follows.

Find $c_0, c_1, \ldots, c_k$ that maximize

$$\frac{(\bar{Y}_1 - \bar{Y}_2)^2}{\frac{1}{n}\sum(Y - \bar{Y})^2} \tag{12.10}$$

The denominator of this expression is the overall variance of the linear scores $Y = c_0 + c_1 X_1 + \cdots + c_k X_k$, and $\bar{Y}$ is the overall mean score.

We should note that the maximization problem Eq. 12.10 has an infinite number of solutions, for two reasons. First, the coefficient c_0 can take any value because it cancels out in both $\bar{Y}_1 - \bar{Y}_2$ and $Y - \bar{Y}$. Second, if $c_0, c_1, \ldots, c_k$ maximize Eq. 12.10, so do $c'_0 = dc_0, c'_1 = dc_1, \ldots, c'_k = dc_k$, where d is any constant.

The latter is so because the linear scores Y' of the new solution are

$$\begin{aligned} Y' &= dc_0 + dc_1 X_1 + dc_2 X_2 + \cdots + dc_k X_k \\ &= d(c_0 + c_1 X_1 + c_2 X_2 + \cdots + c_k X_k) \\ &= dY \end{aligned}$$

It follows that $\bar{Y}' = d\bar{Y}$, $\bar{Y}'_1 = d\bar{Y}_1$, $\bar{Y}'_2 = d\bar{Y}_2$, $(\bar{Y}'_1 - \bar{Y}'_2)^2 = d^2(\bar{Y}_1 - \bar{Y}_2)^2$, and

$$\frac{1}{n}\sum(Y' - \bar{Y}')^2 = \frac{1}{n}\sum(dY - d\bar{Y})^2 = d^2 \frac{1}{n}\sum(Y - \bar{Y})^2$$

The value of Eq. 12.10 associated with the c'_j is the same as that associated with the c_j, since both the numerator and denominator of Eq. 12.10 are multiplied by the same constant d^2.

In mathematically advanced texts it is shown that *the coefficients $c_0, c_1, c_2, \ldots, c_k$ of Eq. 12.9 maximize Eq. 12.10.* [8] In other words, the coefficients of the linear discriminant function under normality constitute one solution of the problem of this section. It is also shown that another solution is the set of coefficients calculated by statistical programs implementing the so-called canonical discriminant analysis. We describe these solutions next.

EXAMPLE 12.3 (CONTINUED)

Earlier in Section 12.3 we had calculated the following discriminant function under the normality assumption

$$Y = 18.7924 + 0.0483X_1 - 0.1217X_2$$

[8]See, for example, Lachenbruch (1975, pp. 8–11) and Johnson and Wichern (1992, Ch. 11).

The same coefficients ($c_0 = 18.7924$, $c_1 = 0.0483$, and $c_2 = -0.1217$) also maximize Eq. 12.10, the standardized squared difference between $\bar{Y}_1$ and $\bar{Y}_2$. The optimal (in the sense of this section) Y-score of the first policy listed in Table 12.4 is

$$Y = (18.7924) + (0.0483)(23) - (0.1217)(153) = 1.283$$

In Problem 12.4, the reader is asked to calculate the Y-scores of all other policies and to confirm that $\bar{Y}_1 = 3.050$ and $\bar{Y}_2 = -3.041$. The Y-scores of all policies as well as $\bar{Y}_1$ and $\bar{Y}_2$ are plotted in Figure 12.8.

Evidently, the optimal values of the coefficients differentiate the two categories better than the arbitrary ones in Figure 12.6.

To classify a policy with the characteristics of No. 1 in Table 12.4, we determine whether its Y-score (1.283) is nearer $\bar{Y}_1 = 3.050$ or $\bar{Y}_2 = -3.041$. Clearly, the policy should be classified as C_1. Also, in Problem 12.4 the reader will verify that all but one of the 11 policies in C_1 and all but one of the 10 policies in C_2 are correctly classified.

A computer program for canonical discriminant analysis gives the following solution to the maximization problem Eq. 12.10 for the data of this example:[9] $c_1 = -0.0196$ and $c_2 = 0.0493$ (c_0 is not calculated). This seems incompatible with the solution based on the normality assumption until it is realized that c_0 can take any value and that the normal coefficients are equal to the canonical coefficients multiplied by $d = -2.467$ (apart from rounding error). Indeed, we could use as a scoring function

$$Y = -0.0196X_1 + 0.0493X_2$$

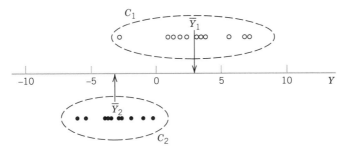

FIGURE 12.8 Optimal linear scores, Example 12.3

[9]Program SAS with the statements `proc candisc ncan=1; class categ; var x1 x2;`.

In Problem 12.5, the reader is asked to confirm that $\bar{Y}_1 = 6.3793$, $\bar{Y}_2 = 8.8476$ and that the classification rule based on the canonical coefficients produces the same results as that based on the normal coefficients. ∎

EXAMPLE 12.4

Which variables influence whether a new product will be accepted for distribution by supermarkets? In a study of 124 new products proposed to supermarket buyers in the Boston area, 18 explanatory variables were considered:[10]

1. Promotion	*10. Competition with private label
2. Company reputation	11. Guarantee of movement
3. Product quality	12. Range of distribution
*4. Newness of product	13. Broker or company presentation
*5. Introductory allowances	*14. Rating of sales presentation
*6. Competition	*15. Category volume
*7. Rating for packaging	16. Category of growth potential
8. Expected gross margin	*17. Shelf space
9. Rating of advertising program	*18. Item cost

The asterisks will be explained later. The products were divided into two categories—those accepted by supermarkets and those that were not. All explanatory variables were either discrete or were made discrete. Lack of space prevents us from listing the codes and definitions of all variables, but the following are representative:

Variable:	*Questionnaire question and code:*
2. Company reputation.	The overall reputation of the manufacturer is
	1 = one of the top four or five companies
	2 = above average
	3 = average
	4 = below average
	5 = poor
8. Expected gross margin.	The expected gross margin is
	1 = above 50%
	2 = 25–50%
	3 = 14–25%
	4 = 7–14%
	5 = less than 7%

[10]D. B. Montgomery, "New Product Distribution: An Analysis of Supermarket Buyer Decisions," *Journal of Marketing Research*, Vol. 12, August 1975, pp. 255–64.

It will be noted that the codes are arbitrary. For example, there is no special reason for rating a "below average" reputation four times lower than a "top" reputation. A linear discriminant function was estimated. Obviously, the use of a linear function cannot be justified on the grounds of normality: the explanatory variables are not continuous, and their values are arbitrary codes. However, the coefficients of the discriminant function Eq. 12.9 maximize the standardized measure Eq. 12.10 of separation between the mean scores of the two samples.

We do not list these coefficients here because they hold little interest in themselves, but we note some results of the study. Of the 124 new products, 37 were accepted and 87 were rejected by the supermarkets. Using all 18 explanatory variables, 73 of the 87 rejected and 34 of the 37 accepted new products were correctly classified; using only the 9 explanatory variables identified with an asterisk in the preceding list, 72 of the 87 rejected and 31 of the 37 accepted new products were correctly classified. ■

12.5   A LOGIT MODEL FOR CLASSIFICATION INTO MORE THAN TWO CATEGORIES

We now consider the general case in which elements are classified into one of m categories $C_1, C_2, \ldots, C_m$ with the help of k known variables $X_1, X_2, \ldots, X_k$.

Let us write P_i for $Pr(C_i|x)$, the probability that an element with the set of characteristics x belongs to category C_i. We assume that each P_i is a function of the variables $X_1, X_2, \ldots, X_k$.

Clearly, the sum of the P_i for all categories must equal one. Therefore, one of the P_i's is redundant and can be calculated from the remaining P_i. Which P_i is deemed redundant is arbitrary; we take it to be P_m, so that

$$P_m = 1 - \sum_{j=1}^{m-1} P_j$$

Let $f_1, f_2, \ldots, f_m$ denote the number of observations belonging to categories $C_1, C_2, \ldots, C_m$, respectively, in a simple random sample of n elements having the same set of characteristics x. f_i/n is an estimate of P_i. The *linear* models

$$P_i = \beta_{0i} + \beta_{1i}X_1 + \beta_{2i}X_2 + \cdots + \beta_{ki}X_k$$

could be used as approximations of the true relationships and estimated by regressing f_i/n against $X_1, X_2, \ldots, X_k$. However, for reasons explained in Section 12.2, it cannot be guaranteed that the forecast probabilities $\hat{P}_i$ will be in the interval from 0 to 1.

Under the *general logit model*, the relationship between each P_i and X_1, $X_2, \ldots, X_k$ is assumed to be

$$P_i = \frac{e^{Y_i}}{1 + \sum_{j=1}^{m-1} e^{Y_j}}, \qquad (i = 1, 2, \ldots, m-1) \tag{12.11}$$

where

$$Y_i = \beta_{0i} + \beta_{1i} X_1 + \beta_{2i} X_2 + \cdots + \beta_{ki} X_k$$

Note that $0 < P_i < 1$, since all $e^{Y_i} > 0$ and the numerator of Eq. 12.11 is one of the terms added in the denominator. Also,

$$P_m = 1 - \sum_{j=1}^{m-1} P_j = 1 - \frac{\sum_{j=1}^{m-1} e^{Y_i}}{1 + \sum_{j=1}^{m-1} e^{Y_j}} = \frac{1}{1 + \sum_{j=1}^{m-1} e^{Y_j}}$$

Therefore, P_m is also in the interval from 0 to 1. Eq. 12.11 becomes Eq. 12.2 when $m = 2$.

The general logit model implies that $P_i/P_m = e^{Y_i}$, and

$$\log \frac{P_i}{P_m} = Y_i = \beta_{0i} + \beta_{1i} X_1 + \beta_{2i} X_2 + \cdots + \beta_{ki} X_k$$

If all f_i are such that $0 < f_i < n$, the parameters of the general logit model can be estimated by regressing

$$\log \frac{f_i/n}{f_m/n} = \log \frac{f_i}{f_m}$$

against the explanatory variables $X_1, X_2, \ldots, X_k$.

EXAMPLE 12.5

A number of shoppers, let us suppose, were surveyed to estimate the relationship between their income and gender, on the one hand, and the probabilities of favoring one of three brands of a product (A, B, and C), on the other. The survey results are shown in Table 12.5.

The 120 shoppers, it is assumed, had only four distinct sets of income values (X_1) and gender (X_2) as shown in the first two columns of Table 12.5.

TABLE 12.5 Survey Results, Example 12.5

Income ($000), X_1	Gender[a], X_2	Number of shoppers, n	Number favoring brand A, f_1	B, f_2	C, f_3	$Y_1 = \log(f_1/f_3)$	$Y_2 = \log(f_2/f_3)$
40	1	25	5	8	12	−0.875	−0.405
50	0	42	8	13	21	−0.965	−0.479
60	1	37	11	7	19	−0.546	−0.998
70	0	16	4	3	9	−0.811	−1.099
		120					

[a] 1 = female, 0 = male.

Using Brand C as the base, the logit model of this example consists of two equations:

$$\log \frac{P_1}{P_3} = \beta_{01} + \beta_{11}X_1 + \beta_{21}X_2$$

and

$$\log \frac{P_2}{P_3} = \beta_{02} + \beta_{12}X_1 + \beta_{22}X_2$$

The parameters of the first equation can be estimated by regressing $Y_1 = \log(f_1/f_3)$ against X_1 and X_2 and those of the second equation by regressing $Y_2 = \log(f_2/f_3)$ against X_1 and X_2. The regression results are as follows:

$$\hat{Y}_1 = -1.613 + 0.012X_1 + 0.298X_2$$
$$\hat{Y}_2 = 1.029 - 0.030X_1 - 0.216X_2$$

Consider now a female shopper with an income of 55 ($000). The probabilities that she favors Brands A and B are estimated by calculating first

$$\hat{Y}_1 = -1.613 + 0.012(55) + 0.298(1) = -0.655$$
$$\hat{Y}_2 = 1.029 - 0.030(55) - 0.216(1) = -0.837$$

and then

$$\hat{P}_1 = \frac{e^{-0.655}}{1 + (e^{-0.655} + e^{-0.837})} = \frac{0.519}{1 + (0.519 + 0.433)} = 0.266$$

$$\hat{P}_2 = \frac{e^{-0.837}}{1 + (e^{-0.655} + e^{-0.837})} = \frac{0.433}{1 + (0.519 + 0.433)} = 0.222$$

The probability she prefers Brand C is, of course, $1 - (0.266 + 0.222)$, or 0.512. ∎

If, for some observations, f_i is equal to zero, $\log f_i$ is not defined and regression cannot be applied. The method of maximum likelihood, however, can be. We do not pursue the topic here but additional information can be found in McCullagh and Nelder (1989, Ch. 5) or Agresti (1990, Ch. 9).

12.6   MULTIPLE CATEGORIES AND NORMALITY

As in Section 12.5, we consider the general case in which elements are classified into one of m categories $C_1, C_2, \ldots, C_m$ with the help of k known variables or attributes $X_1, X_2, \ldots, X_k$. Simple random samples are available selected from among the elements belonging to each category. This general case—without the normality assumption—was examined in Section 11.6.

If the joint probability distributions of the explanatory variables $X_1, X_2, \ldots, X_k$, $p_i(X_1, X_2, \ldots, X_k)$ ($i = 1, 2, \ldots, m$) are all multivariate normal with the same variances and covariances and if the misclassification losses are equal (i.e., all $L_{ij} = L$ for all $i \neq j$, while all $L_{ii} = 0$), the rule that minimizes the overall expected loss takes a simple form, analogous to that for the case of two categories.

1. *Construct a linear classification function for each of the m categories. For category i, this function is of the form*

$$\hat{Y}_i = b_{0i} + b_{1i}X_1 + b_{2i}X_2 + \cdots + b_{ki}X_k + \log q_i \qquad (12.12)$$

The coefficients of these functions are given numbers, calculated from the sample observations; $\log q_i$ is the natural logarithm of q_i, where q_i is the probability (the "prior probability") that an element belongs to category i.

2. *Given an element with characteristics $X_1, X_2, \ldots X_k$, calculate the score $\hat{Y}_i$ for each category and classify the element into the category associated with the highest score.*

Note that the assumptions for the case of m categories are more restrictive than those for two categories, since the misclassification losses are required to be equal. As in the case of two categories, the coefficients b_{ji} are calculated by computer programs.

EXAMPLE 12.6

Suppose that the insurance company of Example 12.1 classified automobile policies into three categories:

C_1: No accident
C_2: Minor accident
C_3: Major accident

It was found that 85% of the policies were C_1, 10% C_2, and 5% C_3. The same two explanatory variables are used as in Example 12.1, namely, the number of years of driving experience of the principal driver (X_1) and the horsepower of the automobile (X_2). Random samples of sizes 11, 5, and 5 were taken from among policies belonging to categories C_1, C_2, and C_3, respectively. The sample observations are shown in Table 12.6.

TABLE 12.6   Data and Classification Scores, Example 12.6

Policy no.	Driving experience, X_1	Horsepower, X_2	Category[a]	Classification scores, $\hat{Y}_1$	$\hat{Y}_2$	$\hat{Y}_3$
1	23	153	1	37.7829*	35.1173	32.1068
2	18	142	1	31.6525*	27.9659	24.8485
3	16	184	1	47.4541	48.3239*	47.3863
4	25	105	1	19.6209*	11.7569	6.2792
5	32	160	1	43.7821*	41.5847	38.1535
6	8	142	1	28.0465*	24.6719	22.3945
7	15	129	1	25.4565*	20.4725	16.9844
8	2	128	1	20.3753*	15.6899	13.2459
9	27	120	1	26.2431*	19.9217	14.9945
10	28	138	1	33.6849*	29.2583	25.1093
11	23	108	1	20.0799*	12.5993	7.4333
12	18	170	2	42.6677*	41.9771	40.2009
13	22	194	2	53.5517	55.3043*	54.3417
14	23	160	2	40.5367*	38.6201	35.9449
15	8	174	2	40.6353	40.6847*	39.9401
16	12	181	2	44.8315	45.5051*	44.7598
17	15	181	3	45.9133	46.4933*	45.4960
18	4	186	3	43.9137	45.3719	45.5381*
19	2	205	3	50.6671	54.2207	55.4650*
20	14	204	3	54.6009	57.6731	57.8615*
21	18	193	3	51.7159	53.4863*	52.8118

[a] 1 = No accident, 2 = Minor accident, 3 = Major accident. Asterisks explained in text.

SOURCE: File discr2.dat

The natural logarithms of $q_1 = 0.85$, $q_2 = 0.10$, and $q_3 = 0.05$ are -0.1625, -2.3026, and -2.9957, respectively. The coefficients of the three classification functions were calculated by a computer program as follows:[11]

$$\hat{Y}_1 = -30.5386 + 0.3606X_1 + 0.3934X_2 - 0.1625$$
$$= -30.7011 + 0.3606X_1 + 0.3934X_2$$
$$\hat{Y}_2 = -46.7175 + 0.3294X_1 + 0.5004X_2 - 2.3026$$
$$= -49.0201 + 0.3294X_1 + 0.5004X_2 \tag{12.13}$$
$$\hat{Y}_3 = -54.4316 + 0.2454X_1 + 0.5483X_2 - 2.9957$$
$$= -57.4273 + 0.2454X_1 + 0.5483X_2$$

For an applicant having X_1 years of driving experience and a car with horsepower X_2, we calculate the three scores $\hat{Y}_1$, $\hat{Y}_2$, and $\hat{Y}_3$ and classify the applicant into that category associated with the highest score. For example, policy no. 1 in Table 12.6 has $X_1 = 23$ and $X_2 = 153$. Substituting these values into $\hat{Y}_1$, $\hat{Y}_2$, and $\hat{Y}_3$, we find $\hat{Y}_1 = 37.7829$, $\hat{Y}_2 = 35.1173$, and $\hat{Y}_3 = 32.1068$. The highest score is $\hat{Y}_1$, and the policy is classified as C_1. The scores of this and all other observations are shown in Table 12.6. Asterisks identify the highest scores.

On the basis of these calculations, we construct the following table showing the number of correct and incorrect classifications:

Actual state	Action: Classify as			Total
	C_1	C_2	C_3	
C_1	10	1	0	11
C_2	2	3	0	5
C_3	0	2	3	5
Total	12	6	3	21

For example, of the five observations known to belong to C_2, three were classified correctly and two were misclassified as C_1. ∎

As we observed in Section 12.3, the assumption of multivariate normality is seldom strictly satisfied in practice. The linear classification functions, however, are often used because of their very appealing simplicity. In such situations, it should be kept in mind that the classification rule is simply convenient, not optimal. The performance of the linear classification functions, however, can be measured by examining the proportions of correct and incorrect classifications.

[11]Program SAS with the statements proc discrim; class categ; var x1 x2; priors '1' = 0.85 '2' = 0.10 '3' = 0.05;.

EXAMPLE 12.7

For a study of delinquency and foreclosure in residential mortgage loans in the state of Connecticut, information on a total sample of 545 mortgages was obtained from 24 granting institutions (commercial banks, savings banks, and savings and loan associations).[12] The mortgages were divided into three categories by status of payment:

C_1 : "Current"—mortgages that are current
C_2 : "Delinquent"—mortgages that are 90 or more days delinquent
C_3 : "Foreclosure"—mortgages that are in foreclosure

Within each category, the sample observations were randomly divided into an "analysis" sample and a "holdout" sample, approximately in the ratio 3:1, as follows:

Sample	Current	Delinquent	Foreclosure	Total
Analysis	224	126	86	436
Holdout	55	32	22	109
Total	279	158	108	545

The analysis sample was used to estimate the coefficients of the classification functions, and the holdout sample was used to estimate the probabilities of misclassification.

For each mortgage loan in the sample, data were gathered on 35 explanatory variables as shown in Table 12.7.

These variables represent characteristics of the borrower (profession, marital status, number of dependents, age, the existence or not of other debt payments, and the payment-to-income ratio), loan characteristics (maturity, purpose, junior financing, whether the loan was insured, and the ratio of the loan amount to the appraised value of the property), and property characteristics. Several of these variables are dummy (0 or 1) variables; for example, if the loan was given for construction purposes, variable 2b is coded 1 and the remaining dummy variables relating to the purpose of the loan (2a, 2c, and 2d) are coded 0.

Not all the variables were retained. It was found that the subset of 11 variables shown in Table 12.8 classifies nearly as well as the full set of 35 variables. Table 12.8 also shows the coefficients of the three linear classification functions.

---

[12]T. G. Morton, "A Discriminant Function Analysis of Residential Mortgage Delinquency and Foreclosure," Report No. 14, Center for Real Estate and Urban Economic Studies, School of Business Administration, University of Connecticut, Storrs, Conn., August 1974.

TABLE 12.7   Variables Included in Classification Study, Example 12.7

	Variable		Variable
1	Original maturity of mortgage	6a	Borrower's age: 18-24
2a	Purpose of loan: Purchase	6b	Borrower's age: 25-29
2b	Purpose of loan: construction	6c	Borrower's age: 30-34
2c	Purpose of loan: repair and	6d	Borrower's age: 35-39
	remodeling	6e	Borrower's age: 40-44
2d	Purpose of loan: refinancing	6f	Borrower's age: 45-49
3a	Profession: self-employment	6g	Borrower's age: 50-59
3b	Profession: sales	6h	Borrower's age: 60+
3c	Profession: clerical	7	Other debt payments
3d	Profession: unskilled labor	8	Junior financing
3e	Profession: professional	9	Loan insured
3f	Profession: skilled labor	10a	Type of property: one-family
3g	Profession: service, etc.	10b	Type of property: two-family
4	Marital status	10c	Type of property: three-family
5a	No dependents	11	Loan amount/Appraisal
5b	One dependent	12	Annual payment/Annual income
5c	Two dependents		
5d	Three dependents		
5e	Four dependents		
5f	Five plus dependents		

TABLE 12.8   Classification Functions, Example 12.7

			Coefficient in classification function		
#	Variable		Current	Delinquent	Foreclosure
1	3a.	Profession: self-employment	4.617	5.510	6.089
2	3b.	Profession: salesman	4.724	4.674	6.101
3	3d.	Profession: unskilled	0.890	2.166	2.047
4	3e.	Profession: professional	4.390	3.767	4.307
5	5f.	Five plus dependents	1.405	2.266	2.891
6	6b.	Borrower's age: 25-29	0.376	−0.534	0.036
7	6g.	Borrower's age: 50-59	3.010	1.971	2.816
8	7.	Other debt payments	2.649	3.291	3.489
9	8.	Junior financing	3.128	4.922	6.465
10	10c.	Type of property: three-family	0.879	0.858	3.058
11	11.	Loan amount/Appraisal	26.016	27.391	28.684
	Constant		−12.728	−14.132	−16.316

All the variables in Table 12.8 except the last are dummy variables and take the values 1 or 0 depending on whether or not the indicated characteristic is present; the last variable (the loan-to-appraisal ratio) is continuous and is in the range from 0 to 1.

A proposed mortgage loan with a given set of characteristics would be classified into the category in which it receives the highest score. For example, if the borrower is in sales, has five or more dependents, is 35 years old, and does not have any other debts, if there is no junior financing, the property is one-family, and the loan-to-appraisal ratio is 0.80, the classification score for the "Current" category is

$$\hat{Y}_1 = -12.728 + 4.724 + 1.405 + (26.016)(0.8) = 14.214$$

Similarly, we find the scores for the "Delinquent" and "Foreclosure" categories $\hat{Y}_2 = 14.721$ and $\hat{Y}_3 = 15.623$, respectively. A mortgage loan with these characteristics, therefore, would be classified as a loan that is likely to be foreclosed.

Based on the classification functions of Table 12.8, the frequencies of classification in the analysis and holdout samples are shown in Tables 12.9 and 12.10.

These results illustrate a bias in favor of the classification rule if the estimates of the probabilities of correct and incorrect classification are obtained from the analysis sample. In the analysis sample, the proportions of the sample observations in each category that are correctly classified are 66.5%, 45.3%, and 40.7%. In the holdout sample, the corresponding proportions are 60%, 31.2%, and 27.3%. ■

TABLE 12.9 Classification Results for Analysis Sample, Example 12.7

Actual state	Current	Delinquent	Foreclosure	Total
	Number of loans classified as			
Current	149 (66.5%)	51 (22.8%)	24 (10.7%)	224
Delinquent	44 (34.9%)	57 (45.3%)	25 (19.8%)	126
Foreclosure	19 (22.1%)	32 (37.2%)	35 (40.7%)	86

TABLE 12.10 Classification Results for Holdout Sample, Example 12.7

Actual state	Current	Delinquent	Foreclosure	Total
	Number of loans classified as			
Current	33 (60.0%)	12 (21.8%)	10 (18.2%)	55
Delinquent	15 (46.9%)	10 (31.2%)	7 (21.9%)	32
Foreclosure	5 (22.7%)	11 (50.0%)	6 (27.3%)	22

12.7 AN ALTERNATIVE DISCRIMINANT CRITERION

The alternative discriminant criterion introduced in Section 12.4 can be extended to the case in which elements are classified into any number m of categories $C_1, C_2, \ldots, C_m$.

Given any set of coefficients $c_0, c_1, c_2, \ldots, c_k$, the linear score of an element with characteristics $X_1, X_2, \ldots, X_k$ is

$$Y = c_0 + c_1 X_1 + c_2 X_2 + \cdots + c_k X_k$$

Let $\bar{Y}_i$ be the average of these scores for all elements in C_i, and $\bar{Y}_o$ the average of these averages,

$$\bar{Y}_o = \frac{1}{m} \sum_{i=1}^{m} \bar{Y}_i$$

The greater the variance of the $\bar{Y}_i$ about $\bar{Y}_o$, the greater can be said to be the differentiation between the categories. We could thus search for the values of the coefficients that maximize this variance, standardized to ensure a finite solution. Specifically, the problem can be stated as follows.

Find $c_0, c_1, c_2, \ldots, c_k$ that maximize

$$\frac{\frac{1}{m} \sum_{i=1}^{m} (\bar{Y}_i - \bar{Y}_o)^2}{\frac{1}{n} \sum (Y - \bar{Y})^2} \tag{12.14}$$

The denominator of Eq. 12.14 is the ordinary variance of all Y-scores.

By extension of the classification rule for two categories, an element with characteristics $X_1, X_2, \ldots, X_k$ is classified into category C_i if its Y-score is closest to $\bar{Y}_i$.

Eq. 12.14 is the extension of the similar criterion Eq. 12.10 for two categories.

To see this, note that when $m = 2$ the numerator—call it Z—of Eq. 12.14 is

$$Z = \frac{1}{2} [(\bar{Y}_1 - \bar{Y}_0)^2 + (\bar{Y}_2 - \bar{Y}_0)^2]$$

where $\bar{Y}_0 = (\bar{Y}_1 + \bar{Y}_2)/2$. Expanding, substituting for $\bar{Y}_0$, and simplifying, we get

$$2Z = \bar{Y}_1^2 + \bar{Y}_2^2 - 2\bar{Y}_0^2$$
$$= \bar{Y}_1^2 + \bar{Y}_2^2 - 2[\frac{1}{2}(\bar{Y}_1 + \bar{Y}_2)]^2$$

$$= \frac{1}{2}(\bar{Y}_1^2 + \bar{Y}_2^2 - 2\bar{Y}_1\bar{Y}_2)$$

$$= \frac{1}{2}(\bar{Y}_1 - \bar{Y}_2)^2$$

Therefore, $4Z = (\bar{Y}_1 - \bar{Y}_2)^2$ and, apart from a constant, Eq. 12.14 is Eq. 12.10 when $m = 2$.

As in the case of two categories, there is an infinite number of solutions to the maximization problem Eq. 12.14. This is so because the constant c_0 can take any value, and if a set of c_j's constitutes a solution, so does the set $c_j' = dc_j$ where d is any constant. *One solution to the problem Eq. 12.14 is provided by statistical programs for canonical discriminant analysis.*

EXAMPLE 12.6 (CONTINUED)

A computer program was applied to the data in Table 12.6.[13] The coefficients maximizing Eq. 12.14 give the following linear scoring function

$$Y = -0.03210X_1 + 0.050134X_2$$

For example, the score of the first policy in Table 12.6 is

$$Y = -(0.03210)(23) + (0.050134)(153) = 6.931$$

It is straightforward to verify that the average score of all policies in C_1 (no accident) is $\bar{Y}_1 = 6.243$ and that $\bar{Y}_2 = 8.280$ and $\bar{Y}_3 = 9.375$.

To determine the category into which to classify a policy with the characteristics of the first one listed in Table 12.6, we calculate $(Y - \bar{Y}_1)^2 = (6.931 - 6.243)^2 = 0.688$, $(Y - \bar{Y}_2)^2 = (6.931 - 8.280)^2 = 1.349$, and $(Y - \bar{Y}_3)^2 = (6.931 - 9.375)^2 = 2.444$. As the Y-score of such a policy is closest to $\bar{Y}_1$, the policy should be classified as C_1.

Repeating such calculations for all other policies in Table 12.6, we arrive at the following table showing the number of correct and incorrect classifications.

Actual state	Action: Classify as			Total
	C_1	C_2	C_3	
C_1	10	1	0	11
C_2	0	4	1	5
C_3	0	1	4	5
Total	10	6	5	21

In other words, all but 3 of the 21 policies are classified correctly. ∎

[13]Program SAS with the statements `proc candisc ncan=1; class categ; var x1 x2;`.

The method for solving the maximization problem Eq. 12.14 is described in mathematically advanced texts.[14] These references also describe extensions of the method that yield more than one linear scoring function, and the conditions under which the classification based on this method produces the same results as the normal classification rule.

12.8   TO SUM UP

- This chapter dealt with special cases of the classification problem in which additional information or a different criterion is utilized to simplify the classification rule.

- The *logit*, *CLL*, and *probit models* in two-category situations are special functions relating the probability that an element with a given set of characteristics is a member of a category to the explanatory variables and attributes. These functions are designed to avoid a shortcoming of the *linear probability model*, which may produce probability estimates outside the range from 0 to 1.

- If the joint distribution of the explanatory variables in each category is *multivariate normal* and the variances and covariances of the explanatory variables are the same in both categories, then the optimal classification rule (one that minimizes the expected overall misclassification loss) takes the form of a *linear classification function* for each category, giving a "score" in favor of that category; an element is classified into the category with the maximum score.

- The same classification rule can also be expressed in terms of a single *linear discriminant function*. An element is classified into one category if its discriminant score is high and into the other if it is low. The cutoff between high and low scores depends on the proportions of population elements falling into the two categories and on the misclassification losses.

- The normal linear discriminant function is also optimal under a different criterion that aims to maximize the separation of the mean linear discriminant scores of the elements in the two categories. Another solution to this last problem, related to the normal one, is the *canonical discriminant function*. The extension of this criterion to situations involving more than two categories is described in Section 12.7.

- In situations involving more than two categories, the optimal classification rule is linear if the joint distributions of the explanatory variables in all categories are multivariate normal with the same variances and covariances and the misclassification losses are equal.

[14]See, for example, Lachenbruch (1975, Ch. 1), Johnson and Wichern (1992, Ch. 11), or Rencher (1995, Ch. 8).

PROBLEMS

12.1 Using a suitable statistical program, confirm the results presented in this chapter.

12.2 A study was conducted to estimate the relationship between the probability of owning a sports car, on the one hand, and age and household income, on the other. Twenty persons were selected from among those having each of nine combinations of age and household income and asked whether or not they owned a sports car. The data are shown in Table 12.11.

(a) Estimate the (i) linear, (ii) logit, and (iii) CLL models using regression.

(b) Determine the fit of a probit model having the parameter values of the linear model (a, i).

(c) Using a suitable computer program, estimate by the method of maximum likelihood the (i) linear, (ii) logit, (iii) CLL, and (iv) probit models.

(d) For each of the preceding models estimate the probability that a 40-year-old person with household income in the 30 to 60 ($000) range owns a sports car.

(e) Which of the preceding models best describes the hypothesized relationship?

(f) Does the method of sample selection (e.g., simple random, stratified, etc.) matter?

12.3 Refer to Table 12.3, showing for each of 21 automobile insurance policies the number of years of driving experience of the principal driver (X_1), the horsepower of the insured car (X_2), and whether or not an accident took place. The data are in the file `discr1.dat`.

(a) Let $Y = 1$ if there was an accident and $Y = 0$ otherwise. Regress Y against X_1 and X_2. Interpret the results. Is this model different from the linear probability model?

(b) Can the logit and CLL models be estimated in this case using regression? Explain.

(c) Determine the fit of a probit model with arbitrary but reasonable parameter values.

(d) Using a suitable statistical program, estimate by the method of maximum likelihood the (i) logit, (ii) CLL, and (iii) probit models.

(e) For each of the preceding models estimate the probability that a driver with 10 years of experience and a car with 160 horesepower will have an accident.

(f) Compare the results in (a) to (e) with those presented in Sections 12.3 and 12.4.

TABLE 12.11 Data for Problem 12.2

Age	Household income ($000)	Number selected	Number owning sports car
20	Under 30	20	3
20	30-60	20	4
20	Over 60	20	4
30	Under 30	20	2
30	30-60	20	3
30	Over 60	20	4
50	Under 30	20	1
50	30-60	20	1
50	Over 60	20	2

12.4 Refer to Example 12.3 of Section 12.4. Calculate the discriminant scores $Y = 18.7924 + 0.0483X_1 - 0.1217X_2$ for all policies in Table 12.3 and show that $\bar{Y}_1 = 3.050$ and $\bar{Y}_2 = -3.041$. Verify that all but one of the 11 C_1 policies and all but one of the 10 C_2 policies are correctly classified.

12.5 Refer to Example 12.3 of Section 12.4. Calculate the scores based on the canonical discriminant function $Y = -0.0196X_1 + 0.0493X_2$ for all policies in Table 12.3. Show that $\bar{Y}_1 = 6.3793$ and $\bar{Y}_2 = 8.8476$ and that the classification based on the canonical discriminant function produces the same results as that based on the normal one (Problem 12.4).

12.6 A study was made of the characteristics of buyers and nonbuyers of Stuart's, a brand of marmalade. Investigators interviewed a number of shoppers who were observed buying Stuart's and other brands in the stores of a cooperating supermarket chain. The current market share of Stuart's is about 23%. For the purpose of this problem, assume that five buyers and five nonbuyers were interviewed, with the results shown in Table 12.12.

The variables have the following interpretation:

X_1: Shopper's household income ($000)

X_2: Number of persons in shopper's household

X_3: $= 1$ if shopper had purchased same brand before; $= 0$ otherwise

Y: $= 1$ if shopper purchased Stuart's; $= 0$ otherwise

(a) Assuming that the joint distribution of the X's among both buyers and nonbuyers is approximately multivariate normal with the same variances and covariances and that the misclassification losses are equal, determine and interpret (i) the classification functions and (ii) the discriminant function with the help of a statistical program.

(b) Determine the performance of the classification rule and the overall probability of misclassification.

TABLE 12.12
Data for
Problem 12.6

X_1	X_2	X_3	Y
73	4	0	1
97	3	1	1
97	1	0	1
71	3	1	1
47	5	1	0
35	2	0	0
62	2	0	0
51	2	0	0
41	4	1	0
84	2	0	1

SOURCE: File
stuarts.dat

(c) Do (a) and (b), but assume that the loss of misclassifying a Stuart's buyer is considered three times higher than that of misclassifying a nonbuyer.

(d) With the help of a statistical program, determine and interpret the canonical discriminant function implementing the criterion of Section 12.4. Interpret this function. Determine its performance. Compare the results with those in (a) and (b).

(e) Of what possible use is this type of study? How would you improve its design?

12.7 A brief questionnaire was sent to recent buyers of three makes of mid-sized cars.

> *On a scale from 0 (low) to 9 (high), rate the importance you attach to the following factors when buying a car:*
>
> **1.** *Economy of operation* ___
> **2.** *Reliability of manufacturer* ___
> **3.** *Friendliness of the salesperson* ___

Fifty percent of recent sales were of Make 1, 20% of Make 2, and 30% of Make 3. For the purpose of this problem, suppose five buyers of each make responded. The responses to the three preceding questions are shown under Q1, Q2, and Q3 in Table 12.13. The last column of Table 12.13 shows the make purchased.

(a) Determine the linear classification functions for distinguishing *Make 1 buyers and non-buyers* assuming multivariate normality, equality of variances and covariances, and equal misclassification losses. Interpret these functions. Determine their performance and the overall misclassification rate.

(b) Same as (a), except that the purpose is to distinguish *Make 2 buyers and nonbuyers*.

(c) Same as (a), except that the purpose is to distinguish *Make 3 buyers and nonbuyers*.

TABLE 12.13 Data for Problem 12.7

Q1	Q2	Q3	Make
5	5	7	1
5	6	7	1
5	6	6	1
6	5	7	1
6	6	7	1
6	9	6	2
7	7	6	2
8	6	7	2
8	6	8	2
7	7	7	2
6	8	8	3
7	7	8	3
8	9	6	3
9	6	7	3
8	7	7	3

SOURCE: File cmakes.dat

(d) Estimate and determine the performance of the canonical discriminant function described in Section 12.4 for the purpose given in (i) (a), (ii) (b), and (iii) (c).

(e) Determine the three classification functions for distinguishing buyers of makes 1, 2, and 3. Interpret these functions and determine their performance.

(f) Compare the results in (e) with those in (a) to (d).

(g) Apply to this problem the alternative discriminant criterion described in Section 12.7. Determine its performance. Compare these results with those obtained in the previous questions.

(h) Of what possible use is this type of study? How can it be improved?

12.8   Refer to Example 12.5, but suppose that the data are as given in Table 12.14 rather than Table 12.5.

(a) Estimate the relationship between the probabilities of favoring brands A, B, and C, on the one hand, and income and gender, on the other, assuming the relationship is approximately linear. Forecast the proportions of male shoppers with income $55,000 that favor each brand.

(b) Same as (a), except use the general logit model described in Section 12.5.

(c) Of what possible use is this type of analysis? How would you improve the study?

12.9   In a certain region, there are three educational TV channels that rely in part on member donations. Recently, the three channels pooled resources and conducted a survey of their members. A database of members and their characteristics was thus established. To investigate the nature of the relationship between channel membership and some personal characteristics of the members, a number of members were selected from the database with the combinations of age, gender, and years of formal education shown in Table 12.14.

Table 12.14 also shows the total number of selected members and the number of members of channels A, B, and C.

(a) Estimate the linear models expressing the probability of membership to channels A, B, and C as a function of age, gender and years of education.

(b) Forecast the proportions of 30-year-old female members with 18 years of education that are members of channels A, B, and C.

(c) Do (a) and (b), except apply the general logit model described in Section 12.5.

(d) Of what possible use is this type of analysis? How can the study be improved?

TABLE 12.14   Data for Problem 12.8

Income ($000), X_1	Gender[a], X_2	Number of shoppers, n	Number favoring brand		
			A, f_1	B, f_2	C, f_3
40	1	40	16	14	10
50	0	30	12	10	8
60	1	20	5	11	4
70	0	10	3	5	2

[a] 1 = female, 0 = male

TABLE 12.15   Data for Problem 12.9

Age	Gender[a]	Years of education	Members selected	Members of A	B	C
25	1	10	17	10	2	5
25	1	16	13	7	3	3
25	0	10	15	9	2	4
25	0	16	15	8	4	3
50	1	10	11	6	2	3
50	1	16	12	6	3	3
50	0	10	11	6	2	3
50	0	16	19	9	5	5

[a] 1 = male; 0 = female.

SOURCE: File edutv.dat

12.10 Refer to Example 12.6. The classification rule (Eq. 12.13) can also be written in a different way. According to the rule, policies with characteristics X_1 and X_2 should be classified as C_1 if $\hat{Y}_1 > \hat{Y}_2$ and $\hat{Y}_1 > \hat{Y}_3$; as C_2 if $\hat{Y}_2 > \hat{Y}_1$ and $\hat{Y}_2 > \hat{Y}_3$; and as C_3 if $\hat{Y}_3 > \hat{Y}_1$ and $\hat{Y}_3 > \hat{Y}_2$ (ties can be broken arbitrarily). That is, classify as C_1 those policies that satisfy $\hat{Y}_1 - \hat{Y}_2 > 0$ and $\hat{Y}_1 - \hat{Y}_3 > 0$; as C_2 all policies that satisfy $-(\hat{Y}_1 - \hat{Y}_2) > 0$ and $\hat{Y}_2 - \hat{Y}_3 > 0$; and as C_3 all policies that satisfy $-(\hat{Y}_1 - \hat{Y}_3) > 0$ and $-(\hat{Y}_2 - \hat{Y}_3) > 0$.

The classification rule can therefore be expressed in terms of three *discriminant functions* $\hat{Y}_1 - \hat{Y}_2, \hat{Y}_1 - \hat{Y}_3$, and $\hat{Y}_2 - \hat{Y}_3$. There is one classification function for each category but one discriminant function for each *pair* of categories.

(a) Determine the three discriminant functions.

(b) Plot these functions in a diagram. Show that they divide the (X_1, X_2) space into three regions, R_1, R_2, and R_3, such that all points (X_1, X_2) in R_1 are classified as C_1, all points in R_2 as C_2, and all points in R_3 as C_3.

12.11 One of the services provided by DEF Inc., a market research firm, is a forecast of business's hiring intentions. DEF maintains a panel of personnel managers from a number of companies. The companies were originally selected at random from a list of all public companies in the country. The personnel managers of those that agreed to participate in the panel respond at the beginning of each quarter to the following question:

> *On balance, I expect my company's workforce next quarter to*
>
> **1.** *Increase* ___
> **2.** *Remain about the same* ___
> **3.** *Decrease* ___

For the purpose of this problem, assume that the panel members' responses for next quarter and some characteristics of their companies are as shown in Table 12.16.

TABLE 12.16 Data for Problem 12.11

Id. no.	Assets ($million)	Revenue ($million)	Industry[a]	Hiring intentions[b]
1	686	831	1	1
2	110	328	0	3
3	427	637	0	1
4	401	347	1	3
5	1322	700	1	1
6	1270	329	0	2
7	676	473	1	2
8	1474	562	0	2
9	1218	790	0	2
10	107	543	1	3
11	385	502	1	2
12	485	483	0	1
13	368	314	0	3
14	316	739	0	2
15	546	498	1	3

[a] 1 = Industry A, 0 = Industry B
[b] 1 = Increase, 2 = Stable, 3 = Decrease

SOURCE: hirint.dat.

In answering the following questions, pretend that the number of participating companies and industries to which they belong are large.

(a) Assuming that the panel of participating companies can be treated as a simple random sample from the population of all public companies in the country and that the assumptions of Section 12.6 are satisfied, estimate and interpret the three linear functions for classifying a company with given characteristics as one that will increase, keep constant, or decrease its workforce. Determine the performance of the classification rule and the overall misclassification rate.

(b) Explain the meaning of the assumptions of Section 12.6 in this case. Are these assumptions likely to be satisfied in reality? If not, how should your interpretation in (a) be changed?

(c) Same as (a), except apply the alternative discriminant criterion of Section 12.7.

12.12 (Due to Mr. Nadeem Siddiqi) The file bankrupt.dat contains financial information regarding 21 companies that became bankrupt during a four-year period and 46 nonbankrupt companies matched to the former by industry, size, and time period. The file is partially listed in Figure 12.9.

The variables have the following interpretation.

IDNO: Company identification number

BANKR: $= 1$ if bankrupt; $= 0$ otherwise

TA: Total assets

TAL1: Total assets, prior year

INDO	BANKR	TA	TAL1	LTD	EQU	EQUL1	SALES	NI	CURA	CURL
1	1	512862	568462	9585	-84271	-7664	504483	-105351	646303	587548
2	1	45473	44351	24629	9233	14934	54246	-9862	22525	11611
3	1	1277	831	105	522	307	1745	-461	754	650
4	1	657327	242762	423363	10124	10472	167488	280	2133690	218840
5	1	3811	3241	1080	365	1457	5643	-1329	1822	2366
6	1	20610	19031	2317	6706	8235	31307	622	11703	11587
7	1	16221	11128	2990	7668	7189	19874	251	9624	5563
8	1	6438	5506	1706	-6177	281	199	-7446	3055	10909
9	1	58526	64789	18910	33312	34743	19835	-6854	4224	6304
10	1	513	145	55	-138	-200	426	-407	322	596

FIGURE 12.9 File `bankrupt.dat`, partial listing

LTD: Long-term debt

EQU: Equity (net worth)

EQUL1: Equity, prior year

SALES: Sales

NI: Net income after taxes

CURA: Current assets

CURL: Current liabilities

All data are in thousands of dollars. With the exception of TAL1 and EQUL1, the data come from the financial statements of each company published one year prior to bankruptcy or selection for the sample; TAL1 and EQUL1 refer to the year prior to that.

A classification model very similar to that of Altman and Lavallee was estimated assuming normality, equal variances and covariances, equal prior probabilities, and mis-classification losses.[15] The explanatory variables were as follows:

X_1: Total sales / Total assets (SALES / TA)

X_2: Long-term debt / Total assets (LTD / TA)

X_3: Current ratio (Current assets / Current liabilities, CURA / CURL)

X_4: Net income after tax / Long-term debt (NI / LTD)

X_5: rate of growth of equity *minus* rate of growth of total assets [(EQU-EQUL1)-(TA-TAL1)]

Using the data in the file `bankrupt.dat`, the two linear classification functions were estimated as follows:

$$Y_1 = -2.23354 + 2.29976X_1 + 3.56992X_2 + 0.72524X_3 - 0.02353X_4 + 0.000011X_5$$

[15]E. I. Altman and M. Y. Lavallee, "Business Failure Classification in Canada," *Journal of Business Administration*, Vol. 12, No. 1, fall 1980, pp. 147–64. The only difference is that Altman and Lavallee use total debt rather than long-term debt as in the model of this problem.

$$Y_2 = -2.12166 + 2.05740X_1 + 4.97716X_2 + 0.42176X_3 - 0.01804X_4 - 0.000002X_5$$

Y_1 gives a score "in favor of" nonbankrupt, and Y_2 one in favor of bankrupt, firms.

(a) Interpret these results. Comment on the assumptions made.

(b) Calculate and interpret the implied linear discriminant function. Describe the classification rule based on this function.

(c) Confirm the estimated classification functions.

(d) Determine the performance of the preceding classification rule using the data in `bankrupt.dat`.

(e) Determine the contribution of X_1, X_3, X_4 and X_5 over that of X_2 alone.

(f) Redo (a) to (d) assuming that approximately 1% of companies become bankrupt in a four-year period.

(g) Improve the classification models you just estimated.

12.13   (Due to Mr. J. Palombo) You are invited to determine if and how financial characteristics of a company can be used to predict whether or not the company will merge or be taken over.

The file `merger.dat` contains financial data for 40 of the top 500 firms that merged or were taken over in a three-year period and for a sample of 40 top-500 firms that were not merged or taken over during the same period. The data for the former firms were obtained from the most recent annual financial statements prior to the merger, while those for the latter group were the most recent prior to the study. A partial listing of the data file is shown in Figure 12.10.

The interpretation of the variables is as follows:

ID: Identification number

CR: Current ratio (current assets / current liabilities)

QR: Quick ratio (current assets - inventory / current liabilities)

INVT: Inventory turnover (sales / inventory)

ID	CR	QR	INVT	FAUT	TAUT	ACRT	WCAT	DETA
1	2.44	19.00	5.38	18.67	0.39	142.20	0.19	0
2	2.37	0.76	2.57	2.42	0.88	7.78	0.29	22
3	1.69	0.90	5.80	5.13	1.31	5.32	0.20	35
4	1.08	0.41	0.18	1.04	0.08	34.16	0.05	4
5	4.25	3.70	21.86	2.02	0.71	4.76	0.19	17

DETE	TIER	ROA	GM	PM	ROE	PER	GRP	NAME
0	0.00	27	113	69	31	8.84	T	DOME
48	5.07	7	18	8	16	8.42	T	H-WALKER
77	2.63	3	9	2	7	9.50	T	HUDRAY
14	4.80	5	21	6	20	3.70	T	IVSTGRP
23	20.40	13	46	19	18	6.82	T	KOFFLER

FIGURE 12.10   File `merger.dat`, partial listing

FAUT: Fixed asset utilization (sales / fixed assets)

TAUT: Total asset utilization (sales / total assets)

ACRT: Accounts receivable turnover (sales / accounts receivable)

WCAT: Working capital turnover (working capital / total assets)

DETA: Debt to total assets (long-term debt / total assets)

DETE: Debt to equity (long-term debt / shareholders' equity)

TIER: Times interest earned (profit before taxes and interest charges / fixed charges)

ROA: Return on assets (net income after tax / total assets)

GM: Gross margin (profit before taxes and interest / sales)

PM: Profit margin (net income after tax / sales)

ROE: Return on equity (net income after tax / shareholders' equity)

PER: Price earnings ratio (price of stock / earnings per share)

GRP: =T if merged or taken over; =A otherwise

NAME: Company name

(a) A computer program for canonical discriminant analysis (SAS `proc candisc ncan=1; class grp; var taut roa dete;`) was used to implement the criterion of Section 12.4. The linear scoring function was estimated as

$$Y = -0.6715TAUT + 0.1263ROA + 0.0059DETE$$

Determine the performance of the classification rule. Interpret the scoring function and rule.

(b) Can the classification rule be improved? Explain your reasoning carefully and in detail.

12.14   (Due to Ms. Patricia Bottomley) Mr. Andrew Baker, a young man of many qualities and considerable promise, recently joined the credit department of a major credit card company. The department looks after two types of accounts: (a) exception (out of pattern; having, for example, an unusually high balance or unusually frequent charges) and (b) delinquent (canceled due to a poor payment record). About 70% of the accounts handled by the department are exception and 30% delinquent.

Mr. Baker was anxious to establish his reputation and demonstrate his quantitative skills. On his own inititative and time, therefore, he proceeded to select a simple random sample of exception, and another of delinquent accounts from among those currently investigated in the department. He then retrieved the original applications for the selected accounts and recorded the following information.

AGE: Applicant's age in years

OWNH: = 1 if applicant owned residence; = 0 otherwise

YRES: Number of years in same residence

INC: Annual income ($000)

YJOB: Number of years at same job

TYPE: = 1 if exception; = 0 if delinquent

The data can be found in the file `ccard.dat`, a partial listing of which is shown in Table 12.17. The samples consist of 38 exception and 41 delinquent accounts.

(a) Indicate how you would analyze this information if you were in Mr. Baker's position.

(b) Acting as Mr. Baker, analyze the information in the file `ccard.dat`. Describe the method used, the findings, and any potential applications of the results. You may wish to recognize that Mr. Baker has a vested interest in producing useful results.

(c) What advice would you give Mr. Baker regarding future initiatives while in the credit department?

TABLE 12.17   File `ccard.dat`, Partial Listing

Id. no.	AGE	OWNH	YRES	INC	YJOB	TYPE
1	38	1	2.0	48.0	15.0	1
2	44	1	6.0	130.0	20.0	1
3	43	1	4.0	40.0	6.0	1
4	36	0	1.0	50.0	0.2	1
5	55	0	4.0	141.0	10.0	1
...	...	...	...	...	...	...

MODELS OF SYSTEMS

13.1 INTRODUCTION AND SUMMARY

Until now, our attention has been directed toward a single dependent variable or attribute, which is considered to be determined by a number of explanatory variables or attributes. The values of these explanatory variables have to be known if the model is to be used for forecasting.

Frequently, one or more of the explanatory variables must themselves be explained and forecast. There is then a need for one or more additional equations to explain these variables. The set of relationships forms a system of equations, all of which must now be estimated if forecasts are to be made.

There are thus two types of variables. Those explained by the equations can be described as internal to the system. The remaining, external variables are assumed to be determined outside the system.

The simplest approach is to estimate each equation in turn by applying OLS or another method appropriate for that equation. Then, by successive substitutions, each internal variable can be expressed as a function of the external variables only, and forecasts of all internal variables for given values of the external variables can be calculated.

Realizing that the external variables "drive" the system of equations and the forecasts, we also consider an alternative approach, according to which each internal variable is directly estimated as a function of the external variables only.

In this chapter, we consider the merits of these two forms for expressing systems of equations and the properties of OLS and other estimation methods for each form.

13.2 THE NORGAS CASE REVISITED

We begin with a simple example to illustrate the manner in which systems of equations are created. We shall use this example throughout the chapter.

EXAMPLE 13.1

In Example 2.2 we examined the case of Norgas, a utility serving residential, commercial, and industrial users of natural gas in a large metropolitan area. Columns 4 to 6 of Table 13.1 show the actual temperature, wind speed, and gas consumption (abbreviated as *TEMP*, *WIND*, and *GASCON*) for the area served by Norgas each Monday during a six-month period from October 1 to March 31. The data were first listed in Table 2.4 and are reproduced here for convenience. Columns 2 and 3 will be explained shortly.

TABLE 13.1 Forecast and Actual Weather Characteristics, Gas Consumption, Example 13.1

| | Forecast | | Actual | | Gas |
Date (1)	Temperature, *FTEMP* (°C) (2)	Wind, *FWIND* (mi/hr) (3)	Temperature, *TEMP* (°C) (4)	Wind, *WIND* (mi/hr) (5)	consumption, *GASCON* (000 m³) (6)
10/01	6.7	11	7.8	8	16,733.0
10/08	8.1	13	6.2	11	16,595.8
10/15	8.5	11	10.1	6	14,665.8
10/22	3.7	5	1.2	5	22,620.9
10/29	7.1	11	4.3	6	20,198.5
11/05	9.4	8	9.4	6	14,848.6
11/12	−0.7	7	−2.0	1	24,085.9
11/19	2.6	10	3.2	9	21,747.5
11/26	5.1	13	3.8	16	24,394.6
12/03	2.6	4	0.4	5	24,035.5
12/10	−5.4	13	−5.3	16	32,919.1
12/17	−7.9	9	−8.0	6	31,712.4
12/24	−5.9	10	−3.9	10	25,435.5
12/31	3.0	10	1.7	14	23,243.3
1/07	−19.3	17	−17.2	14	37,280.6
1/14	−6.6	5	−8.3	8	33,338.5
1/21	−4.8	16	−5.1	7	29,773.4
1/28	−8.1	10	−6.8	5	29,835.6
2/04	−18.1	14	−17.8	13	40,360.6
2/11	−7.3	21	−8.1	20	32,602.4
2/18	7.5	7	7.4	4	18,333.6
2/25	2.9	17	1.4	16	24,628.1
3/04	0.0	14	0.0	7	26,051.5
3/11	−4.4	8	−1.8	9	25,794.6
3/18	−9.8	8	−8.1	4	30,198.4
3/25	4.4	12	2.6	5	21,262.4

SOURCE: File gascon1.dat

Using the data of Table 13.1 and the method of (ordinary) least squares (OLS), we had estimated the following relationship between gas consumption, on the one hand, and temperature and wind speed, on the other:

$$\widehat{GASCON} = 22952 - 862.72TEMP + 162.574WIND \qquad R^2 = 0.957 \atop (-20.90) \qquad\qquad (2.53) \qquad\qquad S = 1463 \qquad (13.1)$$

We had noted at the conclusion of Example 2.2 that in order to forecast tomorrow's (or any future day's) gas consumption, Norgas would need to know the actual temperature and wind speed for that day. These weather characteristics, of course, cannot be known at the time the forecast is made. The estimated model, in other words, provides insight into the relationship between the three variables but is not useful for forecasting.

Forecasts are available, however, of temperature and wind speed made one day in advance by a commercial weather forecasting service. For the dates used in this study, these forecasts are shown in columns 2 and 3 of Table 13.1 under the labels *FTEMP* and *FWIND*.

The forecasts are shown alongside the date to which they refer, but they were made one day earlier. For example, the forecasts of temperature and wind speed for 10/08 (8.1 and 13) were actually made on 10/07; the actual temperature and wind speed for 10/08 were 6.2 and 11, respectively.

In order to forecast a given day's gas consumption one day in advance, Norgas could use the estimated model but with the forecast (rather than the actual) temperature and wind speed. For example, if the forecast of tomorrow's temperature is −10°C and that of tomorrow's wind speed is 10 mi/hr the forecast of tomorrow's gas consumption would be

$$\widehat{GASCON} = 22952 - (862.75)(-10) + (162.574)(10) = 33,205.2 \quad (000\text{m}^3)$$

This approach would be ideal if the service's forecasts were perfect predictors of the weather characteristics. Figures 13.1 and 13.2, which plot actual and forecast temperature and wind using the data of Table 13.1, indicate that this is not the case.

Figures 13.1 and 13.2 show there is a fairly strong relationship between actual and forecast temperature but a weaker one between actual and forecast wind speed. The results of regressing *TEMP* against *FTEMP* and *WIND* against *FWIND* are as follows:

$$\widehat{TEMP} = -0.326 + 0.914FTEMP \qquad R^2 = 0.96 \atop (-1.17) \qquad (25.68) \qquad\qquad S = 1.41 \qquad (13.2)$$

$$\widehat{WIND} = -0.145 + 0.827\,FWIND \qquad R^2 = 0.50 \atop (-0.07) \qquad\quad (4.95) \qquad\qquad S = 3.41 \qquad (13.3)$$

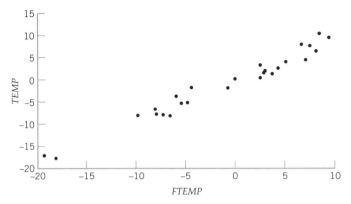

FIGURE 13.1 Actual and forecast temperature, Example 13.1

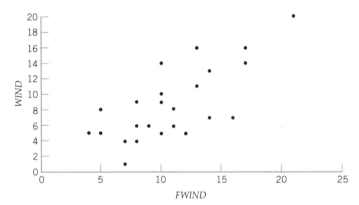

FIGURE 13.2 Actual and forecast wind speed, Example 13.1

If the relationships were perfect, the coefficients of the forecasts would be equal to 1 and the intercepts equal to 0. The OLS estimates of these parameters indicate that the forecasts tend to overestimate the actual temperature and wind speed.[1]

To forecast tomorrow's gas consumption, therefore, Norgas could first estimate the actual temperature and wind speed using Eqs. 13.2 and 13.3 and the weather service's forecasts and then apply these estimates to calculate the forecast gas consumption.

---

[1] The estimated relationships are not, of course, intended to suggest cause and effect—FTEMP does not cause TEMP, nor does FWIND cause WIND—but only an association between the variables.

For example, if the service's forecast of tomorrow's temperature is -10 and that of tomorrow's wind speed $+10$, the estimates of tomorrow's temperature and wind speed are

$$\widehat{TEMP} = -0.326 + 0.914(-10) = -9.466$$
$$\widehat{WIND} = -0.145 + 0.827(+10) = 8.125$$

and the forecast of tomorrow's gas consumption

$$\widehat{GASCON} = 22952 - 862.72(-9.466) + 162.574(8.125) = 32,439.4 \quad (000\text{m}^3)$$

It is clear by now that the forecasts of $TEMP$, $WIND$, and $GASCON$ rely entirely on the values of $FTEMP$ and $FWIND$. The latter variables are not explained by the system of equations but are externally determined. $FTEMP$ and $FWIND$ can be said to "drive" the system of equations, in that forecasts of $TEMP$, $WIND$, and $GASCON$ rely entirely on their values. It seems reasonable, therefore, to estimate relationships that directly link the internal (or *endogenous*, as they are also called) to the external (or *exogenous*) variables. We already have in Eqs. 13.2 and 13.3 the results of regressing $TEMP$ against $FTEMP$, and $WIND$ against $FWIND$. Running a regression of $GASCON$ against $FTEMP$ and $FWIND$ we get

$$\widehat{GASCON} = 23608 - 791.81\,FTEMP + 97.7\,FWIND \qquad R^2 = 0.894$$
$$(-13.12) \qquad\qquad (0.83) \qquad\qquad S = 2298 \qquad (13.4)$$

This approach, it will be noted, does not give exactly the same forecast. Using Eq. 13.4, the forecast gas consumption for a day with $FTEMP = -10$ and $FWIND = 10$ is 32,503.1 (000 m^3).

There are two ways, therefore, of describing the system. The first is by a set of equations, each of which expresses one of the endogenous variables as a function of the variables that determine it (these could be endogenous or exogenous); in the present example, this description is given by Eqs. 13.1, 13.2, and 13.3. The second is by a set of equations, each of which expresses one of the endogenous variables as a function of exogenous variables only; in our example, this description is given by Eqs. 13.1, 13.2, and 13.4.

Two questions arise: (a) which is the better description? and (b) given a choice for (a), which is the best method for estimating the parameters of the system of equations? Of course, in this illustration we estimated both systems by OLS, but as we shall soon see OLS is not the best estimation method in all situations. ∎

13.3 FIRST GENERALIZATION

Let us recapitulate and, at the same time, introduce the notation and terminology employed in the study of systems of equations.

There were three variables of interest in this example: *TEMP*, *WIND*, and *GASCON*. Three linear relationships were proposed to explain these variables, and these can be written as follows:

$$TEMP \approx () + ()FTEMP$$
$$WIND \approx () + ()FWIND$$
$$GASCON \approx () + ()TEMP + ()WIND$$

The symbol $\approx$ ("approximately equal to") indicates that the relationship is not exact; () stands for a parameter that is left unnamed for the moment.

TEMP, *WIND*, and *GASCON* are the three variables explained by the system of equations. They will be called *endogenous*. *FTEMP* and *FWIND* are two variables determined outside the system of equations. They will be called *exogenous*.

The system of equations can be written so that all endogenous variables appear on the left-hand side and all exogenous variables on the right-hand side:

$$TEMP \approx () + ()FTEMP$$
$$WIND \approx () + ()FWIND$$
$$GASCON + ()TEMP + ()WIND \approx ()$$

Let us now introduce symbols for the parameters and an error term for each equation. The latter operation allows us to replace $\approx$ by $=$ and write

$$TEMP = \gamma_{10} + \gamma_{11}FTEMP + \varepsilon_1$$
$$WIND = \gamma_{20} + \gamma_{22}FWIND + \varepsilon_2 \quad (13.5)$$
$$\beta_{31}TEMP + \beta_{32}WIND + GASCON = \gamma_{30} + \varepsilon_3$$

A variable that is missing in an equation can be assumed to be there but with a zero coefficient.

The system of equations Eq. 13.5 can also be specified in the form of a table:

Endogenous			Exogenous			Error
TEMP	WIND	GASCON	CONST	FTEMP	FWIND	
1	0	0	γ_{10}	γ_{11}	0	ε_1
0	1	0	γ_{20}	0	γ_{22}	ε_2
β_{31}	β_{32}	1	γ_{30}	0	0	ε_3

The table should be interpreted as the set of Equations Eq. 13.5. *CONST* can be thought of as an exogenous variable that always takes the value 1.

A system of equations written in one of the preceding forms is said to be in *structural form*. We say that a system is in structural form if each equation expresses an endogenous variable as a function of exogenous and other endogenous variables.

Each endogenous variable can be expressed solely in terms of the exogenous variables and errors. *TEMP* and *WIND* are already so expressed. If their defining equations are substituted in the *GASCON* equation, we get

$$
\begin{aligned}
GASCON &= \gamma_{30} - \beta_{31}(\gamma_{10} + \gamma_{11}\, FTEMP + \varepsilon_1) \\
&\quad - \beta_{32}(\gamma_{20} + \gamma_{22}\, FWIND + \varepsilon_2) + \varepsilon_3 \\
&= (\gamma_{30} - \beta_{31}\gamma_{10} - \beta_{32}\gamma_{20}) - \beta_{31}\gamma_{11}\, FTEMP \\
&\quad - \beta_{32}\gamma_{22}\, FWIND + (-\beta_{31}\varepsilon_1 - \beta_{32}\varepsilon_2 + \varepsilon_3)
\end{aligned}
$$

Renaming the coefficients and error terms, the system can be written as

$$
\begin{aligned}
TEMP &= \delta_{10} + \delta_{11}\, FTEMP & &+ \tilde{\varepsilon}_1 \\
WIND &= \delta_{20} & + \delta_{22}\, FWIND &+ \tilde{\varepsilon}_2 \\
GASCON &= \delta_{30} + \delta_{31}\, FTEMP & + \delta_{32}\, FWIND &+ \tilde{\varepsilon}_3
\end{aligned}
\tag{13.6}
$$

where $\delta_{10} = \gamma_{10}$, $\delta_{11} = \gamma_{11}$, $\delta_{20} = \gamma_{20}$, $\delta_{22} = \gamma_{22}$, $\delta_{30} = \gamma_{30} - \beta_{31}\gamma_{10} - \beta_{32}\gamma_{20}$, $\delta_{31} = -\beta_{31}\gamma_{11}$, $\delta_{32} = -\beta_{32}\gamma_{22}$, $\tilde{\varepsilon}_1 = \varepsilon_1$, $\tilde{\varepsilon}_2 = \varepsilon_2$, and $\tilde{\varepsilon}_3 = -\beta_{31}\varepsilon_1 - \beta_{32}\varepsilon_2 + \varepsilon_3$.

Eq. 13.6 describes the *reduced form* of the system of equations, which can also written in tabular form as follows:

Endogenous variable	CONST	Exogenous FTEMP	FWIND	Error
TEMP	δ_{10}	δ_{11}	0	$\tilde{\varepsilon}_1$
WIND	δ_{20}	0	δ_{22}	$\tilde{\varepsilon}_2$
GASCON	δ_{30}	δ_{31}	δ_{32}	$\tilde{\varepsilon}_3$

We say that a system of equations is in reduced form if each equation expresses an endogenous variable as a function of exogenous variables only.

As noted earlier, we can take as the description of the system either the structural or the reduced form. Which form should be used? And, given a choice of form, by which method should the parameters be estimated?

Two remarks must be made before we address these questions in the following sections.

First, the system of structural equations in this illustration has a special structure that will later be found to have desirable properties. A system is called *recursive* if its equations can be arranged so that the first is a function of exogenous variables only, the second a function of exogenous and the first endogenous variable only, the third a function of the exogenous and the first two endogenous variables only, and so on.

In this example, the first endogenous variable (*TEMP*) is a function of *FTEMP* only, the second (*WIND*) a function of *FWIND* only, and the third (*GASCON*) a function of the first two endogenous variables only. The system, therefore, is recursive.

When the system is recursive, the table ("matrix") of coefficients of the endogenous variables in the tabular representation of the structural form is *triangular*. That is, the β's located above the diagonal are equal to zero:

Endogenous		
TEMP	**WIND**	**GASCON**
1	0	0
0	1	0
β_{31}	β_{32}	1

Second, in Example 13.1 we distinguished two types of variables—endogenous (explained by the system of equations) and exogenous (explained outside the system). In other situations, however, a third type appears—the *lagged endogenous* variable. For example, the model explaining gas consumption could have included the temperature of the previous day, $TEMP_{-1}$, in addition to *TEMP* and *WIND* (it could be argued that because buildings tend to retain heat or cold the gas consumption on a day with given temperature and wind speed depends also on the previous day's temperature). In this case, $TEMP_{-1}$ would be a lagged endogenous variable.

In the following sections, we examine the properties of OLS and other methods for estimating structural or reduced form equations. These properties are essentially the same whether or not lagged endogenous variables are treated separately from exogenous variables. It is simpler, therefore, if we modify our earlier distinction to be one between endogenous and *predetermined variables*, the last type to include both exogenous and lagged endogenous variables. This distinction will be followed from now on.

13.4 SYSTEMS OF EQUATIONS

In general, the *structural form* of a system of equations for l endogenous variables $Y_1, Y_2, \ldots, Y_l$, and $m + 1$ predetermined variables X_0 (a variable consisting of 1's), $X_1, \ldots, X_m$, can be written as follows:

Endogenous				Predetermined				Error
Y_1	Y_2	$\cdots$	Y_I	X_0	X_1	$\cdots$	X_m	
1	β_{12}	$\cdots$	β_{1I}	γ_{10}	γ_{11}	$\cdots$	γ_{1m}	ε_1
β_{21}	1	$\cdots$	β_{2I}	γ_{20}	γ_{21}	$\cdots$	γ_{2m}	ε_2
$\cdots$	$\cdots$	$\cdots$	$\cdots$	$\cdots$	$\cdots$	$\cdots$	$\cdots$	$\cdots$
β_{I1}	β_{I2}	$\cdots$	1	γ_{I0}	γ_{I1}	$\cdots$	γ_{Im}	ε_I

For example, the first line is meant to be read as the structural equation

$$Y_1 = -\beta_{12}Y_2 - \cdots - \beta_{1I}Y_I + \gamma_{10}X_0 + \gamma_{11}X_1 + \cdots + \gamma_{1m}X_m + \varepsilon_1$$

Through successive substitutions, each endogenous variable can be written as a linear function of predetermined variables only. This leads to the *reduced form* of the system of equations, which can also be specified in tabular form as follows:

Endogenous variable	Predetermined				Error
	X_0	X_1	$\cdots$	X_m	
Y_1	δ_{10}	δ_{11}	$\cdots$	δ_{1m}	$\tilde{\varepsilon}_1$
Y_2	δ_{20}	δ_{21}	$\cdots$	δ_{2m}	$\tilde{\varepsilon}_2$
$\cdots$	$\cdots$	$\cdots$	$\cdots$	$\cdots$	$\cdots$
Y_I	δ_{I0}	δ_{I1}	$\cdots$	δ_{Im}	$\tilde{\varepsilon}_I$

For example, the first line can be translated as the reduced form equation

$$Y_1 = \delta_{10}X_0 + \delta_{11}X_1 + \cdots + \delta_{1m}X_m + \tilde{\varepsilon}_1$$

It is understood that some (possibly, many) of the β's, γ's, and δ's are equal to zero, reflecting the exclusion of variables from the equations as a result of theoretical considerations. It is also understood that the δ's are related to the β's and γ's; in general, these relationships are nonlinear and may be quite complicated.[2]

13.5 STRUCTURAL OR REDUCED FORM?

The answer to the first question we raised earlier is fairly simple. If all that is needed are forecasts of the endogenous variables for given values of the

---

[2]Readers familiar with matrix algebra may refer to Appendix B.10 for the relationship between structural and reduced form parameters.

exogenous variables, the reduced form equations are adequate. The reduced form equations, however, are a blend of the underlying structural relationships, and their coefficients represent the net effect of the structural parameters. If the goal of the study is to sort out the separate relationships and effects, then the structural form is more suitable.

13.6 ESTIMATION OF REDUCED FORM PARAMETERS

We may wish to estimate the reduced form of the system of equations mainly for one of two reasons:

- the main purpose of the study is to forecast the values of endogenous variables—there is no particular interest in the structural equations;
- the system studied is already in reduced form—there are no structural equations to estimate.

As in Chapter 3, the properties of estimation methods are determined by the features of the process that is assumed to generate the errors $\tilde{\varepsilon}_i$. If it is assumed that the error values $\tilde{\varepsilon}_i$ of the Y_i equation are generated as if by random draws with replacement from a certain population of $\tilde{\varepsilon}_i$-values having mean 0 and variance σ_i^2, it can be shown that *the OLS estimators of the parameters of each reduced form equation are unbiased and consistent.* If, in addition, the distribution of $\tilde{\varepsilon}_i$-values is normal, *tests and confidence intervals for a parameter as well as interval forecasts can be calculated in the manner described in Section 3.5.* In other words, OLS is a perfectly satisfactory method of estimation and inference concerning the parameters of the reduced form equations.

Thus, the OLS estimators of Eqs. 13.2, 13.3, and 13.4 not only fit best the values of *TEMP*, *WIND*, and *GASCON* (in the sense of least squares) but have the additional desirable properties of single-equation OLS estimators.[3]

However, another method for estimating the parameters of a reduced form equation is preferred to OLS when the errors $\tilde{\varepsilon}_1, \tilde{\varepsilon}_2, \ldots, \tilde{\varepsilon}_l$ are correlated and the number of observations is large. This method is known as SUR, for *seemingly unrelated regression* equations estimation.

---

[3]Since the δ's are related to the β's and γ's and hence also to one another, a case can be made that constrained rather than ordinary LS ought to be applied. For example, it may be that, say, δ_{42} is equal to $2\delta_{13}$; therefore, the estimation method should ensure that the estimate of the latter is twice that of the former parameter. In practice, however, these constraints are seldom observed.

Refer again to Example 13.1, and note that the reduced form errors, $\tilde{\varepsilon}_i$, are related to the structural form errors, ε_i, since

$$\tilde{\varepsilon}_1 = \varepsilon_1$$
$$\tilde{\varepsilon}_2 = \varepsilon_2$$
$$\tilde{\varepsilon}_3 = -\beta_{31}\varepsilon_1 - \beta_{32}\varepsilon_2 + \varepsilon_3$$

$\tilde{\varepsilon}_1$ and $\tilde{\varepsilon}_3$ are related because both depend on ε_1. So are $\tilde{\varepsilon}_2$ and $\tilde{\varepsilon}_3$ because both depend on ε_2. If the ε's are independent, according to Appendix A.12 $Cov(\tilde{\varepsilon}_1, \tilde{\varepsilon}_2) = 0$, $Cov(\tilde{\varepsilon}_1, \tilde{\varepsilon}_3) = -\beta_{31}\sigma_1^2$, and $Cov(\tilde{\varepsilon}_2, \tilde{\varepsilon}_3) = -\beta_{32}\sigma_2^2$, where σ_1^2 and σ_2^2 are the variances of ε_1 and ε_2, respectively.

The $\tilde{\varepsilon}$'s, we conclude, are functions of the ε's and may be related to one another even when the latter are independent. In some applied studies, when the reduced form equations are estimated by OLS and the residuals, $\hat{\tilde{\varepsilon}}_i = Y_i - \hat{Y}_i$, of each equation are calculated, sizable correlations are sometimes observed between some pairs $(\hat{\tilde{\varepsilon}}_i, \hat{\tilde{\varepsilon}}_j)$, suggesting that the corresponding pairs $(\tilde{\varepsilon}_i, \tilde{\varepsilon}_j)$ are correlated.

The SUR method proceeds in three steps. First, OLS is applied to each reduced form equation Y_i and the residuals $\hat{\tilde{\varepsilon}}_i$ are calculated. Second, the variance of each $\tilde{\varepsilon}_i$ and the covariance of each pair $(\tilde{\varepsilon}_i, \tilde{\varepsilon}_j)$ are estimated by $Var(\hat{\tilde{\varepsilon}}_i)$ and $Cov(\hat{\tilde{\varepsilon}}_i, \hat{\tilde{\varepsilon}}_j)$, respectively. Last, these estimated variances and covariances are used to apply GLS to the entire system of equations.[4] Although difficult to execute by hand, the SUR method can easily be implemented with the help of a computer program.

It can be shown that *the SUR estimators are not unbiased, but they are consistent and have smaller variances than the corresponding OLS estimators when the number of observations is large.* SUR is not necessarily superior to OLS when the number of observations is small or moderate. As intuition may suggest, *SUR and OLS estimators are identical when all the estimated covariances in the second step are equal to zero.* It can also be shown that *SUR and OLS estimators are identical when all reduced form equations employ the same predetermined variables.*

---

[4]For a more detailed description of the SUR method and its properties, see, for example, Johnston (1984, Ch. 8) or Pindyck and Rubinfeld (1991, Ch. 11). GLS is the generalized least squares method described in Section 9.6.

EXAMPLE 13.1 (CONTINUED)

In Table 13.2, we compare OLS and SUR estimates for the Norgas example using the data in Table 13.1. The SUR estimates were obtained using proc syslin of program SAS.[5]

The numbers in parentheses are t-ratios (that is, ratios of the estimate of the parameter and its estimated standard deviation). In the case of OLS, the t-ratios have the familiar interpretation. In the case of SUR estimates, however, the estimated standard deviation of a parameter is calculated using a formula that is valid only when the number of observations is large. This is not the case here (the number of observations is 26), so the t-ratios should not be relied upon excessively. ∎

EXAMPLE 13.2

Country S has about one-tenth the population of neighboring Country L. At present, there is free trade in Commodity X between the two countries. The two countries trade X only with each other and not with any other country. In what follows, we shall develop a simple model to explain the price, demand, and supply of X in country S, as well as the net exports (the difference between

TABLE 13.2   Estimates of Reduced Form Equations, Example 13.1

Endogenous variable	Method	CONST	FTEMP	FWIND	R^2	S
TEMP	OLS	−0.326 (−1.17)	0.914 (25.67)		0.965	1.410
	SUR	−0.329 (−1.18)	0.912 (25.88)			
WIND	OLS	−0.145 (−0.07)		0.827 (4.95)	0.505	3.406
	SUR	−0.165 (−0.09)		0.828 (5.01)		
GASCON	OLS	23608 (17.59)	−791.813 (−13.12)	97.704 (0.83)	0.894	2298
	SUR	23152 (37.91)	−855.421 (−20.91)	141.061 (2.28)		

NOTE: t-ratios shown in parentheses.

[5]The SAS statements are proc syslin sur; endogenous temp wind gascon; instruments ftemp fwind; model temp = ftemp; model wind = fwind; model gascon = temp wind;.

exports and imports) from S to L. The situation is illustrated in Figure 13.3, where D indicates a demand and S a supply function.

Let us begin in Country L and imagine that in a certain period the price is P. Because of the free trade in X, the price in S (at the prevailing exchange rate) must be the same. At price P, the quantity demanded in S is Q_d and the quantity supplied Q_s. The difference $Q_s - Q_d$ is exported to L.

If the price in L were P', the quantity demanded in S is Q_d' and the quantity supplied Q_s'. The difference $Q_d' - Q_s'$ is imported from L.

Of course, any exports to or imports from S will change the domestic supply in L and the price there in the next period. But if the quantity exported or imported is very small in relation to L's domestic supply, this "ripple" effect can be overlooked and it may be assumed that the price P is determined entirely by the domestic demand and supply in L. Under these conditions, therefore, variations in P will trace the demand and supply functions in S.

A linear model of demand and supply in S can be written as follows:

$$Q_d = \delta_{10} + \delta_{11}P + \tilde{\varepsilon}_1 \quad \text{(demand)}$$
$$Q_s = \delta_{20} + \delta_{21}P + \tilde{\varepsilon}_1 \quad \text{(supply)}$$

Q_d and Q_s are the two endogenous variables, and P is the single predetermined variable. The system equations describe the reduced form of the model, which, in this example, is identical to the structural form.

By way of illustration, consider the hypothetical data shown in Table 13.3.[6]

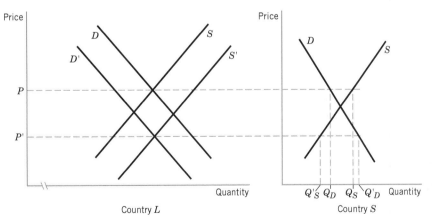

FIGURE 13.3 Demand, supply, and net exports, Example 13.2

---

[6]The data of this example are fictitious, but an application of the method illustrated will be found in Section 13.8.

TABLE 13.3 Data for Example 13.2

Year	Consumption (million lbs.) D	Production (million lbs.) S	Net exports (million lbs.) NE	Price ($ S) P
1	441	450	9	29
2	413	492	79	33
3	461	437	−24	25
4	431	465	34	29
5	454	458	5	28
6	500	424	−76	23
7	490	434	−56	24
8	463	468	5	29
9	479	444	−34	26
10	499	418	−81	22

The commodity X is—let us say—potatoes, and D and S represent, respectively, the year's consumption and production in S. Positive values of NE indicate exports to L, negative values imports from L.

Under the assumptions of this example, the demand function in S can be estimated by regressing D against P and the supply function by regressing S against P. The OLS results are as follows:

$$D = 679.83 - 8.087\,P \qquad R^2 = 0.875$$
$$(23.31)\ (-7.48) \qquad S = 11$$
$$S = 276.20 + 6.448\,P \qquad R^2 = 0.951$$
$$((19.82)\ (12.49) \qquad S = 5$$

The estimated consumption ($\hat{D}$), production ($\hat{S}$), and net exports ($\widehat{NE} = \hat{S} - \hat{D}$) for the observed prices P are shown in Table 13.4. Actual and estimated net exports are plotted in Figure 13.4.

The estimated demand and supply functions can also be used to calculate the price that would prevail in S if for some reason trade between the two countries were halted (for example, by imposing a ban on exports and imports in S or L). The market clearing price in S is that price at which the quantity demanded equals the quantity supplied, or

$$679.83 - 8.09\,P = 276.20 + 6.45\,P$$

or

$$14.54\,P = 403.67$$

TABLE 13.4   Estimated Values, Example 13.2

Year	P	$\hat{S}$	$\hat{D}$	$\widehat{NE} = \hat{S} - \hat{D}$
1	29	463.192	445.307	17.885
2	33	488.984	412.959	76.025
3	25	437.400	477.655	−40.255
4	29	463.192	445.307	17.885
5	28	456.744	453.394	3.350
6	23	424.504	493.829	−69.325
7	24	430.952	485.742	−54.790
8	29	463.192	445.307	17.885
9	26	443.848	469.568	−25.720
10	22	418.056	501.916	−83.860

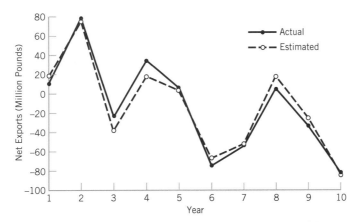

FIGURE 13.4   Actual and estimated net exports, Example 13.2

which yields $P = 27.76$. At that price, 455.25 (million lbs.) of commodity X would be produced and consumed in country S. ∎

13.7   ESTIMATION OF STRUCTURAL FORM PARAMETERS

The structural equations express beliefs about the system under study. Estimates of their parameters are desired primarily in order to check the model's agreement with prior expectations. For example, in the Norgas example, it is believed that the coefficient of *TEMP* in the *GASCON* structural equation is negative and that of *WIND* positive; it is expected that the estimates of these coefficients will agree with these beliefs.

It would again appear that the straightforward estimation method is OLS applied to each structural equation separately, as was illustrated with Example 13.1. The properties of OLS, however, as well as those of other methods we shall describe shortly, depend on the nature of the structural errors ε_1, ε_2, ..., ε_I. We shall distinguish two situations, depending on whether or not these errors are independent of one another.[7]

(A) Independent $\varepsilon_1, \varepsilon_2, \ldots, \varepsilon_I$

The simplest situation is that in which there is no relationship between any given error term ε_i and any other error ε_j. It is assumed that the error values for the ith structural equation are generated as if by random draws with replacement from a population of ε_i-values having mean zero and a certain variance σ_i^2.

Ordinary Least Squares (OLS)   For the situation just described, it can be shown that *the OLS estimators are neither unbiased nor consistent in general, but are consistent if the system of equations is recursive.*

Thus, the OLS estimators of Eqs. 13.1, 13.2, and 13.3 are consistent because the system of Example 13.1 is recursive. These estimates are repeated in Table 13.5 and will be compared to estimates obtained by other methods.

When the system is not recursive, there is no known method that gives unbiased estimators, but there are two methods producing consistent ones—indirect least squares and two-stage least squares.

Indirect Least Squares (ILS)   The method involves two steps. In the first, OLS is used to estimate the parameters of the reduced form equations. In the second step, the ILS estimates of the parameters of the structural equations are calculated by applying the known relationships between the β's, γ's, and δ's and their estimates.

EXAMPLE 13.1 (CONTINUED)

Eqs. 13.2, 13.3, and 13.4 utilize the OLS estimates of the parameters of the three equations of the reduced form in the Norgas example. The relationships between structural and reduced form parameters were listed after Eq. 13.6. Denoting by b, c, and d the ILS estimate of a β-, γ-, and δ-coefficient, respectively, we

---

[7]For more details concerning the results summarized in this section see, for example, Johnston (1984, Ch. 11), Theil (1971, Ch. 10), or Pindyck and Rubinfeld (1991, Ch. 11).

TABLE 13.5 Estimates of Parameters of Structural Form, Example 13.1

Dependent variable	Method	CONST	TEMP	WIND	FTEMP	FWIND
TEMP	OLS[a]	−0.326 (−1.17)			0.914 (25.67)	
	3SLS	−0.329 (−1.18)			0.912 (25.85)	
	FIML	−0.329 (−1.23)			0.912 (26.91)	
WIND	OLS[a]	−0.145 (−0.07)				0.827 (4.95)
	3SLS	−0.127 (−0.07)				0.825 (4.99)
	FIML	−0.127 (−0.07)				0.825 (5.19)
GASCON	OLS	22952 (36.59)	−862.72 (−20.90)	162.574 (2.53)		
	ILS	23342 (*)	−866.313 (*)	112.092 (*)		
	2SLS	23357 (26.97)	−861.137 (−19.60)	117.236 (1.25)		
	3SLS	23354 (27.87)	−856.925 (−20.07)	118.080 (1.31)		
	FIML	23355 (30.15)	−857.006 (−21.94)	118.038 (1.42)		

[a]OLS = ILS = 2SLS. t-ratios in parentheses.
*Not calculated by computer program.

find: $c_{10} = d_{10} = -0.326$, $c_{11} = d_{11} = 0.914$, $c_{20} = d_{20} = -0.145$, $c_{22} = d_{22} = 0.827$, and

$$b_{31} = -\frac{d_{31}}{c_{31}} = -\frac{-791.81}{0.914} = 866.313$$

$$b_{32} = -\frac{d_{32}}{c_{32}} = -\frac{97.7}{0.827} = -112.092$$

$$c_{30} = d_{30} + b_{31}c_{10} + b_{32}c_{20}$$
$$= 23608 + (866.313)(-0.326) + (-112.092)(-0.145)$$
$$= 23342$$

Thus, the ILS estimate of the GASCON structural equation is

$$GASCON = 23342 - 866.313\,TEMP + 112.092\,WIND$$

In Example 13.1, each structural parameter is uniquely determined as a function of the reduced form parameters. All structural equations are said to be *exactly identified*. In general, however, the relationships may yield one, many, or no solutions for a structural parameter in terms of the reduced form parameters. In the latter two cases, the structural parameter and the equation in which it is embedded are said to be *overidentified* and *underidentified*, respectively.[8]

The ILS method can be applied to estimate identifiable parameters and traditionally is used only for exactly identified parameters, although, technically speaking, any one solution of an overidentified parameter is a consistent estimator of that parameter.

Two-Stage Least Squares (2SLS) This second method for obtaining consistent estimators of an identifiable structural equation involves—as the name suggests—two stages. In the first stage, OLS is applied to regress each endogenous variable Y_i against all predetermined variables and to obtain the estimated values, $\hat{Y}_i$, of that variable. In the second stage, any other endogenous variable Y_j appearing in the structural equation for Y_i is replaced by its estimated value $\hat{Y}_j$, and OLS is again applied to the modified equation.

EXAMPLE 13.1 (CONTINUED)

Regressing *TEMP* against *FTEMP* and *FWIND*, we find

$$\widehat{TEMP} = -0.2837 + 0.91377\,FTEMP - 0.00396\,FWIND$$

Regressing *WIND* and *GASCON* against the same two predetermined variables, we get

$$\widehat{WIND} = 0.056 - 0.04209\,FTEMP + 0.8043\,FWIND$$
$$\widehat{GASCON} = 23608 - 791.81\,FTEMP + 97.7\,FWIND$$

In the second stage, we regress *GASCON* against $\widehat{TEMP}$ and $\widehat{WIND}$ to find

$$GASCON = 23357 - 861.14\,\widehat{TEMP} + 117.2\,\widehat{WIND}$$

This is the 2SLS estimate of the *GASCON* structural equation. The other two structural equations for the endogenous variables *TEMP* and *WIND* have only predetermined variables on the right-hand side, so the 2SLS estimates are the same as the OLS estimates given by Eqs. 13.2 and 13.3.

---

[8] In the literature of econometrics, the conditions under which a structural equation is exactly identified, overidentified, or underidentified are studied under the heading of *the identification problem*.

Computer programs implementing 2SLS also produce estimates of the standard deviations and *t*-ratios of the parameters. Those shown in Table 13.5 were obtained using `proc syslin` of program SAS.[9]   ■

2SLS estimators are not unbiased. When a structural equation is a function of predetermined variables only (as happens with the *TEMP* and *WIND* equations of Example 13.1) OLS, ILS, and 2SLS estimators are identical.

(B) Dependent $\varepsilon_1, \varepsilon_2, \ldots, \varepsilon_I$

It is now assumed that the error values of $\varepsilon_1, \varepsilon_2, \ldots, \varepsilon_I$ are generated as if by random draws with replacement from a joint distribution of the ε's having the property that the mean of the distribution of each ε_i is zero. The most widely used methods in this situation are three-stage least squares (3SLS) and full information maximum likelihood (FIML).

Three-stage least squares (3SLS)   The method can be thought to involve three stages, although computer programs perform the calculations in one stage. In the first stage, 2SLS is applied to each structural equation Y_i, and the residuals $\hat{\varepsilon}_i = Y_i - \hat{Y}_i$ are calculated. In the second, the covariance of each pair $(\varepsilon_i, \varepsilon_j)$ is estimated by the $Cov(\hat{\varepsilon}_i, \hat{\varepsilon}_j)$. Finally, in the third stage, GLS is applied to the entire system of equations.

3SLS is a complicated estimation method and is quite difficult to execute by hand. However, computer programs can perform the calculations with speed and ease.

It can be shown that *3SLS estimators are not unbiased but are consistent and, when the number of observations is large, have smaller variances than 2SLS estimators.* It can also be shown that 3SLS and 2SLS are identical when all the estimated covariances in the second stage are zero.

EXAMPLE 13.1 (CONTINUED)

The 3SLS estimates of the three structural equations of the Norgas example, obtained using `proc syslin` of program SAS, are shown in Table 13.5.   ■

Full information maximum likelihood (FIML)   This method requires that the joint distribution of $\varepsilon_1, \varepsilon_2, \ldots, \varepsilon_I$ be multivariate normal. The FIML estimators are the values of the structural parameters that maximize the probability of obtaining the observed values of the endogenous variables (see Appendix B.7 for an outline of this method). From the computational point of view, it is the most expensive of all the methods presented in this chapter.

---

[9]The SAS statements are the same as for the SUR estimates, except that the first statement is `proc syslin 2sls;`.

EXAMPLE 13.1 (CONTINUED)

The FIML estimates of the structural equations in the Norgas illustration, obtained using `proc syslin` of program SAS, are shown in Table 13.5.[10] ∎

FIML estimators can be shown to be consistent. When the number of observations is large, the variances of FIML and 3SLS estimators are approximately equal. Since the 3SLS method does not require the normality assumption and is computationally cheaper, it is preferred to FIML in this situation.

13.8 CASE: THE CANADIAN MEAT PROCESSING INDUSTRY

In the early 1970s, the Canadian meat processing industry was the focus of great public concern because of the rapid rise in meat prices. Since Canada was a net exporter of beef and pork, it was argued that meat prices could be reduced by curtailing exports, thereby forcing the producers of livestock and meat to sell their entire supply in the domestic market. Undoubtedly, prices would have beeen reduced in the short run in order to allow the additional domestic supply to be absorbed. However, the magnitude of this reduction and the long-run effects of this policy would depend on the producers' as well as the consumers' reactions—and these were not obvious. A multiequation model of the industry was used to estimate the effects of a no-trade policy in beef and cattle. Specifically, the question was, What would have been the Canadian prices of cattle and beef, the per capita consumption of beef, the cattle inventories and beef supply if—other things being equal—a ban on exports and imports of cattle and beef were in effect for a number of years?

The model consisted of 16 equations explaining the Canadian prices of cattle and pigs, the wholesale and retail prices and the per capita consumption of beef and pork, the wages and level of employment in the meat processing industry, the inventories and supply of cattle and pigs, and the production of beef and pork. Net exports was estimated as the difference between domestic production and demand.

In view of the proximity of and the close economic ties and low tariffs between the United States and Canada—and the fact that the former is a market more than ten times the size of the latter—it was hypothesized that U.S. prices determine Canadian prices. The most important exogenous variables, therefore, were the U.S. prices of cattle and pigs; others were the tariff rates on meat exports and imports, the deflated Canadian per capita personal disposable income, the prices of feed and of commodities and services used by

---

[10]The SAS statements for 3SLS and FIML are the same as for the SUR estimates, except that the first statement is `proc syslin 3sls;` and `proc syslin fiml;`, respectively.

farmers, and the prices and consumption of veal and lamb. The model formed a nearly recursive system of equations, and its structural equations were estimated primarily by OLS using data for the period 1950 to 1970.

We do not present here the estimated equations because the numbers are many and of little interest in themselves.[11] Figures 13.5 to 13.9, however, give an idea of the degree of success of the model in explaining the endogenous variables in the period 1950–70 and forecasting their 1971 values (the estimates and forecasts were calculated using the estimated equations and the values of the exogenous variables only). The net exports of beef and pork shown in Figures 13.8 and 13.9, in particular, deserve attention; they are estimated as the difference between Canadian production and consumption, both of which quantities are large in relation to net exports. Even small errors in estimating production and consumption magnify errors in net exports.

It was assumed that a no-trade policy in beef came into effect in 1960. In the manner of Example 13.2, the quantity of beef produced can be expressed as a function of the price of cattle and other variables. Similarly, the domestic demand for beef can be expressed as a function of the price of cattle and other

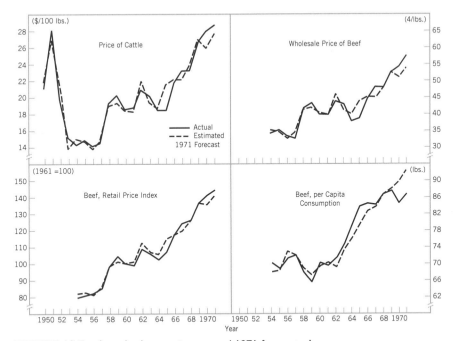

FIGURE 13.5 Actual values, estimates, and 1971 forecasts, I

[11] These can be found in P. Tryfos, *An Economic Model of the Canadian Red Meat System for Policy Analysis*, Ottawa: The Agricultural Economics Research Council of Canada, 1974.

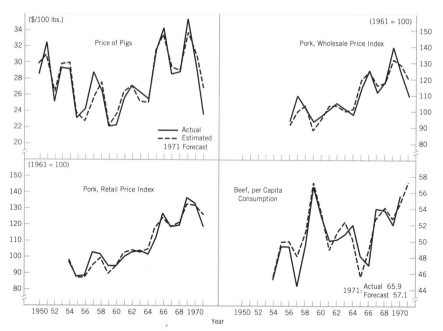

FIGURE 13.6 Actual values, estimates, and 1971 forecasts, II

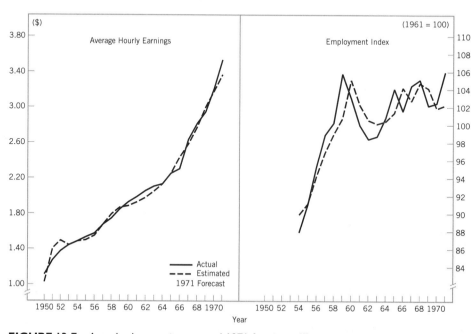

FIGURE 13.7 Actual values, estimates, and 1971 forecasts, III

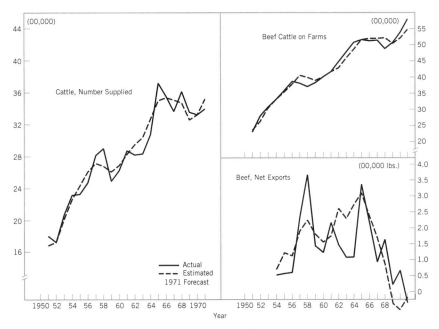

FIGURE 13.8 Actual values, estimates, and 1971 forecasts, IV

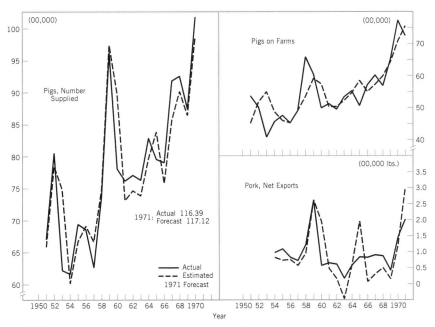

FIGURE 13.9 Actual values, estimates, and 1971 forecasts, V

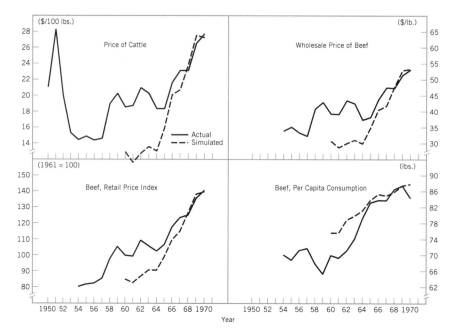

FIGURE 13.10 Simulation of no-trade policy, I

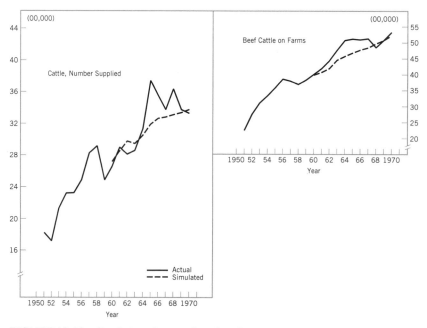

FIGURE 13.11 Simulation of no-trade policy, II

variables. Under the no-trade policy, the market clearing price of cattle is that price at which Canadian demand equals production. Backward substitution yields estimates of wholesale and retail prices as well as of consumption and inventories. All other variables are assumed to take their actual values. The results of this simulation are shown in Figures 13.10 and 13.11.

Prices, it will be noted, are reduced drastically in 1960, the year the no-trade policy is initiated. In relation to the actual 1960 values, the price of cattle is reduced by 30%, while the wholesale and retail prices of beef are reduced by 22 and 16%, respectively. The period of low prices, however, is short lived. Beginning in 1965, prices rise rapidly until by 1970 they reach the levels actually observed. As can be seen from the simulation results, the price increase can be attributed mainly to the relative decrease in supply due to a reduction in the rate of increase of cattle inventories.

13.9 TO SUM UP

- A variable is called *endogenous* if it is explained by one of the system's equations, and *predetermined* if it is determined outside the system or is a lagged endogenous variable.

- A system is in *structural form* if each equation expresses an endogenous variable as a function of predetermined and other endogenous variables. It is in *reduced form* if each equation expresses an endogenous variable as a function of predetermined variables only.

- A system in structural form is called *recursive* if its equations can be arranged so that the first is a function of predetermined variables only, the second a function of the predetermined and the first endogenous variable only, the third a function of the predetermined and first two endogenous variables only, and so on.

- Normally, the reduced form is estimated when (a) the main purpose of the study is to forecast the endogenous variables and there is no particular interest in the structural equations, or (b) the system is already in reduced form and there are no structural equations to estimate.

- If the error term of each reduced form equation satisfies the assumptions of linearity, constant variance, and independence, the OLS estimators of the parameters of each equation are unbiased and consistent. If the normality assumption is also satisfied, tests and confidence intervals for a parameter as well as interval forecasts can be calculated in the usual manner.

- The method of *seemingly unrelated regression (SUR)* equations is preferable to OLS if the reduced form errors are correlated and the number of observations is large, in which case the SUR estimators are consistent and have smaller variance than the OLS estimators.

- The structural equations express beliefs about the system under study. Estimates of their parmaters are desired primarily in order to check the model's agreement with prior expectations.

- When the error terms of the structural equations are independent, the OLS estimators are neither unbiased nor consistent in general but are consistent if the system is recursive. When the system is not recursive, there is no known method giving unbiased estimators; consistent estimators, however, are given by either *indirect least squares (ILS)* or *two-stage least squares (2SLS)*.

- When the error terms of the structural equations are dependent, consistent estimators are given by the methods of *three-stage least squares (3SLS)* or *full information maximum likelihood (FIML)*.

PROBLEMS

13.1 Using a suitable computer program and the data in the file `gascon1.dat`, confirm the OLS, SUR, 2SLS, 3SLS, and FIML estimates shown in Tables 13.2 and 13.5.

13.2 In Example 2.4, OLS was applied to estimate the per capita demands for beef (QB) and pork (QP) as functions of the deflated retail prices of beef (DPB), pork (DPP), and other meats (DPOM) and the per capita personal disposable income (DPDI):

$$QB \approx () + ()DPB + ()DPP + ()DPOM + ()DPDI$$
$$QP \approx () + ()DPB + ()DPP + ()DPOM + ()DPDI$$

The data are listed in Table 2.6 and can be found in the file `bfpk.dat`. (The data and demand functions are indeed a part of the model of the Canadian meat processing industry described in Section 13.8.)

(a) Identify the endogenous and exogenous variables. Is the system of equations in reduced or structural form?

(b) Is there any advantage to estimating the system equations by the SUR method? Explain.

(c) Determine the SUR estimates of the parameters of the demand equations and compare them to the OLS estimates.

(d) Same as (c), except assume DPP does not influence QB, and DPB does not influence QP. Is this assumption warranted?

(e) Would you consider estimating the demand functions by ILS, 2SLS, 3SLS, or FIML in this case? Explain.

13.3 The file `airline.dat` partially listed in Table 6.17 includes the values of two variables each month from January 19X1 to December 19X5:

TATL: Average daily number of passengers on transatlantic flights

TCONT: Average daily number of passengers on transcontinental flights

(a) In Example 6.2 and Problem 6.12, each variable was expressed as a linear function of time and dummy variables representing the months and the Easter holiday. The resulting equations were estimated by OLS. Under what conditions is SUR a better estimation method?

(b) Determine whether or not SUR is a better estimation method than OLS.

(c) Estimate the two equations in (a) by the SUR method. Compare the OLS and SUR estimates.

13.4 (Due to Mr. Zaimin Lu) Table 13.6 shows a partial listing of the file `liquor.dat`. The file contains 60 observations from January 19X0 to December 19X4.

The variables have the following interpretation:

MONTH: Month number

DSHIP: Shipments of distilled spirits, in current $000

BSHIP: Shipments of beer, in current $000

WSHIP: Shipments of wine, in current $000

DIND: Price index of distilled spirits

BIND: Price index of beer

WIND: Price index of wine

The same data were used in Problem 6.20, where the shipments of the three types of spirits were analyzed by time series methods. Unlike Problem 6.20, consider the following system of equations:

$$DSHIP/DIND \approx () + ()DIND$$
$$BSHIP/BIND \approx () + ()BIND$$
$$WSHIP/WIND \approx () + ()WIND$$

TABLE 13.6 File `liquor.dat`, Partial Listing

MONTH	DSHIP	BSHIP	WSHIP	DIND	BIND	WIND
1	44400	68321	8415	148.1	242.8	196.0
2	40515	75213	8538	147.8	257.8	196.0
3	48001	87297	9772	149.1	257.8	198.6
4	46574	103200	12309	158.9	259.7	212.4
5	51948	121061	12668	158.8	260.8	212.8
...	...	...	...	...	...	...

In other words, the index of real shipments of each type of spirits is assumed to be a linear function of its price index.

(a) Identify the endogenous and predetermined variables. Is the above system in structural or reduced form? What are the expected signs of the coefficients of the explanatory variables?

(b) Determine whether OLS or a different estimation method is appropriate, and estimate the equations by that method.

13.5 Same as Problem 13.4, except the system of equations is as follows:

$$DSHIP/DIND \approx () + ()T + ()M2 + \cdots + ()M12$$
$$BSHIP/BIND \approx () + ()T + ()M2 + \cdots + ()M12$$
$$WSHIP/WIND \approx () + ()T + ()M2 + \cdots + ()M12$$

where T is time in months, and $M2$ to $M12$ are dummy variables representing the months February to December. Compare the model of this problem with that of Problem 13.4.

13.6 Same as Problem 13.4, except the system of equations is as follows:

$$DSHIP/DIND \approx () + ()T + ()M2 + \cdots + ()M12 + ()DIND$$
$$BSHIP/BIND \approx () + ()T + ()M2 + \cdots + ()M12 + ()BIND$$
$$WSHIP/WIND \approx () + ()T + ()M2 + \cdots + ()M12 + ()WIND$$

where T is time in months, and $M2$ to $M12$ are dummy variables representing February to December. Compare the model of this problem with those of Problems 13.4 and 13.5.

13.7 Refer to Problem 6.21. Consider the following model for forecasting simultaneously the weekly number of pharmacy (RXNO) and nonpharmacy (FSNO) customers:

$$FSNO \approx () + ()WEEK + ()AUG + \cdots + ()JUN + ()SWEEK + ()NOCIGS + ()RXNO$$
$$RXNO \approx () + ()WEEK + ()AUG + \cdots + ()JUN + ()FSNO$$

Forecast FSNO and RXNO in week no. 83 (the first week of April), assuming SWEEK=1 and NOCIGS=1.

13.8 In Problem 7.4, you were asked to consider the possibility that in the Lydia E. Pinkham case described in Example 7.3 the correlation between advertising and sales was not due to advertising influencing sales but vice versa. There is, of course, another possibility, namely, that this period's sales are influenced by current and past advertising *and* this period's advertising is determined by past sales. A simple version of this model is described by two equations:

$$SALES \approx () + ()ADV + ()ADV_{-1} + ()D1 + ()D2 + ()D3$$
$$ADV \approx () + ()SALES_{-1},$$

where $()$ denotes an unnamed parameter. ADV_{-1} and $SALES_{-1}$ are, of course, the previous year's advertising and sales. $D1$ to $D3$ are dummy variables defined in Example 7.3. The data for this problem are contained in the file `lydia.dat`.

(a) Identify the endogenous and predetermined variables of this model. Is the system of equations in recursive or structural form?

(b) What are the properties of the OLS estimators in this case? Explain.

(c) Estimate the system equations using OLS.

(d) Estimate the equations using 2SLS. Compare the results with the OLS results.

(e) Estimate the equations using (i) 3SLS and (ii) FIML. Compare the results with those in (c) and (d).

(f) Revise the equations so as to improve the model, and estimate the parameters using the most appropriate method.

13.9 The file `housing.dat`, partially listed in Table 7.6, contains the number of housing permits issued (*PERMITS*), the number of housing units started (*STARTS*), and the number of housing units completed (*COMPLETIONS*) in each of 312 consecutive months. A simple model of the relationship between the three variables is

$$STARTS \approx () + ()PERMITS + ()PERMITS_{-1}$$
$$COMPLETIONS \approx () + ()STARTS + ()STARTS_{-1}$$

where () indicates an unnamed parameter.

(a) Identify the endogenous and predetermined variables of this model. Is the system of equations in recursive or structural form?

(b) What are the properties of the OLS estimators in this case? Explain.

(c) Estimate the system equations using OLS.

(d) Estimate the equations using 2SLS. Compare the results with the OLS results.

(e) Estimate the equations using (i) 3SLS and (ii) FIML. Compare the results with those in (c) and (d).

(f) Revise the equations so as to improve the model, and estimate the parameters using the most appropriate method.

PART II

CASES

THE EQUAL BILLING PLAN

A natural gas utility is promoting an Equal Billing Plan (EBP) for its residential customers. The plan is described in Figure 1.

As the person responsible for the successful operation of the EBP, you are asked to consider exactly how the EBP monthly installment for a given customer should be determined.

Your recommendations must be sufficiently detailed that they can be implemented by the staff without confusion. You have considerable freedom in determining the best course of action but must respect the following guidelines.

- EBP must be—despite apparent claims to the contrary—a break-even operation.
- The EBP monthly installment for each participating customer will be reviewed each August and will be fixed from September to August of the following year. No mid-year adjustments are allowed. Also in August, any deficit or surplus accumulated over the preceding 12-month period will be billed to the customer.
- Customers will not be charged or credited with interest on accumulated balances.

The accounting department of the gas utility maintains records of the quantity of gas used each month in each home served by the company over the past ten years. The records also show the number and type of gas-utilizing appliances in use in each home over this period (e.g., furnace, water heater, etc.).

♠ WHAT IS THE EQUAL BILLING PLAN?

It is a system of 12 equal billing payments that allows you to know in advance what your monthly gas bill will be, so you can budget accordingly.

How do we arrive at the specific monthly payments for your home? Well, we estimate your annual consumption based on several factors: size of your furnace. . . consumption of similar homes in your neighborhood. . . or on actual meter readings we have on your account. We put all this information together and work on the equal billing plan for your home.

♠ WHY SHOULD YOU SAY "YES"?

If you would like to know what your charges are going to be with no surprises, then EBP is for you. Each month your bill will be the same. Your monthly budget calculations are made easy with EBP.

We'll review your account on a regular basis and if your EBP is out of line with your actual gas usage, your monthly installment will be revised. In addition, if there is any adjustment up or down between the actual cost of gas and the total of your Equal Billing Plan instalments at the end of 12 months, that adjustment will appear in your August gas bill.

♠ A TYPICAL CUSTOMER'S MONTHLY BILLS FOR GAS USED

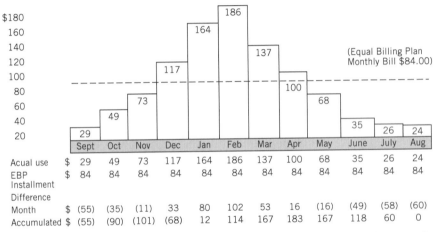

	Sept	Oct	Nov	Dec	Jan	Feb	Mar	Apr	May	June	July	Aug
Acual use	$ 29	49	73	117	164	186	137	100	68	35	26	24
EBP Installment	$ 84	84	84	84	84	84	84	84	84	84	84	84
Difference Month	$ (55)	(35)	(11)	33	80	102	53	16	(16)	(49)	(58)	(60)
Accumulated	$ (55)	(90)	(101)	(68)	12	114	167	183	167	118	60	0

Does the gas company make money on the EBP customers' payments, because it seems they are paying for gas before they use it?

Using the typical customers bill as an example, you can see (below) that the customer is in a credit position (ahead of gas use) for only the first four months of an average heating season, but the Company must then pay interest on borrowing the money the customer owes for the remaining 8 months of the year.

	Sept	Oct	Nov	Dec	Jan	Feb	Mar	Apr	May	June	July	Aug	Accum. total
Interest at 9% p.a.	(.41)	(.68)	(.76)	(.51)	.09	1.15	1.25	1.37	1.25	.88	.45	0	$4.08

In this example it would cost the Company $4.08 in interest charges to maintain the customer on EBP.

We consider this cost well worthwhile since it enables the Company to accurately forecast its cash flow, and reduces customer bad debts.

Remember, to say "yes" to the Equal Billing Plan, complete the postage paid card below, and mail it to us. We make it easy for you to say "yes."

FIGURE I   The Equal Billing Plan

CORPORATE COMPENSATION AND DISCRIMINATION

Inequities in the compensation of women and members of minority groups have led to the establishment of federal legislation requiring fair and equitable employment practices, including equal pay for work of equal value and fairness in promotional opportunities. To comply with this legislation, companies must develop objective and quantifiable criteria under which compensation for all positions is based on the skill, effort, responsibility, and working conditions required of the job.

The following is the verbatim text of an internal report assessing the compliance of a federally regulated corporation in its compensation practices.[1]

You are invited to comment on this report and, if necessary, to revise it. The data used are in the file compens.dat. *A partial listing of this file is given in Figure ?? at the end of this case.*

PURPOSE

The purpose of this study is to analyze the various effects of certain explanatory variables on the dependent variable, annual salary. Given that discrimination of protected groups in any form is a punishable offense, it is imperative that compensation be based on nonbiased criteria.

It is this corporation's policy to compensate employees based on their job level, length of service, time on post, performance assessment, and educational background. Therefore, these factors and these factors only should determine what an employee receives as annual salary. Using statistical analysis will help to show the effects of certain variables and attributes on annual salary. Specifically, running a regression using a variety of explanatory variables will help to determine if annual salary in this corporation is based on the criteria as outlined in its policy or if indeed other factors play a role. Of immediate interest is the influence of attributes that by law are not considered as compensable factors.

---

[1]This case is based on a project by Mr. Andre Craig.

METHOD

The environment consists of 106 employees who work in a variety of departments, ranging from clerical to managerial and from technical to customer service related. Employee profiles for each employee were printed off with all the relevant variables and attributes listed on each.

The annual salary (SALARY), job level (LEVEL), length of service (LENSERV), time on post (TOP), most recent performance appraisal rating (PAR), last PAR (LPAR), second last PAR (SLPAR), sex, whether the employee was a high school graduate or university graduate, racial origin (described as white, asian, black, and other), and age (AGE) were recorded.

The job levels ranged from 10 to 39, length of service and time on post were measured in years, PARs were measured by the corresponding merit increase based on performance rating (i.e., a performance rating of 5 corresponds with a 5% annual salary increase, 6 corresponds with a 6% increase, 4 corresponds with a 4% increase, and so on), age is measured in years, and the remaining variables were input as dummy variables as follows: 0 for male and 1 for female under SEX, 1 for graduate and 0 for nongraduate under high school (HG) and university (UG), 1 if the employee was from a specific racial origin and 0 if not.

RESULTS

A variety of statistical calculations were carried out. Of immediate interest was the resulting regression equation of the dependent variable, salary, upon all the explanatory variables. As the racial origin categories are collectively exhaustive, the category Other was omitted and therefore used as a comparator. From the regression equation the influence of each explanatory variable on salary was estimated.

Predictor	Coeff.	Std. Dev.	t-ratio	p
Constant	−6949	3093	−2.25	0.027
LEVEL	1536.22	59.81	25.68	0.000
LENSERV	−152.38	78.67	−1.94	0.056
TOP	349.4	182.8	1.91	0.059
PAR	221.2	354.5	0.62	0.534
LPAR	−180.9	308.4	−0.59	0.559
SLPAR	259.1	256.8	1.01	0.316
SEX	−25.0	816.4	−0.03	0.976
HG	−1055	1217	−0.87	0.388
UG	648.6	870.8	0.74	0.458
WHITE	1050	1332	0.79	0.432
ASIAN	1969	1419	1.39	0.169
BLACK	1248	1461	0.85	0.395
AGE	238.90	50.34	4.75	0.000

$S = 3536$ $R^2 = 91.1\%$ $R^2(adj) = 89.9\%$

The job level has a positive effect on salary, where as the level increases by 1 salary increases by $1536. Length of service has a negative effect on salary as a service increase of one year results in $152 less in annual salary. Time on post has a positive effect where as time increases by one year salary increases by $349. The last performance appraisal rating has a negative effect on salary with a reduction in the amount of annual salary of $181 for each merit increase of 1%. The current and second-last PAR have positive effects of $221 and $259. If the employee is female she receives $25 less per annum. High school graduation decreases, while university graduation increases salary by $1055 and $649, respectively, over elementary school education. White, asian, and black receive $1055, $1969, and $1248 more than other employees, respectively. Lastly, as age increases by one year, salary increases by $239, possibly indicating the value of previous external experience.

The explanatory variables in this regression explain the total variation of the dependent variable, salary, very well in that R-squared is 91.1%.

CONCLUSION

It seems that the compensation policy of this corporation is not complying with internal equity or federal legislations. This company is compensating employees for job level, time on post, and educational background, but recent PAR and length of service have a negative effect. Moreover, there appears to be discrimination in compensation based on gender and racial origin.

OBS	SALARY	LEVEL	LENSERV	TOP	PAR	LPAR	SLPAR	SEX	HG	UG	WHITE	ASIAN	BLACK	OTHER	AGE
1	28100	19	8.2	1.2	6	6	6	0	1	1	1	0	0	0	26
2	25350	16	1.5	0.6	5	0	0	0	1	1	1	0	0	0	24
3	43200	26	18.9	6.9	5	5	4	1	1	1	1	0	0	0	48
4	43400	26	19.5	4.9	6	6	7	1	1	0	0	0	1	0	47
5	57150	33	7.2	3.2	6	6	6	0	1	1	0	1	0	0	34
6	59400	32	4.5	2.0	4	4	7	0	1	1	1	0	0	0	43
7	32200	23	8.5	0.6	6	5	5	0	1	1	0	0	0	1	31
8	51200	30	18.7	1.5	5	6	6	1	1	0	1	0	0	0	42
9	60400	33	22.6	2.5	5	5	7	0	1	0	1	0	0	0	49
10	32200	23	16.7	1.3	6	6	6	0	1	0	0	0	1	0	38

FIGURE I Data file compens.dat, partial listing

THE ABC MANUFACTURING COMPANY

The goal of Pay Equity[1] is to ensure that the pay of women is the same as that of men for work of equal value. Employment Equity was created to remove barriers in hiring, promotion, and training of persons in four designated groups: native people, people with disabilities, members of racial minorities, and women.

The ABC Manufacturing Company has 238 full-time employees. The file abc.dat contains the following information concerning these employees.

IDNO: Employee identification number

SEX: = 0 if male; = 1 if female

VMINOR: = 1 if member of visible minority; = 0 otherwise

DISAB: = 1 if disabled; = 0 otherwise

SERVICE: Years of service at ABC

AGE: Age of employee

EDUC: Level of education

   = 0, not a high school graduate

   = 1, high school graduate

   = 2, attended college

   = 3, has college degree

   = 4, has master's degree

SALARY: Annual salary ($)

PERF: Most recent performance rating:

   = 0, unacceptable

   = 1, below average

   = 2, average

   = 3, above average

   = 4, excellent

---

[1]The case is based on a project by Ms. Anna Mischinger.

JCLASS: Job class (ranges from 8 to 28 and reflects responsibility level, accountability, and job requirements)

There are no native people employed at ABC. A partial listing of the file `abc.dat` is shown in Figure 1. In the file, missing data are indicated by a period (.).

IDNO	SEX	VMINOR	DISAB	SERVICE	AGE	EDUC	SALARY	PERF	JCLASS
1	1	0	0	9	64	1	28756	2	10
2	1	0	0	20	43	1	29475	2	10
3	0	0	0	4	32	2	59750	2	20
4	1	0	0	3	31	4	82390	4	24
5	0	1	0	4	51	3	29524	2	11
6	0	0	0	1	32	2	50301	3	21
7	0	1	0	2	56	1	31559	2	14
8	0	0	0	17	43	0	47500	4	17
9	1	1	0	4	38	2	33700	4	14
10	1	1	0	4	40	1	28444	2	10

FIGURE I   Partial listing of file `abc.dat`

QUESTIONS

(1)   Determine whether or not there is pay equity at ABC. Identify any areas requiring adjustment to meet pay equity standards.

(2)   Determine whether or not there is employment equity at ABC. Identify any areas requiring adjustment to meet employment equity standards.

(3)   Comment on any other aspects of the case not covered in the preceding questions.

USED CAR PRICES

Automobile dealers[1] purchase and sell cars at weekly auctions held in various places throughout the city. These auctions are strictly for wholesale dealers; the public is not permitted to participate. The prices established at the auctions influence the prices at which used car dealers sell to the public as well as the amount of loans by banks and other financial institutions for automobile purchases.

Table 1 illustrates the format in which the established prices are reported in the industry.

The prices shown in Table 1 are for *one* model only: the Ford LTD Model 63, four-door sedan, with automatic transmission, power steering, and a V8 engine. They depend on the age and condition of the car. According to the brief explanatory notes accompanying these prices, "Extra Clean" means that the car is like new, considering its age and model; "Clean" means good overall condition; "Average," means acceptable condition; and "Rough," when the interior is acceptable (however, the car should not be a former taxi or police car).

Table 2 shows adjustments to the price for selected "extras" (such as factory air conditioning, vinyl top, stereo, sunroof) or for the absence of certain features included in the standard model (such as no automatic transmission,

TABLE I Used Prices for Ford LTD Model 63 (in $)

Model year	Extra clean	Clean	Average	Rough
19X2	1140	1025	620	–
19X3	1495	1350	870	430
19X4	1930	1800	1290	805
19X5	2405	2275	1825	1355
19X6	3270	3125	2625	2050
19X7	4360	4175	3735	–

[1] This case is based on a project by Bruce Darlington, Robert Redinger, Harry Silberberg, and Mark Zaretsky.

TABLE 2 Price Adjustments, All Ford Cars

Model year	Factory air cond.	Vinyl top	Stereo	Sunroof/ moonroof	No auto. transm.	V6	No power steering
19X2	+225				−250	−150	−75
19X3	+250				−275		
19X4	+275				−300		
19X5	+300	+50	+50				
19X6	+325	+50	+50	+200			
19X7	+325	+50	+50	+200			

no power steering, or a six-cylinder engine). These adjustments are applicable to all Ford cars, not only the Ford LTD.

A study was made of the relationship between used-car wholesale prices, on the one hand, and such characteristics of the cars as price when new, age, mileage, weight, type, and model, on the other. From the records of the two largest automobile auctions, 80 General Motors and 50 Ford medium- and large-sized cars were selected. These cars were sold in the period from January 17 to February 7, 19X8. This is usually a stable period for used car prices; prices tend to fall during September and October when the new car models are introduced and during Christmas and New Year when demand is traditionally weak. For each car in the two samples, the following variables were determined.

RATIO: Ratio of wholesale selling price at the auction to car's original suggested retail list price, expressed as a percentage

AGE: Age of car, in model years

MILES: Mileage of car, in thousands of miles

WEIGHT: Weight of car, in thousands of pounds

AIRCON: = 1, if car has air conditioning; = 0, otherwise

The weight of the car and its accessories is used as a proxy for cost of operation, maintenance, and fuel economy, on the argument that heavier cars tend to be less economical to maintain and operate.

Each car was classified according to its type into one of three categories: two-door, four-door, and other. These categories are represented by the following dummy variables:

TWODR: = 1, if car is two-door; = 0, otherwise

FOURDR: = 1, if car is four-door; = 0, otherwise

OTHERT: = 1, if car is of any other type; = 0, otherwise

All automobiles selected were equipped with power steering, power brakes, eight-cylinder engines, and automatic transmission. All GM cars had radios, but some Ford cars did not. Ford cars were classified into four model categories: LTD, Torino, Custom, and Other. GM cars were similarly classified into five model categories: Chevrolet Monte Carlo, Oldsmobile Cutlass, Chevrolet Impala, Pontiac Grand Prix, and Other.

Ford Cars:

LTD: $= 1$, if car is an LTD; $= 0$, otherwise

TORINO: $= 1$, if car is a Torino; $= 0$, otherwise

CUSTOM: $= 1$, if car is a Custom; $= 0$, otherwise

OTHERM: $= 1$, if car is any other model; $= 0$, otherwise

RADIO: $= 1$, if car has radio; $= 0$, otherwise

General Motors:

MONTEC: $= 1$, if car is a Chevrolet Monte Carlo; $= 0$, otherwise

CUTLAS: $= 1$, if car is an Oldsmobile Cutlass; $= 0$, otherwise

IMPALA: $= 1$, if car is a Chevrolet Impala; $= 0$, otherwise

GRDPRX: $= 1$, if car is a Pontiac Grand Prix; $= 0$, otherwise

OTHERM: $= 1$, if car is any other model; $= 0$, otherwise

The data can be found in two files, `ford.dat` and `gmot.dat`. Figures 1 and 2 provide a partial listing of these files.

The results of some regression models are summarized in Tables 3 and 4. In all regression runs, *log* indicates the natural logarithm of the variable; the

OBS	RATIO	AGE	MILES	WEIGHT	RADIO	AIRCON	FOURDR	OTHERD	TWODR	LTD	CUSTOM	TORINO	OTHERM
1	32.5	2	47	4.144	1	0	0	1	0	0	0	1	0
2	35.3	2	38	4.450	1	0	0	0	1	0	0	1	0
3	33.4	3	40	3.998	1	0	1	0	0	0	0	1	0
4	27.5	3	47	3.998	1	0	1	0	0	0	0	1	0
5	32.0	3	51	4.518	1	0	0	0	1	0	0	1	0
6	25.5	3	63	4.462	1	1	0	0	1	0	0	1	0
7	51.1	2	27	4.303	1	0	0	1	0	1	0	0	0

FIGURE I Partial listing, `ford.dat` file

OBS	RATIO	AGE	MILES	WEIGHT	AIRCON	TWODR	FOUR DR	OTHER	MONTE CARLO	CUTLAS CALAIS	IMP ALA	GRD PRX	OTH ERM
1	62.9	1	24	3.764	1	1	0	0	0	1	0	0	0
2	48.0	2	50	3.965	1	0	1	0	0	1	0	0	0
3	48.2	2	60	3.965	1	0	1	0	0	1	0	0	0
4	60.2	3	62	3.860	1	1	0	0	0	1	0	0	0
5	55.5	3	49	3.860	0	1	0	0	0	1	0	0	0
6	40.8	3	77	3.657	0	1	0	0	0	1	0	0	0
7	44.5	4	36	4.019	1	1	0	0	0	1	0	0	0

FIGURE 2 Partial listing, gmot.dat file

dummy variables representing two-door cars, the Cutlass GM model, and the Custom Ford model were left out.

QUESTIONS

(1) Discuss the merits and demerits of regression as a method for establishing used car prices. What are the alternatives?

(2) Select the best regression model for each make among those summarized in this case. Explain clearly the basis for your choice. Interpret the results. Forecast the resale ratio for the first used car in each file.

(3) Confirm the regression results presented in this case.

(4) Can these models be improved upon? If no, explain why. If yes, estimate your proposed model(s) and compare them with those presented in the case.

(5) Comment on any other aspects of the case not specifically covered in the preceding questions.

TABLE 3 Summary of Regression Results, Ford Cars

Explanatory variables	Dependent variable							
	RATIO		log(RATIO)		log(RATIO)		RATIO	
	Estimate	t-value	Estimate	t-value	Estimate	t-value	Estimate	t-value
AGE	−5.871	−7.34	−0.244	−9.56				
MILES	−0.413	−7.23	−0.011	−5.92				
WEIGHT	−7.204	−3.17	−0.157	−2.16				
RADIO	−0.599	−0.14	−0.148	−1.11	−0.211	−1.15	−3.173	−0.87
AIRCON	0.049	0.02	0.023	0.35	0.023	0.27	0.330	0.19
FOURDR	−2.938	−1.34	−0.081	−1.15	−0.074	−0.77	−2.579	−1.34
OTHERT	2.856	1.10	0.019	0.23	−0.046	−0.40	1.578	0.69
LTD	0.970	0.32	0.009	0.09	0.108	0.82	4.223	1.60
TORINO	−6.724	−2.34	−0.119	−1.30	0.080	0.64	−0.677	−0.27
OTHERM	3.365	1.11	0.165	1.70	0.321	2.44	8.503	3.22
log(AGE)					−0.814	−7.22	−21.887	−9.70
log(MILES)					−0.319	−3.10	−14.059	−6.82
log(WEIGHT)					−0.379	−0.96	−28.159	−3.57
CONSTANT	105.8	9.23	5.547	15.14	6.131	8.34	151.550	10.30
S	5.506		0.176		0.241		4.820	
R^2	0.884		0.899		0.808		0.911	

TABLE 4 Summary of Regression Results, General Motors Cars

	Dependent variable							
	RATIO		log(RATIO)		log(RATIO)		RATIO	
Explanatory variables	Estimate	t-value	Estimate	t-value	Estimate	t-value	Estimate	t-value
AGE	-5.758	-9.96	-0.168	-10.4				
MILES	-0.340	-6.06	-0.007	-4.86				
WEIGHT	-7.883	-2.54	-0.113	-1.31				
AIRCON	-0.129	-0.08	-0.095	-2.15	-0.132	-2.49	-1.667	-1.06
FOURDR	-1.833	-0.96	-0.011	-0.21	0.011	0.18	-1.470	-0.78
OTHERT	0.383	0.13	-0.104	-1.28	-0.220	-2.28	-3.585	-1.26
MONTEC	0.188	0.09	0.009	0.15	0.017	0.24	0.351	0.16
IMPALA	-7.739	-3.52	-0.291	-4.73	-0.385	-5.27	-11.107	-5.15
GRDPRX	1.726	0.64	0.062	0.82	0.048	0.53	1.370	0.52
OTHERM	-8.209	-3.26	-0.250	-3.55	-0.326	-3.98	-10.482	-4.35
log(AGE)					-0.508	-8.05	-18.810	-10.12
log(MILES)					-0.319	-3.27	-14.635	-5.10
log(WEIGHT)					0.297	0.70	-4.997	-0.40
CONSTANT	116.580	10.0	5.280	16.25	5.309	8.50	134.470	7.31
S	5.883		0.164		0.196		5.786	
R^2	0.891		0.889		0.839		0.895	

THE CITY OF WEST YORK

Recent legislation[1] requires that the city of West York—together with other municipalities—switch to the market value system of property assessment (MVA). Under this system, the amount of tax levied against a property is proportional to its market value.

According to a widely used definition, market value is defined as the highest amount that a property can be expected to realize if sold in the open market by a willing seller to a willing buyer, with both parties having full knowledge of all the uses to which the property might be put.

This definition recognizes that some sales are not made in the open market (for example, nominal transfers of property between relatives), or by willing parties (for example, in expropriations), or with full information of alternative uses (for example, when the seller is not aware that an imminent rezoning would drastically affect the value of the property). The definition appears straightforward enough, but its implementation is ordinarily quite difficult. How, for example, is one to determine what the market price would be of a factory, an office building, a dairy farm, a mansion in an exclusive section of the city, a gas station, or a tennis club, when these properties did not change hands recently and the owners have no intention of putting them up for sale?

When the MVA system comes into effect, therefore, each of the 200,000-odd residential properties in the city must be assessed a market value. These assessed values must be maintained and revised in subsequent years to reflect changing market conditions (resulting, for example, from the deterioration of some neighborhoods). The property tax in a given year will be calculated by multiplying the assessed value by the city's "mill rate," a common rate applicable to all residential properties in the city. For example, if two properties have assessed market values of $150,000 and $300,000 and the mill rate is 1%, their annual property taxes will be $1500 and $3000, respectively.

The problem, of course, is how to determine the market values of all 200,000 properties. Recently sold properties present few difficulties, but only a small fraction of properties are usually sold in a short period of time, such as a month, quarter, or year.

---

[1] The case is based on a project by Dwayne Biggs, Bruno Amadi, Morley Boyd, Ralph Badolato, Frank Lippa, and Pat Villani.

To assist assessors in arriving at an estimate of market value of a property, three principal methods are employed.

The *income capitalization method* lends itself best to the appraisal of income-producing properties, such as apartment and office buildings. Under this method, the market value of the property is the present value of the future expected net income (for example, future rental income minus depreciation and other direct expenses), discounted at the rate of return for real estate in the community.

According to the *replacement cost method*, the market value is estimated as the cost of reproducing the property, minus the accrued depreciation. The method is usually applied to the appraisal of buildings. Handbooks are available (giving, for example, the cost of erecting buildings of various types), and these are regularly updated with price indexes of building materials.

The *comparative sales method* is used for assessing most residential properties. The method is based on the premise that similar properties will sell for similar amounts. For example, if a house nearly identical to the one being appraised, built on a similar lot, and located in the same neighborhood was sold recently in the open market for $150,000, it would be reasonable to assess the subject property for the same amount. Unfortunately, the properties sold within a short period of time are usually very few in relation to those that often must be appraised, and they are unlikely to include properties identical in all respects to the ones that must be appraised. The comparative sales method seeks to establish a range of values for the subject property by comparing it to similar properties that have recently changed hands and adjusting their sale prices appropriately to reflect significant differences in their characteristics. The following excerpt describes an approach used by real estate appraisers employing the comparative sales method:[2]

> It has been customary to express adjustments as lump sums when dealing with improved residential properties. A typical residential property is presented here. Subject property is a single-family residence on a site 50×127 in a good neighborhood. The building is a one story, frame dwelling built ten years ago, containing 923 gross square feet on the main floor, partial basement with one car garage. Four comparable sales are used. A grid presentation of the pertinent information is displayed:

[2]International Association of Assessing Officers, *Assessing and the Appraisal Process*, 5th ed., pp. 72–73, Chicago, Ill., 1974.

	Subject	Sale 1	Sale 2	Sale 3	Sale 4
Sale Price	–	$16,200	$16,200	$16,800	$16,900
Date of Sale	–	3 years	2 years	1 year	current
Age of Imps.	10 yrs	9 years	11 years	9 years	10 years
Condition of Imps.	Good	Good	Good	Good	Good
Lot Size	50×127	50×117	50×100	50×156	50×115
Floor Area	923 s.f.	962 s.f.	977 s.f.	1,008 s.f	936 s.f
Full Basements[+]	No	Yes	Yes	Yes	Yes
Garage	Basmt.	None	None	None	None
Quality	Good	Good	Good	Good	Good
Utilities	Average	Average	Average	Average	Average
Site Imps.	Average	Average	Average	Average	Average
Location	Good	Good	Good	Good	Good

[+]Subject dwelling has partial basement due to outcropping of ledge.

The display demonstrates that there are several areas of adjustment necessary. The unit of comparison is the dwelling itself. Adjustments will be required for time, floor area, basement, garage and lot size. From available market data, the following lump sum adjustments are abstracted heeding the principle of contribution:

	Sale 1	Sale 2	Sale 3	Sale 4
Time	+$975	+$650	+$350	–
Lot Size	–	+$100	−$100	–
Floor Area	−$250	−$300	−$400	–
Basement	−$625	−$625	−$625	−$625
Garage	+$500	+$500	+$500	+$500
Total Adj.	+$600	+$325	−$275	−$125
Sale Price	$16,200	$16,200	$16,800	$16,900
Adj. Price	$16,800	$16,525	$16,525	$16,775

The adjustments are based on the following observations:

1. Time—advance in the market of two percent per year.
2. Lot size—depths 115 to 130 feet are typical; $100 less for 100 feet of depth and $100 more for 156 feet of depth; all frontages are 50 feet.
3. Floor area—for significant number of square feet, $4.50 to $6.50 per square foot is contributory value.
4. Basement—sales reveal penalty of $625 for ledge in basement.
5. Garage—$500 contributory value for market data.

All dwellings have two bedrooms.

The value indicators for subject property provide a range from $16,525 to $16,800. Since Sale No. 4 required the fewest adjustments, it should be considered the strongest value indicator. The other adjusted sales bracket this value indicator of $16,775. The range of adjusted sales is narrow. All adjusted sales are generally good value indicators for subject property. They tend to substantiate a $16,775 value, rounded to $16,800.

The amounts of these adjustments are based on "available market data." The same source explains how these amounts may be determined:[3]

The following is a discussion of the various mechanical methods which may be employed to determine the amount of adjustment in several frequently encountered categories. The foundation of adjustments in the real estate market cannot be overemphasized. Where market data are not available for analysis, the assessor must draw upon his experience and the experience of other experts to estimate the amount of adjustments. There is, however, no real substitute for bona fide market data.

1. *TIME ADJUSTMENT.* The principle of change states that change is continually affecting the real estate market. During an inflationary period, the value level tends to rise; during the deflationary times, value levels tend to fall. Perhaps the best evidence of the required adjustment for time is the resale of the same property. Assume a downtown retail property sold as follows:

Original sale (two years ago)	$10,000
Sale of property (present time)	$11,000
Increase in value over two year period	$1,000
Increase: $11,000 ÷ $10,000	10%

The indicated time adjustment is plus five percent per year. This exercise is valid if the assessor assures himself that no other changes, physical or otherwise, have occurred to modify property value. This time adjustment may be applied to other comparable sales data.

2. *LOCATION ADJUSTMENT.* The objective here is to find two similar properties: apartments, for example. The only significant difference is location. Both properties sold about the same time.

Apartment No. 1. better location: sale price per unit	$20,000
Apartment No. 2. poorer location: sale price per unit	$16,000
Difference: $20,000 ÷ $16,000	25%

If subject property has a location similar to Sale No. 1, then a plus 25 percent adjustment to Sale No. 2 is required, if it is to be used as evidence of value for subject property.

3. *PHYSICAL CONDITION ADJUSTMENT.* Two similar light industrial buildings sold at the same time. They are quite similar in size. One has

[3]Ibid., pp. 68–69.

considerable deferred maintenance (curable physical deterioration). Functional utility and location are comparable.

Property No. 1. good physical condition: sale price $30,000
Property No. 2. poor physical condition: sale price $27,000
        Difference: $30,000 ÷ $27,000.   11%

This example demonstrates, in addition to the amount of the adjustment, that the market data approach measures and compensates for accrued depreciation.

4. *CONTRIBUTORY VALUE OF COMPONENT*. Assume two similar single family residences recently sold. Amenities are about the same except that the Residence No. 1 has a detached one-car garage.

Residence No. 1. with garage; sale price $24,500
Residence No. 2. without garage; sale price $23,000
Indicated contributory value of garage $ 1,500

The objective in these examples is to isolate the dissimilar characteristic.

5. *VACANT RESIDENTIAL LAND*. Two residential lots on the same street sold recently. Physically they are similar with 75 front feet. The depths are dissimilar:

Lot No. 1, 120 feet depth; sale price $5,000
Lot No. 2, 100 feet depth; sale price $4,600
    Difference: $5,000 ÷ $4,600   +9%

If several of these sales can be accumulated and analyzed, a depth table may be computed.

It would appear, however, that the market value of a property can also be estimated using regression analysis. The prices of the properties that were sold could be related to such physical characteristics as lot size, age of building, floor area, number of rooms, number of bathrooms, type of construction, style of house, and so on. The estimated regression equation could then be used to forecast the market value of any property with a given set of characteristics, even if the property had not been sold recently.

Regression was the method used in a recent study of house prices in the city of West York. The primary source of information was the database of the regional real estate association, listing sales for the period October through December. A total of 100 sales were selected from this source, four from each of the 25 subdistricts making up the city. The study was restricted to detached and semidetached residential properties; condominium apartments and townhouses and commercial properties were excluded.

The file realest.dat contains the data used in the study. The first 10 observations in this file are listed in Figure 1.

OBS	LIST	PRICE	AREA	LOTSZ	ROOMS	CONST1	CONST2	CONST3	TYPE1	TYPE2	TYPE3	STYL1	STYL2	STYL3	GARAG	BASMT	EXTRA	DRVWY	BATHS	AVESELPR
1	224.5	213.75	740	1854	6	0	0	1	0	1	0	0	1	0	1	0	0	0	1	250.5
2	219.5	195.00	914	1256	7	1	0	0	0	0	1	0	1	0	0	0	0	0	2	250.5
3	274.5	267.50	968	1198	7	1	0	0	0	1	0	0	1	0	0	0	0	1	3	250.5
4	317.0	295.00	1983	2667	9	1	0	0	0	1	0	0	1	0	1	0	1	0	2	250.5
5	317.5	307.50	1142	3276	8	1	0	0	1	0	0	0	1	0	1	0	0	1	1	281.5
6	274.5	225.00	848	1980	7	1	0	0	1	0	0	0	1	0	0	0	0	1	1	281.5
7	279.5	245.00	976	2500	6	0	0	1	1	0	0	0	1	0	1	1	1	1	2	281.5
8	572.5	540.00	1355	2220	8	1	0	0	0	1	0	0	1	0	1	0	1	0	2	281.5
9	437.5	415.00	1823	6452	14	1	0	0	1	0	0	0	1	0	1	1	1	1	3	366.0
10	875.0	825.00	2361	7900	12	1	0	0	1	0	0	0	0	1	1	0	0	1	3	366.0

FIGURE I File realest.dat, partial listing

The definition of the variables is as follows.

LIST: List (asking) price of property ($000)

PRICE: Selling price of property ($000)

AREA: Floor area, in square feet; approximate total floor area, excluding bathrooms, closets, porches, and basement

LOTSZ: Size of the lot, in square feet

ROOMS: Number of rooms in the house, excluding bathrooms, hallways, and rooms located in the basement

CONST1-CONST3: Construction of the house, as follows:

    CONST1: = 1 if the house is constructed of brick; = 0, if otherwise

    CONST2: = 1, if aluminum siding; = 0, otherwise

    CONST3: = 1, if other construction category; = 0, otherwise.

TYPE1-TYPE3: Type of the house, as follows:

    TYPE1: = 1, if detached; = 0, if otherwise

    TYPE2: = 1, if semidetached or townhome; = 0, otherwise

    TYPE3: = 1, if other type; = 0, otherwise

STYL1-STYL3: Style of house, as follows:

    STYL1: = 1, if a bungalow or backsplit; = 0, otherwise

$STYL2$: $= 1$, if house is $1\frac{1}{2}$ or 2 stories high; $= 0$, otherwise

$STYL3$: $= 1$, if house is more than 2 stories high; $= 0$, otherwise

$GARAG$: $= 1$, if the property has a garage; $= 0$, otherwise

$BASMT$: $= 1$, if the house has a finished or partially finished basement; $= 0$, otherwise

$EXTRA$: $= 1$, if the value of the "extras" (stove, refrigerator, air conditioner, fireplace, etc.) exceeds \$4000; $= 0$, otherwise

$DRVWY$: $= 1$, if the house has a private or shared driveway; $= 0$ otherwise

$BATHS$: number of separate baths in the house

$AVESELPR$: Average selling price in subdistrict during the period January through September (\$000)

One regression model was estimated with the following results:

$$
\begin{aligned}
PRICE = \quad & 55.072 && + 0.126\,AREA && + 0.013\,LOTSZ && - 0.515\,ROOMS \\
& (0.91) && (3.99) && (3.11) && (-0.07) \\
& + 28.086\,CONST1 && + 30.209\,TYPE1 && + 14.817\,STYL2 && + 153.442\,STYL3 \\
& (0.84) && (1.28) && (0.66) && (2.77) \\
& + 12.683\,GARAG && + 32.141\,BASMT && + 38.800\,EXTRA && + 4.303\,DRVWY \\
& (0.60) && (1.56) && (1.91) && (0.14) \\
& + 34.334\,BATHS && - 68.667\,ASP1 && - 20.071\,ASP2 \\
& (2.16) && (-2.31) && (-0.75) \\
& R^2 = 0.72; && S = 85.932; && n = 100
\end{aligned}
$$

The numbers in parentheses are t-ratios. In the model, ASP1 - ASP3 are dummy variables based on the AVESELPR, as follows:

$ASP1$: $= 1$, if less than 300 (\$000); $= 0$, otherwise

$ASP2$: $= 1$, if from 300 to 400; $= 0$, otherwise

$ASP3$: $= 1$, if greater than 400; $= 0$, otherwise (base)

QUESTIONS

(1)   Discuss critically the comparative sales method of property valuation.

(2)   Comment critically on regression as a method for property valuation.

(3)   Discuss the similarities and differences of the preceding two methods. Which method, in your opinion, is better for the assessment of the residential properties in the city of West York?

(4)   Comment on the results of the regression study. In particular, consider how the model can be improved, and carry out your recommendations using the available data.

(5)   Discuss any other aspects of the case that were not covered in the preceding questions.

THE ENERGUIDE PROGRAM

Ever since the rapid escalation of energy prices in the mid-1970s, consumers have been frequently advised and encouraged to reduce energy consumption by eliminating waste, by improving the efficiency of existing energy-consuming products, by altering lifestyles and behavior toward lower energy usage, and by choosing products at least in part on the basis of their energy consumption patterns. In the electrical appliance sector, an important vehicle for stimulating energy conservation is the Energuide program.

The program requires that various household appliances give prominent display to a label indicating their monthly electricity consumption in kilowatt/hours under standardized test conditions.

The principal objectives of the Energuide program, as announced at the start of the program and repeated several times since, were to

- enable consumers to compare the energy consumption of available models and to choose from comparable models the one that consumes least energy;
- allow retailers to assist their customers in making purchase decisions based in part on the energy consumption of the featured models;
- encourage appliance manufacturers to improve the energy efficiency of appliances through research, design, and development.

The Energuide program first applied to refrigerators. The following year it was extended to freezers; the next year to clothes washers, dishwashers, and electric ranges; and, in the year after that, to clothes dryers.

The determination of the appliances' monthly electricity consumption is the responsibility of the CSA, the national standards association. Annual directories are published listing the monthly electricity consumption for each model tested.

If the energy used by domestic appliances is to be reduced, however, two things must happen. Manufacturers have to make available energy-efficient appliances, and consumers (perhaps influenced by retailers) have to buy them.

In the fifth year of the program, a study was commissioned to assess the performance of Energuide. The question put to the researchers was simply this:

Had there been any improvement in the energy consumption of appliances since the introduction of the Energuide program?

To address this question, six data files were created based on information in the Energuide directories. These six files correspond to the six types of electrical appliances covered by the program: refrigerators, freezers, ranges, clothes washers, dishwashers, and clothes dryers. Each file lists the models made available to consumers since the start of the Energuide program by brand name, model number, selected features, year of introduction of the model, and Energuide rating (the monthly electricity consumption of the model in kilowatt/hours).

QUESTIONS

(1) Explain in detail how you plan to address the question put to the researchers.

(2) You are asked to assume the role of research director and determine just what improvement—if any—has taken place in the energy consumption of appliances since the inception of the Energuide program.

DATA

Six data files are available. Their names, descriptions, partial listings, and the names of the variables they contain are as shown in Figures 1 through 6.

1. *Refrigerators (file* `engrfg.dat`*, 1251 observations).*

MODEL: Model number

BRAND: Brand name code

TYPE: Type code

1 = Single-door, manual defrost

2 = Single-door, no freezer, defrosting automatically on unit off-cycle

3 = Two-door refrigerator/freezer with top-mounted freezer and automatic defrost

4 = Two-door refrigerator/freezer with top-mounted freezer and manual defrost

5 = Two-door refrigerator/freezer with bottom-mounted freezer and automatic defrost

6 = Two-door refrigerator/freezer with side-mounted freezer and automatic defrost

7 = Three-door refrigerator/freezer with two-door side-mounted freezer and automatic defrost

RVOL: Refrigerator volume (in cubic feet)

FVOL: Freezer volume (in cubic feet)

ENER: Energuide rating (kwh/month)

YR: Code for the year of introduction of the model (= number of years after the start of the Energuide program)

2. *Freezers (file* engfrz.dat, *508 observations)*

MODEL: Model number

BRAND: Brand name code

TYPE: Type code

      1 = Upright, manual defrost

      2 = Upright, automatic defrost

      3 = Chest, manual defrost

OBS	MODEL	BRAND	TYPE	RVOL	FVOL	ENER	YR
1	AR581	1	2	15.50	0.00	87	4
2	BINS2479	1	7	15.16	8.45	165	1
3	BINT2179	1	3	14.79	6.60	137	1
4	BN580	1	6	11.48	3.89	136	3
5	CDNS22A9	1	7	15.16	6.51	168	2
6	CDNS24A9	1	7	15.16	8.45	165	2
7	CDNS249T	1	7	15.16	8.45	165	2
8	CINS2279	1	7	15.16	6.51	168	1
9	CINS229T	1	7	15.16	6.51	168	1
10	CINS2479	1	7	15.16	8.45	165	1

FIGURE I File engrfg.dat, partial listing

OBS	MODEL	BRAND	TYPE	FVOL	ENER	YR
1	CF12	1	3	12.1	64	2
2	CF18	1	3	18.1	77	2
3	CF25	1	3	24.8	115	2
4	GFC 0720	1	3	7.1	43	4
5	GFC 1520	1	3	15.0	59	4
6	HV 812	1	1	12.4	95	3
7	WCF 1581	1	3	15.0	59	3
8	WCF 2281	1	3	22.1	76	3
9	WCF 781	1	3	7.1	43	3
10	C 158-1	2	3	15.0	87	3

FIGURE 2 File engrfz.dat, partial listing

FVOL: Freezer volume (cu. ft.)

ENER: Energuide rating (kwh/month)

YR: Code for the year of introduction of the model (= number of years after the start of the Energuide program)

3. *Ranges (file* engrng.dat, *682 observations)*

MODEL: Model number

BRAND: Brand name code

WDTH: Width (inches)

TYPEOV: Type of oven

  1 = Self-cleaning

  2 = Regular

TYPTP: Type of cooktop

  1 = Conventional

  2 = Smoothtop

  3 = Modular

OVSPL: Usable oven space (liters)

ENER: Energuide rating (kwh/month)

YR: Code for the year of introduction of the model (= number of years after the start of the Energuide program)

4. *Clothes Washers (file* engwsh.dat, *254 observations)*

MODEL: Model number

BRAND: Brand name code

CAPAC: Tub capacity (liters)

OBS	MODEL	BRAND	WDTH	TYPEOV	TYPTP	OVSPL	ENER	YR
1	E2A81	1	24	2	1	60.8	56	3
2	E2B81	1	24	2	1	60.8	56	3
3	E2D81	1	24	2	1	60.8	59	3
4	E2G81	1	24	2	1	60.8	61	3
5	E2P81	1	24	2	1	60.8	62	3
6	E3B81	1	30	2	1	77.9	66	3
7	E3C81	1	30	2	1	77.9	68	3
8	E3E81	1	30	2	1	77.9	66	3
9	E3G81	1	30	2	1	77.9	66	3
10	E3J81	1	30	2	1	77.9	66	3

FIGURE 3 File engrng.dat, partial listing

OBS	MODEL	BRAND	CAPAC	TYPE	TEMP	CYCLE	ENER	YR
1	WA479	1	90	1	8	1	95	3
2	WA481	1	55	1	7	1	104	3
3	WA579	1	90	1	8	1	95	3
4	WA679	1	90	1	7	1	118	3
5	WA681	1	55	1	7	1	104	3
6	WA779	1	90	1	7	1	118	3
7	WA781	1	55	1	7	1	104	3
8	WA879	1	90	1	1	1	128	3
9	WA881	1	55	1	1	1	121	3
10	5200	4	77	1	13	2	75	3

FIGURE 4 File engwsh.dat, partial listing

TYPE: Type code

  1 = Top loader

  2 = Front loader

TEMP: Wash/rinse temperature selections (13 types, codes 1–13)

CYCLE: Special cycle

  1 = None

  2 = Maximum water level

  3 = Suds saver

ENER: Energuide rating (kwh/month)

YR: Code for the year of introduction of the model (= number of years after the start of the Energuide program)

OBS	MODEL	BRAND	CONTROL	CAPAC	ENER	YR
1	67010	4	3	168	92	4
2	64030	4	2	168	111	4
3	65030	4	2	168	111	4
4	66030	4	2	168	111	4
5	62010	4	1	168	94	4
6	63030	4	1	168	94	4
7	60200	4	1	76	42	4
8	60208	4	1	76	42	4
9	60410	4	1	110	42	4
10	60418	4	1	110	42	4

FIGURE 5 File engdry.dat, partial listing

5. *Clothes Dryers (file* engdry.dat, *112 observations).*

  MODEL: Model number

  BRAND: Brand name code

  CONTROL: Drying control code

   1 = Timed

   2 = Automatic (ts)

   3 = Automatic (ms)

  CAPAC: Capacity (liters)

  ENER: Energuide rating (kwh/month)

  YR: Code for the year of introduction of the model (= number of years after the start of the Energuide program)

6. *Dishwashers (file* engdsh.dat, *301 observations).*

  MODEL: Model number

  BRAND: Brand name code

  HTDRY: Heat/dry cycle code (1 = No, 2 = Yes, 3 = Optional)

  HWCON: Hot water consumption (liters in normal cycle)

  ENER: Energuide rating (kwh/month)

  YR: Code for the year of introduction of the model (= number of years after the start of the Energuide program)

OBS	MODEL	BRAND	HTDRY	HWCON	ENER	YR
1	DC2496E	1	3	54.7	134	3
2	DC2498E	1	3	54.7	134	3
3	DC416	1	3	45.6	111	4
4	DC418	1	3	45.6	111	4
5	DU2415	1	3	45.6	111	3
6	DU2496E	1	3	54.7	134	3
7	DU2498E	1	3	54.7	134	3
8	DU414	1	3	45.6	111	4
9	DU416	1	3	45.6	111	4
10	DU418	1	3	45.6	111	4

FIGURE 6 File engdsh.dat, partial listing

CARLSEN'S BREWERY

To the sales manager[1] of Carlsen's Brewery, a formal model to explain and predict beer sales seemed worth a try. The manager assigned the job to two business school graduates who were recently hired as assistants in the belief that this assignment would also help the two graduates become familiar with the industry. Carlsen's Brewery is one of the major breweries, with sales in all parts of the country, but the study itself was to be confined to one metropolitan area.

In discussing the assignment, the manager pointed out that weather conditions obviously are responsible for most of the short-run variation in beer consumption. "When it is hot," the manager said, "people drink more—it's that simple." This was also the main reason for confining the study to one area; since weather conditions vary so much across the country, there was no point in developing a single, countrywide model for beer sales. It was the manager's opinion that a number of models should be developed—one for each major selling area—and the total sales forecast calculated as the sum of the area forecasts.

Fifty-nine monthly observations on the following variables were used in the study, starting in January 19X4:

SALES: Monthly beer sales (tons)

TEMP: Average monthly temperature (°F), Mon.-Sat.

*PR*1: Monthly precipitation (inches), Mon.-Wed.

*PR*2: Monthly precipitation (inches), Thu.-Sat.

SUN: Monthly total hours of sunlight

The data can be found in the file beer.dat and are partially listed in Table 1.

In their later report, the two assistants explained their choice of variables:

1. *Temperature, TEMP.* Daily temperature readings were divided into two categories: one for the first half of the week (Monday-Wednesday) and the second for the last half of the week (Thursday-Saturday), with Sunday readings being ignored because Sundays are not selling days. The reason

---

[1]The case is based on a project by Mr. J. Doyle and Mr. M. Krebs.

TABLE 1   File beer.dat, Partial Listing

MONTH	SALES	TEMP	PR1	PR2	SUN
1	2312.000	31.000	0.038	0.074	104.8
2	2580.500	28.900	0.062	0.142	108.3
3	3079.900	32.800	0.143	0.010	153.0
4	3031.000	47.700	0.066	0.105	214.3
5	3361.800	70.300	0.069	0.007	261.7
...	...	...	...	...	...

for this breakdown is that sales for the Thursday-Saturday period account for approximately 70% of total weekly sales. Upon examining the data, however, it was clear that there was virtually no difference in the monthly mean temperatures for both parts of the week. Therefore, monthly means for all days (Monday-Saturday) were used as our data for *TEMP*.

2. *Precipitation.* Using the same procedure as that described above, we divided the daily precipitation readings into two categories and then calculated a monthly total for each category. However, differences in the monthly totals were significant. Two variables for precipitation were therefore used: *PR1* for total monthly precipitation in the Monday-Wednesday period and *PR2* for total monthly precipitation in the Thursday-Saturday period.

3. *Sunlight, SUN.* Once again, two measures for sunlight were calculated but were found to be virtually identical, and we therefore decided to use only one measure referring to the total number of hours.

Other variables, such as population, income, advertising, tastes and preferences, the composition of the population by age and ethnic origin, etc., influence beer sales only in the long run, and can be omitted.

They added,

It should be noted that these variables display some interdependence. For example, the amount of sunlight will likely be inversely related to precipitation. Also, there may be some relationship between precipitation or sunlight and the mean monthly temperature. One such relationship is that precipitation may be most abundant in the spring and fall when the temperature is neither very high nor very low. Therefore, the use of all these variables may violate one of the basic assumptions of a regression model, namely that the explanatory variables should be independent of one another. It will then become necessary to examine the level of multicollinearity between these variables to determine whether or not they are independent of one another.

In their report, the analysts described two of the models they had estimated as follows:

We began with a model relating *SALES* to *TEMP*, *PR1*, *PR2*, and *SUN*. The regression results were as follows:

$$SALES = 2021.4 + 21.766TEMP + 29.445PR1$$
$$(14.42) \qquad (6.26) \qquad (0.04)$$
$$+202.091PR2 - 0.496SUN \qquad R^2 = 0.68$$
$$(0.32) \qquad\qquad (-0.49) \qquad\quad S = 274.639$$

Clearly, this is not a satisfactory model, since only 68% of the total variation in beer sales is explained. In addition, as the low *t*-ratios show, three of the four explanatory variables may be dropped. We did not want to drop precipitation entirely. We thought that the two precipitation variables should be combined into a single variable ($PRT = PR1 + PR2$). However, dropping or combining variables is not going to improve the fit of the model. Additional explanatory variables are needed. For this reason, we introduced 12 dummy variables (*JAN*, *FEB*, ..., *DEC*), one for each month of the year. One of these (*JAN*) was dropped for technical reasons. The regression results were approximately as follows.

$$SALES = \quad 1994 + \quad 15TEMP - 584PRT + 200FEB + \quad 497MAR$$
$$(9.43) \qquad (2.63) \qquad (-1.49) \qquad (1.61) \qquad (3.51)$$

$$+ 349APR + 544MAY + 751JUN + 609JUL + \quad 536AUG$$
$$(1.94) \qquad (2.25) \qquad (2.53) \qquad (1.90) \qquad (1.74)$$

$$+ 249SEP + 278OCT + 407NOV + \quad 878DEC \qquad R^2 = 0.87$$
$$(0.93) \qquad (1.40) \qquad (2.94) \qquad (6.19) \qquad S = 194$$

This appears to be the best explanatory model. The model, however, is not good to forecast the future, because it is totally built on weather, and weather is only predictable over a day or two. One example would be the unexpected hot weather last Easter, when the sales of beer increased drastically.

QUESTIONS

Comment on the excerpts just quoted. Interpret the estimates of the two models. Put yourself in the manager's shoes: How would you rate this study? Do you agree with the approach used? Do you think that the last is indeed the best model? If not, can you improve it? Forecast beer sales for each month of next year.

AUTOMOBILE INSURANCE

An automobile insurance policy[1] consists of three separate policies combined in one, providing coverage for third-party liability, accident benefits, and loss of or damage to the insured

Third-party liability coverage provides indemnity against liability to others due to death, bodily injury, or property damage resulting from the operation of the vehicle.

Accident benefits coverage is for loss of life, ambulance, medical and hospital costs, loss of income, and rehabilitation. Insured under this coverage are the occupants of the insured vehicle, the insured and the members of the insured's family while occupants of any other automobile, and other persons specified in the policy.

Various forms of coverage for *loss of or damage to the insured automobile* are available: "comprehensive," "specified perils," "all perils," "collision/upset," each providing coverage for particular types of damages.

Insurance companies generally set limits on the coverage up to which they are responsible.

An automobile insurance company makes a separate calculation of the required premium for each of the three types of coverage; the total premium of the policy is equal to the sum of the individual premiums. The procedure used to arrive at a premium is similar for all types of coverage; to avoid repetition, we shall concentrate on one type of coverage, that for third-party liability.

The premium for third-party liability coverage depends on the class into which the policy is assigned.

It is perhaps a fundamental principle of insurance that the premium of a policy in a given class be related to the expected claim of that class. In fact, the principal reason for dividing the population of policies into classes is to allow the imposition of such differential premiums. If, for example, the expected annual cost per policy in Class X (consisting of, say, young single male drivers) is $750, while that in Class Y (consisting of, say, middle-aged married men or

[1]This case is based on a project by Mr. Zhanshun Wei.

women drivers) is $250, it is fair (or so it is argued) that the premium of Class X drivers be three times (or 300%) that of Class Y drivers.

In some jurisdictions, the classification system is legislated. In others, it is commonly used by agreement of the insurance companies. In still other jurisdictions, insurance companies are free to determine the classification criteria and the number of classes.

The principal source of information concerning the expected claim of a policy in a given class is the past claim experience of that class. Some insurance companies are large enough to rely on their own experience only, but in most jurisdictions insurance companies find it advantageous (or are required by law) to pool their experience through an industry organization or government agency.

In the jurisdiction dealt with in this case, third-party liability up to a certain limit is compulsory, although motorists are free to purchase additional insurance and to choose their insurer. Insurance companies are required to report their claim experience to an industry association on the basis of the classification system described next, but they are not required to use that system for determining the class premiums.

The current classification criteria are the sex, age, and marital status of the principal and occasional drivers, the use to which the automobile is put, and the claim record of the insured drivers.

Fourteen sex/marital status/age/use classes ("sex/use" classes, for short) are distinguished, as shown in Table 1.

TABLE 1   Classification by Sex, Marital Status, Age, and Use

Principal driver's			Use[a]			
Sex	Marital status	Age	A	B	C	D
Male	Single	16-18	10	10	10	10
		19-20	11	11	11	11
		21-22	12	12	12	12
		23-24	13	13	13	13
		25-29	04	04	04	07
		30+	01	02	03	07
	Married	16-20	08	08	08	08
		21-24	09	09	09	09
		25+	01	02	03	07
Female	Single or	16-20	18	18	18	18
	married	21-24	19	19	19	19
		25+	01	02	03	07

[a]See text.

The description of the four use categories A, B, C, and D shown in Table 1 is as follows:

A: Pleasure only; no drive to work; annual mileage less than 10,000; no male driver under 25; no more than two drivers per auto in the household; each driver has held license for at least three years.

B: Pleasure only; drive to work less than 10 miles one way; no male driver under 25; no more than two drivers per auto in the household.

C: Pleasure only; drive to work over 10 miles one way; no male driver under 25.

D: Used for business purposes; no male driver under 25.

For example, if the principal driver is 23 years old, male, and single, the policy is classified into Class 13; if the car is used for pleasure and is driven only by a husband and wife who are both 40 years old, and if the distance to work is over 10 miles, the policy is classified as 03.[2]

Policies are also classified according to the claim record under the policy, as follows:

Class	Claim record
5	Five years or more claim-free experience
3	Three or four years of claim-free experience
2	Two years claim-free experience
1	One year claim-free experience
0	At least one claim in the year prior to the effective date of the policy.

The claim record code is applied as a suffix to the sex/use code to form a three-digit code; for example, 043 signifies policies falling into sex/use Class 04 and claim record Class 3.

The experience of all insurance companies in the jurisdiction in the past 15 years is summarized in Appendixes A and B. Appendix A shows the "claim frequency" (the total number of claims divided by the number of policies) for each sex/use and claim record class. Appendix B shows the average claim amount (that is, total claim amount divided by the number of claims) for each sex/use and claim record class.

The product of the claim frequency and the average claim amount is, of course, the average claim per policy. As can be seen from Figure 1, the overall average claim per policy has been increasing steadily during the past

---

[2]If any of the use categories A to D has an occasional male driver under 25, this driver is added to the policy as Class 06, but the principal driver retains the class given in Table 1.

15 years, although its two components have been moving in opposite directions (Figures 2 and 3).

On the basis of this experience, the industry association has established a system of "differentials" for each sex/use and claim record classification. These differentials are listed in Table 2.

The industry association recommends to the participating companies the use of these differentials in establishing their class premiums.

The differentials are expressed in relation to two "base classes": Class 02 is the base class in the sex/use classification and Class 3 is the base class in the claim record classification. For example, the recommended premium for

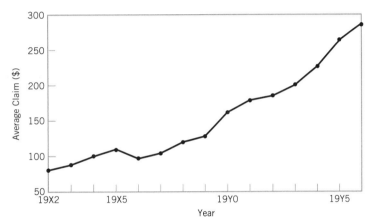

FIGURE 1

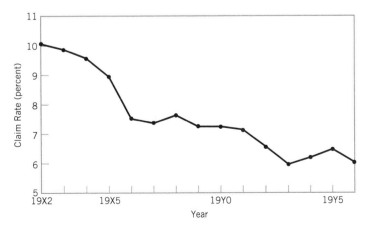

FIGURE 2

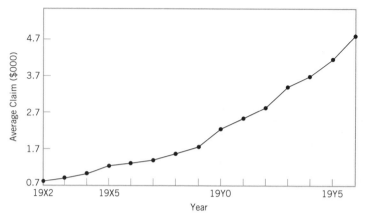

FIGURE 3

TABLE 2   Premium Differentials by Sex/Use and Claim Record Classification

Sex/use class	Differential	Claim record class	Differential
01	84%	5	85%
02 (Base)	100	3 (Base)	100
03	109	2	126
04	159	1	144
07	122	0	178
06	75		
08	139		
09	139		
18	118		
19	118		
10	263		
11	263		
12	197		
13	159		

sex/use Class 10 should be 263% that of Class 02, the premium for claim record Class 5 should be 85% that of Class 3, and so on.

The combined base class is thus Class 023, which consists of policies falling into sex/use Class 02 and claim record Class 3. It is a frequent practice for insurance companies to estimate the expected claim cost in the combined base Class 023 by projecting recent trends in the claim frequency and the average claim amount. This amount, the so-called pure base class premium, is then multiplied by a factor intended to cover marketing, administrative, and other costs and to allow for the desired profit rate. The result is the actual base class premium.

Once this premium is determined, the premiums for all other combined classes are established by simple multiplication. For example, the premium for Class 031 will be 1.09 × 1.44, or 156.96% that of base Class 023; the premium for Class 015 will be 0.84 × 0.85, or 71.4% that of base Class 023; and so on.

There are currently approximately 3.1 million automobile insurance policies in force in the jurisdiction. The distribution of these policies by class is shown in Table 3.

It is clear that the bulk of the policies falls into classes 015 and 025. These two classes contain nearly 70% of the policies in force. Tables 4, 5, and 6 show the number of policies, the claim frequency, and the average claim in these two classes and in the base class 023.

TABLE 3   Distribution of Policies by Class (%)

| Sex/use class | Claim record class | | | | | Total |
	5	3	2	1	0	
01	39.51	2.37	0.45	0.51	0.59	43.43
02	29.94	2.54	0.44	0.48	0.46	33.86
03	5.52	0.53	0.10	0.11	0.13	6.39
06	0.94	1.75	0.21	0.27	0.18	3.35
07	3.19	0.29	0.04	0.05	0.07	3.64
08	0.01	0.04	-	-	-	0.06
09	0.85	0.23	0.03	0.03	0.03	1.17
10	0.03	0.19	0.03	0.03	0.02	0.29
11	0.13	0.50	0.04	0.03	0.03	0.73
12	0.89	0.46	0.05	0.05	0.04	1.48
13	1.23	0.32	0.04	0.03	0.03	1.66
18	0.17	0.62	0.06	0.06	0.04	0.96
19	2.19	0.61	0.07	0.07	0.06	3.00
Total	84.60	10.45	1.55	1.71	1.68	100.00

Note: "-" means less than 0.01%.

TABLE 4   Experience for Class 015

Year	Number of policies (000)	Claim frequency (%)	Average claim ($)
19Y4	1,141	5.23	3,388
19Y5	1,201	5.41	3,790
19Y6	1,278	4.97	4,331

TABLE 5 Experience for Class 025

Year	Number of policies (000)	Claim frequency (%)	Average claim ($)
19Y4	1,265	5.62	3,429
19Y5	1,315	5.73	3,901
19Y6	1,398	5.30	4,431

TABLE 6 Experience for Class 023

Year	Number of policies (000)	Claim frequency (%)	Average claim ($)
19Y4	82	9.24	3,809
19Y5	73	9.64	4,500
19Y6	77	9.11	5,506

The data listed in Appendixes A and B can also be found in the files `autins1.dat` and `autins2.dat`, respectively.

QUESTIONS

(1) Analyze the trends in the claim frequency and the average claim for each sex/use and claim record class. Comment.

(2) Calculate the "pure" premium for base Class 023 policies.

(3) Forecast the average claim per policy for each sex/use class and compare the relative claim to the sex/use differentials shown in Table 2. Do the same for each claim record class. Are the two sets of differentials consistent with these relative average claim amounts?

(4) Forecast the average claim per policy for the three-digit combined sex/use and claim record Classes 015, 015, and 023. Compare the relative claim amounts with the products of the corresponding differentials. Comment.

(5) Comment critically on the combined sex/marital status/age/use classification used by the industry. Are there other reasonable classification systems?

(6) In your opinion, which principles should an insurance company follow in determining the number of classes? Should there be more or fewer classes than the 70 presently used?

(7) As a result of becoming involved in an accident and making a claim, the insured is likely to see his or her premium raised. Is this to reimburse the insurer for costs paid in connection

with the accident or because the accident indicates the insured is more accident prone than had been assumed and hence more likely to cause claims in the future? Explain your answer.

(8) Is the entire classification system a good system? Is it fair? How could it be improved?

(9) The industry is under considerable pressure to discard sex, age, and marital status as classificatory variables. It is pointed out that a system using classification criteria over which individuals have no control is inherently discriminatory. Supporters of the present system argue that the past experience of the industry suggests substantial and consistent differences in the claim frequency, the average claim, and the claim per policy among classes formed according to these variables. Comment.

(10) Comment on any other aspects of the case that you consider important, using additional references and data if necessary.

APPENDIX A

The following is a listing of the file `autins1.dat`. *CLMRT*01 to *CLMRT*19 represent the claim frequency (expressed as a percentage) for sex/use Classes 01 to 19 and *CLMRT*5 to *CLMRT*0 the claim frequency for claim record Classes 5 to 0, respectively. *CLMRTTOT* is the overall claim frequency. Claim record Class 5 was first introduced in 19X4.

OBS	YEAR	CLMRT01	CLMRT02	CLMRT03	CLMRT06	CLMRT07	CLMRT08	CLMRT09
1	19X2	8.10	9.90	10.20	6.90	13.80	19.40	12.00
2	19X3	8.00	9.60	9.90	5.80	13.30	20.00	12.10
3	19X4	7.80	9.27	9.68	4.74	12.54	18.72	11.67
4	19X5	7.18	8.77	9.01	4.25	11.89	16.69	10.91
5	19X6	6.25	7.39	7.90	3.57	9.12	14.44	9.01
6	19X7	5.98	7.34	7.50	3.39	8.72	15.51	8.99
7	19X8	5.84	7.89	6.88	3.82	9.23	15.31	9.59
8	19X9	5.56	7.36	6.71	3.43	8.45	15.85	9.33
9	19Y0	5.85	7.06	6.79	3.11	8.35	16.67	9.50
10	19Y1	5.87	6.94	7.12	3.52	8.20	16.40	9.39
11	19Y2	5.53	6.37	6.51	3.28	7.72	16.23	9.28
12	19Y3	5.29	5.91	5.94	2.77	6.64	13.46	8.48
13	19Y4	5.62	6.06	6.24	2.92	7.02	16.33	8.73
14	19Y5	5.73	6.33	6.57	2.89	7.33	17.73	9.19
15	19Y6	5.30	5.97	6.19	3.00	6.47	12.50	9.68

CLMRT10	CLMRT11	CLMRT12	CLMRT13	CLMRT18	CLMRT19
29.70	21.20	16.60	13.10	13.20	10.50
30.90	21.50	15.90	13.20	13.70	10.20
30.73	20.80	15.30	13.01	13.38	9.37
28.27	19.36	13.82	11.83	12.31	8.89
23.94	14.95	11.05	9.51	10.20	7.69
24.66	15.36	11.51	9.56	10.50	7.73
25.28	16.96	12.44	10.10	11.10	8.17

25.45	17.12	12.31	10.10	10.06	7.71
26.13	17.38	12.50	10.14	11.29	7.73
25.27	16.90	12.90	10.29	11.53	7.93
21.71	15.52	12.00	9.96	9.64	7.18
18.45	13.48	10.28	8.71	9.15	6.71
18.57	13.29	10.73	8.58	10.03	7.16
20.10	15.94	11.51	9.82	10.81	7.55
21.10	15.94	11.00	9.58	11.09	7.50

CLMRT5	CLMRT3	CLMRT2	CLMRT1	CLMRT0	CLMRTTOT
.	9.10	12.20	15.00	16.40	10.10
.	8.90	12.30	15.30	17.70	9.90
7.32	9.88	12.12	14.10	19.58	9.61
6.65	9.72	11.46	13.36	18.24	8.69
5.90	8.09	10.10	11.04	14.36	7.46
6.05	7.94	10.16	11.42	12.16	7.33
6.22	8.55	10.79	13.13	15.09	7.59
6.00	8.31	11.24	13.25	13.83	7.22
6.13	8.09	11.30	13.17	15.91	7.19
6.06	9.42	10.18	11.29	15.77	7.11
5.69	8.85	10.22	11.54	10.65	6.51
5.33	8.16	8.65	9.14	9.05	5.92
5.59	8.77	8.70	9.29	9.89	6.14
5.85	8.92	9.05	10.00	10.87	6.37
5.46	8.71	8.52	9.68	10.55	5.99

APPENDIX B

The following is a listing of the file autins2.dat. *AVCLM01* to *AVCLM19* represent the average claim amount (in current dollars) for sex/use Classes 01 to 19 and *AVCLM5* to *AVCLM0* the average claim amount for claim record Classes 5 to 0, respectively. *AVCLMTOT* is the overall average claim amount. Claim record Class 5 was first introduced in 19X4.

OBS	YEAR	AVCLM01	AVCLM02	AVCLM03	AVCLM06	AVCLM07	AVCLM08
1	19X2	748	785	794	865	756	934
2	19X3	816	862	878	1021	834	1035
3	19X4	936	992	1021	1258	947	1182
4	19X5	1094	1190	1178	1642	1164	1552
5	19X6	1188	1304	1244	1891	1279	1318
6	19X7	1280	1395	1304	1825	1271	1804
7	19X8	1459	1499	1720	1808	1393	2151
8	19X9	1685	1671	1864	2199	1627	1898
9	19Y0	2118	2135	2199	2627	1927	2599
10	19Y1	2353	2476	2463	2701	2355	3271
11	19Y2	2592	2880	3033	3062	2684	4127
12	19Y3	3313	3259	3336	4514	3162	3658
13	19Y4	3429	3612	3922	4540	3597	5819
14	19Y5	3901	4045	4037	5020	3980	6421
15	19Y6	4431	4897	4891	6012	4166	4484

AVCLM09	AVCLM10	AVCLM11	AVCLM12	AVCLM13	AVCLM18	AVCLM19
856	1064	1116	1091	1018	862	804
930	1244	1240	1160	1119	951	912
1117	1468	1433	1290	1319	1115	991
1320	1507	1695	1661	1462	1207	1261
1228	1607	1800	1561	1373	1378	1179
1656	1763	1767	1747	1842	1407	1409
1725	1963	2028	1797	1820	1487	1403
1881	2177	2152	1995	2126	1682	1701
2128	2950	2865	2527	2488	2426	2130
2571	2654	3355	3683	2600	2618	2244
3086	3575	3497	3032	2961	2612	2541
3271	3720	4195	3872	4329	3070	3332
3869	3845	4504	4309	4568	3723	3689
4872	4224	5008	5294	5573	4060	4072
4590	5145	6175	5384	5076	4940	5409

AVCLM5	AVCLM3	AVCLM2	AVCLM1	AVCLM0	AVCLMTOT
.	770	900	987	952	815
.	850	1023	1048	1065	900
921	1030	1199	1175	1262	1040
1114	1228	1386	1453	1424	1234
1267	1283	1456	1421	1425	1306
1348	1423	1504	1625	1508	1413
1477	1585	1798	1744	1826	1567
1713	1759	1795	1879	2051	1766
2125	2334	2305	2410	2650	2234
2363	2764	2780	2800	2927	2517
2697	3105	3178	2807	3157	2819
3239	3704	3890	3424	4021	3370
3549	3891	3886	3937	4433	3648
3954	4713	4523	3933	5265	4110
4567	5382	4862	6149	5430	4761

POPULATION PROJECTIONS

The starting point[1] in population projections is the current joint distribution of the population according to age and sex, as shown in Table 1.

Over a given planning period, changes in the population will occur as a result of new births, deaths, and net immigration (the difference between immigration and emigration).

TABLE 1   Population by Age and Sex (000)

Age	Male	Sex Female	Total	Percentage
0-4	905.8	860.0	1765.8	7.8
5-9	1012.9	966.5	1979.4	8.8
10-14	1202.8	1149.3	2352.1	10.5
15-19	1161.6	1115.5	2277.1	10.1
20-24	1022.2	1010.5	2032.7	9.1
25-29	926.5	929.8	1856.3	8.3
30-34	768.4	737.3	1505.7	6.7
35-39	648.0	627.0	1274.9	5.7
40-44	651.4	622.5	1273.8	5.7
45-49	622.9	621.5	1244.4	5.6
50-54	579.0	600.1	1179.1	5.3
55-59	472.1	495.3	967.4	4.3
60-64	417.1	437.4	854.5	3.8
65-69	318.2	354.6	672.8	3.0
70-74	228.6	273.1	501.7	2.2
75-79	142.3	201.0	343.3	1.5
80-84	83.9	128.5	212.3	0.9
85+	53.5	99.4	152.9	0.7
Total	11217.2	11229.3	22446.5	100.0

SOURCE: File `popproj1.dat`

[1] This case is based on a project by Leon Courneya, Richard Dawson, and Harry Ounpuu. The project, in turn, draws from Nathan Keyfitz, "How Crowded Will We Become?" in M. J. Tanur (ed.), *Statistics: A Guide to the Unknown*, San Francisco: Holden-Day, 1972.

Table 2 shows the historical birth rates by female age groups over the past 16 years.

A plot of these birth rates over time will show a consistent downward trend. To forecast the birth rate for each group, a regression model is used of the form

$$\log(\widehat{\text{Birth}} \text{ rate}) = a + b(\text{Year}) \tag{1}$$

where log is the natural logarithm.

These regression models—one for each age group—are estimated using the observed birth rates in the past 16 years. The regression results are shown in upper part of Table 3. The forecast birth rates for the next five years are shown in the lower half of Table 2.

Tables 4 and 5 show the historical death rates by age groups for males and females, respectively. In all but the 0–4 age group, death rates appear fairly constant, suggesting that the current year's death rates could be used as estimates

TABLE 2   Number of Births per 1000 Women by Age Group

Year	15-19	20-24	25-29	30-34	35-39	40-44	45-49
−15	60.4	233.8	226.7	147.7	87.3	28.5	2.7
−14	59.8	233.5	224.4	146.2	84.2	28.5	2.4
−13	58.2	233.6	219.2	144.9	81.1	28.5	2.4
−12	55.0	231.6	214.6	143.1	77.1	27.6	2.1
−11	53.1	226.0	210.6	140.3	75.8	25.9	2.1
−10	50.2	212.8	203.1	134.9	72.0	25.1	2.1
−9	49.3	188.6	181.9	119.4	65.9	22.0	2.0
−8	48.2	169.1	163.5	103.3	57.5	19.1	1.7
−7	45.2	161.4	152.6	91.8	50.9	15.9	1.5
−6	43.0	152.6	148.7	86.3	44.8	13.8	1.4
−5	42.2	147.7	149.8	85.0	42.6	12.5	1.1
−4	42.8	143.3	147.2	81.8	39.0	11.3	0.9
−3	40.1	134.4	142.0	77.3	33.6	9.4	0.6
−2	38.5	119.8	137.1	72.1	28.9	7.8	0.6
−1	37.2	117.7	131.6	67.1	25.7	6.4	0.4
Current	35.3	113.1	131.1	66.6	23.0	5.5	0.4
Forecasts, years 1 to 5							
1	34.4	106.4	119.1	60.2	23.2	5.9	0.4
2	33.2	100.7	114.2	56.5	21.2	5.2	0.4
3	32.0	95.3	109.5	53.1	19.3	4.7	0.3
4	30.9	90.2	105.0	49.9	17.6	4.1	0.3
5	29.8	85.4	100.7	46.9	16.1	3.7	0.3
Total	160.4	477.9	548.5	266.7	97.5	23.6	1.7

SOURCE: File `popproj2.dat`

TABLE 3   Regression Results, Birth, and Death Rates

Age group	a Estimate	t-value	b Estimate	t-value	R^2
		(a) Birth rates			
15-19	3.575	430.49	−0.036	−38.14	0.99
20-24	4.722	194.63	−0.055	−20.14	0.97
25-29	4.822	207.33	−0.042	−16.00	0.95
30-34	4.159	135.06	−0.062	−17.85	0.96
35-39	3.238	79.20	−0.092	−19.89	0.97
40-44	1.885	28.78	−0.116	−15.60	0.95
45-49	−0.725	−7.37	−0.131	−11.68	0.91
		(b) Death rates			
Male, 0–4	1.361	62.10	−0.048	−19.48	0.96
Female, 0–4	1.133	68.48	−0.047	−24.82	0.98

of future death rates. For the 0–4 age group, a semilogarithmic model—of the same type as Eq. 1— is estimated using the historical observations over the most recent 16-year period:

$$\log(\widehat{\text{Death rate}}) = a + b(\text{Year}) \qquad (2)$$

where again log indicates the natural logarithm. The regression results are shown in Table 3. Forecast values using this model are listed in Table 6.

As Figure 1 shows, immigration and emigration fluctuated markedly over the past 11 years. However, as indicated in Table 7, the age distribution of immigrants remained fairly stable.

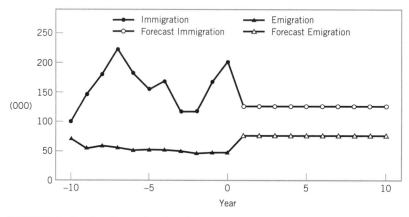

FIGURE I   Immigration and emigration

TABLE 4 Number of Deaths per 1000 Males by Age Group

Year	0–4	5–9	10–14	15–19	20–24	25–29	30–34	35–39	40–44	45–49	50–54	55–59	60–64	65–69	70–74	75–79	80–84	85+
−15	8.0	0.7	0.6	1.2	1.7	1.6	1.7	2.2	3.5	5.8	9.5	15.6	24.0	36.1	55.4	83.3	131.6	221.4
−14	7.7	0.7	0.6	1.3	1.6	1.5	1.6	2.3	3.3	6.0	9.3	15.6	24.0	35.0	54.3	83.2	128.5	217.5
−13	7.5	0.6	0.6	1.2	1.7	1.5	1.6	2.3	3.4	5.8	9.6	15.2	24.0	35.7	54.0	81.8	125.1	208.9
−12	7.3	0.6	0.5	1.1	1.7	1.5	1.6	2.3	3.4	5.6	9.5	15.4	23.9	35.1	54.1	81.0	123.3	209.6
−11	7.0	0.7	0.5	1.1	1.8	1.6	1.6	2.3	3.4	5.7	9.5	15.5	24.1	35.4	53.9	83.2	124.5	214.0
−10	6.6	0.6	0.5	1.2	1.8	1.5	1.7	2.2	3.7	5.7	9.5	15.1	25.0	35.3	53.4	81.3	121.0	200.2
−9	5.7	0.7	0.5	1.2	1.8	1.6	1.7	2.2	3.5	5.6	9.7	15.2	24.2	35.6	53.7	83.3	123.9	211.4
−8	5.4	0.6	0.6	1.3	1.8	1.6	1.7	2.2	3.4	5.7	9.7	15.4	24.0	36.2	53.1	79.9	124.0	213.4
−7	5.1	0.6	0.6	1.3	1.9	1.5	1.6	2.2	3.6	5.8	9.6	15.3	24.0	36.1	52.0	80.2	120.1	209.8
−6	4.9	0.6	0.5	1.3	1.8	1.5	1.7	2.2	3.5	5.8	9.1	15.1	23.4	36.9	52.6	80.5	125.4	211.0
−5	4.9	0.6	0.5	1.3	1.9	1.6	1.6	2.3	3.4	5.7	9.4	15.0	23.0	36.6	53.3	78.2	121.6	205.6
−4	4.9	0.6	0.5	1.3	1.7	1.4	1.6	2.2	3.5	5.6	9.3	14.8	23.7	36.3	53.3	78.2	119.7	197.0
−3	4.7	0.6	0.5	1.4	1.8	1.5	1.6	2.2	3.6	5.7	9.3	14.6	22.9	34.7	51.9	79.0	118.8	198.6
−2	4.5	0.5	0.5	1.6	2.0	1.5	1.7	2.2	3.6	5.6	9.3	14.6	23.0	35.7	53.4	78.9	122.7	213.6
−1	4.0	0.5	0.5	1.7	2.1	1.5	1.6	2.3	3.6	5.8	9.2	15.0	23.0	34.7	52.0	79.6	121.9	218.5
Current	4.0	0.5	0.5	1.7	2.0	1.6	1.5	2.3	3.5	5.8	9.2	14.6	22.7	34.9	53.1	78.3	121.5	217.0

SOURCE: File popproj4.dat

TABLE 5   Number of Deaths per 1000 Females by Age Group

Year	0–4	5–9	10–14	15–19	20–24	25–29	30–34	35–39	40–44	45–49	50–54	55–59	60–64	65–69	70–74	75–79	80–84	85+
−15	6.3	0.5	0.4	0.5	0.6	0.8	1.0	1.5	2.1	3.4	5.6	8.7	13.4	22.0	36.9	63.6	108.9	203.6
−14	5.9	0.4	0.3	0.5	0.6	0.7	0.9	1.4	2.1	3.5	5.3	8.2	13.4	21.3	35.1	60.8	104.1	199.6
−13	5.8	0.4	0.3	0.5	0.6	0.7	0.9	1.4	2.0	3.2	5.3	8.0	12.8	21.4	34.2	59.2	101.2	192.2
−12	5.8	0.4	0.3	0.5	0.6	0.7	0.9	1.4	2.1	3.4	5.1	8.2	12.8	20.7	34.2	57.8	99.5	194.6
−11	5.3	0.4	0.3	0.6	0.6	0.7	0.9	1.3	2.1	3.3	5.2	7.9	13.1	20.6	34.2	58.7	101.9	192.1
−10	4.9	0.4	0.3	0.5	0.6	0.6	0.9	1.3	2.0	3.2	5.1	7.8	12.8	20.0	32.4	56.7	95.3	176.0
−9	4.6	0.4	0.3	0.5	0.6	0.6	0.9	1.3	2.0	3.3	5.3	7.7	12.3	19.5	32.6	56.3	95.5	185.5
−8	4.3	0.4	0.3	0.5	0.5	0.6	0.9	1.3	2.0	3.3	5.0	7.7	12.2	19.5	30.9	53.9	93.6	183.4
−7	4.1	0.4	0.3	0.5	0.6	0.6	0.9	1.3	2.1	3.2	5.0	7.8	11.9	18.9	30.3	51.3	90.3	175.8
−6	4.0	0.4	0.3	0.5	0.6	0.7	0.8	1.3	2.0	3.1	5.1	7.7	11.7	18.7	30.7	50.8	89.3	180.6
−5	3.8	0.4	0.3	0.5	0.6	0.6	0.9	1.3	2.1	3.4	4.9	7.6	11.5	18.4	29.8	50.1	86.4	171.6
−4	3.8	0.4	0.3	0.5	0.6	0.6	0.9	1.3	2.1	3.2	4.9	7.5	11.2	18.3	29.4	48.7	83.9	163.7
−3	3.6	0.4	0.3	0.6	0.6	0.6	0.9	1.3	2.1	3.0	4.6	7.2	11.0	17.3	28.3	48.1	82.4	163.3
−2	3.6	0.3	0.3	0.6	0.5	0.7	0.9	1.4	2.1	3.1	4.9	7.4	11.3	17.7	29.1	48.3	80.8	158.6
−1	3.2	0.3	0.3	0.6	0.6	0.6	0.8	1.3	2.0	3.1	4.8	7.5	11.2	16.9	28.0	47.8	80.8	157.0
Current	3.2	0.3	0.3	0.6	0.6	0.6	0.8	1.2	1.9	3.2	4.7	7.1	11.3	17.3	28.1	46.7	81.3	156.3

SOURCE: File popproj5.dat

TABLE 6 Forecast Death Rates, 0–4 Age Group

Year	Male	Female
1	3.72	2.96
2	3.54	2.83
3	3.38	2.70
4	3.22	2.57
5	3.07	2.45

For the purpose of these population projections it is assumed that immigration and emigration will remain constant at levels of 125,000 and 75,000 persons per year. This implies a net immigration of 50,000 per year, or 250,000 over a five-year period. Applying the joint relative frequency distribution of immigrants to this figure, we obtain the distribution of net immigration by age and sex shown in the last columns of Table 7.

The projection of the total number of births for years 1 to 5 is detailed in Table 8. Of the total 1,445,400 births, 51% of 737,151 are assumed to be male and 49% or 708,243 female. All these persons will fall into the 0–4 age group in years 1 to 5.

The next step is to calculate the number of persons in each age group surviving year 5 and the age distribution of survivors by the end of year 5. This is done separately for males and females, and the details are shown in Tables 9, 10, and 11.

These calculations are fairly straightforward for both sexes in all age groups except the 0–4 age group. In the latter case, it is necessary to calculate a survival rate (=1—death rate) for each year and the cumulative survival rate over the five-year forecast period. The calculations are shown in Table 12.

For all other age groups, the death rate is assumed constant: for example, the five-year survival rate for the 5–9 male age group is $(0.9995)^5$ or 0.9975. The births from Table 8, the survival rates from Table 9, and the immigration figures from Table 7 are combined in Tables 10 and 11 for males and females, respectively.

QUESTIONS

(1) Project the male and female population in year 10, using the year 5 projections as if they were actual figures.

TABLE 7   Net Immigration, Observed and Forecast

Age group	Year −5	%	Current year	%	Unweighted average, %	Net immigration forecast for years 1 to 5 and 6 to 10	
0	7245	4.5	9528	4.4	4.4	11000	M
to 4	6732	4.2	8978	4.1	4.1	10250	F
5	6490	4.0	10620	4.9	4.4	11000	M
to 9	6183	3.8	9800	4.5	4.1	10250	F
10	4344	2.7	7802	3.6	3.1	7750	M
to 14	4072	2.5	7363	3.4	3.0	7500	F
15	5497	3.4	7248	3.3	3.3	8250	M
to 19	6340	3.9	8450	3.9	3.9	9750	F
20	15702	9.7	17028	7.8	8.8	22000	M
to 24	19371	12.0	19518	8.9	10.5	26250	F
25	16086	10.0	21914	10.0	10.0	25000	M
to 29	14487	9.0	18881	8.6	8.8	22000	F
30	9645	6.0	13401	6.1	6.0	15000	M
to 34	7884	4.9	10637	4.9	4.9	12250	F
35	5624	3.5	8385	3.8	3.6	9000	M
to 39	4385	2.7	6397	2.9	2.8	7000	F
40	3028	1.9	4785	2.2	2.1	5250	M
to 44	2582	1.6	3795	1.7	1.7	4250	F
45	1783	1.1	3055	1.4	1.3	3250	M
to 49	1945	1.2	2915	1.3	1.3	3250	F
50	1021	0.6	2036	1.0	0.8	2000	M
to 54	1511	0.9	2606	1.2	1.0	2500	F
55	962	0.6	1350	0.6	0.6	1500	M
to 59	1770	1.1	2236	1.0	1.0	2500	F
60	1066	0.7	1648	0.8	0.8	2000	M
to 64	1706	1.1	2226	1.0	1.0	2500	F
65	782	0.5	1191	0.6	0.6	1500	M
to 69	1214	0.7	1611	0.7	0.7	1750	F
70	732	0.4	1131	0.5	0.5	1250	M
+	1339	0.8	1930	0.9	0.9	2250	F
Total	161528	100.0	218465	100.0	100.0	250000	

TABLE 8   Projected Births, Years 1 to 5

Age group	Current female population	Birth rate	Total births
15 to 19	1115.5	0.1604	178.9
20 to 24	1010.5	0.4779	482.9
25 to 29	929.8	0.5485	510.0
30 to 34	737.3	0.2667	196.7
35 to 39	627.0	0.0975	61.1
40 to 44	622.5	0.0236	14.7
45 to 49	621.5	0.0017	1.0
Total			1445.4

(2)   Plot the distribution of the population by age, and calculate the average age in the current year, year 5, and year 10. Describe the implications of these calculations.

(3)   Discuss the implications of the projections on school enrollments. For the purpose of this case, approximate the elementary- and high school-eligible population by the total population in age group 5–19 and the eligible university population by the total population in age group 20–24. Explain how these projections can be made more accurate.

(4)   Under the country's Old Age Pension Plan, those who work pay the pensions of those who have retired. For the purpose of this case, assume that all persons 65 years old and older receive an annual pension of $1000 and that the burden of these pensions is shared equally by all persons in the age group 25–64. Calculate the individual burden in the current year and in years 5 and 10. Discuss the implications of these calculations.

(5)   Discuss any shortcomings of the methods used in this case and implement any feasible suggestions you may have for the improvement of the forecasts.

TABLE 9 Estimated Survival Rates, Male and Female

Age group	Male			Female		
	One-year death rate[a]	One-year surv. rate[b]	Five-year surv. rate[c]	One-year death rate[a]	One-year surv. rate[b]	Five-year surv. rate[c]
0–4			0.9832[d]		0.9866[d]	
5–9	0.0005	0.9995	0.9975	0.0003	0.9997	0.9985
10–14	0.0005	0.9995	0.9975	0.0003	0.9997	0.9985
15–19	0.0017	0.9983	0.9915	0.0006	0.9994	0.9970
20–24	0.0020	0.9980	0.9900	0.0006	0.9994	0.9970
25–29	0.0016	0.9984	0.9920	0.0006	0.9994	0.9970
30–34	0.0015	0.9985	0.9925	0.0008	0.9992	0.9960
35–39	0.0023	0.9977	0.9886	0.0012	0.9988	0.9940
40–44	0.0035	0.9965	0.9826	0.0019	0.9981	0.9905
45–49	0.0058	0.9942	0.9713	0.0032	0.9968	0.9841
50–54	0.0092	0.9908	0.9548	0.0047	0.9953	0.9767
55–59	0.0146	0.9854	0.9291	0.0071	0.9929	0.9650
60–64	0.0227	0.9773	0.8915	0.0113	0.9887	0.9448
65–69	0.0349	0.9651	0.8373	0.0173	0.9827	0.9164
70–74	0.0531	0.9469	0.7612	0.0281	0.9719	0.8672
75–79	0.0783	0.9217	0.6652	0.0467	0.9533	0.7873
80–84	0.1215	0.8785	0.5232	0.0813	0.9187	0.6544
85+	0.2170	0.7830	0.2943	0.1563	0.8437	0.4275

Notes:
[a] Current death rate, Tables 4 and 5.
[b] Equals 1−(one-year death rate).
[c] Equals (one-year survival rate)[5].
[d] See Table 12.

TABLE 10 Male Population in Year 5

Age group	Current population (000)	Survival rate	Year 5 survivors (000)	Births (000)	Net immigration (000)	Year 5 population (000)
0–4	905.8	0.9832		737.2	11.0	748.2
5–9	1012.9	0.9975	890.6		11.0	901.6
10–14	1202.8	0.9975	1010.4		7.8	1018.1
15–19	1161.6	0.9915	1199.8		8.2	1208.0
20–24	1022.2	0.9900	1151.8		22.0	1173.8
25–29	926.5	0.9920	1012.0		25.0	1037.0
30–34	768.4	0.9925	919.1		15.0	934.1
35–39	648.0	0.9886	762.7		9.0	771.7
40–44	651.4	0.9826	640.6		5.2	645.8
45–49	622.9	0.9713	640.1		3.2	643.3
50–54	579.0	0.9548	605.0		2.0	607.0
55–59	472.1	0.9291	552.9		1.5	554.4
60–64	417.1	0.8915	438.6		2.0	440.6
65–69	318.2	0.8373	371.9		1.5	373.4
70–74	228.6	0.7612	266.4		1.2	267.7
75–79	142.3	0.6652	174.0			174.0
80–84	83.9	0.5232	94.7			94.7
85+	53.5	0.2943	43.9			43.9
Total						11637.2

TABLE 11 Female Population in Year 5

Age group	Current population (000)	Survival rate	Year 5 survivors (000)	Births (000)	Net immigration (000)	Year 5 population (000)
0–4	860.0	0.9866		708.2	10.2	718.5
5–9	966.5	0.9985	848.4		10.2	858.7
10–14	1149.3	0.9985	965.0		7.5	972.6
15–19	1115.5	0.9970	1147.6		9.8	1157.3
20–24	1010.5	0.9970	1112.2		26.2	1138.4
25–29	929.8	0.9970	1007.5		22.0	1029.5
30–34	737.3	0.9960	927.0		12.2	939.3
35–39	627.0	0.9940	734.4		7.0	741.4
40–44	622.5	0.9905	623.2		4.2	627.5
45–49	621.5	0.9841	616.6		3.2	619.9
50–54	600.1	0.9767	611.6		2.5	614.1
55–59	495.3	0.9650	586.1		2.5	588.6
60–64	437.4	0.9448	478.0		2.5	480.5
65–69	354.6	0.9164	413.2		1.8	415.0
70–74	273.1	0.8672	325.0		2.2	327.2
75–79	201.0	0.7873	236.8			236.8
80–84	128.5	0.6544	158.2			158.2
85+	99.4	0.4275	84.1			84.1
Total						11707.5

TABLE 12   Calculation of Five-Year Survival Rate for 0-4 Age Group

Year	Male Death rate	Male Survival rate	Female Death rate	Female Survival rate
1	0.0037	0.9963	0.0030	0.9970
2	0.0035	0.9965	0.0028	0.9972
3	0.0034	0.9966	0.0027	0.9973
4	0.0032	0.9968	0.0026	0.9974
5	0.0031	0.9969	0.0025	0.9975
	Product: 0.9832		Product: 0.9866	

ELECTRIC POWER CONSUMPTION

As an analyst[1] for an electrical utility, you are given the task of formulating a model to explain and forecast the *hourly* consumption of electricity over a year.

A time series will be available for estimating this model showing the consumption of electricity in the area served by the utility each hour over the past five years. This series may be assumed to have the following format:

Year	Date	Day	Holiday	Hour	Consumption (000 kwh)
19X1	Jan. 1	Tue.	Yes	01	10,500
19X1	Jan. 1	Tue.	Yes	02	10,600
. . .	. . .	. . .	. . .	. . .	. . .
19X5	Dec. 31	Thu.	No	24	13,200

This time series, however, has a large number of observations and cannnot be provided to you. As an aid in formulating your model, three data files are available for analysis.

(a) The first (`elec1.dat`) has 744 observations and contains the hourly consumption of electricity in January of a given year. A partial listing of the observations in this file is shown in Table 1. The series is plotted in Figure 1 (*TIME* in this figure is in hours).

(b) The second (`elec2.dat`) has 720 observations and contains the hourly consumption of electricity in June of the same year. A partial listing of this file is shown in Table 2. The series is plotted in Figure 2 (*TIME* in this figure is also in hours).

(c) The third (`elec3.dat`) has 365 observations and shows the average hourly consumption of electricity each day of the same year. A partial listing of this file is shown in Table 3. The series is plotted in Figure 3 (*TIME* in this figure is in days).

It is the practice in the industry to use the terms demand and consumption interchangeably, a practice followed in the labeling of Tables 1 to 3. The variable *HOL* in the first and third files indicates whether or not the day is a holiday.

---

[1]The case is based on a project by Ms. Patricia Yim.

TABLE I   File `elec1.dat`, Partial Listing

DAY	DOWEEK	HOL	HOUR	DEMAND
1	THU	YES	1	10963
1	THU	YES	2	10608
1	THU	YES	3	10246
1	THU	YES	4	9940
1	THU	YES	5	9753
1	THU	YES	6	9701
1	THU	YES	7	9788
1	THU	YES	8	9922
...	...	...	...	...

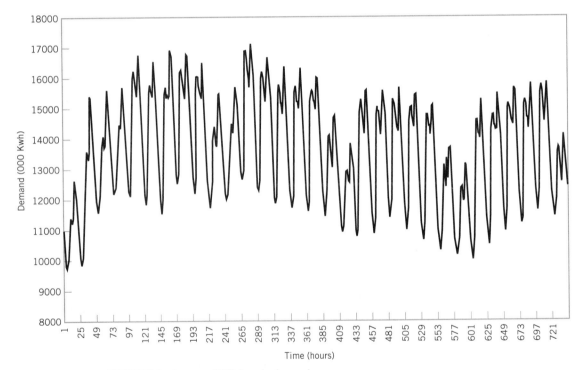

FIGURE I   January 19X1 hourly demand

QUESTIONS

(1)   Develop a model to forecast the consumption of electricity at a given hour of a given day of the week in January. Use that model to specifically forecast the electricity consumption between 1 and 2 A.M. on January 1 (a Thursday and holiday).

TABLE 2 File `elec2.dat`, Partial Listing

DAY	DOWEEK	HOUR	DEMAND
1	MON	1	8384
1	MON	2	8274
1	MON	3	8243
1	MON	4	8237
1	MON	5	8429
1	MON	6	9092
1	MON	7	10842
1	MON	8	12093
...	...	...	...

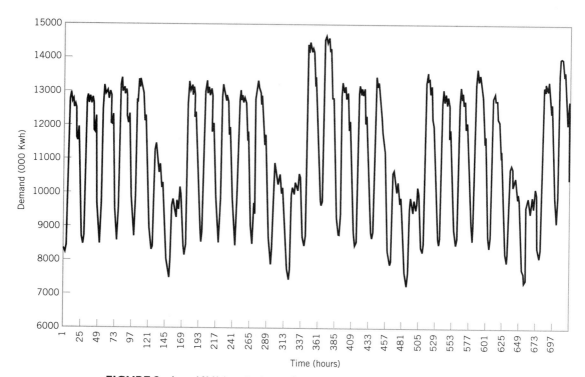

FIGURE 2 June 19X1 hourly demand

(2)   Develop a model to forecast the consumption of electricity at a given hour of a given day of the week in June. Use that model to specifically forecast the electricity consumption between 1 and 2 A.M. on June 1 (a Monday).

TABLE 3 File elec3.dat, Partial Listing

MONTH	DAY	DOWEEK	HOL	DEMAND
JAN	1	THU	YES	11363
JAN	2	FRI	YES	13825
JAN	3	SAT	NO	14060
JAN	4	SUN	NO	14129
JAN	5	MON	NO	15079
JAN	6	TUE	NO	14869
JAN	7	WED	NO	15248
JAN	8	THU	NO	15080
...	...	...	...	...

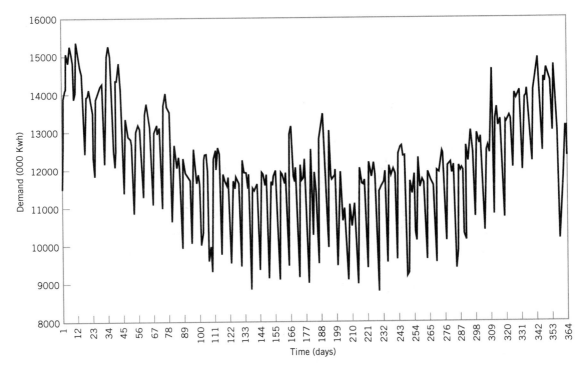

FIGURE 3 19X1 average hourly demand by day

(3) Develop a model to forecast the average hourly consumption of electricity for a given day of the year. Use that model to specifically forecast the average hourly electricity consumption on January 2 (a Friday and holiday).

(4) Given your analysis regarding Questions 1 to 3, outline the form of a model for forecasting the hourly consumption of electricity next year. Your model, in other words, should be able

to forecast the electricity consumption between, say, 4 and 5 P.M. on March 12 (a Friday) of next year.

(5) Comment on any other aspects of the case not specifically covered in the preceding questions.

THE EMERGENCY DEPARTMENT

Nurses at the emergency department[1] of the City General Hospital work in three eight-hour shifts of six nurses each. The shifts start at 6 A.M., 2 P.M., and 10 P.M.

The hospital is reviewing its records and considering a change to staggered shifts to balance the ratio of patients to nurses during the day and the week. With staggered shifts, 18 nurses will work each day in eight-hour shifts, but each nurse's starting time may be different.

The file `emerdep.dat` contains the date and time of arrival, length of stay, severity level and type of emergency for each of 2838 patients admitted to the emergency department during the month of April. A partial listing of this file is given in Table 1.

The definition of the variables is as follows:

DATE: Date of admission (in the format *yymmdd*)

TIME: Time of admission (in the format *hhmm*)

TYPE: Type of emergency; code ranges from 01 (cardiovascular arrest) to 19 (fracture)

SEVERITY: Severity level (A = minimal, B = moderate, C = complex, D = extensive, E = critical)

LOS: Length of stay in emergency department (hours)

TABLE I File `emerdep.dat`, Partial Listing

DATE	TIME	TYPE	SEVERITY	LOS
940401	0002	16	C	8.72
940401	0013	14	B	12.54
940401	0026	14	D	11.82
940401	0100	08	B	2.25
940401	0116	04	A	0.90
...	...	...	...	...

[1] This case is based on a project by Ms. Alice Peter.

QUESTIONS

(1) Determine the seasonal pattern of the number of patients *admitted* to the emergency department hourly.

(2) Determine the seasonal pattern of the number of patients *receiving care* in the emergency department hourly.

(3) How should the nurses' shifts be staggered so as to make the ratio of patients to nurses as uniform as possible?

(4) Comment on any other aspects of the case that were not specifically addressed in the preceding questions.

NORTHERN HYDRO

Northern Hydro is a utility, the principal objective of which is to generate and transmit the electricity required in the region it serves. It owns and operates about 80 hydraulic, fossil, and nuclear generating stations with a total generating capacity of about 34 gigawatts (GW) as well as an extensive power grid across the region.

Hydraulic generation supplies about 24%, fossil-fueled generation about 24%, and nuclear generation about 47% of the electricity required to meet customer demand. The remaining 5% of the requirements are met through purchases from neighboring utilities. For cost and environmental considerations, hydraulic power is used first, nuclear power second, and fossil power (first coal, then oil) last.

Northern Hydro sells wholesale electric power to municipal utilities in urban areas that, in turn, retail to customers in their service areas. Northern Hydro also directly serves more than 100 large industrial customers and about 836,000 rural retail customers in areas or communities not served by municipal utilities. Approximately 3,350,000 customers are currently served by Northern Hydro and the affiliated municipal utilities.

Electricity is used in the home and industry for lighting, heating, cooling, and power; Figure 1 shows the relative importance of the various uses.

Because electricity cannot be stored in large quantities, it must be produced as it is consumed. During any period of time, therefore, there must be sufficient capacity to meet the peak demand during the period. In fact, the system capacity must be substantially greater than the peak demand to allow for disruptions due to equipment breakdowns, repairs, maintenance, labor strikes, and bad weather. Northern Hydro estimates that in order to maintain the present level of service, the peak demand must not exceed 80% of the system's capacity. The difference between this "effective capacity" and actual capacity is a reserve to meet the contingencies just mentioned.

Existing generating plants and transmission lines are subject to physical deterioration. New generation and transmission facilities to replace the old ones and to meet increased electricity demand take 5 to 15 years to complete. In view of this long lead time, Northern Hydro's plans must extend 15 to 20 years into the future. A critical element of these plans is the forecast of the demand for electricity in the region.

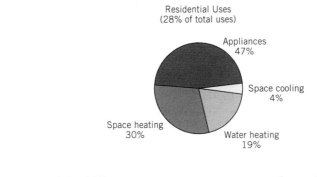

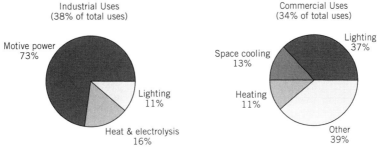

FIGURE 1 Uses of electricity

The importance of this forecast is illustrated in Figure 2, which shows Northern Hydro's current forecast of electricity demand and capacity for the next 25 years.

The forecast peak demand is expected to increase from about 27 GW 5 years hence to about 39 GW 25 years hence. The capacity of the present generating system is expected to decline gradually to about 22 GW 25 years from now. The effective capacity of the present facilities (80 percent of actual capacity) falls short of peak demand in six years.

As shown in Figure 3, about 22 GW of additional effective capacity (about 28 GW of additional actual capacity) will be required to meet the forecast peak demand of 39 GW 25 years from now. To put these numbers in perspective, consider that the total capacity of all hydraulic generating stations on the Niagara River is 1.6 GW and that the largest operating nuclear station has a capacity of 3.5 GW.

Northern Hydro must now begin to plan how best to obtain this additional capacity—a huge task, requiring the consideration of numerous options and constraints. These include the distribution of capacity among hydraulic, fossil, and nuclear generation; the size and location of any new generating plants and their transmission lines; the extent of purchases from other utilities; and—last but not least—the effects of the plans on the environment.

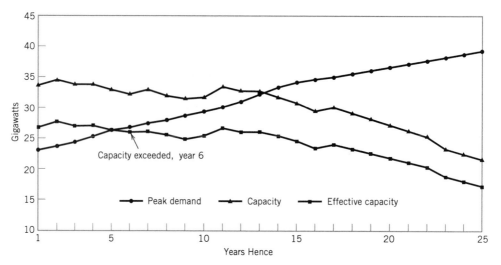

FIGURE 2   Forecast peak demand and capacity

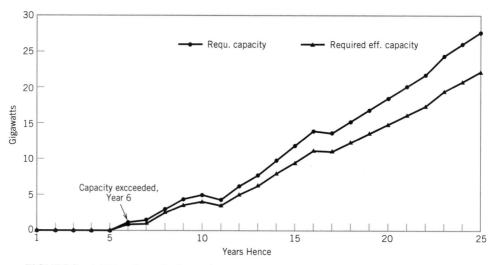

FIGURE 3   Additional required capacity

Evidently, the demand forecasts play a crucial role in shaping future requirements for facilities and the large funds needed for their construction and maintenance. It is not surprising, therefore, that the forecasting methods used by Northern Hydro are carefully scrutinized and often criticized by the media, politicians, and other interested parties.

Northern Hydro's forecasting methods appear to have changed significantly over time.

Until the early 1970s, forecasts were made essentially by assuming that the most recently observed growth rate would continue in the future. These projections were adjusted for the effects of special events, such as the Vietnam War, an economic recession, or changes in nickel production.

Figure 4 shows the 10-year-ahead forecasts made from 1966 to 1970 as well as the actual peak demand for the period 1955 to 1970.

When these series are plotted using the logarithmic scale of Figure 5, it is clear that the forecasts tend to assume a constant growth rate. The 1970 forecast projection of the peak demand in 1990 is 45 GW, while that for the year 2000 is 90 GW.

During the 1970s, these projections were replaced by estimates from a single equation model. In 1978, for example, the following model was estimated on the basis of data for the period 1957 to 1978:

$$PEAKD = c(ROE)^{1.34}(EMP)^{1.26}(PEAP)^{-0.465}$$
$$\times (ENER)^{-0.167}(OILP)^{-0.100}(GASP)^{-0.041}$$

where $PEAKD$ is the annual peak demand, c a constant, ROE the real output per employee, EMP employment, $PEAP$ the "peak charge," $ENER$ the "energy charge," $OILP$ the price of oil, and $GASP$ that of natural gas.[1] The forecast of the

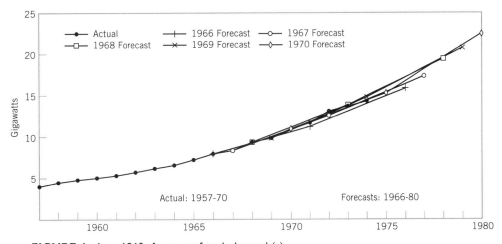

FIGURE 4 Late 1960s forecast of peak demand (a)

[1] Roughly, the peak charge is the price per unit of peak use and energy charge the price per unit of total electricity used.

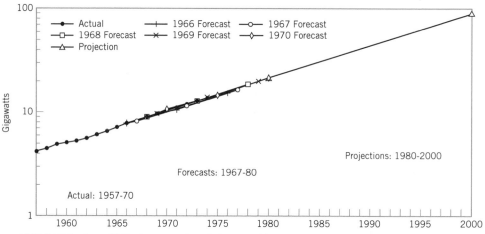

FIGURE 5 Late 1960s forecast of peak demand (b)

peak demand in a future year was calculated by substituting in the preceding equation the forecast values of the explanatory variables *ROE* to *GASP*.

Since the early 1980s, Northern Hydro's forecasting methods have increased in complexity.

In the first place, the forecast is a "judicious blend" of the forecasts of *two* models—an "end-use" model and a multiequation econometric model.

At the latest count, the econometric model contained about 170 equations and identities:

> [The model] takes as inputs forecasts of 13 final demand categories for the regional economy (for example, consumption of durable goods and nonresidential investment). These are processed to derive forecasts of total energy requirements for each of the industrial and commercial sectors on the assumption that technology and productivity remain constant. . . . This static forecast is then adjusted to reflect the impact of changing technology and prices. Forecasts of electricity prices and other fuel prices contribute to determining electricity's future market shares. The product of electricity market share and total energy requirements determines electricity demand for each sector. Demographic forecasts are important in determining the total energy requirements in the residential sector.

The end-use model employs

> a "bottom-up" approach to energy analysis. It starts with the initial stock of energy using devices and an estimate of future demand for the services required of these devices. The energy conversion efficiency of existing

equipment, customer adoption of new technologies, typically with higher efficiency, and relative fuel share for each end use are analyzed. Trends in electricity use per household, per square foot of commercial floor-area and by industrial process are combined with forecasts of activity for each sector to arrive at the final demand estimate.

Each of the major energy using sectors is modelled separately. This analysis requires forecasts of sectoral activity levels such as residential housing stock and commercial floor space by building type and industrial output in physical units. Factors such as population, labour force, disposable income, and detailed forecasts for service and industrial sector economic growth are considered.

A second element of complexity is the introduction of "bandwith" forecasting. There is a lower- and an upper-bound forecast, in addition to the point forecast of electricity demand. The band formed by these bounds is expected to contain the true demand with a probability of 80%.

One of the key lessons of the 1970's was that it is extremely risky to plan on the basis of a [point] forecast. The dramatic volatility of [demand] growth since the first oil price shock has made it clear that plans that did not consider the full range of uncertainty were vulnerable. . . . There is need for bandwidth forecasting and plans which are flexible. . . . The [end-use and multiequation] models used to produce the [point] forecast are not suitable for generating uncertainty bands. A much simpler econometric model is used to produce a median forecast and a probability distribution around it. [This] probability distribution . . . is derived from the probability distribution of [gross domestic product] and the statistical properties of the equation using "Monte Carlo" simulation techniques. The 80% bandwith forecast is then determined by taking the 10% and 90% values from the probability distribution for each year of the forecast. The median forecast is not the same as the recommended one resulting from the integration of the two large model forecasts. Therefore, it must be lined up with the recommended median forecast. The bandwiths generated by the simple model are scaled in a similar way to derive the bandwiths for the recommended long-term forecast.

The third element of complexity in the forecasting process since the early 1980s is the explicit recognition that Northern Hydro can influence the peak demand for electricity. By means of financial incentives or otherwise, for example, it can encourage the use of energy-efficient appliances, the shifting of demand from high- to low-use periods, and the integration in the public system of private and municipal power producers. Northern Hydro must forecast the effect of this "demand management" on the level of demand that would have prevailed in the absence of the policies. Currently, the forecast effects start with 0.8 GW one year hence and increase to about 5.6 GW twenty-five years hence.

Figure 6 shows the actual peak demand for electricity in the past 43 years and the current 25-year forecasts of Northern Hydro.

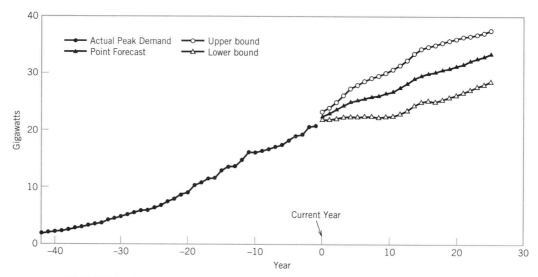

FIGURE 6   Actual and forecast peak demand

A. F. B. Jones is an energy analyst and a vocal critic of Northern Hydro forecasts. "In many ways," says Jones, "Hydro has not yet lived down its past forecasting errors. The excessive forecasts of the early 1970s and the drastic reductions made since then have cost Hydro the confidence of the public. In 1974, Hydro was forecasting a peak demand of about 42 GW in 1990, and 83 GW in 2000. To meet the predicted demand, it would have been necessary to increase the total capacity of the system by the equivalent of one nuclear station per year, at a cost of about $5 billion per year. The actual peak demand in 1990 was about 24 GW."

"In 1980," Jones continues, "Hydro was forecasting a peak demand of about 32 GW for the year 2000, a number conveniently matching the capacity installed once the plants then under construction were completed. In 1986, the regional Energy Board heard evidence that an unpopular forecast which had implications inconsistent with corporate Hydro plans could be changed. The board expressed concern that Hydro was cutting the forecasting suit to fit its own cloth; it felt that the corporation should respond to meet the forecast, and not vice versa. The board was also concerned about the total number of people devoted to forecasting activities and the sizable costs involved. Consequently, the board declared that it was not satisfied with Hydro's forecasting process."

"To be fair," Jones appears to concede, "forecasting is not an easy task. However, it is not made easier by obscuring the process behind an ink cloud of technical detail. Hydro seems to have concluded that its troubles in the 1970s were in part due to the fact that its forecasting method was transparent and could be understood by every one. The current point forecasts are the 'integrated' output of two huge multiequation models that few can understand, while the bandwidth comes from an independent single-equation model which must somehow be stretched to fit the point forecasts. Effectively, then, the relatively simple problem of forecasting one variable, peak demand, is transformed into the far more complex problem of forecasting all the independent variables of the single-equation model and all the exogenous variables of the multiequation models."

QUESTIONS

(1) Using models utilizing *only* the time series of peak demand known at the time the forecasts are made, form point and 80% confidence interval forecasts of the peak demand beginning 15 years ago for each of the following 25 years. Start, in other words, at the end of Year −15 and assume you know only the peak demand for years −42 to −15; form point and 80% confidence interval forecasts for years −14 to 10. Next, assuming you know only the peak demand for years −42 to −14, form point and interval forecasts for the peak demand in years −13 to 11. Proceed in the same fashion until you form forecasts for years 0 to 25 on the basis of the observed peak demand for years −42 to −1. You may report these calculations at the end of years −15, −10, −5, and −1 if the more frequent forecasts do not differ appreciably from one another. Compare your forecasts with those of Northern Hydro.

(2) Examine the advantages and disadvantages of the three forecasting approaches described in this case (projection of past trends, single- and multiequation modeling).

(3) Assess A.F.B. Jones's criticism.

(4) Comment critically on any other aspect of the case not addressed by the preceding questions.

DATA

The data file `norhydro.dat`, listed in Figure 7, contains the actual peak demand (PEAK, in GW) in the past 42 years (YEAR −42 to −1).

YEAR	PEAK
-42	1.771
-41	2.036
-40	2.262
-39	2.393
-38	2.443
-37	2.753
-36	3.063
-35	3.247
-34	3.442
-33	3.665
-32	4.183
-31	4.468
-30	4.737
-29	5.093
-28	5.510
-27	5.699
-26	5.903
-25	6.247
-24	6.751
-23	7.164
-22	7.818
-21	8.566
-20	8.964
-19	9.995
-18	10.555
-17	11.289
-16	11.535
-15	12.739
-14	13.605
-13	13.538
-12	14.512
-11	15.895
-10	15.901
-9	16.246
-8	16.365
-7	16.808
-6	17.189
-5	18.124
-4	18.791
-3	18.896
-2	20.473
-1	20.668

FIGURE 7 Peak demand, in *GW*, file norhydro.dat

ACCS INC.

ACCS Inc. is considering how best to forecast the redemption rates of future coupon issues for the company's clients.

Shoppers are familiar with *coupons*, which entitle them to a price discount on the next purchase of a particular product.

Coupons constitute one form of brand promotion. Other forms include advertising, trade promotion, refunds, contests, and sweepstakes.

Coupons are used to generate trial and first-purchase users among non-users of the brand, to speed acceptance of a new brand, to encourage current users to purchase the same brand again, to encourage users in the same product category to switch brands, to bring back former or lagged brand customers, to increase the effectiveness of brand advertising, to encourage multiple purchases of the same brand, and to encourage trading up to larger sizes of the brand.

> A key objective of most, if not all, product managers is to *create and maintain* a customer. This is frequently referred to as developing a brand's Consumer Franchise through the building of a body of consumers who, through experience and awareness, tend to more or less regularly buy *that brand* when they are in the market for a product of that type.
>
> To develop a franchise for a brand, consumers need to be constantly reminded of the benefits of the brand through advertising and then persuaded to actually buy the brand rather than a competing one. . . .
>
> Couponing provides the extra impetus to get consumers to buy, and is particularly effective in persuading a consumer to buy that brand rather than that of a competitor. Couponing can also help position a brand in the marketplace, establish a brand's key benefits, provide a unique selling feature at the point of sale, remove the risk inherent in trying to buy a new product or brand, create a theme around which a seasonal or special sales effort can be built, or gain effective in-store brand displays. (ACCS, *A Product Manager's Guide to Consumer Promotions*)

Coupons are distributed to consumers in a number of ways, including direct mail, newspapers, magazines, in-store displays, and on the products themselves. Appendix A describes in more detail these methods of distribution.

ACCS provides a variety of services to marketers. Prominent among these are coupon clearing and information services.

ACCS acts as a clearinghouse for coupons. On the one hand, it receives redeemed coupons periodically and in bulk from retailers and reimburses them. On the other hand, ACCS invoices and is reimbursed by companies issuing the coupons. A fee is charged for this service.

In addition to providing clearinghouse services, ACCS collects and stores information for each coupon issue handled. The information includes the face value of the coupon, the price of the product, the number of coupons distributed and redeemed, the area where the coupons are distributed, the date of issue and the period of time in which the coupon is valid, the name of the company and product, the retailer, the medium of distribution, and details depending on that medium. At present, such information is available for more than 50,000 different coupon issues of the past five years. This information may be retrieved and summarized in various forms to allow ACCS clients to learn, for example, the proportion of coupons redeemed by brand, product class, or year of issue; the number of coupons redeemed through particular retailers or in particular areas; and so on. In addition, the information helps ACCS clients design the features of a new issue and forecast the redemption rate of an issue with these features.

Coupon redemption rates depend on the method by which they are distributed. The following table was compiled by ACCS and shows the range and median redemption rate for the standard distribution methods. (The range excludes the 10% of offers that exhibit the highest redemption rates and the 10% with the lowest.)

Medium	Range %	Median (%)
In Pack—Self	1.5-44.3	13.6
On Pack—Self	2.8-33.8	12.4
Instantly Redeemable	19.2-89.2	43.9
In Pack—Cross	1.2-14.3	5.1
On Pack—Cross	0.6-30.4	3.0
Co-op Direct Mail	1.7-12.4	4.7
Freestanding Inserts	1.2-30.4	3.3
Newspapers	0.1- 3.9	1.0
Magazines	0.2- 5.7	0.9
Selective Direct Mail	3.1-36.3	15.1
Selective in Store	0.3-18.2	N/A
In-Store Handout	3.7-75.2	25.1
In-Store Shelf	4.3-39.8	17.3
Retailer In-Ads, large-sales products	0.1- 3.2	0.7
small-sales products	0.1- 1.2	0.3

Apart from the method of distribution, other factors influencing the coupon redemption rate are the expiry period (the time period during which the offer remains valid), the coupon's face value (the price discount) in relation to the product's selling price, the geographic area in which the coupons are distributed, the number of coupons distributed, the size of the product category to which the couponed brand belongs, the frequency of product purchase, the brand's market share, the design of the coupon, the brand's availability at the retail level, the number of purchases required by the coupon offer (for example, buy two units, get one free), and the effectiveness of the advertising accompanying the coupon.

For other than Retailer In-Ad coupons, the first three or four factors are generally considered the most important. However, even the terms of an offer could become the most important factor: for example, if an offer was limited to a nonstandard size of the product or was conditional on the purchase of so many units of the product that a typical buyer would not be able to buy them.

For Retailer In-Ads, the most important factors influencing the coupon redemption rate are thought to be the brand being promoted, the retailer or wholesale group distributing the offer, the size of the coupon and its placement in the advertisement, and the face value of the coupon in relation to the feature price of the product.

Special factors acquire importance for some distribution methods: for example, for On Pack coupons, the redemption rate depends on the ease with which the coupons can be removed and on whether the coupon is on the exterior or the interior surface of the package.

All these factors are interdependent. That is, a change in one can offset the effect of a change on another factor. For example, changing the face value of a coupon from 25 to 50 cents could offset the negative effect of reducing the expiry period from 12 to 3 months.

Coupons are not redeemed all at once—for each distribution method there is a particular redemption time pattern. For example, the following table compiled by ACCS shows the cumulative percentage of coupons redeemed for a "typical" In and On Pack—Self coupon issue with no expiry period:

Months after issue	Cumulative percentage redeemed
3	9
6	32
9	53
12	67
15	76
18	83
21	88
24	94

A successful coupon issue should be profitable. Obviously, a coupon issue cannot be considered successful if it results in no higher sales than would prevail in the absence of the coupon, if additional sales are achieved at the expense of sales of similar company products, or if the additional sales in the period in which the coupon is valid represent sales that would be realized in a later period. And, of course, any additional net revenue realized from a coupon issue must offset the cost of the issue. This cost consists of the face value of the coupon, plus retailer and ACCS handling fees, and postage multiplied by the number of coupons redeemed.

Product managers rely on other sources of information to determine if a coupon issue was successful. ACCS cites a case in which

> a prepared food manufacturer had been using retailer-in-ad coupon programs extensively and wanted to find out: did in-ad coupons successfully attract new users to the brand? did sales after the coupon promotion stay in line with pre-coupon levels, or did they drop below normal levels until pantry stock was depleted?

Period	Brand sales per week (volume index)
Pre in-ad	100
During in-ad	662
Post in-ad	119

> A [special analysis] found that brand sales during the in-ad coupon week increased significantly compared to pre-coupon sales (almost seven times). Household purchase panel data ... also revealed that a substantial portion of incremental sales were from consumers who had not bought the brand in the previous six months—thus the "new user" objective was also satisfied. Sales in the weeks after the in-ad coupons were also maintained above pre-coupon levels, thus meeting the objective to maintain normal sales levels. (ACCS, ibid.)

The past approach to forecasting coupon redemption rates is described in Appendix B.

Stephen Brown, the general manager of ACCS, and Wade Smith, ACCS vice president and manager of analytical services, believe this approach could be improved and forecasts of coupon redemption rates made more accurate. They intend to have the better approach incorporated in a special computer package that will allow ACCS clients to forecast the redemption rates of planned issues for different combinations of features, such as face values, valid periods, number of coupons distributed, or method of distribution. This package is intended to be interactive and user friendly, utilizing windows, graphics, and colors. In addition to the forecasts, the package will calculate the cost of an issue with given features and will allow the client to access the stored information on the client's past coupon issues and get a bar code for the new issue.

QUESTIONS

(1) Comment on the past approach, in particular the use of multipliers for adjusting the basic estimates.

(2) If you think the past approach can be improved, describe in detail the method you recommend.

(3) Using the available data described below, carry out your recommendations and illustrate how your suggestions would be implemented.

DATA

Two computer files are available to assist your analysis and recommendations. The first, accsfsi.dat, is a sample of 500 observations from the company's data on Freestanding Insert coupon issues. The second, accsria.dat, is a sample of 1000 observations from the company's data file on Retailer In-Ad issues. Samples, rather than the original files, are provided because the original files are too large to be conveniently handled in the time and with the computing facilities available to you. However, for the purpose of this case, you may treat the sample files as if they contained all available information. The names of clients and products were replaced by codes to preserve the confidentiality of the sources.

Table 1 provides an explanation of the variables in the data files. Figures 1 and 2 show a partial list of the two data files.

**TABLE I Explanation of Variables, Files
accsria.dat and accsfsi.dat**

Variable	Interpretation
CLCODE	Client code
PRCODE	Product code
FACEVAL	Face value of coupon ($)
PRICE	Regular price of product ($)
NODISTR	Number of coupons distributed (000)
EXPIRY	Number of months coupon was valid
YEAR	Year of issue (last two digits)
RETAILER	Retailer name
AREA	Code for region in which coupons were distributed
RATE	Redemption rate (percentage)

The variable *AREA* distinguishes 10 regions, coded A to K. Combinations of these codes indicate that the coupons were distributed in more than one region; for example, the code *ABC* means the coupons were distributed in regions A, B, and C. The code *NAT* indicates distribution in all 10 regions. Missing values in the data files are indicated by a period (.).

OBS	CLCODE	PRCODE	FACEVAL	PRICE	NODISTR	YEAR	RETAILER	AREA	RATE
1	2	1	0.5	3.29	1000	89	FD CITY	E	0.9
2	18	2	0.3	3.11	1000	90	A&P	E	0.6
3	18	2	0.3	3.11	1000	90	A&P	E	1.4
4	11	3	0.3	2.98	3000	89	OSHGRP	E	0.1
5	16	4	0.3	4.76	450	91	ATL WHLS	H	0.3
6	7	5	0.2	1.34	2000	90	A&P	E	0.2
7	7	5	0.2	1.34	800	90	DOM	E	0.1
8	7	5	0.2	1.34	1500	90	FD CITY	E	0.6
9	7	5	0.2	1.34	1500	90	IGA	E	2.7
10	7	6	0.3	3.63	426	90	A&P	E	0.3

FIGURE 1   File accsria.dat, partial listing

OBS	CLCODE	PRCODE	EXPIRY	FACEVAL	PRICE	NODISTR	AREA	YEAR	RATE
1	6	1	18	0.40	1.70	510	F	87	3.2
2	6	1	15	0.40	1.70	2976	NAT	87	2.3
3	24	2	13	0.40	7.55	3500	NAT	91	4.0
4	2	3	7	0.50	2.96	2300	DEF	87	4.0
5	2	4	7	0.15	2.07	1250	F	90	0.3
6	2	5	36	0.30	0.85	550	F	88	5.9
7	2	5	36	0.30	0.85	1803	DEF	88	3.7
8	24	6	13	0.35	3.97	345	A	87	3.0
9	12	7	13	0.15	1.35	3516	NAT	85	5.0
10	12	7	13	0.15	1.35	3516	NAT	85	5.0

FIGURE 2   File accsfsi.dat, partial listing

APPENDIX A

In Pack—Self coupons are redeemable on the brand *in* which they are carried. The product is usually flagged to advise the consumer that inside there is a cents-off coupon that can be used on the next purchase of the brand.

On Pack—Self coupons are redeemable on the brand *on* which they are printed. These coupons can be printed on the outside of the package label or on the interior or inside the label or package.

In and On Pack—Cross are coupons that are redeemable on a product or brand other than the brand carrying the coupon offer. The coupon-carrying product is usually flagged to advise the consumer that there is a cents-off coupon inside, which can be used on the purchase of another brand.

Instantly Redeemable Coupons (IRCs) are special On Pack—Self coupons that are attached to the product in such a way that they can be easily removed and used by the consumer at the time the product is purchased. IRCs include many varieties such as peel-off label, neck collar, and neck hanger coupons, as well as regularly printed coupons that are taped to the product by the retailer's sales force.

Cooperative Direct Mail coupons are delivered to households in selected postal walks or areas by nonaddressed mail. These coupons share the envelope with other coupons on noncompeting brands and other promotional offers to reduce costs. This service is provided by direct mail houses on a regularly scheduled basis.

Freestanding Insert coupons are printed with other coupons, promotion offers, and associated advertising in a four-color, magazine-quality, tabloid-size supplemental newspaper insert.

Run-of-Press Newspaper coupons are printed as part of an advertisement carried by the newspaper.

Magazine coupons can be placed either directly on the page as part of the brand's advertisement or they can be placed as "pop-up" coupons adjacent to it.

Selective couponing identifies the product/brand use and/or demographic profile of individual consumers and then uses this profile to determine what coupons, if any, the consumer is to receive. The two most frequently used selective couponing methods are *selective direct mail* and *selective in store*.

In-Store Handout coupons are distributed in store by a product demonstrator or host/hostess. *In-Store Shelf* coupons are distributed in special dispensers or "ad pads" at shelf level near or at the brand product displays.

Retailer In-Ad coupons on branded products appear in retailers' weekly newspaper or flyer advertisements. These coupons are placed by the retailer in cooperation with the brand's marketer, who is responsible for the coupon redemptions.

APPENDIX B

COUPON REDEMPTION RATE ESTIMATING GUIDELINES

Introduction

These guidelines are meant to help you, as Client Service Representatives, provide coupon redemption forecasts for your clients by providing relational guidelines for such factors as different media, face values, valid period, and area of distribution.

In the next three sections, I have prepared a list of indexes, which I call "multiplier adjustment factors" to help adjust estimated rates for differences in face value, valid period, and medium. These factors are meant to be applied to rates from the client's existing issues in order to come up with a rate for the proposed new issue.

These factors are guidelines only and, of course, need to be used with discretion.

Common-Sense Factor. When estimating anything, however, nothing takes the place of Common Sense. Look at other issues for the brand and at the typical median rates and ranges, *not just those in the medium the client plans to use*, to make sure that what you are saying makes sense.

Also, no matter what the adjustment factors say, a client won't get more than 100% of distribution, unless he runs into a counterfeit problem, and it is not up to you to predict this.

When using the adjustment factors, if you calculate a rate that does not make sense, before giving anything to the client please bring the estimate request to me for review.

Estimating with Similar Issues Available

It's relatively easy to come up with a budget estimate for a planned issue if a client has conducted similar programs before.

Refer to the client's file for that brand and medium. Use the rates shown there to determine a budget estimate.

For example, if a client wants to know what rate to budget on a 25-cent FSI coupon issue on Brand "A" with a six-month valid period, go to the file for that client and look up the FSI issues on that brand.

If the brand had three similar, or nearly similar, issues in the past four years, and these issues pulled in 4.3%, 5.7%, and 6.0%, I would advise the client to budget between 5% and 6%.

Important—also consider the trend in rates. The one restriction would be if there appeared to be a downward or upward trend in redemption, for example, if the most recent issue pulled 4.3%; I would then tend to advise the client to budget between 4% and 5%.

Different Media

What to do if issues are available on brand but they are in another medium.

If you go to the brand record in the client file and find the previous issues were placed in media different from the one the client wants to use, here's what you do.

Select any similar issues from either Direct Mail or Freestanding Insert (FSI) and determine what the rate for either direct mail or FSI would be for the proposed issue. Adjust this rate using the following factors to come up with a rate for the new medium:

Multiplier Adjustment Factors

Proposed medium	Redemption rate determined from	
	Direct Mail	FSI
Direct Mail	1.00	1.80
FSI	0.55	1.00
Magazine	0.45	0.80
Newspaper	0.25	0.45
. . .	. . .	. . .

For example, your client wants to know what rate to use for a 25-cent Magazine coupon with a six-month valid period on its brand. You find in the file that a similar Direct Mail coupon achieved between 6% and 7%.

To determine the rate for the Magazine issue, go to the adjustment chart. Since you are basing your estimate on a direct mail rate, go to the Direct Mail column. In the row for magazines you will find a multiplier adjustment factor or 0.45. Simply take this factor and apply it to the 6% – 7%, $0.45 \times 6\% = 2.7\%$, $0.45 \times 7\% = 3.2\%$. Therefore, you would advise the client to budget between 2.7% and 3.2% for the Magazine issue. (If your best historical data were based on FSI issues, you would apply the 0.8 factor for magazines from the FSI column.)

Different Valid Periods

What to do if issues are available on brand but they have significantly different valid periods.

Here are some multiplier adjustment factors, using *a coupon without an expiry date* as a base:

No Expiry	1.00
18–30 months	0.92
12–15 months	0.80
6–9 months	0.75
2–5 months	0.75
Less than 2 months	Who knows—use 0.65

Let us look at an example in which your client wants to use a six-month valid period. If you have established a rate of 2% for a similar issue with No Expiry, then use the 6–9 month adjustment factor. In this case, the 6–9 month adjustment factor of 0.75 is applied to the 2% No Expiry rate to come up with a 1.5% rate.

If the 2% was based on a 12–15 month valid issue and you needed to establish a six-month rate, you would have to adjust the 2.0% rate up to a No Expiry rate first before applying the six-month factor:

Step One: Adjust 12-month rate to No Expiry, 2%/0.8 = 2.5%.
Step Two: Adjust No Expiry rate to 6 month, 2.5% × 0.75 = 1.875%.

Note: Even though this example shows only one redemption rate figure, always give the client a range.

THE GREAT WALL BANK

The commercial lending department of the Great Wall Bank[1] is developing a quantitative scoring system for the assessment of a company's creditworthiness. It is hoped that such a system will enable the department to better target companies, better focus its marketing efforts, and better utilize the account managers' scarce resources.

The department has identified the most significant factors affecting the creditworthiness of a company. These factors, which reflect the distinctive economic and business environment of the region, are grouped into three categories: (a) financial and operational, (b) management-related, and (c) industry related.

The intent of the department is to create a scoring system whereby each factor level is assigned a number of points. The creditworthiness of a company will then be measured by the sum of all points associated with its factor profile.

The factors in the first two categories are listed in Appendix 1. An industry score is determined by the bank's chief economist, who takes into account the growth, prospects, and risk of the major industries in the region. All companies in the same industry are assigned the same score. The industry scores range from 0 (least creditworthy) to 40 (most creditworthy).

A great deal of time and effort was spent attempting to analyze the importance of each factor to a company's creditworthiness and to determine the appropriate number of points for each factor level. However, there remain considerable differences of opinion on these issues among the members of the department.

To help resolve these differences, it was decided to select a sample of 40 companies from among the bank's current customers and rank them according to their creditworthiness. That was not an easy task either, but a consensus was reached relatively easily and quickly. It was agreed that, whatever scoring system was adopted, the scores of the selected companies would have to be consistent with these ranks. The ranks and characteristics of the selected companies are listed in Appendix 2. The most creditworthy company is ranked 1, the least 40.

Some members of the department experimented with different scoring systems until by trial and error they found one that produced scores consistent

---

[1]The case is based on a project by Mr. Gregory Pau.

with the ranking of the companies. This scoring system is described in Appendix 1. The scores of the selected companies are given in Appendix 2 under the label SCORES. The maximum number of points under this system is 200 (most creditworthy), while the minimum is −96 (least creditworthy).

Other members of the department advocated a scoring system based on a regression of the ranks against the factors. The regression results (obtained with program SAS) are shown in Appendix 3.

The explanatory variables with the prefix *DUM* are dummy variables corresponding, in order, to the categories of the attributes listed in Appendix 1. For example, *DUMAS1* is a dummy variable taking the value 1 if *ASSOCIAT* is coded 1, or 0 if otherwise; *DUMAS2* takes the value 1 if *ASSOCIAT* is coded 2, or 0 if otherwise; and so on. Dummy variables representing the base categories or those with no observations are left out of the regression.

QUESTIONS

(1) Appraise the first scoring system described in Appendix 1. Describe with care the appealing and objectionable features of this system. Explain how a company other than one of the 40 listed in Appendix 2 will be rated.

(2) Appraise the second scoring system based on regression. Describe with care the appealing and objectionable features of this system. Explain how a company other than one of the 40 listed in Appendix 2 will be rated.

(3) Can the first or second system be modified so as to avoid at least some of their objectionable features? Justify your suggestions.

(4) Comment on any other aspect of the case not specifically covered in the preceding questions.

APPENDIX 1

The following is an explanation of the labels of variables used in the study. Shown in *italics* are the number of points under the proposed scoring system.

OBS: Company identification number

COMPANY: Company code

RANK: Rank of company

SCORES: Total score of company according to the scoring system

ASSOCIAT: Ownership by controlling conglomerate/group

= 1, between 51% and 100% owned (*5*)

= 2, between 20% and 50% owned (*3*)

= 3, less than 20% owned (*0*)

YEARS: number of years in core business (*3 points if more than 10, 1 if 5 to 10, 0 if less than 5*)

STATUS: Percentage of shares publicly owned (*5 points if 50% or more, 2 if otherwise*)

PLACE: Place in market

= 1, leader (one of top three in market share) (*10*)

= 2, follower I (second tier) (*4*)

= 3, follower II (third tier) (*1*)

= 4, fringe (*-10*)

PRODUCT: Product diversification. Number of products contributing less than 35% of total sales each

= 1, 4 or more products (*5*)

= 2, 3 products (*1*)

= 3, 2 or fewer products (*-5*)

CUSTOMER: Customer diversification. Number of customers contributing less than 35% of sales each

= 1, 10 or more customers (*5*)

= 2, 5 to 9 customers (*3*)

= 3, 3 or 4 customers (*1*)

= 4, 2 or fewer customers (*−5*)

SALES: Revenue ($million) (*8 points if more than 2000, 6 if 1000 to 2000, 4 if 500 to 1000, 2 if 200 to 500, -5 if less than 200*)

NETWORTH: Net worth ($million) (*15 points if more than 2000, 10 if 1000 to 2000, 6 if 500 to 1000, 4 if 200 to 500, 2 if 50 to 200, 0 if 25 to 50, -10 if less than 25*)

PROFIT: Last year's profit ($million) (*12 points if profit is more than 500, 8 if 250 to 500, 6 if 100 to 250, 4 if 50 to 100, 2 if 10 to 50, 0 if less than 10, -5 if loss is less than 10, and -10 if loss is greater than 10*)

RECORD: Number of consecutive profitable years; negative values denote number of consecutive losing years (*6 points if more than five, 3 if four to five, 0 if 3 or less, -5 if there was a loss in past two years*)

AUDITOR: Financial statements are audited by an

= 1, approved auditor (*3*)

= 2, auditor with no negative record (*0*)

= 3, auditor with negative record (*-3*)

OPINION: Auditor's opinion is

= 1, unqualified (*3*)

= 2, with minor qualifications (*0*)

= 3, with material qualifications (*-10*)

TIC: Times interest covered, i.e., ratio of Operating Income to Interest Expense (*10 points if greater than five, 5 if two to five, 0 if one to two, -5 if less than one*).

LEVERAGE: Leverage ratio, i.e., ratio of Total Liabilities to Total Net Worth (*10 points if less than 1, 5 if 1 to 1.5, 0 if 1.5 to 2.5, -2 if 2.5 to 4, -10 if greater than 4*).

EXPER: Experience of key management personnel

= 1, all have more than 10 years' experience (*5*)

= 2, all have from 5 to 10 years' experience (*2*)

= 3, at least one has less than 5 years' experience (*0*)

DEPTH: Quality of management

= 1, can meet complex needs (*15*)

= 2, can meet general business needs (*10*)

= 3, can meet needs of line of business (*5*)

= 4, weak (*-5*)

TRACK: Reputation and track record of management

= 1, excellent (*10*)

= 2, good (*5*)

= 3, satisfactory (*2*)

= 4, unsatisfactory (*-5*)

PLANNING: Corporate strategy and planning

= 1, clear and formal long-term goals (*10*)

= 2, informal long-term strategies or goals (*5*)

= 3, short-term goals and strategies (*3*)

= 4, no goals or strategies (*0*)

RISK: Management attitude toward risk

= 1, conservative and risk averse (*10*)

= 2, occasional risk taker but under plan (*5*)

= 3, aggressive risk taker, speculation oriented (*-5*)

SYSTEM: Management system

= 1 Systematic management with well-established and professionally run operation. Corporate policies, operating procedures, and reporting systems are well in place (*10*)

= 2 Adequate system and guidelines exist in major operations. Management relies more on individual manager than on system (5)

= 3 Lack of systematic management. Unsatisfactory operating procedures and reporting system. Slack operating control and policies (-5)

INDUSTRY: Industry score

APPENDIX 2

The data listed below can also be found in the file `wbank.dat`.

```
                 A              C        N                        L        P       I
         C              S        P  U        E              A  O    E        L       N
         O      S    S      S   R  S        T     P    R  U  P    V        A    S   D
         M      C    O    Y  T  P  O  T  S      W     R    E  D  I    E    E  D  T    Y   U
     P   R   O    C    E  A  L  D  O    A     O     O    C  I  N    R    X  E  R  N  R  S
  O  A   A   A    R    I  T  A  U  M    L     R     F    O  T  I  T   A    P  P  A  I  I  T
  B  N   N   E    A    R  U  C  C  E    E     T     I    R  O  O  I   G    E  T  C  N  S  R
  S  Y   K   S    T    S  S  E  T  R    S     H     T    D  R  N  C   E    R  H  K  G  E  M  Y

 1 HKL   1 165 1 22 90 1 2 1 2600 4400  615  4  1 1  6.2 0.83 1 1 2 1 1 2 20
 2 CKG   2 160 1 13 80 1 1 1 3200 5600  720  8  1 1  7.8 0.76 1 2 2 1 2 2 20
 3 CAT   3 152 1 15 90 1 2 1 1200 1600  340  4  1 1  6.3 0.72 1 2 2 2 1 2 30
 4 WIN   4 152 2 12 35 1 2 2  750 1800  220  6  1 1  9.6 0.24 1 2 1 2 1 2 35
 5 SHK   5 148 1 11 75 1 2 1 1300 1700  600  2  1 1  1.4 1.24 1 2 2 2 1 2 40
 6 LCR   6 142 2 24 25 2 1 1  850  870  280  8  1 1  6.8 0.66 1 2 1 2 1 2 25
 7 WEC   7 129 2 11 55 1 1 1  820 1650  130  2  1 2  1.7 1.22 1 3 2 2 1 2 35
 8 UNI   8 127 1  6 70 1 1 1 1300 1680  360  7  1 1  1.8 1.75 1 2 2 1 2 2 20
 9 CYA   9 126 1 16 43 2 2 1 1120 1870  450  4  1 1  2.2 2.34 1 2 2 2 1 2 28
10 MYE  10 126 3  8 60 1 2 1  640  800  180  7  1 1  3.2 1.72 1 2 2 1 2 2 31
11 CRY  11 123 3  7 35 1 1 1  760 1150  265  3  2 1  4.2 1.08 1 3 2 2 2 2 35
12 SFH  12 120 3 25 30 2 1 2  360  470  334  7  2 1 55.0 0.15 1 3 3 3 1 2 30
13 JCP  13 119 1 14 80 1 2 1 1600 3400  240  8  1 1  0.6 5.71 2 1 1 2 1 1 16
14 LIF  14 117 3 28 40 1 1 3  340  460   85  5  2 1  4.8 0.74 1 3 2 1 2 1 30
15 TSL  15 113 2  8 35 1 2 1  680  820   72  5  1 1  3.6 1.22 2 3 2 2 2 2 31
16 MTR  16 112 1  6 90 1 1 1 1800 5600 -200 -5  1 1 -2.2 3.45 1 1 1 1 1 1 16
17 MRX  17 111 2 12 45 2 3 2  640  840   70  1  1 2  5.4 1.42 2 2 3 2 1 2 35
18 PEN  18 111 2 13 68 2 2 1  470  720  110  4  1 1  3.7 1.34 1 3 2 2 2 2 35
19 SEL  19 106 2 16 80 2 1 2  380  700  135  8  1 1  4.1 1.19 1 2 3 3 1 2 15
20 ASC  20 105 1  8 80 2 2 1  660  950  170  4  2 1  2.6 1.78 1 3 2 2 2 2 30
21 PHI  21 105 1  8 80 2 2 1  400  860   46  5  1 1  2.1 1.63 1 2 1 2 1 2 15
22 SHP  22 105 1 24 90 1 2 1 1400 1850  240  7  1 1  1.4 1.87 2 1 2 1 2 1  0
23 HOP  23 104 3 17 80 2 2 1  820 1300  125  2  1 1  2.7 1.20 1 3 2 2 2 2 20
24 UOR  24 103 3  7 30 1 1 1  640  180   60  2  2 1  2.1 2.35 2 2 2 2 2 2 30
25 INT  25 102 1  6 80 2 2 1  370  790   45  2  1 1  2.6 1.96 2 2 3 2 2 2 28
26 SIN  26 102 2  7 60 2 1 1  960 1600  360  3  1 1  4.4 1.21 3 3 2 3 2 2 20
27 DOD  27  98 2 18 30 3 2 1   45   60    6  2  1 1  2.8 1.32 2 2 2 2 1 2 35
28 EST  28  97 3  6 20 2 2 1  160  230   12  5  2 1  3.1 1.47 1 3 2 2 2 2 30
29 WHB  29  95 3  4 55 3 2 3  120  140   26  4  2 1  4.6 0.84 3 3 2 2 2 2 35
30 CHP  30  92 1 14 65 2 1 2  175  250   91  7  2 1  3.5 1.41 1 3 2 2 2 2 15
```

```
31 EDW 31  92 3   7 40 2 2 1  140  220   60  2 2 1  4.6 1.08 1 3 2 2 2 2 30
32 REM 32  92 1   6 60 2 3 2  360  700  110  5 2 1  2.3 2.15 3 3 3 2 2 2 30
33 WAR 33  92 1   4 45 3 2 1  140   34   13  1 2 1  3.7 0.78 2 2 2 2 1 2 28
34 UNI 34  91 1  14 70 1 2 1  680 1840 -140 -4 1 1 -1.2 1.44 2 2 1 2 1 2 15
35 MBO 35  84 3   7 20 4 1 2  430  125   60  2 1 1  2.3 1.46 1 3 3 2 2 2 35
36 COP 36  81 3   4 15 2 1 2  120   20   12  2 2 1  6.8 0.45 2 2 2 2 1 2 20
37 WON 37  79 3   6 20 2 2 3  150   27   21  1 1 2  5.6 0.85 1 3 2 2 2 2 20
38 KOW 38  78 3   2 65 2 2 3  110   14    7  4 1 1  2.7 1.42 1 3 3 2 2 2 35
39 LAF 39  66 3   2 10 2 2 3   85   27    8  2 1 1  4.2 1.37 2 3 2 2 2 2 20
40 OAK 40  41 1   8 70 2 3 1  470  380  -20 -6 1 2 -1.2 5.41 2 2 2 2 2 2 15
```

APPENDIX 3

Regression results (output of SAS proc reg):

Model: MODEL 1
Dependent Variable: RANK

Analysis of Variance

Source	DF	Sum of Squares	Mean Square	F Value	Prob>F
Model	30	5083.20452	169.44015	6.179	0.0035
Error	9	246.79548	27.42172		
C Total	39	5330.00000			

Root MSE	5.23658	R-square	0.9537
Dep Mean	20.500000	Adj R-sq	0.7994
C.V.	25.54427		

Parameter Estimates

Variable	DF	Parameter Estimate	Standard Error	T for H0: Parameter=0	Prob > |T|
INTERCEP	1	44.071831	23.87000630	1.846	0.0979
DUMAS1	1	2.336046	5.45415455	0.428	0.6785
DUMAS2	1	-5.029955	5.62190915	-0.895	0.3942
YEARS	1	-0.013344	0.26053615	-0.051	0.9603
STATUS	1	-0.056310	0.09830728	-0.573	0.5808
DUMPL1	1	-0.829671	15.44314364	-0.054	0.9583
DUMPL2	1	7.214755	15.59115949	0.463	0.6545
DUMPL3	1	11.673095	18.93254145	0.617	0.5528
DUMPR1	1	5.059289	9.05263369	0.559	0.5899
DUMPR2	1	7.566214	9.36819223	0.808	0.4401
DUMCU1	1	-3.843662	4.61111472	-0.834	0.4261
DUMCU2	1	4.788191	7.57549244	0.632	0.5431
SALES	1	0.012244	0.01568926	0.780	0.4552
NETWORTH	1	-0.007103	0.00617440	-1.150	0.2796
PROFIT	1	-0.013703	0.02373599	-0.577	0.5779
RECORD	1	-0.601771	0.84336941	-1.899	0.0900
DUMAU1	1	-1.236314	4.55807524	-0.271	0.7923

DUMOP1	1	0.875596	5.62840691	0.156	0.8798
TIC	1	-0.443569	0.29622546	-1.497	0.1685
LEVERAGE	1	-0.205693	1.86913321	-0.110	0.9148
DUMEX1	1	-0.330182	6.46859764	-0.051	0.9604
DUMEX2	1	4.839854	9.06661933	0.534	0.6064
DUMDE1	1	-13.215044	9.40117563	-1.406	0.1934
DUMDE2	1	-7.987554	5.55605843	-1.438	0.1844
DUMTR1	1	2.391370	9.92157302	0.241	0.8149
DUMTR2	1	-3.491677	6.58007034	-0.531	0.6085
DUMPN1	1	-1.681801	13.13690694	-0.128	0.9009
DUMPN2	1	-9.395444	12.64263904	-0.743	0.4763
DUMRI1	1	-2.714971	4.47778031	-0.606	0.5593
DUMSY1	1	1.674778	7.46606102	0.224	0.8275
INDUSTRY	1	-0.189834	0.46474000	-0.408	0.6925

JOHNSON & PHILLIPS

Four times a year, Johnson & Phillips (J&P), a market research company, selects a national sample of persons 18 years old or older.[1] The selection method is a combination of stratified and multistage sampling. First, telephone area codes are grouped by region. From each region, a random sample of area codes is selected. From each selected area code, a random sample of households is drawn from among those having a telephone, using random-digit dialing. Finally, in the last stage, one person 18 years old or older is selected at random from each selected household.

The selected adults are invited to complete a questionnaire. Some of the questions are common in all J&P surveys, while others are included at the request of the organizations that subscribe to or purchase the results of the surveys.

There were 1518 responses to the most recent questionnaire. The responses to questions concerning ownership of personal computers and other electronic equipment and some characteristics of the respondents can be found in the file jandp.dat. Figure 1 shows the first 10 observations in that file.

The definition of the variables and their codes is as follows.

HBUS: Whether respondent runs business from home*

HSIZE: Number of persons in respondent's household

$= 1$, one

$= 2$, two

$= 3$, three

$= 4$, four

$= 5$, five or more

CHILD: Whether there are children under 19 in respondent's household*

HOME: Whether respondent owns home or rents

$= 1$, owns

$= 2$, rents

GEND: Respondent's gender

[1]The case is based on a project by Mr. Kaan Yigit.

```
                                R                               A       C
                H   C           E   C                       V   P       P
        H   S   H   H   G   L   G   S       E   H   E       H   G   H       H
 0      B   I   I   O   E   A   I   I   A   D   I   M   F   S   A   O       O
 B      U   Z   L   M   N   N   O   Z   G   U   N   P   A   C   E   M   N   P   N
 S      S   E   D   E   D   G   N   E   E   C   C   L   X   D   C   E   E   C   E

 1      2   1   1   2   2   1   1   2   2   3   2   2   2   1   2   2   2   2   2
 2      2   1   1   2   1   1   1   2   3   2   1   2   2   1   2   2   1   2   2
 3      2   2   1   2   2   1   1   2   3   2   3   6   2   1   2   2   2   2   2
 4      2   1   1   1   1   1   1   2   3   2   3   4   2   2   2   2   2   2   2
 5      2   2   1   1   2   1   1   2   5   3   .   1   2   2   2   2   2   2   2
 6      2   1   1   1   1   1   1   2   5   3   4   5   2   1   2   1   2   1   2
 7      2   2   2   2   2   1   1   2   3   3   2   2   2   2   2   1   2   2   2
 8      2   4   2   1   1   1   1   2   3   3   3   5   2   1   2   1   2   1   2
 9      2   3   2   2   2   1   1   2   3   3   3   2   2   1   2   2   2   1   2
10      2   3   2   1   1   1   1   2   2   2   .   4   2   1   2   2   1   1   2
```

FIGURE 1 Partial listing, file `jandp.dat`

> = 1, male
> = 2, female
>
> *LANG*: Language of interview
> > = 1, English
> > = 2, other
>
> *REGION*: Location of household
> > = 1, northeast
> > = 2, southeast
> > = 3, central
> > = 4, northwest
> > = 5, southwest
>
> *CSIZE*: Size of community where respondent lives
> > = 1, over 1,000,000
> > = 2, 100,000 to 1,000,000
> > = 3, 50,000 to 100,000
> > = 4, 10,000 to 50,000
> > = 5, other
>
> *AGE*: Age of respondent
> > = 1, 18–24 years old
> > = 2, 25–34 years old

      = 3, 35–44 years old

      = 4, 45–54 years old

      = 5, 55–64 years old

      =6, 65 or more years old

EDUC: Highest level of education attained by respondent

      = 1, elementary

      = 2, secondary

      = 3, postsecondary

HINC: Annual household income

      = 1, less than $20,000

      = 2, $20,000 to $40,000

      = 3, $40,000 to $60,000

      = 4, more than $60,000

EMPL: Employment status of respondent

      = 1, not employed

      = 2, clerical, sales or service

      = 3, manual labor

      = 4, semiskilled or skilled

      = 5, technical or professional

      =6, supervisory or management

FAX: Whether there is a fax in household*

CD: Whether there is a CD player in household*

HSEC: Whether there is a security system in household*

VGAME: Whether there is a video game in household*

APHONE: Whether the household phone has advanced features*

CPHONE: Whether there is a cellular phone in household*

PC: Whether there is a personal computer in household*

      * = 1, Yes; = 2, No.

In the file, missing values due to nonresponses are indicated by a period (.).

At the urging of management, the staff of J&P is preparing a demonstration of possible uses of the survey data. The demonstration is intended for potential clients. It should involve more sophisticated methods than mere cross-tabulations but at the same time its thrust should be clear to most clients.

After some discussion, the staff decided on an application of discriminant analysis demonstrating how to differentiate households with a personal computer from those that do not have one.

A computer program was used to routinely process the data file `jandp.dat`. The misclassification costs were assumed equal, in part because the program provided no alternative. The probabilities that a household has or does not have a PC were set equal to the corresponding sample proportions on the reasoning that the sample could be treated as "representative" of the population of adults. The program produced the two linear classification functions based on the normality assumption and the misclassification results. Some 221 observations had missing values and were not processed. The edited output of the program is shown in Figure 2.

```
CLASSIFICATION FUNCTIONS:
                                      PC
                           HAVE (1)        HAVE NOT   (2)

         CONSTANT         -70.76559          -68.13054
         HBUS              17.50513           18.23067
         HSIZE              2.38320            2.17965
         CHILD              4.85854            4.78587
         HOME              12.77584           13.01287
         GEND               6.03749            6.23553
         LANG               6.07691            6.24227
         CSIZE              2.61094            2.67991
         AGE                4.67750            4.66352
         EDUC               8.82406            7.96693
         HINC               3.64430            3.17586
         EMPL               1.56733            1.48828

CLASSIFICATION RESULTS:

Number of Observations and Percentage Classified into PC:

From PC              1                2              Total

      1            217              231              448
                 48.44            51.56           100.00

      2            136              713              849
                 16.02            83.98           100.00

Total              353              944             1297
Percent          27.22            72.78           100.00

Priors          0.3454           0.6546
```

FIGURE 2 J&P, output of discriminant analysis

QUESTIONS

(1) Interpret the results of the discriminant analysis. Discuss the appropriateness of the method used and of the explanatory variables employed. Are the results consistent with prior expectations? How useful are the results? Should J&P make use of these results as a "sophisticated demonstration"?

(2) Using the data in the file `jandp.dat` and a suitable computer program, examine whether or not a more judicious selection of explanatory variables improves the credibility of the model. (In this and subsequent questions, you may use a subset of the data if the size of the data file exceeds your computing capacity.)

(3) Would another classification method have been more appropriate? If so, determine the classification rule and its performance using the file `jandp.dat`.

(4) Using the data file `jandp.dat` and a suitable computer program, estimate a model expressing the probability that a household has a PC as a function of selected characteristics of the household.

(5) The data file for this case also contains information regarding the presence in the household of a (i) fax machine, (ii) CD player, (iii) security system, (iv) video game, (v) phone with advanced features, or (vi) cellular phone. Bearing in mind the lessons learned from Questions 1 to 4, prepare a demonstration of the utility of J&P's survey to potential clients who are interested in one or more of the products (i) to (vi).

(6) Comment on any other aspects of the case that were not specifically covered by the preceding questions.

NORGAS DISTRIBUTING COMPANY

INTRODUCTION AND OVERVIEW

The Norgas Distributing Company is the sole distributor of natural gas in the Kingstown metropolitan area and the surrounding region. The region, located along the northern shores of the Great Lakes, has an area the size of Rhode Island and a population of about 3.5 million.

Your task will be to manage the operations of Norgas for a period of one fiscal year, beginning on April 1, 19Y5, and ending on March 31, 19Y6.

The management of operations involves a number of irrevocable commitments, to be made by April 1, 19Y5. A contract has to be arranged with suppliers, specifying the minimum total quantity of natural gas that will be purchased during the year. A contract has to be arranged with the pipeline specifying the maximum quantity to be transported on any day. A decision has to be made whether or not to purchase weather forecasts; if this decision is affirmative, one of two firms providing weather forecasts must be selected and a binding contract signed with the chosen firm. Commitments must also be made concerning the method by which the daily demand for natural gas will be forecast and the order for next day's gas supply determined. Once these commitments have been made, the year's operations can be carried out automatically and the resulting profit calculated.

BACKGROUND

The Norgas Distributing Company is a corporation with assets of $1.8 billion and shareholders' equity of $560 million. It employs about 2800 people. For the 19Y5–Y6 fiscal year, the company projects a gross profit (i.e., difference between gas revenue and cost) of about $475 million. Total expenses for 19Y5–Y6 (including operating expenses, financial charges, and depreciation) amount to $420 million. The forecast is thus for a net profit before taxes of $55 million and a return on shareholders' equity of about 9.8%.

PURCHASE AND TRANSPORTATION

Norgas buys natural gas from a major western gas marketing organization and has this gas transported to its central distribution facility by pipeline. Figure 1 illustrates this arrangement.

As in past years, Norgas intends to contract with the supplier and the pipeline to ensure enough gas will be available to meet its customers' requirements during the year beginning April 1, 19Y5.

Purchasing and transportation are governed by two different contracts, but together these essentially stipulate two key quantities:

A = the minimum quantity of natural gas that Norgas must purchase during the year (in thousand cubic meters, Km^3);

D = the maximum quantity that Norgas may transport on any day during the year (in thousand cubic meters, Km^3).[1]

Norgas cannot have more than D delivered on any day and must purchase no less than A during the year. If the actual annual purchases are less than A, Norgas must pay for the difference at the end of the year.

The cost of transporting Q Km^3 of natural gas on any day from the supplier's gate to Norgas's central distribution point is given by $aQ + bD$ where $a = \$13.32$ and $b = \$26.51$.

The unit purchase cost of gas at the western supplier's gate, c, depends on the annual purchase commitment. It is $92 per Km^3 if A is less than 8 million

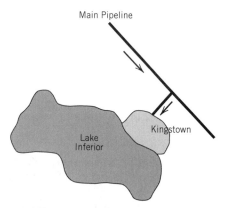

FIGURE I   Norgas, location and gas transportation

[1] All gas quantities in this case are measured in thousands of cubic meters, abbreviated as Km^3.

Km^3; \$90 per Km^3 if A is greater than 12 million; and, if A is between 8 and 12 million Km^3, is given by

$$c = 96 - 0.5A'$$

where A' is A expressed in million Km^3. For example, if A=9,100,000 Km^3. $c = 96 - (0.5)(9.1) = 91.45$.

It follows that the cost of purchasing Q Km^3 of gas on any day and having it transported to Norgas's central distribution point is $(a + c)Q + bD$.

DAILY DEMAND

Natural gas is used throughout the year for cooking and water heating in residences and as a source of power in industry. In the winter months, natural gas is also used for space heating. The daily demand for space heating depends on the weather. The daily demand for other uses depends mainly on household habits and the level of industrial activity.

The retail price of natural gas is regulated and must remain constant throughout the next fiscal year at an average of $r = \$211.78$ per Km^3.[2]

In the short run, therefore, the daily demand for natural gas is a function of such weather characteristics as temperature, wind speed, hours of sunshine, humidity, and the like.

It is the practice of Norgas to relate gas demand, not to the daily temperature, but to "degree days," in the belief that gas demand is more closely related to degree days than to temperature. Degree days is equal to the number of degrees below a given base temperature if the day's temperature is below the base or to zero if the day's temperature exceeds or is equal to the base temperature. In symbols,

$$DDAY = \begin{cases} t_0 - TEMP, & \text{if } TEMP < t_0 \\ 0, & \text{if } TEMP \geq t_0 \end{cases}$$

where $TEMP$ is temperature and t_0 the base temperature. Practice varies concerning the base temperature used. Norgas uses 18°C, but other gas utilities use base temperatures in the range from 15°C to 20°C.

---

[2]The retail price of gas varies with the conditions of service provided, the type of user, and the volume purchased. Numerous "tariffs" exist, but the average just given is considered satisfactory for planning purposes.

CONSEQUENCES OF EXCESS DEMAND OR SUPPLY

Norgas does not have access to gas storage. At the beginning of every day, it must place an order with its suppliers for delivery of the quantity of natural gas that will be required during the next day. For example, at the start of a Tuesday, an order must be placed for the quantity expected to be required during Wednesday.

If, as the day progresses, it becomes clear that the demand for the day is greater than the quantity ordered, Norgas curtails the demand by notifying and shutting off gas to interruptible customers.[3] Interruptible customers are generally large industrial and commercial users who can switch to another source of energy (e.g., oil) on short notice. Interruptible customers are compensated by paying a considerably lower rate than customers on "firm service."

If, on the other hand, the demand for the day is less than the quantity ordered, Norgas must refuse delivery of the excess but pay for the entire quantity ordered.

WEATHER FORECASTS

Two commercial weather forecasting services are available, Orion and Polaris. Both provide forecasts at the start of each day of the average hourly temperature and of the average hourly wind speed during the following day. For example, forecasts of the average hourly temperature and wind speed for a Wednesday will be available at the start of the preceding Tuesday.[4]

Both Orion and Polaris supply forecasts on an annual subscription basis only. The cost of an annual subscription to Orion is $60,000 and to Polaris $50,000.

By April 1, 19Y5, Norgas must decide which one of the two weather forecasting services will be its supplier of weather forecasts for the year. Of course, Norgas may elect not to buy weather forecasts at all if it believes such forecasts are not necessary or accurate.

DAILY OPERATIONS ILLUSTRATED

As noted earlier, a number of additional commitments must be made by April 1, 19Y5, including

---

[3]For the purpose of this case, it can be assumed that the entire excess demand can be interrupted at no higher cost than the lost revenue. In practice, there is a limit to interruptible demand and severe consequences to a gas utility that cannot satisfy uninterruptible demand.

[4]In the gas industry, a day starts at 8 A.M. and ends at 8 A.M. of the following calendar day. For example, "Wednesday" is the 24-hour period from 8 A.M. Wednesday to 8 A.M. Thursday.

- determine A, the minimum quantity of gas to be purchased during the year;
- determine D, the maximum quantity of gas to be carried on the pipeline on any day of the year;
- decide how to forecast the next day's temperature, wind speed, and gas demand;
- decide how to determine the quantity of gas to be delivered the next day.

The daily revenue, purchase and transportation cost, and gross profit, as well as the totals of these variables for the fiscal year, depend on these commitments, the actual demand for gas, and other events beyond the control of Norgas. The spreadsheet shown in Table 1 illustrates the calculations.[5]

The numbers used are purely for illustration. Several rows of the spreadsheet are hidden. It is assumed that Norgas contracted to buy a total of A=900,000 Km^3 of gas during the year, agreed to have no more than D=35,000 Km^3 of gas transported on any day of the year, and decided to subscribe to the Polaris weather forecasts.

The purchase commitment implies that $c = 92$ and that the cost of purchasing Q Km^3 of gas on any day and having it transported to Norgas's central distribution point is $(92 + 13.32)Q + (26.51)(35000)$, or $927850 + 105.32Q$.

At the start of any given day, Norgas will have available the Polaris forecast of temperature and wind for the following day.

The spreadsheet shows the forecasts on the day for which they were intended, even though they were made at the start of the previous day. For example, the forecasts of temperature and wind for April 2 were actually made at the start of April 1.

It is further assumed that Norgas, despite having subscribed to the Polaris forecasts, decides to ignore them (this is not an especially good business decision, but the artificial example is intended to show variety rather than good judgment). Instead, Norgas has no use for wind forecasts and uses as its forecast of temperature the actual temperature of two days before. It can be noted in the spreadsheet, for example, that Norgas's temperature forecast for April 3 is the actual temperature of April 1 (which is available at the start of April 2) and its temperature forecast for April 4 is the actual temperature of April 2 (available at the start of April 3).

In Table 1, Norgas forecasts the demand for gas using the formula $8000 + 910DDAY$, where

$$DDAY = \begin{cases} 18 - FTEMP, & \text{if } FTEMP < 18 \\ 0, & \text{if } FTEMP \geq 18 \end{cases}$$

---

[5]The spreadsheet (in Microsoft Excel format) is stored in the file `norgas1.xls`.

TABLE 1 Spreadsheet Illustrating Daily Operations

A =	900,000	Minimum annual quantity to be purchased and transported (in Km^3)
D =	35,000	Maximum daily quantity to be purchased and transported (in Km^3)
r =	211.78	Revenue per Km^3
a =	13.32	Transportation cost per Km^3 of Q
b =	26.51	Transportation cost per Km^3 of D
c =	92.00	Purchase cost per Km^3

| Year | Month | Day | Day of week | Orion forecast Temp. | Wind | Polaris forecast Temp. | Wind | Norgas forecast of Temp. | Wind | Demand | Quantity ordered, Q | Temp. | Wind | Actual Demand | Sales | Revenue (000) | P&T Cost (000) | Gross profit (000) |
YEAR	MO	DAY	DOW	FTO	FWO	FTP	FWP	FTEMP	FWIND	FDEM	Q	TEMP	WIND	DEMAND	SALES	REV	PCOST	GPROF
												−7.8	3					
												−1.2	7					
19Y5	Apr	1	Sat	9.2	11.3	2.7	10.1	−7.8	10.1	31478	31478	−10.8	8	33573	31478	$6,666	$4,243	$2,423
19Y5	Apr	2	Sun	6.7	7.8	4.8	8.6	−1.2	8.6	25472	25472	−5.4	11	29406	25472	$5,394	$3,611	$1,784
19Y5	Apr	3	Mon	5.2	10.4	−0.6	4.3	−10.8	4.3	34208	34208	−7.5	14	31668	31668	$6,707	$4,531	$2,176
19Y5	Apr	4	Tue	6	9	4.5	7.6	−5.4	7.6	29294	29294	−14.5	4	36139	29294	$6,204	$4,013	$2,191
19Y5	Apr	5	Wed	3.7	10.8	−0.9	13.2	−7.5	13.2	31205	31205	−0.2	8	24390	24390	$5,165	$4,214	$951
19Y5	Apr	6	Thu	9.6	11.7	9.4	8.1	−14.5	8.1	37575	35000	2.8	16	23110	23110	$4,894	$4,614	$280
19Y5	Apr	26	Wed	8.1	9.2	10.7	5.3	−10.4	5.3	33844	33844	−11.0	1	32596	32596	$6,903	$4,492	$2,411
19Y5	Apr	27	Thu	12.7	14.9	9.2	10.6	−5.1	10.6	29021	29021	−8.7	11	32267	29021	$6,146	$3,984	$2,162
19Y5	Apr	28	Fri	20.2	12.1	11.2	11.4	−11.0	11.4	34390	34390	−8.2	6	30978	30978	$6,561	$4,550	$2,011
19Y5	Apr	29	Sat	9.2	6.1	12.3	12.4	−8.7	12.4	32297	32297	−6.1	10	29857	29857	$6,323	$4,329	$1,994
19Y5	Apr	30	Sun	6.1	13.2	3.2	13.9	−8.2	13.9	31842	31842	2.8	8.9	26933.6	26933.6	$5,704	$4,281	$1,423
											891270		8.9	26933.6	26933.6			$43,899

Shortfall: 8730

Adjustment for shortfall:	($803)
Minus operating and financial expenses:	($420,000)
Minus forecasting subscription charge:	($50)
Net profit:	($376,955)

and *FTEMP* is Norgas's forecast of temperature. For example, the forecast of gas demand for April 1 is

$$(8000) + (910)[18 - (-7.8)] = 31,478 \text{ Km}^3$$

as shown in the spreadsheet.

The quantity to order, Q, is made equal to the forecast demand if the latter is less than or equal to the maximum daily quantity, D, or to D otherwise. It can be noted, for example, that the order quantity is equal to the forecast demand on April 1 to 5 but to 35,000 on April 6.

The spreadsheet next shows the actual temperature, wind, and gas demand (these events are, of course, beyond the control of Norgas).

Given Norgas's policies and these actual events, the day's sales, revenue, purchase and transportation cost, and gross profit are calculated, as shown in the last columns of the spreadsheet. Sales equals the smaller of the quantity ordered and demanded.

Pretend that the planning period is the month of April 19Y5 rather than the entire fiscal year. The total purchases over this period were less than the minimum quantity contracted for (900,000). The shortfall must be paid for at the rate of $92 per Km^3; the adjustment reduces total gross profit by the amount shown in Table 1. The other reductions of gross profit are for expenses ($420 million) and the cost of the Polaris subscription ($50,000).

DATA

Table 2 shows the total gas demand (in million m^3) by month and year during the period from April 1, 19X5, to March 31, 19Y5. The data can also be found in the file `norgas1.dat`.

In addition, two years of data are available in the file `norgas2.dat` concerning the daily demand for gas, temperature, wind, and forecasts of the latter variables. Figure 2 is a partial listing of this file.

The variables are defined as follows:

TEMP = Actual daily average of hourly temperatures, in degrees centigrade (°C)

WIND = Actual daily average of hourly wind speed, in miles per hour

DEMAND = Gas demand, in thousand cubic meters (Km^3); equals the sum of the quantities consumed and curtailed

FTO and *FWO* are the Orion and *FTP* and *FWP* the Polaris forecasts of the day's temperature and wind speed, respectively, measured in the same units as TEMP and WIND. These forecasts are made, of course, at the start of the

TABLE 2 Gas Demand by Month and Year (million m³)

MONTH	19X5	19X6	19X7	19X8	19X9	YEAR 19Y0	19Y1	19Y2	19Y3	19Y4	19Y5	Total
Jan	0.0	1217.5	1234.9	1142.3	1175.3	1103.6	1306.7	1140.5	1244.7	1400.5	1350.9	12316.7
Feb	0.0	1052.4	1175.5	1101.0	921.1	1030.6	952.5	1098.3	1076.4	1177.2	1084.2	10669.5
Mar	0.0	1097.5	879.7	931.3	1120.7	1094.7	1116.9	1116.9	1054.3	1004.5	1073.5	10489.9
Apr	657.5	450.3	661.6	875.6	700.6	688.0	595.3	630.8	619.6	720.3	0.0	6599.6
May	314.6	308.3	460.2	355.7	321.2	519.9	323.0	429.6	419.4	467.5	0.0	3919.3
Jun	231.8	229.6	248.9	229.9	221.2	278.1	281.6	279.9	314.5	357.7	0.0	2673.2
Jul	190.6	197.9	199.7	209.2	235.8	259.7	274.7	286.9	302.6	337.7	0.0	2494.8
Aug	192.1	229.4	223.1	219.7	245.7	254.0	283.5	293.5	289.6	317.5	0.0	2548.2
Sep	181.9	365.0	277.8	214.9	334.3	294.8	296.9	373.9	353.6	327.6	0.0	3020.8
Oct	327.0	647.2	395.0	537.2	464.5	481.8	565.7	679.2	637.9	472.6	0.0	5208.0
Nov	800.9	779.0	690.7	732.6	756.7	811.4	774.5	1011.2	919.4	1026.6	0.0	8303.0
Dec	1215.4	1106.2	1038.6	1174.1	1107.8	1101.8	1234.1	1098.7	1015.4	1149.3	0.0	11241.3
Total	4111.8	7680.3	7485.6	7723.6	7605.0	7918.5	8005.3	8439.3	8247.4	8758.9	3508.6	79484.3

YEAR	MONTH	DAY	DOW	FTO	FWO	FTP	FWP	TEMP	WIND	DEMAND
19Y3	Apr	1	Thu	-5.2	6.2	-3.7	13.3	-4.5	5.4	41809.9
19Y3	Apr	2	Fri	-7.2	9.8	-1.5	20.6	-4.8	11.9	40223.9
19Y3	Apr	3	Sat	2.4	12.1	3.5	14.1	2.2	13.5	31462.5
19Y3	Apr	4	Sun	-0.9	11.3	-1.3	15.3	-0.7	11.0	29374.2
19Y3	Apr	5	Mon	4.0	10.7	-4.3	21.5	2.5	13.8	32646.9
19Y3	Apr	6	Tue	5.4	8.7	1.7	14.6	3.7	11.3	28449.4
19Y3	Apr	7	Wed	14.8	12.2	11.8	10.5	13.5	11.4	15618.4
19Y3	Apr	8	Thu	17.5	13.3	15.8	21.4	14.7	11.8	7730.5
19Y3	Apr	9	Fri	11.5	13.0	6.8	14.4	10.0	10.7	16209.9
19Y3	Apr	10	Sat	10.2	11.8	11.6	24.5	11.8	11.8	15781.6

FIGURE 2 File norgas2.dat, partial listing

day prior to the one with which they are listed. For example, the Wednesday forecasts are made at the start of Tuesday.

QUESTIONS

(1) In a report addressed to the management of Norgas, (a) state if Norgas should subscribe to (i) the Orion forecasts, (ii) the Polaris forecasts, or (iii) neither forecasting service, and (b) fully explain the reasons for your recommendation.

If your recommendation is (1, iii) or if your forecasts of temperature and wind speed are to be different from those of the selected weather forecasting service, explain precisely how your forecasts will be formed. The forecasts should not make use of information that is not known at the time the forecasts are made.

(2) In a report addressed to the management of Norgas,

(a) state your decisions concerning

A = the minimum quantity of gas (in Km^3) to be purchased during the 19Y5–Y6 fiscal year;

D = the maximum quantity of gas (in Km^3) that will be transported on the pipeline on any day of the 19Y5–Y6 fiscal year; and

(b) fully explain the reasons for your decisions.

(3) In a report addressed to the management of Norgas,

(a) state clearly the method you recommend for

(i) forecasting the daily demand for gas (in Km^3),
(ii) determining the daily order quantity (Q, in Km^3); and

(b) fully explain the reasons for your recommendations.

Recall that the order quantity, Q, is the quantity of gas ordered at the beginning of a day for delivery on the following day. Q, of course, can vary from day to day.

The methods in (3, a) should be stated in the form of formulas that can be implemented in a spreadsheet program. These formulas should not make use of information that is not known at the time the forecasts and decisions are made.

As a result of your decisions in Questions 1 to 3, and given the actual gas demand each day from April 1, 19Y5, to March 31, 19Y6, the daily revenue, purchase and transportation cost, and gross profit, as well as the total profit for the year can be calculated. This last figure measures the performance of Norgas under your directions.

PART III

APPENDIXES

STATISTICAL ESSENTIALS

A.I   THE SUMMATION NOTATION

The summation notation is a convenient shorthand that is very helpful for reducing the size of certain mathematical expressions.

For example, suppose we wish to indicate the sum of n observations $X_1, X_2, \ldots, X_n$. We can write this sum either as

$$X_1 + X_2 + \cdots + X_n \tag{A.1}$$

or, in summation notation, more simply as

$$\sum_{i=1}^{n} X_i \tag{A.2}$$

$\sum$ is the summation symbol, i is the index of summation, and Eq. A.2 is read as "the sum of the X_i for i taking values from 1 to n." Clearly, Eq. A.2 is a much more compact way of writing a sum than Eq. A.1.

When there is no danger of misunderstanding, even simpler notation is sometimes used in place of Eq. A.2:

$$\sum_{1}^{n} X_i, \qquad \sum X_i, \qquad \sum X.$$

All these expressions translate into Eq. A.1.

The summation notation can be used for writing the sums of any expressions identified by subscripts. Some examples are shown below (c is a constant):

$$\sum_{i=1}^{n} X_i^2 = X_1^2 + X_2^2 + \cdots + X_n^2$$

$$\sum_{i=1}^{n} (X_i - c)^2 = (X_1 - c)^2 + (X_2 - c)^2 + \cdots + (X_n - c)^2$$

$$\sum_{i=1}^{n} X_i Y_i = X_1 Y_1 + X_2 Y_2 + \cdots + X_n Y_n$$

$$\sum_{i=1}^{m} f(Y_i) = f(Y_1) + f(Y_2) + \cdots + f(Y_m)$$

$$\sum_{i=1}^{m} Y_i f(Y_i) = Y_1 f(Y_1) + Y_2 f(Y_2) + \cdots + Y_m f(Y_m)$$

The particular index used does not affect the sense of the summation:

$$\sum_{i=1}^{n} X_i = \sum_{j=1}^{n} X_j = \sum_{k=1}^{n} X_k = X_1 + X_2 + \cdots + X_n$$

The sum from 1 to n of a constant is simply n times that constant:

$$\sum_{i=1}^{n} c = \underbrace{c + c + \cdots + c}_{n \text{ terms}} = nc$$

The sum of terms each multiplied by the same constant equals the constant times the sum of terms:

$$\sum_{i=1}^{n} cX_i = cX_1 + cX_2 + \cdots + cX_n = c \sum_{i=1}^{n} X_i$$

The summation of a sum of terms is the sum of the summation of the terms:

$$\sum_{i=1}^{n} (X_i + Y_i) = (X_1 + Y_1) + (X_2 + Y_2) + \cdots + (X_n + Y_n) = \sum_{i=1}^{n} X_i + \sum_{i=1}^{n} Y_i$$

and more generally,

$$\sum_{i=1}^{n} (X_i + Y_i + \cdots + Z_i) = \sum_{i=1}^{n} X_i + \sum_{i=1}^{n} Y_i + \cdots + \sum_{i=1}^{n} Z_i$$

From the last results we see, for instance, that

$$\sum_{i=1}^{n} (X_i - c)^2 = \sum_{i=1}^{n} (X_i^2 - 2cX_i + c^2) = \sum_{i=1}^{n} X_i^2 - 2c \sum_{i=1}^{n} X_i + nc^2$$

Double summation is shorthand for sums of expressions that can be identified by two subscripts. For example, suppose we wish to write the sum of mn observations arranged in a table with m rows and n columns, as follows:

Rows	Columns			
	1	2	$\cdots$	n
1	X_{11}	X_{12}	$\cdots$	X_{1n}
2	X_{21}	X_{22}	$\cdots$	X_{2n}
$\cdots$	$\cdots$	$\cdots$	$\cdots$	$\cdots$
m	X_{m1}	X_{m2}	$\cdots$	X_{mn}

The first subscript identifies the row and the second the column. Thus, X_{ij} represents the observation in the ith row and jth column (or, in the ijth *cell*) of the table.

The sum of all mn observations can be written in full as

$$(X_{11} + X_{12} + \cdots + X_{1n}) + (X_{21} + X_{22} + \cdots + X_{2n}) + \cdots + (X_{m1} + X_{m2} + \cdots + X_{mn})$$

or, more compactly, as

$$\sum_{i=1}^{m}(X_{i1} + X_{i2} + \cdots + X_{in})$$

or, even more compactly, as

$$\sum_{i=1}^{m}\sum_{j=1}^{n}X_{ij}$$

One also sees this last expression written even more simply as $\sum X$ when it is clear that the sum is over all cells of the table.

A.2 THE MEAN, VARIANCE, AND STANDARD DEVIATION OF A VARIABLE

Available are four observations on a variable X, as shown in the first column of the following table:

X	X^2	$X - \bar{X}$	$(X - \bar{X})^2$
2	4	0.75	0.5625
−3	9	−4.25	18.0625
1	1	−0.25	0.0625
5	25	3.75	14.0625
5	39	0	32.7500

The *mean (average)* of X, denoted by $Ave(X)$ or $\bar{X}$, is

$$Ave(X) = \bar{X} = \frac{1}{n}\sum X \qquad (A.3)$$

The *variance* of X (the average squared deviation of X from its mean), denoted by $Var(X)$ or S^2, is

$$Var(X) = S^2 = \frac{1}{n}\sum (X - \bar{X})^2 \qquad (A.4)$$

For the data of our example,

$$Ave(X) = \frac{1}{4}(5) = 1.25$$

and

$$Var(X) = \frac{1}{4}(32.75) = 8.1875$$

Alternatively, the variance may be calculated from the following equivalent expression,

$$Var(X) = S^2 = \frac{1}{n}\sum X^2 - \bar{X}^2 = \frac{1}{4}(39) - (1.25)^2 = 8.1875$$

The *standard deviation* of X, denoted by $StD(X)$ or S, is the square root of the variance

$$StD(X) = S = \sqrt{Var(X)} \qquad (A.5)$$

In our example,

$$StD(X) = S = \sqrt{8.1875} = 2.8614$$

When dealing with several variables, their means and variances may be denoted as $\bar{X}_1, \bar{X}_2, \ldots, S_X^2, S_Y^2$, and so on, or S_1^2, S_2^2, and so on.

A.3 THE MEAN AND VARIANCE OF A LINEAR FUNCTION OF A VARIABLE

Suppose that a variable Y is a linear function of another variable X:

$$Y = a + bX$$

where a and b are constants. It can be shown that the mean and variance of Y are functions of the mean and variance of X, as follows:

$$\bar{Y} = a + b\bar{X} \tag{A.6}$$

$$Var(Y) = b^2 Var(X) \tag{A.7}$$

To confirm these results, suppose that $Y = 2 - 3X$ and the X-values are as shown in the first column of the following table:

X	Y
2	−4
−3	11
1	−1
5	−13

The corresponding values of Y are shown in the second column.

The mean and variance of X were calculated in Section A.2 as $\bar{X} = 1.25$ and $Var(X) = 8.1875$.

According to Eqs. A.6 and A.7,

$$\bar{Y} = (2) + (-3)(1.25) = -1.75$$
$$Var(Y) = (-3)^2(8.1875) = 73.6875$$

EXERCISE A.1 Confirm these results by direct calculation using the Y-values shown in the last table.

A.4 FREQUENCY AND RELATIVE FREQUENCY DISTRIBUTIONS

When the number of observations is large, it is often convenient to list the distinct values of the variable and the number or proportion of observations with these values. Such a list is called the *frequency* or *relative frequency distribution* of the variable.

Consider, for example, five observations on variable X with values 1, −1, −1, 1, and −1. The data can be grouped as follows:

X	$f(X)$	$r(X)$
(1)	(2)	(3)
−1	3	0.6
1	2	0.4
	5	1.0

The frequencies are denoted by $f(X)$ and the relative frequencies by $r(X)$. Columns 1 and 2 show the frequency distribution and Columns 1 and 3 the relative frequency distribution of X.

When the data have been so grouped, the calculation of the mean and variance can be simplified. If X takes m distinct values $X_1, X_2, \ldots, X_m$ with frequencies $f(X_1), f(X_2), \ldots, f(X_m)$, the mean is

$$
\begin{aligned}
Ave(X) &= \frac{1}{n}[X_1 f(X_1) + X_2 f(X_2) + \cdots + X_m f(X_m)] \\
&= \frac{1}{n}\sum Xf(X) \\
&= \sum \frac{f(X)}{n}X \\
&= \sum r(X)X
\end{aligned}
$$

that is,

$$
Ave(X) = \bar{X} = \frac{1}{n}\sum Xf(X) = \sum r(X)X \tag{A.8}
$$

The same reasoning shows that the variance of X is given by

$$
Var(X) = S^2 = \frac{1}{n}\sum (X - \bar{X})^2 f(X) = \sum (X - \bar{X})^2 r(X) \tag{A.9}
$$

We illustrate the calculations using the relative frequency distribution of this section.

X	$r(X)$	$Xr(X)$	$X - \bar{X}$	$(X - \bar{X})^2$	$(X - \bar{X})^2 r(X)$
-1	0.6	-0.6	-0.8	0.64	0.384
1	0.4	0.4	1.2	1.44	0.576
	1.0	$\bar{X} = -0.2$			$S^2 = 0.96$

EXERCISE A.2 Verify the preceding calculations using the ungrouped data for the example of this section.

It should be clear that Eqs. A.8 and A.9 are different versions of Eqs. A.3 and A.4, respectively, *not* different definitions of the mean and variance of a variable. It should also be clear that the results of Section A.3 concerning linear functions of a variable hold whether the calculations are based on ungrouped or on grouped data.

EXERCISE A.3 Assuming $Y = 1 - X$, determine the frequency and relative frequency distributions of Y. Verify that Eqs. A.8 and A.9 hold whether applied to the ungrouped or the grouped data of this section.

A.5 PROBABILITY DISTRIBUTIONS

According to one definition, the *probability* of an event is its expected relative frequency in a large number of repetitions of the process that generates the event. If it is expected, for example, that a "6" will show up in 1/6 of a large number of rolls of a die, then 1/6 is the probability that a "6" will show up in any one roll.

The *probability distribution* of a variable is a list showing the possible values of the variable and the associated probabilities. For example, the probability distribution of the number of dots, X, showing up in a roll of a die is usually assumed to be as follows:

X	$p(X)$
1	1/6
2	1/6
3	1/6
4	1/6
5	1/6
6	1/6
	1

In view of the correspondence between expected relative frequencies and probabilities, it should not be surprising that all the preceding definitions and results hold for probability distributions as well, except that probabilities $p(X)$ replace relative frequencies $r(X)$ in all expressions.

EXERCISE A.4 Calculate the mean and variance of the number X showing up in a roll of a die. Assuming that another variable is linearly related to X, $Y = 1 + 2X$, determine the probability distribution of Y and calculate its mean and variance.

These definitional and operational identities should not be obscured by established notational conventions. It is common, for example, to denote the mean of a probability distribution by μ, μ_X, or $E(X)$. These conventions are so firmly established that we yielded to them in this text, even though common sense urged uniform notation. The following are some commonly used symbols for the mean and variance of a variable X:

Context	Mean	Variance
Ungrouped or grouped data, sample	$\bar{X}$, $Ave(X)$	S^2, S_X^2, $Var(X)$
Probability distribution or population	μ, μ_X, $Ave(X)$	σ^2, σ_X^2, or $Var(X)$

A.6 COVARIANCE AND CORRELATION COEFFICIENT OF TWO VARIABLES

Suppose four observations are available on two variables, X_1 and X_2, as shown in the first two columns of the following table.

X_1	X_2	$X_1 X_2$
2	1.1	2.2
−3	−1.5	4.5
1	0.6	0.6
5	2.4	12.0
5	2.6	19.3

In Section A.2, it was shown that the mean, variance, and standard deviation of X_1 were 1.25, 8.1875, and 2.8614, respectively.

EXERCISE A.5 Show that the mean, variance, and standard deviation of X_2 are 0.65, 1.9725, and 1.4045, respectively.

The *covariance* of X_1 and X_2, denoted by $Cov(X_1, X_2)$ or S_{12}, is

$$Cov(X_1, X_2) = S_{12} = \frac{1}{n}\sum(X_1 - \bar{X}_1)(X_2 - \bar{X}_2) = \frac{1}{n}\sum X_1 X_2 - \bar{X}_1 \bar{X}_2 \quad \text{(A.10)}$$

For our example,

$$Cov(X_1, X_2) = S_{12} = \frac{1}{4}(19.3) - (1.25)(0.65) = 4.0125$$

The *correlation coefficient* of X_1 and X_2, denoted as $Cor(X_1, X_2)$ or R_{12}, is

$$Cor(X_1, X_2) = R_{12} = \frac{Cov(X_1, X_2)}{StD(X_1)StD(X_2)} = \frac{S_{12}}{S_1 S_2} \qquad \text{(A.11)}$$

For our example,

$$Cor(X_1, X_2) = R_{12} = \frac{4.0125}{(2.8614)(1.4045)} = 0.9984$$

The covariance and correlation coefficient of a pair of variables are, of course, symmetric. That is, $S_{12} = S_{21}$, $R_{12} = R_{21}$, and so on.

Two variables are said to be *uncorrelated* if their covariance (and correlation coefficient) is equal to zero.

The covariance is best thought of as the numerator of the correlation coefficient. As for the latter, its properties are best understood with the help of Figure A.1, which shows six types of scatter diagrams and the associated approximate value of the correlation coefficient:

(a) The value of the correlation coefficient is always between -1 and $+1$.

(b) When all the pairs of values of X_1 and X_2 lie on a straight line, R_{12} is equal to $+1$ if the line is upward sloping (Figure A.1[a]) or to -1 if the line is downward sloping (Figure A.1[d]).

(c) When the pairs (X_1, X_2) of values tend to cluster along an upward-sloping line, the value of R_{12} will be a positive number between 0 and 1; the closer the points cluster around the line, the closer R_{12} will be to $+1$ (Figure A.1[b]). Similarly, the closer the points cluster around a downward-sloping line, the closer R_{12} will be to -1 (Figure A.1[c]).

(d) When, as shown in Figure A.1(e), there is no relationship between X_1 and X_2, R_{12} will tend to be near zero. Note, however, that R_{12} may be near 0 also for certain types of curvilinear relationships, as, for example, in Figure A.1(f).

The correlation coefficient, therefore, may be described as a standardized measure of the degree to which two variables are linearly related.

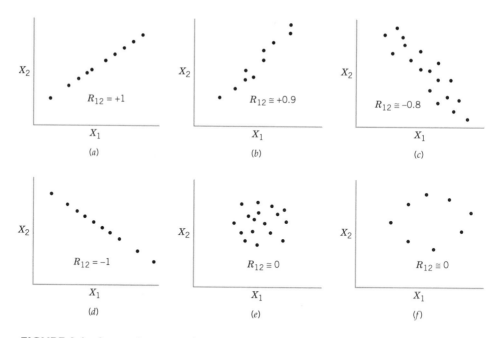

FIGURE A.I Scatter diagrams and associated correlation coefficients

A.7 THE MEAN AND VARIANCE OF A LINEAR FUNCTION OF TWO VARIABLES

Suppose that a variable Y is a linear function of two other variables X_1 and X_2

$$Y = a + b_1 X_1 + b_2 X_2$$

It can be shown that the mean and variance of Y are related to the means, variances, and covariance of X_1 and X_2 as follows:

$$\bar{Y} = a + b_1 \bar{X}_1 + b_2 \bar{X}_2 \tag{A.12}$$

$$Var(Y) = b_1^2 Var(X_1) + b_2^2 Var(X_2) + 2b_1 b_2 Cov(X_1, X_2)$$
$$= b_1^2 S_1^2 + b_2^2 S_2^2 + 2b_1 b_2 S_{12} \tag{A.13}$$

To confirm this result, suppose that $Y = 2 - 3X_1 + X_2$ and the observations on X_1 and X_2 are as shown in the first two columns of the following table:

X_1	X_2	$Y = 2 - 3X_1 + X_2$
2	1.1	−2.9
−3	−1.5	9.5
1	0.6	−0.4
5	2.4	−10.6

In preceding sections we showed that $\bar{X}_1 = 1.25$, $\bar{X}_2 = 0.65$, $S_1^2 = 8.1875$, $S_2^2 = 1.9725$, and $S_{12} = 4.0125$. According to Eqs. A.12 and A.13, we should have

$$\bar{Y} = 2 - 3\bar{X}_1 + \bar{X}_2 = 2 - (3)(1.25) + (1)(0.65) = -1.1$$

and

$$Var(Y) = (-3)^2(8.1875) + (1)^2(1.9725) + (2)(-3)(1)(4.0125) = 51.585$$

EXERCISE A.6 Confirm these results by calculating directly the mean and variance of the Y-values given in the third column of the last table.

A.8 JOINT DISTRIBUTIONS

When the number of observations is large, it is often convenient to group data on two variables into a table or list showing all distinct *pairs* of values of the variables and the corresponding frequencies or relative frequencies. Such a table or list is called the *joint frequency* or *relative frequency distribution* of the two variables. Consider, for example, the following table:

X_1 (1)	X_2 (2)	$f(X_1, X_2)$ (3)	$r(X_1, X_2)$ (4)
−1	1	3	0.30
−1	2	2	0.20
2	1	1	0.10
2	2	4	0.40
		10	1.00

Of the 10 observations on X_1 and X_2, 3 or 30% had the pair of values ($X_1 = -1$, $X_2 = 1$), 2 or 20% the pair ($-1, 2$), and so on. Columns 1, 2 and 3 show a joint frequency distribution, while columns 1, 2 and 4 show a joint relative frequency distribution. Alternatively, the joint relative frequency distribution may be presented as follows:

	X_2		
X_1	1	2	Total
-1	0.3	0.2	0.50
2	0.1	0.4	0.50
Total	0.40	0.60	1.00

The calculation of the covariance can be simplified by taking advantage of the fact that the same pair of values is taken by more than one observation:

$$
Cov(X_1, X_2) = S_{12} = \frac{1}{n} \sum (X_1 - \bar{X}_1)(X_2 - \bar{X}_2) f(X_1, X_2)
$$
$$
= \sum (X_1 - \bar{X}_1)(X_2 - \bar{X}_2) r(X_1, X_2) \qquad \text{(A.14)}
$$

where the summation is over all distinct pairs of (X_1, X_2)-values. The correlation coefficient is calculated by substituting Eq. A.14 into A.11.

We illustrate this with the numerical example of this section. It is straightforward to verify that $\bar{X}_1 = 0.5$, $\bar{X}_2 = 1.6$, $S_1 = 1.5$, and $S_2 = 0.49$. The covariance is calculated as follows:

X_1	X_2	$r(X_1, X_2)$	$X_1 - \bar{X}_1$	$X_2 - \bar{X}_2$	$(X_1 - \bar{X}_1)(X_2 - \bar{X}_2) r(X_1, X_2)$
-1	1	0.30	-1.5	-0.6	0.27
-1	2	0.20	-1.5	0.4	-0.12
2	1	0.10	1.5	-0.6	-0.09
2	2	0.40	1.5	0.4	0.24
		1.00			$S_{12} = 0.30$

The correlation coefficient of X_1 and X_2 is therefore

$$
Cor(X_1, X_2) = \frac{0.30}{1.5 \times 0.49} = 0.408
$$

The *joint probability distribution* of two variables is a list showing the possible pairs of values of the two variables and the associated probabilities. All the definitions and results concerning joint relative frequency distributions apply to joint probability distributions as well except that relative frequencies, $r(X_1, X_2)$, are replaced by probabilities, $p(X_1, X_2)$.

A.9 CONDITIONAL DISTRIBUTIONS AND INDEPENDENCE

The similarity between relative frequencies and probabilities should be evident by now. To avoid repetition and redundancy, we shall explain the concepts of conditional distributions and independence in the context of probabilities, but very similar definitions apply to relative frequencies as well.

A conditional probability distribution is a list showing the possible values of a variable and associated probabilities for *given* values of the other variable.

To illustrate, suppose that the accident records of a large number of insured drivers over two consecutive years were examined. Let X_1 represent a driver's number of accidents in the first year (Year 1) and X_2 the number of accidents in the second year (Year 2). The joint relative frequency distribution of X_1 and X_2 was as follows:

Number of accidents in Year 1, X_1	Number of accidents in Year 2, X_2		Total
	0	**1**	
0	0.5	0.1	0.6
1	0.1	0.3	0.4
Total	0.6	0.4	1.0

Thus, 50% of the drivers had no accidents in Year 1 *and* none in Year 2, and so on. If it is reasonable to suppose that this pattern will hold in any future pair of years, the preceding table also provides the joint probability distribution of X_1 and X_2, where X_1 and X_2 now refer to any pair of consecutive future years.

To form the conditional probability distribution of the number of accidents "next" year given that the driver had no accidents "this" year, we could argue as follows. Out of every, say, 100 drivers, 60 are expected to have no accidents this year; out of these 60, 50 are expected to have no accidents (and 10 to have one accident) next year. Therefore, the chances are 50/60 or 0.833 that a driver with no accidents in a given year will have no accidents in the next year; the chances are 10/60 or 0.167 that such a driver will have one accident next year. This conditional probability distribution is shown in Columns 1 and 2 of the following table.

Number of accidents next year, X_2 (1)	Conditional probabilities, $p(X_2\|X_1 = 0)$ (2)	$p(X_2\|X_1 = 1)$ (3)
0	0.5/0.6 = 0.833	0.1/0.4 = 0.25
1	0.1/0.6 = 0.167	0.3/0.4 = 0.75
Total	1.000	1.00

Columns 1 and 3 show the conditional probability distribution of X_2 for drivers with one accident this year. (The conditional distributions of X_1 for each value of X_2 can also be calculated but are obviously of little practical interest in this example.)

Two variables, X_1 and X_2, are said to be *independent* of one another if all the conditional distributions of one variable are identical. Simply put, two variables are independent if the conditional probability that one variable will take any specified value does not depend on the value of the other variable.

It can be shown that if two variables are independent, their covariance and correlation coefficient are zero. That is, if X_1 and X_2 are independent, then

$$Cov(X_1, X_2) = Cor(X_1, X_2) = 0$$

The reverse, however, is not always true: that is, the covariance or correlation coefficient of two variables may be zero without the variables' being independent.

A.10 THE COVARIANCE MATRIX OF A SET OF VARIABLES

The *covariance matrix* (also called the *variance covariance matrix*) of a set of variables is a table containing the variances of the variables in the diagonal cells and the covariances in the off-diagonal cells. In the case of, say, three variables X_1, X_2, and X_3, the covariance matrix has the form

$$\begin{pmatrix} S_1^2 & S_{12} & S_{13} \\ S_{12} & S_2^2 & S_{23} \\ S_{13} & S_{23} & S_3^2 \end{pmatrix}$$

For example, suppose there are four observations on variables X_1, X_2, and X_3:

X_1	X_2	X_3
2	1.1	0.5
-3	-1.5	1.0
1	0.6	-0.5
5	2.4	0.0

EXERCISE A.7 Show that the covariance matrix of these variables is

$$\begin{pmatrix} 8.1875 & 4.0125 & -0.9375 \\ 4.0125 & 1.9725 & -0.4750 \\ -0.9375 & -0.4750 & 0.3125 \end{pmatrix}$$

A.11   THE MEAN AND VARIANCE OF A LINEAR FUNCTION OF A SET OF VARIABLES

The results of Section A.7 generalize to the case where Y is a linear function of any number of variables $X_1, X_2, \ldots, X_k$,

$$Y = b_0 + b_1 X_1 + b_2 X_2 + \cdots + b_k X_k$$

It can be shown that the mean and variance of Y are

$$\bar{Y} = b_0 + b_1 \bar{X}_1 + b_2 \bar{X}_2 + \cdots + b_k \bar{X}_k \tag{A.15}$$

and

$$Var(Y) = b_1^2 S_1^2 + b_2^2 S_2^2 + \cdots + b_k^2 S_k^2 + 2b_1 b_2 S_{12} + 2b_1 b_3 S_{13} + \cdots$$
$$+ 2b_{k-1} b_k S_{k-1,k} \tag{A.16}$$

Eq. A.16, despite its formidable appearance, can be easily understood. Suppose $k = 3$ and imagine "bordering" the covariance matrix of X_1, X_2, and X_3 with a row and column of the b's, as follows:

	b_1	b_2	b_3
b_1	S_1^2	S_{12}	S_{13}
b_2	S_{12}	S_2^2	S_{23}
b_3	S_{13}	S_{23}	S_3^2

The variance of Y is equal to the sum of all terms obtained by multiplying each cell entry by the product of the row and column b-coefficient.

To illustrate, suppose that $Y = 2X_1 - X_2 + 1.5X_3$, and the four observations on X_1, X_2, and X_3 are as shown in the first three columns of the following table:

X_1	X_2	X_3	Y
2	1.1	0.5	3.65
−3	−1.5	1.0	−3.00
1	0.6	−0.5	0.65
5	2.4	0.0	7.60
5	2.6	1.0	8.90

The corresponding Y-values are shown in the last column.

In Section A.10, we had calculated the covariance matrix of X_1, X_2, and X_3, which we reproduce in the following table bordered by a row and column of the coefficients of the linear function.

	2	−1	1.5
2	8.1875	4.0125	−0.9375
−1	4.0125	1.9725	−0.4750
1.5	−0.9375	−0.4750	0.3125

According to Eq. A.15, the mean of Y should be

$$\bar{Y} = (2)(1.25) + (-1)(0.65) + (1.5)(0.25) = 2.225$$

According to Eq. A.16, the variance of Y should be

$$Var(Y) = (2)(2)(8.1875) + (2)(-1)(4.0125) + \cdots + (1.5)(1.5)(0.3125) = 15.1756$$

EXERCISE A.8 Confirm these results by calculating directly the mean and variance of the Y-values.

In the special case where the variables X_1, X_2, ..., X_k are *independent* (that is, when the covariances of all pairs of X's are equal to zero), Eq. A.16 simplifies to

$$Var(Y) = b_1^2 S_1^2 + b_2^2 S_2^2 + \cdots + b_k^2 S_k^2 \tag{A.17}$$

A.12   THE COVARIANCE OF LINEAR FUNCTIONS OF UNCORRELATED VARIABLES

Suppose two variables, Y_1 and Y_2, are each a linear function of the same un-correlated variables $X_1, X_2, \ldots, X_k$,

$$Y_1 = b_0 + b_1 X_1 + b_2 X_2 + \cdots + b_k X_k$$
$$Y_2 = c_0 + c_1 X_1 + c_2 X_2 + \cdots + c_k X_k$$

It can be shown that the covariance of Y_1 and Y_2 is given by

$$
\begin{aligned}
Cov(Y_1, Y_2) &= b_1 c_1 Var(X_1) + b_2 c_2 Var(X_2) + \cdots + b_k c_k Var(X_k) \\
&= b_1 c_1 S_1^2 + b_2 c_2 S_2^2 + \cdots + b_k c_k S_k^2
\end{aligned}
\tag{A.18}
$$

It can be observed that the covariance is a sum of terms obtained by multiplying the variance of each variable by the product of its coefficients in the two linear functions.

To illustrate, suppose

$$Y_1 = 3 + 2X_1 - X_2 + 1.5X_3$$
$$Y_2 = -5 - X_1 + X_2 - X_3$$

There are eight observations on X_1, X_2 and X_3, as shown in the first three columns of the following table:

X_1	X_2	X_3	Y_1	Y_2
1	−1.0	0.0	3.00	−2.0
1	−1.0	1.5	5.25	−3.5
1	0.5	0.0	1.50	−0.5
1	0.5	1.5	3.75	−2.0
2	−1.0	0.0	5.00	−3.0
2	−1.0	1.5	7.25	−4.5
2	0.5	0.0	3.50	−1.5
2	0.5	1.5	5.75	−3.0
12	−2.0	6.0	35.00	−20.0

The corresponding Y_1- and Y_2-values are shown in the last two columns.

EXERCISE A.9 Show that X_1, X_2 and X_3 are uncorrelated.

EXERCISE A.10 Show that the variances of X_1, X_2 and X_3 are equal to 0.25, 0.5625, and 0.5625, respectively.

Given the results in Exercises A.9 and A.10, the covariance of Y_1 and Y_2 should be

$$Cov(Y_1, Y_2) = (2)(-1)(0.25) + (-1)(1)(0.5625) + (1.5)(-1)(0.5625) = 1.90625.$$

EXERCISE A.11 Confirm this result by calculating directly the covariance of Y_1 and Y_2.

MATHEMATICAL NOTES

The following statements and derivations of selected results presented in the text are for the benefit of readers familiar with calculus and linear algebra.

B.I   DERIVATION OF THE LEAST SQUARES ESTIMATORS

The values of $b_0, b_1, b_2, \ldots, b_k$ that minimize

$$Z = \sum_{i=1}^{n}(Y_i - \hat{Y}_i)^2 = \sum_{i=1}^{n}(Y_i - b_0 - b_1 X_{1i} - b_2 X_{2i} - \cdots - b_k X_{ki})^2$$

are found by taking the partial derivatives of Z with respect to $b_0, b_1, b_2, \ldots, b_k$; setting these equal to zero; and solving the resulting equations. (The second-order conditions for a minimum can be shown to be satisfied.) The partial derivative of Z with respect to b_0 is

$$\frac{\partial Z}{\partial b_0} = -2\sum_{i}(Y_i - b_0 - b_1 X_{1i} - \cdots - b_k X_{ki})$$

$$= -2\left(\sum_{i} Y_i - nb_0 - b_1 \sum_{i} X_{1i} - \cdots - b_k \sum_{i} X_{ki}\right)$$

The partial derivative of Z with respect to one of the other b's, say, b_j, is

$$\frac{\partial Z}{\partial b_j} = (2)\sum_{i}(Y_i - b_0 - b_1 X_{1i} - \cdots - b_k X_{ki})(-X_{ji})$$

$$= -2\left(\sum_{i} X_{ji} Y_i - b_0 \sum_{i} X_{ji} - b_1 \sum_{i} X_{ji} X_{1i} - \cdots - b_k \sum_{i} X_{ji} X_{ki}\right)$$

for $j = 1, 2, \ldots, k$. If we set these partial derivatives equal to zero, we get the system of $(k + 1)$ linear equations in $(k + 1)$ unknowns $(b_0, b_1, b_2, \ldots, b_k)$ described in Section 2.4.

B.2 THE GENERAL LINEAR MODEL IN MATRIX NOTATION

It is easy to verify that the system of linear equations yielding the OLS estimators can be written as

$$(X'X)b = X'Y, \tag{B.1}$$

where

$$Y = \begin{pmatrix} Y_1 \\ Y_2 \\ \cdots \\ Y_n \end{pmatrix} \quad X = \begin{pmatrix} 1 & X_{11} & X_{21} & \cdots & X_{k1} \\ 1 & X_{12} & X_{22} & \cdots & X_{k2} \\ \cdots & \cdots & \cdots & \cdots & \cdots \\ 1 & X_{1n} & X_{2n} & \cdots & X_{kn} \end{pmatrix} \quad b = \begin{pmatrix} b_0 \\ b_1 \\ \cdots \\ b_k \end{pmatrix}$$

and X' denotes the transpose of X. Thus, Y is a $(n \times 1)$ vector, X is a matrix of dimension $n \times (k+1)$, and b is a $(k+1) \times 1$ vector.

If the matrix $(X'X)$ is nonsingular, the solution of B.1 is given by

$$b = (X'X)^{-1}X'Y \tag{B.2}$$

or

$$b = WY \tag{B.3}$$

where $W = (X'X)^{-1}X'$ is a matrix of dimension $(k+1) \times n$. From this it can be seen that the least squares estimators are linear functions of the Y-values:

$$b_j = \sum_{i=1}^{n} w_{ji}Y_i \qquad (j = 0, 1, 2, \ldots, k)$$

B.3 COVARIANCE OF OLS ESTIMATORS AND FORECASTS

The covariance matrix of $b_0, b_1, \ldots, b_k$, denoted by $Var(b)$, is by definition

$$Var(b) = \begin{pmatrix} Var(b_0) & Cov(b_0, b_1) & \cdots & Cov(b_0, b_k) \\ Cov(b_1, b_0) & Var(b_1) & \cdots & Cov(b_1, b_k) \\ \cdots & \cdots & \cdots & \cdots \\ Cov(b_k, b_0) & Cov(b_k, b_1) & \cdots & Var(b_k) \end{pmatrix}$$

and can be shown to be equal to

$$Var(\mathbf{b}) = \sigma^2 (\mathbf{X'X})^{-1}$$

The forecast value of Y for given values of the explanatory variables is $\hat{Y} = b_0 + b_1 X_{10} + b_2 X_{20} + \cdots + b_k X_{k0}$ and can be written as

$$\hat{Y} = \mathbf{b'X}_0$$

where $\mathbf{X}_0' = [1, X_{10}, X_{20}, \cdots, X_{k0}]'$.
The variance of this forecast can be shown to be

$$Var(\hat{Y}) = \sigma^2 [1 + \mathbf{X}_0' (\mathbf{X'X})^{-1} \mathbf{X}_0]$$

and its estimator

$$S_f^2 = S^2 [1 + \mathbf{X}_0' (\mathbf{X'X})^{-1} \mathbf{X}_0]$$

B.4   A REGRESSION MODEL WITH NO EXPLANATORY VARIABLES

The value of b_0 that minimizes

$$Z = \sum_{i=1}^{n} (Y_i - b_0)^2$$

is found by taking the derivative of Z with respect to b_0 and setting it equal to zero:

$$\frac{dZ}{db_0} = (-2) \sum (Y_i - b_0) = 0$$

From this we obtain

$$nb_0 = \sum Y_i$$

or

$$b_0 = \frac{1}{n} \sum Y_i = \bar{Y}$$

B.5 ANALYSIS OF VARIANCE

For a one-way classification with the same number of observations in each category, the problem is to find those values of $b_0, b_1, b_2, \ldots, b_J$ that minimize $Z = \sum_{i=1}^{I} \sum_{j=1}^{J} (Y_{ij} - \hat{Y}_{ij})^2$, subject to the constraint $\sum_{j=1}^{J} b_j = 0$, where

$$\hat{Y}_{ij} = b_0 + b_1 X_{i1} + b_2 X_{i2} + \cdots + b_J X_{iJ}$$

The X's are dummy variables such that $X_{ij} = 1$ for observations in the jth category and $X_{ij} = 0$ otherwise. Consequently, $\hat{Y}_{i1} = b_0 + b_1$, $\hat{Y}_{i2} = b_0 + b_2, \ldots,$ $\hat{Y}_{iJ} = b_0 + b_J$. In general, $\hat{Y}_{ij} = b_0 + b_j$, and

$$Z = \sum_i \sum_j (Y_{ij} - b_0 - b_j)^2$$

Ignoring temporarily the constraint $\sum_j b_j = 0$, for Z to be minimized its partial derivatives with respect to $b_0, b_1, \ldots, b_J$ must equal zero. For example, the partial derivative of Z with respect to b_1 is

$$\frac{\partial Z}{\partial b_1} = (2) \sum_i (Y_{i1} - b_0 - b_1)(-1) = (-2)\left(\sum_i Y_{i1} - Ib_0 - Ib_1\right)$$

In general, the partial derivative of Z with respect to b_j ($j = 1, 2, \ldots, J$) is equal to $(-2)(\sum_i Y_{ij} - Ib_0 - Ib_j)$. Equating this to zero and rearranging terms we get

$$b_j = \frac{1}{I} \sum_i Y_{ij} - b_0 = Y_{\cdot j} - b_0 \qquad (j = 1, 2, \ldots, J) \tag{B.4}$$

The partial derivative of Z with respect to b_0 is

$$\frac{\partial Z}{\partial b_0} = (2) \sum_i \sum_j (Y_{ij} - b_0 - b_j)(-1) = (-2)\left(\sum_i \sum_j Y_{ij} - IJb_0 - I\sum_{j=1}^{J} b_j\right)$$

Equating this to zero and rearranging terms we find

$$b_0 = \frac{1}{IJ} \sum_i \sum_j Y_{ij} - \frac{1}{J}\sum_{j=1}^{J} b_j = Y_{\cdot\cdot} - \frac{1}{J}\sum_{j=1}^{J} b_j \tag{B.5}$$

Observe that there are an infinite number of solutions to B.4 and B.5. For *any* value of b_0, Eq. B.4 has the solution $b_j = Y_{\cdot j} - b_0$. The sum of these equations for $j = 1, 2, \ldots, J$ satisfies B.5. However, if we require that $\sum_{j=1}^{J} b_j = 0$, then, from B.5, $b_0 = Y_{..}$, and Eq. B.4 yields $b_j = Y_{.j} - Y_{..}$, as claimed in Section 4.5. It can be shown that the second-order conditions for a minimum are satisfied.

Exactly the same approach is followed in the case of a two-way classification with one observation per cell to minimize $Z = \sum_i \sum_j (Y_{ij} - \hat{Y}_{ij})^2$, $\hat{Y}_{ij} = b_0 + b_j + c_i$, subject to the constraints $\sum_{j=1}^{J} b_j = 0$ and $\sum_{i=1}^{I} c_i = 0$. Setting the partial derivatives of Z with respect to b_0, the other b_j, and the c_i equal to zero, yields a system of equations with an infinite number of solutions, but only one of these solutions (Eq. 4.13 of Section 4.6) satisfies the constraints.

B.6 THE OLS ESTIMATOR OF A SIMPLE MODEL WITH ZERO INTERCEPT

Suppose $\hat{Y}_i = bX_i$. Let $Z = \sum_{i=1}^{n}(Y_i - bX_i)^2$. Taking the derivative of Z with respect to b, we find

$$\frac{dZ}{db} = (2)\sum_{i=1}^{n}(Y_i - bX_i)(-X_i) = (-2)[\sum_{i=1}^{n} X_i Y_i - b \sum X_i^2]$$

which yields the solution $b = \sum_{i=1}^{n} X_i Y_i / \sum X_i^2$ when this derivative is made equal to zero.

B.7 THE MAXIMUM LIKELIHOOD METHOD OF ESTIMATION

The maximum likelihood method seeks those values of the parameters that maximize the "likelihood function" of the observations.

Perhaps the simplest way to explain the method is in the context of sampling with replacement from a population, the elements of which belong to one of two categories, C_1 and C_2. Let P $(0 < P < 1)$ be the proportion of elements that belong to C_1, and $1 - P$ the proportion belonging to C_2. We shall derive the maximum likelihood estimator of P and show that it is none other than the ordinary proportion of sampled elements that belong to C_1.

Let Y be a variable representing the category of an element selected at random from the population and taking the value 1 if the element belongs to C_1 or the value 0 if it belongs to C_2. The probability distribution of Y, that is, the list of possible values of Y and the associated probabilities, is given in the following table.

Category	Y	Probability
C_1	1	P
C_2	0	$1 - P$
		1

The probability distribution of Y can also be described by the formula

$$p(Y) = P^Y(1 - P)^{1-Y}, \qquad (Y = 0, 1)$$

For it is easy to verify that $p(Y = 1) = P^1(1 - P)^{1-1} = P$ and $p(Y = 0) = P^0(1 - P)^{1-0} = 1 - P$, exactly as shown in the table.

Now, imagine planning to select a simple random sample with replacement of two elements from this population. Let Y_1 take the value 1 if the first sampled element belongs to C_1, or 0 if it does not. Likewise, Y_2 takes the value 1 if the second sampled element belongs to C_1, or 0 if it does not. It can be verified that the joint probability distribution of Y_1 and Y_2 is

$$p(Y_1, Y_2) = [P^{Y_1}(1 - P)^{1-Y_1}][P^{Y_2}(1 - P)^{1-Y_2}]$$
$$= P^{Y_1 + Y_2}(1 - P)^{2 - (Y_1 + Y_2)}$$

For example, the probability that both sampled elements belong to C_1 is $p(Y_1 = 1, Y_2 = 1) = P^2$, and so on.

More generally, if the sample is of size n, we let Y_i $(i = 1, 2, \ldots, n)$ take the value 1 if the ith sampled element belongs to C_1, or 0 if it does not. The joint probability distribution of $Y_1, Y_2, \ldots, Y_n$ is given by

$$L = p(Y_1, Y_2, \ldots, Y_n) = [P^{Y_1}(1 - P)^{1-Y_1}][P^{Y_2}(1 - P)^{1-Y_2}]$$
$$\cdots [P^{Y_n}(1 - P)^{1-Y_n}]$$
$$= P^{\sum Y_i}(1 - P)^{n - \sum Y_i}$$
$$= P^{n_1}(1 - P)^{n-n_1} \qquad (B.6)$$

where $n_1 = \sum_{i=1}^{n} Y_i$ is the number of sampled elements belonging to C_1. Note that L has the same value for all sets of values of the Y's yielding the same value of n_1.

For given values of P and n, Eq. B.6 gives the probability that $Y_1, Y_2, \ldots, Y_n$ will take specified values. For example, if $n = 2$ and $P = 0.4$, the probability that $Y_1 = 1$ and $Y_2 = 0$ is

$$(0.4)^1(0.6)^{2-1} = 0.24$$

But Eq. B.6 can also be viewed as a function of P for given n and n_1. In this context, L is called the likelihood function. We can thus determine the value of P

that maximizes L (that is, which maximizes the probability of the given value of n_1); this is the maximum likelihood estimator of P. It is mathematically more convenient to maximize $\log(L)$ than L (the value of P that maximizes $\log(L)$ also maximizes L). To do so, we take the derivative of $\log(L)$ with respect to P:

$$\frac{d\log(L)}{dP} = \frac{n_1}{P} - \frac{n - n_1}{1 - P}$$

Equating to zero and simplifying, we find after some algebra that the solution is

$$P = \frac{n_1}{n}$$

It can be verified that the second derivative is negative, so that the preceding solution does indeed maximize L. We conclude that the maximum likelihood estimator of P is the proportion of sampled elements that belong to C_1.

In general, maximum likelihood estimators are derived by maximizing the appropriate likelihood function with respect to the parameters of that function. The procedure is very similar to that just illustrated, but the mathematics can become quite complicated for the situations examined in the text. It can be shown (see, for example, Wilks [1962, Ch. 12]) that the maximum likelihood method yields *consistent* estimators of the parameters and that, when the sample size is large, the probability distribution of a maximum likelihood estimator is approximately normal.

B.8 GENERALIZED LEAST SQUARES (GLS)

We state next without proof the expression for the *generalized least squares* or *Aitken estimators*:

$$\mathbf{b}_{gls} = (\mathbf{X}'\mathbf{C}^{-1}\mathbf{X})^{-1}\mathbf{X}'\mathbf{C}^{-1}\mathbf{Y}$$

where $\mathbf{C}$ is the $n \times n$ matrix of known constants C_{ij} described in Section 9.6. When all $C_{ii} = 1$ and all $C_{ij} = 0$ for $i \neq j$, the case under the classical linear model, $\mathbf{C}$ is the identity matrix and $\mathbf{b}_{gls} = \mathbf{b}_{ols}$.

B.9 DERIVATION OF THE CLASSIFICATION RULE UNDER NORMALITY

What follows is just an outline of the derivation of the linear classification functions, Eq. 12.8, under normality in the case of two categories.

In the case of a population consisting of two categories, an observation with the set of characteristics $\mathbf{x}' = [X_1, X_2, \ldots, X_k]'$ is classified into C_1 if (cf. Eq. 11.6)

$$\frac{p_1(\mathbf{x})}{p_2(\mathbf{x})} \geq \frac{q_2 L_2}{q_1 L_1}$$

or, in what amounts to the same thing, if

$$\log \frac{p_1(\mathbf{x})}{p_2(\mathbf{x})} \geq \log \frac{q_2 L_2}{q_1 L_1}$$

If $p_1(\mathbf{x})$ and $p_2(\mathbf{x})$ are both multivariate normal with mean vectors $\boldsymbol{\mu}_1$ and $\boldsymbol{\mu}_2$ and the same covariance matrix $\boldsymbol{\Sigma}$, then by definition

$$p_i(\mathbf{x}) = \frac{1}{(2\pi)^{k/2}|\boldsymbol{\Sigma}|^{1/2}} exp\{-\frac{1}{2}(\mathbf{x} - \boldsymbol{\mu}_i)'\boldsymbol{\Sigma}^{-1}(\mathbf{x} - \boldsymbol{\mu}_i)\} \qquad (i = 1, 2)$$

It follows that

$$\log \frac{p_1(\mathbf{x})}{p_2(\mathbf{x})} = -\frac{1}{2}[(\mathbf{x} - \boldsymbol{\mu}_1)'\boldsymbol{\Sigma}^{-1}(\mathbf{x} - \boldsymbol{\mu}_1) - (\mathbf{x} - \boldsymbol{\mu}_2)'\boldsymbol{\Sigma}^{-1}(\mathbf{x} - \boldsymbol{\mu}_2)]$$

$$= -\frac{1}{2}\boldsymbol{\mu}_1'\boldsymbol{\Sigma}^{-1}\boldsymbol{\mu}_1 + \boldsymbol{\mu}_1'\boldsymbol{\Sigma}^{-1}\mathbf{x} + \frac{1}{2}\boldsymbol{\mu}_2'\boldsymbol{\Sigma}^{-1}\boldsymbol{\mu}_2 - \boldsymbol{\mu}_2'\boldsymbol{\Sigma}^{-1}\mathbf{x}$$

since $\boldsymbol{\mu}_1'\boldsymbol{\Sigma}^{-1}\mathbf{x} = \mathbf{x}'\boldsymbol{\Sigma}^{-1}\boldsymbol{\mu}_1$, and so on. Therefore, classify into C_1 if

$$-\frac{1}{2}\boldsymbol{\mu}_1'\boldsymbol{\Sigma}^{-1}\boldsymbol{\mu}_1 + \boldsymbol{\mu}_1'\boldsymbol{\Sigma}^{-1}\mathbf{x} + \log q_1 L_1 \geq -\frac{1}{2}\boldsymbol{\mu}_2'\boldsymbol{\Sigma}^{-1}\boldsymbol{\mu}_2 + \boldsymbol{\mu}_2'\boldsymbol{\Sigma}^{-1}\mathbf{x} + \log q_2 L_2$$

which is in the form of Eq. 12.8,

$$b_{01} + \sum_{j=1}^{k} b_{j1}x_j + \log q_1 L_1 \geq b_{02} + \sum_{j=1}^{k} b_{j2}x_j + \log q_2 L_2$$

The unknown population means $(\boldsymbol{\mu}_1, \boldsymbol{\mu}_2)$ and common covariance matrix $(\boldsymbol{\Sigma})$ are estimated by the sample means $(\bar{\mathbf{x}}_1, \bar{\mathbf{x}}_2)$ and pooled covariance matrix $(\mathbf{S})$.

B.I0 STRUCTURAL AND REDUCED FORM EQUATIONS

The system of equations in structural form in Section 13.4 can be written as

$$\mathbf{By} = \mathbf{\Gamma x} + \mathbf{\epsilon},$$

where $\mathbf{B}$ is the matrix of the β-coefficients, $\mathbf{\Gamma}$ that of the γ-coefficients, $\mathbf{y}' = [Y_1, Y_2, \ldots, Y_l]'$ is the vector of endogenous variables, $\mathbf{x}' = [X_0, X_1, \ldots, X_m]'$ the vector of predetermined variables, and $\mathbf{\epsilon}' = [\epsilon_1, \epsilon_2, \ldots, \epsilon_l]'$ is the vector of error terms.

Provided the matrix $\mathbf{B}$ is nonsingular, premultiplying the structural equations by the inverse of $\mathbf{B}$, $\mathbf{B}^{-1}$, gives the system of equations in reduced form:

$$\mathbf{y} = \mathbf{B}^{-1}\mathbf{\Gamma x} + \mathbf{B}^{-1}\mathbf{\epsilon} = \mathbf{\Delta x} + \tilde{\mathbf{\epsilon}},$$

where $\mathbf{\Delta} = \mathbf{B}^{-1}\mathbf{\Gamma}$ is the matrix of δ-coefficients and $\tilde{\mathbf{\epsilon}}' = [\tilde{\epsilon}_1, \tilde{\epsilon}_2, \ldots, \tilde{\epsilon}_l]'$ is the vector of error terms of the equations in reduced form.

The estimates and forecasts of the endogenous variables for given values of the predetermined variables can also be written in the same notation. Let $\mathbf{B}$ and $\mathbf{C}$ be the matrices of the estimates of the β- and γ-coefficients of the structural equations. The forecast of the endogenous variables is given by

$$\hat{\mathbf{y}} = (\mathbf{B}^{-1}\mathbf{C})\mathbf{x},$$

where x is the vector of values of the predetermined variables. Alternatively, if $\mathbf{D}$ is the matrix of the estimates of the δ-coefficients of the reduced form equations, the forecasts are given by

$$\hat{\mathbf{y}} = \mathbf{Dx}.$$

1

SELECTED REFERENCES

There is a very large literature concerning the topics introduced in this text. The following selected references provide additional information at a more advanced mathematical level. Many other books can be located with the help of an electronic library search for such subjects as *regression analysis, linear models, least squares, analysis of variance, time series analysis, experimental design, discriminant analysis,* and *econometrics.*

Agresti, A. *Categorical Data Analysis.* New York: Wiley, 1990.

Atkinson, A. C., and A. N. Donev. *Optimum Experimental Designs.* London: Oxford University Press, 1992.

Belsley, D. A. *Conditioning Diagnostics: Collinearity and Weak Data in Regression.* New York: Wiley, 1991.

Box, G. E. P., and N. R. Draper. *Empirical Model-Building and Response Surfaces.* New York: Wiley, 1987.

Box, G. E. P., G. M. Jenkins, and G. C. Reinsel. *Time Series Analysis: Forecasting and Control.* 3d ed. Englewood Cliffs, N.J.: Prentice-Hall, 1994.

Chatterjee, S., and A. S. Hadi. *Sensitivity Analysis in Linear Regression.* New York: Wiley, 1988.

Cox, D. R., and E. J. Snell. *Analysis of Binary Data.* 2d ed. London: Chapman & Hall, 1989.

Draper, N., and H. Smith. *Applied Regression Analysis.* 3d ed. New York: Wiley, 1987.

Gruber, M. H. J. *Regression Estimators: A Comparative Study.* Boston: Academic Press, 1990.

Gujarati, D. N. *Basic Econometrics.* 3d ed. New York: McGraw-Hill, 1995.

Hinkelman, K., and O. Kempthorne. *Design and Analysis of Experiments: Volume 1, Introduction to Experimental Design.* New York: Wiley, 1994.

Janacek, G., and L. Swift. *Time Series: Forecasting, Simulation, Applications.* New York: Ellis Horwood, 1993.

Johnson, R. A., and D. W. Wichern. *Applied Multivariate Statistical Analysis*. 3d ed. Englewood Cliffs, N.J.: Prentice-Hall, 1992.

Johnston, J. *Econometric Methods*. 3d ed. New York: McGraw-Hill, 1984.

Lachenbruch, P. A. *Discriminant Analysis*. New York: Hafner Press, 1975.

Malinvaud, E. *Statistical Methods of Econometrics*. 3d ed. Amsterdam: North-Holland Elsevier, 1980.

McCullagh, P., and J. A. Nelder. *Generalized Linear Models*. 2d ed. London: Chapman & Hall, 1989.

McLachlan, G. J. *Discriminant Analysis and Statistical Pattern Recognition*. New York: Wiley, 1992.

Montgomery, D. C., L. A. Johnson, and J. S. Gardiner. *Forecasting and Time Series Analysis*. 2d ed. New York: McGraw-Hill, 1990.

Myers, R. H., and D. C. Montgomery. *Response Surface Methodology: Process and Product Optimization Using Designed Experiments*. New York: Wiley, 1995.

Nelson, C. R. *Applied Time Series Analysis for Managerial Forecasting*. San Francisco: Holden-Day, 1973.

Neter, J., W. Wasserman, and M. H. Kutner. *Applied Linear Statistical Models: Regression, Analysis of Variance, and Experimental Designs*. 3d ed. Homewood, Il: Irwin, 1990.

Pindyck, R. S., and D. L. Rubinfeld. *Econometric Models and Economic Forecasts*. 3d ed. New York: McGraw-Hill, 1991.

Pukelsheim, F. *Optimal Design of Experiments*. New York: Wiley, 1993.

Raktoe, B. L., A. Hedayat, and W. T. Federer. *Factorial Designs*. New York: Wiley, 1981.

Rencher, A. C. *Methods of Multivariate Analysis*. New York: Wiley, 1995.

Scheffé, H. *The Analysis of Variance*. New York: Wiley, 1959.

Seber, G. A. F., and C. J. Wild. *Nonlinear Regression*. New York: Wiley, 1989.

Tatsuoka, M. M. *Discriminant Analysis: The Study of Group Differences, Selected Topics in Advanced Statistics No. 6*. Champaign, Ill.: Institute for Personality and Ability Testing, 1970.

Theil, H. *Principles of Econometrics*. New York: Wiley, 1971.

Wilks, S. S. *Mathematical Statistics*. New York: Wiley, 1962.

INDEX